Miscellaneous Verdicts

Also by Anthony Powell

NOVELS

Afternoon Men
Venusberg
From a View to a Death
Agents and Patients
What's Become of Waring
O, How the Wheel Becomes It!
The Fisher King

A DANCE TO THE MUSIC OF TIME

A Question of Upbringing
A Buyer's Market
The Acceptance World
At Lady Molly's
Casanova's Chinese Restaurant
The Kindly Ones
The Valley of Bones
The Soldier's Art
The Military Philosophers
Books Do Furnish a Room
Temporary Kings
Hearing Secret Harmonies

BIOGRAPHY

John Aubrey and his Friends

PLAYS

The Garden God and *The Rest I'll Whistle*

MEMOIRS

To Keep the Ball Rolling
Vol. I. Infants of the Spring
Vol. II. Messengers of Day
Vol. III. Faces in My Time
Vol. IV. The Strangers All Are Gone

ANTHONY POWELL

Miscellaneous Verdicts

WRITINGS ON WRITERS 1946–1989

HEINEMANN: LONDON

William Heinemann Ltd
Michelin House, 81 Fulham Road, London SW3 6RB

LONDON   MELBOURNE   AUCKLAND

First published in Great Britain 1990
Copyright © Anthony Powell 1990

A CIP catalogue record for this book
is available from the British Library
ISBN 0 434 59928 X

Typeset in 11/12pt Linotron Baskerville by
Hewer Text Composition Services, Edinburgh
Printed and bound in Great Britain by
St Edmundsbury Press, Bury St Edmonds, Suffolk

For
Roy Jenkins

ACKNOWLEDGMENTS

The pieces which follow were published in *Apollo, The Balliol Register*, Burke's *Landed Gentry, Brief Lives and Other Selected Writings of John Aubrey* (Cresset Press), The *Cornhill Magazine* (in which quotations from Amiel's *Journal Intime* are taken from the Macmillan edition of 1892, the Macmillan Company of New York's edition of 1935, and the Constable edition of *Philine*, 1933), *The Complete Imbiber* (Hutchinson of London), the *Daily Telegraph* (most of the pieces here), *Novels of High Society from the Victorian Age* (Pilot Press), *Punch* (many of the pieces here), the *Radio Times*, the *Spectator*, the *Times Literary Supplement, Marcel Proust: A Centenary Volume* (Weidenfeld & Nicolson). I am grateful to editors and publishers of these for permission to reprint them here; also to Tessa Davies, Roland Glasser, and Violet Powell, for making photocopies, when that was necessary.

CONTENTS

Contents

My Contemporaries

Proust and Proustian Matters

INTRODUCTION

This selection from occasional writing going back more than forty years is mainly, though by no means wholly, made up from reviews. There are also general articles, introductions, a few lighter pieces. Reprinting reviews, perhaps rightly, is apt to be accompanied by some sort of an apology. Assuming this to be made, I should like, however, to say a word on the subject of reviewing itself, a craft not without all intrinsic interest.

So long as I can remember I have been an avid reader of reviews – a condition which persists – and have been writing them almost as long. Reviews can be well or badly written (sometimes scarcely recognized), and the odd thing is that gifted people are often incapable of writing good ones; the hacks sometimes making a better job of it than bright boys summoned from outside, simply because the hacks have, at least should have, a sense of what they can get into the space allotted, and the sort of tone the public they are writing for expects.

Even assuming the ideal reviewer remains uncorrupted by prejudice – a pretty big assumption – reviewing must always remain a far from just estimate of the worth of any book of real merit. All books (most of all novels), if they are in at all a high rank, require rereading and digesting. Going straight through a book, probably in a hurry to get copy off in time, is bound to be unsatisfactory.

This does not mean that reviews *per se* are never worth a second glance. On the contrary, they can reveal all kinds of shifting in literary fashion, individual style, even proclaim the age of the reviewer. I make these comments only to indicate my own relatively strong feelings about the responsibilities of undertaking a specialized form of writing in the first instance, at the same time attempting some excuse for the many examples to be found here. So much for reviewing as such.

After I had gone through the mass of material to be sorted out, some sort of a pattern, or patterns, seemed to emerge, but when attempts were made to transfer these patterns to paper the images became elusive, threatening various forms of boredom or unassimilability. It appeared desirable to reflect variety, but in an ordered manner.

In the end it seemed best to confine the headings in this collection to four. I wanted one that I thought of in my own mind as *Old England*; one

1

about Americans; one about contemporaries; one about the French.

At first this might be thought easy enough. *Old England* covered people like Robert Burton (who gave opportunity for a small touch of autobiography), John Aubrey (introduction to an edition of his *Brief Lives*), Speed's maps, Leland's surveys, Anthony Wagner's magisterial *English Genealogy*, the House of Lords, and so on; slightly weighty fare lightened by Maundy Gregory's sale of honours. The heading did not seem right for some of the rest of the first section: Dickens, Hardy, Conrad, Kipling, even though Isaac D'Israeli offered an unexpected link-up with the Victorians and Kipling. Conrad and others made the sub-title inappropriate. I shall return to this problem of nomenclature in a moment.

There was a lot of American stuff. This particularly well illustrated what has been said above about reviews dating. For example, not many years after the war I wrote a notice of Arthur Mizener's pioneer biography of F. Scott Fitzgerald. I was particularly interested in Fitzgerald, whom I had met in Hollywood, and it was then possible to say in the review that his books were just beginning to be known in Great Britain. Since then endless works have been published about Fitzgerald on both sides of the Atlantic, the newspapers perpetually refer to some criminal as a Gatsby-type, and the name Gatsby may be seen above a shop, aiming at chic, in a small provincial town. In other words what was said in the reviews had lost all relevance, but other books about Fitzgerald appear here, and many fellow American writers.

The section on my own contemporaries also presented difficulties. Who exactly were they? Strictly speaking, I suppose five or six years each way might be considered reasonable, but the age was often much wider among writers I wanted to include. In the end I chose about twenty names, beginning with Ivy Compton-Burnett, who was a good deal older than me, which I excused by her biographer, Hilary Spurling, who was a good deal younger, being in any case a writer I wanted here. In short, I have treated them both as contemporaries. Among these Constant Lambert and Julian Maclaren-Ross were to some extent models in my novel *A Dance to the Music of Time* for Moreland and Trapnell. That represents about the age span covered, roughly in chronological order, but not when chronology proved inconvenient.

Then there was a pile of French material. This, on examination, turned out to contain quite a lot about Marcel Proust, some not directly concerned with Proust himself. Proust, of whom I've always been a great admirer, has many tentacles. For instance, André Gide spoke of the echoes of Benjamin Constant to be found in *À la Recherche du Temps Perdu*. As it happened, I had done a longish piece on Constant, so that it occurred to me he might be swept in as a Proustian forerunner.

Having established that principle, I was able to apply it also to the Swiss diarist Henri-Frédéric Amiel, whose concern with individual psychology, especially his own, often takes a Proustian turn, not least in examination of his sexual instincts, though these were very different from Proust's. Amiel was also interested in the romantic feelings people had about 'High Life'.

If there were these precursors, there were also Proustian contemporaries and friends. The Triestine novelist Italo Svevo has a Proustian side to his self-examination in *The Confessions of Zeno*. I had written about the biographies of figures in the Proust world like Robert de Montesquiou and Winaretta de Polignac; also novelists Proust admired, such as George Sand, Anatole France, Pierre Loti. In short all these persons, together with Harold Pinter's screenplay of Proust's novel, could be accommodated under the Proustian umbrella.

Here I should like to add a word about Amiel, who remains surprisingly unknown throughout the United Kingdom. I was introduced to Amiel's Diary during the war by Alick Dru, when we were both Military Liaison Officers with the Allied forces. Dru, authority on the Danish philosopher Kierkegaard, thought Amiel 'rather my kind of writer'. Dru was absolutely correct. I not only found Amiel absorbing, but, in consequence of reading the Diary, contributed (while still in uniform) two articles about him (here dovetailed) to *The Cornhill*.

These pieces seem to have had a small political repercussion. They appeared at a moment (1946) when the Soviet Union's foreign policy was abandoning all pretence of being anything but openly antagonistic towards the Western powers; in short marking the beginning of what was to be known as the Cold War.

Clement Attlee was then Prime Minister. In perhaps the first of his speeches beamed at attempting to reverse the adulation of Stalin, to which wartime propaganda had been so disastrously slanted in Great Britain, the Prime Minister, calling him a 'wise old Swiss philosopher', quoted at some length Amiel's views on certain sinister aspects of Russian national character, which had appeared in *The Cornhill*.

Amiel (as may be read here) says: 'What terrible masters the Russians would be if ever they should spread the night of their rule over the countries of the South! They would bring us a Polar despotism – tyranny such as the world has never known, silent as darkness, rigid as ice, insensible as bronze, decked with an outward amiability and glittering and with the cold brilliancy of snow, slavery without compensation or relief; this is what they would bring us.'

Amiel's Diary was familiar to Conrad, when he spent some time in Geneva recovering from the experiences related in *Heart of Darkness*. Indeed, Conrad borrowed a remark of Amiel's for an epigraph, and some of the Diary's subject matter is to be found in *Under Western Eyes*: thereby providing a link with the first section here.

I have sometimes run more than two pieces together to widen the field, added a word or sentence to what may have become obscure with the passing of years, but not altered views expressed, which do not necessarily represent what I think now. I have also abandoned use of 'Mr', good manners requiring that at the time, at a later date sounding rather stilted.

Finally – to forestall criticism – I am aware that in his more mature incarnation Bloch, by then a successful dramatist, changed his name to Jacques de Rogier, wore an eyeglass, affected anglicisms. His appearance, therefore, at the Proust Exhibition in Bond Street, in spite of white hair, must have been a throw-back to Bloch's earlier Homeric period; one of those typical inconsistencies of dreams or *revenants*.

Anthony Powell

The British

ROBERT BURTON

When I was a young man working in a publisher's office, I shared with the manager a room surrounded by bookshelves that were closely packed with file-copies of the books the firm had brought out since its foundation at the turn of the century. In the rare moments when all production was in the pipe-line, there were no more manuscripts to report on, no ads to be made up, no authors dropping in to enquire about their sales, I used to read the less uninviting of these file-copies. Sometimes – to tell the truth – I used to read them in preference to business activities.

One of the firm's rather uncharacterstic publications of the early 1900s was a three-volume edition of Robert Burton's *The Anatomy of Melancholy*, a much reprinted classic, first issued in 1621. On an idle afternoon I took the first volume down; in due course getting through the whole of *The Anatomy*, a longish work, in that way. There are perhaps worse places to read about Melancholy than a publisher's office.

Burton (about a dozen years younger than Shakespeare) spent most of his life as an Oxford don; in those days, therefore, of necessity unmarried. He was a parson, with a small living at Oxford; later a second one in Leicestershire. Burton had a great affection for Leicestershire, his own county, but he did not often visit his church there.

Burton himself says he suffered from melancholy. It seems to have been in the family, because his maternal uncle 'died of melancholy', after failing to be given command of the Leicestershire Militia in 1588 on threat of the Spanish Armada. At Oxford, when plagued with melancholy, Burton, who seems always to have enjoyed a joke, used to go down to the bridge over the river, and listen to the bargemen swearing at each other. That would always make him laugh, and at once feel better.

Pondering on his own condition, Burton came to the conclusion that melancholy was 'an inbred malady in every one of us'. He set about to define this malaise; where possible, suggest a cure. In doing this Burton covered an enormous amount of ground. He deals not only with such well-known aspects of melancholy as those brought on by Love, Religion, definable oppressions of the spirit, but also with the whole field, from *angst* – irrational worries about nothing in particular – to really serious disturbances of the mind to be classed as madness. *The Anatomy of Melancholy* is an early treatise on psychological derangement.

It is not unknown for people to find Burton heavy going. Reading him in the office – a little at a time – was probably the best way to extract maximum enjoyment. Nevertheless, Burton is never a bore. Not only a scholar with a good deal of satirical humour, he was also a bit of a poet. Read the section on palm-trees falling in love with each other; while what could give more sense of life (recalling Proust too) than the comment: 'A boy singing some ballad tune early in the street, alters, revives, recreates, a restless patient that cannot sleep in the night.'

The Anatomy of Melancholy, reprinted several times in Burton's lifetime, was an immediate success. Whenever it was reissued, the author revised what he had written, adding more quotations, more apt instances, more extraordinary anecdotes. In consequence he built up a kind of storehouse to be raided by all sorts of other writers (including myself) for the treasures to be found there.

Burton's importance, so it seems to me, is not in being proprietor of this Old Curiosity Shop, but as one of the first writers to grasp the innate oddness of human nature. He called this Melancholy, but what he meant really covered all behaviour. He was keenly aware of the manner in which personal existence can be put out of gear by some utterly trivial matter; the unconventional treatment that may sometimes set things right: for example, 'A gentleman of Senes [Sienna] in Italy, who was afraid to piss, least all the town should be drowned; the physicians caused the bells to be rung backwards, and told him the town was on fire, whereupon he made water, and was immediately cured.'

At the time when I was reading *The Anatomy of Melancholy* in the office, I was also planning to write a novel; perhaps I had begun the novel already. The projected book had no title. One day in Burton I came across just what was required: 'as if they had heard the enchanted horne of Astolpho, that English duke in Ariosto, which never sounded but all his auditors were mad, and for fear ready to make away with themselves . . . they are a company of giddy-heads, afternoon men.' *Afternoon Men* (published 1931) seemed an ideal title for a novel dealing largely with characters who started their mornings with a hangover.

I now regret this Burton quotation did not at once send me to Ariosto, whose *Orlando Furioso* – especially in the translation by Sir John Harington (godson of Queen Elizabeth I, and pioneer of the water-closet) – is very good reading, some of it, but I did not tackle Ariosto until years later.

I did, however, make a note (in about 1927) of a passage from Burton which might come in useful at some future date: 'Now come tidings of weddings, maskings, mummeries, entertainments, jubilees, embassies, tilts and tournaments, trophies, triumphs, revels, sports, plays; then again as in a new shifted scene, treasons, cheating tricks, robberies, enormous villainies in all kinds, funerals, burials, deaths of Princes, new discoveries, expeditions, now comical, then tragical matters; today we hear of new Lords created; tomorrow of some great men deposed, and again of fresh honours conferred; one is let loose, another imprisoned; one purchaseth, another breaketh; he thrives, his neighbour turns bankrupt; now plenty, then again dearth and famine; one runs, another rides, wrangles, laughs, weeps, &c.'

Nearly fifty years passed before I was able to make use of this wonderful epitome of what life is like. It comes at the end of my twelve-volume novel sequence, *A Dance to the Music of Time*, the first volume of which appeared in 1951, the last in 1975.

The narrative of this novel is told by a man who has lived the same sort of life as myself, without our having necessarily shared every experience; a method intended to give consistency to the point of view – all novels must have a point of view – by looking at things from an angle always familiar to the writer.

In 1948 a book of mine appeared about the seventeenth-century antiquary and biographer, John Aubrey, born fifty years later than Burton, but not wholly unlike him through imaginative interest in human behaviour. Historical research has an undeniable effect on one's daily life and approach to things. It seemed right, therefore, that at one stage of the Narrator's story I should represent him as engaged in research. Writing a novel, say, or a travel book, would not be the same.

I had always been interested in Burton, and he seemed a suitable substitute for Aubrey in *A Dance to the Music of Time*. An American, who was interviewing me some years ago, made an interesting comment on that bracketing. He said: 'but Aubrey's a figure of Life, Burton of Death'. I'm not sure that I agree, but I see what he meant.

Possibly the American professor had in mind the legend – never confirmed – that Burton had taken his own life to prove himself right in the calculations of a horoscope he had cast to indicate the hour of his death. Such an act might certainly have fitted in with Burton's sometimes black humour, but I feel the call of listening once again to the swearing of the bargemen would somehow have prevented that.

Tolerant in matters of religion, politics, daily life, Burton wrote: 'Let us drive down care with a cup of wine, though I drink none myself.' He thought Education one of the main causes of melancholy; especially when conducted by 'undiscreet, passionate, Bedlam tutors'. In fact the reader who does not mind taking a little trouble will find in *The Anatomy* much that seems not at all out of date.

1977
Radio Times

JOHN SPEED

These two volumes of early maps of the English counties done in facsimile are such a grand conception and so beautifully reproduced that it is hard to speak of them with moderation. John Speed (1552–1629), well known in his own day as an historian and genealogist, is now chiefly remembered, if not as the first atlas-maker of England and Wales, at least as the one who produced at an early date, in his *Theatre of the Empire of Great Britaine*, the most popular and intelligent work of this kind. He was also the first to show the counties marked out in their old divisions of 'hundreds'. In spite of the many editions of Speed's volume, copies have become increasingly rare because plates are removed and framed – not surprising when the extraordinarily decorative quality of Speed's maps is examined. This lack is now made good.

The publishers rightly emphasize that these maps are not some highly specialized production for expert geographers or pedantic research students. They are something to be enjoyed by everyone who is interested in the English scene, and who possesses some sense of its wonderful past. The little pictures of battles, palaces, cathedrals, famous monuments, or coats of arms, are worked into the general design of the maps with immense skill, and for each county there is a page of description of its history and characteristics together with a gazetteer of the places.

The first volume contains *Hampshire*, the *Isle of Wight*, *Dorset*, *Devon*, *Cornwall*, *Somerset*, *Wiltshire*, *Gloucestershire*, *Herefordshire* and *Monmouthshire*; the second volume, *Kent*, *Sussex*, *Surrey*, *Berkshire*, *Middlesex*, *Essex*, *Suffolk*, *Norfolk*, *Hertfordshire* and *Buckinghamshire*. The rest of England is billed to appear in two more volumes next year. John Arlott has admirably edited the whole production.

The maps themselves are scarcely to be described, because their charm lies in their colour and design, but a word or two may be said of them individually. *Hampshire* shows a small hunting scene in progress in the New Forest, and, elsewhere, the Empress Maud being carried in a horse-litter from Winchester to Ludgershall. Off the *Isle of Wight* (or '*Wight Island*') sea monsters rise from the waves, as they do also on the coasts of *Dorset* and *Devon*. Arlott thinks the map of *Cornwall* one of the least successful, because the pictures of the ancient stones, the Hurlers and the Cheesewring 'weaken the design'. Here I find myself in disagreement. The pictures of the stones, and the mysterious inscription, seem to me to make a striking and surrealist effect against the deep blue of the sea and the 'prospect' of the town of Launceston, showing how Speed can suddenly vary his style with complete success. The fact that Cornwall is a peninsula surely justifies the hard line of termination on the east.

Wiltshire has a delightful picture of Stonehenge being explored by ladies and gentlemen in Elizabethan dress, while *Gloucestershire* contains an illustration of the single combat between Canute the Dane and Edmund Ironsyde, King of the English Saxons. Below this the battle of Tewkesbury is depicted. *Herefordshire* shows the battle of Ludlow and contains two fine figures of geographers (have these some reference to Richard Hakluyt's family coming from Herefordshire?) holding measuring instruments. The description of the county is also notable for an event in Speed's own remembrance 'when *Marcley Hill* in the East of this Shire rouzed it selfe out of a dead sleepe, with a roaring noise removed from the place where it stood, and for three days together travelled from her first site, to the great amazement and feare of the beholders . . . The ground thus travelled was about twenty-six acres.'

Of *Somerset*: 'Yet how delightfull so ever it is in the time of Sommer, with change of season it may well change her pleasing name, and borrow some winterly denomination; so full of wet, so miry and moorish is it; insomuch that the Inhabitants can hardly travell too and fro without their great encombrance. Howbeit they passe over all this with patience, knowing their ensuing seasonable profits farre to exceed present detriments and displeasures: for as it is foul, so it is fruitfull, which makes them comfort themselves with this proverb, that *What is worst for the Rider is best for the Abider.*' *Monmouth* has a picture of King Henry V.

Kent shows a prospect of Rochester with ships sailing up the Thames; *Sussex*, the battle of Lewes; *Surrey*, the palaces of Richmond and Nonsuch; *Berkshire*, the long walls of Windsor Castle; *Middlesex*, Westminster Abbey and old St Paul's. *Essex* has some Roman coins, *Suffolk* fine 'supporters' for the ground plan of Ipswich. *Norfolk* is marked by the insurrection of Ket the Tanner, and *Hertfordshire* by several battles of the Wars of the Roses. The heraldry of *Buckinghamshire* is particularly fine.

John Speed's England: A Facsimile   1953
of the First Edition of 1610. Vol. I: *Punch*
Western and South-Western
Counties. *Vol. II:* Eastern and
Home Counties. Phoenix House.

JOHN LELAND

Henry VIII is commonly thought of as a monarch who had a lot of wives and dissolved the monasteries. The tremendous importance of his reign as a time of intellectual expansion, some of which was undoubtedly owed to the King himself, is often overlooked.

To speak of the Renaissance as if it were a compact historical period is now unfashionable, but much of what can still be conveniently thought of as the Renaissance in this country had been held in check by the Wars of the Roses. It flowered under Henry VIII's tough but modernizing rule.

John Leland's Itinerary of England and Wales, which took place in or about the years 1535–43, is one of the most remarkable examples of this new point of view. Leland was a clever young man who had taken minor religious orders and made some name for himself as a poet. In 1533 – the last year of the Pope's authority in England – he was given a papal dispensation to hold four benefices to provide him with funds for a search in the libraries of monasteries and colleges for 'monuments of ancient writers'; a work with which he had been charged by the King.

The result of his rambles during the years that followed supply the first guidebook to England and Wales – and a very good guidebook it is. The five volumes, as produced here, cover the country with a thoroughness that is really impressive. One of the points of these journeys was to acquire for the King's Library the manuscripts of the religious houses that were to be no more.

Many manuscripts were unhappily destroyed in this process (already begun in the previous reign), but Leland, passionately keen on these antiquities, had studied 'British, Saxon and Welsh' better to equip himself in his task.

One of the various difficulties in performing it successfully was, characteristically, that 'the Germans' had entered the market and liked to snap up valuable medieval manuscripts for their own libraries. It is perhaps not surprising that the strain of his labours finally drove poor Leland out of his mind, but, before that happened, he had perambulated the country from Northumberland to Cornwall, and Kent to Pembrokeshire.

As may be imagined, the editing of Leland's work was a formidable job. Certain portions of the original writing were 'imbesiled and gone', while some of what remained had become 'moth-eaten, mouldie and rotten'. However, Lucy Toulmin Smith, fifty-odd years ago, produced an admirable edition of *The Itinerary of John Leland*, of which this is a reprint, to be universally welcomed. It is newly introduced by Sir Thomas Kendrick.

Such an undertaking as the particular description of England, the features of town and country interspersed with historical notes, was unheard of (wrote Miss Toulmin Smith in 1910); it was a thing of magnitude demanding learning, months of laborious travel, and much expense; it was a mark at once of the increasing desire for information and of the growing pride of Englishmen in their country, of what we should now call 'imperial' spirit.

Oh dear, we mustn't call it that any longer, or Leland will not be allowed in progressive institutions.

Leland travelled through Wales just after the Act of 1535–36 had united that country with England, abolishing the old marcher lordships and creating the new counties of Monmouth, Brecknock, Radnor, Montgomery and Denbigh. While in Wales, Leland noted: 'Hoele communely called in Englische Poele'; his spelling suggesting that in neither country, in that day, was there any tendency to rhyme the name with 'towel'.

There are so many good things to be found in the Itinerary that one can only suggest a few, here and there, to indicate the riches. For example, at Bath he describes how Roman statuary was to be observed embedded in the walls of that city:

There be divers notable antiquitees engravid in stone that yet be sene in the walles of Bathe betwixt the south gate and the west gate: and again betwixt the west gate and the north gate . . . I saw two nakid imagis lying a long, the one imbracing the other . . . then I saw a gray-hound as running . . . then I saw a two images, whereof one was of a nakid manne grasping a serpent in eche hand, as I tooke it . . . I much doubte wither these antique workes were sette in the tyme of the Romans dominion in Britayne in the waulles of Bath, as they stand now.

In Bristol, 'Thereby in the same lane dwellyd the Jewes, and theyr temple, or sinagoge, is yet sene there, and now is a ware howse.' In Burford, 'There was a place caullyd the Priorie. Horman the Kyng's barbar hathe now the landes of it.'

Quotations of this sort could be continued endlessly. It is really astonishing how, if you look up a place, Leland seems always to have passed that way, a feature of the Itinerary that makes it as enjoyable to the general reader as to the scholar.

The Itinerary of John Leland, 5
vols, Lucy Toulmin Smith, ed.,
Centaur Press.

1964
Punch

JOHN AUBREY

A story of Rudyard Kipling's, belonging to the *Stalky & Co.* group, describes how Beetle found Isaac D'Israeli's *Curiosities of Literature* in the headmaster's library, and from it dispensed selected tags for his friends' use in an examination. The housemaster, Mr King, taken aback at unexpected familiarity with literary by-ways consequently displayed, remarks to a colleague: 'Stalky had dug up something by Aubrey on Tom-a-Bedlams from some unknown source. Aubrey of all people! I'm sure I only alluded to him once or twice.'

These words, natural enough at the beginning of the 1880s, imply an essentially obscure figure; for, although never wholly forgotten, Aubrey was then little known except to those concerned more or less directly with historical research. Even today, among a score of persons familiar with the name of Pepys or Evelyn, scarcely one might remember more of Aubrey than the phrase that so often occurs in footnotes – 'Aubrey says . . .' After his death, the *Miscellanies: A Collection of Hermetic Philosophy*, had kept Aubrey's memory afloat for a century, though in a manner on the whole mischievous to his reputation, since this album of occult phenomena represented the depths of superstition to the rationalism of the next epoch; while disciples of the Romantic Movement conceived its author as 'Old Aubrey', a kind of amiable Rosicrucian, browsing over black-letter among artificial ruins.

Except for the folk-lore contained there, the *Miscellanies*, though often entertaining, have little importance among Aubrey's work, in which the collection of short biographies, usually known as *Aubrey's Brief Lives*, holds by far the highest place. He wrote other things that are of value, but the *Lives* give him a claim to be considered the first English biographer, and set him beside Boswell as an equal – though on the whole very different – master of the biographical art. In accumulating for his *Miscellanies* omens, dreams, and transportations by invisible power, Aubrey, not more credulous than most of his contemporaries, was only more systematic (if the word can be used of a man with so little system) in desiring to codify prodigious tales: but the book explains Dr Johnson's caustic reference to Aubrey* (to whom he was at least

---

* Life of *Roscommon*, in which Johnson, after quoting a passage from Aubrey's *Miscellanies*, remarks: 'The present age is very little inclined to favour any accounts of this kind, nor will the name of Aubrey much recommend it to credit.'

15

indirectly much indebted) in the *Lives of the Poets*. Byron quotes a phrase from it in *A Vision of Judgment*; and Scott a passage in *The Antiquary*.

Kipling's schoolmaster (represented in the story as the omniscient Balliol man of the period) possibly knew the *Miscellanies*, a reprint of which had appeared in 1857; and he had probably read *Letters Written by Eminent Persons in the Seventeenth and Eighteenth Centuries*, published in 1813, which reproduce, not very accurately, many of the *Lives* to which his 'allusions' almost certainly referred. He is unlikely to have been aware of John Britton's *Memoir of John Aubrey*, produced by the Wiltshire Archaeological Society in 1845. If he knew Britton's work, Mr King probably owned connections with that county, and he might have studied the Society's further Aubrey volumes, *The Natural History of Wiltshire*, issued in 1847; and Canon J. E. Jackson's edition of *A Description of the Northern Division of Wilts*, of 1862. These topographical collections could in turn have led him to Aubrey's *Perambulation of Surrey*; and he might even have happened casually, in recent months, on *The Remains of Gentilism and Judaism*, printed from Aubrey's manuscript by the Folklore Society in 1880.

To credit Mr King with knowledge of Aubrey's work as extensive as this, would be to suppose him an Aubrey enthusiast, a standpoint which the expression, 'Aubrey of all people!' seems clearly to repudiate. Indeed, any such specific interest would have been likely to have taken him, before Beetle, to *The Curiosities of Literature*, one of the few general works of the first half of the nineteenth century – apart from some encyclopaedias – in which Aubrey finds a place. There remains the remote possibility that Aubrey's name had cropped up in the course of discussions between boys and masters regarding *John Inglesant*, the popular romance about the Civil Wars and Little Gidding, which had come out in 1881. The author, J. E. Shorthouse, Quaker convert to the Church of England, in order to supply his hero with background, had, without acknowledgment, helped himself from Aubrey's autobiographical notes. Apart, however, from these descriptive labels – borrowings hardly revealed at this date – John Inglesant bears little or no resemblance to John Aubrey, some of the circumstances of whose career it may be convenient to recall.

He was born on 12 March 1626, at a house in North Wiltshire called Easton Pierse, near the village of Kington St Michael, about halfway between Chippenham and Malmesbury. The Aubreys, who justifiably claimed Norman descent, had been of some standing in Wales and the Marches since medieval days, though none of them could be considered in any way eminent until the time of Aubrey's great-grandfather, Dr William Aubrey, LLD, a distinguished legal figure of Queen Elizabeth I's reign. Dr Aubrey made a large fortune, and repurchased his ancestral estate in Brecon. One of his sons married a member of the powerful Danvers family, which seems to account for the Aubreys' Wiltshire association. Richard Aubrey, child of this marriage, became husband of Deborah Lyte, whose forebears (a branch of the Lytes of Lytescary in Somerset) had lived in Wiltshire for two or three generations and owned Easton Pierse. John Aubrey was the eldest child – by fifteen years – of Richard and Deborah Aubrey, who were twenty-two and sixteen, respectively, when their son was born.

Aubrey had a lonely childhood. He used to amuse himself by drawing, or watching workmen on the estate. From his earliest years he showed an intense interest in the past, questioning his grandfather, Isaac Lyte, who had known some of the famous Elizabethans, about Malmesbury Abbey and life before the dissolution of the monasteries. His health was bad (he had nearly died at birth) and he suffered from some slight stutter or impediment in his speech. After a good start at lessons with Mr Latimer, a capable local parson (who many years before had taught the philosopher, Thomas Hobbes, a native of Malmesbury and later Aubrey's lifelong friend), he fell into the hands of indifferent teachers. At about twelve years old he was sent to board at Blandford School, then regarded as the best place of education in the West Country for the sons of gentlemen. Life at Blandford was rough, though Aubrey made some friends, and was the best scholar of his time there.

At home intellectual interests were discouraged. English antiquarianism was scarcely a hundred years old, and such tastes were inexplicable in a child. Aubrey says little about either of his parents. His mother possessed a copy of Bacon's *Essays*, and circumstances suggest that her side of the family was more cultivated than the Aubreys. There was some lack of sympathy between Aubrey and his father, a sick man, harassed by financial and political worries, who had no doubt hoped for a practical son, who might put the family fortunes on a firmer basis. It is not altogether clear why the Aubreys' money affairs were in so unsatisfactory a state. Richard Aubrey had suffered a long minority, during which properties had been left in disrepair; and at some stage in Aubrey's childhood Easton Pierse appears to have been expensively transformed from a Gothic manor house to an Italianate mansion. It is possible that the trade depression of the first quarter of the seventeenth century may have adversely affected their income. Exceptional business ability – certainly not forthcoming – may have been required to cope with changing economic conditions.

In May 1642, when he was seventeen, Aubrey went up to Trinity College, Oxford. Here at last he found friends and a life that appealed to him. His time at Oxford was disturbed by the outbreak of the Civil War, in which the Aubreys took no active part, though Royalist in sympathy. Richard Aubrey had to 'compound' with the parliamentarians for his estate, an additional strain on his resources. During his intermittent Oxford residence, disturbed by smallpox, Aubrey arranged for a drawing to be made of the ruins of Oseney Abbey, which ultimately appeared as one of the plates of Dugdale's *Monasticon*. On account of the unsettled state of the country, Richard Aubrey insisted on his son's return home, where for three years he lived, bored and melancholy. In 1642 he persuaded his father to allow him to become a student of the Middle Temple. Afterwards he regarded these two years in London as the happiest of his life; and it was then that he laid the foundations of his vast acquaintanceship – writers, scientists, artists, courtiers, soldiers, wits, astrologers, parsons, dons, and an army of eccentrics of one kind or another. He was never called to the Bar.

At the end of 1648, his father became so ill that Aubrey had to revisit the country; and, while hunting near Marlborough, he happened upon the prehistoric remains of Avebury. His immediate appreciation of the overwhelming historical interest of the stones (which he supposed to be Druidical) shows that by the age of twenty-three, in grasp of such matters he was far in advance of contemporary – and many subsequent – archaeologists. Meanwhile, in intervals of 'soliciting' his father's business affairs, he was carrying on correspondence about scientific, antiquarian, and occult subjects – the latter mostly in connection with what would now be called poltergeist phenomena. There were marriage projects, of which nothing came; and he fell in love with Mary Wiseman, daughter of a former Groom of the Privy Chamber to Charles I. Little is known of this love affair, except that it disturbed Aubrey for at least five or six years, and the girl seems to have died soon after marrying a Wiltshire neighbour.

In October 1652, Richard Aubrey died. He left his son property in Wiltshire, Hereford, Brecon, and Monmouth. There was £500 to be paid to each of the younger sons – William and Tom – and debts amounting to £1,800. Aubrey was immediately plunged into a morass of lawsuits and financial embarrassment (he was in any case eighteenth name in his great-grandfather's entail, which brought him into the Chancery Courts), from which he finally emerged with the loss of all but a few shreds of his fortune, which should have reached the then substantial income of £700 a year. There seems no evidence to suggest that Aubrey was particularly extravagant, though he was generous and easy-going, and liked to spend money on books and manuscripts. For a time he lived on at Broad Chalke, avoiding creditors, and working on notebooks he had begun to keep of 'philosophical and antiquarian remarques'. He used to visit Wilton and other houses in the neighbour-hood where good company was often to be met. His mother (as she appears to have done also on an earlier occasion) dissuaded him from taking a trip to Italy; and in later life for some reason Aubrey regarded the abandonment of this projected tour as a turning point in his career, the 'procatractique cause' of his ruin. Soon after this he was involved with some woman at the cost of contracting venereal disease, a connection he may have intended to break by leaving England for a time, though there seems no reason to suppose that the infection was serious. This was in 1657. In the same year he hoped to marry a young heiress, Katherine Ryves, a friend of his family, with a portion of more than £2,000. She died suddenly, leaving him £350 in her will.

During the Commonwealth, several of Aubrey's friends were working against the Cromwellian dictatorship; but, rather to his regret, he could remember little of their intrigues to record when those days were over. He became a member of the republican Harrington's 'Rota Club', the politico-philosophical debates of which at Miles's Coffee House he used to enjoy enormously. In 1659–60 at a meeting of Wiltshire gentlemen at Devizes to choose the Knights of the Shire it was decided that a history of their county should be compiled, Aubrey agreeing to write the section dealing with the Northern Division. By the time of the Restoration, he was established as one of the *virtuosi* – a group who had to endure some ridicule – and, in 1662, was elected a Fellow of the newly formed Royal Society, soon to possess about 250 members, including an astonishing number of famous men. Dryden, Wren, and Hooke were nominated at the same time as Aubrey, who was brought in contact with the King by his membership; and at the royal command, he showed Avebury to Charles II.

Aubrey visited Ireland, and, some years later, France. Business worries continued, and an episode now took place which caused his final *débâcle*. This was his entanglement with Joan Sumner, sister of a Wiltshire clothier, a woman of about thirty with money of her own and a taste for litigation. To Joan Sumner Aubrey became engaged. The series of lawsuits with her in which he was consequently involved turned on the question of the settlement, as a jointure, of Easton Pierse, free of encumbrance. She herself was to bring £2,000 as marriage portion – some of which was, in fact, to be used to pay off the existing Easton Pierse mortgage. These negotiations are obscure, and Aubrey may well have been confused and dilatory. Joan Sumner's dealings, however, leave an impression of deliberate dishonesty, and the Bill-Books record other cases of questionable complexion in which she was plaintiff. It seems possible that she was also the tool of various evilly-disposed persons who hoped to accelerate Aubrey's bankruptcy, and divide his property among themselves. After three years of legal battles, Aubrey declared himself still prepared to take Joan Sumner to wife, if an agreement could be reached – perhaps a necessary legal fiction. In the end he seems to have won his case, but not before he had had to undergo arrest, and an unconscionable amount of wear and tear.

This affair ruined Aubrey financially. He sold Easton Pierse in 1671 (in the same year Joan Sumner married a Somerset gentleman, dying, presumably in childbirth, nine months later) and, although he retained some interest in Broad Chalke until the end of his life, the property was certainly mortgaged to the hilt. 'I was in as much affliction as mortall could bee, and never quiett till all was gone.' He even discussed, with the head of a Jesuit institution in Belgium, the prospect of entering the cloister. Loss of his money freed him of many worldly worries, but did not relieve him of the necessity of earning a living. Friends came forward: Nicholas Tufton, Earl of Thanet, was helpful in his pompous way; Edmund Wyld, a rich eccentric, formerly Member of the Long Parliament, who owned several houses, was always well disposed – partly on account of the fondness of his mistress, Jane Smyth, for Aubrey; Sir Christopher Wren did what he could; Sir James Long and his wife used to send presents, and have Aubrey to stay. There were numerous others who gave their help.

Some urged emigration to America, or the Antilles; Holy Orders seemed the obvious solution to many. There was the Navy Office (where he might have become the colleague of Pepys) and – as Aubrey himself observed – there were 'peaceable places among soldiers'. Secretarial posts sometimes hovered near his grasp. The fact was that he was unwilling to take a job; he had plenty to engage him in his own work. In 1673 he acted as deputy to the King's Cosmographer, and composed his *Perambulation of Surrey*, but found himself out of pocket over this employment. All the time he was attempting to avoid duns and arrest. He worked hard at his notes on Avebury and Stonehenge (which grew into his *Monumenta Britannica*), and he wrote two comedies for his friend Shadwell. One of these is lost: the other, a fragment called *The Country Revel*, contains scraps of amusing dialogue, satirizing rural life. However, there was more absorbing work on hand, to understand the development of which it is necessary to return to August 1667, when, with far-reaching consequences, Aubrey had first sought out Anthony Wood.

In spite of having been at Trinity with Wood's younger brother, Aubrey had never met the famous antiquary himself, although he must have known for some time of Wood's activities, which were by then publicly recognized. This strange and, in many ways, disagreeable man, after an unsatisfactory academic career at Merton College, had defeated efforts on the part of relations to make him take up a profession. His fairly well-to-do family hired out a tennis-court, let rooms, and possessed other business interests in Oxford, where Wood lived in their house, devoting himself to records of the past – notably the editing of an earlier archaeologist's survey of the City and University of Oxford. Aubrey was about six years older than Wood. Their friendship is interesting, not only on account of its literary consequences, but also as a study of human relationship. Wood cuts so poor a figure in the course of their alliance that it is easy to overlook his quite unusual gifts; but unless his good points are recognized, the moving nature of their final quarrel cannot be properly appreciated. Wood had a passionate love of antiquity, enormous energy, a real understanding of the Middle Ages, and considerable aesthetic appreciation: at the same time he was egotistical, cantankerous, ungrateful, and consumed with envy. His journal and correspondence show him as a superlatively prolific but at times singularly unhandy writer.

Wood's record – he used to touch up his diary at a later date – of Aubrey's first visit speaks of 'a shiftless person, roving, and magotie-headed, and sometimes little better than crazed', and complains of Aubrey's 'foleries and misinformations' which sometimes guided Wood himself 'into the paths of errour'. There is evidence that he was in fact glad enough, even in the early stages, to have the help that Aubrey offered. When, in 1669, the University Press accepted Wood's treatise, a development took place which made this help invaluable; for Dr Fell, the formidable Dean of Christ Church, in whose hands the matter lay, suggested that biographies of writers and bishops educated at Oxford should be added to this volume. Aubrey's wide acquaintance in London and the country, his innumerable relations, his membership of the Royal Society, his knowledge of history, his love of gossip, and – above all – his genius for the apt phrase, made him the ideal collaborator for an industrious recluse, awkward at expressing himself on paper, and almost universally unpopular. This was the foundation of the *Athenae Oxonienses*. Aubrey, who had already toyed with biography in the form of a projected life of Hobbes, now settled down to twenty-five years of meetings and correspondence with Wood; and to the work which was to be his contribution to history.

Wood had many tussles with Dr Fell, powerfully placed for inter-ference, and a worthy rival in irascibility. Aubrey's domestic worries continued, but he was delighted with his work on the *Lives*, sometimes interrupted by the effects of wine and late hours, an inevitable adjunct of an existence spent in friends' houses. The manuscript notebooks passed backwards and forwards between Aubrey and Wood, and Aubrey's letters were also full of information for the *Athenae*. In 1684 he also completed his essay on schools, *The Idea of the Education of a Young Gentleman*. Meanwhile, as years went by, Aubrey often showed concern in his letters at the political situation. Although little interested in affairs of State, and infinitely tolerant in matters of religion, Aubrey sometimes found himself placed in positions that caused him anxiety. Thus, he managed to be staying with a wealthy Roman Catholic at the time of the 'Popish Plot', and to be visiting the West Country, a year or two later, at the moment of Monmouth's rebellion. The Bishops wanted to burn his old friend Hobbes for an atheist, while other cronies, like Ned Bagshaw, were imprisoned for dissenting. More serious still, Wood was on all sides believed to be in secret a Roman Catholic, and Aubrey, increasingly preoccupied as he grew older with the post-humous fate of his writings, feared that Wood's papers – and his own in Wood's keeping – might be stolen or destroyed by government agents or anti-papistical mobs.

Ashmole's new museum at Oxford seemed to offer a suitable repository for Aubrey's manuscripts. Wood, whom age and bad-health made no easier to handle, showed unwillingness to disgorge what he held. He was deaf as well as suffering from noises in the head, and his peevishness and persecution-mania were more than ever in evidence. Aubrey – whose uncompleted *Life of Hobbes* Wood had made difficulties about restoring as early as 1675 – he treated in the most peremptory manner. After some discord between them, Aubrey's papers seem to have reached the Ashmolean about the beginning of 1689. Lawsuits were again breaking out in a most unhappy dispute with Aubrey's brother William (his other brother, Tom, had died a few years before) over whatever rights survived in Broad Chalke. This was apparently the outcome of the death of their mother in 1686. Aubrey, without informing his brother, seems to have pledged the remaining property in return for an annuity, an arrangement much on his conscience. Although William Aubrey, a land-agent and militia officer in Wiltshire, does not appear to have shown any great good sense in his dealings (after his brother's death, he lost the second volume of the *Wiltshire Collections*), this is the one episode in which Aubrey seems, under stress, to have behaved with less than his usual generosity.

All this time he was moving about among different friends, staying at various taverns in London, or with Robert Hooke at the Royal Society's rooms – in secret, to avoid arrest for debt. He still worked on the Wiltshire and Surrey topographical manuscripts, as well as on the *Lives*, and compiled *An Interpretation of Villare Anglicanum* – a list of English place-names which had 'escaped the fury of the Saxon Conquest'. Voluminous correspondence continued: with John Ray, the naturalist; Edward Lhwyd, Keeper of the Ashmolean; Thomas Tanner, a Wiltshire antiquary, who later became a bishop and who added material to Aubrey's notes on the county; and also with many others.

The first volume of Wood's *Athenae Oxonienses* was published in 1691; the second, a year later. Both created a stir, not only on account of the information communicated by them about the living and the dead, but equally because of the tendentious wording employed by Wood, who often went out of his way to cause vexation. In his biography, for example, of David Jenkins, a Cavalier Welsh judge, Wood had repeated a story, supplied by Aubrey, to the effect that Jenkins might have obtained preferment 'would he have given money to the then Lord Chancellor' – Edward Hyde, First Earl of Clarendon. On account of this, at the instance of Clarendon's son, the second earl, Wood was cited to appear in the Court of the Vice-Chancellor of the University to answer a charge of *scandalum magnatum*.

The affair of the libel was widely discussed, and Lord Abingdon, a patron and distant connection of Aubrey's, teased him by pretending that Wood had entangled Aubrey in his own predicament. Wood did not stoop to that meanness, but, in his fright, he destroyed some forty-odd pages from Aubrey's manuscript of the *Lives*; and, although Aubrey's nineteenth-century editor, Andrew Clark, considered that in one way or another all the missing material was eventually incorporated into the *Athenae*, there is no way of being certain of this. There appear to have been 'Lives' of James I and of the Duke of Monmouth, for example, in the loss of which one sadly regret's Aubrey's personal mode of expression. It can be said in Wood's defence that he was, in the first instance, editor of whatever was sent him by Aubrey, who, according to the ideas of the age, sometimes undoubtedly played with fire. On the other hand, Aubrey had shown his own pride in the *Lives* in many letters to Wood. His surprise, indignation, and grief at the mutilation show how confident he had been of Wood's appreciation of this. They continued to see each other after this episode, but friendship in the old sense was gone for ever.

When brought before the court, Wood made the technical defence that there was no proof of his having written the culpable passages. Bribery, in fact, had been one of the charges officially alleged against Clarendon on his dismissal. Wood probably felt that there would be little use in pleading justification; and, even at the present day, formal assertion of corruption on the part of some public figure, recently deceased, however notoriously venal, would be likely to involve the accuser in much unpleasantness. Wood was found guilty, fined, and expelled the University. His designation of Aubrey as 'magotie-headed' no doubt dates from this period. In 1695 he was allowed to return to Oxford; and he died in the same year.

Aubrey, too, had been in his own words 'surprized by age'. For some years his health had been deteriorating, and he suffered attacks of giddiness and fever, although in 1692 he had survived an assault by thieves and fifteen wounds in his head. In 1694 there was a fit of apoplexy. He continued to get through a remarkable amount of work, considering his circumstances, and the *Miscellanies*, the only one of his books published in his lifetime, appeared in 1696. It was perhaps a repetition of the apoplectic fit that caused his death in his seventy-second year – by tradition, on his way to stay at Draycot in Wiltshire with his old friend, the widow of Sir James Long. He was buried on 7 June 1697, in the church of St Mary Magdalene, Oxford.

The outline of Aubrey's career given here does the barest justice to his intelligence, modesty, friendliness – and good sense where anyone but himself was concerned. His own writing is the best index to his character. He found difficulty in sustaining narrative – the summarized history of England at the beginning of this selection is an example of one of his longer pieces – but his style is inimitable. Most of what is now reproduced was only intended to be unsifted material, scored in the original with '*quaere*' or 'from so-and-so' to show Aubrey's own uncertainty. When reporting first-hand, he sometimes confuses dates, but his good faith can be relied upon absolutely. He is notably fair to political opponents, or to persons who had quarrelled with himself or his friends – Dr John Wallis, for example. He makes some mistakes, certainly – such as the note that Ben Jonson was 'a Warwyckshire man', and that he killed Marlowe, the sources of both erroneous statements being supplied in the manuscript. There is, of course, no means of checking the enormous amount of word-of-mouth tradition which he passes on, and of which so much seems to bear the stamp of truth.

The greater or lesser degree of his historical accuracy is perhaps not the main consideration. There is, however, a point regarding Aubrey's stories that should be emphasized. Aubrey's peculiar gift of writing conveys the flavour of his subject so powerfully that his anecdotes have been used a little recklessly by some historians. When these anecdotes are diluted with extraneous elements they are indeed capable of giving a bias, far less admissible than when Aubrey himself mistakes a name or a date. One example will be sufficient. In *Elizabeth and Essex*, Lytton Strachey writes of Francis Bacon: 'an old man, disgraced, shattered, alone, on Highgate Hill, stuffing a dead fowl with snow'. The story of stuffing the hen with snow is Aubrey's, and may be read here. Bacon was certainly an old man at the time of the incident; he was 'disgraced'; he may have been 'shattered'; no doubt at times he was 'alone'; but Aubrey's story of stuffing the fowl on Highgate Hill shows Bacon, accompanied by the King's Physician, conducting a serious experiment to test the preservative properties of snow; and, on becoming indisposed, finding accommodation in the house of the Earl of Arundel. If Aubrey's story suggests anything, it is that Bacon's intellectual faculties were anything but 'shattered' and that he was not 'alone'. This is a trifling instance, though it illustrates how a fragment of a 'Life', combined with juxtaposition of epithets, may be used to convey an oblique hint; a method, incidentally, never employed by Aubrey himself.

Aubrey, without the least conceit, possessed an exceptional sense of his own existence as part of history; and it is perhaps appropriate that he should have been subjected to history's mechanical processes in a marked degree. For a long time he was not much thought of, partly on account of his deprecatory attitude towards himself. Humility is a rare quality. Those who possess it sometimes encounter neglect in life and run some risk of oblivion after death; but in the end history grinds exceeding small. Aubrey's *Lives* are his final monument; and they hand down as striking a record of Englishmen and English ways as has ever been written.

1949
Aubrey's Brief Lives, Cresset Press

I I

As the founder of British field archaeology, which he has every claim to be called, Aubrey is insufficiently known, because his great work, the *Monumenta Britannica*, has hitherto been available only to those who visited the Bodleian Library at Oxford with the express object of studying its manuscript. Even then (I speak from experience) they were confronted with a formidable task.

The first point that should be made about this magnificent facsimile copy of Aubrey's 'Miscellanie of British Antiquities' – to use the subtitle of his pioneer archaeological study, which took the best part of thirty years to assemble – is that here is no mere 'fine book' or 'collector's item'. To make a facsimile with printed transcript on the opposite page (or sometimes set in the appropriate position on the actual facsimile page) is literally the only practical method of dealing with Aubrey's jigsaw of notes, not one of which should be missed.

John Fowles (curator of the Lyme Regis museum as well as novelist) and Rodney Legg (editor of the *Dorset County Magazine* and writer about the Cerne Abbas Giant), are to be congratulated on presenting historians and archaeologists with a real prize.

Aubrey's interest in archaeology, even as a hobby scarcely at all known in that era, began as an undergraduate. Later, as a young man out hunting, he came on the prehistoric temple of Avebury (like Stonehenge described in Part One of this volume) and at once recognized the importance of the Stones, which he supposed to be Druidical: that was a perfectly reasonable guess at the period, when Stonehenge itself was generally thought to be Danish.

Part Two of the present volume deals with camps, Roman towns, walls, and the like, more than 1,000 items in all. Two additional parts of the *Monumenta Britannica* remain.

The advantage of having a facsimile of what Aubrey brought together is that his own drawings (by no means bad) are included, together with letters from correspondents (including the address on the outside, often of interest), prints and pages from contemporary books that have been added by him as having bearing on the subject.

There are also all the relations, friends, persons met by chance during investigations, who make up so essential a part of the Aubrey canon. His life was spent in such an appalling confusion of lawsuits and flights from creditors, losing all his money and existing somehow on the goodwill of patrons and friends, that it is extraordinary how much work he managed to get through:

At Sunbery I saw horses ford this river [Thames] very well . . . Here are some of the 'sharp stakes' [mentioned by Caesar] to this very day, three of them are yet visible on a clear day when the water is low, avowed to me by Dr Peacock minister here, and several of his neighbours. And this summer [1668] the Lord Mayor's water-bailie took up one of the stakes because it hindered barges and was like to split them . . . Venerable Bede sayeth these stakes were to be seen in his day (which was at least 500 years after they were first there) and fishermen still avoid to cast their nets there, for they say something stays them.

In addition to other difficulties was the indifference of most people to such researches as Aubrey's:

At the west end of Cranbourne Chase (anciently belonging to Mortimer Earl of March) on Hambledon Hill is a camp . . . Old Captain Rivers of Ranston told me that he once knew Roman coins digged or ploughed up on the top of Hambledon Hill, which he gave away, and forgot what Emperors' inscription they had.

It would be nice to think that Old Captain Rivers was at least a collateral ancestor of the great archaeologist Gen. Pitt-Rivers, who also lived in Cranborne Chase and excavated the Roman remains there, but the likelihood seems somewhat remote.

'I will grant that the Romans had their camp at Wimborne,' wrote Aubrey, 'which is a place conveniently well sited for aquation [water transport]; to which the Romans had always a main regard.' This supposition of Aubrey's was confirmed in the 1960s with extensive Roman discoveries at Wimborne.

Aubrey's note about Caerphilly Castle in Glamorganshire is a little hard to believe. But, if not Roman, what were the busts? He wrote:

It is greater than any castle that I have seen in England, except Windsor Castle. No History reaches it. It is a most stately Ruine; and true Roman Architecture; and there doe yet [1656] remain in the Hall several Busts, *scilicet* Roman heads and bodies to the waist in the Roman habit.

Was it Renaissance sculpture, but, if so, how did it get to Caerphilly?

In Winchester Cathedral, so he tells us: 'At the beginning of the late Civil War, the soldiers opened the marble coffin of King William Rufus, which lies in the choir here: they found on his thumb a ring of gold which – Wallop of – in Hampshire (the chief of the family and then a Parliament man) bought of a soldier . . . the family have it still.'

The editors rather oddly refer to Garter King of Arms as 'the office of an order of chivalry', when it simply means here the chief herald of the College of Arms. A reader who knows what 'Garter' does probably also knows he is officer of an order of chivalry, but not vice versa. It is by no means certain that Sir Thomas Malory, author of *Le Morte D'Arthur*, was the man imprisoned in Newgate. William Matthews's *The Ill-Framed Knight* (1966) makes a good case for another Sir Thomas Malory, who may have been prisoner-of-war in France: a question Aubrey himself would have loved. These are small criticisms of a noble work.

1980
Daily Telegraph

III

The first facsimile volume of John Aubrey's *Monumenta Britannica* dealt among other things with Stone Circles, Camps, Castles, Roman Towns, and all sorts of archaeological odds and ends, notably giving Aubrey's views on Stonehenge.

Like all his writings it owed a great deal of the interest to the author's incidental comments. This second volume treats of Barrows, Urns, Sepulchres, Ditches, Highways, Roman Pavements, Coins, Embanking and Drainage. As with its predecessor much of the enjoyment comes from material that is sometimes only marginally relevant. Even so – and in spite of the fact that Aubrey was working on and off on this particular collection of information most of his life – it is astonishing how much useful archaeological data he put on to paper for the first time, all quite new.

John Fowles provides an Introduction intended in the first instance for American readers not already familiar with Aubrey's name. I think Fowles does not go too far in speaking of Aubrey as a genius, not least in mastery of poetic prose, even in a day when an ordinary country gentleman or his wife will bowl one over with the beauty of a chance phrase in a letter. One cannot be too grateful to Rodney Legg for begetting the *Monumenta Britannica* project – only to be properly tackled in this manner.

Aubrey was specially interested in where Roman roads ran. One of these was quite near his own house at Broad Chalke in Wiltshire. In Surrey there was:

> Stane Street causeway, 10 yards broad, but in most places seven. It runs from Belingsgate [Billingsgate] to Belinghurst [Billingshurst, near Horsham] and so to Arundel . . . It goes through Dorking churchyard, which they find by the digging of graves. This causeway is eminent in Ockley parish which in winter is extremely wet. Here are no flints nearer than seven miles.
>
> The common people do say it was made by the Devil, that the Devil made one of the causeways for a fair lady, a great man's daughter, whom he should have, if he could make it before the sun rising. And then they made a great fire to make the Devil believe the sun was up; and the Devil then let fall a lapful of stones, which made a hill at one of the causeways . . .
>
> This causeway aforesaid is a yard and a half deep in stones, which they discover by cutting passages to let in water. It runs in an exact straight line. This way is retrieved, or found, by making of ditches between Stansted and Dorking upon the hills.

Aubrey gives one of his characteristic descriptions of Avon Gorge, Clifton Down, near Bristol:

> St Vincent's Rock [where the Observatory now stands] is of prodigious height, I believe much higher than St Nicholas's steeple at Bristow. It is a most romancy place and affords a most pleasant prospect, both from below, as well as from above, from whence you may see the reflection of the rocks and boscage in the water; and tall ships sailing a great way beneath you, and by reflection in the water, topsy turvy, with their keels upwards. So that a bolder orator than I am would say that he did see through to the Antipodes; and ships sailing with their keels upwards.
>
> In short, it is a subject fit for a philosopher, poet or painter. The coy nymph Echo nowhere returns her voice more, the cried commands of the mariners, and the sound of the trumpets.

This sort of book is inevitably to some extent a record of destruction, but even in that Aubrey has his own inimitable way of making notes: 'Mr Anthony Ettrick [an old Oxford friend of Aubrey's who lived in Dorset] had a Roman sword in the castle/camp [Badbury Rings] digging of a burrow found about 1665. It was of the Roman length and fashion, but it is now spoiled and lost. They used it for a cheese-toaster.'

There are a few points that should be put right if there is a question of reprinting: Aubrey's younger brother William is for some reason described in the chart pedigree as 'LLB, Fellow of New College, Oxford'. That was not at all his form. William Aubrey appears to have been a militia officer in Wiltshire, and occasionally helped Aubrey with his researches, although latterly he was furious, probably rather justifiably, with his elder brother's financial muddling.

The 'Mr Sumner' who 'hath writ a "Discourse of Forts, and Ports"', which Aubrey was told about, was certainly not 'John, possibly who became head of Eton College' – the Headmaster being born in 1705, some years after Aubrey's death. He was probably related to Joan Sumner, with whom Aubrey had an unfortunate entanglement. Giraldus Cambrensis (Gerald the Welshman), the chronicler, was Archdeacon of Brecon. He never became a 'Welsh bishop'; that fact was indeed the tragedy of his life.

The editors are to be congratulated on this speedy following up of the first *Monumenta Britannica* volume. There is hardly a corner of the British Isles about which some item is not to be found in Aubrey's researches.

Brief Lives and Other Selected   1982
Writings of John Aubrey, Cresset   *Daily Telegraph*
Press.
*John Aubrey's Monumenta
Britannica, Vol. I*, John
Fowles, ed., annotated by
Rodney Legg, Dorset
Publishing.
*John Aubrey's Monumenta
Britannica; Part Three and Index*,
John Fowles, ed., annotated by
Rodney Legg, Dorset
Publishing.

ENGLISH GENEALOGY

I

The title *English Genealogy* may have a forbidding ring for some people. At best it suggests a highly technical subject; at worst, all kinds of boring, snobbish, possibly bogus matters. Anthony Wagner, Richmond Herald at the College of Arms, by thus naming his book, allows no clue to be revealed of the extraordinary inner richness it contains.

In fact, this title has a double meaning, first the genealogy of the English people, as drawn from known family pedigrees; secondly, the study of such pedigrees, its history, sources and method.

We have here, in short, a social history of England, beginning a few decades before the Norman Conquest, written not only with scholarship and knowledge of the rarest order, but also with ease and fluency of style – by no means a common gift among authors in this particular sphere – together with a great deal of quiet humour.

If genealogy is anything else but simply and solely the truth about ancestors, it is worthless. This may sound an obvious statement, but it is one that has not always been taken to heart. The truth, however, often produces a most surprising picture in this, as in many other branches of study. Commonly thought of as a pursuit best adapted to keeping the various classes of society apart, it is scarcely too much of a paradox to say that the chief lesson of genealogy is to show how extraordinarily close the classes are – and have always been – together. This might almost be called Anthony Wagner's theme.

The story begins, of course, with the military aristocracy who owned their lands by service to the King, heavy cavalrymen expected to turn out in person, the knights as troopers, the barons as officers. Yet even in those days in England there were 'no legal and absolute class barriers', such as existed or developed in other countries.

> It will be seen [writes Wagner] how differences of rank, wealth and education have reacted on one another, each in turn modifying and contributing elements to the whole pattern, while the passionate English interest in social niceties has luxuriated in the consequent complication.

The idea of a 'gentleman' appears to have taken shape about the middle of the fifteenth century. The elasticity of this term, even 500 years ago, is illustrated by a pardon issued to one John Thame in 1459,

30

described as 'husbandman, alias merchant, alias gentleman, alias woolman, alias yeoman'. Similar medieval instances of uncertain social status abound.

Contrary to what the Victorians supposed, a tradesman could be a 'gentleman'. Indeed, Sir John Oglander wrote in 1632, 'It is impossible for a mere country gentleman ever to grow rich or raise a house. He must have some other vocation with his inheritance, as to be a courtier, lawyer, merchant or some other vocation.' Some gentleman had arms; some, Wagner freely admits, did not.

After the Civil Wars and the Revolution of 1688, the great Whig lords were in the saddle, 'whose concept of the social order was that a gulf should yawn between themselves and the mere gentry'. Wagner thinks this may account for the decline of heraldic authority in the eighteenth century, since these magnates 'had little interest in the strict regulation of a privilege – that of bearing arms – which they and the poorest gentry shared'.

In this connection, it is of interest that the peak year at College of Arms for the registering or granting of arms was 1945, which saw the advent of a Labour Government.

The kindred matters dealt with in Wagner's book are so varied that it is possible only to suggest their scope. For example, the grades and professions are considered individually, and also the background of Flemings, Dutch, Germans, Huguenots, Jews and Gypsies who immigrated to England – the last now thought to be wandering tribes of low-caste Indian origin.

Conversely, something is said of places overseas populated by English stock. We hear often enough about the shipments to the West Indies after Monmouth's rebellion; but less of a similar episode, referred to here, Cromwell's disposal of Royalist prisoners virtually as slaves, Barbados rising in population from 20,000 to 30,000 from this source between 1645 and 1650.

Fletcher Christian, the *Bounty* mutineer who found his way to Pitcairn Island with other sailors and some Tahitian women, was, it now appears, descended from Edward I, 'so that it is doubtful whether any British community contains so large a proportion of descendants of our early kings'. However, Wagner, in spite of his generally genial tone, will stand no nonsense where genealogy is concerned. Australians are exhorted to cast away any inhibitions they may feel as to the possibility of discovering a transported ancestor.

> For the genealogist [writes Wagner firmly] a convict ancestor has the outstanding merit that his collision with the law will be the subject of record, so that far more personal information may be available about him than for the average of settlers.

At the end of the volume are several chart pedigrees illustrating improbable family connections. One of these shows a group of individuals allied by marriage, whose grandchildren (all first cousins) were: King James I; Lady Arabella Stuart; the ancestors of, respectively, the Dukes of Norfolk, the Dukes of Kingston, the Dukes of Newcastle and Portland, the Dukes of Devonshire. Finally, the last first cousin is Ferdinando Bainton of Salisbury, Innkeeper, who produced descendants who went to live in New England.

Another of these tables illustrates distant kinsmanship between Samuel Johnson and Lord Chesterfield – although there seems no reason to suppose that, even if the relationship had been known at the time, the Doctor would have been kept waiting less long in his cousin's ante-room. Incidentally, this Johnson–Chesterfield relationship is through the Quaker family of Crowley of Worcestershire. It would be interesting to know if the late Aleister Crowley, magician, was a scion of this stock. His father was a Quaker of Warwickshire.

English Genealogy, Anthony Richard   1960
Wagner, Clarendon Press: OUP.   *Daily Telegraph*

II

These essays by Garter Principal King of Arms mostly deal with the different aspects of 'social mobility' that are illustrated by his own genealogical studies. He points out how much this field has been neglected and misunderstood, and that it is often the only way in which certain historical changes can be properly studied.

Anthony Wagner begins by drawing attention to the amusing paradox that misunderstanding has been connived at by the corresponding views of two opposing factions – these he calls, for want of a better term, the 'conservatives' and the 'revolutionaries'. The former based their views on belief in an unchanging aristocracy, and thought that a 'good thing'; the latter, equally convinced that no one ever altered their social position, found this supposed immutability of the classes unjust to a degree.

The conclusions of a scientific approach to genealogy show this assumption, good or bad, to be entirely wrong. Genealogy teaches the complexity and unexpectedness of society, especially in this country, where impassable social barriers have never existed, and where, incidentally, genealogical researches can be pursued with more effectiveness than anywhere else in the world, owing to our wealth of historical documentation in this field.

It is, of course, undeniable that genealogists have always had a natural desire to make the best of their own family, not to say glorify it, if the latter were at all possible. In consequence there was always a tendency for less successful branches to be quietly forgotten. That did not prevent them from existing, and Wagner is certain that there is scarcely a family, if fully studied, that would not reveal a remarkable variation in social pattern.

One of the essays is devoted to the subject of 'The Recruitment of the English Upper Classes'. Various points are made here, one of which is the law which declared daughters, rather than brothers, to be the heirs of men who died without sons. There is heraldic evidence that marriage with these heiresses considerably added to an infusion of new names.

The old idea that the Wars of the Roses killed off all the old Norman Conquest families was greatly exaggerated, the Conquest families having many of them simply died out. Another erroneous notion (probably arising from Wolsey or Thomas Cromwell being self-made men) was that all those who did well out of the Dissolution of the Monasteries were 'new men'. On the contrary, many of them were already established landowners, and the gradual decay of the monasteries had begun long before Henry VIII's Act.

Wagner considers that an important step in creating a new – and on the whole beneficial – class was the granting of permission to the clergy to marry. Married clergy had, of course, existed throughout the Middle Ages, notwithstanding papal edicts, but (though the Wife of Bath may have prided herself on being an ecclesiastic's daughter) the situation was obviously easier for those concerned when marriage was recognized. Then clergy families produced a solid flow of industry and talent.

English records often make it possible for some of the poorest families to be traced back three or four hundred years. An interesting example of use of names is quoted here, a parish register entry of 3 July 1596: 'Buried, William, servant to Arthur Carew, Esq., commonly called William Carew'; and Pepys mentioned that his servant lad Wareman was often known as 'young Pepys'. Nevertheless, Sir Anthony expresses the view that it often does turn out that families of the same surname are related, sometimes at an immense distance of time.

The points that Wagner makes are illustrated by a selection of pedigrees at the end of the book. For those with the rather dissipated taste of tracing authentic genealogical links far back into antiquity, there are some very remarkable examples going back to the time of Alexander the Great; not less in 'wide', rather than 'long' pedigrees, one of which links Shakespeare with Queen Elizabeth.

Wagner believes that a fluid society has advantages over an imposed egalitarian one; and, indeed, examples of the latter are not easy to find in which such equality that exists is not imposed by a class of officials 'more equal' than anyone else. He thinks it true that the English have always had something of a tendency for social hair-splitting among themselves, and – if a date must be given when they began to develop that – he would choose the Norman Conquest.

Pedigree and Progress: Essays in the Genealogical Interpretation of History, Anthony Wagner, Phillimore.

1975
Daily Telegraph

THE HOUSE OF LORDS

I

This book should be compulsory reading for everyone, in or out of Parliament, who ventures to hold forth on what is to be done about the contemporary House of Lords. It is, in any case, a prodigious piece of scholarship and exposition; clear, to the point, unprejudiced, laced with the occasional shaft of wit.

Enoch Powell's political activities need no introduction, but it should perhaps be recalled that, as well as being a writer on English history, he is author of works on Herodotus, Thucydides and Greek papyri. He is also a poet. To add good measure to this study, his collaborator, Keith Wallis, is an authority on fifteenth-century baronies.

'I first began to concern myself with the history of the House of Lords in 1947–48,' writes Powell, 'in the course of the reform controversy which preceded the passage of the Iron and Steel Act, 1949.' This interest naturally took him back to the Saxon Witenagemot, from which the present House of Lords has some claim to derive.

The point of the story, an absorbing one, is how a slapdash council of Saxon, then Norman, territorial magnates gradually evolved into a governing body, limited in number and hereditary in composition. In the early stages, due to all kinds of reasons, not least the violence of an age that often brought early death, such assemblies were merely a varied collection of the most powerful men of the moment.

In due course, the status of those who attended consistently hardened into a 'dignity' that gave certain powers of government, based first on the ownership of land, then adjusting to more contemporary forms of power, the hereditary principle eventually merging with 'life-peerages'. The remarkable survival of the system is illustrated by the fact, not to be forgotten when reading about the House's early history, that just about half the titles of the present House of Lords were created after 1900.

Enoch Powell emphasizes that only an examination of the historical facts gives a true picture. The generalizations of constitutional historians are often entirely misleading. There is no easy way out. You must look at what actually happened to given individuals. Accordingly, with such a vast amount of material before him, the reviewer can only pick out a few points to indicate the scope and richness of the book.

The first 'peers' to be created were earls, and very few of them. Barons – of whom in the present House of Lords there are now about a third more than all the rest of the peers put together – were, in the first instance, no more than 'men', in the feudal sense, who took an oath of fealty. Indeed, the name derives from Latin forms of 'dunce' or 'servant'.

The term 'barony' as an extent of land took a meaning, if an inexact one, which could later be held to give the owner status, but the first king of England to 'create' a baron was Richard II, in 1387. He did it with fatal results to himself. Incidentally, one notices here what enormous developments took place in Richard II's reign, and the early 1400s, in the direction of a less crude approach to life and government. Those involved in public affairs might be just as violent, themselves always running the risk of death, but language and forms became far more elaborate and precise.

No doubt this tendency had been growing for a long time, and one notes the ever-increasing appeals made to history, even if the history leant rather heavily on myth. For example, Geoffrey of Monmouth – the chronicler, whatever his faults, to whom we chiefly owe, among other things, King Arthur and King Lear – turns up as a relatively important figure, Bishop of St Asaph, in 1152. Nearly 200 years later, in 1337, we find Edward III creating his son Duke of Cornwall, 'over which in past ages, dukes had successively presided'. This was certainly because of the familiarity of the King, or at least his advisers, with Geoffrey of Monmouth's book. Edward, no doubt for the same reason, also had his own 'Round Table'.

The authors show, what is easily forgotten, how the medieval House of Lords was very largely and essentially an ecclesiastical affair. William the Conqueror had taken a firm line with the Pope from the beginning, removing a bishop he considered unsatisfactory. Much of the story consists in the adjustment of lay and ecclesiastical interests, not always harmonious. Abbots attended the earlier parliaments, but in due course dropped out. One of the aspects of the history of the 'House of Lords', as it took shape, is the balance between attendance there being an undesired burden, and determination to attend in order to force some issue.

The first man who was made an earl and did not take the title from a county or county town was Roger Mortimer, earl of March in 1328. This is interesting because although he may have had in mind his descent from the ancient counts of La Marche in France, there would also be the obvious implication of his being a great landowner on the borders of England and Wales – the Welsh March. If one excepts certain doubtful examples from the fourteenth century and before, Thomas Cromwell, to whom so much of the country's basic administration is owed, was probably the first man of genuinely humble origins to be made a peer. His father had been a blacksmith and innkeeper. The rest of Henry VIII's 'new men' tended to be from established, if obscure, families.

Extraordinary as it may seem, the origins and growth of the House of Lords have never before been made the subject of a single study.

The House of Lords in the Middle   1968
Ages: A History of the English   *Daily Telegraph*
House of Lords to 1540, J. Enoch
Powell   and   Keith   Wallis,
Weidenfeld & Nicolson.

II

In 1826 John Burke, then about forty, first produced the *Peerage* associated with his name. He was by no means the first editor of a work of this sort; but alphabetical arrangement, the manner in which pedigrees were set out and interspersion of baronets among peers gave his record some of its novel features. This last commixture was a convenient, though questionable, innovation, because, the Baronetage being something quite other than the Peerage, there is much to be said for its confinement to a separate portion of the book. Baronets well deserve examination on their own account. Here there is space to say no more of them than to remark that the established peers – with their many poets of distinction – have only Byron and Coleridge among the heavy-weights to pit against Dryden, Shelley and Swinburne from Baronetage families: and, although the former can play Fielding as a novelist, the latter have Congreve (the title became extinct in 1941) as a playwright.

Talent shown before and after conferment of title on a family might be worth study; and an examination of Burke's *Peerage* (edited by L. G. Pine), after a lapse of ten years, suggests almost unlimited speculation on social history and changing habits of the country; and, indeed, on human behaviour generally. One of the first reflections that occur to the mind is the manner in which power readjusts itself, landed-interest giving place to company-directing (Vicary Gibbs lists 167 peers as company directors so far back as 1896); company directors yielding in turn to high-salaried executives, often in official or quasi-official appointments; and – turning over Burke's pages – the reader muses on the ever-widening gap between the popular concept of a peer and the existing reality.

This time-lag in public consciousness may be noted in novels or plays, where peers, nothing like so numerous as in the nineteenth century, still crop up fairly frequently; and where a lord, silly or sinister, handsome or grotesque, is rarely allowed to strike a balance between extremes of conduct. Ancient lineage is almost always implied, and even when an ancestral castle has been sold its former owner is

inclined to talk and act oddly. Rare indeed in literature are noblemen
like Belloc's Lord Heygate:

> The sort of Peer who well might pass
> For someone of the Middle Class.

Burke supplies information calculated to correct undisciplined imagery
on this subject and to clear the mind regarding an order of society
which even the best of writers sometimes find difficulty in approaching
soberly.

The main elements of the Upper House (summarized in an account
slightly shortened from that in earlier editions) may be briefly recalled.
Baronies by writ, vaguely associated with the *barones majores* of Magna
Carta, represent a conception gradually developed by legal judgments
from the fifteenth century, under which the individual summons of a
man to one of the early Parliaments was held to vest in him a peerage
inheritable by heirs general in perpetuity. Under this doctrine, which is
now acknowledged to be an historical fiction, peerages still subsisting
enjoy 'precedence' as high as 1265; and in this sense baronies by writ
may be regarded as the oldest surviving creations. As the dignity
became more personal, gradually moving away from the implications
of feudal service in the fifteenth century, creations were by Letters
Patent, the first in 1387. Under the Act of Union in 1707 no further
peerages of England or of Scotland could be created, peerages of Great
Britain coming into being, henceforward the Scottish peers electing
sixteen of their number to sit in the House of Lords.

In Ireland, peerages, with a few exceptions, were created by charter
or patent, rare before 1500. The Act of Union in 1801 laid down that
there should be twenty-eight Representative Peers of Ireland (of whom
only seven now remain) and the Irish Free State Act of 1922 abolished
the Office of the Crown and Hanaper, so that no machinery now exists
for further elections. After the Union, peerages were normally of the
United Kingdom, though some peers of Ireland were created, having
no connection with Ireland and taking their titles from places in
England, by a legal fiction no English county being mentioned in the
patent.

Since 1876 certain judges – at present less than a dozen – have been
made life peers. There are twenty-six Spiritual Lords and four Royal
Dukes. This makes in all about 930 holders of hereditary peerages, of
whom about 100 do not possess a seat in the House. The analysis does
not do justice to the immense intricacies of peerage history and
practice, but it gives some idea of the round figures. About two dozen
peers are minors (and eighty octogenarians), about 840 members,
including bishops, having a seat in the Chamber.

When such records as Burke's are surveyed, peerages dating from the Middle Ages, whose annals have often become part of the nation's history, are, naturally, those accustomed to receive most attention. Today they represent a small minority in the House of Lords. Only about forty peerages (apart from creations submerged in those of higher rank) are earlier in date than 1500. More than half of these are baronies by writ, descending in the female line to heirs-general; the majority of the twenty-four peeresses in their own right (who do not possess a seat) belong to this category.

At one time or another most of these ancient baronies have been in abeyance, sometimes for centuries, their lands long alienated from the heirs. G. E. C., expressing the disapproval felt by many eminent peerage authorities for the doctrine that allowed such revivals, speculated on the future in the words of Sir Guy le Scroope in the Ingoldsby legend:

> What can delay
> De Vaux and De Saye?
> . . . .
>
> And De Nokes and De Styles and Lord Marmaduke Grey,
> And De Roe?
> And De Doe? –
> Poynings and Vavasour? – where be they?
> Fitz-Walter, Fitz-Osbert, Fitz-Hugh, and Fitz-John,
> And the Mandervilles, *père et filz* (father and son)?

Recommendations of select committees, not to mention changes in the social structure, make it unlikely that the absentees of the poem will now appear in the House of Lords, any more than they appeared at the party. Indeed, some may fear promise of new arrivals more comparable to those who substituted for Sir Guy's guests. Barham's comic list of names parodies – probably intentionally – those muster-rolls in the *Poly-Olbion*, token even in Jacobean times of the passing of the great medieval houses. The account of the battle of Evesham is characteristic:

> Young *Humphrey Bohun* still, doth with great *Le'ster* goe,
> Who for his Countries cause becomes his father's foe.
> *Fitz-John, Gray, Spencer, Strange, Rosse, Segrave, Vessey, Gifford,*
> *Wake, Lucy Vipount, Vaux, Clare, Marmion, Hastings, Clifford.*
> . . . .
>
> Amongst the slaughtered men that there lay heap'd on pyles:
> *Bohuns* and *Beauchamps* were, *Basets* and *Manderviles*;
> *Segraves* and *Saint-Johns* seeke, upon the end of all,
> To give those of their name their Christian buriall.

A few traces still remain, certainly, of the names invoked by Drayton, though they have undergone much chopping and changing of descent. Norfolk, Shrewsbury, Derby, for example, represent in the male line a distant period; but on the whole even the more venerable surviving creations date from the sixteenth and seventeenth centuries: though many of these are, of course, lineally connected, often through heiresses, with the more ancient Peerage.

The Ingoldsby Legends, with their satirical though fervent enthusiasm for the gods of the Gothic Revival, are a reminder that *Burke*, too, was a child of this epoch in its later stage. The Red Book has been excoriated for the inaccuracy and pretensions of its pedigrees. 'You should study the *Peerage*, Gerald . . .,' says Lord Illingworth (from whom, incidentally, innumerable stage peers descend) in *A Woman of No Importance*. 'It is the best thing in fiction that the English have ever done.' If Wilde was thinking of Burke's volume, he should have remembered that he was speaking of the compendium of a fellow Irishman; but, be that as it may, sarcasm was often amply justified; the mythology being additionally deplorable since Royal Arms and Garter on the cover seem to claim some, at least semi-official, status. The best that can be said in apology is that the Gothic Revival drew attention to much historical material in due course put to good use by exponents of a more critical attitude towards history. A certain amount of nonsense was the almost inevitable accompaniment of sudden widespread interest in family origins; while another aspect of the Romantic Movement – that which proclaimed all men brothers – set a premium on what might appear evidence supporting a contrary view.

These things do not in any way excuse genealogical excesses (certainly not their prolonged survival), though they may to some extent explain them. It might even be perversely argued that, if an hereditary peerage is to exist at all, it is more consistent for its members to show – even misplaced – anxiety to establish a pedigree than wholly to disregard ancestry. For example, in the present edition, not even the grandfather of the first Earl Lloyd-George of Dwyfor is recorded, though predecessors are surely known at least to the beginning of the nineteenth century; and there are other cases where the reader cannot help feeling that a trifle more historical interest in a distinguished man's forebears might have been shown. The fact that the type has been entirely reset has given the editor opportunity to clear away a great many though not all the imperfections. The Abercorn, Bedford and Fingall pedigrees, to particularize three, still begin with unhistorical or irrelevant material: Stanley of Alderley leaves unfilled the generations between Edward IV and Elizabeth: Broughshane starts off the lineage with a tall story – to put it mildly – for anyone even rudimentally familiar with methods of spelling in the seventeenth century: Monmouth's wife, Anne, Countess of Buccleuch, is rather quaintly stated to have been 'esteemed the greatest heiress and finest woman of her time': and the sixth Lord Falkland is oddly described as having been created Earl by 'the Old Pretender James III'.

However, when all is said and done, *Burke* does supply a vast amount of well-arranged material, and often much trouble has been taken to present this briefly and accurately. If one may take a concrete instance without seeming invidious, Merriman well indicates the course of a family's rise, beginning in the middle of the sixteenth century – weaver, inn-holder, Cromwellian major of horse, two brewers, a cheese-factor, an attorney, and a doctor, grandfather of the present peer. Such an account, considered with collaterals, gives concisely an admirable piece of social history. Many other individual articles would be interesting to discuss if space allowed. It is necessary, however, to return to the subject of dates of creation.

Out of some 520 hereditary baronies (about 480 with seats) some 280 (all with seats) were created since 1900. Add to these creations in the higher ranks (excluding peers promoted in grade) and the number comes to over 350. Very nearly half the number of peerages with seats, therefore – and well over one-third of all peerages – date back, so far as their present titles go, only fifty years. During the previous 100 years about 140 baronies had been created, so that titles later than 1800 easily pass the halfway mark for all peerages and represent about two-thirds of peers with seats. These figures give some indication of how remote from reality is the cartoonist's vision of an assembly whose last practical activities took place at the time of the Crusades.

Two categories notable in the new *Burke* are the dozen or so war commanders raised to the peerage, and the fifty or more creations made to strengthen the present Administration in the Lords. Of the former, Alexander, Douglas, and Portal (of fifteenth-century French descent) derive from Peerage families, and Alanbrooke from the Baronetage: Wavell is of an English family tracing to the sixteenth century, the Field-Marshal's father and grandfather having both been Generals: Cunningham records an undetailed descent from a seventeenth-century Scottish minister: Montgomery, north of Ireland commercial stock, going back to the beginning of the eighteenth century and showing the Field-Marshal to be the grandson of a notable Indian administrator: Mountbatten has its origins, of course, in the German house of Battenberg. Only the briefest details are given regarding Dowding and Tedder.

In the First World War earldoms were granted in cases parallel to those for which viscountcies have recently been given (the Wavell and Mountbatten earldoms being for viceregal services) and it would be interesting to know the reason for this. The public debt was certainly no less, and the difference in 'keeping up' the higher dignity could hardly be a consideration.

Profuse creations for political reasons have been known in the past. All the same, the Labour peers and their families, by no means insignificant in number, make a decidedly interesting addition to the social order of the country. A few of the latest of these creations have not been in time to be included in this volume, but there is already plenty of evidence to show that in general male issue exists to carry on these titles. Their circumstances, for a number of reasons, are undoubtedly somewhat different from peerages of earlier periods and call for a word of comment. In the past public figures without considerable means were inclined to refuse the honour; and comparatively poor men – soldiers and sailors, for example – were normally voted money by Parliament to enable them to live in a manner considered appropriate. This practice has been abandoned in the case of leaders of the Services (though, perhaps rather inconsistently, not in the case of inventors), while political peerages, for obvious reasons – and on both sides of the House of Commons – have tended to fall to those not of the first rank in their party. One may speculate or know the future of these latest peerage families, who might not ineptly be compared to the *noblesse* created by Napoleon. Will there be a tendency in several generations for descendants of Labour peers to identify themselves with an older aristocracy, and by degrees to become absorbed in what has always been something of a family affair? More unlikely things have happened.

Burke's Genealogical and Heraldic 1949
History of the Peerage, Baronetage *Times Literary Supplement*
and Knightage, Privy Council and
Order of Precedence, 99th edn,
Burke's Peerage.

BURKE'S LANDED GENTRY

A characteristically English love of paradox is displayed in preserving the title *Burke's Landed Gentry* into an age when a large proportion even of the heads of families here listed, though they may still live in the country and own a few acres, are certainly no longer 'landed' within the former meaning of the term; while 'gentry', if not entirely outmoded, has become in the contemporary world an awkward word to use indiscriminately. The short answer to any such demur might be made under three heads: first, that a surprising number of families to this day retain their ancient lands, in spite of the upheavals of a thousand years: secondly, that the earlier editions of this work, under cadet branches, equally record persons not themselves 'landed', though stemming from 'landed' stock: thirdly, that in the past, no less than today – though for rather different reasons – argument was far from unknown regarding pretensions to the second qualifications specified. This last extenuation touches, of course, on issues both deep and delicate, at the same time indicating the difficulty of providing any one definition at all satisfactory for the persons to be found in the pages that follow.

If it is agreed then that, with all the ramifications of relationship included, the large majority of the living set down here are not 'landed', it is reasonable to enquire further. Who are these people? It is an interesting question. Is this, for instance, something like a 'Social Register' in the American manner? Decidedly not. Apart from excluding the Peerage, names that would no doubt figure in any such volume are not necessarily found, while others present might not be at all appropriate in that more worldly context.

Are they all rich? Far from it, though some could certainly be so described. Not only are they not all rich, but one would not be surprised to find amongst them, materially speaking, some of the least prosperous of the 'affluent society'. Do they possess long pedigree? Some do; some, on the other hand, do not. Pedigrees of any length are recorded, though only ones which every effort has been made to set out accurately.

Are they all armigerous? Certainly not. Some, indeed, descend from 'disclaimers', persons who deliberately disavowed at the Heraldic Visitations the right to bear arms, marginal cases who did not wish to pay the fees, or preferred not to be bothered with such matters.

43

Anyway, they all reside in this country? Nothing could be further from the case. Australians, New Zealanders, Canadians, South Africans, Americans, are often to be found.

At least they are all of British descent? Not even that is true. Quite a sprinkling of these families originated abroad: France, Germany, the Low Countries, Poland, Greece, India.

No doubt it is possible to exaggerate the complex nature of our own social structure in comparison with that of other countries. In France, for example, the facts, when examined historically, are less logical, systematized, hierarchical than is sometimes supposed.

A book like Stendhal's autobiographical *La Vie de Henri Brulard* shows the family connections, and social pretensions, of a 'bourgeois' French provincial family on the eve of the Revolution, as not so very unlike – however differently handled by the author – those of the same sort of English family described by Jane Austen.

The lower echelons of the French *noblesse* were in many ways indistinguishable from the higher of the *bourgeoisie*, with whom they intermarried. In the far from simple social situation of pre-Revolutionary France it was, among other complications, possible to be 'noble' without a title, to have a title and not be 'noble'. The fact remained that, however blurred the line of demarcation, a *noblesse* existed – as in most other European countries – enjoying privileges derived from the legal fiction that they performed military service in the feudal manner for the monarch in time of war. In other words, it was in principle possible – though the picture is confused and borderline cases seem to have been not uncommon – to say whether or not an individual belonged to the *noblesse*.

Such an arrangement was never true of England. That fact has often been stated before, but must always be borne in mind if the English social system of the past is to be understood. England did not possess a 'caste' society. Whig lords in the eighteenth century may have been relatively successful in creating a gulf between themselves and the 'mere gentry', but even the Peerage did not restrict marriage by any means to its own families. Accordingly, there never grew up here an *haute bourgeoisie*, which in other countries balanced a 'nobility', some-times setting up serious competition in the political and intellectual fields; especially if the 'nobility' allowed themselves to relinquish power and property at the price of marriage only within their own order.

In the English 'landed gentry' are to be found elements of the continental *noblesse* and also its *haute bourgeoisie* – with others, too, peculiar to this country, like the 'yeomen' from whom so many of the families here derive – but the differences remain more remarkable than the similarities; most of all the absence of all rule as regards entering the class that on the Continent would be the *noblesse*.

In England, such a position always rested on 'living like a gentleman'; and, for persons coming up in the world, there can be no doubt at all that individual acceptability among neighbours played an enormous part. This is perhaps why England is so particularly taxed with 'snobbishness', the more exact and definitive rules of other social systems putting less strain on personal behaviour. A patent of nobility was handed out once and for all in most countries, and that was the end of it. There were no heart-burnings about doing, or not doing, the right thing. Again, such a generalization can obviously be carried too far, French noble families, both before and after the Revolution, possessing long memories for dates of ennoblement and *mésalliances*. At the same time, ennoblement had to take place sooner or later. It was the lack of rule in England which caused foreigners to despair, and, if the truth be known, was at times not without its embarrassment even domestically.

'Landed gentry', undefined yet vigorous, was in itself an essentially English development. In Wales, on the other hand, a caste system did exist, the *bonheddig* ('men with pedigrees', estimated at some three-quarters of the population) being in the past the only class who could inherit land.

Welsh law, before Henry VIII's Act of 1536 imposed primogeniture, divided inheritance equally within a family, specifying in detail potentially complicated situations in administering the system. This naturally required carefully kept genealogies for legal processes. These documents disregard everything but birth, so that it is not unknown, in Welsh pedigrees going back to remotest antiquity, to find persons described as 'labourer', 'pedlar', or even 'pauper'. 'Landed gentry' in anything like the English sense of the phrase did not take shape in Wales until the late seventeenth or even eighteenth centuries, although the land itself often remained in the hands of its immemorial owners. Indeed (as Major Francis Jones, Herald Extraordinary for Wales, has pointed out), in 1957 the Lords Lieutenant of three adjacent Welsh counties possessed estates their chieftain-ancestors had owned in the eleventh century.

In Scotland, too, the clan system operated a different machinery, a common surname not necessarily implying a blood relationship, no sharp line existing between peer and chieftain. In *Kidnapped*, Stevenson amusingly illustrates something of what was felt about these things:

'Why, then,' said he, 'what's your name?'
'David Balfour,' said I: and then thinking that a man with so fine a coat must like fine people, I added for the first time, 'of Shaws.'
It never occurred to him to doubt me, for a Highlander is used to see great gentlefolk in great poverty; but as he had no estate of his own, my words nettled a very childish vanity he had.

'My name is Stewart,' he said, drawing himself up, 'Alan Breck, they call me. A King's name is good enough for me, though I bear it plain and have the name of no farm-midden to clap to the hind-end of it.'

However, these widely differing aspects tended to be ignored by Victorian writers, inclined to seek in Great Britain's 'landed gentry' something akin to the continental *noblesse*, even at times going so far as to hint that they were the same thing.

The Press notices quoted in the 1852 edition of *Burke's Landed Gentry* supply some of these contemporary views. The *Examiner*, for example, says:

The landed gentry of England are a more powerful body than its peerage. The office of peerage is hereditary, it is true; but when the strict line of succession terminates, the Crown substitutes a new family. The new peers are selected from the landed gentry, or from successful adventurers in law, commerce, arms, and divinity, who having acquired wealth, contrive to get themselves adopted into the landowning class. In the identification of the peers with the great landowning class lies their strength. As an isolated body they could not exist for a year . . . a mere peerage conveys a very inadequate notion of the position and consequence of the peers.

The tone is characteristic of the period, not least in its insistence that the peerage should not be allowed to get away with too much prestige. The landed gentry, the reviewer implies by his words – so one feels – might live less spectacular lives than the lords – no bad thing perhaps – but they were solid, commendable, unpretentious, their descents by no means shorter than those of the Upper House, their acres possibly even wider.

That the 'landed interest' was politically powerful in the first half of the nineteenth century is, of course, undeniable. At the same time, we should not be impressed by Victorian rhetoric to the extent of misunderstanding what these people were really like. There were other sides to the 'landed gentry' than portentous rivalry with the peerage, since human beings cannot be reduced exclusively to figures plotted on a political or economic graph. For example, if we turn to the novels of Surtees (who occurs, himself in the 1852 *Burke's Landed Gentry, Mr. Sponge's Sporting Tour* being published the following year), we find another sort of material for showing how life was lived by persons of this kind. The scenes of the novel are certainly no less true, and decidedly livelier, than the picture the *Examiner* adumbrates.

To begin with, the Earl of Scamperdale, living in the servants' quarters of his ancestral mansion and dining off beefsteak and batter pudding, is by no means unthinkable today, though he might come under the *Examiner*'s heading of one of those 'mere peerages' which 'convey a very inadequate notion of the peers' position'. Lord Scamperdale is, of course, outside the scope of this article, but the 'landed gentry' who surround him are no less striking than himself in their way of life.

Their variety is unexpected and picturesque. Nothing could be less hidebound or further from the picture of Victorian country life popularly envisaged today. Money is often lacking. Masters of Foxhounds are City tea-brokers, or live in rooms over a chemist's shop: Miss Lucy Glitters, her reputation of the frailest, finds beauty and dash quite sufficient introduction to local society: everyone drinks to their heart's content. In fact the panorama Surtees presents is in many respects crammed with the very circumstances so often lamented now as symptomatic of a world in decay; yet Surtees wrote at a time when the world he describes was at its peak. This point is worth making, simply because it is so often forgotten. No one suggests that vast changes have not taken place since those days, nor that everyone who lived in the country a century or more ago spent their time in the Surtees manner. The picture is a composite one. There were large, thriving estates: there were also small ones; and estates, both large and small, which hardly throve at all. There were 'landed gentry' of the most miscellaneous origins rubbing shoulders with those of antedeluvian standing. All this should be remembered if a sense of proportion is to be maintained.

If we move on a hundred years, some of the statistics from the 1952 edition of *Burke's Landed Gentry* may be of interest in relation to this earlier picture. To estimate the number of living individuals named in the 1852 volume is not easy, because in those days typographical blobs were not yet used to indicate survival. However, their number might be guessed at something like 20,000. A century later, four times that figure – rather less than 80,000 – would probably be near the mark. One hundred consecutive pages, taken at random and analysed in a rough-and-ready manner, reveal some 116 families. It is hard to speak with greater precision, owing to changes to name, or because some are branches of the peerage, or another *L.G.* family. However, this approximation should not be far from the mark. From it certain averages may be inferred for the whole volume.

Of these 116 families, thirty-seven (say an average of a third) are described as 'formerly of' their original country seat: the 'seat' itself varying greatly in length of possession and status as a dwelling, the grander houses not always having been owned for the longest series of generations. Seventy-four families (say an average of half) are shown as bearing arms. The inclusion of these arms here, if not an absolute guarantee of registration at the College of Arms, would certainly denote at least 'bearer' standing of the most respectable order.

With regard to pedigrees, some approximation must again be made as to how far a family may be said to go back. Some families, for example, will name two or three persons of their name and residence, who cannot be fitted on to the earliest known generation, although obviously earlier members of the same family. For statistical purposes these have been ignored, the dates that follow indicating the century to which the earliest connected ancestor belongs. Following this rule, therefore, one family traces back to the twelfth century, two to the thirteenth, two to the fourteenth, eleven to the fifteenth, eighteen to the sixteenth, thirty-five to the seventeenth, thirty-four to the eighteenth, thirteen to the nineteenth. The documentation of these dates can be regarded as trustworthy. It will be noted 70 per cent record no further back than the seventeenth century, though no doubt this is often as much due to lack of a genealogically-minded member of the family as to impossibility in achieving an earlier direct forebear. On the other hand nearly 14 per cent may be said to have their roots in the Middle Ages – one would say an unexpectedly high proportion.

The question of professions is also of interest. That of the heads of these 116 families is not always stated. Probably they are less often 'country gentlemen', pure and simple, than omission of any other calling might be held to imply, though one mentions farming activities and another designates himself 'agriculturalist'. Half a dozen or more heads of families are represented by ladies. The stated professions of others include twenty-five officers retired from, or serving with, the regular army (several Indian Army, one Royal Army Medical Corps), but several of these only served for a few years as subaltern, so that to regard the army as representing nearly a fifth of the whole would probably be deceptive. Four are naval officers (one Royal Indian Navy, one Royal Canadian Navy), one from the Royal Air Force, thereby bringing the average of the Services, on paper at least, up to over a quarter of the whole. Nine are, roughly speaking, Civil Servants (three Foreign Office, one Forestry Commission, two former Indian Civil).

There are two Members of Parliament (one Conservative, one Liberal), two company directors (probably more of these exist undeclared), two barristers, a parson, a surgeon, a mining engineer, an underwriter at Lloyd's, a schoolmaster, an accountant, a bank manager in the Far East, an author of works on 'history, mythology, philosophy and psychical research', a celebrated writer of travel books. Seventy-one heads of families (over 60 per cent) are shown as having served in the armed forces (excluding Home Guard) during the First or Second World War (some in both), one of these as 'an other rank' in the Army Dental Corps. It should perhaps be added that the second fifty of the consecutive hundred pages worked out about the same as regards seats and arms, but increased the number of regular soldiers by twenty-one (as opposed to four in the first fifty), so that number can scarcely be looked upon as average. The second fifty pages also produced both MPs. There is, of course, much more diversity of professions in cadet branches where a calling is stated.

It is clear even from this rapid glance that we are dealing with nothing like a closely integrated category of hereditary landowner. Investigation of the pedigrees confirms this. Indeed, the records here are on the whole more interesting than those of such a narrowly defined class would be, certainly far more varied. They are, in fact, a kind of chronicle of those families who, for one reason or another, have kept their history intact, usually, though not always, against a background of land.

Many of the pedigrees support the conclusion of Sir Anthony Wagner, Garter King of Arms's study *British Genealogy*, in which the extreme social fluidity of families in this country was remarked. Side by side with a steady and unexplosive rise and fall is to be noted the really amazing survival of certain families – or perhaps one should say branches of families, for some of the same name are to be found in less exalted positions – who continue to live where they have lived for centuries, producing over long periods representatives of distinction and even eminence. There is much talk these days of the stratification of our social structure. It might be thought that a book of this kind confirms such a view. In certain respects perhaps it does; in others, strangely illustrates the contrary. The English approach to such matters continues in many ways to defy rationalization. Have we a deeply rooted, even ineradicable, taste for drawing social distinctions for their own sake and then disregarding them? It is worth considering.

In Domesday Book, for instance (when about 200 magnates found place in a population of perhaps a million and a half, the lord of a manor possessing about 7,000 tenants), nothing is more remarkable than the varied status of members of the lower-middle class in England before the Norman Conquest: freemen, sokemen, holders of Thegnland, holders of commendation land, radmen, drengs (or drenches), and finally the *miles*, for whom the style 'soldier' is too low, 'knight', too high. There is not a village in England that does not still reflect these subtle, labyrinthine relationships to this day. Is it something innate, a subtlety in human contacts due as much to appreciation of special circumstances, even friendly diffidence, rather than to less desirable characteristics sometimes put forward in explanation?

Burke's Landed Gentry is an enormous and unique repository of the history of individual families – something unlike anything else to be found in Europe, or probably in the world.

1965
Introduction to *Burke's Landed Gentry*. Vol. I, Burke's Peerage.

OF THAT ILK

I much regret not having known Sir Iain Moncreiffe of that Ilk. The only occasion when we came into brief contact, he was pretty tight and, in spite of my respect for him as a genealogist, seemed rather too much of a good thing.

Hugh Montgomery-Massingberd, in his admirable Introduction, says Moncreiffe was in reality the kindest and gentlest of men, which, after reading this book, one wholly believes; although readers should be warned that there are moments in these collected essays when hackles may begin to rise. It is well worth pressing ahead in spite of that. You will be entertained.

Moncreiffe was 11th baronet 'of that Ilk', which simply means that the surname is the same as that of the estate. The term should only be used in that sense; *not* as in 'persons of that ilk'. He was a herald, QC, soldier, well-known social figure, but above all scholar, who played an incomparable part in putting life into the study of genealogy; not least in showing, in his own words, that genealogy is 'great fun'.

As Hugh Montgomery-Massingberd emphasizes, Moncreiffe met the charge of snobbery head on. So far from denying it, he delighted in the self-designation of Master Snob; though in fact, as his Editor equally points out, a snob was the last thing he truly was. He might take pleasure in the probability that his property in Perthshire had belonged to Pictish ancestors (in the female line) in the third century; he was no less keen to draw attention to how, on his mother's side, an Admiral turned out to be a Sergeant, and a Hungarian ancestress tops the list for murder in the *Guinness Book of Records*.

What interested Moncreiffe was continuity in history, and the Y-chromosome, which scientists say can only be given to a man by his father. In an age which has gone to the furthest lengths in suggesting that almost all behaviour is attributable to the parents, or lack of sense of parentage in a child, it is really extraordinary that people are still found to sneer at genealogy.

In case anyone remains doubtful about Moncreiffe's abilities as a scholar, let me draw attention to the piece here on Ravaillac's dagger. When Ravaillac assassinated Henry IV of France in 1610 he was overpowered by a nobleman whose descendants, the family of Caumont La Force, still possess the dagger.

Ravaillac would say no more of the dagger, embossed with a coat of arms, than that he had stolen it near the Rue de Rivoli. Moncreiffe, staying with the owners, was asked to identify the arms. This he did, as those of Ramsay; initials, added to the dagger later, made clear it had belonged to a certain Sir John Ramsay.

The Gowrie Conspiracy is a notoriously obscure affair, but it is known that, on a visit to Gowrie House, in 1600, James VI of Scotland (not yet James I of England) retired to an upper room with the notably good-looking Master of Ruthven, brother of the Earl of Gowrie. John Ramsay, one of the King's homosexual boyfriends, heard a shout. Rushing upstairs, he found the King struggling with the Master of Ruthven, who appears to have planned to kidnap James.

The King cried out that Ruthven was wearing a mail doublet, and to strike him low. This Ramsay did with his hunting knife, killing him. Ramsay, subsequently knighted for this act, advanced to Viscount Haddington and finally Earl of Holdernesse. These augmentations of rank were crudely marked with initials on the dagger.

In other words, Moncreiffe was able to show a strong presumption that the weapon used to slay Henry IV in France was the same one that had settled the Master of Ruthven.

Moncreiffe, an immensely patriotic Scot, was also a passionate Unionist, and, as a lawyer, convinced that, even if a Jacobite stance is taken, George III was the undoubted heir of Cardinal York. He also draws attention – for the benefit of those who seek to diminish the Prince of Wales's Scottish affiliations – that Prince Charles is descended from Mary, Queen of Scots, through twenty-two lines.

Another interesting point he makes is why Darnley should always be inexplicably referred to as Lord Darnley, a name that was never rightfully his, especially when he became an earl, a duke, finally a king, whose name, Henry, actually appeared on the coinage. Moncreiffe also thinks that Mary, Queen of Scots's protégé Riccio (murdered by the grandfather of the Master of Ruthven above) was, far from merely an innocent musician, being groomed to become the sort of royal minister promoted from low rank like Thomas Cromwell or Cardinal Wolsey.

Moncreiffe explains that the reason for the Nine of Diamonds being called 'the Curse of Scotland' has nothing whatever to do with the Duke of Cumberland and Culloden, the alleged order written on a playing-card, but refers to the Nine of Diamonds (heraldically speaking, Lozenges) on the arms of the Master of Stair who organized the massacre of Glencoe. He also objects to a favourite cliché, in which some Tory is described as 'to the Right of Ghengiz Khan', logically insisting that, in his destruction of existing institutions, Ghengiz Khan was a Leftist of recognizable type.

Lord of the Dance: A Moncreiffe
Miscellany, Hugh Montgomery-
Massingberd, ed., Debrett's.

1986
Daily Telegraph

PRICE OF A PEERAGE

There are really two sides to this enthralling book: first, the whole question of the sale of honours; secondly, the personal life of Maundy Gregory (1877–1941), the subject of the biography. The first matter is not quite so simple as might at first sight appear. To put the situation in its simplest form, it was only during the reign of Queen Victoria that the idea grew up that a peerage was a definite reward for public service. Before that a man of very large estate automatically wielded a great deal of political influence, and could expect, if he so wished – William Beckford provides an eighteenth-century example – to become a peer without unreasonable difficulty, though not without money passing hands.

Baronetcies were, of course, actually instituted by James I for the specific purpose of raising funds for certain enterprises; though it was laid down that they should be offered only to persons of appropriate wealth and position. As the party system grew up it became a natural element of helping a political party (not necessarily the only help given) to contribute to its chest. Accordingly, certain rich men who became peers largely by contributing to party funds continued what was to some extent an historical tradition of, in some sense, 'buying' a peerage.

Whether the promotion, in this manner, of various rich nonentities to the Upper House had in a general way any worse results than the promotion of various nonentities of modest means put there in our own day, not because they 'deserve' peerages but simply to strengthen a given party, must rest a matter of opinion. There can, however, be no doubt whatever that the methods employed by Lloyd George, when Prime Minister, passed all bounds in the scandalous and utterly cynical manner in which honours (ranging from viscountcies downwards) were hawked round literally for sale: sometimes to men of the most dubious reputation.

Maundy Gregory was one of the touts – no doubt by far the most picturesque – used as a go-between for those who wished to purchase an honour and swell the Liberal – or rather the Lloyd George – Party fund.

That brilliant novel of Scott Fitzgerald's, *The Great Gatsby*, describes how the narrator finds himself involved with Gatsby, the boundlessly rich and romantic gangster, who gives huge parties to which the whole world of New York comes.

Maundy Gregory was Gatsby in real life. He was a mad aspect of the 1920s incarnate. Unfortunately he was not good-looking, like Gatsby, and he did not have a romantic passion for a beautiful lady (instead he collected 'several hundred' statuettes of Narcissus), but he lived the same career of reckless spending – and, like Gatsby, he too had the Montenegrin Order of Danilo.

He owned a club called the Ambassador. Those who enjoy a good laugh should read the list of guests (given here in the appendix) at the club's Derby Eve Dinner in 1931. Major-General 'Jack' Seely (later Lord Mottistone) was in the chair, but it was really Maundy Gregory's party. He certainly may be said to have 'brought them in'.

Gerald Macmillan has collected together a great deal of material about this extraordinary man, but much remains to be discovered. The author's general account of what might be called the political side of the story is well and succinctly told (an index would have been acceptable), but Gregory himself, and some of his associates, do not come alive quite as they should. The fact is that a large chunk of Gregory's life remains wrapt in mystery.

Making quite a successful start as a theatrical manager, he left the stage after the failure of a play. What he did between then – about 1909 – and the end of the First World War no one seems to know. Already he had a good deal of money. Was he really ever in some form of the Secret Service? His period in the Army (on paper) as trooper in the Household Battalion (Reserve) and private in the Irish Guards at Caterham (he was five-foot-eight) certainly seems mysterious enough. I can remember his paper the *Whitehall Gazette*, 'under the patronage of the Hetman of the Ukraine', and a very extraordinary periodical it was.

Finally, did Gregory murder his friend Mrs Rosse? There can be no doubt that she left him £18,000 at a very opportune moment. Gerald Macmillan sets out the evidence, and everyone must judge for himself. After his two months in Wormwood Scrubs Gregory retired to France, where, with remarkable moderation, he styled himself Sir Arthur Gregory. He had by that time become a Roman Catholic. His accountant later went to gaol for writing menacing letters to the Latin Patriarch of Jerusalem regarding the Knighthood of the Order of the Holy Sepulchre conferred on Gregory.

Honours for Sale, Gerald   1955
Macmillan, Richards Press.   *Punch*

ISAAC D'ISRAELI

If Benjamin Disraeli had never entered politics he would still have some name – perhaps more name – as a remarkable novelist. If he had never existed at all, his father, Isaac D'Israeli, would still be remembered as author of *Curiosities of Literature*.

James Ogden's study of Isaac D'Israeli (1766–1848) was well worth doing: modifying the rather over-idealized portrait presented by his son; enlarging our picture of the literary activities of the period, providing interesting sidelights on Jewish life in England at the end of the eighteenth and beginning of the nineteenth centuries.

Dizzy's grandfather, also called Benjamin, was of Jewish-Italian origin, as was his grandmother. They were not of romantic Venetian-Hebrew extraction, as Dizzy himself supposed, though respectably placed in life. Benjamin, the grandfather, who emigrated to England in 1748, was one of the founder-members of the London Stock Exchange, and left an estate valued at £35,000 in 1816.

Isaac seems to have been a classic case of a young man given every opportunity for making a successful business career who for no particular reason decided he wanted to 'write'. His home appears to have offered opportunities for fairly wide reading, and, although his mother (according to her grandson) was 'a demon . . . only equalled by Sarah Duchess of Marlborough, Frances Anne (Marchioness of Londonderry), and perhaps Catherine the Great of Russia', and 'foresaw for her child only a future of degradation', Isaac was allowed to have his own way and 'write'. He made some sort of impression on the literary world by his middle twenties.

D'Israeli started with a great admiration for Johnson, and in a sense he himself always remained a man of the eighteenth century, in spite of occasional attractions exercised by changing literary fashion.

He wrote a great many other books – poems, novels, stories, essays – as well as the *Curiosities of Literature* which was to be his *chef d'oeuvre*. It passed into endless editions, became a favourite of Byron's, and was introduced into one of the *Stalky & Co.* stories by Kipling, and into a novel by Gissing.

At the time of the French Revolution D'Israeli was mildly infected with the contemporary literary 'jacobinism', and he seems to have been

56

one of the earliest customers for Blake's illuminated books. On the whole, however, he stuck to Dryden, Pope and Gray. Chaucer and Shakespeare he found a shade quaint; Richardson, Fielding and Sterne not to be taken too seriously; but French authors, Montaigne, Racine, Boileau, Voltaire, Rousseau were especially to be recommended.

Benjamin Disraeli liked to picture his father a scholar absorbed in research, but he was really a popularizer, who did a lot of useful work in presenting little-known sides of history or literature to a wide public. For example, the seventeenth-century antiquary, Anthony Wood, was a great writer in whom D'Israeli delighted, but he never, although he mentions John Aubrey, grasped the fact that it was Aubrey who produced all the good stories in Wood's Collections.

There are indications that D'Israeli was regarded at times as a bit of a bore in his ceaseless asking of questions at dinner-parties. He was also capable in his novels, notably *Flim-Flams* (in which he caricatured the female astronomer Miss Herschel, whose prototype is represented as giving birth to an ape), of displaying less than the 'philosophic sweetness of disposition' ascribed to him by his son.

D'Israeli contributed liberally to synagogue funds and had certainly caused Benjamin to be given instruction in the Jewish faith, but he was not ardent in his religious observances. Accordingly, the governors of the synagogue, as a call to order and much to his own annoyance, elected him as Warden; when he refused, they tried to fine him £40. This appears to have been the reason why Benjamin Disraeli was baptized at the age of twelve.

D'Israeli was an early member of the Athenaeum Club and a Fellow of the Royal Society of Antiquaries. Maclise did an amusing drawing (frontispiece to this book) which shows him sitting in front of the fire in his slippers, a pen in his hand and wearing spectacles. He was attacked, it is interesting to note, for giving too much prominence to unpleasant aspects of history.

Like his own father, D'Israeli, perhaps because he was a literary man himself and knew its disadvantages, had doubts about his son turning to that career. He wanted to make a solicitor of him, with a firm promise to marry the daughter of the head of the business. All the same he was reasonable, again like his own father, when Ben insisted on going his strange way. It is an unusual, yet oddly complete story, that comes over vividly.

1969
Daily Telegraph

BENJAMIN DISRAELI:
G. A. LAWRENCE: OUIDA

The three novels contained in this volume have not been chosen at random. They cover more than forty years of Queen Victoria's reign, and, although all deal with the same kind of people, they represent three very different stories and points of view. Each is the work of an author of unusual talent, whose own life explains to some extent his or her approach to 'society', and whose success tended to form a pattern to be followed by lesser writers.

Benjamin Disraeli was born in 1804. His political career is well known and does not here concern us, except in so much as it showed by its achievement that his understanding of society was of a thoroughly practical sort. He was leader for many years of the Conservative Party – indeed restated for his age the philosophy of Conservatism – became Prime Minister, was created Knight of the Garter, and raised to the peerage as Earl of Beaconsfield. When *Henrietta Temple* appeared in 1837, the year of Queen Victoria's accession and his own first election to the House of Commons, he was still making his way in the world. As an author he had already something of a reputation – this was his eighth book apart from lesser writings – and although his status as a novelist cannot be separated entirely from his fame as a statesman, there can be no doubt that the latter has done something to eclipse the former. He came of a good Jewish family [outlined earlier under Isaac D'Israeli]; so although not brought up in the circles described in his own novels, was in a position to hear of them at second hand from men who knew society well; in some ways a most advantageous situation for the development of a writer. Literature provided his stepping-stone into the world of action.

In spite of his superlatives, his Asiatic delight in luxuriant description, his disregard for anything like a naturalistic method in dealing with human behaviour, the conscious artificiality of his dialogue, and the improbability of much of his plot, Disraeli has a grasp of human motives that makes his novels far more 'true to life' than many laborious essays in realism. This is because, paradoxically enough, he is a classical and not a romantic writer. As fashion dictates, his characters may run up the flag of Byronism; but their feet are firmly planted on the ground. The tone of *Henrietta Temple* (though death may sometimes threaten its characters) is never allowed to become too serious; yet Ferdinand Armine's money troubles and his entanglements with girls are convincing enough. Armine is an attractive, thoughtless, worldly, good-natured, and thoroughly selfish young man of ancient family, who obtains a commission in a regiment of the line (a hero, for once, outside the ranks of the household troops), and he is torn between the conflicting attractions of love and money, incarnate in the persons of Henrietta Temple and Katherine Grandison. The name and his debts suggest his creator – the young '*Benj*-Armine' – and Disraeli had visited Malta some years before (when the Royal Fusiliers had indeed been stationed there) at a time when, as his letters show, he himself was oppressed by disappointment in love. Armine does not behave with undue scruples in his dealings with these two young ladies; but the author wastes no time in moralizing, relating the incidents as they occur, interesting only as a tricky problem to be solved. Disraeli's picture is alive because he makes no demands on society as an institution. His is a world where people want to get on and to be amused, where birth and money and beauty and wit, all have their place as commodities; and no one behaves, or is expected to behave, with disregard for material values. The psychology is unaccentuated but shrewd (the female characters are perhaps too faintly traced), and the final exchange of partners and friendship of the two families, in which the husbands 'both honestly confess that they are a little in love with each other's wives' is not so unlikely as might appear at first sight. Disraeli alone of the trio of authors collected here shows no disappointment in his acceptance of society. In spirit *Henrietta Temple* (dedicated to D'Orsay, who appears in it as Count Mirabel) belongs to the eighteenth century – one of its characters, Lady Bellair, had indeed been painted by Reynolds and had chatted with Dr Johnson – and on the whole the Victorian novel branched away from its type, though there were minor contemporary imitators, few of whom possessed the detachment concealed under Disraeli's exuberant style. He has few literary descendants today, though traces of his fluent manner can be detected in the novels of Evelyn Waugh.

From *Henrietta Temple*, we jump twenty years to *Guy Livingstone, or Thorough*, published anonymously in 1857, a first novel of a very different type, which had a tremendous contemporary success. The Victorian Age had now begun to take shape, classicism had been left far behind in the conception of this neo-Gothic Lifeguard officer with a moustache 'that fell over his lip in a black cascade'. The author, George Alfred Lawrence, was born in 1827. Surprisingly little is known of him considering the popularity of his books, of which about a dozen appeared, all anonymously. What remains suggests that he was an interesting figure. His father, a parson, had married Lady Emily

Finch-Hatton, sister of the tenth Earl of Winchelsea, whose contemporary at Christ's College, Cambridge, the elder Lawrence had been; and where the connection between the two families had probably begun. The Revd Alfred Charnley Lawrence had been born at Camberwell, a district then inhabited by prosperous business-men, and it seems clear that Lawrence's grandfather, who owned one of the fine villas there, had made his pile in the City. Of the many violent emotions expressed in George Lawrence's novels, a contempt for the abject bearing and demeanour of the clergy, solicitors, and other members of the professional classes, is the most outstanding; while this contempt reaches a pitch of almost Marxian abhorrence when the story necessitates the mention of persons engaged in commercial enterprise. It must be assumed that the example of his father and grandfather generated some of the heat of this sentiment, which can be transmuted into almost tearful adoration, by unquestioned membership of the higher ranks of the aristocracy; or by a commission in the regular army, supported by a sound record of active service. Few who cannot be included in these latter categories escape the author's scathing sarcasm, administered with a wealth of quotation and metaphor. Lawrence's uncle, Lord Winchelsea, was no doubt a relation more to his taste than those on the paternal side of his family, for he had fought a duel with the Duke of Wellington, whom he charged with 'introducing popery into every department of the state'.

Lawrence was educated at Rugby and was a Balliol exhibitioner, both school and university providing backgrounds for the earlier scenes in *Guy Livingstone*. The incident of the headmaster's wife – an early appearance of the now familiar Young Woodley triangle – is reported to have been autobiographical, the victimized husband being Dr Tait, who had recently succeeded Arnold as headmaster. On coming down from Oxford, Lawrence read for the Bar but abandoned the law for writing; and he indulged his taste for martial activities by serving for a time with the Northampton Militia in the rank of lieutenant. He married a lady, said to have been beautiful and of saintly disposition, who belonged to an Irish landed family, the Kirwans of Cregg in Galway – a region where some of the scenes in *Guy Livingstone* are laid. At the time of the American Civil War, he set out from England to join the Confederate forces; but on the way there he was captured by the Northern authorities, who locked him up for a short time, and then sent him back to this country. He wrote a book describing this episode, and we may guess that – like so many other passionate worshippers of action – his efforts to become himself a participant in deeds of violence were, as on this occasion, always doomed to failure. He was fond of gambling, and enemies spoke ill of his reputation; but on his death in 1876, George Augustus Sala, in his weekly column in the *Illustrated*

London News, commented on the sparseness and unfriendly nature of Lawrence's obituary notices and spoke highly of him as a friend.

Guy Livingstone, the hero of the book, is the bearer of an ancient name, with a handsome balance at the bank (a brother officer, filling in Livingstone's blank cheque for a loan of £1,000, elicits no more than a dry comment on the payee's modesty), of dauntless courage in the saddle or with duelling pistols at fifteen paces, intelligent and even well-read, but contemptuous of the things of the mind – in short the embodiment of the century's beefy romanticism. He is of the nineteenth century but he belongs to that section of the community against which Victorian puritanism was aimed. In literature he derives partly from such figures as the Corsair, but there is much originality in the creation of his type; and, in spite of its occasional absurdities, the book remains lively and readable to a high degree. Like the hero of *Henrietta Temple*, Livingstone becomes involved with two girls at the same time, but this situation is treated with very different emphasis from that used by Disraeli. Livingstone may be prepared to smash men's noses and ladies' hearts with an equal lack of compunction, and he represents in his love affairs a kind of Stendhalian determination to be bound by no moral or bourgeois law; but at the same time he is too prudent a man to take on Flora Bellasys as a wife. He feels, no doubt rightly, that notwithstanding her passion for religious ritual, Constance Brandon is the better bet; and the breaking off of his engagement would soon have been cleared up in the apparently more emotional, but actually far cooler, atmosphere of Disraeli's novel. Lawrence's hero may be in revolt against Victorian conventions, but he cannot elude the *zeitgeist*; and, a Victorian of the Victorians, he makes heavy weather with the best of them when he feels that his own *amour propre* is concerned.

Guy Livingstone has had many literary descendants. In a somewhat watered-down form his bulky image recurs again and again in the novels of the latter half of the century. He can be dimly recognized even so far afield as 'Taffy-the-Laird' in *Trilby;* for, as the Yellow Dwarf remarked in his review of that book, Taffy and the Laird are indistinguishable. Kipling, too, was obsessed with these hard, masculine, sardonic, unintellectual supermen; though in Kipling's hands Livingstone would have had his pedigree shortened, his income cut, and his sense of public responsibility increased. More recently the type – with appropriate adjustment – has reappeared from across the Atlantic and we find the heroes of Ernest Hemingway drinking, womanizing, fighting, and brawling, with the same volcanic sentimentality, they too the victims of disaster in love and war, no less unfortunate than Livingstone in his hunting accident; a brood on the whole less companionable and even more egotistic than their English forebears. Lawrence's cult is said to have had a noticeable effect on the young men of his day, and it was the Aesthetic Movement of the 1880s that at last offered a challenge to the aristocratic, athletic, military prodigy, finally making fiction safe for the weedy, intellectual, middle-class heroes of the twentieth century. The social atmosphere is conveyed on the whole with conviction. Unlike Disraeli's broad canvas, we are shown only a small 'set', a group of people, who, in spite of wealth and title are apparently in process of becoming quickly *déclassé*. It is hard to say how much this impression is intended by the author; and in his other books there is a tendency to be less insistent on riches and rank, perhaps in order to avoid extreme contrasts of position and behaviour on the part of the *dramatis personae*.

Among the writers who deliberately modelled their work – at least in its early stages – on *Guy Livingstone* was Ouida, the third and last of the authors collected here, whose novel, *Moths*, appeared in 1880, at the height of her fame as a popular writer. If Disraeli was born within sight of the world to which his ambitions attracted him, and Lawrence possessed close family connections with the same world, Ouida, with similar aspirations, found herself in her early days far less propitiously placed. She was born at Bury St Edmunds in 1839 and christened 'Louise', of which name 'Ouida' was a childish corruption. Her father was Louis Ramé, a French schoolmaster, who (though he disapproved of the *coup d'état* of 1852) is believed to have been involved in the intrigues of Prince Louis Napoleon, while the latter was exiled in England. Ramé had married an Englishwoman with a little money of her own, but he did not spend much of his time in her company, putting in an appearance intermittently as the mood took him; and eventually vanishing for good about the year 1871. When she was eighteen Ouida came to London, accompanied by her mother, her grandmother, and her dog, Beausire. Almost immediately she began to sell her writings successfully. By the time she was twenty-six she was an established author, known for her eccentricity, though some still persisted that her books were written by George Eliot under another pseudonym. In 1867 she began her habit of staying at the Langham Hotel, then under the management of an ex-colonel of the Confederate Army – a force which has provided fiction with many punctilious characters from the ranks of its demobilized senior officers, and which, as has been seen, exercised an attraction for the imagination of George Lawrence. The Langham was patronized by many American clients (among them Longfellow), and Ouida and her mother used to give parties there for men only; Lady Burton, the wife of an explorer, constituting the sole female exception. So far as can be judged from what traditions have been handed down, these gatherings consisted for the most part of authors and journalists possessing, as war-correspondents or suchlike, claims to some more or less military background. George Lawrence used to be among her guests. As her notoriety increased, Ouida, whose dreams were of social eminence, uncontaminated by any hint of bohemianism, attempted progress into more pretentious and conventional circles. In 1871 she settled in Florence, where the society she sought seemed available on not too stringent terms; and she lived in Italy until her death in 1908.

Ouida is the most tragic of the authors here discussed. In spite of the sales of her books, she was perpetually in deep water about money; and, in her old age, the embarrassments and humiliations she had to suffer on account of her extravagance and folly are painful to investigate. She was a kind of monstrous incarnation of the female novelist of caricature, egotistical almost to the point of insanity, consumed with snobbishness, egregiously bad-mannered, unattractive in appearance, with a voice 'like a carving-knife', and habitually surrounded by a herd of pet dogs of doubtful temper. She supposed that the expression of her political opinions (she was a Liberal) could shake cabinets, and that her prejudices were banners to be followed by the statesmen of Europe. Yet with all her failings and futilities she is a writer to be taken into account when the novels of her time are considered. Although scarcely aware at all of the principles of form in constructing a plot, she achieves an extraordinary vitality in the presentation of her narrative. The reader of *Moths* should note the pace of the book's opening pages, the *tempo* of which seems at first impact either too slow or too fast – one feels that the author will either sink into dullness, or be compelled to accelerate the action, if our attention is to be held. Neither of these changes takes place. Like a confident Marathon runner, Ouida bowls along at a velocity she knows she can maintain; and at the end of the course she and her readers are no more (if no less) breathless than at the start.

Since all but purely snobbish considerations were rejected by Ouida in her approach to society, she naturally depicts a somewhat unpleasing world, the disagreeable features of which are in no way ameliorated by the fact that they are drawn largely from her imagination. Her position as a well-known novelist allowed her opportunities of meeting and mixing with many of the people whom it was her ambition to know; but her faculty of balance was not sufficiently developed for a prolonged performance on her self-chosen tight-rope. For Disraeli, society was the glittering battlefield on which personal and political fame might be won; for Lawrence, a select stage upon which to play out the calamitous dramas in which the superhumanly strong, brave, and nobly-born found themselves inexorably ensnared; but for Ouida, society was the firmament of the charity-bazaar, the gossip-column, and the illustrated papers, the promised land of those who could dream only of its splendours. Although she never ceased to deplore the fact that the world after which she hungered had lowered its standards – and was indeed accustomed to describe herself, in her own inimitable fashion, as '*laudator tempori acti*' – she never shows the faintest insight into the roots of human conduct, high or low. Her idea of doing good is bounded by taking flowers to the invalid father of a poor seamstress, and, although she hints of vices 'shut up between the pages of Suetoneus and Livy', the face of evil is expressed in her fantasy by the carriage of a mulatto *cocotte* drawn by white mules with Spanish trappings. Her *naïveté* was proverbial and W. H. Mallock (a novelist and snob of a far more sophisticated order) wrote:

> Ouida was sitting after dinner between Mrs. ——, the mistress of one of the greatest houses in London, and a vulgar little Irish peeress who was only present on sufferance. Ouida treated the former with the coldest and most condescending inattention, and devoted every smile in her possession to an intimate worship of the latter.

However, this deficiency in appreciating realities, social or otherwise, makes her no less entertaining as a novelist, and the very crudity of her situations sometimes gives them an unexpected force.

Moths is the *via dolorosa* of a young, innocent, and indisputably priggish girl, Vere (or Vera) Herbert, who, to save the honour of her mother, Lady Dolly Vanderdecken, accepts a husband, insupportable even for a Russian. Vere loves Corrèze, opera-singer and prototype of one, Mario, for whom Ouida cherished a passion. (This infatuation was not so overpowering as that Ouida possessed later for the Marchese Lotteringhi Della Stufa, a gentleman-in-waiting at the Italian Court; though it should be added that there was never in the course of her life the slightest question of her entering into what her biographer calls 'an irregular union'. Vere has to endure tribulations of the most arduous kind, but she wins her tenor in the end, however not before he has been shot in the throat – a fate to which such paragons are foredoomed; and, after all, a lighter nemesis than Guy Livingstone's paralysis from the waist down. *Moths* was later turned into a play and enjoyed a good run. Its picture of Trouville and elsewhere reflects all the bitterness suffered by its author in the pursuit of her mirage; and at the time of its publication she wore the white gown – and in general sustained the *rôle* – of its martyred heroine. Ouida's literary descendants are legion. Even the early novels of Bernard Shaw suggest her influence, certainly more than that of Disraeli or Henry James, writers noted by that author himself as 'badly assimilated' models. The persecuted wives of John Galsworthy have much in common with poor Vere's afflictions; and D. H. Lawrence's discontented women mark her reappearance in a more aggressive form. *The Rosary* is in the direct succession, and to this day an ever-rolling stream of novelettes and magazine stories echo Ouida's florid yet intimate style.

*

Novels that deal with a specialized form of life inevitably pose the question of how successfully or otherwise their author has presented the background against which the characters play their part. How much do the surroundings approximate to the outward realities of this particular world; how much has the author, deliberately or otherwise, allowed his or her imagination to diversify the scene in order to accommodate with greater convenience a certain favourite idea? Fashions in literature change. Factory or Saloon bar in these days often provide a backcloth for popular romanticisms that the Victorians preferred to set in the drawing-room or the hunting-field; but whatever solecisms may pursue the painter of proletarian or gangster landscape – and there is ample evidence of the hazards that surround such an undertaking – there can be no doubt that the writer who decided to describe 'society' had, at any period, a task that laid him open to criticism of a peculiarly searching kind. A society novel, by its very nature, treats of a form of existence unfamiliar to a large proportion of its potential readers. An explanation to the uninitiated of the doings of the elect undertaken by one of the latter, even if the grosser forms of vulgarity are avoided, can at best hardly fail to escape a note of patronage, not to mention some reproach of 'giving the show away'; while, at worst, the definitions risk downright contradiction on the part of those readers who consider themselves in a position to be as well, or better, informed. Alternatively, the narrator may speak as a social inferior, a point of observation accepted without demur by so pre-eminent a writer in this *genre* as Marcel Proust. In England the ramifications of the social hierarchy have been always of infinite complexity and even in the nineteenth century, when the professional classes made little or no pretension to inclusion in 'society', few authors were prepared to disclaim familiarity with its habits. A sociological criticism to which novelists lay themselves open (Proust again is the exception) might be aimed at their almost invariable disregard for the network of family connections, by which, as the strawberry-leaves recede, ducal families can tail off into obscurity; and they are also inclined to neglect the ceaseless assimilation of would-be recruits pushing their way into a world for which few might be chosen but whither many felt themselves called. The activity of both these forces is of course difficult to convey in a book. One suspects that their unpopularity with writers may have had something to do with the former making society seem too select – a family party to which a mere author might not aspire – and the second, implying a goal of too easy achievement – an awkward reminder of energetic fellow-climbers. The Victorian social scene can now be observed with comparative impartiality. Deprived of its more exaggerated features, we recognize its 'society' as small and based for the most part on hereditary possession of land, coupled with the occupation of a London house for entertaining during 'the season'. For two hundred years or more it had been largely infiltrated by families with commercial interests, and the fabulous lineages stretching to the Conquest which no novelist could resist, were almost wholly imaginary, few enough pedigrees going back to the 1400s, and even a progenitor recorded in the Heraldic Visitations of the sixteenth century becoming every year more rare. As the manifestation of an aristocracy which did not represent a caste, like the nobilities of the Continent, access was in fact always achievable for those with outstanding personality or pertinacity.

That *Henrietta Temple*, *Guy Livingstone*, and *Moths* have their silly moments, all of them, it would be hard to deny; but at their worst they soar into an empyrean of absorbing theme, acute psychology, and workmanlike narration, when compared with many novels of the last twenty years that have been hailed on their first appearance as works of genius. It is easy to laugh at much in these Victorian romances that now seems stilted and ludicrous, but, even so, the reader is constantly reminded that they depict a dignified and mature civilization, though often in its most unattractive form. Before ridiculing Victorian 'society', or disparaging those who enjoyed reading about it, it is well to recall the slavish adulation of our own day paid to the business-boss or to the commissar; and to consider whether snobbery of the old-fashioned sort did not sometimes act as a brake on power-worship in its purest form.

1947
Introduction to *Novels of High Society from the Victorian Age*, Pilot Press.

ROBERT SURTEES

Born in 1805, of an ancient Durham family that had already produced an antiquarian writer of some standing, Robert Smith Surtees was a younger son articled to a solicitor. He soon abandoned the Law for sporting journalism, but he lived in London for some fifteen years and few knew its seedy aspects better. In due course he inherited Hamsterley Hall, and returned to his native county, where he spent the rest of his days undertaking, with notable conscientiousness, the local duties of a country gentleman of his time. His most famous character, the fox-hunting tea-merchant of Great Coram Street, Jorrocks, first appeared in sketches done during his period as a journalist, but the novels were written after his retirement to the country. He married in 1841 and died in 1864.

Surtees is a writer somewhat uncomfortably placed for the approach of serious criticism. His comic genius, though not without occasional moments of sentiment, contains no grain of sentimentality, and there is often a tendency for contemporary opinion to underrate writing of this kind, especially when, as with Surtees, the narrative is inclined to tail off into farce. In addition to this, he wrote as a specialist: a specialist, that is to say, in fox-hunting. From this fact there is no escape. Although in his own manner Surtees scrutinizes life closely, the hunting-field always provides the ultimate reason for existence. The result of this preoccupation is to make him an author with devoted admirers in circles not otherwise much given to reading; while persons to whom hunting is of subordinate interest, or indeed no interest at all, are sometimes legitimately reluctant to explore his pages.

This is a pity, because Surtees is a writer of rare and powerful gifts, to whom justice has never properly been done. The article about him in the *Dictionary of National Biography* shows a lamentable inadequacy in appreciating his status as a novelist, and, although a certain number of miscellaneous studies have grown up round his name, he has never yet been treated biographically and critically in the way he deserves.

Surtees himself is certainly not above facetiousness and the use of the cliché, and his own determination to behave in a thoroughly unprofessional manner makes his defence, as a writer, sometimes difficult. Besides this, it is almost impossible to separate him entirely from the

67

tangle of usually rather second-rate sporting journalism, and its literary images, that surrounds him. Perhaps some persons might even think it undesirable to make this effort, since these must have provided the atmosphere of much of his life as a young man. Leonard Cooper struggles manfully to present a coherent picture, but in the last resort he seems almost unwilling, in spite of his admiration, to accept much of the manner in which Surtees looked at life. Or perhaps it would be fairer to say that he cannot at times reconcile the occasional savagery of the writer with the good sense of the man.

If we turn to *The World of Henry Alken* we are immediately supplied, in a series of loosely connected chapters, with an example of the kind of book which, so far as Surtees is concerned, merely clouds the landscape. Aubrey Noakes begins his volume with some account of the Alken family, several of whom, in different generations at the beginning of the nineteenth century, painted sporting subjects in an individual and attractive style. From the Alkens the author follows on to a general account of sporting life at the time of the Regency and later. He touches in a chatty, discursive way on the Lambtons, Jack Mytton, Assheton Smith, Nimrod, the Midnight Steeplechase, rackety life at Melton Mowbray, and so on. Among others, Surtees is mentioned, described, not without justice, as 'a dour, cantankerous north country squire', and treated as if he were just one more eccentric figure in this pageant of sporting oddities.

Now it is precisely from such a position that Surtees's reputation must be rescued, if only because the people in Noakes's book do not, any of them, bear close examination as possessing characters that are of any true literary interest; and Cooper cannot be entirely exonerated from treating Surtees at times somewhat in the Noakes manner. There is no reason whatever why persons like Jack Mytton, who set fire to his nightshirt to cure hiccups, or Captain Barclay, who walked one thousand miles in one thousand hours, should not be discussed in an easy-going tone, as they are here, but the moment such individuals are considered at all seriously they must stand revealed for what they are. Mytton, for example, driven mad by his own insensate egotism, must have been one of the greatest bores of all times; while a figure like Squire Osbaldeston was notoriously corrupt in the field of sport in spite of his prominence there. Other well-known personages here chronicled are sufficiently shabby in behaviour when investigated. This does not mean, of course, that the anecdotes about them are not entertaining. In fact they make admirable material for light reading. The point is that Surtees stands apart, as a very considerable novelist, from this mob of hard-riding, port-drinking paranoiacs. In fact, he is really the exemplification of an objective point of view directed towards their particular world; or what was left of it by mid-Victorian times.

It is perhaps fruitless to regret that any writer is what he is, or to hope that he could be otherwise. If Surtees had been different in some respects he might also have been different in others, and we might never have had his best work. His worst fault is his unwillingness to impose some kind of a pattern, not necessarily a plot, on his material. The fact that he wrote primarily for his own amusement, though it gives him zest, perhaps removes also an element of discipline. Even if it were not clear from his novels that he must have been inwardly a melancholy man, his portraits show a sad, handsome face that indicates his nature clearly enough. It was one of his notable traits that he was able to see the unpleasant side of the things he liked and still continue to like them. In this connection it is possible to disagree with Cooper in some of his conclusions regarding Surtees's point of view.

It is suggested that Surtees disliked the nobility, the regular army, inn-keepers, servants, ambitious mammas, lots of other categories. He was subject to irritation with the whole of humanity, combined with a relenting in the case of pretty girls. Otherwise he was sunk in the deepest melancholy, for which the only alleviation was the theory and practice of fox-hunting. Accepting for the moment this proposition, exactly the reverse conclusion might be drawn. The extraordinary skill with which Surtees depicts an irascible peer or a blundering butler is because in his heart he loved, or at least understood, them both. Hatred is on the whole an unsatisfactory inspiration for a novelist. Understanding is the key to successful character drawing and within the limitations he set himself Surtees possessed this gift to a high degree.

A similar scepticism might be expressed towards the statement that Surtees was not interested in women. Again allowing for the background, he could surely be extraordinarily successful in lightly suggesting his female characters. Lucy Glitters (whom Cooper freely grants as an unqualified success) is, of course, masterly; and is there any reason why he should be taken to task for making jokes about girls looking for husbands? After all, it is a matter that must be allowed, like so much else of the serious business of life, to have its funny side.

Above all, Surtees is a remarkable antidote to the too prevalent notion that everything which happened in Victorian times was strait-laced and conventional. Indeed, he seems almost to go out of his way to drive a coach and horses through what is nowadays almost the accepted view of the kind of life he describes. The class distinctions have little of the rigidity now popularly attributed to the period. An MFH will be living in rooms over a chemist's shop; an earl inhabits the servants' quarters in his mansion and dines modestly on beefsteak and batter pudding. To make Jorrocks himself, a retired Cockney business-man, the mouthpiece of classical views of hunting is a brilliantly original conception. It is scarcely necessary to add that Surtees's publisher wished Jorrocks much reduced or, better still, removed entirely from *Handley Cross*.

As a writer Surtees at times a little resembles Gogol, and *Mr Sponge's Sporting Tour* (translated into French as *La Tournée Sportive de Mr Sponge* by the author of *Les Villégiatures de Jorrocks*) is in some ways not unlike Chichikov's pilgrimage from country house to country house in *Dead Souls*. Both heroes, in their different ways, are presented as irredeemably dull in all respects save in satisfaction of their ruling passion, and there can be little doubt that if Mr Sponge's favourite reading, Mogg's *Ten Thousand Cab Fares*, had been extended to the droskies of St Petersburg or Moscow, Chichikov would have devoured its information with equal interest.

One should at once add that among the types Surtees detested, fox-hunters themselves come high. He was not interested in 'going hard' in the hunting-field; indeed he disapproved of it. What he liked was the scientific hunting of hounds. In Durham he was never on specially good terms with neighbours who hunted, or the farmers across whose fields he rode.

But why should non-fox-hunting readers endure pages and pages about fox-hunting in shapeless, all but plotless, novels, however well written? There is no answer except that Surtees, at his best, gives far the most convincing picture that exists from early Victorian times of dukes, ostlers and a hundred other types.

Dickens never really got the hang of the upper classes (even if one accepts Cousin Pheenix's reminiscences of Mr Pitt), nor for that matter of his soupily sentimental proletarians. What he wrote of with genius was the lower-middle class. Thackeray was familiar with certain worlds, describing them in a stylized manner, while always tormented by his own social uneasiness. Trollope can deal with a cathedral close or political machinations, but again takes conventional views and is often stodgy. Surtees, with recklessly knockabout humour (that can tail off into farce), strikes an uncanny realism that is always without humbug.

There is also perhaps something rather in the Russian manner about the death of Jack Spraggon at the Grand Aristocratic Steeplechase. His friend, patron and tyrant, Lord Scamperdale, sees that Spraggon's horse has rolled on him, and rushes to the scene of the accident:

> 'Oh, my poor dear Jack!' exclaimed his lordship, throwing himself off his horse, and wringing his hands in despair, as a select party of thimble-riggers, who had gone to Jack's assistance, raised him up, and turned his ghastly face, with his eyes squinting inside out, and the foam still on his mouth, full upon him. 'Oh, my poor dear Jack!' repeated his lordship, sinking on his knees beside him, and grasping his stiffening hand as he spoke. His lordship sank overpowered upon the body.

The thimble-riggers then availed themselves of the opportunity to ease his lordship and Jack of their watches and the few shillings they had about them, and departed. When a lord is in distress consolation is never long in coming; and Lord Scamperdale had hardly got over the first paroxysms of his grief, and gathered up Jack's cap and the fragments of his spectacles, ere Jawleyford, who had noticed his abrupt departure from the stand, and scurry across the country, arrived at the spot. His lordship was still in the full agony of woe; still grasping and bedewing Jack's cold hand with tears.

'Oh, my dear Jack! Oh, my dear Jawleyford! Oh, my dear Jack!' sobbed he, as he mopped the fast-chasing tears from his grizzly cheeks with a red cotton handkerchief. 'Oh, my dear Jack! Oh, my dear Jawleyford! Oh, my dear Jack!' repeated he, as a fresh flood spread o'er the rugged surface. 'Oh, what a tr-treasure, what a tr-tr-trump he was. Shall never get such another. Nobody could s-s-slang a fi-fi-field as he could; no hu-hu-humbug about him – never was su-su-such a fine natural bl-bl-blackguard'; and then his feelings wholly choked his utterance as he recollected how easily Jack was satisfied; how he could dine off tripe and cow-heel, mop up fat porridge for breakfast, and never grumbled at being put on a bad horse.

Leonard Cooper takes the view that this passage is not successful; it is, however, also possible to feel that the episode, one of the rare moments when Surtees is touching tragedy, displays a depth that suggests a writer capable of even greater things than he actually achieved. Lord Scamperdale and his hanger-on are characters who truly live, and the former's agony of regret, and simultaneous awareness of Jack's good and bad points bear all the stamp of reality. Remorse surges up in a man's heart; in the background the race-gang pick the pockets of the living and the dead. There are few of those writers of the present day who specialize in violence who could do the thing so neatly, with so much feeling and yet with so little sentimentality. There is perhaps a touch of Dostoevsky here; and not Dostoevsky at his worst. It might be added that Thackeray, a friend of Surtees, in a letter about the book, singled out Scamperdale and Spraggon for especial praise.

Like most writers of his own, or any other period, Surtees was from time to time involved in literary rows. He quarrelled with Harrison Ainsworth as an editor, who quite unjustifiably published his name in a magazine when he had wished to remain anonymous. He also crossed swords with Nimrod, the sporting writer, C. J. Apperley, whom he guyed in *Handley Cross* as Pomponius Ego. Both Cooper and Noakes are severe with Surtees for caricaturing a friend. Once more it is possible to demur, at least as a reader, if not as a moralist, for the scenes between

Jorrocks, Ego, and the bad-tempered north-country huntsman, James
Pigg, are extraordinarily funny. Moreover, it is hard to feel that
they are unjust to Apperley as a man. Certainly they hit him off neatly
as a writer. Incidentally, Surtees's letter of reply to Nimrod's
protest is a model for any author accused of drawing too closely from
life:

> Sir,
>   Yours of the 27th has just reached me
> where I have been staying. In reply to
> your demand I beg to say the character
> of 'Pomponius Ego' is meant for Nim-
> rod.
>   Your obedient servant,
>   R. S. Surtees.

The matter never came to anything because Apperley died a few
months later. The opinion of friends was that it would in any case never
have come to anything. Perhaps it is true that Surtees behaved rather
unkindly. It is equally true that Nimrod achieves in Ego a personal
immortality his own writings have scarcely brought him.

Since John Welcome is concerned with the sporting world he gives at
some length the vendetta Surtees conducted with Nimrod, author of
The Life of a Sportsman (1842) and much sporting journalism. Surtees, to
tell the truth, does not always appear at his best in what he wrote about
a man twenty-five years older, implying, for example, that Apperley
did not 'go' well in the field when he was known to be a fearless rider
and in fact Surtees himself was not much of a thruster.

My own feeling is that Apperley was snobbish, pompous, unreliable
and a provocation to having his leg pulled. But my objection to
Welcome devoting so much space to him, while emphasizing that
Surtees is sometimes shown in their mutual relations in a bad light, is
that readers might suppose Apperley to be a writer comparable with
Surtees.

That is not so. Just because Surtees cannot be classified other than as
a 'sporting writer' he is not a mere comic Whyte-Melville. Surtees has
an originality as a depictor of Victorian society that is not surpassed
in certain respects – indeed never quite equalled – by Dickens,
Thackeray, Trollope, anyone else you like to name.

When Surtees tries naturalistic writing, it does not come off. He has
to be funny. What would we give to hear more of the lost years (like
Shakespeare's), when he was rubbing shoulders in London with a
disreputable underworld of Sponge and Glitters (the latter 'tolerably
virtuous'). But Surtees was writing with the wind in his face. The

Victorians found him coarse. A hundred years before, a hundred years later, he would have hit the mood.

Surtees's world does, however, indicate what the Victorians were prudish about. There were reasons for that. Who would doubt, for instance, that Jorrocks slept with Mrs Markham, the housekeeper, on that night he stayed at Sir Archey Depecarde's house when his host was absent? By no means all the interesting social touches of Surtees are in this vein. There is – or certainly was until recently – a miners' hunt in South Wales, but it comes as a surprise to learn that there were miners' hunts in Surtees's day.

Finally, a word about illustrations in Surtees, which are as important as Cruikshank and Phiz were to Dickens. Phiz also illustrated Surtees, but it was more often Leech (an equally melancholy fox-hunter). Contemporaries like Alken, Heath, Wildrake, Jellicoe tried their hand, but, capable as Alken can be, he fails when he tries to represent a naturalistic Jorrocks.

The short novel *Young Tom Hall* (unfinished owed to Surtees's row with Harrison Ainsworth) did not appear until 1926, then disastrously illustrated by the *Punch* sporting cartoonist J. D. Armour, whose pictures show just what was to be avoided in illustrating Surtees.

Welcome produces the interesting information that, so far from dashing his novels off, Surtees took great trouble and made many drafts. This suggests that genius for human observation and dialogue was handicapped by some inner inability to give shape to the work. Welcome comments that Surtees's women have no 'life below the waist'. That was inevitably imposed by nineteenth-century censorship, but I always understood that Surtees would write the story as freely as he liked, fully expecting the publisher to make excisions. Certainly some paragraphs read like that.

As a writer there can be no doubt that Surtees had an influence on Kipling, both in his vigorous choice of words, and liking for transcribing them exactly as spoken. He is adept at concentrating atmosphere and character in dialogue, doing this almost in the manner of Ronald Firbank:

'How many children have you, Mr Jorrocks?' now asked the lady [Mrs Muleygrubs] thinking to pay him off for some of his *gaucheries*. ''Ow many chi-e-l-dren 'ave I, mum?' repeated Mr Jorrocks, thoughtfully. ''Ow many chi-e-l-dren 'ave I? Legally speakin', mum, *none*.' – 'Chi-e-l-dren,' continued our master, dry-shaving his stubbly chin, 'are certain cares, but werry uncertain comforts, as my old mother said when I upset her snuff-box into the soup.' 'Oh dear, I'm afraid you've been a very mischievous boy, Mr Jorrocks,' observed the lady, motioning Stiffneck to put the almond-backed sponge-cake rabbit straight on the table.

R. S. Surtees, Leonard Cooper, Arthur Barker.
Mr Facey Romford's Hounds, R. S. Surtees, Folio Society.
The World of Henry Alken, Aubrey Noakes, Witherby.
The Sporting World of R. S. Surtees, John Welcome, OUP.
The Collected Novels of R. S. Surtees, R. S. Surtees Society

1952; 1982; 1988
*Times Literary Supplement,
Daily Telegraph*

CHARLES DICKENS

I

Dickens, whatever anybody may say – and some fairly silly criticism has been devoted to him during the last decade or so – remains a dominating figure. Of course he is not the same sort of novelist as Flaubert or James. You do not have to possess a First in Eng. Lit. to see that.

He is the product of a terrifically powerful imagination, geared to many other strong characteristics, not necessarily those of a novelist. Nevertheless, his influence stretches from Dostoevsky to Proust.

Philip Collins, who has already worked on Dickens's letters, and published a study of *Dickens and Crime*, well describes the present-day acceptance of Dickens as a kind of folk memory. There must be thousands of people nowadays who have never read the books – at least never read them thoroughly – who know about Mr Micawber and Oliver Twist, take for granted a whole canon of Dickensian humour.

The man himself is full of contradictions, and not always a particularly attractive figure. Even by Victorian standards his self-righteousness was colossal, and, if he had a lot to put up with himself, many people had a lot to put up with from him.

Some key to the situation is given by one aspect of the public readings Dickens gave from his novels: readings into which Dickens put all his own bottled-up talent as an actor, giving so much of himself that these performances probably shortened his life. At them it was very generally observed that his imitation of Squeers was beyond praise; his presentation of Smike quite hopeless.

All Dickensian criticism might be boiled down to this fact. Indeed, the whole history of *Nicholas Nickleby* is of great interest, both as a general example of Dickens's method, and a particular one of Collins's theme, *Dickens and Education*.

The Yorkshire schools, of which there were a great many, had been a long-standing scandal when Dickens wrote his novel. There had been a lawsuit in the 1820s about the school belonging to one Shaw, generally accepted as the figure Squeers represents, and Dickens visited the neighbourhood to look for himself.

Collins points out that *Nicholas Nickleby* is an excellent example of a 'committed' novel, but that, paradoxically enough, in quarters where writing 'committed' books is advocated, it has rarely been admired for

75

that reason. The interesting thing is that a novel written in this way –
for a purpose – should have such abounding vitality, and that in
Squeers a great comic character should come to life.

However, Squeers was primarily a bad man, a contrived villain, in
Dickens's eyes, rather than a schoolmaster on the wrong educational
track. It is the irrational emotional force behind the indictment that
carries the narrative on so splendidly, not any clarity of thinking.

It is not difficult to believe that the Yorkshire schools, a convenient
dumping ground for illegitimate children, were very dreadful places.
Most middle-aged men who attended even respectable preparatory
schools forty or fifty years ago could tell some hair-raising stories. At
the same time, there were witnesses who offered a different picture in
certain individual cases, while Dickens himself was not above cooking
the evidence.

For example, in his childhood at Chatham, Dickens says he met a
boy 'with a suppurated abcess . . . in consequence of his Yorkshire
[schoolmaster] guide, philosopher, and friend having ripped it open
with an inky penknife'.

This incident is attributed in *Nicholas Nickleby* to Mrs Squeers. The
original of the story was, as it happened, traced in the 1880s. He
disclosed that he had 'caused the abcess himself by cutting a pimple off
his nose', and his schoolmaster 'had never said an unkind word to him'.

In short, it was the picturesque side of reform that attracted Dickens.
Where his own children were concerned, he cannot be said to have
shown any great initiative in devising their education. His eldest son,
horrible to relate, went to Eton, although it was true he was taken away
for no particular reason after a couple of years. The others were brought
up in a decidedly miscellaneous, even ramshackle manner.

One of the points that recurs in Dickens's interest in education is his
preoccupation with abnormal children. Obviously this is an important
social problem, but it is so often with the deaf-and-dumb or the
mentally deficient that he is found, rather than setting his mind to what
is the best way for a normal child to be brought up.

When it comes to such knotty problems, he falls back on common-
places of the most traditional kind. Collins gives a good and entertaining account of all this, which should amuse everyone interested in
Dickens.

Ivor Brown's profusely illustrated *Dickens in His Time* consists largely
of discursive remarks about the period when Dickens was writing.
Brown gives the Bad Old Days an absolute cannonade in the best
tradition of Whig history, and I am not sure all his generalizations
would stand up to a rather more pedantic historical approach.
However, towards the end of the book he admits that our own age is a
frightful one, too, and seems almost to feel at times a nostalgia for the

tyrannical, unforward-looking goings-on of the first half of the nineteenth century.

Dickens is related to all this material, and a certain amount of the information used in Philip Collins's book inevitably reappears. However, Brown also points out such things as how reticent Dickens was on the subject of ordure, 'with him it came under the polite name of "dust"'. This makes sense of Silas Wegg in *Our Mutual Friend* prodding the 'mounds of dust' with his wooden leg.

Dickens and Education, Philip   1964
Collins, Macmillan.   *Daily Telegraph*
Dickens in His Time, Ivor Brown,
Nelson

II

In 1840, Bartholomew Fair was suppressed. The Fair, a very famous institution, background of two plays by Ben Jonson, had been founded in the twelfth century by the monk Rahere (said to have started life as Henry I's jester), and for centuries had been one of the great jollifications for the poorer classes in London.

It is also true to say that for many years there had been complaints about the Fair on the grounds of the 'debauchery' that took place there. One presumes that there was drunkenness and it made a convenient spot for prostitutes to promenade.

The fair was not prohibited in so many words, but a lot of new regulations were drawn up, of which one was that 'booths for the exhibition of plays, interludes, pantomimes, mimes and all other theatrical representations be henceforth excluded from the Fair'. That amounted to closing down a large-scale entertainment that, in spite of being the scene of rioting and deaths, had even had its royal patrons.

This was only one example, although a striking one, of a process that was taking place all over the country, doing away with the old style of entertainment for the masses while putting nothing in its place. No doubt there had been many disagreeable features among the entertainments of the past, like dog-fighting and bear-baiting, but the new movement to do away with the ancient amusements of an agricultural society was influenced not only by the change-over to an industrial world, but also by the growing puritanism and sabbatarianism of the mid-nineteenth century.

Paul Schlicke's book describes how Charles Dickens was one of the first to recognize what was happening, and in several of his novels took a stand against a process which was to make Victorian England a byword for dullness, especially the dreariness of Sundays, in the eyes of foreigners.

Schlicke's first example comes from *Nicholas Nickleby* with the Crummles theatrical company. Apart from that, the subject of shows and exhibitions is often mentioned. Cruikshank's picture, called *November – St Cecilia's Day*, gives an idea of the London streets of the time and such elements as the Thirsty Woman of Tutbury, the Cock Lane Ghost, the Pig-headed Lady and various Child Phenomenons, not to mention street singing, Highlanders playing bagpipes, Italian organ-grinders, Punch-and-Judy shows, and coach-horns blowing.

Nicholas Nickleby himself is decidedly uneasy about being mixed up with players, and at once adopts a pseudonym. This is of interest, because Dickens had quite seriously thought of taking up the Stage as his own profession. Schlicke suggests that the whole Crummles interlude came to Dickens as an afterthought, and was not originally intended to be part of the novel.

The Old Curiosity Shop has a good many scenes and characters from the entertainment world, included a race-meeting and a metropolitan circus. When it comes to something like a race-meeting Dickens cannot compete with Surtees – every bit as skilful a depicter of nineteenth-century types and masterly where sport is concerned. Here Dickens also provides a gallery of stilt-walkers, performing dogs, conjurers, freaks, jugglers and the like.

Hard Times deals with the circus world in some detail. Here it has to be noted that Thomas Frost, foremost nineteenth-century authority on the circus, dismissed what Dickens says about circus life as 'rot'. Frost objected that the slang is all wrong. What strikes an even more unauthentic note is the versatility attributed to Sleary's artistes. For example, few clowns can ride, few equestriennes can perform rapid bare-back acts, and the majority of wives of performers never appear in the ring themselves.

Schlicke puts this criticism very fairly but, as a Dickens addict, it makes him extremely indignant. He takes the reasonable line that in a novel the author is not bound to give an exactly accurate picture of a given profession; the object is to entertain or to teach, and naturalism may not be the chosen manner of doing those things.

Dickens's popular journalism is full of pleas for more cheap amusement; he was firmly against a sabbatarianism that made Sundays a day to be dreaded; in this last respect Scotland being particularly grim.

Finally there is the question of Dickens's public readings from his own books. As mentioned above, Dickens had considered becoming a professional actor. Macready said Dickens was the only amateur he had ever seen who had the makings of a great actor in him.

There seems no doubt whatever that the readings were truly remarkable. The question was whether that was a medium which a novelist should take on, especially as the energy Dickens devoted to these occasions (which were primarily to make money) seems definitely to have shortened his life.

The answer really must be that Dickens created his own rules. The thought of emphasizing certain salient characters in a novel would be abhorrent to many, probably most, novelists nowadays, but Dickens was not an artist in that sense. His fantastic gifts had to be used in their own way.

Dickens and Popular Entertainment,   1986
Paul Schlicke, Allen & Unwin.   *Daily Telegraph*

III

'Ah, young Copperfield?' said Steerforth, passing a pale hand through curls now flecked with silver as he lay, his head resting on his arm – 'You ask me about young Copperfield? He has become a *very* successful man. Of course he always was a thruster, was young Copperfield. I shan't easily forget his first arrival as a new boy at Salem House. We often talk about it to this day at Old Salemite dinners. He pinned a placard on himself saying: *"Take care of him. He bites."* Do you know, for a long time nobody dared go near, boys or masters. He did no work at all for ages. Even when we got used to his ways everyone was a bit afraid of Copperfield, including the Head, poor Mr Creakle – between you and me rather an old woman, in spite of being a fine scholar.

'There was a boy called Traddles – now Sir Thomas Traddles, QC – whom Copperfield used to bully unmercifully. Made him do all his exercises for him. He'd have bullied me too, if I hadn't been tall for my age – though my health has never been too good. He nearly got me into serious trouble as soon as he arrived by persuading me to get him a lot of currant wine and biscuits and cake for a dormitory feast. Gave me seven shillings, and a great list of things he wanted. Prices were high in those days – the Corn Laws weren't abolished and the Government hadn't started the sliding-scale – so seven shillings didn't go far. Result was I had to produce most of the viands out of my own pocket just at the time when my mother had particularly asked me to be economical before going up to Oxford.

'Salem House wasn't a bad little school in its way. There was one master called Mell I could never get on with. Always playing the flute instead of teaching the boys. Copperfield marked him down at once as a coming man. Poor old Creakle used to put up with Mell because of the difficulty of finding staff, but had to get rid of him in the end. Mell went on from strength to strength and eventually founded a school in Australia. Became a very famous establishment. But it owed all its traditions to Creakle. Mell learnt everything from the dear old Head.

'Full of ambition was Copperfield. That stepfather of his, Murdstone, an able fellow in his way but weak, kept a good opening for him in his firm, one of those old established wine businesses. That wasn't good enough for Copperfield. No, he got hold of an aunt of his, Miss Trotwood. She financed him – and look where he is now.

'Do I remember the Peggottys? I should just about think I do remember the Peggottys, my dear fellow. They caused me a lot of trouble, did the Peggottys. You see, when I was still at Oxford I ran into Copperfield one night at the Golden Cross. He didn't recognize me at first, but I marked down his O.S. tie and buttonholed him. The next thing I knew was he'd whisked me down to Yarmouth to meet these Peggotty friends of his. They were in the fish business – crustaceans – a very flourishing concern. Lived in a house shaped like a boat. Advertising was in its infancy in those days, and you'd hardly believe how brisk trade was as a result of that unusual architecture.

'Well, as you know, the Peggottys had a young lady residing with them they used to call "little Em'ly". What was her exact relationship was nobody ever seemed certain. Young Copperfield was devilish keen on her. Said she needed educating, and ought to see the world. Long and the short of it was Copperfield eventually persuaded me to escort her to the Continent on a kind of Grand Tour. Of course I knew it was an unwise thing to do, but I needed the money. Even so, I wouldn't have taken the job on if Copperfield hadn't been so insistent. I guessed it would lead to trouble and talk. But he wanted her to acquire what he called "a bit of culture", and he knew she'd be safe in my hands.

'Italy wasn't at all what Emily liked. She was vastly bored there. Used to talk to the fishermen a bit, and picked up some of the language, but she hated sight-seeing. Then there were difficulties with my man, Littimer. I know he's not much of a valet, but he does his best. Nothing was ever good enough for Emily. She once told poor old Littimer that she wished she were his wife, and then she would teach him a thing or two. Of course, Littimer is as confirmed a bachelor as myself. Then she decided to travel home alone. I had to go on studying my special subject – navigation – and rather lost touch with her, though I heard she went to Australia (like Mell) not long after, and married very well there – one of the Governor-General's staff, I believe.

'You can't imagine the fuss the Peggotty family made about my allowing Emily to travel home by herself. As a matter of fact I believe she *did* pick up rather a fast girl as soon as she got to London, a Norfolk neighbour, who moved in rather a bad set. I had always suspected Mr Peggotty of being a bit of a Chartist. Even so I was quite unprepared for the attitude he took up. Copperfield did not behave at all well either. Pretended it had been my own idea to take this young woman abroad. Told the most highly-coloured story to a Miss Dartle, an old friend of my mother's. I am inclined to believe that he was also responsible for an extraordinary rumour that I myself had been drowned.

'No,' said Steerforth, with a touch of his old vivacious manner, 'don't mistake me. I like Copperfield. He was one of those strong characters few of us can resist. He has made his way in the world. He is a famous writer. But I sometimes think, "Ah, Copperfield, Copperfield, I wonder whether you ever recall your old friend James Steerforth."'

1953
Punch

THOMAS HARDY

I

The restorers' savage devastation of the churches of England and Wales was in full swing, when, in March, 1870, Thomas Hardy, then an architect in his thirtieth year, came to St Juliot, a remote Cornish parish, as representative of this church-wrecking fury. Hardy himself, a mere subordinate, cannot reasonably be held guilty of what he did there. Decisions had already been taken; the building was anyway in a tumbledown state.

However, something more happened at St Juliot than the reduction in area of the church. The parson's wife had her sister living in the house. They were the daughters of a retired, rather drunken solicitor, who had left Plymouth for Cornwall to economize. Emma Lavinia Gifford was the same age as Thomas Hardy. Four years later she became his first wife.

The marriage was not a happy one. When, in 1917, his wife died at Max Gate, Hardy's house near Dorchester, her husband found among her papers three manuscripts. Two of these are said to have been so painful that he destroyed them. The third, called *Some Recollections*, is reprinted here.

This is not all. These memoirs of his wife's early life – together, probably, with the other writings that were burnt – had such an impact on Hardy that a succession of poems by him appear to have stemmed directly from them. It must be remembered that, in his own eyes, Hardy was primarily a poet. To him his novels were pot-boilers of a superior sort. When they had earned him sufficient money, he settled down to the poetry, which was his true concern.

It will be seen, therefore, that this book is of very great interest in the study of Hardy's life and work. Apart from that, it stands on its own feet as one of those curious little essays in self-revelation that can sometimes be produced so successfully by persons quite unused to writing.

Emma Hardy regarded herself as her husband's social superior, and in later life would make embarrassing references in public to the gap in class that existed between them. In her *Recollections* she conveys with remarkable vividness the social level to which the Giffords in fact belonged in Plymouth – a world recalling the lesser levels of Jane Austen and the ladies of *Cranford*.

More than that, she expresses well her own character. Her delight in her brown riding habit and her brown mare on which she charged about to the admiration of the villagers is both taking and tiresome. One can see how captivated Hardy must have been by her; at the same time, what an appalling bore she must have become in middle age. Her egotism was obviously tremendous. What appeared imaginative energy was mostly an immense concentration on herself.

At the same time, she was not by any means without a turn for expressing herself on paper. There are lively descriptions of the countryside, commonplace things that happened to her, which could only be told by someone who had a certain gift of appreciation of what was happening round her.

Hardy himself did some editing of the manuscript. In the version given here (admirably edited by Evelyn Hardy and Robert Gittings, though it could perhaps have done with an index) we are shown his omissions and additions. There are several places where the great man's alterations did not at all improve his wife's phrase. It must also be mentioned – in the light of the imputations of snobbishness levelled at Emma Lavinia – that he cut out from the text the statement that all were welcome at her brother-in-law's table, the words 'even the dentist from Camelford who called regularly and actually dined with us at our mid-day meal, Mr Holder having much employment for him'.

Here is her account of Hardy's courting:

> I rode my pretty mare Fanny and he walked by my side and I showed him some of the neighbourhood – the cliffs, along the roads and through the scattered hamlets, sometimes gazing down at the solemn small shores where the seals lived, coming out of great caverns very occasionally.

No one could have written that who did not possess some slight talent. This description was re-echoed in Hardy's famous poem *After a Journey*.

> Hereto I come to view a voiceless ghost;
> Whither, O whither will its whim now draw me?
> Up to the cliff, down, till I'm lonely, lost,
> And the unseen waters' ejaculations awe me.
> Where you will next be there's no knowing.
> Facing round about me everywhere,
> With your nut-coloured hair,
> And gray eyes, and rose-flush coming and going.

Some Recollections by Emma Hardy
Together with Some Relevant Poems
by Thomas Hardy, Evelyn Hardy
and Robert Gittings, eds, OUP.

1961
Daily Telegraph

II

'What again and again introduces a note of falsity into Hardy's novels,' wrote T. S. Eliot, 'is that he will leave nothing to nature, but will always be giving one last turn of the screw himself, and of his motives for so doing I have the gravest suspicion.'

Thomas Hardy (1840–1928) remains, nearly half a century after his death, an extraordinarily difficult writer to assess. To begin with, he is one of the very few considerable novelists who was also a considerable poet. To this, as J. I. M. Stewart points out in his illuminating study of Hardy and his work, is added a good deal of deliberate mystification by Hardy himself; notably in saying he was never going to write an autobiography, then leaving one bogusly represented as written by his second wife.

Hardy's own hand-out in later life was, roughly speaking, to the effect that his novels were written merely to earn a living, his important work being his poetry. Stewart shows that this was not wholly true, Hardy having a high regard for his novels, though being at the same time prepared to submit them to a good deal of 'editing' to make them saleable.

Stewart devotes two chapters to Hardy's poetry, which, comparatively speaking, presents far fewer critical problems than the novels. He places him, in respect of a sizeable sheaf of the poems, as a major English poet; pointing out at the same time that *The Dynasts* is at times dreadfully dull, at others, no more than a competent pastiche of Shakespearian verse. I should like to have heard his views on that strange poem *The Revisitation*.

Both poems and novels rest on Hardy's personal myth, at once well defined and enigmatic, the same images recurring again and again. The basis of this myth was, on the one hand, Hardy's picture of himself as belonging to a family that had come down in the world in the course of several generations; on the other, the love of a man for a woman of a higher social class.

The former was reasonably true of Hardy's situation, as well as the latter, but in the case of his marriage, although there had been opposition on the grounds of his own social ineligibility, it was Hardy himself who emerged in middle life as taking great delight in the London Season and a row of smart friends, his wife who settled down to be dim and rather dotty.

'At a certain level of contrivance,' says J. I. M. Stewart, speaking of the novels, 'he is very good indeed at fabricating a plot.' Hardy also had a real grasp of the genuinely grotesque things that happen in life, even if at times these may be clumsily expressed. To this he added an enormous sense of 'seriousness' in the motives of his writing. He wanted to do nothing less than rival Aeschylus and Shakespeare in representing the eternal conflicts of right and wrong, duty and inclination, and so on. At the same time he hoped to propagate the supposed 'new truths' that were making themselves known.

Hardy in his novel-writing practice seems almost unhesitatingly to assume something really far from clear: that the elaborately 'made up' plot of the popular Victorian novel could be manipulated or refined or elevated in such a way as to subserve both these grave intents.

In saying that Stewart states the whole critical situation of Hardy and his novels.

A certain number of the ludicrous situations in the Wessex novels were, of course, caused by Victorian prudery, e.g. girls trapped into mock marriages, because it could not be suggested that they had gone to bed of their own free will; but, even allowing for such necessary evasions, there is much that is impossible to swallow. To the end of his days Hardy insisted on putting his novels through the mill of serial publication, which always increased the need to invent unlikely short episodes, and added to censorship difficulties.

In this field a distinction must be drawn between, say, Clym Yeobright's job in Paris, which may not be very convincing, but stands for some sort of amusing life that a potential husband might offer to a girl like Eustacia Vye, and Little Father Time murdering the other children, which, to be remotely believable, needs something far more elaborate in the way of a build-up.

Eliot, although he somewhat modified the view in later life, always found in Hardy too much of a taste for disagreeable situations that seemed engineered rather than required by the story. Stewart, although he defends Hardy in some directions, accepts the objection in others.

This does not mean that the character of Sue in *Jude the Obscure* is not astonishingly well expressed. The reddleman at the opening of *The Return of the Native* is a marvellous piece of descriptive writing, so are many passages in *Tess*.

Hardy's failing was a total lack of humour, which, one feels, might have prevented some of the absurdities. He could do knockabout up to a point, or irony, but one has only to think of Balzac, Dickens, Dostoevsky, Proust, or Conrad, to see the missing quality that is possessed by most of the great novelists in one form or another.

In this last connection it is interesting to note that not only was Proust a great admirer of some of Hardy's work – to be fair, some of that most open to criticism – but Hardy also read Proust with close attention. Hardy's life is on the whole well documented (the Stevens Cox pamphlets of the Toucan Press should be mentioned here), but it is possible to feel him badly treated by conjectures based on such slender evidence that he had a son by Tryphena Sparks. On the other hand his own mysterious hints about himself and his emotional life justify some speculations of that sort.

Thomas Hardy: A Critical   1971
Biography, J. I. M. Stewart,   *Daily Telegraph*
Longman.

III

When Thomas Hardy was fifty-two he met Florence Henniker, then thirty-seven. Their first encounter seems to have been at the Viceregal Lodge, Dublin, where she was acting as hostess for her widowed brother, who was Lord-Lieutenant of Ireland.

Hardy had not yet published *Jude the Obscure*, which was to give him the reputation of a dangerously outspoken writer, but his other works had already made him famous. Florence Henniker was the daughter of the 1st Lord Houghton – better known as Monckton Milnes. She was married to Arthur Henniker (younger son of the 4th Lord Henniker), an officer in The Coldstream, later promoted major-general. Mrs Henniker, who was childless, had written several novels.

They seem to have taken an immediate liking to each other and this quickly developed into an *amitié amoureuse*. It ran for thirty years. In a collection of Mrs Henniker's short stories, *In Scarlet and Grey*, Hardy even collaborated in one called 'The Spectre and the Real'. The volume was published in John Lane's Keynote Series, though not one of those with an individual Beardsley design on the binding.

Although they contain no striking revelations, these Letters are of great interest. There seems little doubt that Hardy was in love with Mrs Henniker, though this emerges from his poems rather than from any direct evidence here or elsewhere; and such conclusions must always be treated with extreme caution. It has been suggested that she contributed some of the characteristics of Sue Bridehead in *Jude*.

Hardy took considerable pains to provide posterity with material for the picture of himself he hoped to be preserved. This, as so often, was not entirely in accordance with what appear to be the facts, not so much because it was untrue, but as only part of the story. The editors of *One Rare Fair Woman* seem to me to be fighting a rearguard action to sustain this severely stylized view of Hardy, sometimes so much so as to be misleading. They tend to adopt a slightly condescending tone towards Mrs Henniker, and appear positively shocked by Hardy referring to peeresses by their nicknames.

To say, for example, that Florence Henniker's father was 'noted for his extravagant hospitality', yet give no hint of Monckton Milnes's contemporary reputation (erotic library, and so on) is to do less than justice to a remarkable personality. The omission vitiates also the comment: 'It is amusing now to read that Florence was considered rather "fast" by the members of the older Victorian set . . .' No doubt Mrs Henniker was respectability itself, but naturally Monckton Milnes's daughter was expected to be 'fast', not without reason, and she seems certainly far from unwilling to carry on a flirtation with Hardy, even if things stopped there; as no doubt they did.

In the same way, it is a little absurd to write of Hardy as 'mingling' with the aristocracy as if he were an oddity at their parties. He obviously became part of the whole show. He lived a thoroughly 'smart' life, when he was in London ('smarter', one would venture to guess, than James), and was obviously perfectly at ease in a world where much was enjoyable, even if intellectual matters were not an essential medium of conversation.

These points seem worth making to prevent the reader from stepping off on the wrong foot. They are required to understand why Hardy and Florence Henniker at once got on so easily together, quite apart from emotional questions involved. If anyone doubts their validity, the letters to Mrs Henniker should be compared with those Hardy wrote to his first wife, published as *Dearest Emmie* (1963).

The first Mrs Hardy thought Florence Henniker 'poison', but the second Mrs Hardy was introduced to her husband by Mrs Henniker herself; who was perhaps a little taken aback later by her protégée's marriage to the novelist.

Hardy's literary tastes emerge from these Letters. Shelley was his favourite poet. As to other novelists:

> In my enforced idleness, I have been reading H. James's *Wings of the Dove* – the first of his that I have looked into for years and years. I read it with a fair amount of care – as much as one would wish to expend on any novel, certainly, seeing what there is to read beside novels – and so did Em; but we have been arguing ever since about what happened to the people, and find we have wholly conflicting opinions thereon. At the same time James is almost the only living novelist I can read, and taken in small doses I like him exceedingly, being as he is a real man of letters.

Galsworthy did not score so high: 'The author of *A Man of Property* sent me the book, and I began it, but found the people too materialistic and sordid to be interesting.' This surely answers the editors' rhetorical question, 'One wonders what the author of *Jude the Obscure* thought of that,' when Mrs Henniker writes that Galsworthy's 'curious fondness

for the flagrantly immoral women seems to be more marked than ever –
as he now even condones their suffocating their children!'
Of Meredith:

> I am not surprised that you got stuck in *The Egoist*. It is awkward for
> me, of course, to criticize the work of a man I liked and admired so
> much, but I may say that the difficulty of reading – or at least
> enjoying – some of his books arises entirely (as I think) from his
> errors of method. Why he was so perverse as to infringe the first rules
> of narrative art I cannot tell, when what he had to say was of the very
> highest, and what he discerned in life was more than almost any
> novelist had discerned before. A child could almost have told him
> that to indulge in psychological analysis of the most ingenious kind in
> the crisis of an emotional scene is fatal – high emotion demanding
> simplicity of expression above all things – yet this is what Meredith
> constantly did.

In the light of this last comment, it is remarkable that Hardy thought
highly of such of Proust's works as he read.

Julia Peel (p. 13) was the granddaughter, not daughter, of the Prime
Minister; 'Lord Hungerford Crewe' (p. 40) should read Hungerford,
Lord Crewe; 'Hugh Seton Merriman' (p. 55), Henry Seton Merriman.

One Rare Fair Woman: Thomas   1972
Hardy's Letters to Florence   *Daily Telegraph*
Henniker, 1893–1922, Evelyn
Hardy and F. B. Pinion, eds,
Macmillan.

IV

These letters, which take Thomas Hardy just into his fifties, are
overwhelmingly concerned with his business affairs as a writer. They
are not for that reason uninteresting.

Hardy presents two sides in his professional literary life. On the one
hand, in the still chaotic publishing conditions of the period, he had
firm ideas as to what he should be paid, and the extent of copyright; on
the other, he was quite astonishingly unassuming in being prepared to
fit in with what any given periodical wanted for its public, sometimes
telling editors that they could alter whatever they liked in the stories he
sent them.

These two contrasted aspects of Hardy's approach to writing are also
seen in his speaking of an ambition to do no more than produce a 'good
serial', combined with the extreme sensitiveness he showed to adverse
criticism. It was true that the attacks on *Tess*, for example, were of a
particularly irritating kind in their sanctimoniousness, but Hardy

never really accustomed himself to routine contradictions and muddle-headness displayed by reviewers in general. Indeed, when in his sixties, he compiled a list of totally conflicting opinions expressed by critics about his books.

The editors of this volume, Richard Little Purdy and Michael Millgate, do their job very thoroughly and concisely, with notes after each letter. They draw attention to Hardy's extreme discretion on what he committed to paper when writing to friends or relations. Even though these are usually just notes sent during a day or two's absence from home. The letters to his first wife, Emma Gifford, are noticeably bare and brief in tone.

No doubt a great deal was deliberately destroyed. Even so, a remarkable sense of formality is always kept up. This possesses its own element of revealing the man himself, and I think, however little he gives away, one does seem to know Hardy better after reading this volume.

The nearest Hardy comes in these pages to having an easy-going relationship is certainly the one with Edmund Gosse (1849–1928), to whom, in a light-hearted moment, he once headed a letter 'Porta Maxima', instead of 'Max Gate'. This was about the furthest Hardy went in the way of high spirits. In the other direction (30 August 1887), he admitted to Gosse: 'As to despondency I have known the very depths of it – you would be quite shocked if I were to tell you how many weeks & months in byegone years I have gone to bed wishing never to see daylight again.'

This innate gloom is repeated in another letter (undated, but about May 1891) written to thank Rider Haggard for a book. The Haggards had recently lost a child, and Hardy adds: 'Please give my kind regards to Mrs Haggard, & tell her how deeply our sympathy was with you both in your bereavement. Though, to be candid, I think the death of a child is never really to be regretted, when one reflects on what he has escaped.'

These were the days when novels were illustrated, and there are amusing letters on this subject, about which Hardy seems to have felt almost more strongly than about tinkering with the stories themselves. He would offer to send his own drawings of objects mentioned, which might be unfamiliar to the artist.

At the beginning of 1878, for instance, there was some correspondence about *The Return of the Native*, which was to be illustrated by Arthur Hopkins, brother of the poet, Gerard Manley Hopkins. Hardy writes: 'It is rather ungenerous to criticise; but since you invite me to do so I will say that I think Eustacia should have been represented as more youthful in face, supple in figure, &, in general, with a little more roundness & softness than have been given her.' Later (regarding the mummers scene): 'Eustacia in boys' clothes, though pleasant enough to the imagination, would perhaps be unsafe as a picture.'

For *The Trumpet-Major* Hardy wanted Charles Keene, because he drew soldiers well, and he was pleased to get George Du Maurier for *The Hand of Ethelberta* and *A Laodicean*. In connection with pictures, it is notable that Hardy (1 June 1889) writes: 'An exhibition of "impression" pictures by Claude Monet was very interesting – he being the latest exponent of that school. In looking at them you could almost feel the heat of the sun depicted in the painting, & the dazzle of the noon-day.' This seems remarkable appreciation of an Impressionist at that date.

Hardy's literary likings or dislikings are occasionally to be found. He wrote a fan-letter (8 June 1875) to R. D. Blackmore on the subject of *Lorna Doone*. In 1891 he was fairly fulsome in his praise for the poetry of Alfred Austen, William Watson, and Owen Meredith (the second Lord Lytton). In the same year he wrote: 'I have just finished Barrie's *Little Minister*. Up to the 8th or 9th chapter it is excellent – After that it grows second-rate, & the ending is as bad as novel can be.'

The Collected Letters of Thomas   1978
Hardy: Vol. I: 1840–1892,   *Daily Telegraph*
Richard Little Purdy and
Michael Millgate, eds,
Clarendon Press: OUP.

V

When Somerset Maugham's novel *Cakes and Ale* appeared in 1930, Alroy Kear in it was generally recognized as a take-off of Hugh Walpole who was indeed so upset by the book that he fell ill.

Driffield, the recently deceased 'great' writer round whom the plot revolves, although possessing certain aspects of Thomas Hardy, including the fact that he had been twice married, was a far more generalized figure, quite unlike Hardy in singing comic-songs to the banjo and decamping without paying his debts.

It came as news to me, therefore, that the second Mrs Hardy was scarcely less upset by Maugham's novel than Walpole, and because of what she supposed to be the picture of herself there, refused to unveil the stained-glass window put up by her husband in the Hardy family's local church.

Robert Gittings and Jo Manton (Mrs Robert Gittings) have put together a short but absorbing book about Florence Dugdale, Hardy's second wife. It was well worth doing, even after Gittings's two masterly earlier volumes on Hardy. The authors are, I think, sometimes a little hard – in the now fashionable manner – on their subject for wanting to

'better' herself (and for some reason castigate her for patriotism in the
first world war), but they also bring out what an exceedingly trying
time she had throughout most of her life. It is a strangely tragic story,
completely in Hardy's own manner.

Florence Dugdale was one of the children of an energetic headmaster
of a National School at Enfield, a man who had made his own way. His
daughter had literary ambitions, and not very good health. She taught
in her father's school for some years, also managing to do odds and ends
of journalism and write stories for children's magazines. She had an
attractive appearance and one is surprised that proposals did not come
her way. Possibly the men she ran across found the literary ambitions a
shade forbidding.

Alfred Hyatt, with whom she fell in love, and who seems to have
loved her (without hope of marriage, for various reasons), was a
talented editor of anthologies, one of which made selections from the
works of Thomas Hardy. Just how the meeting between Hardy and
Florence Dugdale took place is not clear, but one has the impression
that there was an immediate reaction on Hardy's part, and the
secretarial work for him which Florence Dugdale now took on was,
from the start, coloured by strong physical attractions on Hardy's side.

By this time Florence Dugdale was not without all contact with the
higher levels of the literary world. She had already developed romantic
feelings about the lives of authors when Hardy turned up as answer to
her dreams.

Hardy's uncomfortable relationship with his first wife, Emma, was
no secret, and one of the most piquant aspects of the story is that by
chance Emma Hardy also came across Florence Dugdale (of whose
existence she seems to have been unaware), took a fancy to her, and
invited her to the Hardys' hideous and depressing Dorset home, Max
Gate. Indeed, as the authors suggest, Emma seems to have fallen in
love with Florence scarcely less than had her husband.

What had been happening on Hardy's various jaunts to the country
with Florence Dugdale? They seemed to have been chaperoned, more
or less, most of the time, but it is hard to believe that she became his
mistress only on moving into Max Gate after Emma Hardy's death.
The stages of their relationship are unlikely ever to be known.

When Emma Hardy died it never appears to have occurred to Hardy
that Florence would do otherwise than welcome marriage to him,
although he was then seventy-three, she thirty-four. Certainly there
was something to be said for becoming his wife, not only for worldly
reasons, but because that position satisfied her earlier dream.

One of Hardy's least endearing qualities was his pathological
stinginess, of which Florence Dugdale must already have acquired
some working knowledge before marriage. What she – or anyone else –

could not possibly have foreseen was that after her death Emma Hardy would become enshrined in her husband's memory – and in some of his best poems – as his supreme love. The only jaunts Florence was allowed being visits to Emma's grave or places associated with her.

Hugh Walpole could complain with some justice that Alroy Kear was decidedly like him, but in most respects the second Mrs Driffield was not at all like Florence Dugdale, dedicated to keeping herself in the background, terrified of Hardy rather than managing him. Nevertheless, although Maugham can at best have acquired his information by hearsay, a few horrible half-truths adhered. I think this was just a novelist's instinct, and no mystery.

Florence's character is elusive. She could act with extraordinary bad temper and silliness; the servants at Max Gate did not like her. Even so Hardy's grander friends, using the epithet both in a social and literary sense, do not seem to have found her at all unsympathetic. After his death she appeared to be about to marry J. M. Barrie; then realized herself by devotion to Dorchester hospital and housing, also serving as a J P. In a photograph of her at the age of twenty, the expression of the fox-terrier who poses with her seems to suggest that he well foresees her future fate, with his kinsman, Wessex, Hardy's dog who terrorized all visitors to Max Gate and bit a whole generation of men of letters.

The Second Mrs Hardy, Robert   1979
Gittings and Jo Manton,   *Daily Telegraph*
Heinemann

VI

On the face of it, this book has the air of a pendant to *The Second Mrs Hardy*, by Robert Gittings and Jo Manton, which appeared some few months ago. But Denys Kay-Robinson is not so accomplished a biographer as Gittings, and in attempting a single portrait, he has set himself a far more difficult task.

When Hardy married his second wife, Florence Dugdale, he was in his seventies and famous. The reader can take Hardy himself for granted, concentrating on the husband-and-wife relationship. In addition to that, the authors of *The Second Mrs Hardy* gave an admirably clear account of their subject's family and earlier background. Such explicit treatment is scarcely possible with Emma Gifford, the first Mrs Hardy.

Denys Kay-Robinson, perhaps unavoidably, goes over familiar ground in his first fifty pages or so, and we never really achieve a clear picture (as with Florence Dugdale) of what made Emma Gifford (1840–1912) the woman she was. Let me quickly add that such information may well be not available, or would at least take a lifetime to ferret out, but Emma Gifford's case is not really covered by a page or two of slightly precarious nineteenth-century social generalizations, provided by Kay-Robinson at the beginning of his book.

The established story is that the first Mrs Hardy looked down on her husband for his modest origins (which Hardy certainly took steps to conceal). Her own father was a solicitor (son of a schoolmaster) who seems to have had just enough money to retire early from the job. Retirement may have been hastened by the fact that he was an alcoholic. His daughter describes how he would get drunk, shut himself up in a room with drawn curtains, and recite Shakespeare. At least one of the family ended in an asylum.

The airs assumed by Emma Gifford (whose mother's family were Bristol merchants) were no doubt to a great degree self-protective, but one would like to know more. Was there any reason for Mr Gifford being a drunk? Were there grander earlier generations of Giffords to look back on? Emma Gifford, a considerable fantasist in some respects, does not seem to have invoked the latter.

There are many odd aspects in Hardy's behaviour, one of the most notable the manner in which he prejudiced the happiness of his second wife after marriage by canonizing the memory of his first, with whom he had, in fact, lived far from happily. He did that particularly by a burst of remarkable poems in celebration of that earlier love. In this paradoxical connection it might perhaps be urged that no one objects to Swinburne having written some of the most passionate verse ever composed, while not himself having lived, anyway on a wide scale, a passionate life.

Kay-Robinson thinks that Emma Hardy has been unfairly treated, and one of the aims of his book is to set right the balance. He does convince the reader that Hardy was very much in love when the first marriage took place, and no one would disagree with the view that Hardy was a difficult husband. At the same time, as the list of the witnesses to the first Mrs Hardy's shortcomings are assembled – some of them to a certain degree confused – we begin to wonder whether, if Emma Hardy is to be presented in a sympathetic light, it would have been easier to prove the case without calling on so many people who found her tiresome.

It was undoubtedly a sorrow that the Hardys had no children. Hardy wished for children, and it has been suggested that he had difficulties in a sexual relationship. But evidence that Kay-Robinson produces as to the second Mrs Hardy's correspondence with Marie Stopes points to the second marriage being perfectly normal, in that respect, though by that time Hardy himself did not want a child.

Emma had literary pretensions, not only copying out Hardy's novels

in longhand, but offering advice that seems often to have been helpful –
though at other times to take it would have been disastrous. Kay-
Robinson tries to persuade us that she herself possessed some talent but
I remain unconvinced. Many Victorian ladies could write a good
account of their travels, for instance, at which the first Mrs Hardy
seems to rise to no uniquely remarkable height even if able to do that;
while very useful advice can be given to novelists by those with no
ability at all to write themselves. Nevertheless, Emma Hardy felt her
literary gifts were insufficiently recognized.

Then there was the matter of his first wife trying throughout their
marriage to win Hardy from his agnostic opinions. *Jude the Obscure* was
a particular stumbling-block. Kay-Robinson quotes the memoirs,
hitherto unemphasized, of the dramatist, Alfred Sutro, who lunched
with the Hardys soon after *Jude*'s publication. The vignette is a striking
one.

I was loud in my praises of that work. Mrs Hardy was far from
sharing my enthusiasm. It was the first novel of his, she told me, that
he had published without first letting her read the manuscript; had
she read it, she added firmly, it would *not* have been published, or at
least not without considerable emendations. The book had made a
difference to them in the County . . . Hardy said nothing, and did not
lift his eyes from his plate.

Perhaps the fairest assessment comes from a friend of the Hardys,
Bertha Newcombe, in a letter (1900) to the wife of Edmund Gosse:

I felt a great sympathy and pity for Emma this time. It is pathetic to
see how she is struggling against her woes. She asserts herself as
much as possible and is a great bore, but at the same time is so kind
and goodhearted, and one cannot help realising what she must have
been to her husband. She showed us a photograph of herself as a
young girl, and it was very attractive. I always thought she must
have had a certain *beauté de diable*.

The photographs, even the early ones, make one wonder whether
there may not have been a glandular disturbance, which could have
caused some of the trouble. Desmond McCarthy, by the way, was a
critic not a novelist.

The First Mrs Thomas Hardy, 1979
Denys Kay-Robinson, *Daily Telegraph*
Macmillan.

JOSEPH CONRAD

I

To unravel the secret of Joseph Conrad's racial origin from his novels could provide a fascinating exercise in literary detective work. *The Secret Agent* and *Under Western Eyes* would have to be excluded from the collected edition, because, when ranged with other available evidence, they offer clues that hint too strongly at the truth to make the enquiry sufficiently recondite. Both books, in short, assume a critical familiarity with the organization of revolutionary activities, and a knowledge of the intricacies of Russian temperament, that combine to support a strong *prima facie* case for authorship by a member of some community uncomfortably conversant with Russian methods of administration. Nineteenth-century Poland would immediately spring to mind. It might be argued that the remaining novels offer sufficient data to draw the same conclusion; and – since the peculiarities of Conrad's background took an emphatic part in forming his point of view as a writer – we may consider briefly how such an investigation might proceed.

In the first place, the occasional esoteric phrase indicates fairly plainly (though perhaps not so frequently as is sometimes maintained) that Conrad's upbringing was foreign; while the exotic panorama he unfolds is rarely contrasted, except in the most general terms, with life in England. These mannerisms could, of course, belong to an Englishman, especially an Englishman who had been educated abroad. There is a subtler strain, however, which might be held – almost irresistibly – to establish the author as neither English nor American: an aspect of Conrad's writing that might be overlooked by those who regard him (understandably, but quite erroneously) first and last as a chronicler of the sea. This characteristic is his attitude to the machinery through which government is made manifest – an attitude camouflaged sometimes by florid colours – an instinctive conviction that takes for granted officialdom, corrupt and oppressive to a greater or lesser degree. His is an accepted continental scepticism towards such matters, far removed from the expostulation of, say, Dickens or Trollope, in whose books mischiefs in Parliament or Civil Service are never something almost inherent in public affairs.

Nostromo and *The Arrow of Gold* furnish examples of this scepticism, the former taking misrule almost for its main theme. ('It so happened, however, that the Finance Minister of the time was a man to whom, in years gone by, Mr Gould had, unfortunately, declined to grant some small pecuniary assistance, basing his refusal on the grounds that the applicant was a notorious gambler and cheat . . .'; or, 'No. Bribes were out of the question, he admitted. But there were many legitimist sympathies in Paris. A proper person could set them in motion and a mere hint from high quarters to the officials on the spot not to worry over-much about the wreck. . . .') This apprehension of the abuse of power, especially power in the hands of demagogues and *fonctionnaires*, would on the whole suggest a Latin or Slav, rather than a Teuton, writer; and Conrad is in all respects sufficiently un-German (not to say anti-German) to put any such consideration out of court. It might be advanced, however, at this stage of the investigation that Americans often pride themselves on seeing through the motives of politicians, alien and domestic, and that Conrad – merely on the grounds outlined above – could have been American. A keenly felt sense of European tradition, a knowledge of the ways of peasants, make this classification improbable. Besides, he is rarely, if ever, high-spirited enough for an American. His love for superlatives, in action or in emotion, exists: they are not American superlatives.

Scepticism about official integrity at once hints at a Frenchman; and here for a time the enquirer might pause. He is at his ease in France. An insuperable objection arises. The advocate of French – or any other Latin – derivation would be faced with the difficulty of fitting Conrad's heroines into any Latin novel; and, it might be added, into Scandinavian literature, too; though for different reasons. We are left, therefore, with the probability that he was a Slav; perhaps a Russian with his eyes fixed on the West.

This conclusion – that Conrad was Russian – might satisfy a less persevering investigator; and there is much in his sardonic humour and idealized women for which parallels might be found in the great Russian novels. More penetrating analysts would remain unconvinced. Conrad has neither the credulity nor the despondency of the Russians. His humour has not that touch of caricature that Russian writers can rarely resist, and in which (like the English) they excel. Moreover, his admiration is directed towards tolerance, moderation, discipline: the individual often playing a noble part in a subordinate role (Dominique or Nostromo), but always as an individual, never as avatar of some uncontrollable and mystic force. Alyosha and Bazarov are scarcely conceivable in a Conrad setting: Pechorin, and even Prince Anton, would have to undergo drastic modification. Pondering on the signposts set all over Conrad's novels – a Slav, and yet hardly a Russian – the Polish answer might almost be inferred (though not without ingenuity) even from the stories about the islands and the sea.

This attempt to trace Conrad's beginnings from his writing is intended to emphasize that his standpoint inevitably leads back to these beginnings; and not to insist, because we already know that he was a Pole, that supposedly Polish attributes must be sought in his books. On the contrary, fellow Poles are inclined to deny any specifically Polish orientation there. All the same, opportunities that have arisen in this country since 1940 to observe Polish national character at close range lead inexorably to the conclusion that Conrad's idiosyncrasies are typical of the distinctly Polish frame of mind that nature and history have combined to shape. In crude terms some of its facets might be hazarded: intense nervous force, appreciation of humour and a mercurial approach to life; pronounced taste for political discussion, a disposition to melancholy and devotion to panache; enormous endurance, with some tendency to strain at gnats and swallow camels; somewhat tortuous processes of thought, directed passionately towards enlightenment. These are certainly aspects of character in which Conrad habitually shows himself keenly interested. Are they Polish characteristics, taken so much for granted that their recurrence in his books is imperceptible to his countrymen? Conrad's life suggests that he himself possessed a fair share of them.

The facts are set out in Jean-Aubry's clear and conscientious narrative. Teodor Jozef Konrad Naleçz Korzeniowski was born in 1857. His father, Apollo Naleçz Korzeniowski, amateur of poetry and philosophy, land agent, dramatist, and publisher, was the son of a cavalry officer in Napoleon's Duchy of Warsaw army. The family came of impecunious landed gentry (his mother, Eveline Bobrowska, was of similar stock), 'Naleçz' being the designation of a specific coat of arms, attached to the name, in the Polish manner, to distinguish them from other Korzeniowskis. Apollo Korzeniowski, an engaging but ineffective figure, was implicated in the preliminary activities of the Polish revolt of 1863 against Russian rule and sent into exile; but the relatively easy-going course sometimes followed by Tsarist persecution did not on this occasion demand Siberia. His family was allowed to follow him to a distant province, on condition that his wife accepted the status of a political prisoner. She accompanied him, and died when Conrad was six years old. In 1867 her husband's health was considered to have been sufficiently undermined by his deportation to reconcile the authorities to his release. He was allowed to leave Russia, and settled in Austrian Poland, where he died when his son was thirteen. Conrad was brought up at Cracow by his mother's brother, Tadeusz Bobrowski, who played a great part in his life, not only as a firm – though genial and sympathetic – guardian but also as the antithesis in character of his father. Bobrowski had refused to identify himself with the insurgents of 1863, on the ground that they had no chance of success. He was cautious, honest, clear-headed, an amusing talker: the arch-enemy of romanticism. His shadow falls across the scenes of conflict between idealism and common sense so often illustrated in his nephew's novels: a battle, indeed, never resolved within Conrad himself.

To the surprise of his relations, Conrad announced at fifteen that he wanted to be a sailor. There seems to have been no reason for this decision more valid than an enjoyment of Captain Marryat's tales; and there was much family opposition. Russian, German and Austro-Hungarian navies did not recommend themselves to a patiotic Pole, though there would have been little difficulty in entering the last of these as a cadet. Instead, he went at seventeen to Marseilles, and, living there on a small temporary allowance from his uncle, took steps to acquire experience in seafaring matters. At the age of twenty-one, without a word of English, he landed at Lowestoft. Two years later he passed the examination qualifying him as an officer of mercantile marine, in which capacity, taking British nationality, he served for the next fifteen years; until the publication of *Almayer's Folly*, in 1895.

The Arrow of Gold, a good example of his mature style, portrays his life during the Marseilles period and his entanglement with the Carlist war. To the disenchanted eyes of today the love affair may seem to lack force in comparison with the rest of the book; although the final anti-climax redeems this side of the story from what threatens at times to become an overstrained delicacy. In the verbal fencing, Henry James's influence is noticeable, and also – though far more robustly – in the characterization of Captain Blunt, dashing American, a mother's boy; while Mrs Blunt's plans to unite her son to Doña Rita's money recall a little the atmosphere of *Portrait of a Lady*. However, if Conrad sometimes looks back here to James, he looks forward to Hemingway ('The mistral howled in the sunshine, shaking the bare bushes quite furiously. And everything was bright and hard, the air was hard, the light was hard, the ground under our feet was hard'); and other Americans (Scott Fitzgerald, William Faulkner) have studied his methods of handling action, in which he is supreme.

Although the merest sketch, Ortega, as a revolutionary outwardly of the Right, anticipates the nihilistic side of Fascism. He brings us back to the quality suggested earlier as attesting Conrad's nature to be something other than Anglo-Saxon in his instinctive awareness of the mixed and violent emotions – the personal frustration and desire for power – that attend public affairs and political insecurity. This subject is treated at length in *Nostromo*, a story of a Latin American State, in which the integrity of the Goulds, a local family of British origin, is contrasted with the baseness of politicians and generals, pursuing their evil ways in the name of democracy; another – and romantic – sort of democracy being exemplified by the old Garibaldino, and by Nostromo himself. A *tour de force*, *Nostromo* owes something to *Le Rouge et le Noir* and, less erratically brilliant, suffers from the same diffuseness. Conrad sets out his point of view with greater economy in *Under Western Eyes*, already mentioned as signalizing so unmistakably his Polish ancestry.

Haldin, a Russian student, after committing a political assassination, seeks refuge with another student, Razumov. Razumov, who had no connection with the terrorist movement, seeing his whole career threatened, informs against him. Haldin is executed; and Razumov finds that he himself is left with no future except as a police spy. He is sent to Geneva to report on revolutionary intrigues there, falls in love with Haldin's sister, and, in despair, reveals his identity to the conspirators he has been sent to watch, one of whom deafens him for life by breaking his ear-drums. Published in 1911, *Under Western Eyes* is remarkable for the mixture of humour and horror with which it depicts the anti-European and anti-democratic principles of Russian revolutionary thought. Razumov's predicament – a man forced to play a shabby part through no particular fault of his own – is a favourite theme of Conrad's, and might be compared with *Lord Jim*, in which he perhaps symbolized (by Jim's desertion of the pilgrim ship) his own forsaking of Poland.

This disparagement of himself as a patriot came from the romantic element in his character which he never tamed; though, unlike Heyst in *Victory*, he was no 'utopist'. Indeed, his informed distrust of pretentious claims to idealism and of pursuit of power masquerading as liberalism sets him apart from the mood of his literary contemporaries, most of whom, like H. G. Wells or John Galsworthy, owing to his late start as a writer, were ten years younger than himself. In this divergence he resembles Kipling – an author personally unsympathetic to him – who shares Conrad's respect for a sense of duty, his recognition of the practical difficulties of exercising command, and also, to some degree, his satirical attitude towards officials. Conrad is more sensitive than Kipling in handling the niceties of human character, but he does not possess Kipling's dexterity nor, perhaps, his imaginative powers. On the other hand Kipling – although his dislike for Peter Ivanovitch and his circle would in no way have fallen short of Conrad's – could never have achieved the objectivity of *Under Western Eyes*.

'As if anything could be changed!' thinks Razumov. 'In this world of men nothing can be changed – neither happiness nor misery. They can only be displaced at the cost of corrupted consciences and broken lives – a futile game for arrogant philosophers and sanguinary triflers.' This was the lesson Conrad himself had learnt: not without some inclination to think otherwise. Armed with this knowledge, he has been pictured by Max Beerbohm – pointed beard, eye-glass, and reefer jacket – watching a thin green snake crawling through the eye of a skull that lies by the shore, as he reflects: 'What a delightful coast! One catches an illusion that one might forever be almost gay here.' For Conrad, we feel, that coast was the world of men.

Nostromo. Under Western Eyes. The Arrow of Gold, collected edn, Joseph Conrad, Dent.
Vie de Conrad, G. Jean-Aubry, Gallimard.
Sagesse de Conrad, G. Jean-Aubry, ed., Gallimard.

1947
Times Literary Supplement

II

For those who find Joseph Conrad of peculiar interest these Letters will be a great treat. Others may perhaps think the collection rather heavy going, because the majority are no more than the letters of an uncle to a nephew of whom he is guardian, complaining that the young man has too happy-go-lucky an attitude towards money and lacks in general a practical approach to life.

The letters in *Conrad's Polish Background* are, indeed, such a classical example of this situation that one might put it the other way, and add that those who enjoy studying human nature at close range will find entertainment in them irrespective of the fact that they deal with the early life of a great writer like Conrad.

Conrad came of the Polish nobility – or, as we should say, gentry – a class much larger in relation to the whole population than anything comparable in France, Germany or Great Britain. No one who has had any dealings with Poles on an extensive scale can have failed to notice the 'aristocratic' tradition, good or bad as you choose to think, that regulates the Polish approach to life. It cannot be ignored in Conrad's writing, and is well brought out here.

Conrad was born in 1857, at a time when Poland had ceased to exist as a country. Russia tyrannized over her Polish population, and Germany was not far behind, but in Austria the attitude to Poles was liberal. Conrad's father was a Russian Pole, a poet and dramatist of some local standing, full of patriotic feeling, which resulted in his being imprisoned and sent into exile by the Russian authorities. His wife was sentenced with him (a fact that emerges in this book, it hitherto being thought that she accompanied him voluntarily), and both died as a result of their hardships when Conrad himself was still a small child.

Conrad was sent to Austrian Poland to be brought up by his mother's brother, Tadeusz Bobrowski. Bobrowski is an interesting figure, if only because he had a perfectly clear-cut view of himself and his relations, particularly the Korzeniowskis.

In the eyes of Conrad's uncle, the Korzeniowskis were a crowd of romantic, utterly unpractical dreamers, their heads full of poetry, patriotic sentiments and absurd uplift, high-flown ideas which had landed them just where you might expect.

He himself was a successful lawyer, opposed equally to what he regarded as intellectual or political follies of the imagination. Sound common sense, he proclaimed, was the tradition of his own family, the Bobrowskis. He was always pointing out in his letters, with apparent truth, that far too many of his relations seemed to expect him to be perpetually handing out money and arranging their affairs.

The uncle Bobrowski's generalizations about the two families from which Conrad sprang must not be taken too seriously, but undoubtedly there was an element of truth in what he said. What should also be remembered is that a man who had thought all this out must also be to some extent a man of imagination himself. One is struck by the force of expression in Bobrowski's letters. They could almost have provided the foundation from which literary gifts might emerge.

Conrad, therefore, from the very beginning, can be seen in the characteristic situation of the novelist, pulled in two contrary directions by temperament and upbringing. Other circumstances played even stranger tricks.

As a Russian citizen, son of a convicted political prisoner, Conrad was liable to as much as twenty-five years' conscription in the Russian forces. One of his uncle's hopes was to arrange for his nephew to become the naturalized subject of some country which would put him out of reach.

In Zdzislaw Najder's excellent Introduction he points out Conrad's choice of the sea as a profession was largely brought about by desire to get away from his own melancholy background, coupled with a vague wish for adventure. To make himself a seaman was not in the first instance a dedicated vocation, because other projects and possibilities were evidently often mentioned by him when he wrote to his uncle.

The fact that he did become a Master Mariner in the British Merchant Service by the time he was twenty-nine, and ten years later left the sea to be a writer, does bear out the view of two conflicting strains at work in him. The former was certainly an extraordinary achievement for a young man who appeared to his uncle to be lacking in application.

Bobrowski's letters nag so much that at times one feels that he would positively drive a nephew into undesirable paths, but the fact remains that, however differently they looked at life, Conrad ended by possessing a deep affection for his uncle. That Conrad himself was hard to deal with cannot be denied, his shortcomings including an attempt at suicide the wound from which was passed off as the result of a duel.

The relatively calm manner in which this incident is reported by his uncle (who had been forced to travel to Marseilles to clear up matters) contrasts with chronic grumbling about such things as leaving letters unanswered or wanting an advance on an allowance.

One of the points in which these Letters supplement Jocelyn Baines's *Joseph Conrad: A Biography* (1960) is in revealing that Conrad as a child appears to have suffered from epilepsy. He seems to have grown out of this early in life, but such a condition at one stage in his career would not have been out of keeping with the way he subsequently developed.

Incidentally, in a letter written when Conrad was twenty-three his uncle remarks on his nephew's capacity for expressing himself on paper, suggesting that he should contribute articles on travel subjects to a Polish paper. It is a pity that it is only the uncle's letters that have been preserved. Conrad's own early letters, which appear to have been often full ones, would have been of the greatest interest.

The latter part of this collection includes letters from Conrad himself. One states his views at the time of the South African War.

> That they [the Boers] are struggling in good faith for their independence cannot be doubted; but it is also a fact that they have no idea of liberty, which can only be found under the English flag all over the world. *C'est un peuple essentiellement despotique*, like, by the way, all the Dutch. This war is not so much a war against the Transvaal as a struggle against the doings of German influence. It is the Germans who have forced the issue. . . .
>
> Europe rejoices and is moved because Europe is jealous and here in England there is more real sympathy and regard for the Boers than on the whole continent, which proclaims its compassion at the top of its voice.

After sixty-five years these comments hold up pretty well.

Coward's Polish Background:　　　　　　　　　　　1964
Letters to and from Polish Friends,　　　　　　*Daily Telegraph*
Zdzislaw Najder, ed.,
Halina Carroll, trans.,
OUP.

III

The question of a novelist's material is a complicated one. To the non-professional it seems to take the form of choosing various outstanding individuals known to the writer and setting them in some more or less dramatic relation to each other. 'Is such-and-such a character meant to be so-and-so?' is a question often asked.

This approach is apt to irk the author himself, because, although 'real people' and 'real situations' may form the basis for a story or incident, the moment a novelist gets to work on them it is his own sensibility, not the original model, that motivates the scene.

Having made this plea for the novelist's freedom of action, one has to admit that, in the case of great writers, some documentation of the sources they used can be of very considerable interest. In *Conrad's Eastern World* there is much to hold the attention (not only about Conrad) if you are interested in how novels are put together. One of the side-issues is the influence of these books on Somerset Maugham.

Conrad sailed Eastern waters as an officer in British merchant ships between 1883 and 1888, in an area now very much in the news; roughly Thailand and Vietnam in the North, the Philippines (not 'Phillipines', as in the map provided) to the East, Malaysia and Indonesia to the South.

The novels that derive from his five years in South-West Asia are *Almayer's Folly, An Outcast of the Islands, Lord Jim, Victory* and *The Rescue*, together with the autobiographical volume *The Shadow-Line*, and several short stories like 'Typhoon' and 'Falk'.

Norman Sherry, who is a lecturer in English at the University of Singapore, has done a job to delight those who enjoy the best sort of literary detective work. He really knows what he is talking about, and supplies some excellent illustrations. His abilities in other directions even make one forgive him the horrible phrase 'central to'.

It becomes clear from the start that any effort to protest that novelists do not use 'real people' is doomed to total failure in the case of Conrad. Not only was Almayer actually called 'Olmeijer', but Capt. McWhirr – a novelist's comic name, if ever there was one – was named precisely that, put in bodily by Conrad, just as the Queen of Naples or Princesse Mathilde were put in bodily by Proust.

Amongst a great deal of incidental detail of good value for the Conrad reader, Sherry's job on *Lord Jim* stands out. Lord Jim, it will be remembered, was a young merchant service officer who had been involved in the abandonment of a ship full of pilgrims. The officers had left in the boats, thinking that the ship would go down. She had, in fact, reached port.

After a Court of Inquiry had dismissed Jim from the Service for this lack of integrity, he becomes a 'sea-clerk' – a ship's chandler, rowing out to meet incoming vessels and sell them odds and ends of equipment. Finally, Jim, involved in romantic circumstances with a girl on an island, meets his death through the agency of near-pirates led by the unspeakable Gentleman Brown.

The scandal of the abandoned ship had actually taken place. She was the *Jeddah* taking pilgrims from Singapore to the town of that name. Sherry not only shows who was the model for Jim, but actually supplies a photograph of the man, by name A. P. Williams. He did indeed become a 'sea-clerk' after his débâcle, made a small fortune, lost it in the rubber boom, and had sixteen children.

I have to admit that the photograph of Lord Jim's prototype was rather a shock to me. I had imagined Jim just like Peter O'Toole, peeping shyly from the cover of the current paperback of the novel, and did not at all envisage waxed moustaches, or evening tails with a black waistcoat. Still, this proves how unwise it is to expect an exact portrait when novelists 'put someone in'.

Gentleman Brown seems to derive from a certain Capt. Brownrigg, somewhat less outrageous than Conrad's character, but far from well behaved. Indeed – Conrad apart – the picture incidentally conveyed by this book of South-East Asia about 80 or 100 years ago is remarkable in the violence and adventure that was available.

In this world sea-captains like Conrad were not only expected to shoulder responsibility, show courage and resource and live up to 'the best traditions of the Service' (the words used when the officers of the Jeddah let the side down), but do it all for £14 a month. One hears a good deal about disgracefully low wages at a working-class level, but this sum suggests a certain exploitation of middle-class virtues and enterprise.

Conrad produced *The Shadow-Line* as straight autobiography, but, oddly enough, as Sherry shows, he seems to have used invented material in this book almost as much as in the novels. We also see how he employed books already written about the East to supply detail for his own background.

It is notable that Conrad is quoted as considering his personal equipment as a novelist in some respects inadequate. While the writer who deals with nothing more exciting than social life in London might complain that he had never had opportunities such as Conrad's, Conrad, on the other hand, complained that his own life had excluded him from the subtle relationships of a more sedentary society.

There is an almost perfect example of the way in which 'good writing' exists in the man, not in what he does. In fact, it seems relatively true to say that, given the circumstances of a sea-going life in the 1880s, round and about the China seas, nothing exceptionally outstanding happened to Conrad himself. On the other hand, one cannot help feeling that it was much better he should examine such an incident as the *Jeddah* at second hand, rather than have it colour his whole life by personal experience of it.

Some of Conrad's characters recur in the novels – Capt. Marlow, so often the epic narrator for example – and one could wish that this method had been even more developed by the author. Schomberg, the Alsatian who runs a hotel in what appears to be Bangkok, appears in

Lord Jim, 'Falk' and finally in *Victory*, in the course of which he grows steadily more unpleasant. The female orchestra which played at Schomberg's hotel – its members sitting with the guests during the interval – is traced by Sherry to Singapore.

The final impression derived from *Conrad's Eastern World* is that, so far from being less extraordinary than the one Conrad depicts, it was even more extraordinary. Conrad himself remains an enigmatic figure. The more we read about him, the less we seem to know him. This was probably what people felt who met him in the circumstances here described.

Conrad's Eastern World, Norman   1966
Sherry, CUP.   *Daily Telegraph*

IV

Jerry Allen in *The Sea Years of Joseph Conrad* quotes Conrad as wishing to

> get free from that infernal tail of ships, and that obsession with my sea life which has about as much bearing on my literary existence, on my quality as a writer, as the enumeration of drawing-rooms which Thackeray frequented could have had on his gift as a great novelist.

Although easy to see what Conrad meant by this outburst, it is equally true that, if you are an admirer of his novels, information about the people and places from which he drew his material is of great interest.

In this connection it is impossible not to refer to the protests made by Jerry Allen not long ago on the publication of another book about these sources – *Conrad's Eastern World* by Norman Sherry.

Having now read both books, one feels sympathy with Jerry Allen in finding a fair amount of her subject-matter dealt with before the appearance in this country of *The Sea Years of Joseph Conrad*. At the same time, one must regret the manner in which objection was taken. In the first place, Norman Sherry had specifically gone to the Far East to write *Conrad's Eastern World*, which was finished in 1962, though for various reasons delayed in publication. In the second place *The Sea Years of Joseph Conrad* and *Conrad's Eastern World* are really books of quite a different sort.

Sherry's, detailed and scholarly, has very great appeal for the Conrad fan, but is not, in the usual sense, 'popular'. Jerry Allen, on the other hand, writing in a highly coloured journalistic style, covers much more of Conrad's life, but will suddenly go off at a tangent on some such subject as duelling, as if no one had ever before heard of such an

activity. This does not mean that Jerry Allen is not required reading for
the Conrad-fan too. On the contrary, she provides some excellent
material not yet made public.

How *The Sea Years of Joseph Conrad* and *Conrad's Eastern World*
supplement each other can be seen from Norman Sherry's work on the
identity of the odious Gentleman Brown in *Lord Jim* and Jerry Allen's
discoveries about the model for Kurz in *Heart of Darkness*.

Kurz was, it turns out, based on a sinister British officer belonging to
a distinguished family. The description Allen gives of this man's
background, sadistic goings-on in the Congo, and final murder,
certainly gives point to the otherwise rather enigmatic figure of Kurz.

Besides *Lord Jim* and the abandonment of the pilgrim ship, Allen
deals at some length with the period when Conrad, as a young man of
nineteen, was living in Bordeaux, gun-running for the Carlists, the
events that provided the background for *The Arrow of Gold*.

In this connection she joins issue – indeed has more than one head-on
collision – with Jocelyn Baines, who wrote *Joseph Conrad: A Critical
Biography* (1960). It will be remembered that the hero of *The Arrow of
Gold* had a brief affair with the Carlist Pretender's mistress, Rita, and
was later wounded in a duel with an American soldier of fortune, Capt.
Blunt.

It is not denied that Conrad carried a wound on his chest, but he
explained this to his Uncle Thaddeus, who brought him up, as an
attempt at suicide. Baines accepts this, while Allen believes that all fell
out more or less as in the novel, Conrad being afraid to admit to his
straitlaced uncle that he had been involved in a duel about a woman.

In this difference of opinion, I am inclined to agree with Jerry Allen,
though she seems unduly hard throughout her book on Uncle
Thaddeus, who may have been nagging and parsimonious, but was
not, I think, a kind of Polish Mr Pontifex, for whom Conrad's recorded
affection was merely the sentimentality of later life. I think Conrad
recognized that he was himself a very difficult young man and
appreciated his uncle in spite of failings.

Another serious difference between Jerry Allen and Jocelyn Baines is
whether Rita could have been modelled on the Pretender's mistress,
Paula de Somoggy, of whom an alluring photograph is provided.
Baines says the chronology of events makes this very unlikely; Jerry
Allen is a wholehearted believer, and much that she puts forward is
convincing.

All the same, it does seem a little unlikely – though, of course, not
impossible – that a boy of that age should have lived, even briefly, with
this glamorous lady, especially as Conrad was throughout his life
admittedly neurotic in his dealings with the women who attracted him.

One wonders whether the Pretender had more than one mistress, and, when Conrad came to write the story as a novel, he used the perfectly legitimate device of attaching the characteristics of one lady to another to make a better story.

This was done, so to speak, the other way round, in Benjamin Constant's *Adolphe*, where the famous Mme de Staël is portrayed in her love affair with the author, but given certain easily recognizable outward characteristics of one of his more obscure mistresses.

One of Conrad's oddest habits as a novelist was sometimes to use the actual surname of his model, perhaps changing the first name, e.g. Tom Lingard in *The Rescue* and other works, is drawn from the real man, William Lingard.

Capt. Blunt, and his vividly portrayed mother, in *The Arrow of Gold* were really drawn from a mother and son called Blunt. Jerry Allen gives an entertaining account of them, but does not mention that Capt. Blunt must, in fact, have been a cousin of Scott Fitzgerald. Had he known, Fitzgerald would certainly have appreciated that, both for swagger of the duelling kin and through his own admiration for Conrad.

Jerry Allen sometimes goes a trifle off the rails in things like calling knighthood 'Britain's highest honour', but she does use the word 'careening' correctly – not in the dreadful contemporary American misunderstanding of careering – and one hopes she will impress this on her countrymen.

She pays tribute to information about the Lingards and Olmeyers (*Almayer's Folly*) gleaned from the late Dr J. G. Reed, who was a prisoner of war in Japanese camps for three and a half years, after making a study of Conrad origins.

One should perhaps end with a plea for mutual tolerance among authors writing on the same subject, since so often, as in this instance, both have different matter of value to contribute.

The Sea Years of Joseph Conrad,   1967
Jerry Allen, Methuen.   *Daily Telegraph*

Note
Correspondence took place later between Jerry Allen and Norman Sherry regarding primacy in establishing certain Conradian points. Both agreed that credit should be given to several other researchers in this field.

V

After his investigation of Conrad sources in *Conrad's Eastern World*, particularly on the subject of *Lord Jim* and the Malayan stories, Norman Sherry turns to *Conrad's Western World*, notably *Heart of Darkness, Nostromo* and *The Secret Agent*. He has done another splendid job. In Conrad we find no crude caricature such as, say, D. H.

Lawrence's or Aldous Huxley's but 'reality' worked out with extraordinary skill and industry, life rearranged in the form of art.

A striking aspect of the Conrad books examined in Norman Sherry's
latest study is that three quite different methods are illustrated of
employing documentary matter. *Heart of Darkness* is autobiographical;
Nostromo, derived from works of history and travel; *The Secret Agent*, a
mixture of personal information and press reports.

It seems to have been one of Conrad's principles to try out his themes
first in short stories. For example, 'An Outpost of Progress' explores the
possibilities of Conrad's experiences in the Belgian Congo, to be
expanded in *Heart of Darkness*.

Sherry has a lot of good things to say about the background of *Heart of
Darkness*, a very remarkable work, but there can be no doubt that the
most interesting of these is what seems to be a clear identification of
Kurtz – 'Mistah Kurtz, he dead' – the incredibly active agent for
collecting ivory, idealistic, keen on African folk-lore, yet intensely
sinister.

Jerry Allen in her *The Sea Years of Joseph Conrad* (also well worth
reading) thought Kurtz was the British officer who, apparently losing
his reason in the Congo a year or two before Conrad's arrival, had
behaved with great cruelty and been finally assassinated. This, I think,
must be abandoned in favour of Sherry's candidate, Hodister, agent of
the Katanga Company, who fits at all points, though the sense of utter
horror of what had been done may have also owed something to the
sadistic British officer's goings-on.

In *Nostromo*, thought by some critics Conrad's finest novel, the
author's very slight practical knowledge of South America is aug-
mented by immense reading, so that an absolutely convincing Latin
American country, with a history and geography of its own, is created,
and peopled with living characters. There are splendid things in
Nostromo, but the purely 'documentary' work put into it, immense and
impressive, is also a shade too discernible.

In this last connection, it should be added that Sherry thinks
Decoud, the Parisian Costaguanero of *Nostromo*, has something in him
of Conrad himself; that Decoud's attempted suicide parallels Conrad's
own. This appears to be additional ammunition for those who suppose
it was attempted suicide, rather than a duel in Conrad's early days in
Marseilles.

Finally comes *The Secret Agent*. This first-rate novel, strongly
recommended to all who have not yet read it, is built round Mr Verloc,
the secret agent, proprietor of a rubber-goods shop, and in close touch
with revolutionary movements, chiefly Anarchist, regarding which he
keeps the police informed. Verloc is also in the pay of the Russian
Embassy, which, at the opening of the story, requires the perpetration

of an outrage in Great Britain in order to stiffen the hand of the authorities against foreign terrorists.

Again Conrad tries out the theme in short stories. His final use of the circumstances surrounding the blowing up of a man in the neighbour-hood of Greenwich Observatory – gathered from newspapers and pamphlets of the period – is a masterly example of putting a novel together from actual facts. Conrad pleaded an absolute lack of any first-hand knowledge of Anarchists, but was able to obtain information about a group of London Anarchists – a very modern touch – whose paper was run by the children (the eldest age seventeen) of a 'distinguished government official' in the Inland Revenue. (Inciden-tally, when Conrad was sent a letter by the Prime Minister proposing a knighthood he did not open the envelope until a further desperate enquiry arrived, because he thought it was from the Inland Revenue.)

Sherry seems a little inclined to think that Conrad represents the Anarchists – documented from various sources, including Irish Fenians – as too disagreeable, but their own writings and sayings quoted by him here scarcely bear that out. I would suggest, however, that Conrad rather soft-pedalled what must have been his own dyed-in-the-wool familiarity with the idea of secret gatherings, some-thing that no Pole of his period could have entirely lacked.

Conrad himself said that Mr Verloc's shop was on the site of the former Leicester Galleries in Irving Street, just out of Leicester Square, but I find this difficult to work out, and think it might perhaps have been in Lisle Street.

Conrad's Western World, Norman   1971
Sherry, CUP.   *Daily Telegraph*

VI

This year is the fiftieth anniversary of Conrad's death. He is one of our greatest novelists. In 1960 a biography of him appeared by Jocelyn Baines. So far as the facts were concerned it was a competent piece of work – notable for drawing attention to Conrad's injury as a young man being the consequence of attempted suicide, rather than a wound in a duel – but a book that never closely examined its subject's complex character, and a trifle pedestrian in critical approach to the works.

Since then much attention has been devoted to Conrad, notably Norman Sherry's remarkable detective work on sources in *Conrad's Eastern World* and *Conrad's Western World*, together with an ever growing collection of critical studies. A Joseph Conrad Society has come into being. At the same time Conrad himself remains a man, obviously extraordinary, but in many respects unexplained in certain aspects.

C. B. Cox's *Joseph Conrad: the Modern Imagination* takes the major novels separately – Conrad produced a few relative failures – and has interesting things to say about all of them. Cox has that mark of a good critical writer in that where one disagrees with his findings, one wants to argue.

In principle, I found myself almost always on Cox's side, particularly in his view that Conrad's 'modern imagination' was out deliberately to resist the clarity and consistency that had hitherto been the fashion in novel writing.

> We cannot describe the universe in isolation from an observer [writes Cox]; things are seen relative to some individual, rather than absolutely. By placing this attitude at the centre of his work, Conrad proved himself in accord with the very essence of modern physical thought.

There are moments when it is impossible not to feel that literary criticism has got out of hand. Formerly a novelist wrote a novel. Some liked it; some didn't. There was none of the appalling weight of what it 'meant', its symbolism – let alone what it meant to Freudians, Jungians, Marxians, and so on.

Conrad is particularly difficult to investigate at the symbolism level. Clearly he does use symbolism at some moments – but does he always? It seems to me that he is often merely telling a story describing a peculiar sort of human being – for instance Kurtz in *Heart of Darkness* – and that it is possible to overdo comment on what such a character 'represents'. In short, if you want Kurtz, among many others, to 'represent' something, that is up to the reader. Conrad leaves it open.

Cox is illuminating about *Nostromo* and *Lord Jim*. In the case of *Nostromo*, I have to confess that I got through it only at a fourth attempt. Then, the cure was complete. I enjoyed *Nostromo* enormously; and subsequently reread it with equal pleasure. This seems worth recording just as an example of the discovery that Conrad's powers sometimes lie well below the surface.

I am sure Cox is right, in thinking *Nostromo* should have had another title, the emphasis deflected from Nostromo himself. He may be rather overdone as a character, but I demur a little at some of Cox's doubts about his validity; and about Decoud, too, who seems to me altogether convincing.

Cox seems to me less at ease with *The Secret Agent* and *Under Western Eyes*, though he regards both as the masterpieces they certainly are. *The Secret Agent* has been under Marxian attack because it shows professional revolutionaries as odious – sensual, lazy, callous, venal. Even less prejudiced critics have expressed hurt feelings at such savage treatment of the Extreme Left.

When Cox says that the narrator of *The Secret Agent* is 'uncommitted', that he 'escapes by entertaining himself in ironic detachment', Conrad – for better or worse as an artist – is surely not in the least detached. He loathes terrorists, as much as he loathes Mr Vladimir (obviously of the Russian Embassy) arranging an outrage by *agent provocateur*. The world of the terrorist is one we have come to know much more closely than in Conrad's day and what he says in *The Secret Agent* has absolutely contemporary bearing.

In a somewhat similar connection Cox seems to insist too much that Razumov in *Under Western Eyes* was 'wrong' to betray the fellow student who had thrown the bomb. Surely Razumov is presented as a man caught in the grip of Fate. Certainly Conrad was no lover of Tsarist Russian methods, but Razumov was simply trying to save himself from the consequences of an act he himself did not approve, one that was no less 'wrong' – simply as a murder – than the betrayal.

C. B. Cox touches on Conrad's frequent failure in projecting his female characters. Mrs Gould in *Nostromo* and Mrs Verloc, in *The Secret Agent*, both come over well, and, in spite of the romantic manner in which she is sketched in, Mrs Travers in *The Rescue* (not on the whole a success) possesses some charm. They are exceptions. There seems little hope that we shall ever obtain a clear vision of Conrad's relations with women – to whom he was certainly attracted – but it was undoubtedly of much complication.

Joseph Conrad: the Modern   1974
Imagination, C. B. Cox, Dent.   *Daily Telegraph*

VII

Frederick R. Karl writes at immense length (over 900 full pages), in *Joseph Conrad: the Three Lives*, the 'Three Lives' being Conrad's Polish beginnings, his days at sea, his career as a writer. He is inclined to get out of proportion Conrad's coming of 'aristocratic' stock. Conrad went out of his way himself to point out that he came from 'land-tilling gentry', a very large class in Poland. In fact, Conrad's background was probably not so very different from that of some of the clergymen's sons turned Merchant Service officers, who figure in his own novels.

Unsolved problems are Conrad's attitude to women and his own marriage. There is evidence that he was attracted by somewhat older women, and I put forward the suggestion (so far as I know not mentioned hitherto) that the photograph here of his wife, Jessie, apparently wearing a mantilla, looks decidedly like that of his mother, wearing a head-scarf.

In any case, Jessie Conrad, though apparently quite English, seems to have had a decidedly Polish appearance, both before and after marriage. An interesting sidelight on Conrad and the opposite sex is here given by a lively and efficient drawing by him showing ballet girls exposing their legs on applying for an engagement.

Karl has clearly soaked himself in his subject, but he is dreadfully prolix. I am all for detail, however trivial, but this biography could have been reduced by at least a third by omitting what has little or no bearing on the matter in hand. If it is necessary (which one doubts) to spend a page and a half on Erik Erikson's views on M. K. Gandhi, we do not want Erik Erikson, with several lesser appearances, at equal length again four hundred pages later. The same surely applies to John Stuart Mill's relations with his father; indeed lots more figures no less remote from Conrad.

It may well be that Conrad's particular complexities defy clear definition, but a sea-fog of psychological conjecture does not help at this stage. The sort of thing one would like to know is why Henry James thought Conrad so 'rum', so unfortunate as an individual. Admittedly Conrad had a great deal of bad luck, but James's attitude seems to suggest something quite different from, say, John Galsworthy's feelings about his friend.

Karl gets the sea years into good order, making the point that Conrad soft-pedalled the fact that he had some troubles with passing examinations for promotion. At one moment (although he disliked Melville's *Moby Dick*) he thought of becoming a whaler.

There is much here of interest about Conrad's professional career as a writer, the changes that took place in his language, subjects, creative energy. When Conrad became more familiar with English he did not necessarily write better, the unconventional phrases about which unimaginative reviews grumbled often having a force that was lost when the language flowed more freely.

There is still room for a clear-cut book about Conrad (perhaps an impossible demand), and one is grateful for the story here of his suddenly being sent into wild suppressed laughter by the comedian, George Robey. That sort of thing suddenly lights up the picture far more than pages of psychoanalytical speculations.

Frederick Karl sometimes gets a bit confused by British institutions. When he writes: 'He [Conrad] says that as soon as he became an officer he tried to do his duty by the boys who served under him, some boys from Conway, Wales, others coming from schools on shore,' he seems not only to miss the point that *Conway* was a training ship, but also to suggest that Wales is an island.

Joseph Conrad: The Three Lives,
Frederick R. Karl, Faber.

1979
Daily Telegraph

VIII

There are about 3,500 letters from Joseph Conrad (1857–1924) extant, and this is the first of what are to be eight volumes. Several selections have been made in the past, some of these taking a special aspect of Conrad's correspondence, or, in the case of *Conrad's Polish Background* (1964), reproducing letters to him from that striking figure his uncle and guardian Tadeusz Bobrowski, to which the nephew's replies unfortunately do not survive.

They would have shed much light on the young Conrad during the obscure Marseilles period. In fact, after a letter written with a guided pen at the age of three and a half to his father, the earliest is dated about sixteen months before Conrad passed (after first failing) his examination to become a second mate. By that time he had already served as third mate after just over two years in the British merchant service as an ordinary seaman. In 1886 he became a naturalized British subject and (again after initial failure) passed his master mariner's certificate.

In other words, the letters do not become at all plentiful until Conrad is over thirty in 1889, making plans to leave for the Congo and experience the highly disagreeable interlude from which he subsequently drew *Heart of Darkness*. The next eight years see him established as a writer, taking him to the publication of *The Nigger of the Narcissus*, when Conrad was forty.

There are inevitably a fair number of routine letters in this collection, of interest only as establishing dates and the like but, for the Conrad fan, several relationships are highlighted, both personal and literary. Of the former, that with Mme Poradowska, recipient of many of the letters, is perhaps the most striking.

Marguerite Poradowska, always addressed by Conrad as 'Aunt', was really the wife (in these Letters soon widow) of a first cousin of Conrad's maternal (Bobrowski) grandmother. She was Belgian, an acknowledged beauty, wrote several novels, and was five or six years older than Conrad. He wrote to her with great affection and a touch of flirtatiousness. One feels that she was at once the mother, who had died when Conrad was eight, and the semi-official sweetheart Conrad never seems otherwise quite to have established in early life, though one or two 'understandings' have been suggested.

After the letters to Mme Poradowska had been running for about five years she suddenly ceased to preserve them, though evidence exists that Conrad continued to write to her. Conrad's tone had latterly become appreciably warmer, and it seems not impossible that he proposed, a short time before he actually married Jessie George in 1896. Of the latter Conrad wrote with characteristic realism: 'She is a small, not at all striking-looking person (to tell the truth alas – rather plain) who is nevertheless very dear to me.' The marriage was successful, though Jessie was fated greatly to irritate Conrad's friends and biographers.

After an apparent first trial-run as writer of fiction in a *Tit-Bits* competition, Conrad placed his novel *Almayer's Folly* with the monumentally stingy T. Fisher Unwin.

Fisher Unwin bought the copyright outright for the sum of £20 in 1895, a period by which time eyebrows were beginning occasionally to be raised at such publishers' coups. Conrad's main object, however, was to get into print, and he always referred to Fisher Unwin as the 'Enlightened Patron of Letters'. Publication had come about through the recommendation of Edward Garnett, thereby beginning a friendship which was of immense consequence to Conrad, and supplies some of the most revealing of the letters so far as Conrad's views and methods of writing are concerned.

Conrad is always apologetic about speaking of himself and his doings, so the Letters are not a great repository of detail or pen-pictures of people he came across. He never indulges in gossip, but occasionally touched on politics. When the Liberal Government came to power in 1885 he wrote: 'the International Socialist Association are triumphant, and every disreputable ragamuffin in Europe feels the day of universal brotherhood, despoliation and disorder is coming apace . . . Socialism must end in Caesarism.' It is clearly a relief to his editors when in 1897 he also refers to the 'languid imbecility of the present [Conservative] government', a judgment generally agreed to be true.

On 20 July 1897, Conrad wrote to Fisher Unwin, who had published Somerset Maugham's *Liza of Lambeth* and presumably sent him a copy of the book.

> I've finished reading *Liza of Lambeth*. It is certainly worth reading – but whether it's worth talking about is another thing. I at any rate have nothing to say except this: that I do not like society novels, and Liza to me is just a society novel – society of a kind.
>
> I am not enough of a democrat to perceive all the subtle difference there is between the two ends of the ladder. One may be low and other high – a matter of pure chance – just as the ladder happens to be stood-up. The principal thing is that the story gets on a rung and stays there; and I can't find it in my heart to praise it because the rungs happen to be low. Rungs are artificial things, that's my objection.
>
> There is *any amount* of good things in the story and no distinction of any kind. It will be fairly successful I believe, for it is a 'genre' picture without any atmosphere and consequently no reader can live *in* it. He just looks on – and that is just what the general reader prefers. The book reminds me of Du Maurier's drawings – same kind of art exactly, only in another sphere.

This seems to make a critical point worth bearing in mind. There are plenty of others scattered throughout the Letters, which are excellently annotated and contain a useful chronology and summary of main correspondents.

The Collected Letters of Joseph   1983
Conrad: Vol. 1: 1861–1897,   *Daily Telegraph*
Frederick R. Karl and Laurence
Davies, eds, CUP.

IX

This is far and away the best book about Joseph Conrad that has yet appeared. Conrad may be said at last to have a definitive biography. Zdzislaw Najder, himself a Pole, is author of *Conrad's Polish Background* and became an exile from his country as recently as 1981 when martial law was declared.

Najder (whose book is excellently translated by Halina Carroll-Najder), does not produce a great deal of new material – though there are several items to which at least attention has never been drawn – but he handles what is already known with so much more intelligence and clarity than has been achieved hitherto that new life is infused into Conrad's extraordinary story.

The decks must be cleared (the metaphor is wholly applicable) of many obstacles to truth, some deliberately placed by Conrad himself to give or alter an autobiographical slant, others for which his biographers are responsible, due to that chronic biographers' misconception in assuming that a character in a novel represents what actually happened to the author. For example, it has been supposed from *The Arrow of Gold* that Conrad was engaged in gun-running during the Carlist War in Spain. In fact he was too young to have been in that war, and at best seems to have done some purely commercial smuggling.

Najder considers the fact of Conrad as a boy in Poland wishing for a life at sea is less odd than has been suggested. Long voyages and exploration were very much in the air at the period. It has often been said that Conrad did not join the Russian or Austrian navy for patriotic reasons, but in fact he did not have the choice. As child of parents convicted of political offences he would have been harassed had he lived in Russia at all, while Austria refused to give nationality to a Russian subject liable for conscription.

Najder does, however, point out that there is evidence that Conrad, as an apparently rather unpopular schoolboy, announced that he was going to become a 'great writer'. That is of course at variance with Conrad's own line about himself. Although in one sense the most dedicated of artists, in another he was at times prepared to insist that he was by calling a sailor.

Conrad spent just under eleven years at sea, of which nine months were on steamers. There were decided ups and downs in this sea-going career, such as failing to pass exams, giving information about himself that was far from accurate, and finally having to take a job as First Mate when qualified as Captain. In other words, the Merchant Service was not offering prospects so brilliant that they made a change of profession inconceivable for a man who may always have had an ambition to write – though no doubt such a transformation was obviously hazardous.

All his life Conrad suffered from fearful bouts of depression. Najder thinks Conrad was a depressive in the strictly psychiatric sense. As this book is refreshingly free from amateur (or professional) psycho-analysis, Najder's opinion in this matter carries weight, putting forward the theory that Conrad's fits of gloom were as unavoidable as his attacks of gout.

The female characters in Conrad's novels are apt to be so romantically conceived and shadowy (with the exception here and there of a personality like Mrs Verloc in *The Secret Agent*) that some people have assumed that Conrad's inhibitions about the opposite sex were so oppressive that he just managed to get married and produce two sons, but that was the extent of his sexual commitment. This is a field in which Conrad biographers have been particularly uninformative.

Again, Najder usefully steps in without overdoing unproved conjectures. He just mentions that Ford Madox Ford inserted what appears to be a spiteful caricature of Conrad in a pseudonymous novel; a foreign writer who seduces and marries a typist, which Jessie George certainly was. Whether or not this was true, the origins of the marriage are more convincingly set out here than elsewhere. Incidentally, the photograph of the French girl with whom Conrad had a serious flirtation in Switzerland, and possibly wished to marry, is remarkably like Jessie Conrad on the opposite page.

Evidence is adduced that where sex was concerned Conrad was far from the naive figure sometimes painted (which would certainly be unexpected in a Pole), and R. B. Cunninghame Grahame, no doubt a flamboyant show-off, nevertheless a close friend, wrote about Conrad's son Borys that he 'will be an *homme à femmes* like you and I'. Another friend of Conrad's, J. H. Retinger (who survived to be a member of General Sikorski's retinue during the Second World War), spoke of Conrad's '*affaires louches*'.

It should be added that Jessie Conrad was often *hors de combat* from illness, but she seems to have taken offence in the strange business of Jane Anderson to whom Conrad is alleged to have written an indiscreet letter which his wife found. Jane Anderson was a pushing American journalist who imposed herself on the Conrad family when the novelist was in his sixties and a relatively famous figure. She was later to have an affair with Retinger himself but, stranger still, a note here states that Jane Anderson became a German spy in the 1930s, and spent the Second World War doing pro-Axis propaganda.

Throughout the whole of his life, even at the end when he was making comparatively large sums from books and dramatic rights, Conrad was in fearful monetary difficulties. Friends at all levels, notably John Galsworthy, practically supported him a great deal of the time. Like all persons hopeless at handling money Conrad thought himself rather unusually capable of making financial arrangements.

I wish Zdzislaw Najder had just spared a brief word for the likelihood of Conrad having read Amiel's diary when in Switzerland, in the light of the epigraph to *Almayer's Folly* and the escape from Siberia of Peter Ivanovitch in *Under Western Eyes*.

Joseph Conrad: A Chronicle,   1983
Zdzislaw Najder, CUP.   *Daily Telegraph*

X

By this second volume of these edited Letters (the first appeared in 1983), Joseph Conrad has become an established writer, receiving on the whole respectful reviews, but at best selling no more than 4,000 copies of a novel like *Lord Jim*. He is perpetually hard up.

The period begins with the publication of *The Nigger of the Narcissus*, moving on to *Youth, Heart of Darkness, Amy Foster*, and *Lord Jim*, not to mention various short stories; a fairly rich crop judged by any standards. The Conrads left their farm in Essex – which Jessie Conrad had never liked – moving to Pent Farm near Hythe, which was within visiting distance of a remarkable number of fellow-writers. One cannot help being struck by the houses it was then possible to rent for a song.

Money was a perpetual trouble. Conrad worked immensely hard, but he was often ill; a son had been born to them whose health was sometimes a worry too. Life was not easy. It would be true to say that none of the Letters here could be called cheerful or lighthearted, and many of them deal simply with the business of getting enough to live on from publishers or magazine editors.

One of the crosses Conrad had to bear was that almost all his friends held Leftish views, which were very far from his own – John Galsworthy, R. B. Cunninghame Graham; the Edward Garnetts; in his own particular manner H. G. Wells. The South African War falls into this period, which Conrad was against, not because he felt much sympathy for the Boers – 'they have no idea of liberty, which can only be found under the English flag all over the world' – but because the war would be inconclusive, not one of extermination. In fact leave the Boers in possession.

At the same time Conrad did not accept Kipling's view that the war had been undertaken for the cause of democracy. Incidentally, the notion that Conrad did not admire Kipling's books, which has somewhat taken hold, is entirely wrong. On the contrary, writing to a Polish friend (Christmas 1898) about books which had recently appeared in this country, Conrad puts Kipling (who had recently published *The Day's Work*) at the top of the list.

Conrad had become friends with Galsworthy some years before, when he had still been at sea and Galsworthy, by one of those strange coincidences, had found himself a passenger in the ship Conrad commanded. There is no doubt that a real affection existed between them (Galsworthy more than once helping Conrad out financially), though Conrad's innate irony of mind could never take Galsworthy's didactic sentimentalities altogether seriously. He thought Galsworthy (later to sell in millions and win a Nobel Prize) would always have a limited appeal.

At the period of the Letters, Galsworthy was still writing under the name of John Sinjohn. When he produced *Jocelyn*, a novel about unhappy marriage and adultery, it seems clear that Conrad did not know about Galsworthy's involvement with Ada Galsworthy, his cousin's wife, because Conrad wrote: 'Your book is an analysis of high-minded and contemptible types – and you awaken sympathy, interest, feeling in an impartial, artistic way. It is an achievement.'

He sometimes argues with Galsworthy, who seems to have suggested that Henry James 'did not write from the heart', and tells him that he, Galsworthy, needs 'more scepticism at the foundation of your work'.

One of the writers Conrad detested was John Buchan, then in his early twenties. He thought that Buchan's *The Far Islands*, published in *Blackwood's Magazine*, was a crib of Kipling's 'The finest story in the world', calling Buchan an 'unspeakable impostor'. *Blackwood's* had hoped to bring them together, but clearly that was not on.

The letters here to Edward Garnett, who had been a key figure in Conrad's early career as a writer, are usually of interest. In one of them Conrad speaks of 'that amazing masterpiece', Guy de Maupassant's *Bel-Ami*. One would certainly agree that *Bel-Ami* is a novel of extraordinary skill and adroitness of characterization, but not expect Conrad to pick it out for special praise.

During this period Conrad decided to have his books handled by J. B. Pinker. Literary agents were just beginning to appear on the scene.

Pinker at various times represented Ford Madox Ford (who plays a considerable part in the Letters as Conrad's collaborator in what subsequently became *Romance*), Henry James, Conrad's American friend Stephen Crane (to die in the course of the Letters), H. G. Wells and Arnold Bennett.

In spite of having an agent, Conrad seems to have continued to make a lot of the arrangements for his books himself. Some, one cannot help thinking, might well have been better left in Pinker's hands. There is a wonderfully angry letter from Conrad to his agent, complaining that he is being treated like a 'Grub Street dipsomaniac'. Conrad's tastes in that line were in fact extremely moderate. He writes: 'I drink weak tea and yearn after dry champagne.'

By the way, Sir Redvers Buller was relieved of his command in the South African War, not 'dismissed the Service', as the note here states.

The Collected Letters of Joseph   1986
Conrad: Vol. 2: 1898–1902,   *Daily Telegraph*
Frederick R. Karl and Laurence
Davies, eds, CUP.

RUDYARD KIPLING

I

Kipling's prose is so well adapted to selection, Hardy's so little, that there is a certain unfairness in examining them side by side in their Everyman volumes.

At the same time, to read through both painlessly brings out striking comparisons and contrasts. Hardy was born a quarter of a century before Kipling, but Kipling only survived Hardy by eight years. During that last decade, there can be little doubt that Hardy was generally regarded as the greater writer.

To deal with contents first: Roger Lancelyn Green's Kipling selection is good, if a trifle idiosyncratic. For example, there is nothing from the *Soldiers Three* sequence, strong emphasis being laid on the mystic stories like 'They', 'The Marlake Witches', 'The Gardener'. Green says with truth that no agreement will ever be reached as to what should be included, and there is much to be said for a selection to surprise those – if such there be – who still suppose Kipling only wrote about the Army and India.

The poems, probably deliberately, to some extent adjust the balance in this respect; for example, 'Danny Deever', 'Mandalay', 'Gunga Din', 'Lord Roberts'. I have a weakness for 'Tomlinson' in the verse, 'Mrs Bathurst' (though I never know what happened) among the stories, but bow to an editorial decision that presents a fresh picture. It is, by the way, an excellent short collection of the poetry.

The Hardy selection includes two 'gothick' stories, 'The Withered Arm' and 'The Melancholy Hussar of the German Legion', 'rustic comedy' in 'Tony Kytes, the Arch-Deceiver', and some pieces from the novels and *The Dynasts*. In fact the volume really concentrates on Hardy as a poet, no doubt the wisest course when space is limited.

J. I. M. Stewart, in a sympathetic introduction, draws attention to the difficulty of criticizing a novelist who said in so many words that he wrote the novels simply as a means to financial independence, was always prepared to alter them if that made for better sales, and in any case expressed the view that reading novels was a waste of time.

Stewart believes – one would agree – that there is an element of disingenuousness here. That in a way makes it worse – anyway more disconcerting for the critic. In fact it is extremely difficult to know what is a just assessment of Hardy the novelist. On the one hand, the melodrama, the unlikely situations, atrocious patches of writing, antagonized many of his own contemporaries (George Moore, for example). On the other, during the first half of the century he was spoken of in terms of Shakespeare.

The second approach seems to be going too far, but, given the convention in which Hardy writes, there is an immense vitality in many of his scenes and situations. Above all, the English countryside, even today, is thickly populated with Hardy characters. I do not think *The Dynasts* comes off as a whole, though there are enjoyable lyrics like (not included here):

> When we lay where Budmouth Beach is,
> O the girls were fresh as peaches.

Although many would regard Hardy as primarily a poet, he did not publish any poetry until he was fifty-nine. He had a taste for elaborate, near-Swinburnian metres. There is Housman's attraction for corpses and executions, without Housman's facility. Avoidance of facility is no doubt conscious. The poems written in old age to early loves are often absorbing. Oddly enough, though less at ease with 'Vespasian's Legions' or 'Drummer Hodge', Hardy is sometimes curiously reminiscent of Kipling.

When one reads Kipling and Hardy at a sitting, the force of Kipling's writing is staggering. True, the Everyman volume is handicapped by space, but a story like 'The Withered Arm', by no means without merit, has dated in almost every way; the Kipling stories scarcely at all.

'The Miracle of Purun Bhagat' – the Prime Minister of an Indian state who becomes a holy man – is a masterpiece of narrative and concentrated material. Written when Kipling was twenty-eight, we see here the germ of both *Kim* and *The Jungle Book*. When he wrote 'Beyond the Pale' – the Indian girl who has her hands cut off for having a lover, another wonderful story – he was only twenty-three.

Kipling, no one would deny, has his failings, especially insistence on putting forward his own aggressive literary personality. He pays in various ways for his abundant energy. For instance, in 'The Man Who Was', a British officer, captured in the Crimea, sent to Siberia and brutally treated, turns up in the mess of his former regiment where a Russian officer is being entertained.

They want to ascertain who the man is. 'The rolls! The rolls! Holmes, get the rolls . . . and the adjutant dashed off bareheaded to the orderly-room, where the muster rolls of the regiment were kept.' But surely there was no need for the 'muster rolls' and this drama? All that was required was an Army List. Perhaps they only had the current one.

Kipling Stories and Poems, with an
Introduction by Roger
Lancelyn Green, ed.; *Hardy
Stories and Poems*, Donald J.
Morrison, ed., and with an
Introduction by J. I. M.
Stewart, Everyman: Dent.

1970
Daily Telegraph

II

It is impossible to define Rudyard Kipling's position as a writer in a few sentences. Everything about him is hedged in with infinite complication and contradiction.

After reading a dozen essays on his work, during which one has been blown this way and that, in agreement, disagreement, irritation, admiration, one can do little more than say that Kipling was a writer of very remarkable originality and distinction who rises to greatness in spite of many unsympathetic characteristics, both personal and professional.

Aspects of Kipling's Art by C. A. Bodelsen, Professor of English in the University of Copenhagen, is a good introduction to the other investigations because the author is concerned with the purely technical and aesthetic sides of Kipling's writing, and – although it would be impossible to guess from Bodelsen's study that English is not his native language – he is less troubled than the other essayists, English and American, by the sort of Englishman that Kipling was.

Bodelsen touches on Kipling's extraordinary, even rather embarrassing, accounts of orgiastic laughter, an element that plays a great part in the earlier books especially. He also considers a no less uncomfortable side of Kipling's art expressed in the 'Hymn to Physical Pain'.

One of the points that is made clear once and for all in this study – for those who ever doubted it – is Kipling's extraordinary integrity as an artist. No writer can ever have taken more trouble, been more concerned with technique and experiment, left more hidden clues by which the foundations of any given story can be tested and examined. Kipling's fascination with language more than once recalls Joyce.

The essays in Andrew Rutherford's collection, *Kipling's Mind and Art*, are by W. L. Renwick, Edmund Wilson, George Orwell, Lionel Trilling, Noël Annan, George Shepperson, Alan Sandison, Mark Kinkead-Weekes, J. H. Fenwick, W. W. Robson and the editor himself. They vary a good deal in merit, but all have views to put forward which are of interest.

For example, Renwick's obituary lecture on Kipling in 1936 reflects the defensive, rather condescending tone that a Kipling admirer then felt necessary. He refers to Kipling's 'philistinism' – except in a superficial sense, a totally inappropriate epithet.

In Edmund Wilson's essay, written in 1941, we find what is in some ways the first public acknowledgment (after his fall from grace about 1910) of Kipling's high position as a writer to be made by a well-known American critic. Wilson is never any good at understanding English life, and he puts forward the extraordinary suggestion that Kipling cynically abandoned his status as an artist to champion politics. He also calls him 'snobbish', though Kipling must have been one of the least snobbish of men. All the same, Wilson should be given credit for talking more sense about Kipling than had been uttered for years by anyone of his standing.

In the same year T. S. Eliot published his selection of Kipling's verse. This volume was discussed in a lively essay by George Orwell, in whose mystique Kipling played an enormous part. Orwell came of an English family associated with India, he had himself served in the Burma police, and he was preoccupied with many of the same themes. Kipling's ideas were at once immensely attractive and immensely abhorrent to him.

But what were Kipling's ideas? They are as difficult to define as anything else about him. Edmund Wilson obviously finds it hard simply to accept Kipling as a man who voted Conservative and believed in Imperial expansion; but surely that side of him can, comparatively speaking, be disregarded.

It is much more difficult to say what Kipling thought at a deeper level, when he was not taking part in an election. On the one hand there are the contemptuous references to races of other colour than white, some of which the least squeamish mind finds unpalatable; on the other, Kipling shows more understanding – in *Kim*, for example – of the forces that bind the human race together, whatever their colour, than perhaps any other writer in English.

The only explanation of this paradox seems to be the way Kipling regarded his own writing. He believed in his 'Daemon', the inner power that inspired him, which he always feared might suddenly depart and leave him written-out. Accordingly, in some moods he would write – in a sense quite impersonally – as a man who despised Indians or idealized the most tiresome form of army subaltern.

When another state was on him – like someone under the influence of a drug – he would show extraordinary understanding of the ways of the East or detestation of those material values which at other times he exalts. There seems no other rational explanation for Kipling's split personality.

   Unfortunately for his reputation during his middle and latter years, the less attractive side was taken, quite wrongly, to be the whole Kipling. It would be almost as easy to compose a Kipling anthology representing the precise opposite to the jingoistic, colour-bar-conscious, machinery-mad vulgarian envisaged by Max Beerbohm and others, as to embarrass Kipling supporters with quotations they would prefer unwritten.

   George Shepperson's and Alan Sandison's essays make some particularly good points. Sandison suggests that Kipling's 'Imperialism is offensive not because it is Imperialism, but because it isn't'. In short, Kipling was only interested in a special sort of 'Imperialism' – India, etc. – because it was necessary to him *as an imaginative writer*. This is beginning to get to the root of the whole matter.

   Alan Sandison also describes Kipling as 'half-way between Marx and Sartre', in his hesitation between the retention of self and assimilation by society. (Shepperson has pointed out a few pages earlier that Kipling is the most popular modern British writer in the USSR.) More than once one feels that Kipling could easily have belonged to the extreme Left, though he could never have been a Communist – any more than he could have been a Fascist, of which he is sometimes accused – because he believed implicitly in the 'bourgeois' conception of personal honour.

   It is the measure of Kipling's stature that there are so many aspects of his work to discuss. On the whole, too much attention is perhaps devoted to his theory, not enough to his practice. J. H. Fenwick's close examination of the *Soldiers Three* stories is, for example, well worth reading because it shows the literary development of this particular theme.

   Bodelsen points out that one of Kipling's great disappointments as a writer was that the revolutionary style of his later stories, like 'Dayspring Mishandled', was almost completely ignored by the critics, a style which has its origins in the very interesting short story 'Mrs Bathurst' (*Traffics and Discoveries*, 1904). 'Mrs Bathurst' crops up in several of the essays. I recommend a re-reading.

Aspects of Kipling's Art,   1964
C. A. Bodelsen, Manchester   *Daily Telegraph*
University Press.
Kipling's Mind and Art, Andrew
Rutherford, ed., Oliver & Boyd.

III

It has taken the best part of thirty years since his death for a coherent outline of Kipling to emerge. Even now there are many gaps. All the same, he can be seen today as probably our greatest writer of his generation, a man of extraordinary gifts, uncomfortable failings and, above all, an iron integrity.

J. I. M. Stewart, in *Rudyard Kipling*, gives an account of his subject's life, and a critical examination of his work, to be recommended to everyone who wants to know the facts about Kipling as a man and a writer, without becoming involved in too much complicated material. Stewart is thorough, fair and has a grasp of the essential points.

Louis L. Cornell, Professor of English at Columbia University, New York, is concerned, as the title of the book implies, with the Kipling of India, by no means the whole Kipling, though sometimes taken as such. *Kipling in India* has some interesting things to say, providing among other useful appendices a bibliography of all Kipling's writings while he worked in India between 1882 and 1889.

Both authors begin with the good point that, from his very earliest years, Kipling is on record as being a child so formidably aggressive that even devoted relations practically suffered nervous breakdowns after having Ruddy to stay.

'Auntie Rosa', with whom he and his sister were exiled while their parents were in India, was no doubt an odious woman, but at the same time she must be allowed to have had a tough assignment. The United Services College at Westward Ho! was a cut-price public school, accommodated in seaside boarding-houses found wanting by holiday-makers. It was to some extent recruited from boys found unassimilable by other schools, but the evidence is that, once he had found his feet, Kipling was the one in control there.

Stewart perhaps underestimates the fact that the headmaster, Cormell Price, was, politically speaking, so much what Kipling came to detest. He was a friend of the family, and Kipling liked him personally, but he was in his day the equivalent of a headmaster parading the streets with a board saying 'Stop the War in Vietnam'.

The people who stand out as more than ever dominating in their influence, and unexpected in their behaviour, are the Kipling parents. If the 'House of Desolation' at Southsea was a tenth as bad as their son painted – and they seem to some extent to have accepted his version – it is odd that they continued to allow their daughter to board there.

For his mother to make Kipling spend his holidays at school while she herself met her husband in Italy is, to say the least, on the surface unattractive. We are reminded of Lady Randolph Churchill being too socially engaged to have Winston home for the Eton and Harrow match.

Kipling adored his parents. To the end of their days they constituted the final court of criticism to which he took all his own writing. It seems probable that they made actual verbal alterations to some of the verse.

A fact that comes out with great clarity from the books of both Stewart and Cornell is that Kipling himself was not at all anxious to go to India at the age of seventeen and work as a journalist. If money had been available (or teaching at Westward Ho! good enough to have brought him to scholarship level), he would have much preferred the university. He wrote this at the time to his first cousin, Stanley Baldwin, the future Prime Minister.

Stewart gives a striking description of the extraordinary town of Simla in its heyday. There in the hot months, from a converted shooting-lodge with a tiny staff, the Viceroy 'administered, virtually with an absolute power, a mingling of races more than twice as numerous and 10 times as densely planted as the present population of the United States'.

When Cornell writes about the similar background, one feels that he, as an American, does not always correctly interpret the tone – often misleading enough – that is used in this country. He is also, one would say, disconcerted, like so many American critics, by the form adultery is apt to take in European literature.

For example, he quotes Denis Kincaid as saying that 'Simla society' regarded Kipling as a 'bounder', and draws the conclusion from this that Kipling may have misrepresented life in a Hill Station, 'though no doubt Kincaid exaggerates'.

Kincaid is, of course, at once stating a fact, and himself laughing about it. It is, I think, true to say that Kipling was never accepted by Anglo-Indians (as they were then called) or the Army, as the voice of Anglo-Indians and the Army. He was never truly popular with those two communities even if, at last, they came to see that he preached many of their own views.

Kipling as a great artist in fact created an Anglo-Indian and Army 'image' that had its own validity. It was not necessarily 'naturalistic'. All the same, one of the least of our critical worries is to question the existence of ladies like Mrs Hauksbee or the general goings-on Kipling portrayed in Simla.

Flora Annie Steel, in a different manner, confirms the same picture. Though she was older by twenty years than Kipling, he got into print before her, but she should perhaps have been included by Cornell in the list of writers who dealt effectively with the Indian scene, since some literary cross-fertilizing between them could have taken place.

Cornell also seems to me to suffer from sheer inexperience of the way the English talk. Discussing 'The Story of Muhammad Din' (also referred to by Stewart), he writes: '"They have no stamina, these brats," says the doctor *callously*.' I do not think in the context – especially a Kipling context – there is any reason to think the doctor spoke 'callously'. Indeed, we may have been an inch off an embarrassing emotional display like that when they read The Boy's letters in 'Thrown Away'.

Both authors note Kipling's rejection of the French Realist School as 'unwholesome'. This is one of the strangest things about him, because, contrary to what is sometimes said, Kipling could in certain respects face facts about sex that were brutal enough.

We do not know – probably shall never know – some of the key things in Kipling's life. The manner in which he seems to have fallen deeply in love with a girl a year or so older when he was fourteen himself, and the subsequent way in which he seems, so to speak, to have given up the struggle where women were concerned, suggests a side that may to some extent always have inhibited a tremendous talent.

Rudyard Kipling, J. I. M.   1966
Stewart, Gollancz.   *Daily Telegraph*
Kipling in India, Louis L.
Cornell, Macmillan.

I V

Kipling's 'Barrack-Room Ballads' fall roughly under three heads: a first book of verse given that name published in 1892 (when the poet was twenty-six); a second series, 1896; a third series, dealing with the South African War, 1903.

To the present volume has been added the anthology of soldiers' epitaphs composed by Kipling during the First World War. They do not altogether harmonize with the earlier mood, though they can be regarded as a fitting conclusion.

Charles Carrington has some excellent things to say in his Introduction, both about the poems themselves, and the background against which they were written. He notes that his own problems as editor were not so much to decide what was a Barrack-Room Ballad, as the linguistic and historical questions which these verses raise.

The Ballads are 'about' what it was like to be what was very generally termed in my childhood 'a tommy'. No writer until Kipling had dealt seriously with the soldier since Shakespeare. Carrington makes the point that even by the period of the Boer War the British Army had changed greatly from the men Kipling describes in his opening Barrack-Room verses, by the total war of 1914 unrecognizably so.

Two characteristics are common to all the Barrack-Room Ballads proper: they are told from the point of view of the soldier himself – not that of the poet – and they are told in dialect, usually London Cockney. Objections may be put forward as to speaking 'from the inside' about a character – especially if the author comes from a different background –

but this has often been done, from Browning to Joyce. Some readers find all dialect tedious, others are never satisfied that it is correct.

In a stimulating, if at times somewhat perverse, essay on Kipling, George Orwell expresses a preference for cutting out dialect altogether. He gives examples of how the poems read in ordinary spelling. This is a perfectly reasonable taste, but Orwell goes on to make the astonishing statement: 'Kipling ought to have known better . . . to have overridden the impulse to make fun of a working-man's accent.'

It would be just as reasonable to complain that Robert Burns was 'making fun' of Scotland, or William Barnes of Dorset. Carrington rightly points out that (setting aside poetic merits) the dialect preserved in the Ballads is of particular interest, not only from the aspect of development of language, but also for the fact that the army slang, much of it by now all but unintelligible, is usefully put on record. He adds that to assume that verses like 'Loot' (in which a soldier beats an Indian with a ramrod) represent Kipling's own point of view is like insisting that 'Mr Sludge, "The Medium"' represents Browning's.

One hesitates to use Orwell as an example of getting the Kipling myth wrong, as Orwell himself, in his way a great admirer, played a notable part in the enormously increased recognition of Kipling's genius (over and above his steady sales). But to read through this edition of the Ballads is to see the flaws in Orwell's generalization: 'Kipling idealises the army officer, especially the junior officer, and that to an idiotic extent, but the private soldier, though lovable and romantic, has to be comic.'

This is wholly untrue of Barrack-Room Ballads. In almost the only two Ballads in which officers play the main part, they are drunk. The first – a very funny one – is 'The Shut-Eye Sentry', where the Orderly Officer has got tight in the mess, and kisses the sentry on his rounds:

> The moon was white on the barracks,
> The road was white and wide,
> An' the Orderly Orf'cer took it all,
> An' the ten-foot ditch beside.

The second example is 'The Jacket', where a gunner officer, celebrating promotion to the Royal Horse Artillery, loads up with liquor, rather than shells, and has to charge the enemy with the empty guns.

In the same way many, if not most, of the Ballads could not possibly be regarded as making the private soldier 'comic'. One might instance 'Back to the Army Again', 'Shillin' a Day', 'Mandalay', 'Danny Deever', 'The Married Man', together with those two remarkable poems 'Wilful-Missing' and 'Bridge-Guard in the Karroo'. The latter deals with troops doing boring, uncomfortable, but not dangerous jobs:

Few, forgotten and lonely.
Where the empty metals shine –
No, not combatants – only
Details guarding the line.

Another poem not widely known is the 'Half-Ballad of Waterval'
(Boer POW camp for British prisoners):

When by the labour of my 'ands
I've 'elped to pack a transport tight
With prisoners for foreign lands
I ain't transported with delight.
I know it's only just an' right,
But yet it somehow sickens me,
For I 'ave learned at Waterval the meanin' of captivity.

Much imitated, the Barrack-Room Ballads, like most of what
Kipling wrote, could not have been produced by anyone else. He
learned from many, but is himself unique.

The Complete Barrack-Room   1974
Ballads of Rudyard Kipling,   *Daily Telegraph*
Charles Carrington, ed.,
Methuen.

V

Born 100 years ago today, Rudyard Kipling might be claimed by the
astrologers as a typical Capricornian. Outwardly at least, he was
practical, straightforward, down to earth, not without ruthlessness and
a nagging persistence.

When he is examined closer such simple terms turn out to be
inadequate; while his work, critically speaking, presents a tangle of
contradictions to anyone who hopes to make a brief, trenchant exposé.
Indeed, Kipling's centenary cannot better – nor more enjoyably – be
celebrated than by re-reading his books during the New Year, thereby
overhauling the whole question.

One thing at least is clear. He was a writer of the first rank, a genius,
though perhaps even in that category, a genius of rather a peculiar
kind. 'His talent I think quite diabolically great,' said Henry James,
disinclined as a rule to commit himself so bluntly. In such matters
James knew what he was talking about.

Why, then, a century after his birth, is it so difficult to assess Kipling
quite in the manner most writers can be assessed? There seem two
answers to this: first, the strength of his largely – though not wholly –
erroneous popular 'image', always obtruding, always requiring to be

explained away; secondly, the fact that at least a dozen different Kiplings exist, all demanding a separate consideration.

T. S. Eliot, with good reason, canvassed him as the predominant writer of his age, and also provides one explanation of the difficulty in coming to grips with Kipling's work. Kipling wrote intuitively, not intellectually. Accordingly, his books present at one moment, one view of life; at the next, another. This method, suggests Eliot, may explain some of the disesteem Kipling arouses among non-intuitive intellectuals.

Strange as it may seem, Kipling – this incredibly productive creator – always feared he might write himself out, since he could compose only under the direction of a powerful, yet fickle, inner force that might one day abandon him.

The difficulty of nailing down any writer who works in this intuitive way – Dostoevsky offers another example – may be seen if we approach the question of Kipling's 'imperialism'; perhaps with a view to venturing some defence of such opinions within their historical context. Why, it might be asked, should Kipling be excoriated for being keen on the British Empire, any more than Virgil for being keen on the Roman Empire, or Gogol on the Russian Empire?

However, when we turn to Kipling's books to confirm just what he did say, a paradox emerges. Kipling, in fact, we find putting out some of the most damaging anti-British, anti-imperialist propaganda imaginable – if you like to look at books in that particular committed way.

We know, of course, that Kipling did, in truth, hold strong political views of an 'imperialist' kind; could describe with enthusiasm aspects of British rule in India that now strike, to say the least, an unsympathetic note. On the other hand, there is much ('Lisbeth' or 'Without Benefit of Clergy', to name just a couple of examples) which presents another picture altogether.

It should be added that no rival 'imperialism' came anywhere near competing with India in Kipling's imagination. The idea of India overwhelmed him completely.

> Hard her service, poor her payment – she
> In ancient tattered raiment –

His own lines, expressing one of those uncomfortable truths (some find unpalatable) in which Kipling's verse abounds, supply the explanation:

> We've only one virginity to lose,
> And where we lost it there our hearts will be

'He has seen marvellous things through keyholes,' wrote Wilde, and there is unquestionably something about Kipling's stories, verses and gnomic utterances that invokes the picture of a man intently inspecting a scene vividly outlined in a small circle of light.

When it comes to telling what he had seen, he cannot write a sentence without betraying his own passionate interest in words and language, a preoccupation that at times – as with Joyce – gets the better of his writer's instinct, imposing an almost intolerable strain on the reader.

George Orwell pointed out that Kipling's determination to express dialect exactly as spoken is often more than flesh and blood can stand. To prove his point, Orwell transmuted some of the Cockney poems into plain English; on the whole, one would say, with good effect.

Nevertheless, Kipling must be remembered as one of the great revolutionaries where writing is concerned. Dialogue was never the same after him, while his powers of compressing required, and at the same time picturesque, information into a short paragraph are unequalled.

Stalky & Co. shows as absolute an originality in tackling the subject of schoolboys, as does *Soldiers Three* of the Army. The latter stories are also an early example of getting away from 'bourgeois' life as subject matter. The sheer virtuosity of *Kim* is dazzling. 'Mrs Bathurst' (1903) is a masterpiece of narrative unrolled in a totally 'modern' manner. One of the features of this last story – used with astonishing technical effect – is the introduction of a sequence in a cinema film, adding a dimension to other elements of the story, variously told in the first person, that would be ingenious even today.

Kipling is sometimes blamed for allegedly bogus realism, and it is true that his taste for professional detail sometimes becomes obsessive. The answer is that 'naturalism' in a novel or short story is merely one of the available forms. It cannot be too often repeated that a naturalistically written narrative does not necessarily convey what happened better than the employment of, say, rhymed couplets or interior monologue. It is just the method the author prefers. If Kipling is to be read, his world – like that of all great authors – must be accepted; but we can agree that its 'naturalism' is often open to argument.

That his gifts were not always used to the most admirable effect is equally undeniable. Most writers have a personality, not necessarily attractive, that must be accepted over and above their writing, as such – D. H. Lawrence, for example. In Kipling's case, this personality was unusually strong; to some more pungent than was tolerable.

Max Beerbohm's Kipling parody in 'A Christmas Garland' (Father Christmas arrested emerging from a chimney) hits off this less engaging side. The story is elaborately mannered, the epigraphic lines from 'Police Station Ditties':

'Wot, 'e *would*, would 'e? Well,
Then yer've got ter give 'im 'Ell,
An' it's trunch, trunch, truncheon does the trick.'

The implied criticism is savage, and not undeserved; but, when all is said and done, if Kipling had more than a strain of sadism in him, so had Baudelaire and Proust. If he were a nationalist, so were Dostoevsky and Yeats. If he was vulgar, what about Balzac and Hugo?

It was oddly supposed, when Kipling first appeared, that a new writer like Dickens had entered the lists. In fact, of course, Kipling did not possess that kind of objectivity required by a novelist. He was not interested in people in a novelist's way. All the same, there are notable things in *The Light that Failed*, chiefly the opening pages in the mud flats, even though the scene is only an extension of 'Baa, Baa, Black Sheep' and the horrible days as a child at Southsea.

This lack of objectivity was turned to full advantage in Kipling's poetry, where the intensity to be found in his prose (observable if read aloud) was given full rein. Here, again, the range is extraordinary, derivations from Swinburne and Browning becoming lost in a fantastic and original talent that often refuses to accept relegation to a secondary place.

'Tomlinson', to pick an example at random, is always worth re-reading, and, for acute comment, the little known 'An American'. Lest 'Recessional' has become hackneyed by repetition, Jules Castier's French version affirms the magnificence of its sombre and prophetic gloom:

> *O Dieu de jadis, ô Dieu de nos pères,*
> *Seigneur tout-puissant des combats lointains,*
> *Sous la main de Qui nous tenons, prospères*
> *Le sol des palmiers et le sol des pins,*
> *Dieux des Armes, sois avec qui Te prie,*
> *De peur qu'on n'oublie – hélas, qu'on n'oublie!*

1965
Daily Telegraph, Centenary Tribute

VI

The ingenuity of Jules Castier's 1953 French translation of Kipling's verse is, at times, almost startling. Not only is the sense accurately conveyed, but as often as not the metre itself is retained, or at least closely matched. Painters at work will sometimes hold up an unfinished picture to a looking glass to consider its form and colours from a new angle. Translation has a somewhat similar effect. An author's – even a whole country's – idiosyncrasies are suddenly revealed in a different light. Here, for example, what fascinating trains of thought are evoked by the changes required to turn Kipling material into a medium intelligible in France.

How would you render 'gentleman-ranker'? Few of us would have thought of '*le troupier fils de famille*', with its suggestion of such a different kind of social exile; while the Absent-minded Beggar as '*le mendiant distrait*' becomes a sad, almost pierrot-like figure. (Curiously enough a French poster is mentioned in *Ulysses* announcing: *Hamlet: où le distrait*, at which Stephen comments: 'The Absent-minded Beggar'.) In 'The "Mary Gloster"' the phrase 'for I lunched with his Royal 'Ighness' is expressed by '*j'ai reçu le ministre à dejeuner*' which has a far more practical air about it than the royal luncheon. The 'flannelled fools at the wicket' and the 'muddied oafs at the goals' develop, in addition to their thoughtlessness, a kind of ludicrous male vanity:

> '*De vos crétins sportifs exhibitant leurs flanelles,*
> *De vos oisifs boueux qui surveillent les "goals".*'

'Mandalay' loses some of its nostalgia, but in matters of love the French tongue will not accept emotional *gaucherie*:

> 'Plucky lot she cared for idols when I kissed 'er where she stud!'

is transformed to:

> '*Elle s'fichait bien d'tout's les idols, quand j'l'ai eu embrassée tout d'bout!*'

'McAndrew's Hymn' falls completely into place:

> 'Lord, Thou hast made this world below the shadow of a dream,
> An', taught by time, I tak' it so – excepting always Steam.'

> '*Seigneur, Ton monde d'ici-bas, c'est l'ombr' d'un rêv' trompeur.*
> *Comm' l'experienc' me l'enseigna – sauf, toujours, la Vapeur.*'

But Castier can tackle more difficult problems than McAndrew, the sonorous tones of which find an obvious parallel in certain kinds of French formal verse. Look at this:

> 'So one shall Baltic pines content,
>   As one some Surrey glade,
> Or one the palm-grove's droned lament
>   Before Levuka's Trade.
> Each to his choice, and I rejoice
>   The lot has fallen to me
> In a fair ground – in a fair ground –
>   Yea, Sussex by the sea!'

> '*Pour l'un, les pins de la Baltique,*
> *Pour l'autre, un bosquet du Surrey,*

Ou bien le frôlement discret
Des longs palmiers sous le tropique.
Chacun sa voie –
Mais c'est ma joie
D'aimer sans nul destin amer,
Le sol charmant, où tout rougeoie –
Le Sussex bercé par la mer.'

We may regret the removal of Levuka's Trade, but how neat is the rest. Is there even a touch of Laforgue in the fourth line? However, here and there alliteration and the pounding of the metre has proved too much, as in 'The Song of the Banjo', where something has undoubtedly been lost:

'But the word – the word is mine, when the order moves the line
And the lean, locked ranks go roaring down to die!'

'*Mais je suis le signal, après l'ordre banal,*
Quand les rangs vont en plein vers la Mort qui les happe!'

Rather in the same manner:

'Daughter am I in my mother's house,
But mistress in my own.'

becomes a trifle flat as:

'*Je suis l'enfant en maison maternelle,*
Mais je suis maîtresse chez moi.'

While in 'Tomlinson':

'"And this I ha' got from a Belgian book on the word of a dead
French lord."'

'"*Et puis, ceci encor', j'ai appris tout d'abord*
'*D'un Belg', qui l'tenait d'un Français.*"'

is a rendering that misses the apparent reference to the Divine Marquis, though the final line of the poem is excellent:

'"And . . . the God that you took from a printed book be with you,
Tomlinson!"'

'"*Et . . . ce Dieu chapardé dans un livre imprimé,*
Qu'il te protège, Tomlinson!"'

In the same way perfect ease is found in:

'*C'est Tommy-ci, et Tommy-ça, et "Tommy, fous-moi l'camp";*
Mais c'est "Merci, monsieur Atkins" dès que l'concert reprend.'

'O Blanc, reprends ton lourd fardeau — '

'A la tienn', Fuzzy-Wuzz, à ton pays, l'Soudan!
T'es un bougre d'païen, mais un fier combattant!'

'J't'ai battu, rossé, en effet —
Mais, par Dieu vivant qui t'a fait,
Tu vaux mieux qu'moi, mon vieux, et j'te l'dis, Gunga Din!'

'Sir Richard's Song (A.D. 1066)', 'Harp Song of the Dane Women', and 'If – ' all pass almost effortlessly into French through Jules Castier's skill. Perhaps 'Recessional' is best of all.

Kipling: Poèmes choisis par T. S.   1953
Eliot, Jules Castier, trans.,   *Punch*
Robert Laffont.

VII

The title of Philip Mason's book is taken from a quotation of R. L. Stevenson, which refers to a bottle in which 'something obscurely moved like a shadow and a fire'. This is the Bottle Imp, and Mason uses the image to express the nature of Kipling's writings, so difficult to pin down in a critical way.

Philip Mason himself is, by definition, almost all that Kipling himself might have chosen as a sympathetic interpreter of his own work: twenty years in the Indian Civil Service, both in district administration and the Defence Department, followed by appointment as Secretary to the Chiefs of Staff Committee. And yet – as Mason himself more than once indicates – you can never be certain about Kipling. All that might be held against him.

It is equally likely that Mason would be treated by Kipling as an obstructive bureaucrat, as a public servant dedicated to selfless duty. This almost complete ambivalence on Kipling's part is one of the subjects of this most interesting study.

In fact, and this is a good fault, Mason is hard – sometimes it seems to me rather unnecessarily hard – on the side of Kipling that might be supposed to make the most appeal to him, the stories about India. Even that statement must be qualified. He thinks *Plain Tales* flashy, but finds 'William the Conqueror' moving.

Of course *Plain Tales*, though of astonishing originality for a writer of not much more than twenty, are flashy, but I like them; while I find the heroine of 'William the Conqueror' just a shade embarrassing or perhaps I should say the author's approach to her.

Mason's personal history as a Kipling reader is that he was brought up as a great admirer, went through a stage of dislike when Kipling seemed wrong intellectually, and returned to him enthusiastically in later life. He finds Mulvaney's stage Irish hard to bear, and 'The Brushwood Boy' appallingly coy. He does not much care for 'The Finest Story in the World', but likes 'Wireless', with which the former surely links up in type.

He approves of 'On the Gate' and 'Uncovenanted Mercies' (Heaven treated as military headquarters), but disapproves of 'My Sunday at Home' (the workman who is given the emetic). I feel the reverse about these last, and (happening to dislike anthropomorphic stories about animals) am less warm towards the *Jungle Books*, but warmer towards *Puck of Pook's Hill*. This just to clear the ground, and show that Mason is no uncritical admirer, and neither am I.

When Kipling first appeared on the scene he was thought to be a new Balzac or Dickens. This was perhaps a pardonable mistake, but, as he himself said more than once, he was unable to write a long novel. *The Light that Failed* might just pass as such, but *Kim*, with its many brilliant passages, is really something different.

This incapacity in Kipling is additionally extraordinary since many of the short stories are, in fact, miniature novels. Philip Mason points out that the absorbing story 'Mrs Bathurst' is in truth a novel, and might well have been treated at greater length.

One of Kipling's strangest characteristics as a writer was to continue throughout his life to produce examples of good, bad and indifferent works. Some of his very best stories were written when he was quite young, and equally good stories also occur at the end of his life; yet late in life he was also capable of producing altogether inferior stuff.

This variation was to some extent due to Kipling's absolute faith in writing intuitively. No doubt all the best imaginative writing is largely intuitive, but Kipling frequently stated his own entire dependence on his 'Daemon'.

There are probably still people who suppose that Kipling only wrote stories like *Soldiers Three* and verses like *Barrack-Room Ballads*; and very good both of these can be. At the same time Mason is rightly more concerned with the stories like 'The Wish House', 'The Gardener', and 'Mary Postgate', in which Kipling enters into the mind of a middle-aged woman confronted with emotional crisis arising from moral or physical pain. The last of these three is uncompromisingly disagreeable, but certainly represents one of Kipling's recurrent attitudes of mind.

'The Wish House' and 'The Gardener' show astonishing technical skill. The same quality applies to 'Dayspring Mishandled' and 'Friendly Brook'. Mason draws attention to the manner in which Edmund Wilson, a lively but far from sensitive critic (who wrote about

Kipling when that was an unfashionable thing to do), has often missed the point of a story's subtlety in the conclusions he draws.

One side of Kipling is concerned with work and discipline, the overwhelming importance of order, but this is only in relation to the individual's own integrity. He is also much weighed down by certain secret horrors, particularly those of nightmare.

In his summing-up Mason contrasts the stiff-upper-lip teaching to which Kipling was subjected, which he thinks stemmed the emotion required of an artist. Here, for once, Mason seems to me slightly at fault. Surely 'artists' have to show discipline, and (as Robert Graves objected) the Kipling hero cannot be wholly cleared of saying he is not going to be sentimental, and then being very sentimental.

There are other points that one might like to argue with Philip Mason, but the wish only emphasizes the force of his book, which throws fresh light on many aspects of a great, but infinitely convoluted writer. One remarkable suggestion Mason makes is that Kipling refers to himself and his marriage in the lines: 'I had loved myself, and I/ Have not lived and dare not die!'

Kipling: The Glass, the Shadow   1975
and the Fire, Philip Mason, Cape.   *Daily Telegraph*

VIII

This is a brilliant book. Kipling has been extensively written about, and Charles Carrington's official biography is an excellent piece of work, but the subject is so various that plenty of room remains for further examination.

Angus Wilson in *The Strange Ride of Rudyard Kipling* has pulled the whole picture together in an admirable manner, producing a certain amount of new material, while putting into perspective much that has been said already.

From childhood Kipling's life falls into well-defined phases, each with its own particular drama or emphasis. Wilson is very good, for example, on the miserable period with the Holloways at Southsea, when Kipling, aged six, and his sister were sent home from India; the tribulations described in 'Baa, Baa, Black Sheep'.

He makes the point that Capt. Harry Holloway represented the less successful end of a relatively successful family, starting as midshipman, RN, at Navarino, but transferring to the merchant service ('captain of mercantile marine', perhaps a preferable phrase to 'captain of marines' which suggests a Royal Marine officer). This may have additionally embittered his wife, the horrible 'Aunt Rosa'.

One of the best sides of Wilson's study lies in his modification of the Kipling myth; he shows that Kipling's parents may have been less to blame for this unfortunate situation than has sometimes been assumed. Although a cat-lover, Wilson can even speak with moderation of Kipling aged sixteen, walking in Kensington Gardens with the young Gilbert Murray, and throwing stones at a cat. He recognizes that Kipling's more unattractive characteristics, especially his early philistinism, are an essential part of him, and indeed are in themselves of interest, it being rare to find such a personal point of view portrayed through the eyes of a gifted writer.

Wilson sees Kipling as an artist rather than a thinker, who was always to be anti-highbrow in spite of his own artistry. Indeed Kipling, writing for his public in India, underplays his exceptional knowledge of, say, French literature in a manner that stops not much short of humbug. A contrast to his boasting of technical terms and phrases.

This attitude resulted in an uninstructed view of Kipling – which even today to some extent persists – as a crude jingo. It has been shown that almost every view that Kipling himself expresses can be countered by one in the opposite direction. Wilson gives a striking example of this in the same passage of Kipling's writing, describing erotic sculpture in the ruined city of Chitor: 'What is visible is finely and frankly obscene,' but later on: 'the loathsome Emblem of creation . . . It came upon me that I must get quickly out of this place . . .'

Even Angus Wilson does not attempt to probe at all deeply into what seems to me the central mystery of Kipling's nature: this boy of admittedly exceptional physical maturity at school, who, when fourteen, fell passionately in love with a girl of the same age (something comparatively rare), yet apparently kept himself going with platonic loves until (and after) marriage; including a surrogate mother, to whom he wrote letters beginning 'Dearest Mater,' signed 'Your own graceless boy.'

Wilson firmly – one would suppose rightly – says:

> I think it likely that Kipling was very much in love with Wolcott [Balestier, brother of his future wife]. Worry about the nature of his feelings may have played some part among all the anxieties crowded in on him in those brief London years. Yet I believe it to be more probable that he did not allow himself to glimpse anything that was unorthodox in his feelings for his friend.

Again one would agree. Kipling, for all his rebellion, remained an intensely 'Victorian' figure, resolutely refusing to look into himself. Wilson, credibly, makes this attitude the explanation of Kipling's unexpected lack of interest in the origins of his own family, in spite of his fascination with the individual in history. In early middle age he had already begun to object to an Edwardian looseness of talk. This puritanical closing of eyes to certain things is probably the explanation of limitations that now seem strange in a man who knew so much, and so often expressed what he knew so subtly.

Wilson thinks that Kipling would certainly have married Carrie Balestier anyway, even if one disregards his feelings for her brother. He makes the perceptive comment that (the Balestiers coming from Martinique) Mrs Kipling is to be thought of more as a French woman than an American. He emphasizes that, however trying people found her – and there can be no doubt people *did* find her trying, even her own family – she performed a wonderful job in seeing her husband through the difficulties and tragedies of their life together.

The book includes some good critical remarks on Kipling's work, considering him not so much a realist but as the creator of a world of his own, which the reader has to accept. In this Kipling is not much short, if at all, of the very best. Wilson is anti-'Mrs Bathurst', a story that has received much praise. I would agree that it is unnecessarily obscure, but surely its merits are in depicting this wonderfully convincing 'nice woman'.

When Kipling originated the expression 'It' I think he meant 'niceness', not sexual attraction to which Elinor Glyn (in my opinion) perverted the sense for her own public. In addition, the obsessive watching of Mrs Bathurst for a split second on a news-film night after night by Vickery does seem to me a remarkable image, and an altogether original one.

The Strange Ride of Rudyard   1977
Kipling: His Life and Works,   *Daily Telegraph*
Angus Wilson, Secker &
Warburg.

IX

Quite by chance – with no eye to the fact that it was just fifty years since Rudyard Kipling's death – I finished a re-read of *Kim* (1901) last week. It is an astonishing book, a mixture of naturalism and improbability from which Kipling managed to exclude all his less endearing mannerisms.

Once the convention of the narrative is accepted, it carries you with triumphant speed through more than 400 pages of what is for most people the utterly unfamiliar background and happenings of a century or so ago. One is staggered by the novel's sheer originality.

I have been surprised by the comparatively apologetic and condescending tone, even in some of the pieces which have celebrated this Kipling half-centenary. Surely he is up with, say, Dickens as one of the country's greatest writers. Of course Kipling wrote dreadful things, for instance about dogs, motor-cars, children like Wee Willie Winkie, while he had a disagreeable strain of rather schoolboyish sadism. But what writer can be named who does not possess certain bad habits?

It is this originality which has made Kipling so hard to place, since a great deal of (mostly rather third-rate) literary criticism consists in comparing one writer with another. There is no one with whom Kipling may be aptly compared, even though his verse was plainly influenced by at least a dozen other poets.

It is, for example, strange to find Henry James (no bad critic, and one of the first to recognize Kipling's genius) supposing Kipling would be a British Balzac. One can hardly think of a single point in which Kipling resembles Balzac – setting aside a few characters like Soldiers Three, Mrs Hawksbee, Strickland of the Police, who recur from time to time.

When Kipling, three months short of seventeen, began to work on the Lahore *Civil and Military Gazette* in 1882, the paper was edited by a rather dreary fellow called Stephen Wheeler, who totally failed to grasp the abilities of his subordinate. It was not until about two years later, when Wheeler was replaced by the brighter E. K. Robinson, that Kipling was allowed to produce original stuff. The sketches collected here represent authentic Kipling material, not always easy to identify because Kipling himself, understandably, discouraged republication of his immature writings.

Thomas Pinney (an American), who edits these articles, makes no great claim for them. This is a very proper attitude for their editor but, speaking as a reviewer, I think that even without knowing their origin, one would be conscious of a quite unusual energy and fluidity of language on the part of a young journalist under twenty – in this volume never more than twenty-two.

For those concerned with the mature Kipling there is much here to observe, both the early appearance of views and methods that were to last a lifetime and the manner in which other characteristics of approach have not yet developed. In short, the smooth narrative conventions of *Kim*, referred to above, have not been fined down for use.

Mahbub Ali, the Afghan horse dealer in *Kim*, makes his first appearance here in 1886, as Afzul of the Sultan Serai, the latter somewhat cleaned up as the Kashmir Serai of the novel. This laundering process is often particularly noticeable in later Kipling. For example, one of the Uncollected Sketches entitled 'The City of Evil Countenances' describes Peshawar – apt to be more romantically spoken of later – where at least one comment would never have appeared: 'Women of course are invisible in the streets, but here and there, instead, some nameless and shameless boy in girl's clothes with long braided hair and jewellery the centre of admirers.'

Any such local colour as the last would in any case have had to be treated with the greatest delicacy in *Kim*, to say the least, where Mahbub Ali's womanizing is always insisted upon, in spite of the friendly interest the horse dealer had always taken in the hero. Even Hurree Babu, somewhat improbably, seems perhaps to have had a brief affair with the Woman of Shamlegh; though that may be a mistaken reading of the passage in question.

The Uncollected Sketches are valuable in showing what an exceedingly uncomfortable time Kipling underwent in these early Indian years, which also supplied him with such a capacious stock-in-trade. In *Something of Myself* Kipling recalls reporting 'an inquiry into the percentage of lepers among the butchers who supplied beef and mutton to the European community of Lahore'. If he actually wrote such an article it has not been found, but 'Typhoid at Home', an account of the dairies and production of milk in the city, is quite sufficiently hair-raising.

Several pieces deal with the Amritsar Horse Fair, a perfect example of Kipling's journalistic ability, and, it might be added, delight in displaying his own knowingness. The Fair was visited by Remount Officers ('remount' being the term used in the army for a horse), where they appeared usually to have been made to pay a high price. Kipling, in fact, was by no means at ease with horses himself, and after marriage his wife usually drove. One would never for a moment guess that.

The account of suffering from fever (which antedates later descriptions of breakdowns and hangovers in prose and verse) is a remarkable passage of sustained writing at nineteen, and there is an interview with an adventurous dentist who had treated the Amir of Afghanistan (including the extraction of a tooth), in the midst of continuous Durbars.

Kipling's India: Uncollected   1986
Sketches: 1884–1888, Thomas   *Daily Telegraph*
Pinney, ed., Macmillan.

X

Hal o' the Ministry

Rudyard Kipling's daughter, Mrs Elsie Bambridge, is fighting to recover the requisitioned land round her seventeenth-century home in Cambridgeshire occupied by the United States Air Force

Dan had come to grief over his Civics, and was kept in to see the psychiatrist; so Una went alone to Far Wood Camp. Dan's space-gun that Colonel Dwight K. Hobden, USAF, had made for him was hidden in an old broken ice-box that someone had thrown away on the west of the wood. Una passed Top-Sergeant Schnapperkratz who is not quite right in the head, but can pick up swarms of broads by just raising one eyebrow; and Top-Sergeant Schnapperkratz gave her some gum.

Una slipped through their private gap in the barbed wire, and sat awhile chewing the gum as 'mericanly as she knew how. Then she took Dan's space-gun from its secret place and fired it towards the Quonset hut right away on the horizon, where a squad of enlisted men were unloading stores for the sanatarium. She heard a grunt.

'Aw hell!' she said aloud, and that was something she had picked up from Dan. 'I b'lieve I've tickled up a GI.'

'Are you aware you are trespassing on Government property,' a voice cried, 'and can be prosecuted under the Act?'

She looked from behind the ice-box most cautiously, and saw a middle-aged man in a dark suit and bowler hat, with a shiny black brief-case under his arm with the Royal cipher on it in gold, and glowing among the late broom.

'I'm not trespassing,' said Una stoutly. 'We've been given permission to come here. We've lived here for years – why my family even lived here before the land was requisitioned.'

'Oh yes, I understand,' said the man. 'Your parents or grandparents, or their legal representatives, were the requisitionees at the time of the finalization of the negotiation.'

He smiled.

'I'm most awfully sorry I plastered you with the space-gun,' said Una. She felt herself blushing.

'Didn't the local representative of Folklore and Ancient Institutional Life inform you that my visit had been arranged by telephonic communication? We spoke.'

'Not if you mean Puck. I thought you were a GI. I – I didn't know you were a – a — What are you?'

He laughed outright, flashing a pair of splendid horn-rimmed glasses and taking off his hat. His hair was thinning beautifully on top.

'They call me Sir Henry Bureauboard. I have been for some years now Chairman of the Commission for Property Exaction, a mobile branch of the Anti-Derequisition Office – it has been called the Pride of the Civil Service.'

There was a rustle among the briars. He rose to his feet and listened, beginning to open his brief-case and feel for his fountain-pen. Dan and Puck stumbled through the copse.

'Passed to ye! Passed to ye!' Puck cried. 'See what it is to go through the correct channels. Sir Henry Bureauboard – pardon, Hal – says I am the very image of a Public Relations Officer.'

'Are you a Civil Servant, sir?' asked Dan. 'That's what I want to be when I grow up.'

'I was just the same at your age,' said Sir Hal. 'Good families are very much alike. Mother would sit listening to a wireless talk on Economic Theory – those were days before the Third Programme, you must remember – while Father worked on his Allowances and Income Tax Rebate, and we four looked through old Civil Service Examination Papers and asked each other questions. I shall never forget the news coming that I'd passed.'

'It must have been wonderful,' said Una, her eyes dancing. 'When did you begin to actually requisition people's property in a big way?'

'Why, in those days,' interrupted Puck, 'private citizens thought they owned the place. I can even remember in your grandfather's time he behaved just as if he could do what he liked with his own property.'

'But it still does belong to us in a way, doesn't it — ' Una paused as Puck held up one of his gnarled fingers, inky with decades of filling up forms.

'Naturally, it belongs to you, or your legal representatives, within the terms of the Act,' said Sir Hal quietly.

'Exactly,' said Puck, 'but a few generations ago people were not nearly so aware of the need to grant wider powers to the Requisitioning Authority, whichever it might be.'

'Well, as I was saying,' continued Sir Hal, 'it was a great day for me when I first took my seat at the Ministry. And do you know my very first task was to requisition *this property*. Of course I saw at once that it was not going to be at all easy. The owners' great-great-grandchildren, or their heirs, might easily get it back unless I did my duty properly. I believe I wrote thirty or forty minutes – many of them interdepartmental – before the end of that afternoon. I had filled my out-tray, and sent one of the messengers for the necessary form to obtain another one, when the young man at the next desk, Pending-Partly – now Sir John Pending-Partly – said "Come and have a mug of cocoa, Bureauboard." "Not till I've tied up this bit of requisitioning, Pending-Partly," I said.

'I felt angry and ashamed that he should speak of cocoa when my work was still unfinalized.

'"Oh you'll soon outgrow that sort of nonsense," he answered. "It is not nearly so easy for the public to get back their property from the Government as you seem to think."'

'What a shame,' said Una, 'after you had written all those minutes. But did you feel happy?'

'Happy?' said Sir Hal. 'When the cleaners came in to dust the office the following morning I was still writing. I felt a bit faint and took some Vitamin B tablets, but I had tied up the requisitioning. After what I had done there was little or no hope of the so-called owners getting it back for four or five generations, if then.'

'And did you ever speak to Mr Pending-Partly again,' asked Dan, 'after he'd been so beastly?'

'Oh yes we made it up,' said Sir Hal, laughing his rich laugh. 'He wasn't a bad fellow really. It was just that he went about requisitioning in a different way. He was really very efficient at it. We got our "K" the same year as a matter of fact.'

'You've no idea how the place has improved since those days,' said Puck. 'Notices up everywhere, a sewage farm, lots of barbed-wire. We've even been promised two 12,000-gallon oil tanks in the grounds. I'm hoping they will cut down some of those awful old trees that have been an eyesore to me for two or three hundred years.'

'And you've improved your position too, Puck,' said Sir Hal. 'You weren't a Civil Servant yourself in those days.'

'Nor was I,' said Puck, grinning.

As he gave the children the Oak, Ash and Thorn, chanting the magic-making words 'Passed to ye, passed to ye,' they could scarcely hear their own voices gently echoing 'We concur,' as they raced by Pook's Hill Centre on the way home to tea.

1955
Punch

The Americans

PRESIDENTIAL ORIGINS

The 200th anniversary of American Independence comes up next year. This volume, giving the origins of the families of all the Presidents of the United States, provides a remarkable commemoration.

It is packed with documentary material of great interest. Reading the book through is one of the best – and easiest – ways of learning American history. The contents include an essay on the Presidency by Denis Brogan; individual essays on the Presidents (with portraits of them and their wives) by Marcus and Lesley Hume Cunliffe; and pedigrees showing descendants, compiled by David Williamson.

The direct male line ancestry of every President is traced back to the earliest recorded origins of the family. A detailed account is provided of all progeny, living and dead, in male and female lines, and of step-children and adopted children of Presidents. Where a President – like Washington – had no issue, the descendants are given of his brothers and sisters.

There have been, up to and including Gerald Ford, 37 Presidents of the United States; plus one President of the Confederate States during the Civil War, who has also been chronicled here. Of these, 18 unquestionably have their family origins in England; Andrew Johnson, Harry Truman, and Gerald Ford himself (whose family name was formerly King) quite possibly coming from England, too.

Scotland – so to speak directly – produced 4 Presidents; by way of Northern Ireland, 5 more. The Kennedy family came, of course, from Southern Ireland, and Richard Nixon's forebears were from Ireland too (1731). Wales can claim the Confederate President, Jefferson Davis.

Of the Presidents of Continental origins, the forebears of Van Buren and the two Roosevelts came from the Netherlands; Hoover's immediate immigrant ancestor crossed from Germany, but earlier Hoovers were from Switzerland; the Eisenhowers were also from Germany.

An aspect of the information found here that surprised me was the early date at which most of the families of the 'English' Presidents had arrived in America. Sixteen of them were there earlier than 1677, 12 before 1640. Researchers on President Ford's ancestry have at present proceeded no further than his grandfather. Apart from him, the only Presidents whose families arrived after the Declaration of Independence were Buchanan, 1783 (the year of Truman's first ancestor's birth in Virginia, so Truman may be given the benefit of the doubt); Arthur, 1815; Kennedy, 1848.

The industry devoted to George Washington's background is probably second only to that on Shakespeare's, and, so far as pedigree is concerned, has produced far more concrete results. Washington's lineage is an astonishing one. It is absolutely watertight, father to son, back to the grant of the manor of Washington, near Sunderland, about 1180 – in itself no small genealogical achievement when fully documented.

There is, however, more to come. The compilers of the pedigree here show self-discipline in giving only a modest note to the effect that the first Washington was probably descended (details given) from a tenth-century historical figure Crinan, a lay abbot of the Western Isles. They restrain themselves from adding that Crinan is likely to stem in the male line from Niall of the Nine Hostages (died 438), ancestor of the O'Neils.

The fact that Washington himself had no children made things much easier for those who did not want an American semi-royal dynasty to be founded. As it was, his wife was normally called 'Lady' Washington, and the 23rd President, Benjamin Harrison, remarked in his book, *This Country of Ours*, that he, Harrison, would sometimes be addressed by letter-writers as 'His Majesty' or 'His Lordship'; that was as late as the 1890s. The Adams family also produced two Presidents, the 2nd and the 6th.

Marcus and Lesley Cunliffe's brief essays on the Presidents themselves – and their wives, an important adjunct to the office – are excellent (better than Denis Brogan's slightly condescending piece on the Presidency itself). The Cunliffes quite often offer something rather different in tone from the generally accepted view of the man. Lincoln, for example, is pointed out to have been at times something less than the saintly figure now established in clichés; while Harding, even if he spent some of his nights at the White House sitting up late drinking and playing poker, did useful things too.

Coolidge's prim ways were a contrast to Harding's dissipations – Groucho Marx, catching sight of the President at a theatre, shouted out: 'Isn't it past your bedtime, Calvin?'

In the appendix are charts showing the royal descents of some of the Presidents. These are interesting not so much as proving this or that President was 20th from Edward III, as for the more various family connections they bring in. For example, that Washington's descent from the Talboys heiress (1566) put him 'in remainder' (though admittedly a lot of people were that) for the barony (formerly regarded as merely in abeyance) of Kyme.

Presidential Families of the United States of America, Hugh Montgomery-Massingberd, ed., Burke's Peerage.

1975
Daily Telegraph

FIRST LADIES

The wives of the Presidents of the United States of America are in a position unlike that of any other women. Royalty may be criticized, even have its head cut off, but everyone, even its detractors, knows where Royalty stands. Presidential wives have as often as not married a local young man without any particular prospects (it is striking how frequently, anyway in the past, parental approval was initially lacking), then found themselves First Lady.

In addition, Americans are the first to admit that they believe in a 'dream'. It would perhaps be truer to say they believe in a soap opera; though a 'dream' is the ideal that Presidential candidates can appeal to even today. This belief is not combined with willingness to pay for dreamlike glamour at the top (we perpetually read here that the White House needs redecoration for which no money is available), and the glamour has to be skilfully acted out (for instance, Jacqueline Kennedy), or a charge is levelled of being 'undemocratic'.

The subject of class is one apt to make Americans dreadfully uneasy. Paul F. Boller Jr refers more than once to 'middle-class Americans', but you can't be in the middle unless someone is above you and below you. In one case, John Quincy Adams is so designated; his family made him, one would think, decidedly 'upper class' in American terms, especially as he was Minister to Russia at the time. Clearly Adams did not belong to the same class as, say, Abraham Lincoln. One makes these comments to emphasize the extreme difficulties with which First Ladies were, and are, faced.

Boller has a rather unexciting style, and the anecdotes which follow the story of each First Lady are, to say the least, sedative – no doubt in a commendable wish not to be scandalous, which a chronicle such as this might easily have become. We are told, for example, that Florence Harding (née Kling) definitely did not poison President Harding (whose own rackety tastes are somewhat soft pedalled), whatever Gaston B. Means may have written in his book.

However, after a while Boller exercises a certain fascination, and one reads on compulsively through what is really an extraordinary narrative of how human beings behave when placed in an unexpected social situation.

150

George Washington had many excellent qualities, but history has failed to invest him with the smallest sparkle of glamour. It was characteristic of him to marry a rich widow. Martha Washington (known as 'Lady Washington') seems to have been a thoroughly sensible woman, relieved when her husband retired and she could once more live the life of a country squire's wife. She had offspring by her first marriage, her background was 'Tory', but she was always a support to the General.

Dolley Madison (née Payne) made some show of Presidential smartness. She is reputed to have cut Gilbert Stuart's portrait of Washington from its frame, to escape with it when British troops were about to burn Washington in the war of 1812. Margaret, wife of Zachary Taylor, was popularly believed to smoke a corncob pipe. Others denied this imputation, saying she had 'the artlessness of a rustic and the grace of a duchess'.

Abigail Powers, wife of Millard Fillmore (1850, a fairly obscure President), was the first to point out that the White House was totally bookless. No one before that had noticed. Congress was induced to vote a library.

Mary Ann Todd, wife of Abraham Lincoln, has passed into legend as a terror, and for once legend turns out to be perfectly correct. One also feels that Lincoln himself is deservedly remembered as an admirable man. They were the first Presidential couple from the Middle West. It told against them (one is struck how many of the earlier Presidents had Southern origins).

From the first Mrs Lincoln could do nothing right. She was blamed for wearing low-necked dresses, spending money renovating the run-down White House, accused of traitorously sympathizing with the Confederate cause; the Civil War by then having broken out. The virulence of the press against Mrs Lincoln was unequalled before or since. She disliked her husband's associates, gave Abe an awful time. After Lincoln's assassination the unhappy woman, incapable of handling money, grew increasingly impossible to deal with, being for a time before her death confined as insane.

The first couple at the White House to have any real style were Theodore and Edith (née Kermit) Roosevelt (1901). Roosevelt had been married before (his first wife died young), and both marriages were outstandingly happy. Roosevelt, so often referred to as Teddy, hated being called that after his first wife's death. The Roosevelts were known as a Presidential couple outside America, which made a great change.

From here on Paul Boller deals with twentieth-century history. Eleanor Roosevelt, wife of Franklin D., was the nearer related to Theodore Roosevelt, whose widow was always at pains to emphasize that Franklin D. was a *very* distant relation. She was the first wife to be a big operator. We end with Mrs Reagan, 38th in the line, also something of an operator.

Presidential Wives: An
Anecdotal History, Paul F. Boller
Jr, OUP.

1988
Daily Telegraph

AMERICA IN ARMS

This account of American military organization between the Declaration of Independence and the Civil War is full of good things. On the face of it the subject might seem specialized and relatively obscure, but Marcus Cunliffe, covering a great deal of ground, and disposing of a great many legends, is both entertaining and instructive.

First and foremost, *Soldiers and Civilians* provides at close range a perfect example of the conflict, so apparent in almost every branch of American life, between a peculiarly American high-minded idealism and the claims of practical life and government. For that reason alone it should be read by all interested in the American Idea. On the more general side there are also lessons to be learnt – if they could ever be learnt – about some of our own forms of opposition to preparedness that culminated in 1914 and 1939.

When the American Revolution had become an accomplished fact, liberal feeling in the United States was against having a 'standing army' at all, a sentiment inherited from Great Britain, largely deriving from the acts of Cromwell and James II. This was found to be impracticable, if only because force was required to dispossess Indians. A small American standing army accordingly came into existence – at first only one regiment – together with a militia, theoretically compulsory, enrolled on a State basis.

The American moral approach required constant political attacks on the regular army, chiefly on the grounds that it was officered by 'heedless aristocrats', at their worst and most sinister educated at the United States Military Academy at West Point. The militia, on the other hand, were praiseworthy citizen-soldiers. Since in former days they provided their own arms, it is theoretically on account of the militia that any American can to this day order a rifle by post.

Passionate belief in the 'plain man', as against the expert, has led, for example, to the widespread American belief that the forces of Sir Edward Pakenham (not 'Lord' Pakenham) were defeated by 'backwoodsmen', before New Orleans in the war of 1812; whereas the action was settled, in fact, by Andrew Jackson's efficient artillery dispositions. Cunliffe might have added that 'Col Pakenham' has now passed into

American popular ballad (for instance those of Lonnie Donegan) as an *American* partisan leader on that occasion.

In the first half of the nineteenth century, between a probably reasonably efficient, if ungratefully treated regular army, and a tumbledown, finally inoperative militia, grew up the Volunteer movement. This represented the characteristic American reaction against a self-imposed puritanism of one kind or another – this time reaction against disapproval of well-equipped, well-drilled, well-dressed soldiers.

Most of the big cities produced these 'Territorial' units, with titles like the Philadelphia Lancer Guards and uniforms to match, kilted regiments and zouaves in baggy trousers being only two of the many variations in turn-out and designation. Visitors to America were surprised to find cavalry and infantry parading to bands wherever they went, and were on the whole full of praise for the demeanour and drill of the troops they saw. Here we have one of those typical antitheses of American life.

Cunliffe has many interesting comments when we come to the Civil War itself. It has almost always been accepted that the South provided most of the officers for the American army, or at least most of the officers who made the army their career, as opposed to serving briefly as young men.

Although this is stated in many history books, Cunliffe shows that statistics hardly substantiate the view, except perhaps in the cavalry. Moreover, it was in the North that 'military schools' first came into being, and on the whole Volunteer companies were a more prominent feature of the North than the South.

The legend of 'the South' – chivalry, feudalism, plantations, pillared manor houses – has taken some hard knocks lately, and it would be agreed that, so far from being a relatively old 'feudal' civilization, much of the land by the time of the Civil War was owned by speculators of the 1840s. Cunliffe points out that certain aspects of the military legend were encouraged by the North, attracted by the thought of military glory, but transferred into terms that might be romantic, but could not be overtly approved.

In point of fact, Cunliffe suggests the Northern army was led by more 'aristocratic', anyway richer and better educated officers than the Southern. He quotes a West Point cadet as saying that a fellow cadet from the South told him that 'plantations' meant no more than 'farms', and he himself was accustomed to work in the fields beside the Negroes. Cunliffe adds that 'Stonewall' Jackson, for example, apart from his military genius, was not a planter-aristocrat but a rather crochety enthusiast for dietary reform, more in the manner of New England crankiness.

Is the price that America pays for the unpopularity of her army – and it would be hard not to agree that it is still relatively unpopular with the Americans – an unfortunate lack of accord between it and the civil administration? It would at least be true to say that Sandhurst and Woolwich combined cannot easily rival West Point in producing a poet like Poe or a painter like Whistler.

Soldiers and Civilians: The Martial Spirit in America: 1775–1865, Marcus Cunliffe, Eyre & Spottiswoode.

1969
Daily Telegraph

THE GENTEEL TRADITION

In America at the moment there is tremendous interest in the subject of the sources of American civilization. Books are pouring from university presses all over the Republic explaining why Americans are what they are. The difficulty, of course, as in all such investigations, is to agree about the existing situation that has to be explained.

Obviously America presents sociological problems of immense complexity. It is, however, generally conceded in the United States and elsewhere that, both in theory and practice, the American Woman is from certain aspects something rather different from the European Woman.

William Wasserstrom tackles this question by taking as his foundation 'The Genteel Tradition'. This is a recognized phrase to describe the aspirations, literary and to some extent social, of the period in America between about 1830 and 1920.

According to this tradition 'A true, noble woman [writes Wasserstrom] was guided by something called the Eternal Feminine' which yearned 'to integrate itself in the companionship' with something else called the Secular Manly, a companionship that 'is strongest and most blessed after the passions have ceased to heat the blood'. Emphasis was laid on the purity, remoteness, sacredness, of a woman as such.

The natural result of this idealization of women – which our own country's Victorian literature by no means wholly escaped – was a growing, if unspoken, fear that, if women were really so unapproachable as all that, perhaps they were also less attractive than had hitherto been supposed.

The English disregard for logic as usual carried them through after a fashion. If Dickens's Dora was a bore, there was Surtees's Lucy Glitters as a foil; while Thackeray could draw Becky and Amelia in contrast in the same book without too deeply committing himself as to women in general. In America, on the other hand, there is always a tendency to work any given idea threadbare.

However, another ideal, that of an immensely independent, self-possessed, sex-conscious female, was, so to speak, added to the original conception of the immaculate goddess.

If I understand Wasserstrom rightly, his contention is that, deep down in the national consciousness, America has never in truth given an inch where the Genteel Tradition in relation to the American woman is concerned. Yet at the same time America wants to have all the fun of being able to claim the very same woman as the embodiment of sexual fulfilment, indeed often of sexual licence. This paradox has led, in his eyes, to a great deal of confused writing, and perhaps some unhappy social results.

The American Dream – freely referred to as such in American writings – took its first bad knock at the time of the Civil War. A spate of novels followed, usually of the form 'in which the chaste Northern girl personifies virtue and the fiery Southern man personifies vice'. James, in *The Bostonians*, used a variation of this, and 'displeased his audience because he separated passion from idealism'.

The period of reconstruction after the Civil War, the classic age of American toughness and money-making, led in due course to the epoch of the American heiress who found a husband in Europe:

> Princes, to you our western breeze
> Bears many a ship and heavy laden.
> What is the best we send in these?
> The free and fair young Yankee maiden.

The Yankee maiden of the verse was symbolized by the drawings of Charles Dana Gibson – the Gibson Girl. She now took the place of the young lady of the steel engraving who had delighted an earlier generation, but in a sense even the Gibson Girl still clung to the pretensions of that more innocent ideal.

One of the many curious aspects of Wasserstrom's subject is the cult of the 'Dad's girl'. Once again we find Henry James contriving his own version of a generally popular subject in *Washington Square* and *The Golden Bowl*.

This preoccupation with a rather sultry relationship between father and daughter runs through the whole history of American novel writing. It is perhaps a direct and logical result of the insoluble problem posed by the Genteel Tradition of how to make a woman passionless and yet at the same time involve her in love.

Finally, the First World War delivered the death blow – at least on the surface – to the Genteel Tradition; although in writers like Scott Fitzgerald and Edith Wharton the 'Dad's girl', for example, clung on, herself now hopelessly compromised. In other respects the heroine of that age was 'the Hot Number' – Clara Bow in the films, Temple Drake in Faulkner's novel *Sanctuary*.

Wasserstrom becomes at times a trifle diffuse, but he has some amusing ideas to ventilate. His thesis gives him the opportunity to make a quick, and at times witty, survey of the whole extent of

American literature. It is a field in which there are some notable figures, but not an infinite number of them. The critical weight to which these distinguished American writers of the past are now being subjected is certainly a heavy one.

Heiress of All the Ages: Sex and   1959
Sentiment in the Genteel Tradition,   *Daily Telegraph*
William Wasserstrom, OUP for
Minnesota.

EDGAR ALLAN POE AND
THOMAS HOOD

At first sight Edgar Allan Poe (1809–49) and Thomas Hood (1799–1845) do not seem to have much in common except what comparative closeness of date inevitably gives, although Poe wrote a poem called 'The Haunted Palace' (not 'House', as John Clubbe quotes the title), and Hood 'The Haunted House'.

'The Haunted Palace' in *The Fall of the House of Usher* (1839), was possibly read by Hood, though there is no evidence of it. Hood's poem was admired by Poe, who also expressed appreciation for:

> O saw ye not fair Ines?
>   She's gone into the West,
> To dazzle when the sun is down
> And rob the world of rest . . .

One might think Poe immensely out of fashion at the moment, but in fact his complete works, in seventeen volumes, have quite recently been reissued in the United States (together with Woodberry's biography), so clearly interest in him exists. If reading his poetry in bulk is rather heavy going, that is true of all but very few poets, and the good bits are certainly remarkable for their peculiar individuality. Baudelaire and Yeats thought highly of Poe and it is hard to feel that they were mistaken.

Hood, on the other hand, has come into his own with contemporary emphasis on 'social criticism'. 'The Song of the Shirt' remains a powerful piece in its own genre, and 'The Bridge of Sighs' was also admired, indeed translated, by Baudelaire:

> Look at her garments
>   Clinging like cerements;
> Whilst the wave constantly
>   Drips from her clothing;
> Take her up instantly,
>   Loving, not loathing.

It might be priggishly suggested that the suicide of an ill-favoured and middle-aged prostitute could, morally speaking, be just as tragic as that of a young and good-looking one, and there is no doubt that sentimentality of just that sort does flaw Hood's work in a manner that Poe, for all his dead child-loves (his own wife was only thirteen when they married), manages to avoid.

John Clubbe mentions the difficulty of categorizing Hood's verse, and the divisions of his selection into Romantic, Comic, Domestic, Narrative and Social Protest work well. Among these 'Miss Kilmansegg and Her Precious Leg', taking up eighty pages, has a section to itself. These verses tell how Miss Kilmansegg, a very rich young lady, lost her leg in a traffic accident, had it replaced by a leg of gold, married a foreign count who ill-treated her, and was eventually done in by the count with this leg, the verdict being suicide as it was her own limb.

'Miss Kilmansegg' is much too long and immensely boring, but it does show the odd surrealist side of Hood, of which his Joycean puns were also part. It illustrates too his sado-masochist strain, which made it possible for him to write a comic poem describing how a man, born blind, married, had his eyes opened 'like oysters, with a knife', murdered his wife because she turned out to be so ugly, and was hanged.

In Hood's sado-masochism and surrealism we seem to have a closer link with Poe than in the purely romantic element the two poets share in common – Hood's efforts to write like Keats were disastrous. Poe was, of course, hailed as one of their masters by early writers of a surrealist sort like Jarry and Apollinaire.

It is true that André Breton, the prophet of Surrealism, said that 'in questions of revolt, none of us should need ancestors' and 'let us spit in passing on Edgar Poe', but that was later on. By then Surrealist obeisance had already been made. The Surrealists do not seem to have discovered Hood, who certainly has something to offer in their line.

Accordingly, it is interesting that this republication of Poe's poems have the Heath Robinson illustrations. It may not be generally known that Heath Robinson – later famous for his caricatures of incredibly complicated mechanical devices – started life drawing romantically in the Walter Crane/Beardsley manner. Although obviously derivative, Heath Robinson's work is never offensively so and has a certain charm of its own.

A not uncommon paradox is suggested by Heath Robinson's change from an extreme romanticism to a technique based on mechanism, that is to say the short step from the romantic to the grotesque. One cannot help playing with the idea of an edition of Poe's poems illustrated in Heath Robinson's *later* manner. For example:

> By a route obscure and lonely,
>   Haunted by ill angels only,
> Where an Eidolon named Night,
>   On a black throne reigns upright,

I have reached these lands but newly
From an ultimate dim Thule
From a wild weird clime that lieth, sublime
Out of Space – out of Time.

Surely Heath Robinson would have done a splendid surrealist picture of that?

John Clubbe's Hood selection must be commended for giving the poet's own original illustrations. They are in the Leech/Thackeray manner, a shade scratchy, but add to the understanding of Hood's personality. He was typical of one kind of English literary figure, deeply imbued with middle-class respectability, hard working, always pressed for money. His 'Pauper's Christmas Carol' is typical:

Ring the Day of Plenty in!
But the happy tide to hail
With a sigh or with a tear,
Heigho!
I hardly know –
Christmas comes but once a year!

Poe was a not uncommon American literary type (rather in the Scott Fitzgerald manner), just as hard-up, but approaching life with a reckless, erratic violence which led to a bad end. He and Hood make an interesting couple.

The Poems of Edgar Allan Poe,
illustrated by W. Heath
Robinson, Bell.
Selected Poems of Thomas Hood,
John Clubbe, ed., OUP for
Harvard.

1970
Daily Telegraph

JAMES McNEILL WHISTLER

The Gentle Art of Making Enemies now appears, in facsimile, in its thirteenth edition. First published in 1890, it is a kind of scrapbook recording the public quarrels of the painter James McNeill Whistler. Of these the best known is his libel action in 1878, when Ruskin, referring to Whistler's picture, *Battersea Bridge*, wrote: 'I have seen, and heard, much of cockney impudence before now; but never expected to hear a coxcomb ask two hundred guineas for flinging a pot of paint in the public's face.' Whistler, awarded a farthing's damages by the court, went bankrupt as a result of legal expenses. Other minor rows are included here: prolonged skirmishing with Wilde; polemics with Swinburne; Whistler's 'Ten o'clock' lecture, delivered in London, Oxford, and Cambridge, in 1885, expressing his own views on art.

How is it that *The Gentle Art* has survived? Endless silliness and triviality is enlivened by an acid, though far from copious wit. The atmosphere is that of undergraduate badinage. Yet obviously this volume has been read, and pilfered by generations of writers – from the poems of Aleister Crowley to the script of Graham Greene's *The Third Man* (where the joke about the chief achievement of the Swiss being the cuckoo clock is repeated). What is the secret of its vitality?

The Gentle Art is important because it crystallizes certain constituents from which we have suffered ever since its period. These may be summarized as the Advertising Artist, the Oppressive Critic, and the Facetious Public. Its hard core is the *Whistler* v. *Ruskin* case; in its different way, a kind of rehearsal for the Wilde trial. The participants are worth examination.

Whistler (*b.* 1834), an expatriate American, is a painter of considerable charm, but it would be hard to find anyone who would now attempt to claim for him anything approaching the first rank. He is not to be compared, for example, with Degas or Manet. At the same time, it would be generally conceded that he was 'on the right side' where painting was concerned. As a wit his position is more difficult to estimate. He enjoyed a great contemporary reputation, and it is probably true to say that to the generation born about 1880 he was – and is – regarded (chiefly on the strength of 'You will, Oscar, you will', if he ever said that, which seems extremely doubtful) as habitually scoring off Wilde. The fact remains that Wilde's sayings have stood the test of time better than Whistler's, many of whose verbal fireworks (like those of Bernard Shaw, whom he sometimes resembles) have become hopelessly damp.

In opposition, stands Ruskin (*b.* 1819), the apostle of Gothic architecture. Of late years some effort has been made to re-establish Ruskin as an art critic of supreme eminence. Those who feel tempted to accept this view of him would do well to cast their eye over his sayings quoted in the margin of *The Gentle Art*. They are certainly extraordinary enough. That Ruskin had no opinion of Rembrandt or Velasquez is sufficient to go on, so far as the conflict with Whistler is concerned.

Turning once more to Whistler, we find him propagating two general laws, put forward perhaps for the first time: that only a painter may criticize a picture; that 'artists' are persecuted by the public. It would be interesting to know whether evidence exists for such views being urged at an earlier date. They seem to belong essentially to the middle of the nineteenth century, not according at all with the thought of the two previous centuries or Renaissance times.

Obviously certain technicalities of painting, as of writing or music, are unfamiliar to those who do not practise those arts. True, Ruskin involved himself deeply in this technical side. ('It is physically impossible, for instance, rightly to draw certain forms of the upper clouds with a brush . . .') But the weakness of Whistler's position seems to be that (with Tom Taylor, Editor of *Punch*) two painters, Frith and Burne-Jones, *did* testify against his work; while, if an 'established' critic is not to be allowed to say what he likes about a 'modern' painter, how can a 'modern' critic say what he likes about an 'established' painter? The latter right is in some respects surely a more important one to defend. Swinburne, for example, comes out of his bout with Whistler very well, liking Whistler's painting but not liking his nonsense – in which Whistler was, after all, involving himself in the mysteries of writing.

That certain artists have a taste for cheap publicity we know in our own day only too well. It does not mean that they are necessarily bad artists. Such artists do, however, have the undesirable effect of making the public think that art is 'funny'. How infinitely wearisome here, in the pages devoted to the libel action, are the remarks about art of the Attorney-General (probably a reasonably capable man at his job, though now quite forgotten). 'What was the structure in the middle? Was it a telescope or a fire-escape? etc., etc., etc.' And yet it was not the Attorney-General's fault that he had to stand up and, intellectually speaking, make an ass of himself; it was Whistler's and Ruskin's.

This brings us to the final point: the persecution of artists. If Whistler were persecuted, he was persecuted not as an artist but as a publicity-hound. His extreme aggressiveness suggests, indeed, a form of persecution mania. The Pennells in their biography admit that, every allowance being made, he was not normally balanced. Whether Ruskin was ever quite sane at any stage of his life is equally arguable. Between the two of them, on that day, they did little to benefit painting in this country. *The Gentle Art of Making Enemies* has claims to be regarded as the first milestone on its own particular melancholy road.

The Gentle Art of Making Enemies,   1954
James McNeill Whistler,   *Punch*
Heinemann.

MARK TWAIN

Mark Twain looms over American literature. In *Huckleberry Finn* he produced a masterpiece of its kind; in *Tom Sawyer* something not quite so good, at the same time a classic.

The rest of his innumerable works are all but unreadable today. *A Yankee at the Court of King Arthur*, for example, is pitiful stuff.

At the same time, it is not so much the question of whether he is writing well or badly that makes Twain of interest, as the manner in which he always, in all circumstances, represents the American idea in its most extreme form, carried to its logical conclusions.

The Autobiography of Mark Twain now under review – printed in notably unattractive type – is stated to be the first volume to put his writings in correct sequence. One approaches it with interest.

Twain was born in Missouri in 1835. After being apprenticed to a printer, he became a pilot on the Mississippi. This job came forcibly to an end when the Civil War broke out. He tried a couple of weeks as a soldier, when he was 'hunted like a rat'. Then he earned his living as a miner, returned to journalism, and finally emerged as the best-known American writer of his day.

He is the voice of the new American writer, bursting with hatred of European literary domination as represented by Edgar Allan Poe, whom Twain found as unreadable as Jane Austen. Cocksure, materialistic, anti-religious, anti-capitalist, he could not avoid in due course – like so many persons of his kind – becoming involved in truckling to the causes he was ostensibly attacking.

His agnosticism had to be soft-pedalled because it was bad for sales. When he became famous he was inevitably associated with systems of which he had loudly disapproved. His wife, to whom he was devoted, was mortal enemy of that very coarseness of speech that was an essential part of his approach. For her he modified his natural roughness.

This would all make very good material for an autobiography. Unfortunately Twain had little or no gift for objectifying such experience. He had no power whatever of self-examination. He cannot tell you what he himself is like; he cannot tell you what other writers are like.

Bret Harte, for example, occurs at some length in these pages. We learn that Harte was unreliable, borrowed money from his friends, deserted his wife, was in general a nuisance; but Bret Harte, the man, never emerges. Twain's account of it all is like a bore grumbling about an acquaintance in a railway carriage.

After an attack – possibly quite justified – on phrenology, Twain goes on to say:

Two years ago Col. Harvey took prints of my two hands and sent them to six professional palmists of distinguished reputation here in New York City; and he also withheld my name and asked for estimates. History repeated itself. The word humour occurred only once in the six estimates and then it was accompanied by the definite remark that the possessor of the hands was destitute of the sense of humour.

Twain is naturally ironical about this finding. After closing his *Auto-biography* one has an uneasy feeling that the palmists were absolutely right – especially the one who affirmed his specific lack of humour.

He can brilliantly describe violent, grotesque, savage situations, e.g., the Royal Nonesuch in *Huckleberry Finn*, but they are not, so it seems to me, humorous ones. In fact they are desperately melancholy. Indeed both *Tom Sawyer* and *Huckleberry Finn* owe their greatness to their intense melancholy, which is the melancholy of the persecuted child escaping into a world of dreams.

Twain worshipped adolescence in a characteristically American manner. He himself shows always the egotism of an adolescent. The strait-laced aunts of his books about boys seem a ghastly prophecy of the strait-laced wife he loved, who bossed him in a world that had nothing in common with the adventurous Mississippi.

In saying this, I do not, of course, mean that Twain could never tell a funny story; merely that his approach to life was not individual enough, not objective enough, to be truly humorous. There is here, for instance, the enjoyable anecdote of Bret Harte correcting the obituary notice in the provincial paper which stated of some deceased lady, 'Even in Yreka her chastity was conspicuous'. This was a misprint for 'charity'. Harte saw a mistake had been made and, underlining the word, put a query. As a result the passage appeared as 'Even in Yreka her *chastity* was conspicuous (?)'

There are passages of real poetry in Twain at his best, and he can be moving when he tells in this *Autobiography*, quite simply, how his carelessness in taking his first child out in bitterly cold weather led to its death. But he is also liable to speak of emotional matters in a manner to suggest that they are always simple and uncomplicated, so that his protestations lose all force.

Above all, when you read Twain you hear echoes of every modern American writer – Pound, Hemingway, Salinger, Capote even. In fact there are moments when one wonders whether it would not be a good thing for American writing if someone could make a mighty effort and forget about Mark Twain altogether for a while.

The Autobiography of Mark Twain,   1960
Charles Neider, ed., Chatto &   *Daily Telegraph*
Windus.

HENRY JAMES

I

For some reason – perhaps largely on account of Sargent's well-known portrait – Henry James lives in the mind as elderly and rotund, an Edwardian sage, irretrievably expatriate, and of infinite verbal anfractuosity. We have almost forgotten that he was born an American, and it comes as a surprise that it was ever necessary for him to take British nationality. But American he was once; a good-looking, intelligent, witty, though always rather serious, young man whose photograph at nineteen strangely resembles the young Proust's. Leon Edel's book is the first volume of a series to cover James's life. It provides an enthralling opening to the story.

The family background is full of interest. William James, the grandfather (1771 – 1832), an Irish Protestant of excessive puritanical rectitude, had emigrated to the United States and made a large fortune. His son Henry (the novelist, somewhat to his chagrin, was known for the first forty years of his life as 'Henry James, Jr.') was a man of very different stamp. He had a cork leg, consequence of an accident in a fire, and his tastes were at once philosophical and frivolous. A breathless letter survives in which his own father speaks of him as having

> so debased himself as to leave his parents' house in the character of a swindler, etc. etc. – details presented to-day – are the order which I enclose as a specimen of his progress in arts of low vileness – and unblushing falsehood . . . a fellow from Schenectady was after him to-day for fifty or sixty dollars (in a note I understand), for segars and oysters.

The novelist, with more moderation, later alluded to this episode as a 'misunderstanding if not . . . a sharp rupture'.

William James left an estate valued at $3,000,000. His will was so cantankerous that his eleven children had it broken, and Henry the elder's share was a parcel of real estate in Syracuse that yielded about $10,000 a year. For the rest of his days he was able to live a life of leisure and indulge the undoubted eccentricity of his tastes. Mainly a Swedenborgian, he took a keen interest in all religions, and was determined that intellectually his children should never endure the parental domination of his own youth. One of the results of this catholicity, and of his wandering, vaguely literary life, was that the novelist suffered much embarrassment at school from being unable to state precisely either the profession or religion of his father.

The elder James spent much of his time in Europe where, in France and Switzerland, the greater part of Henry James's education took place. Mrs James, a woman of quiet good sense, was also of unbending will, and it is clear that, if one kind of parental domination was expelled from the home, another, and perhaps more insidious sort, was much in evidence. There were five children: William, later famous as a philosopher, Henry, the novelist, two younger brothers, and a sister.

Henry seems perpetually to have felt the undue preponderance of the apparently more brilliant and successful William. Edel points out how often in his stories a second son triumphs morally over an aggressive elder brother. An additional twist was given to the complications of family relationship by the American Civil War. Although strongly Abolitionist politically, their father also held that 'no young American should put himself in the way of death until he has realized something of the good of life'. However, his two younger sons went off to the war, thereby unexpectedly stealing prestige from William and Henry.

This situation left a lifelong impression on Henry James. True, he was hardly cut out to be a soldier, and there were plenty of reasons why he had no need to become involved. One of these was the mysterious 'accident' which happened to him at about this time, apparently a strained spine. Edel effectively disposes of the legend of sexual hurt resulting in physical inadequacy. James's back gave him pain all his life, and one of his letters on this subject 'in the history of literature may well be the most elaborate account of the ailment extant'. The two younger brothers, after their moment of glory, led unsuccessful lives; the sister became a neurotic. Henry, though apparently not William, was left with a sense of guilt about the war.

The book takes Henry James as far as his return to Europe as a man of twenty-six, already making a reputation as writer. He arrives in England armed with excellent introductions; he tours Italy, that 'dishevelled nymph'. London enchanted and horrified him. Although scarcely able to remember his sojourn there as a small child, he was familiar with many of its salient features from the pages of *Punch* (a periodical to which he was eventually to contribute), read assiduously from the age of seven in the James home on 14th Street. While abroad, he heard of the death of Minny Temple, an attractive consumptive whose image was to figure in his books, with whom he had some sentimental understanding, though it could scarcely be called a love affair. Indeed, this last emotion remains a mystery, perhaps to be

unravelled in subsequent volumes. Nor are we offered any solution yet
to the dark undercurrent of so much of James's thought.

Henry James: The Untried Years:　　　　　　1953
1843–1870, Leon Edel, Hart-　　　　　　*Punch*
Davis.

II

Here we have James a successful and relatively famous writer in his
forties, a little tired of the social life that had formerly so much attracted
him, anxious to make more money, possibly by writing plays.

James remains an absorbing, oddly mysterious figure. On the face of
it, he pottered about, working hard all the time, but living a life without
adventure, without passion, mild by almost any standards. He himself
was far too intelligent not to be aware of this lack of impact. His novels
suggest that at least one side of him deplored it.

At the same time, no one was more keenly aware of what was going
on around him. Nothing could have been less like the real James than
H. G. Wells's bad-mannered, trivial caricature of him as a bumbling,
pompous literary bore. Again and again in Leon Edel's book the reader
is brought up short by James's direct, almost brutal judgments,
expressed in the clearest terms.

Although this is only a section of the whole biography, Edel has
planned it to some extent with the shape of a novel, James's friendship
with Constance Fenimore Woolson providing a framework and
characteristically Jamesian theme.

The niece of Fenimore Cooper's wrote novels herself. James
described her, rather unkindly, as a 'deaf and *méticuleuse* old maid'. But
he obviously found her a great support. Edel suggests, with good
reason, that on Miss Woolson's side this friendship was allowed to take
on an emotional tinge. In the end it led, if not directly, perhaps
indirectly to tragedy and suicide.

So often, reading James's novels, one is tempted to ask what all the
fuss that the characters are making is about. Did people ever go to the
lengths there represented for the artificial reasons put forward? To
some extent the story of James and Miss Woolson seems to answer that
question. They did. This tenuous, unexpressed, well-behaved relationship led to violence and horror.

James's view of the novel, as such, was that 'the laws imposed upon
novelists by aesthetics resolve themselves into this: to give a personal
impression of life'. He did not 'put people into novels', but he certainly
transmuted the characteristics of persons he knew, through the
medium of writing, into his books.

There is here, for example, a striking photograph of his friends the Boott family, of whom the father, Francis Boott, certainly provided one of the models for Mr Verver in *The Golden Bowl*. There was also perhaps a little of Boott's daughter, Lizzie, to whom James was much attached, in Maggie Verver. Lizzie Boott's death fifteen months after her marriage was another sad story, typically Jamesian in many respects.

We are given several glimpses of James through the eyes of others. Violet Paget, who had some name in her own day as a writer under the pseudonym 'Vernon Lee' – a figure neither greatly talented nor very sympathetic – speaks of his 'absolute social and personal insincerity and extreme intellectual justice and plain-spokenness'. Others mention his great liveliness in conversation.

Through his familiarity with the Parisian world of fashion, James knew Robert de Montesquiou, one of Proust's models for M. de Charlus, and it is even possible that he may have met the young Proust himself.

Throughout this period James depended on his writing for money. Admittedly he liked living comfortably and staying at good hotels. This was becoming increasingly difficult with small sales for his novels. He toiled away at short stories for magazines, but here, too, the idiosyncrasies of editors often made such work unsatisfactory. That was why James turned his attention to the theatre. He did this quite cold-bloodedly. Indeed, his lack of success in that field was perhaps due to his regarding the medium of the play with so little respect.

However, the picture that has survived of James as a dramatist is not altogether a true one. Edel corrects it. I had myself imagined James working away at one play, which was at last put on stage, then booed off the first night. On the contrary, there were several years of close association with the theatre, which, even if they did not produce dazzling success, resulted in an undoubted claim for James to have had his plays put before the public. In the last resort, one feels that the point about James was his extreme intelligence. He knew himself; he knew other people. He was not taken in. Perhaps if he had been less acute, he would have had a less muted life so far as incident was concerned – intellectually it was certainly energetic enough.

One small slip of Leon Edel's: Hyacinth Robinson in *The Princess Casamassima* was not the illegitimate son of an English *peer* and a French seamstress who turned on her seducer and murdered him. Hyacinth's father was a *younger son*, with quite different social and financial implications.

Henry James: The Middle Years: 1884–1894, Leon Edel, Hart-Davis.

1969
Daily Telegraph

III

One might risk saying Leon Edel's chief achievement is showing what a split personality James was, in spite of very strong innate characteristics, and a positive caricaturing of these in his own daily life. When this book opens Henry James, on the verge of sixty, was a famous writer who lived mostly by his writing, notwithstanding what were regarded by the public as obscurities of style. He appears to have drawn about £700 a year from his American capital, making that up to about £2,000 (required by the level of existence he led) in literary earnings. The Edwardians have been much abused for their philistinism, but such royalties for such novels are worth considering, also the extreme 'aliveness' of writing as a profession at that period.

A word should be said of Edel's technique in handling the formidable number of writers and others who abutted on James's life. Muddle might easily have resulted from dealing with them in purely chronological manner, but Edel, with inconspicuous art, sketches James's relations with, say, Conrad, or Stephen Crane, in such a way that the reader is given a portrait, all of one piece, that can be carried through the narrative. James, priding himself on his insights, found the Pole unfathomable. One would greatly like to know what was his 'realising sense' about Conrad, 'of a rum sort', and if he actually confided that to Edith Wharton.

Edel is rightly very sympathetic to James, who had many admirable points as a man (as opposed to good points as a writer), but he draws attention to a strong desire to dominate, an historic instinct, and an 'aggression' that took the form of forcing people to wait while conversationally he took an interminable time to choose the right word – and woe betide anyone who offered assistance.

These aspects were sharply in counterpoint to the social, courtly old buffer side of tradition. James could also be at times rather silly. His views on Shakespeare, for example, suggest his sense of the past did not include something rather different, a sense of certain historical disconnections from the present. Edel treats with tact and good sense the question of James's homosexuality.

Forty years ago one would be told stories of how James, towards the end of his life, had kissed Hugh Walpole, and how, hearing of that, Wilde's friend Robbie Ross had said: 'If only we had known, we could have found him someone better.' I do not quote this story very seriously, but it is worth recalling as an example of completely missing the point. James was perfectly aware of being homosexual, and it may even have been that its physical expression was not unknown to him. He speaks of not regretting the 'excesses' of his youth.

Here we get back to the strangely divided nature of James's personality referred to above. On the whole one would guess that he preferred – as some do – to live a life in which physical sex played no part. Certainly to talk about such things openly was in general abhorrent to him. What is our surprise, therefore, to find in Edel's pages a letter specifically requiring, in terms as plain as any available in the Jamesian vocabulary, homosexual gossip of the most highly spiced sort.

In this inconsistency, there is perhaps a similar one in James's literary approach, though Edel's book is essentially about the life and aims to keep away from criticism so far as possible. At the same time, if James disliked the novels of Dostoevsky and Tolstoy as 'great, baggy monsters', how could he put Balzac top of all novelists, surely the baggiest monster of all? I know that is not quite fair. Balzac's 'Western' mind is, of course, quite different from the Russians'. All the same, he far from fits into the James straitjacket. The divided side of James is seen in literature as well as life.

One might very reasonably surmise that the last fifteen years of a successful, deliberately pompous, trifle snobbish, essentially kind (even if he did, horribly, kill a cat with a stick because it disturbed him nocturnally) author's life would be pretty humdrum. Nothing could be further from fact.

An egregrious young woman called Miss Grigsby, American, mistress of a tycoon, put it about that she was model for the heroine of one of James's novels (published before they met), raising such a to-do that even William James, the philosopher, had to be told by his then sixty-year-old brother that there was no truth in newspaper statements that he, Henry, was going to marry her.

An old friend (of all things, representative of *The Times* in Paris) was blackmailed by a woman. James and Edith Wharton, in the manner of a play by Sardou, raised the required sum, and bought off the blackmailer. This gave Edith Wharton an idea. Generously, she secretly paid James (always grousing about his poverty) about £1,500, represesented as startling generosity in his publisher. James never knew, but his agent (who benefited) was not taken in.

The last few weeks of James's life were spent in delirium, in which he dictated in his usual manner to his secretary. What she took down bears that same macabre touch of loss of mental control so strikingly chronicled in Evelyn Waugh's *Pinfold*.

Henry James: The Masters: 1901–   1972
1916, Leon Edel, Hart-Davis.   *Daily Telegraph*

IV

The point about letters – as opposed to biography – is that the reader is allowed to make up his own mind: he is not told what to think. Henry

James's biography has already been admirably set out by Leon Edel. Edel now edits this collection of James's letters with just the right amount of introductory material and notes, though one could have done with a slightly fuller index.

Letters: Henry James: Vol. I covers the formative period of the writer's life: getting away from his loving but somewhat overpowering family – not to mention intellectual Boston society; seeing something of Europe; founding his career as an author. In one way none of the letters is particularly exciting, but the reader gradually gets involved in them, until there is almost a sense of tension as to what is next going to happen to this young man.

Certain things strike one immediately: the early stage at which relations and friends kept letters from James; the power and clearness with which he wrote, even when quite young; the freedom from the convolutions that later overtook his style. This volume brings him to his early thirties, and towards the end it is just possible to see the beginnings of complicated sentence construction, a general thickening of manner, though nothing to what was to come. James was just seventeen when he wrote (13 May 1860) from Switzerland that he had been to see a dissection:

> The subject was a strapping big gendarme who had died of inflammation of the lungs. The smell was pretty bad, but I am glad to say that I was not in any way affected by the things. Willie [James's brother] went the next day to see a drowned man dissected, and although the smell was not bad, one student fainted away, another turned a livid green and was obliged to leave and the rest only stood it by reinforcements of fresh air every little while.

In such a description we seem a long way from *The Golden Bowl*, but James was already preparing to be a professional writer, an end which he slowly, but quite surely, achieves as the Letters unfold. He borrowed money from his father, which was repaid as James himself sold critical pieces and short stories to magazines. The tone of blandness, never relaxed, undoubtedly covered a good deal of severe nervous strain.

James would go off to London, Paris, Rome, stay for months, even years, at these capitals, and work. In London, where he first lived on his own at the age of twenty-four, he had good introductions to the intellectual world of the period (1867), and met people like Ruskin – who some years later wanted to see James appointed to the Slade Professorship of Fine Arts at Cambridge.

All the same, it must have been very lonely, and money was never more than just enough. In Rome there was a considerable society of Americans, but James at times regarded that as an infliction rather than an advantage. These were the years when most men undergo emotional experiences of one sort of another; nothing of the kind is even hinted with James, and there are moments when the eternal blandness threatens to become something not much short of creepy.

His health was not always good, and he suffered tortures from constipation. This was certainly not due to lack of exercise, he walked for miles and, when in Rome, often rode on the Campagna. Edel suggests that nervous tensions may have played a part in these troubles. When James was in England he underwent treatment at Malvern. Food-values were not well understood in those days. He wrote (8 March 1870):

> The narrowness of English diet is absolutely ludicrous. Breakfast cold mutton (or chop) toast and tea: dinner leg or shoulder, potatoes and rice pudding; tea cold mutton again (or chop) toast and tea.

It was not surprising that he did not improve. James was, incidentally, a great beer-drinker.

There are occasional vignettes of individuals which perfectly convey the subject in a line or two – Francis Boott, for example, who lived in Florence and, with his daughter Elizabeth, is thought to have provided some of the material for characters in *Portrait of a Lady*. James writes (9 April 1873): 'Lizzie [Boott] wears better than her father, whose dryness and coldness and tendency to spring back to calling you Mr again like a bent twig, is ineffable.'

James was always friends with his fellow novelist, William Dean Howells, but had no illusions about his literary merits.

> Poor Howells is certainly difficult to defend, if one takes a stand-point the least bit exalted: make any serious demands and it's all up with him. He presents, I confess, to my mind a somewhat melancholy spectacle – in that his charming style and refined intentions are so poorly and meagerly served by our American atmosphere. There is no more inspiration in an American journey than that. Thro' thick and thin I continue however to enjoy him – or rather thro' thinner and thinner. There is a little divine spark or fancy that never quite goes out.

The overall impression of James at this age is one of immense doggedness. At present it is not at all easy to see how this determined young man is going to turn into a distinguished but – there is no avoiding this phrase – mannered old buffer of later years. Fellow writers of every sort will, however, feel sympathy with James when he wrote 'idle vistas and melancholy nooks', and the sentence, when it appeared in print, read: 'idle sisters and melancholy monks'.

Letters: Henry James: Vol. I: 1843–1875, Leon Edel, ed., Macmillan.

1975
Daily Telegraph

V

This second volume of the James Letters begins when the writer was in his early thirties (and decided to live in Paris), and ends with him as a forty-year-old established figure in London, and (significant event) the death of his father.

Even in the first instance James would have preferred London to Paris, but Paris offered a job in the form of a regular Paris Letter to an American paper. He could write his books there as well as anywhere else, and he spoke fluent French. London must wait.

James's Letters bring home things that can never be quite so vividly expressed in a biography. One is astonished how easily James glided into what now seems a fairly sparkling Parisian literary world – Flaubert, Edmond de Goncourt, Alphonse Daudet, Zola, Turgenev.

Still, although he liked Flaubert personally and was devoted to Turgenev, French intellectual life (which he considered vastly inferior to English, chiefly owing to the supremacy of George Eliot) did not really suit him.

James seems to have accommodated himself pretty well to the French habit of not asking people – anyway foreigners – to their houses. He did not mind café life; later he much preferred British hospitality and the weekend house-party. The real trouble with the French was his genuine distaste for easy-going sexual behaviour at too close range.

Writing (2 May 1876) to his Harvard friend T. S. Perry, he says: 'I heard Emile Zola characterize his [Daudet's] manner sometime since as *merde à la vanille*. I send you by post Zola's own last – *merde au naturel*. Simply hideous.' Or again (to the American novelist William Dean Howell, 28 May 1876):

> I went yesterday to see a lady . . . Baroness Blaze de Bury – a (supposed) illegitimate daughter of Lady Brougham . . . She . . . has two most extraordinary little French, emancipated daughters. One of these, wearing a Spanish mantilla, and got up apparently to dance the cachaca, presently asked me what I thought of *incest* as a subject for a novel – adding that it had against it that it was getting, in families, so terribly common. *Basta!*

James wrote to his brother William James, the philosopher (29 July 1876):

> My last layers of resistance to a long-encroaching weariness and satiety with the French mind and its utterance has fallen from me like a garment. I have done with 'em for ever and am turning English all over. I desire only to feed on English life and the contact of English minds – I wish greatly I knew some.

It was not long before he did. James moved to London (rooms at 3, Bolton Street, Piccadilly) the following year. Again one is struck by the speed with which he begins to be asked 'everywhere' (he would certainly have used inverted commas for that term). He became a member of the Athenaeum and Reform Clubs.

Henry James, as we know, was to live the rest of his life in London, and in one respect he is never tired of insisting on his admiration for the British character, the satisfaction he felt for the existence that he had designed for himself. In another he gets from time to time cheerfully bored with British stuffiness, philistinism, lack of imagination.

Without for a moment questioning the abundance of such elements, then or (in contemporary form) at any other time, one cannot help wondering what James expected if he combined his own intellectual sensibilities with liking to dine out two or three times every week. Here, I think, a point about James should be noted. Like Dickens, though unlike, say, Kipling, he never really understood what people, especially the upper-middle class, did in a 'job', or, in James's case, that their minds were occupied with their own profession or business, not with being primarily entertaining guests.

It may be that in the 1870s there was no easy answer in London to James's problem, but again he was up against his own incurable primness. He liked R. L. Stevenson but found him 'bohemian', and Whistler was just a 'queer little Londonized Southerner' who painted 'abominable' pictures. Lord Houghton (Monckton Milnes) asked James to Fryston (where life at times had been anything but stuffy), but Houghton was getting on in years and no doubt his interests had become more solidly political than in his Swinburnian days.

James did take quite a keen interest in British politics and some of his comments on this subject are terrifyingly apt. He saw, just a hundred years ago, that a decline was threatened; that the Government was shilly-shallying about the Eastern Question – Russia's perpetual imperialist expansion, the crumbling of Turkey.

James did not like the Tory support of Turkey (not a very estimable power at that period), nor did he care for Disraeli. But what was the Jamesian alternative? He disliked Russia too, hating the 'equally odious peace-at-any-price "Manchester"-minded party', and 'the absence in the Liberal party, as a party, of the good old-fashioned sentiment of patriotism'. These orientations all sound a trifle familiar.

The phrase to 'take a shine' to a person surprises one at this early date, also James writing to his brother that he was going to 'give himself unseriously to "creative" writing'. He writes from Boston to Lady

Rosebery (16 June 1883): 'Newport indeed is given up to billionaires and "dudes" (I will explain the dude when I see you next).'

Letters of Henry James: Vol   1980
II:1875–1883, Leon Edel, ed.,   *Daily Telegraph*
Macmillan.

VI

Henry James, now in his forties, celebrated as a writer, much sought after for London dinner-parties and country-house visits, was making rather less than more money, and the first glow of being asked 'everywhere' had worn off.

During the dozen years here covered he suffered a series of emotional blows from which in a sense he never quite rehabilitated himself. The death of his sister Alice set her free from an unhappy life, but James had been attached to her. He was particularly devoted to Robert Louis Stevenson, who was to die in the South Seas.

The apparent suicide of 'Fenimore', James's somewhat condescended-to female friend Constance Fenimore Woolson, disturbed him in a horrifying manner. Finally, there was the shattering setback to his plans to be a successful playwright.

At the beginning of this third collection I began to wonder whether I had not had enough of these elaborate phrases and overflowing epistolary courtesies, which often concealed a good deal of melancholy, boredom, and irritation with the English and their ways; though London still remained the place where James felt most at home. Sometimes the images kindled by contorted metaphor get a shade out of hand, as when referring to an article James was writing about Stevenson's short stories:

> I shall finish it by the end of next week – so for these impending days I shall really cohabit with you. Pray for me that I don't offend you. If I do, it will only be by too thick a buttering – and yet I shall try not to be indecently greasy.

Stevenson and the very young Kipling were pretty well the only British writers of the period whose work James admired, and although W. D. Howells was an old friend whom he praised while privately feeling certain reservations, he was equally unenthusiastic about American writing.

> Yes, I have read Trollope's autobiography and regard it as one of the most curious and amazing books in all literature, for its density, blockishness and general thickness and soddenness.

*

The greatest pleasure I have lately had has been the perusal of the last two volumes of Froude's Carlyle. They are of the deepest interest and entertainment. Decidedly Carlyle was a brute, a man of jealous, grudging, sinister, contemptuous, ungenerous, most invidious soul . . . But what a genius, painter, humorist.

Francis Marion Crawford is an American novelist now not much remembered but popular in his day:

What you tell me of the success of Crawford's last novel sickens and almost paralyses me. It seems to me so contemptibly bad and ignoble that the idea of people reading it in such numbers etc.

This is to tell you *that*, in sorrow, and to relieve myself a little further on the subject of the unspeakable [Rider] Haggard. Since I saw you I have finished Solomon and read half of *She*. *Ah, par example, c'est trop fort* – and the fortyieth thousand on the title page.

Stevenson fought back about both Crawford and Haggard.

I grant you Hardy with all my heart and even with a certain quantity of my boot-toe. I am meek and ashamed where the public clatter is deafening – so I bowed my head and let *Tess of the D.'s* pass. But oh yes, dear Louis, she is vile. The pretence of 'sexuality' is only equalled by the absence of it, and the abomination of the language by the author's reputation for style.

Oddly enough, James liked Zola's novels, but when he met Zola himself found him 'very sane and common and inexperienced. Nothing, literally nothing, has ever happened to him but to write the Rougon-Macquart. It makes the series. I admit; still more curious.'
To Gosse he wrote of Ibsen:

I think you make him out a richer phenomenon than he is. The perusal of the dreary *Rosmersholm* and even the reperusal of *Ghosts* has been rather a shock to me – they have let me down, down. Surely the former isn't *good* – any more than the tedious *Lady from the Sea* is?

James in fact revised this view, but his failure to grasp at once the dramatic powers of Ibsen does suggest why his own writing of plays was not a success.

This volume includes a most interesting Appendix of four letters written to James by poor 'Fenimore' (Miss Woolson). She was an intelligent woman and quite a successful novelist, but deaf, lonely and unhappy. She adored James, but in a peculiarly provoking and nagging manner.

James was clearly quite unaware what this tone indicated. These four letters tell the whole story, and one feels that James, in certain respects a complete innocent, could not be blamed for causing a disturbance for which there was probably no remedy.

A small correction should be made to the note on p. 22: James's American friend Mrs Pakenham was married to Lt.-Gen. Thomas Henry Pakenham (as is made clear on p. 214), not Admiral William Christopher Pakenham; and surely to call Mrs Fitzherbert the 'wife' of George IV is to beg a whole series of questions?

Henry James: Letters: Vol.   1980
III: 1883–1895, Leon Edel, ed.,   *Daily Telegraph*
Macmillan.

VII

This final volume of Henry James's Letters deals with the last twenty years of his life, the period of literary eminence (without much financial reward), residence mostly at Rye, a certain loosening up of the novelist's personality. Leon Edel's editing is, as ever, admirable (though the explorer's wife was Lady Stanley, not Lady Dorothy).

The elephantiasis of James's style had by now become fully developed, sometimes to the extent of defeating its object of avoiding clichés by introducing clichés of his own. This becomes very apparent reading letters written over two decades, but by that time extreme elaboration had become James's natural manner of expressing himself. He had no prejudice against the split infinitive, and we must regret when he wrote to ask Asquith (then Prime Minister) to be one of the four sponsors of James's British nationalization, he misquotes 'a poor [*recte* ill-favoured] thing, but mine own'.

The Letters portray an extraordinary figure, unfailingly good-hearted, dedicated beyond all else to his work, a strange mixture of primness and humour, innocence and sophistication. James's capacity for writing unconscious *doubles ententes* is notorious (especially in the novels), yet these years do reveal an increased awareness of sex, even an occasional attempt to use relatively plain language. For example, he writes here to Hendrik Andersen, a sculptor in Rome, and one of the four young men to whom he wrote passionately flirtatious letters:

> Also I sometimes find your sexes (putting *the* indispensable sign apart!) not quite intensely enough differentiated – I mean through the ladies resembling a shade too much the gentlemen, perhaps as in the case of this last *Ballerina*, through your not allowing her a quite sufficiently luxury – to my taste – of hip, or to speak more plainly, Bottom.

James was aware that Andersen was not in the top rank of sculptors and there is an ineffably comic photograph of them together in which the sadly romantic Andersen wears his *atelier* smock and James, in a white tie, looks like the butler.

James's other platonic loves (whom he addresses with quite unbridled affection) were of a very different variety. One, Jocelyn Persse, came of an Anglo-Irish landed family, a man-about-town who liked hunting. He appears to have been altogether heterosexual, and never quite to have known why James liked him so much. Another was the young Hugh Walpole, who certainly knew what it was all about (Somerset Maugham alleging that Walpole made himself available to James though met with shocked if regretful refusal). Since Walpole was himself setting out on a career as a writer, James's letters to him about writing are among the most interesting here.

Finally there was Morton Fullerton, the most complex and sinister of men (he was not all that young) to whom James was strongly attached, and the one who gave him opportunity to peep comparatively first-hand into the darker sides of sexual involvement.

Fullerton, a New Englander, had come to Europe, and almost immediately acquired a job in *The Times* Paris office, later on *Le Figaro*. He was bi-sexual, had a divorced actress wife and daughter, a French mistress who blackmailed him. At different periods Fullerton had affairs with (among others) the sculptor Lord Ronald Gower, the (white) Ranee of Sarawak, and James's friend the talented American novelist Edith Wharton.

Mrs Wharton, a woman of enormous energy whose rich marriage had never been much of a success (her husband finally going off his head) also had an apparently intermittent affair, perhaps platonic, with Walter Berry, President of the American Chamber of Commerce in Paris, a friend of Proust's. James mentions a luncheon in Paris with Edith Wharton, Walter Berry and Morton Fullerton, all of whom he knew pretty well.

One can only say that it must have been a tough party, which absolves James from any imputation that when he wrote about convoluted sexual goings-on he did not know the sort of people familiar with them. James, who was never very well off, relatively speaking, even contributed to alleviate Fullerton's blackmail.

James, in his own manner, can be very funny, especially about himself. When his old friend, the American novelist William Dean Howells sent him an advertisement for an apartment house in Manhattan called The Henry James, James suggested it might better have been named The Edith Wharton, or after the author of *Rebecca of Sunnybrook Farm*. He wrote a rather pompous letter to Violet Hunt when she was the cause of Ford Madox Ford's divorce, saying he did not wish her to come to his house; but that appears to have been at least as much because he found her a bore as for moral reasons.

There are domestic horrors chronicled as when James's married couple of sixteen years' service got so incapably drunk that their own relations had to remove them bodily from the houses. James's boot-boy, subsequently valet, 'the gnome', possessed the wonderfully novelistic name of Burgess Noakes.

The apocryphal legend that James wrote an enthusiastic letter of admiration to Proust seems to have arisen, Leon Edel suggests, through Proust's maid Céleste Albaret confusing Henry James's name with that of the French novelist Francis Jammes.

Letters of Henry James: Vol. IV: 1984
1895–1916, Leon Edel, ed.,   *Daily Telegraph*
Belknap Press of Harvard.

VIII

Henry James left New York in 1883 at the age of forty and did not return to his native country until 1904. *The American Scene* is the record of his personal impressions when he did so.

I had never before read this book, but always thought of it as a work that had given offence in America on account of its outspoken – if James could fittingly be called outspoken – criticism. This is certainly the reputation *The American Scene* bears. It came as a surprise, therefore, to find that it contains some of the most sensitive praise of the American countryside, and best 'evocation' (James's habit of inverted commas is catching) of the American past, anywhere to be enjoyed.

Of course James found not only change, but many things he did not like. Why should he not? I was reminded of the reactions in a recent book very different, yet in some ways comparable, V. S. Naipaul's *An Area of Darkness*, in which much that was critical of India was combined with acute understanding and sympathy.

James travelled round and about: New England in the autumn, New York and the Hudson in the spring, Newport – even in those days a haunt of the antiquated and esoteric – Boston, Concord, Salem, Philadelphia; Washington, where he found that the

> late excellent extensions and embellishments [to the White House] have of course represented expenditure – but only of the refined sort imposed by some mature and portionless gentlewoman on relatives who have accepted the principle of making her, at a time of life, more honourably comfortable.

Then there was the South: Baltimore, Richmond, Charleston, Florida. James had never before been to the South, and he went with all sorts of mixed feelings, for it was no more than a chance that he had not himself been involved on the Union side during the Civil War.

Leon Edel points out that the essential horror James suffered throughout his tour was what Edel calls 'America's cult of impermanence'. James speaks again and again of this 'perpetual repudiation of the past, so far as there has been a past to repudiate.' It frightened and oppressed him.

In a close examination of his country, James could not avoid – indeed there was then no temptation to avoid – the question of 'race'. Accordingly, the peculiar ineptitudes generated by contemporary obsession with this question have resulted in some critics labelling *The American Scene* anti-Semitic. The late F. O. Matthiessen, for example, usually competent, if prejudiced, wrote that James 'drifted dangerously close to a doctrine of racism'.

It is perfectly clear that, so far from being anti-Semitic, James was impressed and fascinated by the traditional inward-looking Jewish-American life he describes. He complains, it is true, that Italian immigrants seem to lose in America the charm they possess in Italy; he even goes so far to say that – to his great surprise – Negro waiters in the South could not remember whether or not he took sugar in his tea or coffee; but it would be hard to find a better example than this book for showing that the 'race' protesters are the ones who are really stirring up 'racist' trouble.

James asks: 'Do certain impressions there [in America] represent the absolute extinction of old sensibilities, or do they represent only new forms of them?' Nearly three-quarters of a century later, the question could still well be put. America seems always fighting against the old classical values, yet always succumbing to them.

James's power of putting his finger on what is wrong is well illustrated by his remarks on the layout of New York:

New York pays at this rate the penalty of her primal topographic curse, her old inconceivably bourgeois scheme of composition and distribution, the uncorrected labour of minds with no imagination of the future and blind before the opportunity given them by their two magnificent waterfronts.

Here it might not be amiss to interpolate that much of what he has to say is now only too true of London, though he goes on to excoriate New York in that city's special terms:

This original sin of the longitudinal avenues perpetually, yet meanly intersected, and of the organised sacrifice of the indicated alternative, the great perspectives from East to West, might still have earned forgiveness by some occasional departure from its pettifogging consistency.

One of the most cogent reasons for recommending *The American Scene* is for the picture it gives of James himself. The point of view of the narrator of the novels is placed more clearly in focus by the extraordinary shrewdness and intelligence of the comments in this book.

In New York he recalls being taken, as a small child, to hear the infant phenomenon Adelina Patti, wearing a 'fan-like little white frock and pantelettes . . . mounted on an armchair . . . and warbling like a tiny thrush'. Such memories brought a feeling that one does not commonly associate with James. 'This impact of the whole condensed past at once produced a horrible, hateful sense of personal antiquity.'

The frightening thing is how much of what is said in *The American Scene* now applies to this country.

The American Scene, Henry   1969
James, Hart-Davis.   *Daily Telegraph*

IX

H. G. Wells met Henry James in about 1898. James was by then a figure of great distinction in the literary world, but his books did not sell widely, and they were destined to sell even less as he approached the later phase of his writing. He had also recently suffered a disaster in the theatre, when his play *Guy Domville* was booed; an occasion, oddly enough, at which Wells himself was present, experiencing his first night as a dramatic critic.

Wells was thirty-two, regarded as a promising writer, but with by far the greater part of the work for which he eventually became known still before him. So far as may be judged by the letters reproduced here – and in spite of their diametrically opposed temperaments – the two authors seem immediately to have got on well together. Wells would send James his books; James, at times critical, was also abundantly full of praise. He would write what were practically private reviews of each Wells novel as it appeared.

Let me put my own cards on the table. I find – and have always found – Wells all but unreadable. I recognize that the 'science fiction' group were remarkable in their day, and have stood up fairly well to the subsequent factual history of scientific development. I can see that certain episodes in nóvels like *Mr Polly* or *Love and Mr Lewisham* are well observed and amusingly told. The fact remains that the bulk of Wells's writing seems to me shoddy; the 'realism' at which he aimed, on the whole, quite unreal. Only for brief moments do his characters live, because – as he himself was the first to proclaim – he was primarily interested not in people as human beings but in the politico-social ideas he himself wished to propagate. Above all, the reader can never escape from the really dreadful cockiness of Wells's own personality, bursting irrepressibly through the printed page.

This is by the way, and only to excuse what may be prejudice against Wells, who appears to me to come out of his relationship with James very badly indeed.

After seventeen years of friendship Wells wrote a story called *Boon* – its appropriate parts are reproduced here – which caricatured James as 'Boon', and also introduced him by his own name. The first thing that strikes the reader about *Boon* is how astonishingly badly James's style is parodied by Wells. It might be thought that nothing would be easier than to pastiche the Jamesian convolutions, but Wells fails lamentably. In addition to saying straight out a number of wounding things about James's character, the dialogue put into James's mouth is (so anyone of even the mildest sophistication can see) full of *doubles ententes*, much more remarkable for crudity than wit.

Wells sent this book to James. James's letter acknowledging it is a masterpiece of dignity and good nature. At this, Wells appears to have lost his head and replied with a letter the silliness and bumptiousness of which make embarrassing reading. James wrote again, but the friendship was, of course, at an end.

The difficulty is to be fair to Wells. It could perhaps be urged that James's letters might have prepared Wells for somewhat kinder, or at least less tortuous treatment, than he received in two long articles on 'The Younger Generation' in *The Times Literary Supplement* of 1914; although the obviously keen interest he showed in Wells's writing should have satisfied the most exigent author's vanity. No doubt James had his absurd side, especially for one of Wells's point of view and manner of existence. Although it might well be urged that he is revealed here as having more grasp than Wells of the humours of life. To have woven into one of his serious novels a full length picture of James, or a brief vignette of him, possibly severely critical, would have been understandable, even if open to objection. To produce, and dispatch, a slipshod, badly written squib, put together in an almost amateurish way seems inexplicable after their years of friendship.

Henry James and H. G. Wells: A   1958
Record of their Friendship and   *Punch*
their Quarrel, Leon Edel and
Gordon N. Ray, eds, Hart-Davis.

X

Just forty years ago *The Notebooks of Henry James* first appeared, edited by F. O. Matthiessen and Kenneth B. Murdock. These had slightly longer comment on the literary consequences of James's outlined plots, but the present volume, *The Complete Notebooks of Henry James*, is updated, reveals many names previously concealed by initials, reproduces several additional odds and ends, including James's pocket diaries 1909–15, giving appointments and luncheon dates, a goldmine for addicts of the laundry-list like myself. This edition possesses also the advantage of part editorship by James's compelling biographer Leon Edel.

André Gide says somewhere (I quote from memory) that James was intelligent but not interesting. Disregarding the possibility that, with the passing of the years, a similar judgment threatens Gide himself, one sees this might be a valid objection to James as a novelist. He faces certain facts, not others. The Notebooks give illuminating instances of this habit.

For example, James notes a piquant situation in January 1884. The heir of the Duke of Sutherland had for several years been deeply in love with Lady Grosvenor, a married woman. Under family pressure he had become engaged to a 'young, charming, innocent girl', Lady Millicent St Claire-Erskine. Contrary to all reasonable expectations, Lord Grosvenor suddenly died. Should the young man marry his longtime love, or remain loyal to his engagement?

James outlines various possibilities of behaviour, adding that 'If I were a Frenchman or a naturalist' the marriage with Lady Millicent would take place (thereby not disappointing her of becoming a duchess), while the widowed Lady Grosvenor would be the young heir's mistress. This admission of not being a 'naturalist' is significant. What James never for one moment contemplated in his theorizing was that here we have the early history of the redoubtable Millicent, Duchess of Sutherland, married three times, living till ninety, a figure of legend in her own right.

In fact James never did very much (only 'The Path of Duty', a short story) with this undoubtedly striking situation. On the same day he noted that he would also try to write about 'the self-made girl', a kind of pendant to *Daisy Miller*. This eventually appeared as 'Pandora', where James beautifully sketches in his friend Henry Adams (author of that incomparable book *The Education of Henry Adams*) and life with the Washington *beau monde* of the period. Here we have James at his most amusing; the Adams figure remarking: 'Hang it, there's only a month left; let us be vulgar and have some fun – let us invite the President.'

Edel emphasizes that note-taking was at the heart of James's method (James was taking notes on his death-bed), but it is character, rather than the 'necessities of plot', with which the material here has to do. One is struck by the sheer number of stories carried in the novelist's head at the same moment, most of which he ultimately brought to birth. Others, of course, were never attempted; some attempted, appeared stillborn.

One of the last kind is adumbrated in two forms. A married couple approach a well-known painter, asking him for a portrait of their child. The painter naturally enquires the child's age, when it will be possibly to have a sitting, etc. It then appears there is no child. The couple have never had a child. What they want is a picture of the ideal child they would have wished. In a similar case a woman who has had adventures, but never married, wants a painter to do an imaginary portrait of her dead husband. This would hang on the wall and impress her visitors.

Perhaps the former of these ideas, the imagined child, generated the frightful 'dream-child' of the academic couple in Edward Albee's *Who's Afraid of Virginia Woolf?* James himself attempted the theme in an unfinished story called 'Hugh Merrow', reproduced here.

In connection with his story, 'The Reverberator', James records that Venetian society had been upset by an American girl staying with some member of it, then writing a chatty account of her experiences for an American paper. James discusses with himself where this gossip-column-type disturbance should be placed. The 'difficulty was where to find people today in Europe who would really be shocked . . . I don't in the least see them in England, where publicity is far too much, by this time, in the manners of society.' That was written, please observe, a century ago, in 1887. Incidentally, about fifteen years later he notes the unhappy condition of a man who subscribes to a press-cutting agency and receives no press-cuttings.

James has sometimes been compared with Proust. A note made in 1894 shows that at times the paths of their ideas certainly crossed:

A clever woman marries a deadly dull man and loses and loses her wit as he shows more and more. Or the idea of a *liaison* suspected of which there is no proof but this transfusion of some idiosyncrasy of one party to the being of the other – this exchange or conversion?

A similar notion crops up more than once in *A la Recherche*.

Finally there are the long lists of names, persons and places which James made for his own use. These are fascinating, especially for the recurrence of surnames that attract novelists. One would say the lists are good, James's ear less good, particularly when it comes to their employment for country houses, for which James's names are awful. No one interested in novel-writing should miss the Notebooks, and their innumerable nuggets.

The Complete Notebooks of
Henry James, Leon Edel and
Lyall H. Powers, eds, OUP.

1987
Daily Telegraph

XI

Alice James, born 1848, was the only sister of Henry James. She was the youngest, a neurotic in the top class of that category. She kept a Diary when living in England between 1889 and her death in 1892. Although not of exceptional interest in itself, it fills in some acceptable details about Jamesian family life, a fascinating subject.

When, aged about thirty, she asked her father if it was a sin to commit suicide:

> He gave Alice his fatherly permission to end her life [says Leon Edel] whenever it pleased her, beseeching her only to 'do it' in a perfectly gentle way in order not to distress her friends.

This absolute tolerance was no doubt as hard to bear as parental domination. At least the result where Alice James was concerned was illness, hysteria, boredom and a very hearty dislike for the human race in general. Efforts were made to find her charitable work to do, but it was no good. Although she was by no means unintelligent, her total self-absorption made her impossible to assimilate into any form of communal life.

Fortunately she possessed a comfortable private income. Her family were altogether unable to cope with her problems, which were to some extent alleviated, if not solved, by an emotional friendship with an energetic New England lady of about the same age, with a sickly sister of her own to care for. It is an absolutely classical picture of feminine neurasthenia of a particular kind.

On the whole, life in England seems to have suited Alice James better than that of her own country, if only on account of her really whole-hearted disapproval of the English, their food, their houses, their ways, and – above all – their upper class and inability politically to satisfy the Irish. Grumbling at the English in her Diary seems to have brought her as near to pleasure as she came in her brief and unhappy life.

Her political Liberalism might be said to be coloured by a touch of Marxism in that she expressed a sense of her dividends making her feel less guilty when they were 4 per cent rather than 5 per cent or 6 per cent.

British expansion in Africa made her particularly incensed, but in the ironical manner by which the progressive views of one age can possess reactionary implications in the next, she wrote: 'Poor little Portugal has succumbed before the Big Bully', an allusion to this country's curtailment of Portuguese ambitions in Mozambique and Angola.

Royalty and aristocracy (having a rough time at this period with Tranby Croft and other scandals) are perpetually incurring the diarist's disapproval. Their regrettable goings-on were not mitigated in her eyes by seeing a lady, obviously of the highest rank, on the way to the park in her beautifully appointed carriage and eating 'a huge, stodgy penny bun'.

In the end, organic disease was diagnosed, and poor Alice James died at the age of forty-four. One cannot help wondering whether, if it had been possible to put her right in herself, this trouble might never have developed.

One of the last entries in the Diary dealt with her father's end:

> A week before Father died, I asked him what he should like to have done about his funeral. He was immediately very much interested, not having apparently thought of it before; he reflected for some time, and then said, with the greatest solemnity and looking majestic: 'Tell him to say only this, "here lies a man who has thought all his life, that the ceremonies attending birth, marriage and death were all damned nonsense." Don't let him say a word more.'

Alice James also had to put up with a father who held exceptionally strong views on the nobility and purity of womanhood. He did things like helping his children to find, and look at, the Christmas presents their mother had very naturally hidden before Christmas Day. Her brothers alternately petted and bullied her.

One knows at once that Jean Strouse is the right sort of biographer when she points out that the Civil War was just as much about Free Trade and Protection as about Slavery.

She writes well and pulls together the story behind the Diary. Alice James was undoubtedly an intelligent and gifted woman, even if the Diary shows her principally as a neurotic grumbler with an almost pathological dislike of the English.

I had not realized quite how physically ill she was for most of her life, apart from the most appalling mental breakdowns. It was thought that the trouble had some basis in gout, but the family history suggests heredity was mainly responsible, whatever the additional influences of her own conscious frustrations.

To indicate Alice James's capabilities as an observer, also what life in the James home was like, nothing could be more vivid than this letter written when she was about seventeen:

> The scene is laid in the dining room, time, dinner:
> Harry [Henry James, the novelist, then about twenty-four] to the mother: 'May I have some of those brown rolls that were left this morning at breakfast?'
> Mother: 'Yes, certainly, but do you wish to eat them with your soup?'

> Harry: 'You can't certainly expect me to minutely explain what I intend to do with them.'
> Laughter from the family.
> Harry: 'I was coming over the bridge this afternoon and stopped a runaway-horse.'
> You may imagine the shouts of the family at this.
> Aunt Kate: 'I hope you did not try and stop him by the bridle.'
> Harry: 'Would you prefer to have me take hold of his legs?'
> Aunt Kate: 'But you should not not run after horses and stop them.'
> Harry: 'Would you rather have me run before them?'
> You must let your imagination supply the manner of this Harry, a good deal of eyebrow, nostril and shoulder affectation.

Even Leon Edel's five volumes scarcely give a more vivid vignette of the young Henry James than this. Had she ever managed to write a novel, what a book about her own family circle Alice James might have written. 'The sharpened points of Alice's wit held venom when she was jealous,' write Jean Strouse. 'She anatomized feminine flaws and scrutinized connubial financial arrangements as if she were narrating a Jane Austen novel.' Jean Strouse also speaks sagely of 'Alice's sense of competition, her objection to being compared with Henry, and the old James notion that one person's success must be balanced with another person's failure'.

I had imagined from Alice James's Diary (by which time she had developed the emotional friendship with Katherine Peabody Loring, dynamic New England lady of about the same age) that she was temperamentally inclined towards her own sex.

That does not seem to have been so. When Alice was younger she had greatly desired to find a husband, and makes no secret of that fact in her letters. At the same time, she never seems to have taken in the rudiments of what marriage would actually have been like – even allowing for the conventional manner in which it was looked on in her day – and the men she speaks of as finding attractive sound more like schoolgirl crushes.

Although not outstandingly pretty, Alice might well have found a husband, Jean Strouse implies, had she made rather more effort to make herself agreeable to men. They were clearly afraid of her. Female friendships of her sort with Katherine Loring were so common at that time as to be known as 'Boston marriages'. Alice James also felt very strongly towards her eldest brother, William James, some of whose letters to her were most odd. She had a fearful breakdown when William James married, and again when her father died.

When, aged about six, Alice James saw Kean in *Henry VIII*, she was enthralled, 'and all her life remembered Cardinal Wolsey on his way to execution'. But, unless Kean altered Shakespeare's play radically, it was surely Buckingham who was executed.

The Diary of Alice James, Leon
Edel, ed., Hart-Davis.
Alice James: Biography. Jean
Strouse, Cape.

1981
Daily Telegraph

EDITH WHARTON

There have been good books by Millicent Bell and Louis Auchincloss about certain aspects of Edith Wharton (1862–1937). Now R. W. B. Lewis presents a long and full account of her life, which covers the ground in a most interesting and workmanlike manner. Lewis also produces some lively new material.

Edith Wharton went through a stage of being out of fashion, but it is hard to offer a more convincing candidate as the greatest American woman novelist. (I am not prepared to except Willa Cather.) She was attacked in her own day for writing about the affluent society into which she was born. In fact, some of her best work, notably *Ethan Frome* (1911), has quite another setting. *The House of Mirth* (1905), *The Custom of the Country* (1913) and *The Age of Innocence* (1920) remain as readable as the day they were published.

The Jones family of New York had arrived in America at the beginning of the eighteenth century (from Cornwall), and, although not among the richest of their social level, thought a good deal of themselves. Their world was a ruthlessly philistine one, and the fact that, from her earliest childhood Edith Wharton (née Jones) wrote stories and poems, represents one of those inexplicable flowerings of talent in unexpected places.

The epithet even her closest friends applied to Edith Wharton was 'formidable'; a reputation to some extent due to shyness. To her abilities as a writer, she added immense energy; a professional grasp of such matters as interior decoration; a mastery of languages that made it possible for her to write books in French and be scarcely less fluent in Italian and German.

She showed the same power when operating as an energetic hostess in the aristocratic circles of the Faubourg St Germain, or the equally tough intellectual environment of Berenson and Cocteau.

To these often alarming characteristics, Edith Wharton undoubtedly added the love of a good joke, and it is clear that the jokes she herself made were excellent ones. Perhaps the most extraordinary thing about her was a capacity for living the high-powered social life, while at the same time getting her work down on paper, never showing any sign of drying up imaginatively as a writer – though all her books are not at the same high level.

Critics, rather obtusely, have compared Edith Wharton with her great friend Henry James. Lewis gives an example of her efforts to parody the style of James (when he had momentarily annoyed her) and points out with great truth that the parody could hardly be worse done. Edith Wharton could not write like James even when she tried.

Her many gifts were not combined with good luck in achieving a happy married life, though it seems possible that her years with Teddy Wharton were less lacking in mutual sympathy than has sometimes been put forward. Wharton, a good-natured, good-looking, well-born New Yorker, was understandably not up to the strain of his wife's fame, especially when it came to living in Paris, which drove him into a manic-depressive state.

The Whartons' marriage appears to have got off to a very bad start so far as their physical relations were concerned. It would seem probable that Teddy Wharton found consolations for this long before he confessed as much; but Mrs Wharton, although a woman of strong passions, seems to have remained without a lover until the age of about forty-five.

Edith Wharton's love affair with Morton Fullerton, an American correspondent of *The Times* in Paris, is already known, but Lewis pungently adds to what is on record. An associate of Henry James (who obviously felt warmly towards him) Fullerton seems to have been specifically involved in homosexual connections in the Wilde circle. He was no less enmeshed with several women (one of whom he married); and, for good measure, his younger sister was passionately in love with him; though in the end she turned out to be only his first cousin.

There was a whiff of blackmail about all this; though exactly who was blackmailing whom is not altogether clear. Leon Edel (in his great biography of James) says Fullerton asked James for advice, not money; Lewis says he asked for money. James certainly produced no substantial amount of money. In the end, by roundabout means, Edith Wharton helped Fullerton out to the extent of about £100; allegedly to buy back some letters.

Perhaps as a kind of souvenir of her affair with Fullerton, Edith Wharton (about seventy-two when she wrote it) left behind the draft of a novel about a man who seduced his daughter; together with a couple of pages of description of specific sex acts during this seduction. The passage seems to me of interest as an example of how unsatisfactory elaborate prose accounts of sexual intercourse can be.

Edith Wharton was a writer of the highest gifts and intellectual integrity, but, critically speaking, I doubt whether this fragment could be said to rise above what is written merely to excite. I see nothing very shocking in it, but it does not seem to me a success as literature.

Lewis's frequent maltreatment of English titles must have made

Edith Wharton (who felt strongly about such things) all but rise from the dead (and I think he should reconsider the statement that Vuillard was 'an artist of about the same gifts' as Jacques-Emile Blanche), but he has produced a good biography of a very considerable novelist, and an absorbing and adventurous personality.

<table>
<tr><td>Edith Wharton: A Biography,</td><td>1975</td></tr>
<tr><td>R. W. B. Lewis, Constable.</td><td>Daily Telegraph</td></tr>
</table>

In an article in *The Times Literary Supplement* (16 December 1988) Marion Manwaring, who provided some of the research for *Edith Wharton*, by R. W. B. Lewis, casts considerable doubt on what is said there about the circumstances of Morton Fullerton, especially in relation to Edith Wharton.

JACK LONDON

George Orwell – who possibly derived the title *1984* from Jack London's *The Iron Heel*, a similar novel in which that date has particular significance – admired London, but thought his books 'well-told' rather than 'well-written'.

Those who have never read them may accept this as an excellent definition of their qualities. American novelists have been said to derive either from Mark Twain or Nathaniel Hawthorne. It is worth considering whether London has not some claim to have been the first of them to introduce a deviation, unconnected with either of those two forerunners, from which flowed the whole school now chiefly associated with Hemingway.

However, London's writing, as such, is far from being the only interest of Richard O'Connor's entertaining biography, which covers a great deal of ground and throws light on aspects of American social life in the early years of the century, not usually given much attention.

London was born in San Francisco in 1876. He was never able to establish the identity of his father, though everything pointed to William Henry Chaney, who originated in Maine, grandson on both sides of Revolutionary War veterans.

Chaney himself always strenuously denied that he was London's father, but his own history bears some resemblance to London's in its early struggles and general oddness. Chaney finally set up as a professional astrologer, married six times and organized a peculiarly discreditable incident which involved the the tarring and feathering of a Roman Catholic priest. Chaney reminds one of Dr Tarrant in Henry James's *The Bostonians*, or Dr Agathon Carver in Edith Wharton's *The Age of Innocence*.

Whether or not he was London's father, Chaney played no other part in London's life. The boy was brought up at starvation level by his dominating, unpleasant mother, and a good-natured step-father, called London.

There can be no doubt whatever that Jack London, however much in later life he might vary the emphasis he put on the depressed conditions of his early life, did have a very hard time. He was a professional oyster-stealer (from their sea-beds, rather than from restaurants), boxer, tramp, and 'stampeder' in the Gold Rush of 1898. However, he managed for a time to attend the University of California at Berkeley.

Although only twenty-two when he set out for the Yukon, London was already avid to learn 'the meaning of life'. From the record he left of the Klondike trail, it is permissible to wonder whether its least endurable hardships were the amateur philosophers giving their views on this subject round the camp fire in the evening.

Although he had won a newspaper essay competition at seventeen, his Klondike experiences – and desperate financial straits, in which he contemplated suicide – seemed to have turned London's attention to the possibility of earning a living as a writer. Before he was twenty-four he may be said to have established himself in this profession.

London's further adventures included being a war correspondent in the Russo-Japanese war in 1905 and attempting to circumnavigate the globe in an unseaworthy ketch. Although never free of money troubles, owing to the manner in which he organized his life, he became a best-seller of extraordinary proportions throughout the world. Royalties poured in.

London was specially popular in Russia, and Lenin's widow relates that he asked her to read London's stories to him when dying. She read one in which a starving wolf eats a starving man, which Lenin greatly enjoyed; but she records that her husband was disappointed by the bourgeois note struck by the tale that followed, in which a sea captain sacrifices his life in order to keep his word. Indeed, this distasteful theme seems to have finished Lenin off.

London himself was a life-long Marxian Socialist, a creed he infused with trimmings of his own such as a fervent belief in the necessity of Anglo-Saxon predominance and dislike for the African and Asian peoples, though he always employed Japanese or Korean valets. He owned a considerable estate in California, where he planned eventually to keep 'seven sages', with whom he would discuss higher thought.

London's life as a Californian landowner is no less interesting than his rise from the social depths and adventurous expeditions. He was fond of practical jokes, in which his guests were expected to join.

A favourite trick of his was to persuade a man to stand facing a doorway, supposedly to have his height measured. While his back was turned, Jack or someone else would hit him over the head with a mallet.

London was notable for patronage of emergent writers. Sinclair Lewis, as a young man, formed part of his entourage. Lewis at one period supplied London with plots, which seemed to have been paid for at a rate unbecoming an ardent social reformer who had campaigned for a living wage. London's interest in psycho-analysis as early as 1912 or 1913 is notable. He died in 1916, of an overdose of narcotics, intended to relieve pain, rather than as suicide.

Jack London: A Biography,   1960
Richard O'Connor, Gollancz.   *Daily Telegraph*

STEPHEN CRANE

Stephen Crane (1871–1900), whose letters are collected together here, was only happy in the saddle, knocking about the Bowery, or working as a war correspondent; although in this last capacity he does not appear to have shown himself a very capable journalist.

R. W. Stallman, one of the editors of the present volume, produced about six years ago a selection of Stephen Crane's writings, *Stephen Crane: an Omnibus*, which gives everything of value that Crane ever wrote. Now we have Crane's letters. Although he has been dead sixty years, he is not an easy writer to assess.

The Red Badge of Courage is certainly looked upon in America as a classic. Here people have heard of, rather than read, this short novel, or greatly swollen short story. Its style, like the rest of Crane's work, is awkward, over-written, expressed with that studied avoidance of elegance which was thought at the time 'natural'; a manner from which the prose of writers like Frank Norris, Jack London, and Theodore Dreiser to some extent derives.

However, whether you like Crane's writing or not – and I don't – it has to be admitted that he brought off a revolution in American literature by treating the Civil War in realistic, rather than romantic, terms. He described low life and prostitution without moralizing at a time when such subjects were scarcely dealt with.

His letters are of considerable interest in helping to understand Crane. A friend described him as 'perhaps the most complete example of a self-absorbed ego that was ever carried on two feet'. For this reason the characters in his books never live as individuals. They are 'the tall soldier', 'the quiet stranger', 'the oiler in the stern', brought to life only momentarily for Crane's own use. In the same way the letters seem perpetually dealing with Crane's own work and the daily administration of Crane's life. They comment far too little on the many interesting people he met.

Crane, a womanizer, settled down towards the end of his life with a lady (whom he may even have married, though this is improbable) who had formerly presided over an establishment in Jacksonville, Florida, with the attractive name of the Hotel de Dream.

They came to England and lived in the old Elizabethan mansion of

Brede Place, near Rye. Here took place house parties which, if at times too much of a good thing, must have had their funny side. A. E. W. Mason (author of *The Four Feathers* and other novels) recalled, for example:

> The house, which frankly was not in a state to be occupied, was sketchily furnished, and I think there was arranged a dormitory in which six or seven men slept. I know that I was given a room to myself, but warned not to open except very cautiously, two great doors which enclosed one side of it. There was no electric light and naturally enough I opened very carefully the two doors. I found that if I had taken one step forward, I should have stepped down about 30 feet into the chapel.

Crane does not emerge from the letters as a particularly attractive person, but there can be no doubt that in the flesh he exercised great charm. Conrad, who was living in the neighbourhood, immediately took a great fancy to him. Henry James was also a visitor who enjoyed Crane's company.

There is a well-known legend to the effect that Crane arrived drunk one night when bidden to dinner with James at Lamb House, Rye, causing embarrassment of a most acute kind. The question of Crane's drinking is a somewhat vexed one. Certainly he had the reputation of a drunkard and drug addict. The more reliable authorities seem to think this unjust, and largely the result of his writing about sordid aspects of life.

Crane is perhaps to be thought of chiefly as an example of the 'Nineties movement, translated into American terms. His portrait certainly suggests comparison with the faces of Beardsley or Dowson. There can be no doubt that Crane burned himself out in much the same way.

He has, perhaps, more in common with Gissing – a violent Gissing, of course – than with Kipling, with whom his contemporaries compared him.

He came from New Jersey stock. His family had arrived in America in the early part of the seventeenth century, and at the time of Revolution one of its members signed the Declaration of Independence. His father, a clergyman, not only held severe views on drinking and smoking, but also recommended a 'rigid iron rule for the guidance of all, young and old, learned and unlearned: *total abstinence from novel-reading henceforth and for ever*'. That was the world from which Crane was reacting.

Finally, I cannot forbear quoting Lincoln's answer (referred to here by Crane himself), when asked how long an ideal soldier's leg should be. The President replied that the soldier's leg should be at least long enough to reach the ground.

Stephen Crane: Letters, R. W. Stallman and Lillian Gilkes, eds, Owen.

1960
Daily Telegraph

ROBERT FROST

Robert Frost is a poet perhaps less well known in Great Britain than he deserves. In America he has been so much accepted as the repository of down-to-earth New England wisdom, and the poetry of the farmyard, that there has been some reaction against a way of looking at life that latterly became with him more of a habit than a daily experience.

Nevertheless, Frost was a considerable technician in writing verse, and his links with the English Georgian poets make him of special interest to readers over here.

Writing his life cannot have been easy. Lawrance Thompson, a friend of many years' standing, editor of Frost's *Selected Letters* and deeply immersed in his subject, has done an excellent job. He never lets the reader forget how extremely difficult Frost was, nor does he hold him up to ridicule, which must have at times have been a temptation. Thompson's tone is set by the opening words of his introduction:

> Robert Frost was so fascinated by the story of his life that he never tired of retelling it. A good raconteur, he naturally varied his accounts, and whenever the bare facts troubled him, he discreetly clothed them with fictions. This imaginative process caused him to mingle self-deceptions with little falsehoods; it even caused him gradually to convince himself that some of these fictions were genuine truths.

Frost's background was in any case calculated to produce something unusual. His father, a New Englander, had wanted to enter the Army, but failing to get into West Point, had a stormy career as an undergraduate at Harvard; then, at the time of the 'War between the States', became a 'copperhead' – a Northerner who supported the South. He finally settled as a journalist in California.

The doctor who came to attend Frost's mother at the time of his birth was met by Frost Senior with a pistol and told he would not leave the house alive if the delivery was unsuccessful. One feels that in some respects it was just as well for Frost that his father died when his son was still a boy. All the same, the problem of how the family was to survive was a serious one.

There were relatively well-off grandparents, but they were not easy to deal with. When Frost grew up, he got occasional financial assistance from them, but made little effort to accommodate himself to their ways. Frost's mother, who had been twelve years old when she arrived in America from Scotland, seems to have been a remarkable woman. She combined a special talent for teaching with total inability to keep order.

It is interesting that Frost at the age of eighteen (he somehow managed to attend briefly both Dartmouth and Harvard) made up his mind to marry, and actually did marry a couple of years later, in 1895. The pattern of early marriage in America is not so modern as might be thought.

Frost's ups and downs were fairly harassing. He attempted to write poetry while earning a living in various ways – working in mills, on farms, journalism, teaching, interlarded with an endless series of rows with employers, colleagues and neighbours.

Then, chiefly on the strength of the modest legacy inherited from his grandfather, Frost, his wife and four children transplanted themselves to England in 1912. Frost was then thirty-seven. Although poems of his had appeared for years, he had achieved no sort of real recognition.

Thompson tells Frost's story up to this point with an amount of detail that gives a convincing picture of what it must have been like to be the sort of person Frost was, trying to earn a living in the America of sixty or seventy years ago.

Inevitably, however, it is more interesting for the English reader when Frost arrives in the country and gets mixed up with the Georgians and Harold Monro's Poetry Bookshop. Thompson's description of Monro as a 'moody Scotsman' is a masterpiece of understatement: at a dinner party Monro gave at an Italian restaurant for W. H. Davies, the 'supertramp' drank so much that he left the room and forgot to return – behaviour that might well have been paralleled by his host.

Frost occasionally attended W. B. Yeats's 'Mondays', but never managed to acclimatize himself to Yeats's approach to life. Yeats told him that William Sharp (Fiona Macleod)

> Walking with his wife in an English lane fell behind just far enough to see Mrs. Sharp running towards him to say she had just seen a little man with goat's hind legs scuttle into the woods. 'A faun!' she said. 'I saw him!' Her husband did not even break stride as he answered, 'It's nothing. Such creatures are all about this part of the country.'

Wilfred Gibson, Lascelles Abercrombie, Rupert Brooke and especially Edward Thomas became friends of Frost's. His first book of poems was published by a Mrs Nutt, on terms of which the best one can say was that they were preferable to having no volume published at all, as had hitherto been the case in America.

An important meeting was with Ezra Pound, who, with his accustomed flair, noted down the abilities of the older man, and made an important contribution to Frost's ultimate success. All this pre-First-World-War London intellectual life, seen through American eyes, makes fascinating reading.

Thompson comes slightly adrift when he says of Edward Thomas that in August 1914, he was 'aware he might be drafted into military service at any time'. There was no 'drafting' at that period. Conscription was introduced in May 1916. Thomas enlisted in the Artists' Rifles nearly a year before that.

In so scholarly and informative a book, one must regret misuse of the word 'careen' (turn a ship on her side for caulking), in place of 'career' (move swiftly). This is a popular American solecism of late years which destroys a useful word to no good effect.

Robert Frost: The Early Years: 1967
1874–1915, Lawrance   *Daily Telegraph*
Thompson, Cape.

EDMUND WILSON

I

Most people (at least in this country) if asked who was the foremost American literary critic would reply 'Edmund Wilson, I suppose.' There might be a touch of Gide's '*Victor Hugo, hélas!*' about this answer, but I doubt whether, at the conversational level, Wilson would find a serious rival.

The Shock of Resignation is a selection of critical pieces produced by distinguished American writers on the subject of other distinguished American writers since American literature came to birth at the beginning of the nineteenth century. A few English opinions (H. G. Wells, D. H. Lawrence) are also included to round off the picture, but these scarcely affect the impact of a record beginning with Lowell on Poe and ending with Sherwood Anderson's correspondence with Van Wyck Brooks. Wilson provides a thread of commentary.

Red, Black, Blond and Olive brings together four studies on the subject of places and people observed: the Zuñi Indians of New Mexico (1947), Haiti (1949), Soviet Russia (1935) and Israel (1954). Here, too, is a great deal of interesting material. The Russian section, much the longest, is of course written in the tone of the period; but the author has – I think rightly – judged that his views should appear un-revised.

One of the first things apparent in Edmund Wilson's approach is that every American writer, of any standing whatever, has influenced him to at least some degree. We find the romanticism of Poe united to the knowingness of Twain, the apocalypticism of Melville side by side with the astringency of Mencken, the egotism of Thoreau with the urbanity of James. One could go for ever – or at least as long as there are American writers to invoke.

This variegation is no bad thing in a critic; but on account of its very wideness of scope Wilson's point of view veers about in what at times seem mutually contradictory directions. One side of him is decidedly sentimental, more than a trifle bad-tempered, intermittently naïve, once in a way rather over-anxious to show himself a dog with the girls; the other is perceptive – not only where writing is concerned in grasping character or appreciating beauties of scene – tolerant of intolerable con-ditions, quite willing to admit his own changes of opinion and mistakes.

He shared, for example, that enthusiasm for Soviet Russia characteristic of the intellectuals of the Thirties. (Surely the true 'Treason of the
Intellectuals', who, after all, had as much opportunity to learn then, as
later, of the methods of a Communist régime.) However, less gullible
and flabby than many who believed as he did, Edmund Wilson not only
lived in Russia for several months but also fell ill there and survived an
interlude of treatment in an Odessa hospital.

One of the best things in *Red, Black, Blond and Olive* is the account of
his Russian friendship in 1935 with the unfortunate Prince Mirsky,
Professor of English and acute critic, who made his peace with
Marxism and returned to his native country. I myself was in Moscow
the following year and often caught a glimpse of that bearded figure,
formerly so familiar in Bloomsbury. The last time I saw him Mirsky
was drinking champagne. It must have been a few weeks – perhaps
even a few days – before his arrest, and liquidation, as here recorded.

But it is not for nothing that Wilson's grandfather was, so he tells us,
a Presbyterian minister. The shadow of that reproving Cynara is ever
in the background. It matters not how Wilson strays from the Strait
and Narrow, the old puritanism can never quite be quelled. Nor can he
wholly conquer that sturdy American belief that all life is odd, except
that in force in the United States. He may grumble about Miami, where
'I had the annoyance of removing encasements of Cellophane from the
toilet-seat and the drinking tumbler,' or the 'steel towns' where you get
menaced if you report a strike; but always in the end he gets back to
American standards and American perfectionism. The disillusion-
ment, if not of Europe, then of individual Europeans, irks him. He is the
least frivolous man imaginable.

What conclusions then? That Edmund Wilson is a person of strong
æsthetic perception, good at hitting off individuals and their eccentricities, passionately fond of literature. To this he has added a bit of an itch
for politics and 'social science'. In these dangerous areas one feels him
far less at home.

He is like a good painter who can never resist making his canvases
'problem pictures'. One is distracted from colour and design by the
triviality of the 'lesson'. Sometimes Wilson seems to be trying too hard;
at others, not nearly hard enough. Often irritating, he is also often
worth reading.

The Shock of Recognition,   1956
Edmund Wilson, ed., W. H.   *Punch*
Allen. *Red, Black, Blond and*
Olive, Edmund Wilson, W. H.
Allen.

I I

One of the acute comments in this well-edited selection of Edmund Wilson's letters is about book reviewing: 'The trouble with most of our American literary journalism is precisely that the literary critic usually doesn't make any effort to understand the writer's point of view' (14 November 1927).

This ideal is not perhaps universally achieved in our own country, nor was Wilson himself always its highest exemplar. All the same he did let light into the literary scene.

Edmund Wilson (1895–1972) was something of a prodigy in his variety of interests, capacity for work, mastery of foreign languages. He combined considerable scholarship with a capacity to make the occasional schoolboy howler, and an immediate grasp of the importance of writers such as Proust, Joyce, Eliot, Hemingway, Cummings, Fitzgerald (a contemporary at Princeton), with a prejudice against Byron, Baudelaire, Conrad, Gide, Aldous Huxley (but he was pro-Lytton Strachey), Hart Crane and a lot more. Although keenly interested in Russia, he did not read *War and Peace* until 1936, and 'except for Lady C.', never read any D. H. Lawrence at all.

In his early passion for literature, politics played a predominant part. He wrote in his younger days about Marxism, and was totally taken in by Stalin, though later agreed he had been mistaken. In a letter (after Wilson's political recovery from this aberration) to the American writer, Malcolm Cowley (20 October 1938) he says:

> I think politics is bad for you because it's not real to you: because what you're really practising is not politics but literature; and it only messes up a job like yours to pretend it's something else and try to use it like something else.

This seems a precise summary of Wilson's own case.

On the other hand, the clarity of Wilson's critical thought where literature is concerned is often keen though he had no grasp of the subtle, or the deliberately blurred edge – always yearning for exactness and some form of direct social comment. For example, to say (28 September 1943) 'The houses and the people that Chichikov visits are not really known and created as the Rostovs and the Bolkonskys are' is to miss the point that Gogol in *Dead Souls* was writing a different sort of book from Tolstoy in *War and Peace*.

Daniel Aarons in his Introduction attempts to refute the charge of Wilson's 'total want of humour'. This defence, by drawing attention to Wilson's own comic writings, really makes matters worse, and it is hard to feel that Wilson's 'unsolemn' side was other than heavyhanded. Of course he liked conjuring, knockabout jokes, and there is one very funny story here (too long to quote) about Hemingway's publishers bowdlerizing one of his novels. But all this does not convince one that Wilson had much humour, if any, to spare.

His pulpit was the *New Yorker* magazine, where for nearly twenty years he wrote critical articles on all sorts of unlikely subjects. He was given a great deal of rope there, dealing at length, for instance, with the Dead Sea Scrolls, an archaelogical and biblical discovery, the importance of which he at once appreciated at a stage when the Scrolls were unknown to any but a few specialists.

The interest Wilson felt in the Scrolls was founded on his own intense anti-religiousness, which had something of the religious bigot about it, the background in Wilson of puritanism. Not only was he 'a little disgusted at first' 26 December 1927 by M. de Charlus's goings-on in Proust, but, when writing a letter of general approval (11 April 1925) to Scott Fitzgerald about *The Great Gatsby*, he complained of the characters' 'unpleasantness'.

Although, on the whole, prepared to listen to criticism of his own works, Wilson never sent a letter to writer friends without telling them, in the most pungent terms, what was wrong with their books. Not everyone took this lying down, an aspect of this volume which makes for enjoyable reading. Nevertheless, Wilson kept his friends, even those like Dos Passos with whom he latterly violently disagreed.

Wilson would develop violent enthusiasms for some subject: the American Civil War; the shabby treatment of American Indians; the iniquities of the Income Tax (which he never, if possible, paid, in spite of socialist views) – throwing all his his energies into their investigation. He himself practised most forms of writing: novels, short stories, plays, verse, but was at his best in the literary essay.

There was a curiously gullible and insensitive side to him. He was admittedly anti-British (though with moments of nostalgia about good times in London), which from time to time caused lack of grasp. For instance (10 March 1944): 'I have never been able to see any Catholic point of view in his [Evelyn Waugh's] novels'; or Wilson supposing that Maurice Bowra (as adept at languages as himself) did not know (28 October 1968) what *baiser* meant in French. Incidentally, Arthur Mizener (biographer of Scott Fitzgerald) is wrongly described by Wilson as not 'making' the Princeton club at which Mizener aimed.

Letters on Literature and Politics: 1978
1912–1972, Edmund Wilson,   *Daily Telegraph*
with Elena Wilson, eds, and
Foreword by Leon Edel,
Routledge.

E. E. CUMMINGS

E. E. Cummings was born in 1894. In the First World War he volunteered for an American ambulance unit and was sent to France. There a close friend of his serving in the same organization wrote some mildly defeatist letters home.

Accordingly, the friend and Cummings (whose worst crime was habitual dirtiness on parade and a taste for fraternizing with the French) were both incarcerated in a kind of French concentration camp for awkward characters. This was the 'enormous room' where Cummings was immured for three months. The account of his stay there, for vivid writing, humour, deep feeling, and a horror all its own, cannot be too highly recommended.

Cummings was descended on both sides from emigrants settled in America in the seventeenth century, his mother's family rather more intellectually distinguished than his father's. His maternal grandfather had indeed been rather too sharp, and had done time for forging one of his own father-in-law's cheques. Cummings's father was a Unitarian minister and minor Harvard don.

Edward Estlin Cummings, although reacting strongly against Harvard, and the Cambridge (Mass.) atmosphere generally, was good at his books, and fascinated at an early age by the Modern Movement in the arts. Richard Kennedy brings out the fact that Cummings, more or less a pacifist, had volunteered for the ambulance unit in which he served simply as an easy way out, as he wished neither to train as an officer nor to be conscripted. In this he was wholly different from Hemingway, who had joined a similar ambulance unit for adventure, or Fitzgerald, who never really got over the disappointment of being in the American army, but not sent to France.

The Enormous Room appeared in England in 1928, six years after American publication. It had a *succès d'estime* and was reprinted twice. Kennedy explains this by saying 'English readers took an avid interest in war memoirs.' Here I think he is mistaken, even though *The Enormous Room* had an Introduction by Robert Graves, and this was certainly the moment when half a dozen war novels did become bestsellers.

I well remember *The Enormous Room* being talked about; the fact that its circumstances were occasioned by the war was marginal. People who liked war books liked descriptions of army life, the trenches, fighting. What attracted readers to *The Enormous Room* was its entirely new literary style – slang, unexpected allusions, scraps of French, scatology – and the totally unusual milieu and personalities to be found in it. All this had nothing to do with the kind of nostalgia for military life which sold real 'war books'.

Cummings, like many intellectuals of his generation, was romantically drawn to Communism and the Soviet Union, but unlike many of his friends a visit to Russia in 1930 caused him to view the USSR and all its works with greatest possible horror. His life-long pacifism was outraged by the United States making no gesture against the Russian invasion of Hungary.

In 1931 Cummings went to Russia, producing in due course *Eimi* (Greek for 'I am'), an account of his month's visit to the Soviet Union. This is a good an account as has ever been written of how Communist life strikes the observer from without.

There are some superbly funny passages. At the same time the author's interest in 'experimental' writing has been allowed free play. In *The Enormous Room* Cummings's revolutionary use of word is like a fresh breeze; in *Eimi*, the style has become excellent, but very rich plum-pudding. Cummings did not take to life in the USSR, which he attacks not for political, but intellectual and aesthetic reasons. This made him unpopular among the highbrows of the 1930s who spent so much time telling everyone what a splendid thing Communism was for authors and artists.

Charles Norman suggests that Cummings's verse has never been popular in England, owing to his innovations. It might be urged in reply that Cummings is no more obscure than some of our own poets. Geoffrey Moore, editor of *The Penguin Book of Modern American Verse,* takes precisely the opposite view of Cummings's reputation, saying 'Prof. Spencer, like most English critics, is inclined to rate Cummings highly.' The style of his material – his taste for playing about with punctuation and distaste for capital letters – has caused critics to compare him with Guillaume Apollinaire. Cummings himself disputes this, and rightly. They are poets of a very different stamp.

Although certain eccentricities may have told against him, it is impossible not to be struck with the fact that he is in many ways a traditional poet, who has been influenced by traditional poets. Norman does not mention Matthew Arnold, but I suspect he was an early favourite.

The original phraseology of *The Enormous Room* was equally apparent in Cummings's poems. In consequence he was hailed as one of the most 'modern' of poets, but it has been pointed out that the content of Cummings's verse is wholly traditional, at times romantic to the point of being banal.

Roy Fuller is one of those who have attacked Cummings for sentimentalities, and there is no doubt that some of his verse lays him open to such objections. At the same time it would be impossible to give any account of poetry in America in the first half of this century without according Cummings a fairly high place, while such lines as 'All in green went my love riding' and 'My father moved through dooms of love' stick in the mind in a manner that cannot be ignored. He wrote of Ernest Hemingway:

> What does little Ernest croon
> in his death at afternoon?
> (kow dow r 2 bul retoinis
> wus de woids uf lil Oinis).

Cummings thought of himself equally as a painter, and family pressures to make him take a job were to some extent dismissed on the plea that he occasionally sold a picture. In this art he was reasonably competent, but it seems to me unpleasing. Still his painting has interest as a key to his own aesthetic personality.

Cummings was hard up all his days, though he latterly managed to make two ends meet by 'non-lectures' and poetry readings at academic institutions. He had three wives, all beauties, and managed to get into an appalling mess *vis-à-vis* his one child, a daughter. Richard Kennedy steers the narrative through these marital involvements both tactfully and without too much covering up, making them interesting to those who want to know about this talented figure.

The Magic-Maker: E. E.
Cummings, Charles Norman,
Macmillan.
Dreams in the Mirror: A
Biography of E. E. Cummings,
Richard S. Kennedy, Norton.

1969; 1980
Daily Telegraph

F. SCOTT FITZGERALD

I

It is eleven years since Arthur Mizener's *The Far Side of Paradise* appeared; the same length of time, as it happens, between Scott Fitzgerald's death and the publication of that biography. Since then a fair amount of new material – notably Sheilah Graham's *Beloved Infidel* – has come to light to add to the picture.

In some ways, for the reader who is simply interested in Fitzgerald as a writer, Mizener's remains the clearer, more balanced book; but for those who want to know as much as possible about Fitzgerald as a man, Andrew Turnbull has collected together an accumulation of intensely interesting facts and memories, at times a shade rambling, but full of information and personalities. (In future editions 'Lady Florence Willerts' should read 'Florence, Lady Willert'.)

The general picture is by now well known. Scott Fitzgerald, born in the Middle West in 1896, of, on the whole, comparatively recently emigrated Irish stock, together with a few glamorous Southern ancestors, went to Princeton; had a big popular sucess with the 'College' novel *This Side of Paradise*; wrote one of the best novels that has ever come out of America – or anywhere else – *The Great Gatsby*; produced another excellent novel in *Tender is the Night* and other works of notable talent; drank too much; died in comparative obscurity in 1940.

Perhaps the most interesting readjustment that emerges from Turnbull's book, apart from the many fascinating sideshows it provides, is in relation to the financial position of Fitzgerald's parents.

His father was an ineffectual, good-looking figure, apparently rather silly; his mother, tactless, eccentric, full of energy. When Fitzgerald's father lost his job, one of the terrible moments of the writer's early life, Fitzgerald himself feared the family would go to the poor-house.

This was in 1908, when Scott was twelve years old. I had previously taken this story quite seriously. It now appears that Fitzgerald's mother was always fairly comfortably off – they never ceased to keep a servant – and, when her own mother died in 1913, their capital amounted to the respectable sum of just over £30,000. This did not, of course, alter the fact that in America it was only thought respectable to live on a wife's income if really huge; also that the early 1900s was the period *par excellence* everywhere when people with perfectly adequate means supposed that ruin faced them at any moment.

However, in spite of these latter points, Fitzgerald's presentation of himself as a poor boy at Princeton was only relatively true. He always liked to dramatize his own life.

One of the most interesting characteristics of Fitzgerald as a writer was that at one level he was the most industrious, the most serious artist imaginable; at another, a hack who could produce popular stories which, almost to the end, earned a reasonable return.

I can think of no other writer of Fitzgerald's kind who brought this off. Giants like Balzac or Dickens wrote a lot of rubbish, together with their first-rate stuff, but their immense vitality made that possible. Their best work was not of Fitzgerald's immensely finished, consciously perfected sort.

Scott Fitzgerald well brings out these two sides of the man by supplying, as it were, an enormous number of vignettes of him at different moments. In this Andrew Turnbull has the particular advantage of having, as a growing boy, himself known Fitzgerald, who lived on the Turnbulls' estate at the time when Zelda Fitzgerald's mental breakdowns caused her to be accommodated in an institution not far away.

The whole tragic story of Zelda is additionally illuminated here. Again, the financial details are of interest. Zelda's father, Judge Sayre, was only earning about £1,500 a year in 1918; in other words not much more than was presumably being produced by the capital of the Fitzgerald parents. No doubt the Sayre background was more distinguished, but Fitzgerald seems, all things being equal, to have been a perfectly reasonable suitor for Zelda, rather than the Gatsby-and-Daisy image.

Scott Fitzgerald, Andrew   1969
Turnbull, Bodley Head.   *Daily Telegraph*

II

To produce another book about Scott Fitzgerald at this stage, and for it to be readable, is something of an achievement. Aaron Latham's *Crazy Sundays*, an account of Fitzgerald in Hollywood, throws new light on several aspects of the novelist's life. It should also be studied by everyone who aspires to write film scripts.

Fitzgerald, in contrast with many, probably most, serious writers who went to Hollywood, had as his aim not merely to earn enough money to get back to novel writing; he was interested in the film-making technique as such. It was almost his highest ambition to write the script for a great film.

What could be better than that? No one could deny Fitzgerald's remarkable inventive powers, ability to create convincing dialogue, an approach to his story making little or no demands on a public who liked a straightforward plot. It is indeed one of Fitzgerald's skills that he can include an astonishing subtlety within a narrative like *The Great Gatsby*, a work that in lesser hands would have been no more than a melodramatic extended magazine story.

The fact was that Fitzgerald approached Hollywood, like everything else in his life, in a spirit of pure romanticism. The natural instinct, hard work, powers of observation, which he brought to his novels, made romanticism an effective method. In Hollywood it was no good whatever.

It has been suggested that the Hollywood bosses became at last worried at their 'image'. They were right to be. It is hard to think of a less attractive collection of human beings. Grasping, stupid, wasteful, procrastinating collectively in their business, the fact that their own individual morals were rarely to be held up as an ideal standard did not prevent them from being hypocritical, unctuous, Pecksniffian in the highest degree. It would not be going too far to say that the rubbish gurgled out by the Hays Office (the Hollywood authority imposing moral censorship), by its determination to prevent realistic representation of life, pointed the way to the contemporary appetite for four-letter words and wearisomely erotic situations.

All this emerges from Latham's book. Let us take one instance of how authors were created in Hollywood. Fitzgerald had done most of the work on a certain film, admittedly then handed on to other script-writers, who no doubt tinkered about with it to some small extent. Fitzgerald received $5,000, or some proportion of that sum (probably less), at that time about £1,000. The script was then sold by the studio to another larger studio, *which had already sacked Fitzgerald*, for $100,000, say £20,000 (then enough to set an author up for life) of which Fitzgerald never saw a cent.

Fitzgerald himself sentimentalized a film executive as hero of his unfinished novel *The Last Tycoon*, where Irving Thalberg appears as Monroe Stahr. This incomplete work has many merits, but one often feels that Stahr himself needs a kick in the pants. It is hard to believe that did not apply to Thalberg too.

One of the most interesting facts produced by Latham (so far as I know for the first time) is the help given to Fitzgerald in writing *Tender is the Night* by the seventeen-year-old song-writer Bill Warren, whose real first names 'Charles Marquis' were used in the first edition of the novel as those of the heroine's father.

Aldous Huxley appears in Latham's pages, not as the withdrawn intellectual brahmin he was considered anyway in his earlier days, but as a slick writer of film scripts, a great deal nimbler at handling the business side of the 'industry' than Fitzgerald himself. The story Huxley produced of Mme Curie and her young scientist lover hanging a picture of her husband, Curie, over their bed is a good one of its kind, and an antidote to the honeyed film about the Curies that was produced.

We have a vignette of Dorothy Parker throwing up the window of the writers' block at MGM, and shouting 'Let me out – I'm as sane as you are!'; of Fitzgerald renting a villa from the actor Edward Everett Horton and being dismayed at finding it named 'Belly Acres'.

I have elsewhere described my own meeting with Fitzgerald in Hollywood, and stick to it that he did not seem the broken man there he is so often represented. It was, however, a lucky day. He could undoubtedly behave appallingly. I have also stayed at The Hanover Inn at Dartmouth, New Hampshire, but only learnt from Latham's book that it was from the steps of this old world hostelry that Walter Wanger fired Fitzgerald and Budd Schulberg, after the devasting drinking spree from which Fitzgerald's final downfall might be said to date.

Calvin Tomkins's long essay *Living Well is the Best Revenge* might perhaps have been more sensibly called *The Murphys*. It describes convincingly Gerald and Sara Murphy, friends of Fitzgerald and many other writers and painters of the period. On the Murphys and their entourage some of the characters in *Tender is the Night* are modelled.

The Murphys were well off, though not enormously rich. They were among the first Americans to grasp that the South of France life could be enjoyable in the summer. It is clear that both of them, Gerald Murphy especially, had remarkable talents. Although I do not find his paintings sympathetic, they are certainly gifted and one more indication of the out-of-dateness of so much current Pop Art.

That Satie found a musical performance by the two Murphys amusing enough to make suggestions as to its improvements indicates their ability in that field too. They were a remarkable couple and Calvin Tomkins defines them well.

With all their charm, tolerance (heaven knows how they put up with the Fitzgeralds) and intelligence, there is also something a shade macabre about the picture, even apart from the tragedy that overcame two of the Murphys' children.

Crazy Sundays: F. Scott Fitzgerald in Hollywood, Aaron Latham, Secker & Warburg.
Living Well is the Best Revenge: Two Americans in Paris, 1921–1933, Calvin Tomkins, Deutsch.

1972
Daily Telegraph

III

It might be thought saturation point had been reached in books about Scott Fitzgerald, but, strangely enough, isolation of the letters between him and Maxwell Perkins – his editor in the old-established New York publishing house of Scribner – makes a remarkably interesting book.

The interest arises partly from the fact that Fitzgerald is here shown simply as a professional writer, all other aspects of his complicated life taking a back place, and partly from the way that the letters illustrate the general author/publisher relationship.

La Rochefoucauld said there were happy marriages, but no charming ones. A similar reflection crosses the mind reading these letters, which begin July, 1919 (when Fitzgerald had just written the novel to appear as *This Side of Paradise*) and continue until the week before his death in December 1940. Perkins and Fitzgerald got on extremely well during these twenty years, but Fitzgerald's constant need for money did not make things easy.

Perkins, as well as Fitzgerald, was an unusual man. Descended from a 'Signer' (of the Declaration of Independence), he represented in all respects the old America, in which the Civil War blew such an appalling hole. As the Editors of *Dear Scott/Dear Max* point out this background was one of the sides of Perkins that appealed to Fitzgerald, who could claim certain relatively distinguished Southern connections himself.

The moderation of tone that made Perkins a 'great' publisher has its less sympathetic side in the years leading up to the Second World War (in *Editor to Author*, a selection of his Letters published in 1950 he seems determined to keep a fair balance between Hitler and the Allies), and here, when Fitzgerald writes (6 June 1940) 'The Allies are thoroughly licked, that much is certain . . .'. and later (15 August 1940) 'The only cheerful thing is the game scrap the British are putting up,' Perkins replies sedately: 'People hereabouts are very much alive to the war and anxious we should get prepared and should help England in all ways "short of war" in the meantime.'

Perkins, as his particular pets at Scribner's, ran Fitzgerald, Hemingway and Thomas Wolfe – his 'sons', Fitzgerald called them – amongst whom Wolfe turned out badly, and put two rather unflattering portraits of Perkins into his novels.

One of the facts that emerges from these Letters is how extraordinarily well Fitzgerald behaved towards Hemingway (apart from always spelling his name 'Hemmingway', whenever he wrote it), from the first moment of coming in contact with the writer's work, doing his best to get it recognized. He never lost interest in the writing, in the face of much unpleasant behaviour from Hemingway himself. Fitzgerald was altogether without envy.

One cannot help being struck by the way in which Fitzgerald knew what he was aiming at from the very beginning. *This Side of Paradise* is full of absurdities, and Fitzgerald himself wrote of it as 'now (April 1938) one of the funniest books since *Dorian Gray* in its utter spuriousness'. Nevertheless his Letters – more than the novel itself perhaps – show the germ of talent that was there.

A good deal of literary comment is interspersed between business dealings. Fitzgerald is always worth hearing, even, as below, on the subject of forgotten writers. The inarticulate, of whom he complains in 1925, were to continue for many a long day; indeed are going yet, and in a hippy form:

> I hear he has written a very original and profound novel. It is said to be about the inarticulate farmer and his struggles with the 'soil' and his sexual waverings between his inarticulate wife and an inarticulate sheep. He finally chooses his old pioneering mother as the most inarticulate of all but finds her in bed with our old friend THE HIRED MAN CHRISTY!
>
> CHRISTY HAS DONE IT!

The Editors note that in 1962 this letter of Fitzgerald's to Perkins was sold at Christie's – '(not old man Christy)' – for £7,000.

Dear Scott/Dear Max: The   1973
Fitzgerald–Perkins Correspondence,   *Daily Telegraph*
John Kuehl and Jackson R.
Bryer, eds, Cassell.

IV

It is just over thirty years ago since I reviewed Arthur Mizener's *The Far Side of Paradise* (1951) and remarked that Scott Fitzgerald was just beginning to emerge from the decline that his books had long suffered in America.

I said that his work was rapidly beginning to be known in this country where hitherto he had been the admired writer only of a few enthusiasts and added, what I think now, that *The Great Gatsby* is a novel in the top class.

Mizener's biography relates the Fitzgerald story in all its essentials, but since its appearance books have poured out on every aspect of that subject, adding information and clearing away a certain amount of myth, some generated by Fitzgerald himself. Matthew J. Bruccoli's definitive work, *Some Sort of Epic Grandeur*, is very acceptable. Bruccoli is thorough, scholarly and writes in an excellent no-nonsense style which never involves the reader in a lot of phoney psychology.

It was to some extent Fitzgerald's misfortune that he was almost universally looked upon as the archetypal figure of the 1920s, even though up to a point he took that view of himself. As Bruccoli says:

> The identification of Fitzgerald with the Twenties – which represented half his professional life – has contributed to the distorted popular impression of him as the totemic figure who embodied or was even somehow responsible for the excesses of the boom and the punitive Depression. The ways in which his career duplicated the national moods are almost too neat – like something inept novelists invent.

At the same time *The Great Gatsby* is pervaded by an atmosphere of the period that no other novel conveys in quite the same manner. It is a sad serious book about people who are on the whole not themselves serious, and treats of romantic love in purple passages that somehow never become absurd, while in the many funny scenes Fitzgerald is unrivalled for wit and irony. *Tender is the Night* is a pretty good novel. *The Last Tycoon*, if completed, might have been pretty good too; some of the short stories are accomplished but *The Great Gatsby* is in a class by itself.

Apparently Gatsby was partly inspired by a Long Island figure called Max Gerlach or von Gerlach, said to be a 'gentleman bootlegger'. The identification is supported by a newspaper photograph in the Fitzgeralds' scrapbook, dated July 1923, and captioned in Gatsby's own characteristic idiom: 'En route for the coast – Here for a few days on business – How are you and the family old Sport? Gerlach.'

Bruccoli is skilful in dealing with the complicated and usually painful relationship between Fitzgerald and his wife Zelda. It is tempting to speculate on what Fitzgerald's life would have been had he married someone else. His own alcoholism was of a thoroughly unpleasant sort, but Zelda's characteristics, combined with their undoubted mutual love, were geared peculiarly to upset him.

That Zelda's madness was hereditary can scarcely be doubted. There was a marked history of mental disturbance in her family background. At the same time, in addition to her beauty, she had her own kind of brilliance. It is even possible to wonder whether her phraseology did not contribute something to Fitzgerald's own literary style, when one reads the letters she was writing as a girl of nineteen. It is customary to represent Zelda as bitterly envious of her husband's success in his writing, but Fitzgerald clearly had feelings about her too that went beyond sexual jealousy.

An interesting small point that emerges is that Fitzgerald's father – whom his son disprized as a failure in life but liked as a man, especially for his claims to relatively glamorous 'Old Southern' forebears – so far as he had any ambitions for Fitzgerald would have liked him to be an army officer; something very rare, one would say, in American families not already connected with the army.

Bruccoli gives much financial information, which is needed in chronicling a hero who looked upon riches with respect that approached awe. The Fitzgerald parents appear to have had the equivalent of about £1,200 a year in the early 1900s, and at his lowest point before his death Fitzgerald himself never earned less than £2,000 to £3,000 as year, sometimes much more, though he had very considerable expenses. Bruccoli rightly emphasizes that Fitzgerald did not (repeat not) say to Hemingway: 'The rich are different from us' nor Hemingway reply: 'They have more money.' On the contrary the occasion when some such exchange had involved Hemingway was one at which the joke went against him.

One feels that only Fitzgerald could have employed a lawyer (a Princeton contemporary) called Edgar Allan Poe, Jr. The term 'flapper', which plays a great part in Fitzgerald's early books, deserves a word of explanation. In America at that period 'flapper' meant a débutante, but one probably flaunting unconventional behaviour. In this country 'flapper' was simply used for a girl who had not yet 'put her hair up'. I mention that because John O'Hara (author of *Appointment in Samarra*) is quoted in Matthew Bruccoli's book as giving a totally incorrect definition of the English use as a 'society girl who has made her début and hasn't found a husband'.

Some Sort of Epic Grandeur: The   1982
Life of F. Scott Fitzgerald,   *Daily Telegraph*
Matthew J. Bruccoli, with
Genealogical Afterword by
Scottie Fitzgerald Smith,
Hodder. ·

V

As Matthew Bruccoli's comprehensive biography of Scott Fitzgerald cleared up several points that needed qualification, there cannot be said to exist a pressing need for another Fitzgerald biography. At the same time André Le Vot is no less thorough than Bruccoli and, as he is Professor of American Literature at the Sorbonne, interest certainly attaches to seeing what aspects of the Fitzgerald story chiefly strike a Frenchman.

In his Introduction Le Vot speaks of Fitzgerald as 'virtually unknown in Europe twenty years ago'. In his bibliography he says 'not until 1960, however, were all of Fitzgerald's novels made available in a new hard-cover series'. If he equates Europe with France (not unheard of among his countrymen) this is doubtless true. In the 1940s here the Grey Walls Press began to reprint all the Fitzgerald novels, running on into the early 1950s, and when Arthur Mizener's biography appeared in 1951 it was already possible to speak of Fitzgerald as becoming widely known in Great Britain.

A non-American, Le Vot pays more attention than usual to the contemporary American political and social scene, apt to be taken for granted by Fitzgerald's compatriots. He obviously thinks – and one would heartily agree – that Fitzgerald stands or falls by *The Great Gatsby* and the pages he devotes to the corruption of that moment in American Hisory are not wasted in defining the qualities of the book. As Le Vot remarks, Watergate seems a peccadillo compared with the accumulated scandals of Elk Hill, the Teapot Dome, the head of the Veterans Association, the Secretaries for the Interior and the Navy – all convicted of fraudulent contracts set against a background of universal disregard for law and order, largely stemming from Prohibition and its attendant evils.

Part of the strength, the extraordinary originality of *The Great Gatsby* is expressed by such extraneous incidents as the immensely comic meeting with the gangster Wolfsheim (whose model, in the phrase of the time, was 'rubbed out' a year or two later), in which gangsterism is shown as no less sinister on account of being ludicrous. The novel is usually thought of as the story of a love affair (in fact several love affairs) but Wolfsheim 'fixing the World Series' (baseball) suggests just as much the atmosphere of the Twenties – the Jazz Age – as Gatsby's parties or Buchanan's polo.

Fitzgerald, anyway so far as *The Great Gatsby* is concerned, is one of those remarkable examples of a novelist outstripped by his own novel. This is often true of Fitzgerald, the tawdriness of whose dreams and, one regrets to say, the unpleasantness of whose actions never managed to obliterate the poetry of much of his writing. One side of him was courageous, unbeatable, a dedicated artist, but, even apart from the damage he did, the sheer unfunniness of his behaviour when drunk is unbelievable in a man who could also display such delicate irony in watching human behaviour.

Fitzgerald is impossible to conceive in any country but America. Here, in France, anywhere else in Europe, for that matter in Latin America, he could not have taken quite the same form. Only in the United States does he embody not one, but a whole series of American realities, paradoxes, and fantasies.

On the whole Le Vot's is the gloomiest picture yet given. Although certain periods in Fitzgerald's career might possess a touch of nostalgia when looked back on, the actual living of them was scarcely ever pleasurable. That was in spite of early success, a very reasonable amount of money flowing in, and his meeting everybody an ambitious young writer might want to meet in an epoch when writing was more highly, certainly more romantically, regarded than today.

One wonders not that Zelda Fitzgerald went off her head but that her husband did not go the same way too. After the appalling drinking bouts his physical ability to write at all is staggering. Even if

Fitzgerald's short stories often fall a long way short of his novels he was almost always able to sell them, while much of his best writing was brought off when hangovers must have threatened death's door.

During the latter days in Hollywood things were getting very bad. Again André Le Vot's account emphasizes how uncompromisingly ominous matters had become, how difficult further employment in the movies would increasingly be. Sheilah Graham behaved with truly saintly endurance after one of the ruinous rows that took place. Another on the same lines might well have finished the association. Fitzgerald's end, when it came, was the best possible answer.

Edith Wharton, on the occasion of the disastrous tea party, wrote after Fitzgerald's name in her diary '(awful)', not 'horrible' (no doubt an understandable error in translation). Fitzgerald, great writer as he was at his best, was fairly often awful; comparatively rarely horrible. There is a difference.

F. Scott Fitzgerald: A Biography,   1984
André Le Vot, Allen Lane.   *Daily Telegraph*

VI

Why Sheilah Graham, now a highly paid Hollywood columnist, thought it necessary to co-opt a professional American 'ghoster' of memoirs to help write her autobiography is a mystery. Between them they have certainly brought together a fair number of clichés.

Sheilah Graham was born in the East End of London and brought up in an orphanage. By the age of eighteen, extremely pretty and possessed of enterprise, she obtained a job at a department store demonstrating a new toothbrush. Struck by her appearance and abilities, the owner of a small business offered her a better salary.

Her new employer, John Graham Gillam, who sold costume jewellery, lamps, and leather goods, was in his forties and had risen to the rank of major in the First World War, in which he had been awarded a DSO. Miss Graham married him. This seems to have been about the year 1928 or 1929.

Major Gillam undertook a certain amount of journalism as a sideline. His wife, too, wrote occasional articles, which were accepted. She also trained for the stage, and seems to have had little or no difficulty in establishing herself as one of 'Mr. Cochran's Young Ladies'.

To these triumphs she added that of meeting a lot of lively people of the sort whose names appear in the gossip columns. She was presented at Court, but kept her marriage secret in her professional life. Major Gillam tended to stay at home, trying to sort out his financial worries.

Here the book loses some sense of proportion, and Graham writes about the persons she met and her presentation, rather as if she were the first woman to return from Mars on a space-ship. It is understandable that she should be gratified by the company of such people as A. P. Herbert, Randolph Churchill and various members of the Mitford family, but granted her gifts not particularly surprising she should have come across them.

She was taken aback when someone said: 'You are an adventuress, aren't you?' But surely it was being an adventuress that made her acceptable in the circles she describes.

Sheilah Graham seems to have dovetailed in her mind two quite different approaches to life. Her social values will be confusing to Americans. As a matter of fact, at that period no adventuress need have felt lonely or uncomfortable. There were plenty of them about.

One sees from the start that Major Gillam is not going to stand the pace. It comes as no shock that he is left at home (and later divorced) when his wife transfers herself to America in 1933. Three years later we find her established as a syndicated movie columnist in Hollywood.

From here the book takes on a different, much improved tone. What has previously been a conglomeration of selected autobiographical slices, greatly varying in interest and candour, becomes the story of Sheilah Graham's association with Scott Fitzgerald.

Fitzgerald, although once celebrated as the playboy of 'the Jazz Age', had arrived in Hollywood, forgotten, hard-up, his beautiful wife, Zelda, in an asylum, himself working on the script of *A Yank at Oxford*.

Sheilah Graham's story is here of especial interest to me, for she saw Fitzgerald for the first time on 14 July 1937. I met him a few days later at luncheon in the MGM commissary and found him a most enjoyable contrast to Hollywood life.

Fitzgerald could keep off drink for long periods, but in his bouts he was utterly unmanageable, breaking up the furniture, fighting with his friends, sending offensive telegrams to those he loved, or to those upon whose payroll he figured. During these interludes he could be coped with only by the police. Sheilah Graham stood it for some time, but it was no good.

As it turned out, some sort of reconciliation brought her to Fitzgerald's final hour. Her account of their love affair is vivid; at times even moving. As might be expected from these circumstances she figures to some extent in Fitzgerald's unfinished novel *The Last Tycoon*. Sheilah Graham is, it must be admitted, extraordinarily suited to the world of Fitzgerald's imagination. Indeed, romantically speaking, she might almost be thought of as a kind of female Great Gatsby.

Beloved Infidel: The Education of a Woman, Sheilah Graham and Gerold Frank, Cassell.

1959
Daily Telegraph

MAXWELL PERKINS

In this country it is rare for anyone, let alone a publisher, to take writers seriously.

In America the case is different. There writers are sometimes taken very seriously indeed, fêted for several years, then easily forgotten; a process not necessarily advantageous to the writer, who is expected to develop a kind of film-star personality, and becomes for ever anxious about his, or her, public – on that account often at risk of going off his, or her, rocker.

Maxwell Perkins (1884–1947) was a celebrated 'editor' in the old-established New York publishing house of Scribner. He took writers immensely seriously, and had a really astonishing record of success in finding and promoting them. He was assisted in this by great energy, an altogether unusual instinct for knowing how a novel should be put together, and absolute personal freedom from any vestige of humour.

Although not very happily married, Perkins lived a life of complete rectitude, lightened emotionally only by a lifelong (undoubtedly) platonic love for a lady who never married. He devoted his seven-day week entirely to doing his duty as he conceived it. His absorbing story, excellently narrated by A. Scott Berg, is a fascinating reversal of the contemporary assumption that only a biography full of sexual adventures is interesting.

Although dozens of names could be invoked of writers Perkins knocked into shape and high circulation his name will always be associated with F. Scott Fitzgerald, Ernest Hemingway, Thomas Wolfe (whose mammoth manuscript was introduced by an agent, and scented by Perkins as a possibility). These three writers were an essential part of Perkins's career, and – although both men were entirely heterosexual – his relations with Wolfe were not much short of a love affair.

Of these three, it seems to me that Fitzgerald was a relatively bad writer, who became an exceedingly good one; Hemingway, an exceedingly good writer, who became a relatively bad one; Wolfe, a literary curiosity, whose unstemmable autobiographical outpourings must be admitted to be out of the ordinary.

The consequence of Fitzgerald becoming a good writer was that his sales dropped to barely subsistence level, while Hemingway becoming a bad writer resulted in an enormous boost. Wolfe's elephantine productions also reached a large market, though nothing like the final Hemingway scale.

In April 1922, Perkins writes (of *The Beautiful and the Damned*) to Fitzgerald: 'It has sold about 33,000 copies actually. I doubt if we can hope that it will be an overwhelming success now, but when you speak of me as being disappointed, you're wrong.'

Perkins was not only publisher and literary adviser of these writers, but banker, lawyer, confidant, comforter. Hemingway needed far the least looking after in all repects, but even Hemingway, when well into middle life, and far more than middle literary success, expected regular letters from Perkins to bolster up his self-esteem. Fitzgerald and Wolfe would be given loans from Perkins's own resources.

Perkins hated taking holidays but would sometimes be induced to go sea-fishing with Hemingway, or squat in the snow in the early hours of the morning to shoot duck. All publishers would not have been up to this. He could also give all these three alcoholic writers a game so far as drinking went, drink being Perkins's only self-indulgence.

Berg, in a longish but never dull book, weaves his way deftly through a web of publishing material that cannot have been easy to handle, though John Hall Wheelock, poet and fellow Scribner's employee, edited a good volume of Perkins's letters, *Editor to Author*, in 1950, which must have been a help.

One often hears the story quoted of Fitzgerald saying to Hemingway: 'The very rich are different from us,' and Hemingway replying: 'Yes, they have more money.' Berg rightly attempts to nail this tale down, but I am not sure that he does so finally.

The exchange between Fitzgerald and Hemingway about the very rich, with Ernest's trumping of Scott's line, survives as one of the notable literary anecdotes from that time. But it is spurious, for, as Max Perkins well knew, the truth was otherwise. Perkins had been present when the rejoinder had been made – in a New York restaurant. Scott Fitzgerald was not there.

Those present were Hemingway, Molly Colum, and Perkins, and it was Hemingway, in fact, who spoke of the rich, 'I am getting to know the rich,' he declared. Whereupon Molly Colum topped him, saying: 'The only difference between the rich and other people is that the rich have more money.' Bested by a woman, Hemingway salved his ego by expropriating the witticism, having it come from his own lips, and making Scott, once again, the victim.

Fitzgerald did write in 'The Rich Boy' (one of the stories in *All the Sad Young Men*, 1926): 'Let me tell you about the very rich. They are different from you and me,' but he did not, as Hemingway wrote when quoting him, begin the story with those words.

Max Perkins: Editor of Genius, A.   1979
Scott Berg, Hamish Hamilton.   *Daily Telegraph*

ERNEST HEMINGWAY

I

Ernest Hemingway, largely through his own fault, occupies an over-dramatized therefore somewhat artificial position in contemporary literature. It should be stated in the clearest terms that what is important about him is whether or not he is a good writer. His experiences in the two world wars, in the Greco-Turkish war, and in the Spanish Civil War, his exploits as a fisherman, as an amateur bullfighter, or flying his own aeroplane, no doubt provided suitable material to make up that seven-eighths of the iceberg which he himself describes every writer as needing. But they are not, in themselves, interesting. Or, rather, if one were interested especially in any of these subjects, there are plenty of other authorities to draw upon, many of them with more serious qualifications to speak of such practical matters.

Indeed, so far from being a great hearty, Ernest Hemingway seems to me a great aesthete: using the word, of course, in its serious sense. He, more than any other novelist, was responsible for clearing the ground of extraneous matter in the Twenties. It is largely due to him that people are not still writing like Hugh Walpole.

But when you come to examine the Hemingway novels, it is not, on the whole, the scenes of violent action that make the lasting impression. Conrad, for example, a novelist whose approach is the extreme reverse from the swashbuckling, self-conscious Hemingway manner, is a far greater master of the violent scene. Hemingway's power lies rather in describing a man unhappily in love (as in *Fiesta*), or small groups of people talking together (like the Italian mess in *A Farewell to Arms*). The short stories ('The Mother of a Queen') provide many good examples of sensitive and satirical observation. There is much good stuff in 'Death in the Afternoon' – again on the discursive rather than the violent side – while the conversation about American literature is perhaps the best thing in 'Green Hills of Africa'. *For Whom the Bell Tolls* seems to me a failure, *Across the River* even worse, and I do not share recent enthusiasm for *The Old Man and the Sea*.

Now Charles A. Fenton comes along with a book that describes Hemingway's life up to the time when he wrote *Fiesta* – or, as it was called in America, *The Sun Also Rises*. It is a most interesting account of

225

the making of a writer, and bears out, what has been said above, that the remarkable thing about Hemingway is not his various excursions into the world of action but his determination, formed at an early age, to produce a powerful technique of writing.

This may sound a dull subject, but Fenton, in a humdrum, unpretentious way, manages to make it extremely interesting – that is if you are interested in how authors begin to write. We are shown Hemingway at school, beginning his journalistic career on the *Kansas City Star*, and gradually finding his way to the famous newspaper the *Toronto Star*, which he worked for in Canada and represented during his early period in Paris. The unhappiness of his early days in Oak Park, Illinois, is hinted at, though never fully explained.

This account of his life as a young and capable journalist shows the foundation of his writing. To the background of highly efficient professional journalism was added the impact of Gertrude Stein, whom Hemingway met in France. That curious woman, whose own works are of such limited interest, undoubtedly acted as an important stimulating force on others. It was so with Hemingway, and the result of her influence on him altered the whole tendency of American and English writing during the next twenty years.

When Hemingway went to France in 1918 it was as a driver (with the rank of honorary second-lieutenant) in an ambulance unit. Fenton quotes a fact, probably not generally known, that Henry James in November 1914 wrote a twelve-page patriotic pamphlet called *The American Volunteer Motor-Ambulance Corps in France*:

> The pamphlet was distinctly in the prose of James's late period. He described the suffering of the wounded. 'Carried mostly by rude arts, a mercy much hindered at the best, to the shelter often hastily improvised, at which first aid becomes possible for them, they are there, as immediately and tenderly as possible, stowed in our waiting or arriving cars, each of which receives as large number as may be consistent with the particular suffering state of the stricken individual.'

Without saying a word against the greatness of James as a novelist, it will be seen that there was certainly something in the way of style for writers like Hemingway to react against.

The Apprenticeship of Ernest Hemingway, Charles A. Fenton, Vision Press: Peter Owen

1955
Punch

II

For those addicted to reading books about Ernest Hemingway, A. E. Hotchner's memoir seems at first to threaten all the most familiar and tedious anecdotes and attitudes that make that particular taste a gruelling one.

The Hemingway myth is totally accepted. Hotchner likes all the things Hemingway liked. He even performed himself in the ring dressed up spuriously as a bullfighter.

However, by the time the last page of *Papa Hemingway* is read, it has to be admitted that an exceedingly interesting, though painful, document has been produced – one of those curiously successful essays in the higher journalism that for some reason only Americans seem able to assemble. The comparison that comes to mind is Malcolm Brinnin's *Dylan Thomas in America*. Mrs Mary Hemingway cannot be blamed for disapproval; Hotchner cannot be expected to have forgone writing his book in the way he has.

He was sent to Havana in 1948 to ask Hemingway to do an article for a magazine. This was their first meeting. Never expecting to get as much as a sight of his prey, Hotchner, on the contrary, embarked on a lifelong friendship, in due course sharing Hemingway's sports and pastimes, acting eventually almost as secretary or literary agent.

At the time of their meeting, Hemingway (born 1899) was a world-famous figure, embarked on a fourth marriage, set in his way of life. Hotchner takes the story from here to Hemingway's death by his own hand in 1961. The book could have done with an index.

The Hemingway legend requires some disentangling. When *The Sun Also Rises* (*Fiesta*) appeared in 1926 it was clear that a new sort of novel had emerged. This was chiefly on account of the bare dialogue and understated descriptive writing.

In addition to these stylistic innovations, the characters tended not only to drink heavily but also to be devoted to sport – shooting, fishing, boxing, bull-fighting. There is no reason why these activities should not play a part in a novel. Indeed, after D. H. Lawrence and Virginia Woolf, they offered a certain exhilaration.

A Farewell to Arms (1929) still reads well, though as much as an adventure story as a serious novel. Many of the earlier short stories are first-rate. 'Death in the Afternoon', a study in bullfighting (1932) and 'Green Hills of Africa' (1935) have also excellent points. These last added greatly to Hemingway's popular reputation. At about this stage – so it appears to me – something went wrong.

Certain writers find the wear-and-tear of the world around them so unsympathetic that they create a 'persona' for themselves which is intended to protect them from it. Evelyn Waugh did this (of course in a totally different manner from Hemingway), and more than once a similarity is glimpsed in Hotchner's book.

We recognize, for instance, that same refusal ever to drop this persona, however inconvenient, the dislike for parties or speaking on the telephone, finally the Pinfold voices – in Hemingway's case a delusion that he was being shadowed by Federal agents.

The danger of assuming this persona appears to be the risk of hardening whatever are the mysterious processes of imaginative production, perceptible at times in Waugh, manifest in Hemingway. It is only necessary to consider later Conrad or later Kipling – writers with whom Hemingway might reasonably be compared – to see how muscle-bound Hemingway ultimately became.

For Whom the Bell Tolls (1940), *Across the River and Into the Trees* (1950) and *The Old Man and the Sea* (1952) are works produced by a naturally talented writer with a lot of will-power, rather than the real stuff – the stuff from inside Hemingway – of which *The Sun Also Rises* was made. The fact that *The Old Man and the Sea* resulted in the award of the Nobel Prize does not convince me that it is a good book.

Hotchner's memoir, though not explaining why this imaginative deterioration took place – indeed, probably no one could – does supply a lot of material to suggest that Hemingway's colossal self-absorption was finally the enemy of his writing.

In certain directions Hemingway's capacity to stand boredom (including boring companions) must have been boundless, but, like Einstein's universe, it was not infinite. It is clear that really terrible tortures of ennui from time to time beset him, for which inscriptions on the bathroom wall in a careful hand of 'dated blood-pressure counts, and weights, prescription numbers and other medical and pharmaceutical intelligence' were no antidote.

So often one feels, reading of Hemingway's drinking or sporting activities, that they may have been enjoyable in themselves, even appropriate as material for literature, but totally inappropriate to boast about all day long. No doubt Hemingway was a gifted sportsman, a splendid shot; but everything in his fishing or boxing is put, so to speak, at a remove from the action itself. It is Hemingway looking at Hemingway catching a fish. This is, of course, to some extent required when writing is in question, but to be deplored on the whole in social life.

In the background there existed also certain emotional complications at which Hotchner hints, though he treats them with what one imagines to be reasonable delicacy. The impression is conveyed that Hemingway liked to have an attractive girl about, in whom he was interested, though not necessarily more than that. Pressures possibly released in this way were built up to a dangerous point in the wilderness of Idaho.

There were also money worries: so far as can be seen, quite unnecessary ones, though Hemingway must have needed a good deal of money to exist in that expensive, if disorganized, manner he did. One suspects that within him a very real desire to be a lonely and dedicated artist was at times in conflict with the commercial writer and celebrated personality.

Hotchner does not attempt to unravel all this. Such comments as he makes are presented in Hemingwayese that tends to get us little further. All the same his account of the last terrible few years is well done, and without undue luridness.

Once in a way we see with a different vision from A. E. Hotchner's as when he describes Hemingway's host in Spain, Bill Davis, as 'Pickwickian'. He must surely mean another Bill Davis or another Mr Pickwick?

Hemingway himself said: 'You know what the French call war: *Le métier triste* . . . Do you know the real *métier triste?* Writing . . .' Certainly this book makes you think so.

<table>
<tr><td>*Papa Hemingway: A Personal*</td><td>1960</td></tr>
<tr><td>*Memoir*, A. E. Hotchner,</td><td>*Daily Telegraph*</td></tr>
<tr><td>Weidenfeld & Nicolson.</td><td></td></tr>
</table>

III

There will no doubt be disagreement about this aspect or that of Carlos Baker's *Ernest Hemingway: A Life Story*. It would be impossible to record so crowded, varied and tempestuous a career without that. Nevertheless it is of absorbing interest, long, but one would not have a word the less.

Consider a few of Baker's problems: Hemingway's four marriages; quarrels at one time or another with almost all friends; books, the relative value of which is in some cases still controversial; a great deal of sport (including bullfighting), not everyone's taste to read about; three wars involving at least a small grasp of military affairs for his biographer.

On top of all this was Hemingway's own character. Those who admire him as a writer – and I am one – have a good deal to put up with in reading about him as a man. It would have been easy to be self-righteous, apologetic, blustering. Baker is none of these. He makes no effort to conceal what were often pretty bad situations. His achievement is that, in spite of much that is appalling, we accept the contention that Hemingway possessed also an extraordinary sensibility and charm.

The best description of his subject is in Carlos Baker's Foreword, where he lists Hemingway's contradictions of temperament and behaviour without trying to explain them. That Hemingway had a kind of shyness in public, contrasted with bombast in private, I can confirm from having heard him introduce his (rather indifferent) film *Spanish Earth* in Los Angeles in 1937. He scraped his foot, was indistinct, seemed not at all at ease.

The way in which Hemingway got off to a good start in life is worth emphasizing. This doctor's son from Illinois was not yet nineteen when badly wounded with an American volunteer ambulance unit on the Italian front. The decoration he received from bringing in another wounded man was well deserved.

He was a war veteran of twenty-three when he arrived in Paris, married, with introductions to Gertrude Stein, Sylvia Beach of Shakespeare & Co. (Joyce's publisher) and Ezra Pound. They were written by Sherwood Anderson, who spoke of 'extraordinary talent' and 'a writer instinctively in touch with everything worthwhile'.

In addition, Hemingway's first wife had an income of about the English equivalent of £500 a year, not great wealth, but certainly enough for a writer to exist on in Paris at that date. This was the far from inauspicious background that in 1926 produced *The Sun Also Rises* (in England *Fiesta*): in my own opinion Hemingway's best novel and a classic.

Baker rightly reduces literary criticism in his biography to a minimum, but it may be observed that the discipline and balance with which Hemingway treats his narrator in that first novel is never really achieved again. *A Farewell to Arms* has many good points, but the old ego is already out of control, to pursue a runaway course towards the dreadful disharmonies of Col. Cantwell in *Across the River and Into the Trees*.

In Hemingway's private life – if it could be so called – the pace ever increased: rows, violence, drinking, more and more fame, with its attendant obstructions to work, a really terrifying proneness to accident (skylights collapsing, guns exploding, aircraft crashing), and, with all these, a tendency to what can only be called paranoia.

It is the feeling of inevitability that makes Baker's book such compulsive reading. Could anything have been done? There can be no doubt, for example, that Hemingway remained all his life a dedicated writer. There was nothing phoney about that, any more than there was about his willingness to risk his life. Yet the decline in his writing was relentless in spite of the immense amount of work he put into it. How many serious critics now, one wonders, would echo the praise that greeted *For Whom the Bell Tolls* in 1940?

Hemingway was quite unreliable in personal reminiscence. Baker is right, for example, in treating with caution his account of meeting George Orwell in Paris in 1945. Apart from the inherent improbability of the incident described, Hemingway left France in March, and Orwell did not arrive there until April. It is unlikely that they even met during the Spanish Civil War, or Orwell would have described it.

Hemingway's first employment in the Second World War was British, rather than American, making flights as a journalist with the RAF. Later, with the American forces, where his indiscipline can only have inconvenienced those seriously conducting operations.

In spite of the seriousness with which he took himself, Hemingway was by no means incapable of being funny. 'Even in the days when Thurber was writing under the name of Alice B. Toklas, we knew he had it in him if he could get it out.' He once referred to William Faulkner as 'Old Corn-drinking Mellifluous', and to a photograph of himself as representing 'a cat-eating Zombie'.

By no means indifferent to social nuances, Hemingway is done an injustice here by Baker's reference to the prototype of the heroine of *The Sun Also Rises* as Lady Duff Twysden 'instead of Lady Twysden' ('"What do you know about Lady Brett Ashley, Jake?' – 'Her name's Lady Ashley. Brett's her own name.'").

Hemingway's end, by his own hand, was not, one feels, inappropriate, nor without a kind of dignity in the circumstances in which he found himself.

Ernest Hemingway: A Life Story   1969
Carlos Baker, Collins.   *Daily Telegraph*

IV

Hemingway's story has been told in such a scholarly manner in the biography of Carlos Baker, and annotated with such personal touches in the book by A. E. Hotchner, his fervent disciple, that it is something of an achievement on the part of Anthony Burgess to dish the facts up again in so concise, readable and lively a manner.

Here is all the general reader requires to know about Ernest Miller Hemingway, together with a lot of pictures which are not at all irrelevant to his publicity-seeking career.

The essential point about Hemingway seems to me to be his phenomenally early start. It is worth pausing a moment over these circumstances. First, a young American had none of the war-weariness with which four years of conflict had infected this country; secondly, the Italian front had a drama lacking in the trenches of France and

Flanders. Hemingway did not return with at all the same sort of feelings as, say, Graves or, for that matter, E. E. Cummings.

Burgess is particularly good in defining in a few paragraphs the period between Hemingway's home-coming and the setting off for Paris at the age of twenty-one as a married man and European correspondent of the *Toronto Star*. He says Hemingway's aim was not so much to write a book as 'to draw the aesthetic disposition of language away from its traditional locations in the head and heart and attach it to the nerves and muscles'.

Hemingway was given the *Star* style-book, 'which, in effect, told him to write in the style of the mature Hemingway'. The interesting conclusion at which Burgess arrives is that, although the all-conquering Hemingway style was founded on journalism, Hemingway himself was not a very good newspaper reporter, certainly not a good war correspondent.

Hemingway's mother (whom he termed 'a bitch') was a failed opera-singer, and it is perhaps not generally known that he was himself relatively musical. He seems to have been a late starter in sex, in spite of Kansas City, where he first worked, having Twelfth Street so full of prostitutes that it was known as Woodrow Wilson Avenue, because you could get 'a piece [peace] at any price'.

Hemingway arrived in the Heroic Age of Paris expatriates with introductions to all the most go-ahead in the world of writing. The result was his classic novel *The Sun Also Rises*.

The Sun Also Rises is Hemingway's sole book in which he takes an interest in other people, while himself, so to speak, participating. Characters like Robert Cohn, Brett Ashley, Mike Campbell, all live. 'To Have and Have Not' or 'Frances Macomber' may be good stories, but their characters can claim none of the earlier novel's intense vitality. This brilliant promise was never truly fulfilled. One cannot help attributing the fact not to any lack of intensity in pondering the words he set down – in certain respects Hemingway always remained a hard-working stylist – but to the gnawing desire to build himself up into an Homeric figure.

Burgess justly excoriates Hemingway for his behaviour in the Second World War. No one doubts Hemingway's bravery; the point is that, having received an assignment as a newspaper correspondent, he collected a kind of private army, which only added to the confusion of the campaign.

He was charged with this and 'impeding the orderly advance of the official forces by acting like one of the personages of his own fiction', but swearing that he had not hidden his non-combatant insignia and otherwise acted in contravention of the Berne Convention, he was white-washed, even shamefully given a decoration. He never forgave the French general Leclerc, a real soldier, for treating him as an impertinent journalist, always referring to 'that jerk Leclerc'.

It is significant that Hemingway's most satisfying work among his latest publications is *A Moveable Feast*. These Paris memoirs, which appeared posthumously, were founded on notes made by Hemingway and rediscovered in the 1950s. They belonged to an earlier, uncorrupted period of his writing.

I demur at only one of Burgess's critical judgments, his admiration for *The Old Man and the Sea*, a story which seems to me sententious and self-parodying.

What went wrong? Burgess offers some suggestions. There must have been moments of doubt between pursuing the virility myth (especially when that showed signs of falling short) and the youthful ideal of total artistic dedication. Besides, says Burgess: 'With fame, anyway, any kind of sense of recognised achievement, the incursion of a chronic melancholy may be expected, expressible as a death urge.' Just an occupational hazard could have done it.

Ernest Hemingway and His World   1976
Anthony Burgess, Thames &   *Daily Telegraph*
Hudson.

V

'Jesus Christ some time I'd like to grow up,' wrote Ernest Hemingway (then aged twenty-six) to Scott Fitzgerald in December 1925. Traversing the 921 pages of these Letters the reader often profoundly echoes that wish.

There are even moments when one wonders whether any writer ever possessed a more tedious and disagreeable personality; then Hemingway says something that makes you laugh; expresses a deep truth about writing itself; is understanding with his children; thereby revealing how people could put up with him – though by no means everybody could.

Hemingway is lucky in having had an admirable biographer in Carlos Baker, who edits the Letters with equal dexterity. They do, I think, add something to knowledge of the man himself in a way that can never quite be conveyed in a book; although their interest is very hit-or-miss. When Hemingway is being to some extent consciously serious – to Bernard Berenson, for instance – he is far from at his best.

By the time the remark quoted at the opening of this review was made Hemingway was on the point of establishing himself as one of the most influential writers in English of his generation. Early success can notoriously create difficulties for a writer. Hemingway's temperament was not one to lessen these. Kipling might be world famous at the age of twenty-four, but Kipling never ran out of steam. Something went wrong with Hemingway in his late thirties. The watershed between on the whole good and (excluding *A Moveable Feast*) relatively bad writing seems to have dated from taking part as a journalist in the Spanish Civil War, together with the break-up of his second marriage.

The Letters well indicate Hemingway's nervous tensions, which get steadily worse as the collection progresses in time. The terrible, ever growing elephantiasis of personality is something that could not possibly do any good to a writer. It was not that Hemingway was 'bogus' in the sense that he was not brave, not good at boxing, fishing, shooting, sailing, bullfighting, drinking, but that these things had nothing to do with his abilities as a writer. In his saner moments he states this himself in so many words.

Hemingway seems to me most regrettably at his worst during the Second World War. His letters on the subject reflect his most deplorable side, and swashbuckling actions contributed nothing to his future books. After the war, terrible deadness begins to be felt. None the less, that Hemingway was an impressive writer is not for a moment to be denied; indeed his unremitting application was in one sense an obstruction to all his later writing. A little more humour about himself might have helped.

The most interesting letters here are those to Scott Fitzgerald and various members of the Scribner firm, the publisher both writers had in common. The mutual feelings of Hemingway and Fitzgerald were like nothing else in the lives of either of them: admiration; contempt; love; hatred; envy – perhaps in both cases a certain gratitude even. Hemingway lived longer and therefore had the last word. Oddly enough he repeats more than once here that he thought (after at first running the novel down) that *Tender is the Night* was a better book than *The Great Gatsby*.

The letters to Max Perkins and the Charles Scribners themselves, father and son, contain much that is worth reading. Hemingway was keen on the business side of being an author, which gives a backbone to the letters, often missing when he is merely wise-cracking. At the same time, when writing to Perkins and the Scribners he mixes in a good deal of amusing gossip about his own current life.

Although Hemingway will quite often praise other writers it is rare for him not to go back on this in some way, and his stories about them always take an absolutely stylized form. Again and again he will tell the same anecdote about Gertrude Stein (he astonishes by saying, apparently seriously, that when he first knew her he would have liked to sleep with her), and about Fitzgerald, Dos Passos, or anyone else he often came across. There is rarely if ever any variation or additional material in the story.

To Fitzgerald (4 September 1929) he makes the very true comment about novel writing: 'The good parts of a book may be something a writer is lucky enough to overhear or it may be the wreck of his whole damn life – and one is as good as the other.'

After writing unexpectedly agreeable letters to Arthur Mizener when Mizener was engaged on the Fitzgerald biography, *The Far Side of Paradise* (1952), he then rounds on him for allegedly saying things he should not have done about Fitzgerald, though Mizener might be thought to have accomplished that difficult assignment with remarkable tact.

In the notes, probably due to a typographical error, Duff Twysden appears as née Byrom rather than Smurthwaite; and, if not too late, one must put in a plea for 'befriend' having a sense of favour or condescension, not just meaning 'to be friends with'.

Ernest Hemingway: Selected   1981
Letters; 1917–1961, Carlos Baker,   *Daily Telegraph*
ed., Granada.

VI

Ernest Hemingway has been worked over fairly closely. His factotum, A. E. Hotchner, provided some piquant close-ups, and Carlos Baker's biography was tactful without undue discretion. Those two books appeared when Hemingway's reputation was somewhat in decline (more, I think, in the US than here, where he had never been a popular hero in the same way), and there is room for Jeffrey Meyers's full and sober reassessment.

Hemingway's life is peculiarly difficult to separate from his works, because so much of the latter was not only straight autobiography, it also took the reader by the throat in insisting that only by drinking, fighting, boxing, bullfighting, and so on, could a man find salvation. Nevertheless Hemingway remains a dominating literary figure. He was a classic by the time he was twenty-six; all the same Jeffrey Meyers sagely remarks that 'though mature in his youth, Hemingway often seems adolescent in middle age'. Meyers deals more fully than Carlos Baker with the latter part of Hemingway's life. He certainly does not beautify the picture.

One is prepared to believe that Hemingway could put over a great deal of charm, was what is called 'a leader of men' (he was never without a court of toadies), possessed a real inner intelligence; and that individuals could meet him at moments and be struck only by his unassuming good sense. This did not prevent his awfulness as a man wrecking his own writing.

Meyers (though he admits Hemingway totally misjudged the situation in Cuba) tries to make a case for Hemingway having some political grasp, but at no stage does Hemingway appear to have understood that, had the Communists taken over during the Spanish Civil War, which might easily have happened, German troops would have had access to Spain during the period of the Nazi–Soviet Pact. Orwell, a far more serious combatant in the war than Hemingway, saw that.

All these things might be unimportant enough had they not had such a deleterious effect on Hemingway as a writer. *Pace* Meyers, who finds a good deal to be said for the Spanish Civil War novel *For Whom the Bell Tolls* (1940), it seems to me the essence of the blockbusting middlebrow Book Club bestseller. No doubt there are goodish passages, but it is the essence of that kind of popular work to possess a few scattered merits that make it readable. One has only to compare a page with *The Sun Also Rises*, or *A Farewell to Arms*, to see what a falling off has taken place.

Jeffrey Meyers is, however, admirably sound on *The Old Man and the Sea* (1952). After the disaster of *Across the River and Into the Trees* (1950), which all the critics had panned, the whole lot of them went down like a row of ninepins in praise of this pretentious little fable. Perhaps they were honourably anxious to reinstate a great writer which Hemingway at his best certainly is. Meyers lists among the novella's gems 'the setting of the sun is a difficult time for all fish' and 'the ocean is very big and a skiff is small.'

The filming of *The Old Man and the Sea* was a problem. No fish big enough could be caught, so at great expense a twenty-foot long artificial fish was created, with internal motors which moved its eyes, mouth and fins (did it say 'Papa'?) The first time it was tried in the sea off Havana, it sank to the bottom. Never mind. *The Old Man and the Sea*, with its fake simplicity and moral uplift, has rather justly settled down to earn $100,000 a year as a textbook for school children learning English.

As the tragic end of his life drew near, Hemingway was obsessed by the anxiety that he was being shadowed by agents of the Federal Bureau of Investigation. This was naturally regarded as a comparatively common form of persecution-mania. Jeffrey Meyers shows that, in fact, it was perfectly true. He was being tailed. During the war Hemingway, with characteristic vanity, had set up his own spy-network in Cuba, thereby displeasing the Head of the Secret Service, who in consequence kept tabs on him.

One hesitates to dish up the fallibilities of a writer one so greatly admires for his early work, but Hemingway was so disagreeable about everyone else, including his greatest friends, that he must be held to deserve all he gets. Meanwhile, I re-read *The Sun Also Rises* about a year ago, and am prepared to do so again in, say, six months' time.

Hemingway: A Biography, Jeffrey
Meyers, Macmillan.

1986
Daily Telegraph

GERTRUDE STEIN

'Gertrude Stein's prose-song is a cold, black suet-pudding,' wrote Wyndham Lewis; 'we can represent it as cold suet-roll of fabulously reptilian length. Cut it at any point, it is the same thing; the same heavy, sticky, opaque mass all through, and all along.'

On the other hand, a little more than a year after their first meeting, Ernest Hemingway wrote to Gertrude Stein 'It was a vital day for me when I stumbled upon you.'

One could go on endlessly quoting diametrically opposed opinions about Gertrude Stein. It is one of the merits of John Malcolm Brinnin's book that he does not content himself with doing that, but makes an immense, an almost successful, effort to resolve the whole problem of her writing. No one who read his *Dylan Thomas in America* could doubt Brinnin's own powerful, at times rather uncomfortable, intelligence. Here it is put to a severe test and emerges with flying colours.

Gertrude Stein was born in 1874 into a fairly prosperous American family of German-Jewish origin. The account given here of the life of the Steins in their early days is enjoyable. Her brother Leo and Gertrude emerge as the two dominating personalities. They both settled in Paris in 1903 to work away at the arts.

It may well be asked, 'What arts?' – a question not so easy to answer. In this connection Leo Stein emerges as a comic figure of colossal proportions – and, like all truly comic types, a deeply tragic figure, too. Leo could not make up his mind whether he was to be a great writer or a great painter. All he knew was that he was a genius. He would hold forth on the arts interminably in their salon.

A friend wrote of him: 'He seemed to need constant reinforcement of his ego, in order to be certain that all was well with the world and that God was in his heaven.' Of his sister, with whom he was finally on bad terms, Leo wrote: 'Gertrude and I are just the contrary. She is basically stupid and I'm basically intelligent.' If a film is ever made of the Gertrude Stein story – and why not? – one feels irresistibly that Leo Stein should be played by Groucho Marx.

However, to get back to Gertrude in Paris in the early 1900s, she and her brother were among the first patrons of Picasso, Matisse, Braque and the school of painting subsequently to be called Cubist. Characteristically, Leo Stein, having shown himself one of the most brilliant connoisseurs of modern art between 1905–7, then turned to violent disapproval.

Meanwhile, Gertrude, whose education had been directed towards philosophy and psychology in her university days under William James, was hard at work. Brinnin writes, with perspicacity: 'Once a particular set of conditions were present, her arrival was inevitable – like an event in chemistry.' He sees that Gertrude Stein was not, in one sense, a 'modern' figure. She was the last stuttering of the Enlightenment.

> She believed exclusively in the power and efficacy of the rational mind when all of her major contemporaries in art and literature were examining with fascination the power of the non-rational as a course of aesthetic communication.

Gertrude Stein's first novel, a story of the emotional relationship of three young women, written when she was twenty-nine, was rediscovered only in 1932. Brinnin can be trusted when he speaks of 'its excellence as an example of conventional fiction'. This manuscript was put away, apparently at the instigation of her brother Leo. She then decided to produce prose that was to be, to previous writing, what Cubism was to previous painting.

To explain this is a big proposition; but, very briefly, the Cubists believed that painting was not 'to try and *reconstitute* an anecdotal fact, but to *constitute* a pictorial fact'. Put another way, Cubism was 'the art of painting new structures borrowed not from the reality of sight, but from the reality of insight'.

This perhaps takes a bit of grasping. It may, or may not, be a mistaken approach; but is patently not the 'rubbish' that it was immediately proclaimed to be. The theory is at least worth considering. However, many people refused to consider it. We learn here, for example, of one lady in Boston who fainted in front of a Cubist picture, and smashed to pieces in her fall a bust of Baudelaire.

Gertrude Stein set out to make literature a matter of immediate sensation, free from history and anecdote, by the impact of words used in a new manner designed to force attention. Her contention was that if you wrote 'a rose is pink,' the phrase had been used so often before that the reader's mind no longer reacted to it. If, on the other hand, you wrote 'Rose is a rose is a rose is a rose' (from which this book takes its title), you obtained a far keener sense of the rose's pinkness. This is, of course, a very crude manner of explaining her method, which is set out with great skill, good sense, and total absence of bigotry by John Brinnin.

Towards the end of her life Gertrude Stein began to write in a manner intelligible to a wider public. Publicity laid its wreaths at her feet, and she revelled in these tinselled garlands. After refusing to consider the possibility of war until the moment of its outbreak in 1939, she approved of Pétain, showed courage in refusing to leave France, and, when American troops finally arrived in her neighbourhood, was overcome with Uncle Sam patriotism.

The Autobiography of Alice B. Toklas, and Gertrude Stein's other 'popular' books, are commonplace, arch, and tedious to a degree. Her insufferably patronizing attitude towards all she writes of – a manner which chronically permeates all her work – is symptomatic of a megalomaniac egotism.

This egotism prevented her from truly examining human relationships and becoming the great artist she aspired to be. Without that handicap, her gifts might have brought her close. Her 'experimental' works are of considerable interest to professional writers, although I suspect they have done more harm than good in America.

Gertrude Stein, to use one of her own phrases, was a 'personality saint'. She charmed many people – and many intelligent and gifted people – who met her. 'She felt what she felt and she did what she did and she worked.'

The Third Rose: Gertrude Stein and Her World, John Malcolm Brinnin, Weidenfeld & Nicolson.

1960
Daily Telegraph

ALICE B. TOKLAS AND
MORLEY CALLAGHAN

Alice B. Toklas was born and brought up in California. The earliest author she met when she was a child was General Lew Wallace, American Ambassador to Turkey, who wrote *Ben Hur*. Her family was of Polish extraction, and when her father first saw his daughter walking with the Stein family he later said: 'Who did you say was the German memorial monument you were with today?'

What is Remembered falls, so to speak, into three periods. The first is that heroic age before the First World War, when Miss Stein and Miss Toklas hobnobbed with Picasso, Matisse, Apollinaire, and all that emergent Paris world of the new approach to painting and writing.

During the war the two ladies worked hard doing things like distributing Red Cross supplies. When peace came the second period began, less heroic than the first, but nevertheless of considerable interest, still closely connected with the painters and post-war movements, and also with American writers like Hemingway and Fitzgerald.

This gradually gives place to a third period, with more English affiliations, mainly social, although of course no less associated with the arts, notably now the ballet. By this time the field of operation had greatly widened from the early Paris days, even though it was less striking in its pioneer work.

This orthodox aspect of Alice Toklas's autobiography seems worth mentioning, because it so much reflects the general tendency of the first forty years of the twentieth century, that is to say the respectable establishment of what first appeared to be the wild paradoxes of the Modern Movement, then the gradual absorption of those concerned into one form or another of fashionable life.

One cannot agree from the photograph which Alice Toklas supplies that 'Marie Laurencin was in those early days plain.' Again, Apollinaire volunteered as a *driver* in the French artillery, of course, not an *officer* – he later became an officer in the infantry.

There is a good account of the famous dinner given by Picasso and others for the Douanier Rousseau, at the end of which Rousseau took his violin from its case and played 'endless dull music'. Later Alice Toklas was asked if she would sing the national song of the Red Indians.

241

The scene of Morley Callaghan's *That Summer in Paris* is set during what has been defined above as the second heroic period. Indeed, it represents what might be looked on as the extreme end of it, when there was still much to be seen that was of interest, but things were already taking a new shape.

Morley Callaghan, novelist and author of some notable short stories, a Canadian, had been friends with Hemingway when they had worked on the same Toronto paper. The title of his book exactly describes what it is about, that is to say a few months in Paris in 1928. The theme is, as the sub-title puts it, *Memories of Tangled Friendships with Hemingway, Fitzgerald and Others*. A great many people are worked into the picture, and the final result is well worth reading.

It would be totally unfair to Callaghan to suggest that his book is built up round one incident, but there can be no doubt that the high spot is the moment when he boxed with Hemingway, Scott Fitzgerald keeping time, and, owing to Fitzgerald being carried away by the fascination of the scene, the round went on unchecked, and Hemingway was knocked out.

This Dostoevskyan incident caused a lot of later trouble. An enjoyable literary competition might be to decide who would be the funniest trio of English or French authors to have acted out a similar drama with the gloves.

Morley Callaghan is modest to a fault. He was visiting Paris with his wife, newly married, and his effective, economical style gives a very good account of their experiences there. One has the feeling that, although blissfully happy, he looked a little wistfully at all the dubious behaviour going on round – which adds a charm to the book. It should, by the way, have had an index, because a great many persons are mentioned to whom one might want to refer again for Morley Callaghan's opinion.

What is Remembered, Alice B. Toklas, Michael Joseph.
That Summer in Paris, Morley Callaghan, MacGibbon & Kee.

1963
Daily Telegraph

AMERICAN BOOKSELLERS AND PUBLISHERS IN PARIS

Sylvia Beach, offspring of nine generations of American Presbyterian clergymen, set her heart when young on opening a bookshop in Paris. She brought off this ambition in 1919. The shop was named 'Shakespeare and Company'. Business began in the rue Duputren, but moved later to 12 rue de l'Odéon, where the place became one of the landmarks of Left-Bank Paris.

Shakespeare and Company almost immediately developed into a kind of club through which the writers of the period – expatriate American, French and, to a somewhat lesser degree, English – inevitably passed at one time or another. However, the concern which brought Sylvia Beach her chief fame, and of which she herself remained most proud, was the publication of James Joyce's *Ulysses*, and its distribution in early days when, even in France, there was doubt whether the authorities might not take a prudish line about some of the contents. The many remarkable people Sylvia Beach ran across are seen here through rose-coloured spectacles; for example, Joyce himself is described as 'extremely scrupulous in money matters', a characteristic hardly confirmed by Richard Ellman's biography. However, even if Paris intellectual life of the 1920s is presented without some of its warts, there remains a lot of acceptable information.

Peter Arno, in the *New Yorker*, once drew a picture of a middle-aged American lady asking a down-at-heel bookseller on the Quais: 'Avez-vous *Ulysses*?'; and there can be no doubt that a lot of the excitement stimulated by Joyce's book was of a non-literary kind.

Accordingly, efforts were made to persuade Sylvia Beach to publish D. H. Lawrence's *Lady Chatterley's Lover*. She remarks – and many will heartily agree – that she found this novel 'the least interesting of its author's productions'. She did not want to get a reputation for publishing books just because they were regarded by the unenlightened as something 'rather spicy'; nor did she have the capital to risk.

It is interesting to note that, although their names are now often coupled together as the two most considerable novelists of their period, Joyce and Lawrence had in fact no high opinion of each other's work.

Sylvia Beach, in spite of a certain outward primness required by those who traffic in serious literary works regarded as too outspoken by the puritanical, can also see the funny side of her profession. When Frank Harris was in a hurry to catch a train, she sold him a two-volume edition of Louisa Alcott's *Little Women*, allowing him to suppose it to be a translation from the French of the most daring sort. The Magician's name, by the way (whose Memoirs were also submitted to Shakespeare and Company), was Aleister, not 'Aleicester' Crowley.

Hugh Ford found some new angles to explore (Joyce does not emerge with enormous credit in the author/publisher relationship), but, as in the case of Gertrude Stein and Ezra Pound, a certain feeling of weariness comes over the reader at the thought of having to hear all these sagas again, even if told in a new way.

Soon, however, the well known names are left behind – or only crop up intermittently – Ford devoting far the greater part of his investigation to the many small publishing companies of Paris, mostly American, occasionally British, that functioned between the wars. They were run by a truly extraordinary crew of amateurs and enthusiasts. These are well worth reading about. Ford treats them as they should be treated, in a scholarly manner where business detail is concerned, but with not too great solemnity when it comes to examining personalities.

Among these Robert McAlmon deserves a high place. McAlmon – when in the vein, a bore altogether unsurpassed, as many bear witness – possessed also a certain amount of money.

Born in Kansas, tenth son of a minister, in 1920 he married 'Bryher' (known for her historical novels written under that name), daughter of the rich shipping tycoon Sir John Ellerman. He is in some ways the embodiment of 'the Quarter', more typical than those of greater fame who lived that life for a time, then lived quite another one. Remove the Dôme and the Select, the Boeuf sur le Toit and the Jockey, the Dingo and the Deux Magots, and there is little of McAlmon left.

The point of McAlmon was that, although far from universally popular, he 'knew everyone'. He helped type the latter part of *Ulysses*, carried Joyce upstairs when dead drunk, went on one of the bull-fighting trips to Spain later depicted in *The Sun Also Rises*, was praised by Ezra Pound, met George Moore, Frank Harris, Yeats and found them all wanting. T. S. Eliot wrote him an interesting letter; Wyndham Lewis hobnobbed with him; Hemingway (a much more powerful man) knocked him down. Scott Fitzgerald, Cocteau, Picabia, Brancusi . . . the roll-call is unending.

His autobiography *Being Geniuses Together* was first published in 1938, an odd mixture of anecdote, *obiter dicta* and literary judgment, most of the latter badly damaged by the passing of the years. Of McAlmon's other writings, *Grim Fairy Tale* (homosexual Berlin) is probably the best. *Being Geniuses Together*, in many ways exasperating, also expresses as no other book the naïvety, impatience, enthusiasm, violence, generosity, seediness, melancholy, all so characteristic of that aspect of American life in exile.

But here's the rub. *Being Geniuses Together* is 'revised and with supplementary chapters by Kay Boyle'. What has in fact happened is that McAlmon's book has been divided up into short sections, interspersed with autobiographical chunks of about the same length by Kay Boyle. One absolutely gasps. Admittedly Kay Boyle is a well-known American writer, lived in France at the same time as McAlmon and was latterly a close friend of his. That surely does not include the right to chop up his book and superimpose her own?

Being Geniuses Together may not have been the greatest autobiography ever written, but it has at least a funny title. So far as it went, it could be read from cover to cover as a coherent whole. Now it is reduced to snippets that totally lose the flow of breathless irritability that animated the original.

There is also evidence of efforts to clean it up, present McAlmon with less of his own innate absurdity. That is to lose the whole point of him. For example, the enjoyable story is omitted of Sir John Ellerman asking two distinguished English literary men to meet his son-in-law, when McAlmon got so drunk at the dinner-table that he kept on saying Kelly and Sheets, when he meant Shelley and Keats.

I have personally no axe to grind. I met Bob McAlmon in London for a minute or two perhaps a couple of times. It merely seems a shame to maul his book about. Besides Kay Boyle has herself a story to tell. This is not at all a satisfactory way to tell it. She married a Frenchman, lived in frightful poverty for a time, did not know who was the father of her baby, worked away to become a writer, met a lot of people. The facts in themselves possess interest. It is just that her deadly serious, carefully written account of her doings requires constant changes of gear from the absolutely different McAlmon story. Justice is done to neither.

McAlmon's 'printery' (as Hugh Ford well designates these freaks of publishing) was called the Contact Publishing Company, and, among other things, issued Gertrude Stein's *The Making of Americans*. This work was more than half a million words long, and Ford Madox Ford was conned into taking it on for the *Transatlantic Review* without knowing its vast length.

McAlmon himself wrote huge slabs of supposedly naturalistic prose, from which it was alleged that Hemingway had learnt something. If so, Hemingway's modification of McAlmon's style was a decided improvement. After his divorce McAlmon was known among his friends as 'McAlimony'.

In the last resort McAlmon was rather a sad figure. He is to be respected for knowing that. A friend remarked that he had 'a genius for life'. McAlmon, commenting on this, wrote: 'If absolute despair, a capacity for reckless abandon and drink, long and heavy spells of ennui which require bottles of strong drink to cure, and a gregarious but not altogether loving nature is "a genius for life", then I have it.' An unrecorded poet, quoted in his book, wrote:

> I'd rather live in Oregon and pack Salmon,
> Than live in Nice and write like Robert McAlmon.

After trying Mexico, Munich, Berlin, Majorca, Barcelona, Strasbourg, Texas, Los Angeles and Paris again, he was given a job by his brothers in their Southwest Surgical Supply Co., as a travelling salesman marketing trusses in the Arizona desert. Sufferers from hernia down in Arizona must have had yet more to bear. He died, it appears, in California. One wonders whether he survived well disposed towards a world of Beats, or, quite likely, strongly disapproving of them.

A rather different small Paris publishing house, at the Sign of the Black Manikin, was run by Edward Titus. Titus, an American of Polish origin (settled in New Orleans as a boy), was married to the celebrated queen of cosmetics, Helena Rubinstein. In spite of Titus's wandering eye where ladies other than his wife were concerned, cosmetics subsidized this avant-garde press. That was not because Helena Rubinstein liked avant-garde writers – very much to the contrary. She detested them.

Titus, on the other hand, reserved and pompous, loved only the highest standards in contemporary literature. He once saw a friend carrying a copy of the *Reader's Digest* and overwhelmed him with remonstrances for a week. Titus published *Lady Chatterley's Lover*. D. H. Lawrence found him a 'nice little man . . . shy . . . with a pushy wife'. Titus also published the memoirs of Kiki, the famous Montparnasse tart. Some of the Black Manikin authors are mentioned as staying in Paris at l'Hôtel du Caveau de la Terreur, an establishment that might be said to put its cards on the table.

The ends of some of the main actors in this carnival were suitably macabre. For instance the beautiful model Kiki, painted and mascara'd like a clown in her palmy days, living with the American photographer Man Ray, found herself selling matches and safety-pins on the terrace of the Dôme.

Different again from anything resembling Sylvia Beach or Edward Titus were Harry and Caresse Crosby, who between them ran the Black Sun Press. Crosby and his wife were a couple in the Scott Fitzgerald tradition, good-looking, rich, full of ideals, almost literally worshippers of the sun. As Ford comments, 'a meeting between D. H. Lawrence and Harry Crosby was foreordained'.

Crosby's business correspondence with Lawrence was couched in such high-falutin language that Lawrence thought Crosby wanted to buy a manuscript, rather than commission a book. Lawrence, not backward in high falutin himself, wrote back that he hated to sell manuscripts, but would make an exception in this case for 'as much gold as Crosby' could 'easily spare'. Later this misunderstanding was sorted out, but Crosby continued to consider himself under an obligation to pay literally in gold.

Crosby packed the requisite sum in a 'small square Cartier box', hurried to the Gare de l'Est, where he arrived a few minutes before the departure of the Rome Express. He saw a 'distinguished Englishman' leaning out of a compartment window, and asked him would he mail the box in Florence; adding: 'It's gold for a poet.' When the gold arrived – as rather surprisingly it did – Lawrence said he felt 'almost wicked'. It was in the inevitable tradition that Crosby should take his own life.

British efforts in the Paris publishing line were represented by Nancy Cunard and her black lover, the musician Henry Crowder, who toiled away together setting type at the Hours Press. Among other works they printed was what Norman Douglas described as the 'only meritorious action in my whole life' (dating from his early years in the Foreign Office), *Report on the Pumice-Stone Industry of the Lipari Islands*, eighty copies of which were produced – a good example of Douglas imposing his will.

Another British effort was Jack Kahane's Obelisk Press, the founder of which died in 1939. Kahane's most momentous contribution was to print the early works of Henry Miller. He also issued the first edition of Cyril Connolly's novel *The Rock Pool*, which, he later complained, was a 'disgrace to his list', as it was not obscene at all. These are just a selection from Hugh Ford's tasty Parisian printers' pie.

Harry Crosby was born in 1898 into a patrician American family, living in Boston (though of essentially Boston descent only on his mother's side). His uncle and godfather was the famous banker, John Pierpoint Morgan. All the boys Crosby went to school with had famous American names. Indeed *Black Sun* is particularly recommended to those – including Americans – who suppose that, unlike decadent Europe, the United States is classless and wholly unaristocratic.

Like so many notable Americans of his age group – Hemingway, Cummings, Don Passos – Crosby, at the age of nineteen, joined an ambulance unit, before America came into the First World War, and served in France. He was at Verdun, won a Croix de Guerre, and seems to have done an unpleasant and dangerous job with notable perseverance and bravery. He also learned to speak fluent French. When he returned home he went to Harvard (which provided 21 out of the 150 ambulance volunteers killed).

Crosby did not much like Harvard, but he seems to have been a fairly conventional undergraduate there, even if wilful and rackety. His future began to take shape more clearly when, after an utterly unsuccessful attempt to make him work in his uncle's bank in Paris, he ran away with a married Boston lady somewhat older than himself. She was called Polly (later Caresse) Peabody. The row in Boston about this divorce was terrific.

The Crosbys now resided for the most part in France – though they also travelled fairly extensively – existing in a manner that makes, say, Scott Fitzgerald (who seems not to have abutted on Crosby life) and the Gerald Murphys, tediously humdrum in their drunken exploits and rowdy parties. Crosby not only drank, drugged, compulsively womanized, poured out reams of poetry, but from an early stage was obsessed with death, and in the 1920s arranged for the suicide of his wife and himself to take place in 1942.

None of this would be very interesting, if unaccompanied by other circumstances. For those at all concerned with merely material considerations, the financial side is not to be completely ignored. This sort of life seems to have been carried on with a basic income, not of untold millions, but about £2,500 a year. No doubt gifts, debts, overdrawing at the bank, cranked up that sum. This, of course, represented at least five times the amount many American couples in Paris lived on comfortably enough in those days.

Crosby was evidently one of those persons who exercised a fascination which cannot be preserved on paper. Women clearly fell easily to his charm (he was occasionally bisexual), and even the powerful hold of a private press does not quite explain the many notable writers who got along well with him. His particular brand of mysticism went down well with D. H. Lawrence, even if Lawrence hedged his bets when he agreed to write a preface for Crosby.

T. S. Eliot was careful too, when it came to preface-writing, but he produced something. Hart Crane, a good poet, could beat Crosby at his own game so far as drinking and bad behaviour went. When he came to stay at the Crosbys' smart country cottage (an old mill belonging to the Rochefoucaulds, where Rousseau and Cagliostro had at different times lived), Crane introduced a chimney sweep into his all-white bedroom with disastrous results.

Hemingway seems to have known Crosby (who accompanied him on one of the Spanish bullfighting trips) at a hearty level, which included a good deal of horse-racing as well as drinking. All this literary life was combined with by a great many purely *beau monde* contacts (agreeable to Caresse Crosby), such as entertaining royalty.

At the end of his life at least it seems doubtful whether Crosby could have been called sane. The best to be said of him as a poet seems to me to be that he was not entirely without any sort of talent. Geoffrey

Wolff's use of French names is sometimes a little reckless; 'Montesquieu-Fezensac', surely 'Montesquiou-Fezensac', and 'Cubourg' probably 'Cabourg', while Prince Carageorgovitch (usually spelt with a 'K'), who learnt to fly with Crosby, was a Serb rather than a Russian.

Shakespeare and Company, Sylvia Beach, Faber.
Being Geniuses Together, 1920–1930, Robert McAlmon, revised and with supplementary chapters by Kay Boyle, Michael Joseph.
Published in Paris: American and British Writers, Printers and Publishers in Paris 1920–1939, Hugh Ford, Garnstone Press.
Black Sun: The Brief Transit and Violent Eclipse of Harry Crosby, Geoffrey Wolff, Hamish Hamilton.
Geniuses Together: American Writers in Paris in the 1920s, Humphrey Carpenter, Unwin Hyman.

1960; 1970; 1977; 1987
Daily Telegraph

JOHN DOS PASSOS

John Dos Passos is perhaps not so well known in Great Britain as he should be. This is not entirely inexplicable, for although in a sense nothing could be more 'American' than Fitzgerald or Faulkner, Dos Passos concerned himself largely with particular American social and political problems which may have become part of American history, but by their nature as the years pass are relatively specialized subjects.

He has now produced an autobiography, *The Best Times*, a very accomplished and interesting book. Its quiet style is deceptive. He has had a lot of adventures, which are exciting to read about; he has also known most of his literary contemporaries pretty well, and he can show them in a fresh light.

The son of a successful lawyer of Portuguese origins (of whom he gives an attractive picture), Dos Passos graduated from Harvard in 1916. He served in France and Italy with the Norton-Harjes Volunteer Ambulance Service, almost a required apprenticeship for spirited young American intellectuals during the period before their country came into the war.

Indiscreet to a somewhat lesser degree than E. E. Cummings, who was arrested for what he wrote home, Dos Passos also provoked official disapproval, and had to resign. Later he served in the US Army Medical Corps, where he experienced frightful boredom though his war also included dangerous and harassing duties.

One wonders if there were ever such a collection of romantic-minded young men as those Americans of that generation. The patriotism of this country, however immense, partook of something altogether different. In that connection it is interesting to note that while he was in the army, Dos Passos read, and was obviously impressed by, Vigny's *Servitude et Grandeur Militaires* (1835). Yet he completely misses the point of this book. He asks (in his diary) what would Vigny, with his dragoon uniforms, have thought of the squalor and boredom of modern war? But Vigny's whole point was that a soldier's life was not only dangerous, but boring, squalid, and controlled. That was why Vigny thought it noble. He praised, so to speak, Northern Ireland, not cavalry charges. It was odd that Dos Passos missed this emphasis because he himself was a man of great compassion and 'social conscience', his books in the main devoted to the sufferings of the underdog.

Dos Passos's war experiences are sometimes very funny. He came out of the army on the crest of the wave of the generation who were going to build a New Heaven and a New Earth. He was involved for quite a long time, and in a quite unamateur manner, with bringing about a Marxist revolution. This attitude led to energetic political interests. He was much concerned, for example, with protests in the Sacco and Vanzetti cases, and similar activities. Dos Passos never joined the Communist Party, but for a long time made no secret of regarding himself as a fellow-traveller.

A visit to the USSR in 1928 did not have so drastic an effect in changing Dos Passos's views as a similar trip had on E. E. Cummings. The parting of the ways, so far as Communism and Dos Passos were concerned, was the Spanish Civil War.

He went to Spain (a country he already knew fairly well) in support of the anti-Franco forces, more particularly to collaborate with Hemingway in his propaganda film. There were disagreements with his fellow novelist about the focus of the film, but a much more serious quarrel took place about José Robles, close friend and translator of Dos Passos. Robles, a Spaniard of liberal views, living in America, was visiting Spain when the Civil War broke out. Working at the Ministry of War (with the equivalent rank of lieutenant-colonel), he was arrested, and done away with, by the Communist extra-legal secret police.

Hemingway was prepared to turn a blind eye to Robles's murder, but, from this episode on, the opposition of Dos Passos to Communism became intense. He remained 'on the Left', but by 1937 was writing:

> I have come to believe that the Communist party is fundamentally opposed to our democracy as I see it and that Marxism, though an important basis for the unborn sociological sciences, if held as a dogma, is a reactionary force and an impediment to progress. Fascism is nothing but Marxism inside out and is of course a worse impediment – but the old argument about giving aid and comfort to the enemy is rubbish: free thought can't possibly give aid and comfort to fascism . . . I now think that foreign liberals and radicals were very wrong not to protest against the Russian terror all down the line.

So strongly did Dos Passos ultimately feel about the successful methods of Communist infiltration that – although he disapproved of the ineptitude of 'unAmerican activities committees' – he refused to sign protests, as it was 'just as much part of Stalin's machine for world conquest . . . to capture the movie industry for Moscow purposes and especially to keep out any writers whom they suspected of working honestly from an American point of view'.

Dos Passos also had amusing adventures in the Middle East, travelling by caravan and being attacked on more than one occasion by bandits. He was informed by a French consul that the British had decided to murder him.

Arriving home from his travels when already an established writer, Dos Passos found a play of his had been staged in New York while he was away. Feeling it would be too much of an embarrassment to explain who he was, he simply bought a ticket at the box-office and waited for the curtain to go up. This is, I suspect, a rather characteristic incident, one of the reasons why people who read him superficially may miss some of his good points.

Cummings and Fitzgerald come to life in his hands. Dos Passos used to stay with the Hemingways at Key West, and is particularly good in describing the moment when Hemingway became a little too aware that he was a great man.

A bust had been made of Hemingway – not of the best sculpture, Dos Passos assures us – and placed in a prominent position in the hall. Dos Passos used to put his Panama hat on it, which did not go down at all well with his host.

Dos Passos remained hard-up all his life, in spite of a considerable reputation as a writer. His literary views are always of interest, strongly held and individual. The Letters are perhaps his best memorial.

The Best Times: An Informal Memoir, John Dos Passos, Deutsch.
The Fourteenth Chronicle: Letters and Diaries of John Dos Passos, Townsend Ludington, ed., Deutsch.

1968; 1974
Daily Telegraph

JAMES THURBER

James Thurber stands alone in his own sphere of humour. I had no idea of the tribulations he suffered, though his work would certainly suggest that he knew a good deal about the painful aspects of life.

Thurber (1894–1961) was the son of a not very successful public official, one perhaps to be thought of over here as having a job in local administration, with the additional hazard of losing it during a change of government. There was a history of eccentricity (coming within hail of madness) on both sides of the family.

At the age of seven, Thurber lost an eye in an accident playing a game with his brothers. The inept medical handling of this mishap eventually resulted in his all but total blindness in middle age. As a boy, and young man, Thurber was neurotic, poor, unhappy, just able to keep afloat as a struggling journalist. This was pretty well his position until his early thirties.

The gradual building up of Thurber's success – which was associated with the, at first, equally struggling *New Yorker* magazine – is an interesting story. It ended by his becoming one of the great figures in writing (and drawing) of a generation in the United States that produced Scott Fitzgerald, Hemingway, Cummings, and several others; hardly one of whom was not galvanized by the experience of war-time or immediately post-war Paris.

Thurber was of too low a medical category to be in the army, but he arrived in France as a cipher clerk – the mysterious word-symbols of ciphering fascinating him to the end of his days. The appointment was typically Thurberian: Col House (Woodrow Wilson's chief of staff, then quite a famous figure) had cabled the State Department for a dozen code-*books*; the word had been misread as code-*clerks*.

Thurber, when success came, was taken to the heart of the United Kingdom scarcely less than in his own country. In America he is sometimes spoken of as the greatest humourist since Mark Twain, but Thurber is, of course, a writer utterly different in sensibility and character from Twain, having more in common with Edward Lear and other creators of purely surrealist Nonsense.

Thurber wrote a great many amusing pieces, and his 'Walter Mitty' nailed down a type of daydreaming that has given an easily expressed definition even to professional psychiatrists. Thurber thought far less of his drawings than his writing – the drawings first appeared through the enthusiasm of friends, rather than of Thurber himself. He would dash them off in a few minutes. Some people (myself among them) find these drawings his strongest claim to be an original genius.

When success came, Thurber's troubles were far from at an end. His first marriage was not happy, and although his second wife behaved in a manner that can only be described as heroic, drunkennesss, rows with friends, and rather sordid infidelities, made him a difficult husband.

In this last field, a single incident will suffice. Thurber, although blind, was having an affair with one of the *New Yorker* secretaries. An eighteen-year-old office boy would take him to the lady's flat. Thurber could undress himself, but the office boy had to dress him. As Mrs Thurber dressed him in the morning, she naturally noticed, when he came home, that his clothes looked different; particularly that his socks were inside out. Thurber was very cross with the office boy, who happened to be the young Truman Capote, in due course author of *Other Voices, Other Rooms*, and so on.

During the 1930s, Thurber was somewhat alienated from several of his writer-friends, who were adopting extremely left-wing views. Thurber at once grasped the fear and hatred of humour felt by Marxists as perhaps their ideology's greatest enemy. He expresses an aspect of what was happening round him in one of his letters to his friend (and collaborator in 'Is Sex Necessary?'), E. B. White:

> This is one of the greatest menaces there is: people with intelligence deciding that the point is to become grim grey and intense and unhappy and tiresome because the world and many of its people are in a bad way. It's a form of egotism, a supreme form. I've toyed with it myself and understand it a little. It's as dangerous as toying with a drug.

Although Burton Bernstein (another *New Yorker* writer) has done a first-rate job, and gives plenty of instances of Thurber being nice and entertaining, as well as odious and boring, the latter characteristics inevitably somewhat dominate the book. It is, therefore, perhaps permissible for me to say a word about my own Life with Thurber.

Let me begin by paying tribute to Herschel Brickell, the American critic (at Holt's, the New York publisher, he took on my first book in 1931), who seems to have been the first to make a serious effort to get Thurber published. In 1938, I met Thurber at a party in London. He and his (second) wife subsequently lunched with us. No one could have been a more charming guest. He drank possibly a shade more than most at luncheon, stayed a shade later, and left behind him a tiny drawing of one of his famous dogs.

Years after, we met again at the *Punch* 'table' in 1958. By then Thurber was blind. Those present were led up to him one by one. It is impossible to express how immediately he took in and gaily replied to the word or two of explanation as to our having met twenty years before. His method of dealing with the problem of eating was also masterly. He would lightly touch the contours of his plate; then no one present could have guessed for a moment that he was blind. Thurber at his best deserves personal recording.

One final vignette: during Thurber's worst periods of illness and gloom, his mind was always working round his obsession with words. This sometimes took the form of inventing palindromes. Burton Bernstein gives an example: '*The noon sex alert relaxes no one. HT.*'

Thurber: A Biography, Burton   1975
Bernstein, Gollancz.   *Daily Telegraph*

DASHIELL HAMMETT

Photographs of Dashiell Hammett suggest a strong element of narcissism. Hammett's drinking and his compulsive womanizing seem to bear out that diagnosis.

Dashiell Hammett (1894–1961) was a Southerner of impoverished but eighteenth-century stock on both sides. He revolutionized the detective novel, in relation to which he might be described as at the more respectable end of the school attacked by Orwell in his essay 'Raffles and Miss Blandish' for its sadistic violence. In Hammett violence can be sadistic, but the writing is in general accomplished.

Hammett was just old enough to be a soldier for a short time in 1918, when his tubercular condition made itself known. In hospital he met the nurse he subsequently married, who remained his wife for many years, behaving extremely well under always trying conditions. On leaving the army Hammett got a job in the Pinkerton National Detective Agency, thereby acquiring what must be unusual qualifications among writers of detective fiction.

The Pinkerton job took Hammett to San Francisco where at one moment he was employed (for the defence) in the Fatty Arbuckle case, when the obese (and extremely funny) actor suffered unjust accusations of rape, which wrecked his screen life. Hammett left Pinkerton's for an advertising post with a jewellery firm. All the time he was doing odd bits of journalism, trying to write poems and short stories.

Hammett had no objection either to being a detective or an ad-man, except that neither brought in much money. In his early thirties there were signs that he was going to make a success of writing, so he packed his wife and children off to Los Angeles (already having an eye on the movies), and went himself to New York. It is notable that Hammett, after leaving San Francisco, was never to replenish the material necessary to a novelist.

Dashiell Hammett's best novels are *The Maltese Falcon* (1930), *The Glass Key* (1931), and *The Thin Man* (1934). After the last of these he never wrote another novel, though he was to live for twenty-seven more years. What happened? Why did his experience cease to have any bearing on his writing?

At one moment Hammett was among the dozen highest-paid writers in Hollywood, and he clearly moved effortlessly into the world of the most publicized stars. There, no doubt, the rot set in. He had always drunk hard, and possessed a taste for prostitutes, as well as casual affairs.

We are given here a macabre account by his secretary (a young married woman doing the job through studio influence) of Hammett lying inertly in bed for weeks at a time, the monotony of the ceaseless playing of *Parlez-Moi d'Amour* broken only by intermittent visits from ladies, usually black or oriental, from the celebrated local establishment of Madame Lee Francis.

Hammett had always taken an interest in left-wing politics, and the Hollywood Section of the Communist Party was founded in his house. Diane Johnson suggests that, although always a Marxist, Hammett did not always accept Communist Party discipline. But until 1941, when Hitler invaded his Soviet ally, the League of American Writers, of which Hammett was President, accepted the official view of the Communist Party that the war was a 'pro-fascist imperialist' struggle.

In 1942, however, when the Communist volte-face had taken place, Hammett, although forty-eight, managed to get enlisted by the army where a dentist removed all his teeth. ('There is a man in my barracks called Edward Extract, but I don't think that is what I am depressed about.') He was sent to the Aleutian Islands off Alaska, where in due course he edited a paper for the American troops. Even then, only Russian victories were reported. When a visiting officer asked the reason Hammett replied: 'This paper does not take advertising.'

Not surprisingly, after the war there was trouble under Senator Joseph McCarthy's régime. Hammett, in 1951, was sent to prison for six months for contempt of court. It does not seem to have been too bad. Most of the inmates actively liked being inside, though the hillbillies were unfamiliar with the use of a lavatory with a seat. When Hammett was given the prison intelligence test he impressed everybody (I am impressed myself) by being able to divide fractions.

This was undoubtedly a regrettable interlude in United States history. Examples are given of Hammett's interrogations. They resemble nothing so much as political trials in Communist countries. There is naturally a certain irony in Hammett's conduct being based on his firm belief in a freedom that no Communist government would ever dream of according. Indeed, by the Communist standards, which he himself had certainly at times advocated, he was hardly punished at all.

It must be added that his offence was the purest non-political legal one of refusing to give information about persons for whom he had stood bail, and then had skipped. It should also perhaps be borne in mind that 1951 was the Burgess-and-Maclean year – an example of too little attention being paid to matters that in the United States were receiving too much.

A very readable, if on the whole melancholy, story, as Hammett died existing on the charity of friends.

The Life of Dashiell Hammett,   1984
Diane Johnson, Chatto.   *Daily Telegraph*

NATHANAEL WEST

In 1933, I recommended Nathanael West's *Miss Lonelyhearts* to the publishing firm for which I was working. They did not do it, but the gesture absolves me from any suggestion of unfriendliness towards West's writing, which, long underrated, now seems to me to be accorded rather too high a place by admirers. All I suggest is that West (who, after all, died when he was only thirty-seven), in spite of undoubted talent and originality, is not really in the Fitzgerald-Hemingway class, and I don't think would ever have achieved that. In certain respects this makes his story at times even more remarkable as a record.

Nathanael West (1903–40) was grandson of a Russian Jew named Weinstein who had emigrated to America. His father was a reasonably successful building contractor, and West had a university education. He turned out to be a classic case of the young man who 'wants to write'. Jay Martin gives a good account of this early stage, not an easy thing to do.

West's family stood him three months in Paris, where the great days of American expatriate life were already pretty well over. In any case West did not find it too easy to get on with professional 'intellectuals'. He returned to New York, where the Depression was well under way. As a vocation he took on being night-manager of a fairly seedy hotel, a job he did conscientiously, and one that offered certain vantage points for a potential novelist.

Although, as Martin allows, West possessed a 'considerable reservoir of self-pity', there can be no doubt that throughout his short life he suffered dreadful blows of ill fortune. *Miss Lonelyhearts*, his most original work, if not necessarily his best, received excellent reviews, but the publisher went bankrupt, so the printer would not release copies of the novel.

'Miss Lonelyhearts' is a male journalist who writes an advice column for persons with emotional problems. These problems are naturally harrowing enough, and his involvement in them leads in due course to the columnist's own murder. The poignancy of the book is that West was perhaps the first writer to pinpoint that peculiarly American popular yearning for success in impossibly romantic terms.

259

West got on to the idea of writing *Miss Lonelyhearts* when a friend doing that very job showed him some of the letters received. Martin gives an example of one of the real letters, and shows West's adaptation of it in his book. Here, I think, we see why West remained out of the top league: the girl who writes to the paper complains that she is lame, will always have to walk with a stick; accordingly, although good-looking, lacks boy-friends. West adapts this to cause the letter-writer to lack a nose. Throughout his work recurs this insistence on dealing always with a worse, rather than a bad, situation.

Inevitably, West fetched up as a script-writer in Hollywood. At first he was unable to get any studio to take him on. This was his most painful experience. He was ill, all but starved. *The Day of the Locust* describes this period, a Hollywood not of glamorous stars and successful writers, but of superannuated stage-cowboys, prostitutes, midgets and Filippino waiters. After an agonizing start, West was a successful script-writer, finding in this hack work none of the effort it was to write his novels.

The oppressive and preposterous treatment of writers devised by the bosses of the film industry not unnaturally drove many of their employees to revolutionary activities. There was quite a strong Communist movement in the film world, shattered by the Nazi–Soviet alliance in 1939, when Germany and Russia combined to attack Poland. West was always on the outskirts of Marxism, but could never take it wholly seriously.

As an example of his chronically bad luck, his anti-war play (remarkably poor stuff, extracts here suggest) actually reached the stage, but coincided with the moment when Hitler's goings-on had convinced Americans of the danger; so that anti-war propaganda, of a not very profound sort, swallowed for years, was suddenly unacceptable overnight.

The great merit of Martin's biography is that it chronicles with notable skill a patch of American life that often escapes notice. The horrors and squalor of (say) business or backwoods life are familiar on the one hand; so on the other is the rise to fame of the successful writer. The struggles of an odd, intelligent, talented figure like West, who knew quite a lot of the American writers of his time, but himself never really made the grade, tend to pass unnoticed. They are well worth reading about, not least as a picture of the period.

I think it a pity that Jay Martin begins his book with what is, in fact, the last chapter – West's death in a motor accident. This is too good a book for that rather cheap device. Nevertheless, West's last disaster was no less typical of him than the rest of his life, as he was famous as a thoughtless driver. He had been happily married for eight months, and his wife was killed too. Incidentally West's brother-in-law, S. J.

Perelman, to whom the Marx brothers owe some of their dialogue, always seems to have behaved with extraordinary kindness to him. The English detective story writer was Francis Iles, not 'Frances Isles'.

Nathanael West: The Art of His
Life, Jay Martin, Secker &
Warburg.

1971
Daily Telegraph

CARSON McCULLERS

This rather sad little collection of short stories, occasional pieces, bibliographical odds and ends, edited by her sister, is not a very satisfying posthumous tribute to Carson McCullers, a writer of talent, but it is better than nothing. At least the Notes on Writing she herself jotted down are worth reproducing, though her gifts were not on the whole of an analytical sort.

Née Lula Carson Smith, daughter of a jeweller in a small town in the state of Georgia, she showed early musical ability, and, so far as possible in the circumstances, was brought up as a 'genius'. This, in the old-fashioned nineteenth-century use of the term, she, broadly speaking, was, even if her books are not flawless.

In 1938 she married Reeves McCullers, a corporal in the US regular army, good looking and reasonably intelligent. The marriage was not a success. They were divorced, he rejoined the army, the war came, he did well in the field, was commissioned. They had always kept in touch, and in due course remarried. They separated again in 1953, and he committed suicide.

McCullers himself had literary ambitions, and the story 'Who Has Seen the Wind?' in *The Mortgaged Heart* clearly has bearing on this side of their married life, also on his drinking; just as 'Wunderkind' has direct reference to its author's earlier hopes of making a career as a musician.

As a girl Carson McCullers was obviously of charming appearance, but suffered from health precarious to a degree. She had to endure strokes; it appears that her illnesses were wrongly diagnosed, and in the end it is remarkable that she managed to go on writing at all; but somehow she did.

An interesting element of the present volume is the inclusion of reports made by an instructress of a 'creative writing' course at New York University, attended by Carson McCullers when she was nineteen. These were valued by the student, but one cannot help wondering whether this sort of practical 'sensible' criticism was not on the whole damaging to a writer of her own intensely subjective order. Similar rather stereotyped political pressures produced traces of 'socially conscious' attitudes, most apparent in her first novel *The Heart is a Lonely Hunter* (title a publisher's choice, one is not surprised to hear the author planning to call it *The Mute*), and her last, *Clock Without Hands*.

In between these two books were *Reflections in a Golden Eye*, dealing with the horrors suffered by a group of American officers and their wives in a peacetime garrison; *The Member of the Wedding*, jealousy of a child of twelve for her brother's impending marriage, endlessly played out in kitchen conversations and card games with her cousin, John Henry, aged five, and the black cook; *The Ballad of the Sad Café*, disastrous love of a tough middle-aged woman for a sinister homosexual hunchback.

From even these brief summaries, the charge of 'gothicism' levelled by early critics against Carson McCullers will be easily understood, and certainly 'gothic' goings-on in the Deep South are something that can easily be overdone. They might be described as a good servant, but a bad master. Carson McCullers does control this background well, though it might be argued that at times excessive drama and exotic character are pushed near the point of sentimentality; usually, if not always redeemed by irony and deep knowledge of the material used.

Although Edmund Wilson, in a *New Yorker* review, called *The Member of the Wedding* 'absolutely pointless', it seems to me, on the contrary, not only the best of the Carson McCullers works, but also a disciplined, finished, delicate example of its genre.

Here we get back to being 'committed'. In *The Member of the Wedding* the children and the black cook – in the areas of their existence as separate characters – never strike a false note. By being treated as a 'work of art' the book is a far more effective judgment on 'poor white' poverty, racial discrimination, any other aspect of life, local or general, than, say, the intelligent black doctor in the *Lonely Hunter*, or the pompous white judge in *Clock Without Hands*. Those two may well be true enough types, but have become less acceptable by over-plugging.

This is, in effect, much what Carson McCullers herself implies in more general terms in 'The Flowering Dream', as the Notes on Writing are called in *The Mortgaged Heart*. She is insistent that her own writing is from the subconscious, that she scarcely knew what one of her novels would be about until it was finished. This approach is borne out by examining her work; the weak examples were always those attempted in a conventional commonplace manner. Fortunately, Carson McCullers wrote most of the time as her instinct taught her.

The Mortgaged Heart: Carson McCullers, Margarita G. Smith, ed., Barrie & Jenkins.

1972
Daily Telegraph

TRUMAN CAPOTE

Truman Capote wrote a good first novel, *Other Voices, Other Rooms* (1948), about an unloved boy living in the Deep South who finds himself confronted by homosexuality in unexpected forms. Capote is quoted by John Malcolm Brinnin in this memoir as complaining that he was himself inaccurately written of in a similarly bizarre strain: 'You've got a talented queer around, you have to tie him in with Oscar Wilde or some other image of the drag queen "exotic".'

None the less the public might be forgiven for not always regarding Capote's dress and demeanour as 'crew-cut butch and high school conservative', though his style proved no handicap to social advancement. From Capote's earliest days there was at least a certain amount of justice in Gore Vidal's denunciation of 'a public relations campaign masquerading as a career'.

The works which followed *Other Voices*, including travel sketches and a musical play set in a West Indies brothel, are of varying merit, somewhat similar in tone. Then in 1966 Capote branched out into what he called a non-fiction novel, *In Cold Blood* (which I have not read), a documentary account, done in the greatest detail, of the murder of a farmer and his whole family in West Kansas by two ex-convicts.

Capote spent four years on this book, which was an immense success and brought him a fortune. It also set the fashion for 'documentaries' of a similar kind. *In Cold Blood* was, however, the last notable piece of writing Capote was to produce, though he planned a long Proustian novel about 'café society'. That proved to be something he was not up to, collapsing into odds and ends of short stories.

When Capote went to Paris in 1948, aged twenty-four, it was no time before Gide gave him a sapphire ring, Cocteau a laurel-leaf costume, Colette 'tea for two, in a boudoir that smelled of sachet and cat pee'. In short Capote knew how to get on, and his aim became finally fixed on what Brinnin calls 'individuals in the international society of the conspicuously rich'.

Capote's fame in that world penetrated even over here, and before reading Brinnin's book I used sometimes to wonder why this dumpy figure in sun-spectacles should be photographed at so many 'fabulous' millionaire parties on the strength of his literary output.

Brinnin makes this very clear in a short, readable book based on friendship going back some forty years, and diaries. The memoir has, indeed, something of *In Cold Blood* about it, being almost a novel in neatness and dialogue, yet founded on fact. It is also dramatically right, even if painful to the author (as it must have been) that at the last Capote publicly denied ever having been a close friend of John Malcolm Brinnin's.

They had first met at Yaddo, 'a residence, not far from Saratoga Springs, New York, for artists – mainly writers – who, upon application supported by prominent figures in their respective fields, may be invited to spend months there without cost'. Capote, on the strength of a few short stories, was already confident that he would be a success. I take this to be after his stint as office boy at the *New Yorker*, where he had undertaken the rather creepy duty of escorting the by then blind artist James Thurber to and from the flat of his mistress in the afternoon.

Apart from describing Truman Capote in a convincing manner, which was certainly worth doing, even if he was not the towering genius he himself supposed, Brinnin gives a vivid picture of that literary-academic-social American life of which there is no precise equivalent in this country. Everyone you have ever heard of who belongs there crops up sooner or later. Also Evelyn Waugh and Cyril Connolly make very brief appearances, neither behaving in the way one might most like to read about of one's countrymen abroad.

To follow up the subject of the English not displaying their best manners to Americans, the sole occasion when I encountered Truman Capote was at a large luncheon party in London in, I suppose, the 1960s given by Lady Pamela Berry. Capote was barely introduced to those present, no one took the least notice of him, certainly showed no sign of treating him as in any way a celebrity.

It fell out that he and I left the house at the same moment and walked up the street together. In the light of the way that British writers are treated in the United States I thought the least I could do was to make an effort to be agreeable, probably on the subject of *Other Voices*. He seemed a rather dull little man. Brinnin's memoir shows that any such efforts were quite unnecessary. Capote's self-esteem was undentable. He finally expired from drink and drugs, perpetually required to stimulate a frantic social round.

Truman Capote: A Memoir, John   1987
Malcolm Brinnin, Sidgwick.   *Daily Telegraph*

My Contemporaries

IVY COMPTON-BURNETT

I

The first time I saw Ivy Compton-Burnett was at a party given to watch the Oxford and Cambridge Boat-race from Chiswick Mall. The setting was appropriate, because this fixture always peculiarly evokes in the mind a sense of the late nineteenth century, and the 'varsity men' of that era, rather than the undergraduates and sporting events of today. In early or later life these are the people, with their womenfolk – one uses that word advisedly – who make up the population of the Compton-Burnett novels, most of which suggest in period the years not long before the turn of the century.

Ivy Compton-Burnett herself was wearing a black tricorne for the Boat-race. She looked formidably severe. I think she was severe. She saw life in the relentless terms of Greek tragedy, its cruelties, ironies, hypocrisies – above all its passions – played out against a background of triviality and ennui. Later we met on two or three occasions, but I never knew her well, and always felt the sort of constraint experienced as a child talking to an older person, who, one suspected, could never understand the complexities of one's own childish problems. This was absurd in a way, because we shared a lot of literary likes and dislikes (she wrote to me of Emily Brontë: 'Posterity has paid its debt to her too generously, and with too little understanding'), and we might be said to have 'got on' together very well.

I think the explanation of my sense of unease was no more and no less than what has been said; Ivy Compton-Burnett embodied in herself a quite unmodified pre-1914 personality, so that one was, in truth, meeting what one *had* encountered as a child. The particular interest and uniqueness of this is in relation to the immense individual revolutions and transformations that must, in fact, have taken place within herself, all without in the smallest degree affecting the way in which she faced the world. No writer was ever so completely of her books, and her books of her.

The Compton-Burnett novels deal with a form of life that has largely, if not entirely, disappeared, though I suspect that even to this day pockets of something very similar could be found; perhaps not so much in the country, where the novels tend to be located, as in residential suburbs and seaside towns. As with all good writers, a fair amount of nonsense has been written about her subject matter, so that one hesitates to generalize for fear of adding to it, especially in these days when so many people are obsessed with the subject of 'class'.

However, let me risk suggesting that, between a still lively aristocracy merging effortlessly into an enormously proliferated middle class, both keenly aware of what is going on round them, large gloomy moderately rich families in largish, though not immense, houses in the country, going as a matter of course to Oxford or Cambridge, interested in acquiring property or money, yet lacking almost all contact with an outer world, living in a state of almost hysterically inward-looking intensity, have become pretty rare. If we add to that the Compton-Burnett conditions that such families take little or no interest in sport, and none of the sons enter the army or navy, the field is again narrowed within the terms of reference.

This is the usual Compton-Burnett set-up, and certainly it had once a being. My reason for thinking it not wholly extinct is partly on account of the vitality of the novels themselves – if people were ever like this, there must be people always like this; partly because one will suddenly be confronted – in a railway carriage, for example – with a great burst of overheard Compton-Burnett dialogue. However, whether or not they remain in any appreciable number, such persons form the core of the novels as they are, a social category accepted without question by the author. The men have a classical education, the women a good knowledge of standard poets. It is a 'cultivated' society, but not, one would say, an 'intellectual' one in anything like the contemporary sense. Professional writers play only a small part, artists none at all, though the children draw and paint.

The matter of 'class' is touched on here chiefly because it is almost always made such a feature by Compton-Burnett reviewers. In fact, she is not a novelist greatly concerned with class differences and nuances, as was, for example, Proust, or even Dickens. All novels must be written from a given point of view. The Compton-Burnett novels concentrate minimally on an aspect that is usually allowed undue prominence in their criticism. They are primarily concerned with human passions, and the ruthless manner in which these are usually satisfied. For an investigation of that sort, an accepted routine of manners must always be a great convenience to any novelist.

The game is played, therefore, in a manner all the players understand. Accordingly, much that is said and done is not made explicit. It might be pondered whether one of the great errors of the present day is the theory that nothing is thought to be 'true' which is not explicit; or, put another way, everything that is 'true' can be explicitly expressed. This is surely a great mistake. Life itself is not explicit. To write of it explicitly on all occasions is just as much an author's convention as any other; possibly a mistaken one. It is not, in any case, the Compton-Burnett method.

Her writing is a complete denial of any such approach. It is also, incidentally, a discommendation of a fashion of the moment, usually immature in conception, not to say half-baked, for supposedly 'showing up' the Victorians for the licence of their lives. Of course much of Victorian life was licentious. Everybody knew that at the time; only the inadequately informed are just beginning to find it out now. However, the particular social technique of that epoch was to deal with such matters obliquely. The Compton-Burnett novels show – satirically, painfully, compassionately – how that method worked out in practice.

This is not the place to argue whether or not there was more seduction, adultery, illegitimacy, incest, lesbianism, homosexuality, not to mention swindling and murder, in those days than now; above all whether there was more, or less, 'fun'. It is, however, a fact that all these subjects are dealt with in the Compton-Burnett novels in a manner, so it seems to me, unlikely to be made more effective or convincing by the recital of elaborate physical details. Nor does it seem of the smallest importance, one way or the other, that the people concerned belong on the whole to the upper-middle class; any more than that a lot of Shakespeare's plays are about kings and queens. In fact, if I were to name a contemporary writer who suggests something of the Compton-Burnett approach, it would be not among the novelists, but in the plays of Harold Pinter. Pinter certainly allows himself more down-to-earth language, but conveys much of the same ironic despair set against drearily humdrum circumstances.

Death is a subject never very far away in Ivy Compton-Burnett's books, and, one may guess, in her imagination too. There had been tragedies within her own family which she never quite got over, and she could not speak of war or read a book about it, because she had lost in war a favourite brother. Nevertheless death, like everything else, is treated by her with a sense of proportion, an awareness that its threat is only for those who fear it.

'Ah, my little hostess, so you are looking after us, are you?' said Godfrey, throwing one leg over the other.

'It is so painful to me to see this house without its mistress,' said Agatha, taking her stand by Rachel and stirring her cup. 'She is in my mind every moment I am here. That things have to go on, and do go on, is of course a ground for thankfulness, but their very going on causes something very near heartache.'

'Very near,' said Rachel. 'That is an excellent way of putting it. We are reminded that things will go on after we are dead, that people will be happy, actually be that, when we are not anything. And yet it would not do to have quite a heartache.'

'I suppose we ought not to feel it. We can do nothing while we are here for those who have passed before.'

'You were thinking what we could do for them before they passed, if we could prove we could never be happy afterwards?'

'They would not feel that, though we cannot suppress a tendency to feel that for them,' said Agatha, and added half to herself:

> Better by far you should forget and smile,
> Than that you should remember and be sad.

I am convinced that would be – that is my dear husband's feeling towards my life.'

'People improve so tremendously when they are dead,' said Rachel. . . .

A final word I think she would like said. When, a long time ago, I once spoke of some novel by 'I. Compton-Burnétt' to the late Roger Hinks – no less astringent as a wit and mimic than in the famed rigour of his Elgin Marbles spring-cleaning – he replied, in a tone of quiet reduction to powder that, although still unmet, I knew must be Miss Compton-Burnett's own: 'Búrnett, we call it.'

1969
Spectator, Obituary Appreciation

II

The novels of Ivy Compton-Burnett (1884–1969), who belonged to a generation of writers not lacking in remarkable talents, can match any of her contemporaries in originality of style and content. I should myself regard her as its outstanding woman novelist.

It is, however, not so much to Compton-Burnett fans that *Ivy When Young* is to be recommended – they will read it in any case. What must be emphasized is that, for those who do not enjoy the Compton-Burnett novels (and some don't), or have perhaps never heard of her (some haven't), Hilary Spurling's book presents a story of extraordinary fascination and drama. This is not only in relation to the novelist herself, but to the historical period it covers.

We begin with a surprise in the discovery of the novelist's origins. If ever a double-barrelled surname carried an almost oppressively patrician ring, it is 'Compton-Burnett' – an assumption certainly not lessened by meeting Dame Ivy herself. In fact both Burnetts and Comptons, at the turn of the eighteenth century, were Hampshire families, apparently dissenting, of the most modest origins: agricultural labourers, blacksmiths, small coal merchants. The founder of his own fortunes was the novelist's father, Dr James Compton Burnett

(1840–1901), who, not without struggles, established himself as a physician.

Dr James Compton Burnett (the hyphen developed gradually) is a figure of considerable interest, Victorian not only in almost exact span of years, but also in the energy, violence, geniality, controversy, which he brought to everything he did. He became professionally converted to Homoeopathic Medicine, which in those days landed a medical man in rows paralleled only by the Guelphs and Ghibellines, or the Wars of Religion.

Dr Burnett married twice, both times to Welsh ladies. By his first wife, daughter of a chemist, he had six children. When she died, he remarried, and fathered seven more, of whom the novelist was the eldest. His second wife, Katharine Rees, fifteen years younger than the Doctor and a beauty – and, as it turned out, a tyrant – was daughter of the Mayor of Dover. Even Dr Burnett's medical rows paled beside his father-in-law's municipal pitched battles, but they got on well together.

Ivy Compton-Burnett's background has been described here in some detail, because this was what provided generous material for her twenty novels. In flashing epigrammatic dialogue, she is always analysing the horrors of family life; domestic tyranny; step-children; the difficulties of the young and the old understanding each other – all formally played out in late nineteenth-century Greek Tragedy.

The oddness of the Compton-Burnetts, whose life was latterly centred on a house in Hove, is suggested by Hilary Spurling with great skill. Their vague shabbiness – though in the end they were by no means poor – combined with intellectual interests at once exuberant and cramped. There were musical talents in the family as well as underground literary strivings.

In days when it was still thought eccentric for a woman to aim at higher education, Ivy Compton-Burnett went to the Royal Holloway College, overlooking Virginia Water and Windsor Great Park, a pile modelled on the château of Chambord, and built round two court-yards. Another surprise for the reader is that such a seat of female learning in the early 1900s might be expected to be fiendishly uncomfortable. In fact, Holloway was rather luxurious, with good food, if prim regulations.

It was apparent at an early stage that Ivy Compton-Burnett was 'good at her books', long before there was any question of her writing novels. It is of interest that, in spite of the 'stratified' nature of English social organization that we are always hearing about, it was not long before this in many ways not particularly eligible family was, in fact, in touch with a great deal of the liveliest intellectual life then available; even if their own household itself was in many ways a grim one.

One of the channels of release for the Compton-Burnetts was the departure of Ivy's brother, Noel, for Cambridge. There he became a favourite of that remarkable don, Oscar Browning, and mixed with the set from whom Bloomsbury was principally drawn. It is notable that, although she knew the Bloomsburies, Ivy Compton-Burnett remained, intellectually speaking, always quite separate from them.

Noel Compton-Burnett was the brother to whom Ivy was very close. He does indeed seem to have been a young man of notable intelligence, charm, and finally heroism. The account of his death, as a soldier, and the appalling blow this was to his always stoical sister is very moving; though Hilary Spurling, in emphasizing its waste of human life, perhaps implies that the war could have been avoided. With the state Europe was then in, it is hard to see that this were possible.

When Ivy Compton-Burnett's mother died, Ivy herself took over the Hove household. It was now she who tyrannized over the younger members of the family. This is one of the dramatic moments in the narrative, as if Ivy was acting in a tragedy which she herself had written. In the year following Noel's death in action came another shattering blow – the joint suicide of two of the younger sisters.

When one reads the life of Dostoevsky, it is possible to feel that his novels play down the circumstances in which he often actually found himself. That is hardly less true of Ivy Compton-Burnett. It is not going too far to say that Hilary Spurling has done a brilliant job.

Ivy When Young: The Early Life of   1974
I. Compton-Burnett, 1884–1919,   *Daily Telegraph*
Hilary Spurling, Gollancz.

III

The centenary of Ivy Compton-Burnett is celebrated this week, and it is ten years since the appearance of the first instalment of Hilary Spurling's life of that accomplished and stylistically unique novelist.

The setting of Ivy Compton-Burnett's novels may be always at the turn of the century; her ruthless originality and technical innovations place her more with the writers born twenty years later. This second volume of biography repeats Hilary Spurling's brilliant handling of the first; for it is brilliant to make a story absorbing, moving, at times helplessly funny, in which in one sense nothing unusual (for a writer) ever happened to its subject.

The First World War left Ivy Compton-Burnett in a state of almost hopeless depression. She had already lost a brother to whom she was greatly attached. Two sisters died in tragic circumstances, another brother she adored was killed in action and his wife attempted suicide. These were only some of the troubles that beset her. She had written one unsuccessful novel, and was satisfactorily placed solely in having a little money of her own.

A large part of Hilary Spurling's book is devoted to the friendship of Ivy Compton-Burnett with Margaret Jourdain, a relationship itself described here with all the subtlety of a first-class novel, above all a novel by Ivy Compton-Burnett. The Compton-Burnett family, with its children by Dr Compton-Burnett's two marriages, its jealousies, its tyrannies, its near-incestuous affections, its rows about money, might well be thought to have provided sufficient material for the action of the Compton-Burnett novels. On the contrary, the Jourdain family, equally numerous, complex, irascible, could give the Compton-Burnetts a game any day – even defeat them in the characteristics listed above, with the possible exception of near-incestuous affection.

The Jourdains were of Huguenot origin and, although the airs they gave themselves were perhaps a trifle inflated, had produced a steady flow of not undistinguished parsons, soldiers, dons, civil servants. None of them had ever made any money to speak of. When therefore, almost by chance, Ivy Compton-Burnett and Margaret Jourdain (eight years the elder) arranged to live together, the latter seemed very much the more advantageously placed as regards social connections and even intelligence.

Margaret Jourdain was the daughter of a clergyman with ten children. Her sister Eleanor (subsequently Principal of St Hugh's, Oxford) had been one of two ladies of 'An Adventure' who claimed to have seen the supposed apparitions at Versailles. Margaret Jourdain, determined to live by writing, existed at one period on £1 a week. She never earned much by her pen but, scholarly and industrious, became an authority on antique furniture, especially Regency.

In the shared accommodation Ivy therefore supplied the money, Margaret the social and intellectual prestige. That, however, was only at the beginning, and one of the most fascinating aspects of Hilary Spurling's narrative is the manner in which Ivy gradually but incontestably became the more celebrated figure of the two, the one people most wanted to meet.

At this point it might be worth remarking that, although the last twenty years have documented love-with-sex to a degree that might almost be called unmerciful, that does not mean that love-without-sex is necessarily lacking in interest. So far as anything of that sort can be certain, it is certain that Ivy Compton-Burnett and Margaret Jourdain were not lovers. When a search was being made for Margaret Jourdain's will, Ivy Compton-Burnett said: 'I have never been into Margaret's bedroom, and I am not going to go in now.' And they used to say: 'Today the lesbians are coming to tea.'

Where their relationship is so striking is that Margaret used to refer to Ivy's 'trashy novels' – once on a bus she saw what was in fact Ivy's publisher reading one and commented to him: 'I write all her books.' Ivy was totally uninterested in furniture or indeed any other artefact though she would occasionally accompany Margaret on professional visits to country houses, expeditions which could have had some significance for a novelist whose scenes were usually given country-house backgrounds.

In short their association had an undoubtedly spiky side; yet when Margaret died Ivy was utterly shattered, in spite of her latterly positive brutality (brought on by her own anguish) to her dying friend.

Ivy's whole life seemed emotionally and actually in ruins. Gradually, however, with the help of her many friends, some sort of recovery was made, and the manner in which her books continued with undimi-nished energy (*A God and his Gifts*, published when she was a few months short of eighty, one of the best) is truly remarkable.

I have paused rather long on the Compton-Burnett–Jourdain relationship because it seems to me the single most interesting aspect of Spurling's book, fascinating in itself, in its ups and downs, in its inherent resemblance to many things in the novels. That does not mean there is not much else to read about in *Secrets of a Woman's Heart* which is unexplored, touching, at times suffused with black humour. For example, at Margaret Jourdain's funeral an eminent museum official was heard to greet a colleague with the words: 'This is the happiest day of my life. Margaret Jourdain is dead, and you've got the sack.'

Secrets of a Woman's Heart: The Later Life of Ivy Compton-Burnett, 1920–1969, Hilary Spurling, Hodder.

1984
Daily Telegraph

THE LAMBERTS: GEORGE,
CONSTANT AND KIT

Dostoevsky (who was particularly interested in heredity) would have found the story of these three generations of the Lambert family perfect material for one of his novels.

There are moments of Dostoevskian irony, knockabout humour, unrelenting horror. George Lambert was even born in Russia. As an alternative to the great novelist, Andrew Motion has done an excellent job as a biographer.

A member of the Lambert family emigrated from Yorkshire to Baltimore in the early years of the nineteenth century. His son worked on the first railways, becoming sufficient of an engineer to be offered employment in Russia. His son, George Washington Lambert (1873–1930), one of the trio of this book, emigrated to Australia as a boy with his maternal grandfather.

After knocking about as a jackaroo in the outback, George Lambert became convinced that his career was to be a painter. He married with reckless impetuosity, and came to England, where, although always desperately short of money, he soon made some sort of name; mixing with contemporaries like Augustus John, Sargent and Orpen, the last of whom he perhaps most resembles in a bravura that only too easily sinks to vulgarity.

Vain, egotistical, utterly imprudent, George Lambert was not without swashbuckling charm. He found himself, to some extent, as a war-artist with the Australian Forces in the Middle East. By that time he had already in principle returned to Australia, leaving his devoted wife, Amy, in England with their two sons, Maurice and Constant.

George Lambert became an RA, which delighted him, was regarded as top painter in Australia, and died at the age of fifty-six from a stroke, his reputation immediately submerged in the rise of Modernism. He drank rather too much, but appears to have been more narcissistic than greatly involved with many women, which I had wrongly supposed.

Amy Lambert, who lived to ninety-two, always remained passionately loyal to her husband, and a dominating figure to her sons and grandson. Maurice Lambert, by no means a negligible character, became an academic sculptor. His brother, Constant (1905–1951), composer and founder of the Sadler's Wells Ballet, is the second of the trio here considered.

Maynard Keynes said that Constant Lambert was 'potentially the most brilliant person I have ever met'. This was certainly praise for someone who never made any secret of his dislike for Bloomsbury and all Bloomsbury's work. I would heartily agree in this estimate of Constant Lambert, who had an unrivalled capacity, amounting to genius, for seizing on the essential point in any of the arts. He combined that brilliance with an extraordinary freedom from the least pretentiousness, also possessing an unmatched wit and sense of fun.

Constant Lambert was the first English composer to be commissioned by Diaghilev. Musical tastes mutate quickly. I think perhaps Motion is already a shade out of date in the degree of unfashionableness he attributes to Constant Lambert's best-known music. *Summer's Last Will and Testament* was performed in Brighton only the other day; *Rio Grande* is frequently on the radio. One would agree, however, that the enormous service Constant Lambert did to Ballet in this country (especially by keeping it going during the war) is still not adequately recognized.

He was a great friend of mine, so that I cannot write about him without prejudice in his favour. Again and again in this book appear tributes from those who worked with him, not only to his exceptional intelligence, but to the manner in which he endeared himself. At the same time he was not without his father's selfishness, and what had been a too excessive taste for drink in the father, in the son became at the end hopeless alcoholism.

None the less Constant Lambert cruised along reasonably well before the Second World War. While it was being fought (he was militarily unfit), as has been emphasized he did wonderful work, in extremely uncomfortable circumstances, preserving the Ballet, and bolstering up the sort of good morale that is of the utmost value in wartime. It was after the war that things began to collapse seriously, and the end was tragic enough.

Kit Lambert (1935–1981), his son, is the third of these studies. He was sent to Lancing and Trinity College, Oxford, which says something for his father's educational efforts, but it must be admitted that in other respects he neglected his son. Kit, from the first a highly intelligent little boy, was left in the hands of a bevy of female relatives, who alternately dominated or spoilt him.

Of the three Lamberts, Kit seems to me the one with the most sinister Dostoevskian traits. He had all his grandfather's ambition and swagger, a great deal of down-to-earth ability (he had, for example, become an officer on his National Service, and served in Hong Kong). At the same time his father's easy-going ways, dislike for convention, had turned in him to hatred of all civilized values to which was joined a fanatical desire to make money.

One of the strangest aspects of the three Lambert generations was the way all of them, contrary to what might be expected, were efficient organizers. Kit Lambert, quite unexpectedly, managed – and for a time made an incalculable success of – the pop group, The Who, celebrated for breaking their instruments after each performance.

He made and lost an immense sum; bought a palazzo in Venice; was homosexual (though always himself ashamed at that condition), hopelessly addicted to both drink and drugs; probably murdered. This was, after all, the logical conclusion to being 'anti-establishment' in the fullest sense. Kit's life makes painful, even gruesome reading.

Constant did actually get as far as giving Anna May Wong dinner at the Savoy; Lady Harrod is Billa, rather than Bella; in Lambert's limerick The Bishop of Sodor and Man (rather than Central Japan) behaved so improperly with a fan.

The Lamberts: George, Constant and Kit, Andrew Motion, Chatto.

1986
Daily Telegraph

GEORGE ORWELL

I

It was an excellent idea to mingle chronologically letters, essays and journalism in these volumes so that they form what is roughly a narrative, and include all George Orwell's writings except the novels. The editing is admirable, with just the notes required and a superlative index. To include a fair amount of quite trivial stuff like reviews was also sound, because Orwell himself set great store by the day-to-day work that earns a living, and such material adds to the picture of him.

We begin with an immensely characteristic letter he wrote at the age of seventeen while still a schoolboy to (Sir) Steven Runciman, an Eton contemporary. Orwell had managed to be left behind at an intermediate station on the way back from an OTC camp. He had enough for his fare and 7½d over. He could stay the night at the YMCA for 6d, but that left only 1½d for food. Orwell bought 12 buns and slept out. Here, we feel, is the germ of the Orwell who later deliberately got drunk in the Mile End Road to see how he was treated when arrested.

This is the first letter, though the reader's curiosity is aroused by a sentence written to Cyril Connolly in 1938: 'What you say about finding old letters of mine makes me apprehensive.' This could hardly refer to the earliest letter to Connolly included here and dated 1936.

Orwell's most effective writing might be said to fall into three main groups, because the early naturalistic novels (which he himself later disparaged) are more interesting for the light they shed on their writer than as novels.

First comes the reportage. This was a genre in which Orwell was particularly skilled. Pieces like 'The Spike' or 'Hop-picking' are written in that deceptive manner that makes you feel you have been brilliantly told exactly what happened, and that the writer has done this without any trouble at all to himself. Secondly, there are the amusing essays like those on Donald McGill comic picture-postcards or the *Gem* and *Magnet* stories about Greyfriars School. These might be said to shade off into Orwell's journalism as a columnist.

As a columnist – or in the London letters to *Partisan Review* – one sometimes feels his innate eccentricity and wilfulness take over, even when the ideas are lively and out of the ordinary. There will be generalizations like 'all writers are lazy' (what about Balzac and Dickens, for that matter, Orwell himself?), or an astonishing supposition that Jews cannot be naval officers.

The fact is that Orwell had so much cut himself off from 'bourgeois' life that he was sometimes out of touch about how it functioned. His love of the past caused one side of him to cling to the idea that nothing ever changed, while his 'clever schoolboy' background did not always keep him entirely free from what might be called the superior sort of historical cliché.

His third group of writing consists of the political fantasies, *Animal Farm* and *Nineteen Eighty-four*. These represent the final stages of Orwell's development , and have a quite peculiar interest in relation to the rest of his life and work.

Animal Farm (begun in 1943) has the rare distinction of being at the same time an attractive and popular children's book, and a savage and damaging satire on Communism. One of the most interesting aspects of these four volumes is the way they show how the left-wing press of the 1930s and 1940s was so Communist-dominated that Orwell's articles were barred from publication. When it came to *Animal Farm* even quite 'uncommitted' publishers were *afraid* to take the book on.

Orwell's exposure of the ruthless, totalitarian nature of Communism is his greatest political achievement. It happens to be chiefly linked with what is also his most accomplished literary work. The interesting point about the manner in which Orwell finally found his expression in fantasy is that he had always rigorously extirpated anything of the sort from his earlier writing, and deprecated it in his criticism. This is well illustrated throughout this miscellaneous collection.

For example, he takes Dickens to task for allowing Magwich, the escaped convict in *Great Expectations*, to threaten Pip with over-picturesque imagery: 'There's a young man hid with me, in comparison with which young man I am an Angel. . . .' One has the feeling that Orwell was always suppressing this side of himself, the childish, imaginative side, which some psychologists say we all need from time to time to allow freedom, and that he did this with some odd results. Oddest of all was that when he released these forces he became a world best-seller.

An instance of a perceptive Orwell comment is that contemporary preoccupation with naturalistic sexual descriptions will seem to later generations like the over-exuberance of the death of Little Nell. These volumes are a mine of enthralling material for those who want to study one of the most notable figures of our time. They prompt the fascinating speculation about what would have happened if – as he at one moment suggested – Orwell had called himself 'H. Lewis Allways'.

The Collected Essays, Journalism and Letters of George Orwell, 4 vols, Sonia Orwell and Ian Angus, eds, Secker & Warburg.

1968
Daily Telegraph

I I

Writing the life story of George Orwell (né Eric Blair, 1903–50) has been complicated by his express wish that no biography should appear. This seems to me unreasonable. Just the same, an old friend, even now, is put in a somewhat delicate position as to how far to simulate disapproval.

The distinction made by Peter Stansky and William Abrahams between 'Orwell' and 'Blair', as excuse, is merely casuistical, *The Unknown Orwell* being quite simply a biography up to the age of thirty. If it had to be, the authors have achieved a very creditable job, making great efforts to get at the truth, avoiding any hint of trying to be sensational, conjectural or psychoanalytical. Orwell might easily have fallen into far worse, less competent, less conscientious hands.

The part of the book open to the charge of being a trifle stereotyped – Orwell himself cannot be held blameless – is the hard-luck story of a family come down in the world, pious horror at scholastic barbarity, and the 'English class system'. There is also, surely, nothing wicked, unnatural, or even peculiarly British, in wanting your children to be a success in life.

'What about' arguments are, in general, to be avoided, but, assessing Orwell's allegedly uncomfortable social position, 'what about' Scott Fitzgerald's disquiet regarding his mother's (comparatively) rich shanty Irish family, in contrast with his (comparatively) impoverished father's glamorous Colonial ancestors? What about obnoxious initiatory rites at American colleges or the social strain of what fraternity you would make – just as harassing as public-school asperities or snobbishness? I suggest this merely to keep a sense of proportion. Most young men, British or otherwise, were likely, at one stage or another, to be subjected to pressures of relative brutality, hard-upness and snobbery, perhaps still are.

Thousands of people like Orwell's father (an Indian civil servant of modest rank, of whom no outline whatever emerges) had to educate their children. What was exceptional was that Orwell was a clever little boy, his mother (French on her father's side), a woman of energy, who got him into a high-powered preparatory school, specializing in winning scholarships. Different results might, of course, have resulted from the current doctrine of 'mixing' him in with backward children.

As it was, Orwell won a scholarship to Wellington, then Eton. It should be emphasized that, if the Blair family, or Orwell himself, had preferred the supposedly less affluent atmosphere, he could have gone to Wellington. In fact, among the seventy King's scholars at Eton, there must have been quite a lot with backgrounds not greatly different; nor, if it came to that, among many of the rest of the school.

Play is made in the early pages of *The Unknown Orwell* with an eighteenth-century forebear, Charles Blair, who, fairly rich (having Jamaican interests), married a daughter of the 8th Earl of Westmorland. Here two points should be noted; first, the fortunes of most English families over several generations rise or decline in a far more continuing process than is generally appreciated; secondly, a minute amount of additional research would have revealed the not uninteresting fact that the Lord Westmorland in question inherited the title at sixty-two from a second-cousin. Up till then he had been a Bristol merchant.

Such family vicissitudes, as it happens, are admirably investigated in *English Genealogy* (recently revised), by a former fag of Orwell's at Eton, Sir Anthony Wagner, Garter King of Arms, who does not find a place here. In general the Eton period has been well documented by Cyril Connolly, Christopher Hollis and others. Orwell did not have at all a bad time there. It does come to light here, however, that, when in the upper part of the school, he switched about rather aimlessly in 'specialist' studies, never getting himself anywhere near the running for a university scholarship.

Here the Blairs' lack of means intervened. The question of an immediate job had to be faced. Orwell himself made no demur about going into the Imperial Police. I think it would be true to say (from my own observation) that his imaginative powers, remarkable in one direction, in another did not run to grasp what any given job was really like.

He chose Burma as his area on account of family connections on both sides. His maternal grandmother still lived there. Orwell served in the Burma police for five years. After little training (none political) a police-officer of nineteen would be pushed off to a station in the wilds; only his sergeant would understand English; the average local murder rate was 300 a year. This was tough, even by the standards of College at Eton.

Orwell's stretch in Burma does him credit, however you look at it. He returned with an overwhelming disapproval of 'imperialism', though Stansky and Abrahams give a reasoned picture of the situation, showing Burmese nationalist aspirations awakened not so much by British oppression, as by attempts at liberalization of administrative methods.

Orwell came back to England on leave (he had been ill) and resigned. He wanted 'to write'. He had as little idea of earning a living as a writer, as earlier of what life would be like in the Imperial Police. The various stages that followed are of considerable interest. Judged by his own severe, not to say puritanical measure, there were certain inconsistencies of behaviour. These probably caused him – in some respects acutely sensitive – to dislike the idea of biography. He was, for example, a charge to his parents for about two years. He may have felt his odd forays dressed as a tramp had their absurd side.

No matter. The books were written. The adjective 'Orwellian' was added to the English language which, in the last resort, was his deepest inspiration and love; his political side was what he felt to be the path of duty.

<table>
<tr><td>The Unknown Orwell, Peter</td><td>1972</td></tr>
<tr><td>Stansky and William</td><td>Daily Telegraph</td></tr>
<tr><td>Abrahams, Constable.</td><td></td></tr>
</table>

III

This second volume of the study of George Orwell undertaken by Peter Stansky and William Abrahams is as good as the first, *The Unknown Orwell* (1972). It is not only both sensible and scholarly but written with the occasional quiet humour that is essentially required by the subject.

A good deal of effort has gone into attempting to find some symbolism in the name Orwell, but its bearer told me that he liked it simply because he had pleasant memories of the river Orwell in Suffolk. He also mentioned on another occasion that in Burma no one uses their own names which are known only to the priest.

Stansky's and Abraham's book begins with the publication of *Down and Out in Paris and London* (1933) which had the then very respectable sale of about 3,000 and put Orwell on the map. That Orwell's account of how sauté potatoes are cooked in some restaurants has entered deeply into the national consciousness is illustrated by it being mentioned in a kitchen scene in a TV programme of the series *Fawlty Towers* recently.

Orwell planned to earn his living as a novelist, keeping himself intermittently by teaching, and work in a bookshop, Booklovers' Corner, in South End Road, Hampstead. (Evelyn Waugh's family lived in the connecting channel, North End Road.) Orwell disliked being a shop assistant, but the work was a useful launching-pad for dating girls, which he took advantage of as described here.

Burmese Days (1934) had somewhat Maugham-like overtones, *A Clergyman's Daughter* (1935) and *Keep the Aspidistra Flying* (1936) deriving more from Orwell's favourite novelist, Gissing. The last of these novels outlines its anti-hero's despair working in a bookshop. The authors of this study point out that although most readers (including, I confess, myself) took this as straight autobiography, Orwell's circumstances were, in fact, decidedly less gruelling, though he was no doubt short of money at the time.

Orwell's method of novel writing meant that he was using up his novelist's material at a reckless rate and he himself realized – if one may speak flippantly – that the Gissing had to stop. In 1936 an opportunity arose of writing some sort of 'documentary' about unemployment and poverty in the industrial areas of the north. That such a book would have a good chance of being made the choice of the Left Book Club was also promised. So Orwell wrote *The Road to Wigan Pier*, which – albeit at a much reduced rate of royalty compared with normal non-Left Book Club sales – sold something like 50,000 copies.

Meanwhile – at one of the literary salons which he excoriated, though it might be argued that he could not know of their horrors unless he attended them – Orwell met Eileen O'Shaughnessy whom he seems immediately to have decided to marry. The authors do justice here to Eileen Orwell, which she was soon to become, who could hold her own as an eccentric and was to show herself an unfaltering support for Orwell, throughout a married life that was rarely easy, right up to her own sad and sudden death in 1945.

The Orwells set up house in a small village in Hertfordshire where, not very seriously, they ran a general shop. Although universally agreed to be fairly rigorous by guests who stayed there, days at The Stores, Wallington, have claims to represent the happiest interlude of Orwell's life. From there, inevitably, he set off at the end of 1936 (soon to be followed by his wife) for the Spanish Civil War.

The authors give a clear account of the exceedingly complex circumstances which encompass Orwell's Spanish experiences. His plan was to get to Spain as a journalist, then join whichever branch of the Left's forces offered at the same time a chance of action and reasonable attraction for his own political views. Those were vaguely Anarchist, a group detested by the Communists.

In Barcelona, the Anarcho-Syndicalists (CNT) were having a power struggle with the Socialists-dominated-by-Communists (PSUC). POUM, which Orwell joined because he thought it offered most chance of fighting (that is fighting Franco), was a splinter group of the Anarcho-Syndicalists with Trotskyist leanings. Paradoxically, the Communists (typically pragmatic) were playing a less Leftist game than POUM, but the Communists also disliked the fact that POUM was making propaganda against Stalin's purges.

The picture that emerges makes the term 'The Loyalists' occasionally used for the Republican forces, seem a somewhat inept one, as they were all harrying each other in Barcelona and also shooting at the Civil Guard barracks, which, so far as it went, was no less presumably pro-Republican. Orwell was shot in the throat. (At Huesca, at a dawn stand-to in the trenches, so I am informed by a fellow-volunteer F. Frankford, who added that Orwell was relating to him his experiences when working in a Paris brothel.) This was in some respects perhaps a fortunate wound, as he just escaped a general arrest of all POUM combatants, which might have meant death. Here the book ends. The authors seem to indicate that they are to carry their study of George Orwell no further, but they have laid a firm foundation for estimating his far from simple character.

Orwell: The Transformation, Peter
Stansky and William
Abrahams, Constable.

1979
Daily Telegraph

IV

When Peter Stansky and William Abrahams wrote *The Unknown Orwell* (1972) and *Orwell: The Transformation* (1979) they drove a coach and horses through the wishes of George Orwell himself that a biography should not appear.

It was quite an elegant coach, on the whole scholarly horses, but the vehicle only travelled as far as 1936, broke down at a few points, and very sensibly the subject's widow, Sonia Orwell, decided to put her papers into the hands of Bernard Crick, Professor of Politics at Birkbeck College, University of London, to assemble information for completing the Orwell story in a coherent and responsible manner.

The account of the Burma police interlude is by far the best yet. In Raymond Asquith's recently published *Letters* Asquith refers to 'a brother of Lord Erroll who for some years took refuge from his creditors in the Burma police'. By the time Orwell arrived in the force twenty years later there were no such picturesque ex-guardsmen and future courtiers (gift for a novelist), and he was apt to be introduced with the words: 'Blair was eaten and brought up, ha, ha, sorry, brought up at Eton.'

This splendidly Joycean pun might have pleased Orwell later, but he had not yet read *Ulysses*. It should be noted, by the way, that Orwell in Burma was very proficient at local languages.

Crick grasps the important point that Orwell's writing always moves within sight of fantasy, founded on a basis of truth. It has never been established with absolute certainty whether he did indeed shoot an elephant or witness an execution, but he certainly knew well the circumstances of those events.

I must admit to finding the story he told Loelia, Duchess of Westminster in the fantasy class (that as assistant-waiter at the Hotel Lotti in Paris he had broken a shop window in the middle of the night to get a peach for her), if only because there is no other reference to his working at the Lotti as a waiter.

One of the funniest howlers made by Stansky and Abrahams in their usually well-documented Orwell works is to describe a school where Orwell taught in 1932 as an establishment of the same sort, only less pretentious, as his own prep school St Cyprian's. In fact this was a confusion with another school in the neighbourhood, and Orwell's school sounds much more like the academy presided over by Dr Smart Alick (as played by the immortal Will Hay), since there were only fourteen boys, Orwell was virtually headmaster, and the last Head had just begun a six-year sentence for indecent assault.

Two things seem to me to emerge from Bernard Crick's book: the first, that Orwell would not have been very different however he had spent his early life. There was an unusual heredity, and from quite a small child he showed indications of the characteristics that made him the man he was.

The second aspect of Orwell's life that comes out so strongly here, not only in the earlier chapters, but right up to the end, is the extraordinary doggedness of his own development as a writer. He was determined to be a writer from the first, and he hammered away until his style was a powerful and individual instrument. He had at first wanted to be a poet. That he did not achieve, but the mastery of manner and matter that can be justly called Orwellian was in a large degree the consequence of sheer hard work.

I don't think Orwell himself would have objected to what is said here. There are bound to be a few minor inaccuracies and, in the case of a figure so eccentric, so habituated to keeping the different sides of his life in separate compartments, everyone who knew Orwell will place a varying emphasis.

Certainly one finishes the book thinking more highly of him, not less, as with so many contemporary biographies. The over-all picture strikes me as remarkably true.

I must point out, however, that I was not in College at Eton (otherwise I should have known Orwell already), and when we were introduced I was wearing the uniform of a regiment of the Line rather than that of the Brigade of Guards.

George Orwell: A Life, Bernard   1980
Crick, Secker & Warburg.   *Daily Telegraph*

V

By this stage it is not easy to say anything new about George Orwell. Peter Lewis's book does not do so, but it puts what is known already in a compact and accessible form, competently handling material that might be looked on as controversial. The copious illustrations are also good.

A double-spread showing Trotsky in military uniform getting out of a train on one page, and on the other Lenin and Stalin having a chuckle about what Bernard Shaw called 'humanely and judiciously liquidating a handful of exploiters and speculators to make the world safe for honest men', strikes just the right 1984 touch. Contemplating the genial countenances of the latter pair one wonders whether one would not, if it came to the dire alternative, choose to be alone on a desert island with Stalin rather than Lenin.

Orwell's *Animal Farm* and *Nineteen Eighty-four*, more especially the former, express in the art of fable the inevitable consequence of Communism and its half-brother Fascism, or under whatever name such governments masquerade. The importance of this method of attack – as opposed to marshalling evidence, political, social, economic to show that Communism in Eastern Europe has been an utter failure – is the manner in which Orwell struck the imagination of millions of people.

Lewis tells the not very edifying story of the vigorous efforts to prevent *Animal Farm* from being published in 1945 – that quiet, bland, stifling censorship that is the British way of dealing with awkward customers. At that particular moment a special fog of pro-Soviet propaganda hung over the country as part of waging war against Hitler. Anyone who wishes to plumb the depths of drooling fatuity in which famous writers and miscellaneous intellectuals had been indulging for years on the subject (indeed some are still doing so) should read the recently published *Political Pilgrims: Travels of Western Intellectuals to the Soviet Union, China and Cuba, 1928–1978* (OUP) by Paul Hollander.

In dispersing at least some of these clouds of rubbish Orwell remains unmatched. His credentials were impeccably of the Left; he had fought in the Spanish Civil War; he had lived at starvation level and never made enough money to do more than just keep going.

Peter Lewis rightly deprecates what he calls an 'immense psychological superstructure' erected to try to prove that the man who wrote under the pen-name of George Orwell was in some manner different from the man whose real name was Eric Blair. There were obvious reasons why *Down and Out in Paris and London* should appear under a pseudonym, and, as the name Eric had always been abhorrent to him, this opportunity gave an additional motive for getting away from it.

That contradictions did exist within Orwell himself is certainly true. They were very violent ones, but not divided between the personalities of Blair and Orwell. Orwell himself would have been the first to admit these contrasts. He would have said that they merely proved that abstract ideas could not be used in government without some admixture of decency and commonsense.

All the same Orwell never manages to harmonize his combined hatred and love of the England of 1910, the world of his own childhood. He wrote about this in *Coming Up for Air*, where that lost Paradise (or Hell) is seen through the eyes of a middle-aged insurance-salesman who has lived into an England made hideous by ribbon-development and shattered by bombs.

Orwell's notions of the sort of individuals or institutions he disliked (for instance, for some reason, Building Societies) are often as strange as his picture of an England represented by 'Old Maids biking to Holy Communion through the mists of the Autumn morning', a picture of which he could not help in his heart approving. No doubt this conflict within himself produced much of his force as a writer. Certainly there is no one at all like him and we may wish that he were here to see what is happening in Poland and Afghanistan.

George Orwell: The Road to 1984,   1982
Peter Lewis, Heinemann.   *Daily Telegraph*

VI

Harry Wharton & Co. stood in a wrathy and worried group. The Famous Five were in the soup. They were landed and stranded, diddled, dished and done. Billy Bunter, his mouth full of cake and treacle, managed to gurgle out the news. 'Have you chaps heard? Greyfriars is to be nationalized!'

'Late as usual, you thumping ass!' echoed Bob Cherry. 'Only just discovered that! Why, next term even the name of the school is to change! The Grey School, it's to be called! The Grey School of Social Significance, of course! More in keeping with Modern Thought!'

'I knew we'd have a lot of bother after that giddy essay George Orwell wrote about us in Connolly's frabjous mag., saying we were what everybody wanted to be!' groaned the fat Owl of Greyfriars, lapping up a mug of cocoa and strawberryade, as he stuffed several back-numbers of the *New Statesman* into the seat of his striped trousers.

'Bunter, you fat ass, what are you doing with that merry paper?' yelled Vernon-Smith, the Bounder of the Remove, whose father was a millionaire.

'Got to see the Head about the disappearance of the soya-bean jam!' Bunter grunted, adding a copy of *Tribune*. It could only just be contained in the space available!

'But he'll twig those at once!' shouted Harry Wharton, planting a hearty kick well and truly on Bunter's ample anatomy.

'The Head is staying on, and he'll be jolly pleased at what I'm reading, and let me off!' Bunter gasped, taking some lollypops and liquorice on board. 'And if he don't notice, that stuff is so thick I shan't feel a giddy thing!'

'Oh gum!' Bob Cherry groaned. 'Here's a go! We'll be losing Gussy anyway! The Honourable Arthur Augustus D'Arcy won't do at all at Greyfriars in the Century of the Common Boy!'

Arthur Augustus adjusted his monocle and began to pummel Cherry's ribs!

'You fearful outsidah!' he gasped. 'Weally, have none of you taken the twoubble to find out that my father, Lord Eastwood, is a Labah peer?'

'Ooogh!'

'Urrggh!'

'What!' expostulated the Bounder of the Remove. 'Then I suppose you thought it a rich jape to boast all these years about your father's old title and broad acres!'

'He's got a seat on the Coal Board! That isn't a bad bizney, is it, bai Jove?' retorted Gussy. 'What about your storwies of your own father's sur-tax? Why is *he* standing at the next election in the Labah interwest, deah boy? I see I've thwown you into quite a fluttah!'

'If anyone goes it will be Fisher T. Fish!' asserted Bob Cherry. 'They won't want a bally American witch-hunting the new masters!'

'I do hope we have some fellow-twavellers!' put in Arthur Augustus. 'I'll wagah the Stinks Beak will be a Party membah!'

'Waal, I guess it won't be me that's quittin' this durned consarn!' drawled the American boy. 'I'm a sartin New Dealer, that's so, and my Pop's currency is cute and hard. If it's any of us guys quittin', it'll be Inky here.'

Hurree Jamset Ram Singh, Nabob of Bhanipur, denied this suggestion vociferously!

'My esteemed Fisher!' Inky reiterated, 'since the implementiveness of the Education Act of 1944, the barkfulness and bitefulness of Privilege had its teeth removed by the painless dentalism of Equal Opportunities. As the English proverb has it, Leftfulness has become Rightfulness. Besides, my esteemed family is far too lovesome with the esteemed Mr Nehru for any troublesomeness.'

'But what a thump!' groaned Harry Wharton. 'Will Prout remain our housemaster? I jolly well hope not!'

'I read a letter on Prout's desk applying for a post at the British Council!' asserted Vernon-Smith, the Bounder of the Remove, 'I 'spect he'll go! The giddy Council's always looking for new personnel!'

The Honourable Arthur Augustus could not contain himself at this!

'Oh cwumbs! You wottah!'

'Go and eat coke!' riposted the millionaire's son and heir. 'If your father's really on the Coal Board, you'll probably get it more easily than the rest of us! As a matter of fact, I bet your Guv'nor just does low-level House of Lords committee work on things like Cost of Living!'

'Ha! ha! ha!'

'Groo!'

'Yarooh!'

'You uttah boundah!'

'Anyway, I'm leaving this term!' groaned Bunter, as he spread wads of marmalade on thick slices of meat loaf. 'I've passed the interview for the Ministry of Food! And the Intelligence test, too! They say the elevenses there are simply frabjous!'

1953
Punch

CYRIL CONNOLLY

I

Cyril Connolly has collected his occasional writings for the past ten years in a volume which contains more than 400 pages: parodies, travel, reviews, thoughts on life.

The total effect of *Previous Convictions* is at once stimulating and soothing, almost too much of both, for Connolly's outstanding quality is his pervasiveness, his determination that you are going to like what he likes.

'Look here, Connolly,' one feels at times inclined to say, 'Do stop talking about wild strawberries and Nebuchadnezzars of Armagnac, Sienese painting and Chinese porphyry, lemurs and snorkels, Villon and Scott Fitzgerald, Boswell and Baudelaire, Hemingway and Saint Simon, e. e. cummings and the Goncourts – in short, about the whole bag of tricks. We know these things are very interesting but we must get on with our own work . . .'

It is, of course, no good. Connolly goes remorselessly on. Work has to be abandoned. We eat and drink and talk too much. We travel too far. The journeys are not always comfortable, the hotels not always clean, but there once more is the world-famous Connolly Collection through which we are led, room after room. The fact is the museum is well worth another visit. One might well describe the most dominating piece there – Antique, Renaissance, Baroque, Modern Art, one is not quite sure – as the Connolleone Statue.

There used to be little boxes containing biblical texts rolled up like cylinders, one of which you could take out each morning to give you a great thought for the day. Some of Connolly's reprinted reviews to be found in *Previous Convictions* might be treated in a similar manner. You read a brief comment on Montaigne or Denton Welch, James Douglas or Diderot, while you are shaving. Few of us would not benefit, educationally speaking.

One of the things Connolly understands very well – and many contemporary critics fail completely to grasp – is that, as Rilke remarked, it is no good approaching a work of art in any spirit but sympathy. It is perfectly easy to make fun of Shakespeare or the Sistine Chapel if you apply only that treatment.

This, of course, does not mean that a critic is inhibited from saying what he thinks. On the contrary. All that is required is for him to understand that he is not simply there to show off and be disagreeable. A good example of the correct method is to be found here in Connolly's treatment of Hemingway. High regard and understanding of Hemingway's work does not prevent him from expressing in the strongest terms the lamentable failure as a novel of *Across the River and Into the Trees.*

Assorted material is hard to discuss in an over-all manner, since different standards are demanded by different subjects. On animals, or 'underwater man', one seems to detect a faint note of obsession, but this is perhaps no more than variance of taste, like feeling that Connolly somewhat overrates D. H. Lawrence as a novelist, or puts Beckford too high in classing him beside Horace Walpole.

The great thing is Connolly's clarity of expression, and the fact that everything is related to his own well-defined point of view. You may or may not like this point of view, but it focuses a hard light on to the people considered. Thus, when Connolly expresses reservations in his admiration for Stendhal, this is at once felt to be reasonable, even to be expected, against the general picture of his own likes and dislikes.

The piece called 'The Breakthrough in Modern Verse' is a really admirable account of the coming into being of Modern Poetry. Connolly shows why there is a reason for supposing there is such a thing – as opposed to the many obscurities of verse that existed in the past – and examines those concerned in the launching of this movement in England. It is a small masterpiece of conciseness and enlightening explanation.

Turning from such things to the parody of Ian Fleming's James Bond, we find some first-rate examples of Bondese, set in a thrilling network of transvestite spy-catching; something perhaps not to recommend to that rather uncomfortable uncle of yours.

And so we must say farewell to the Connolly Grand Tour, to Antibes and Abu Simbel, Rhodes and Ravenna, Munich and Memphis, Delos and Dongola . . .

Previous Convictions, Cyril 1963
Connolly, Hamish Hamilton. *Daily Telegraph*

II

Anyone at all interested in the arts knows, roughly speaking, what 'the Modern Movement' means in his own mind. Presenting the same thing on paper might be a different matter. Cyril Connolly has chosen 100 books covering a period of 70 years as the medium for his personal view.

He briefly introduces the various periods and says a word or two about each book in turn.

This is coming out in the open; and the reviewer feels at the start that, in return for this candour, he should not argue the toss about small points. Obviously where detail is concerned, there must be disparity of opinion.

However, when Connolly outlines his terms of reference, it becomes clear that the title of his volume is open to very grave objection. Because he does not know Russian, Italian or German, no translations are to be included. This is surely carrying intellectual integrity to pedantic lengths. No one fears to quote *Don Quixote* because he has not read it in Spanish.

To attempt to consider the Modern Movement without, for example, a glance at Dostoevsky's psychopaths, Nietzsche's exaltation of the will, the scepticism about human identity itself as expressed so differently by Pirandello and Kafka, is going to be a difficult proposition.

It is therefore wiser to ignore Connolly's title, and confine ourselves to his own definition of 'the modern spirit'. This he derives from the Enlightenment, and calls 'lucidity, irony, scepticism, intellectual curiosity, combined with passionate intensity and enhanced sensibility'. The touchstones are Baudelaire, Flaubert, Rimbaud.

That is all very well, but the more we delve into Connolly's book, the more clear it becomes that he is, in fact, preaching his own private literary religion, rather than examining all the miracles available. Idiosyncrasy is the basis of most good criticism, so there is no objection to that, but it would be a pity if readers – especially young readers – regarded this collection too finally as the Tables of the Law.

Connolly may imply, but he never sufficiently emphasizes the bifurcation of the Movement, even accepting his own limited terms. On the one hand there was aesthetic sensibility, mild social rebellion, pacifism, even at last – to be seen from examples here – a certain old-maidishness. On the other hand there was deliberate perversity, unintelligibility, anarchism, violence (Jarry, etc.) The two Hydra heads were anxious to consume one another.

One feels Connolly is a shade too willing to accept the standards of the pundits of his youth, of Bloomsbury. He is, of course, much too acute to be unaware of these warring elements, but – as seen by his treatment of Wyndham Lewis and others – it is easy to guess where his own sympathies lie.

Furthermore, the path he takes is sometimes hard to plot. Maugham is allowed, but the technical innovations of Kipling are ignored, although Kipling was scarcely less interested in technique and verbal gymnastics than Joyce himself. To class Kipling as 'traditional' is surely inappropriate. After all, Apollinaire – impeccably of the Movement – introduced a Kipling translation into his 1903 magazine.

In rather the same way, one must disagree with Connolly when he says that Firbank's novels owe 'allegiance only to Congreve'. It is clear that Firbank's dialogue owes a good deal to such an unexpected source as Thomas Hardy (also, no doubt rightly, excluded here as a novelist), as examination of the peasants' talk in, say, *The Return of the Native* will show.

The peak period of Connolly's Movement he places between 1910 and 1925. Examining these decades, he is himself at his best, an admirable expositor of Eliot, Joyce, and the rest. He seems to me to overrate D. H. Lawrence, E. M. Forster and Virginia Woolf as novelists, and is clearly most at his ease with poetry of the period to which he is an invaluable guide.

As the date passes 1930, Connolly tends to flounder. I think there is no doubt the collection should have stopped there. Constant Lambert's *Music Ho!* (1934), although dealing primarily with music, touches on writing and painting. It should either have been included, or quoted for the arguments it puts forward for the Modern Movement having, even by then, come to an end.

By attempting to extend the story for another twenty years. Connolly appears to find himself in a dilemma between leaving out 'good' books and putting in ones that have little or nothing to do with the Movement as such.

Auden and Co. seem to me a reaction from the Modern Movement, which always had, at least implicitly, an 'Art for Art's sake' basis, Betjeman, it might be thought, even more. Connolly obviously feels uncertain himself, making excuses that cannot be wholly accepted. In the same way, Ivy Compton-Burnett, with all her distinction as a novelist, has, so it seems to me, reacted away from the Modern Movement.

It might be argued that Hemingway belongs to the Movement, Scott Fitzgerald not. E. E. Cummings is mentioned chiefly as a poet, *The Enormous Room* (1922) not given enough importance. *Miss Lonelyhearts* (and some others) scarcely make the grade. If we are to have no Russians, William Gerhardi's *The Polyglots* (1925), would have been a good indication of Chekhov penetration in the 1920s.

Writing comments on individual authors and their books, Cyril Connolly is always worth reading. His criticism is without fail personal and acute. He is less successful at nominating a team.

The Modern Movement: 100 Key Books: from England, France and America, 1880-1950, Cyril Connolly, Deutsch and Hamish Hamilton.

1965
Daily Telegraph

III

In October, I shall have known Cyril Connolly (who has just celebrated his seventieth brithday) for half a century to speak to; for about two years longer, by sight. When I opened *The Evening Colonnade*, a 500-page collection of his assorted literary journalism, some going back over more than twenty years, I decided to pretend that I had never read anything by Connolly before.

If these pieces had been found in the Commonplace Book of a man of letters, his name associated with various literary circles, who has not published anything, one had never met, what would one's judgment be?

I think there is no doubt that one would be very impressed. Unfortunately, the pretence was impossible to keep up. Indeed, even after a few pages, most readers must feel that they have known Connolly for over fifty years, on account of the pervasiveness of his own personality. He is always anxious to define himself – sometimes perhaps over-anxious, to his own disadvantage – but it is this personality against which, critically speaking, the ball is bounced. On the whole, the more subjective Connolly's judgments the better. If he falters, it is when he has felt that he ought to toe the line.

This also seems to me evident as far back as *Enemies of Promise*, now republished, Connolly's best book. It first appeared in 1938, and was reprinted with minor revisions ten years later, from which the present edition remains unaltered.

To get the maximum enjoyment from *The Evening Colonnade*, the earlier book should be read first. *Enemies of Promise* consists of a breakdown of the literary situation in this country at the time of its appearance, especially in relation to the writer's own literary tastes. This section is followed by an autobiographical one, showing how Connolly's upbringing (until going to the university) was responsible for these tastes.

To deal with these two matters in that order – the general then the particular – was both original and effective. Connolly makes all sorts of good points that would have been lost by putting the autobiographical part first.

After thirty-five years, *Enemies of Promise* holds up astonishingly well. There is perhaps a shade too much schoolboy documentary materials, and it was a pity Connolly was seduced just before the book's completion by the Leftism fashionable at that moment. This not so much politically, but because a sudden veering towards 'committed' writing put in the shade the important critical role Connolly himself had played only a short time earlier.

To give a concrete example, Scott Fitzgerald is barely mentioned in

Enemies of Promise, yet Fitzgerald would have been almost unheard of in Great Britain before the war if Connolly had not propagated his name. It was almost solely Connolly's efforts at that period which laid the foundations of Fitzgerald's post-war success over here. Connolly simply does not do himself justice, owing to momentary infatuation with the view that a novelist like Fitzgerald, uncommitted, was therefore not worthy of attention.

This point seems worth making as some of the best of the pieces in *The Evening Colonnade* are about Fitzgerald, and American writers generally. In fact, American writing is the area in which Connolly perhaps excels. He is understanding and well disposed towards American life (domestic or expatriate) in a way that is not always found in this country's critics.

An occasional lack of adaptability where his fellow-countrymen are concerned is not altogether absent (which critic in his own country can feel himself altogether free from that?), while he is sometimes open to the more serious charge of being over-impressed by the French. The Americans, on the other hand, provide the subject for some of his liveliest and most clearcut pieces.

Our imaginary reader, who approaches Connolly for the first time through *The Evening Colonnade*, would find himself after a thorough study in a position to speak intelligently and forcibly about Henry James, Edith Wharton, Ezra Pound, Hemingway, Fitzgerald, E. E. Cummings, Thomas Wolfe, William Carlos Williams, Henry Miller, Norman Mailer. Even if people disagreed with him (about Pound, for instance), he could give them a game.

About the French he might sound more academic, though he would easily get by on La Fontaine, Voltaire, Sade, Flaubert, Proust, Gide, Valéry, Cocteau, Genet, clearing himself of over-seriousness by declaring the last a bore. If the subject were then changed to the Russians, he would have to talk for the rest of the evening about Solzhenitsyn.

So far as his own country is concerned, the Connolly-student could play Swift, Pope, Boswell, the Dandies (a strong Connolly lead), the Nineties (he would sometimes, on this group, have to make up his own mind) before settling down to Eliot, Joyce, Bloomsbury, the Sitwells.

If his listeners, carried away by what he said of the Twenties, wanted something more up-to-date, they would have to be satisfied with Orwell, Auden, MacNeice, Spender, and Ian Fleming; Basil Bunting is about the only new arrival. There is here no betting on the young, nor on unknown foreigners of any date. In fact talk will then probably be turned to African travels and Big Game parks.

The *London Magazine* has a Cyril Connolly seventieth-birthday Number, with contributions by John Betjeman, Raymond Mortimer and Roy Fuller, and some excellent photographs. It also contains a short piece by Cyril Connolly himself, written in the mid-1930s, in which to gain detachment he turns himself (by an anagram on his own name) into Lincoln Croyle, an American. The latter name will be seen to lose a 'y' and gain an 'e' in the process. Surely neither of these alterations is necessary. Why not 'Lincoln Y. Croyl' – the middle name being, of course, 'Yorick'? Let us, in any case, end by wishing Cyril Connolly Many Happy Returns.

The Evening Colonnade, Cyril   1973
Connolly, David Bruce &   *Daily Telegraph*
Watson.
Enemies of Promise, Cyril
Connolly, Deutsch.

IV

In the autobiographical section of *Enemies of Promise* (1938), Cyril Connolly writes: 'I first saw Nigel by the letter-slab . . . the dream brother . . . that afternoon we played in a knock-up cricket match and each made twenty-five . . . in spite of the year and a half between us in age companionship was possible.'

This was the summer of 1920. Both boys were in college (that is to say had scholarships) at Eton. 'Nigel' was Noel Blakiston, who was, in fact, two years and three months younger than Connolly, and in due course a cricketer of some attainment.

Connolly (who died last year) had a very successful school career, which – as he himself often said later – made all else an anti-climax, though he achieved celebrity as literary critic and unique personality. Blakiston became an official in the Public Record Office, and writer of short stories.

Connolly was right in supposing that he had found a 'dream brother'. The Letters (written roughly between 1924 and 1928 in their most vital form) reveal a deep and fascinating relationship. The title, *A Romantic Friendship*, is a just one. Warm, at times even sentimental (for which Connolly always apologizes to Blakiston), it was not a homosexual one in the true sense. This can be seen by comparing the tone with, say, the Journal of Denton Welch, an accomplished piece of documentation of only a few years later essentially homosexual in flavour; and no doubt there are equally good examples of this contrast in other collections of published letters.

Connolly went to Oxford; Blakiston to Cambridge. The Letters begin in a serious way when both are at their universities. At quite an early stage it seems to have struck Connolly – whose precocious development was phenomenal – that the correspondence might eventually be, if not published, at least a valuable record of their friendship, and what each thought, so that not only are many letters exceptionally long, but they are deliberately leisurely in style.

A warning should be uttered about some of the early letters, where Connolly explains the meaning of life. Connolly had no gifts as a philosopher; and – apart from the occasional rhymed epigram – few as a poet. It would be a pity if the reader were put off by early bursts of philosophy and verse, and the overloading of the letters with Greek and Latin quotations. I can give an assurance that these hazards are soon traversed.

We do not, of course, see Blakiston's letters, but often get some idea of what he said. Up to Connolly's own standard where the classics were concerned, a practising member of the Church of England, with very definite ideas of how he wanted to pursue his life, Blakiston was perhaps the only person who was ever able, relatively speaking, to cope with Connolly. Even Blakiston contrived to do so satisfactorily only for about four or five years.

Much of the interest of the Letters is in the light they throw on the literary tastes of an exceptionally bright young man of that period; one brought up by schoolmasters, rather than acquiring 'culture' at home. There are some surprises. Pater's *Imaginary Conversations* played so great a part that at least one of the characters there became a recognized standard of exchange in these Letters; and for long Milton is invoked as Connolly's favourite poet.

Connolly liked Ralph Hodgson's poems and Flecker's, as well as those of A. E. Housman, whom he was later savagely to attack. Unlikeliest of all is a positive obsession for Margaret Kennedy's *The Constant Nymph*, quoted time and again to illustrate human relationships.

This too has its ironic side, because, when reviewing in 1935 a book called *Antony* (a memoir of Lord Knebworth, an energetic and promising young man killed in a flying accident), Connolly (who had known Knebworth) takes him to task for reading and re-reading *The Constant Nymph*. Of course, it could be reasonably argued from Connolly's point of view that ten years later Knebworth, as Connolly had done, should have progressed in literary tastes.

When he came down from Oxford, Connolly was for about six months tutor to a boy in Jamaica; then he got a job as secretary to the American man of letters, Logan Pearsall Smith. This second job brought him into touch with all sorts of notabilities – for example, Berenson, who was Logan Pearsall Smith's brother-in-law.

Many of the Letters are devoted to making plans for going abroad together, or Connolly's accounts of going abroad by himself. Some of his journeys were quite adventurous for those days, and people who knew only the later Connolly will be astounded by records of riding, going for runs, days of starvation by deliberately missing meals to economize; most of all – in spite of fairly frequent bouts of depression – the general air of high spirits.

In November 1926, Connolly writes:

I feel I have lived such a lot already that there would be hardly any kind of experience that I had not been deprived of, only quantity, and death, though by no means desirable, would not be unjust.

He was then just twenty-three.

By no means all the Letters strike this note, and sometimes the reader laughs aloud. It seems to me that the Golden Bowl of the relationship was broken when Connolly set up on his own in London at the end of 1927. Nothing is said, though, and the correspondence continues intermittently until both writers marry.

A Romantic Friendship: The Letters   1975
of Cyril Connolly to Noel Blakiston,   *Daily Telegraph*
Constable.

V

On one thing everyone was agreed – schoolmasters and dons, patrons and fellow competitors, friends and enemies – Cyril Connolly (1903–1974) was not in the least like anyone else.

The book consists in about equal proportions of a biographical Memoir by David Pryce-Jones and Connolly's own journal between 1928–1937. Although some of the Journal has appeared in print before there is here new material, and, especially for the connoisseur, much that is on no account to be missed.

David Pryce-Jones has done the biographical Memoir well – no easy job. He had the advantage of knowing Connolly as a friend of his father's, Connolly himself being always more at ease with, and better disposed to, the young. The Connolly legend is creditably and compactly handled for the first part of its subject's life, the period up to the war helpfully recorded, the later years summarized.

Few men of letters have ever propagated their personal myth so effectively as Cyril Connolly: success at Eton, the Balliol Scholarship, brilliance subsequently wasted through sloth and love of pleasure. This picture did not tell the whole story because, if Connolly had been altogether unproductive, he would not be found, as he is today, in books of literary reference.

No doubt Connolly was an exceptionally lazy man, but that was not the reason why he never became a novelist or poet (though there are admirers of his novel *The Rock Pool*). The fact was that, good or bad, he was neither novelist nor poet by temperament, which the Journal over and again makes very clear, though (in my own view) he was more nearly a frustrated poet than a frustrated novelist. He was, none the less, an admirable stylist with wit, grasp, power of expression.

The Journal does, however, bear out that his lack of industry in keeping it more fully was a loss to himself and others. There is a certain amount of dead wood here – rather unfunny Joycean ramblings, or too beglamourized social snippets – but also passages of criticism that at worst pinpoint vividly the views of the period: vignettes of individuals, strongly felt impressions of climate and the seasons wherever he happened to be. For instance, the entry about Lily France at Mrs Fitz's (a brothel not nightclub as in the note) perfectly hits off what is evidently the girl's own narrative style.

Where books and writers are concerned Connolly held strong opinions, but often changed them; sometimes, one feels, after due consideration; sometimes influenced by fashion – too much popularity working against a given book as much as too little.

This is also to be seen in his collected criticism – still immensely readable – and illustrated here, for example, by contrasted comments about Aldous Huxley's *Point Counterpoint* or Harold Nicolson's *Some People*, both at moments admired, at moments severely censured.

In much the same way Connolly had, at best, erratic judgment of individuals. Owing to early 'promise' (so fatal to himself as he always asserted, and giving the title to his best book, *Enemies of Promise*) he tended in early days to move among people older than his own contemporaries. Of one after another we read high commendation in the Journal; then a row: Maurice Bowra, Desmond MacCarthy, Harold Nicolson, Aldous Huxley . . . Connolly's intelligence and magnetism were always at risk, for he had an utter disregard of other people's well-being and convenience, and often abominable manners.

There was not exactly a row with Logan Pearsall Smith (with whom Connolly landed a remarkably cushy secretarial job) though things were never quite the same after Connolly married his first wife Jean Bakewell (whose essential niceness comes out extremely well here).

David Pryce-Jones is undoubtedly right in supposing Logan Pearsall Smith's the strongest and most enduring influence; an approach well suited to an elderly American composer of aphorisms, probably damaging to Connolly with whom an excessively critical attitude became a method of avoiding work rather than perfecting it.

Connolly in attack may be seen in relation to Virginia Woolf, 'A female spider by whom I fear to be devoured.' He considered her much overpraised:

She is not really a novelist – she does not care for human beings, her best effects, the mark in the wall, the empty house, are based on the absence of them. This is good, but she shouldn't write novels. Her characters are lifeless anatomical slices, conceived all in the same mood, unreal creatures of genteel despair. They are not human beings, but sections of them which portray the doubts, the tenderness, the half-hopes and half-fears of the human mind. From this same misty backwater of the stream of consciousness she fills up all her puppets through a hole in their heads.

Virginia Woolf fought back (in her letters) with references to 'that little pimp Connolly' and 'a less appetising pair I have never seen out of the Zoo . . . She has the face of a gollywog and they brought the reek of Chelsea with them.'

There was also a disaster when Connolly lunched with the American novelist Edith Wharton (b. 1862 not 1865) in the south of France. Connolly said the luncheon had aged him ten years. It is only to be regretted that he devotes only a line to the occasion, of which he would give an entertaining account.

This book will be used as an authority when it is possible to write a fuller biography and certain small points should be put right. Although Connolly and other undergraduates may have modelled themselves on Maurice Bowra, I don't think it is true in the least to say that Evelyn Waugh did. Waugh and Bowra saw very little of each other at Oxford, as Waugh himself records.

The Duggan who visited Connolly a few days after arrival at Balliol was Alfred, not Hubert, the latter coming up more than a year later and being at Christ Church. Patrick Balfour was at Balliol, not Trinity, and Bowra had served in the war as a Gunner officer, not an infantryman.

In one of Connolly's parodies (which could be first-rate, though this is not a very successful one) 'Miss Saridge' should read 'Miss Savidge' (recalling an indecency case of the period in the park). The unidentified 'Howard (USA)' at the Connolly dinner-party in about 1933 was Tom Howard, a genial New York interior decorator, brought by Elizabeth Bowen.

On the other hand, a dropped comma has resulted in the creation of an imaginary character (p. 246 & Index) called Howard Hardy, a composite figure resulting from the merging (awful thought) of Brian Howard and Eddie Gathorne-Hardy.

Cyril Connolly: Journal and Memoir, David Pryce-Jones, Collins.

1985
Daily Telegraph

VI

Cyril Connolly was a wit, an exceedingly talented literary journalist and a brilliant analyst of his own strange, inconsistent, sometimes far from commendable character. The investigation of himself runs through almost everything he wrote, but is the main subject of his books *Enemies of Promise* (1938) and *The Unquiet Grave* (1944).

The latter, a kind of notebook of maxims and literary gleanings, is really a sequel to the former in its continuation and development of the history of Connolly's melancholy guilt, thwarted hopes, love affairs and favourite books.

Connolly's literary journalism chiefly expressed itself, first, in the editorship of *Horizon*, of which Michael Shelden gives an excellent account here, together with a fair amount of biographical background; secondly, in reviews, particularly his latter years of reviewing regularly for a Sunday newspaper.

Selections of his reviews were later published. They make good reading to this day, though they tend to be discursive rather than strictly speaking critical: one notice on the subject of, say, D. H. Lawrence will mention his good points; another, with Connolly in a different mood, all Lawrence's bad ones.

Connolly had always wanted to edit a literary magazine. In 1939 the chance arose, when Peter Watson, a rich young man primarily interested in modern art, rather than in literature, offered to put up the money. Stephen Spender, who also had a finger in the current publication *New Writing*, was prepared to come in as associate editor. Connolly's volatile nature made that advisable. It was, however, Connolly who set his mark on *Horizon* throughout its publication, giving a personal tone that *New Writing*, for example, altogether lacked.

Horizon appeared between Christmas 1939 and New Year 1950. Whatever other people said about Connolly's failings – and they said a good deal – no one criticized him so savagely as he criticized himself. Even of his own editing he wrote: 'I fall an easy victim to political quacks and neurotic journalists.'

None the less all sorts of then unknown names of notable writers and poets made an appearance in the magazine: to mention only a few, Julian Maclaren-Ross, Angus Wilson, Denton Welch, William Sansom, Alun Lewis. George Orwell contributed some of his best essays. There were many more, whose state of health or some other reason kept them out of full-time commitment to wartime duties. Naturally most young were fully occupied elsewhere.

The editor of *Horizon* graded as a 'reserved' occupation, that is to say Connolly was not liable for conscription into the Services or other governmental employment. The threat always hung over him that, if his magazine did not come up to scratch in the eyes of the bureaucrats, it would no longer be allotted severely rationed paper. From doing a job he actively liked he would be cast into the outer darkness of something like the Fire Service.

It is ironical that, after Connolly's editorial noisily welcoming the Labour Government of 1945 as champion of the art and artists, not only did food rationing become more acute under Labour, but during the fuel crisis of 1947 for the first time *Horizon* was actually disallowed from publication.

Notwithstanding, *Horizon* had been an undoubted success in 'keeping culture alive during the war'. By the end of it Connolly's fame was not only considerable in this country, but also in America. Publishers of both nations enthusiastically signed up contracts right and left for books that never got written.

By this time, in any case, Connolly was bored with editing. Like Toad, in *The Wind in the Willows*, he now had a formidable conceit of himself. Even Peter Watson, who had poured out money, while exerting a minimum of interference in running *Horizon*, complained that 'Cyril's vanity' made him impossible to live with when they travelled together abroad.

That was certainly true during the immediate post-war period. There had been no competition in London during the war. Now he found himself threatened on all sides by demobilized contemporaries.

During the latter part of *Horizon*'s existence it was more or less run by Sonia Brownell (later the second wife of George Orwell). Here it might be added that Michael Shelden, who has to handle a great many of Connolly's relationships, male and female, reduces them all to the simplest possible terms (often no easy matter), the result being an intelligible narrative that may sometimes ignore subtleties but makes good sense.

Connolly was always tortured by the conviction that he ought to have been a great novelist. In fact, he was entirely without the temperament that makes a novelist, good or bad, and those who suppose otherwise show ignorance of novel-writing. Strange as it may seem, Connolly himself was intelligent enough to know that he did not possess the necessary characteristics.

In *The Unquiet Grave* he notes: 'If we have no appetite for the idiosyncracies of minor personalities, then we must fight shy of the novel'; again: 'Never will I make that extra effort to live according to reality which alone makes good writing possible.' My own feeling is that Connolly ought to have been a poet, but somehow he wasn't that either.

Several very small points: the material of *The Unquiet Grave* dates back at least as early as 1927, about the time when Connolly showed me a collection of quotations and comments of that type which he had brought together; Connolly liked to describe his first wife, Jeanie Bakewell, as 'from Baltimore' (possibly from romantic feelings about the 'Old South'), but in fact only her stepfather lived there. Jeanie (and her sister) were irritated by that label, because their family came from Philadelphia, of which they were proud.

It would be a pity if the cliché that the traitor Guy Burgess was 'charming' became rooted in legend. I met him in 1939, and am on record at the time as thinking him one of the most repulsive specimens that ever came my way.

Friends of Promise: Cyril   1989
Connolly and the World of   *Daily Telegraph*
Horizon, Michael Shelden,
Hamish Hamilton.

VII

Night-Thoughts From a Day-bed – by Cyr*l C*nn*lly

Most of the articles that follow are reprinted from *Perimeter*, the only magazine of its kind that has ever appeared, or is ever likely to appear. I wish to express my indebtedness to those writers who answered my questionnaire: 'How much money have you got, how much of it was earned on *Perimeter*, and how much more would you like to have?' This material is to be found collected together at pp. 47–193. Its lesson is more than ever paramount. Those who were kind enough to send gifts during our days of florescence are reminded that these can still be forwarded c/o the bank named at the end of this volume. Presents should be dispatched, carriage paid, in non-returnable wooden cases containing units of a dozen. Single bottles may also be left, securely packed and clearly addressed, c/o the publishers.

Perimeter ran its course for ten years without interference from the censors in spite of our ceaseless advocacy of better conditions for magazine-editors. Those of us to know the bitter taste of Algerian caking on the palate at 4 a.m. must be thankful for at least that small mercy. Once we had hopes of something more. '. . . but to be young was very heaven'. Such dreams are past in a world where sponsored TV threatens to make even an editor no more than a father-figurine to his public. Already the chill gales from Vienna can be felt whistling through the Brenner, bringing their Freudian message, as we shuffle along the deserted Bloomsbury streets, toes through patched galoshes, long pants darned with unmatching wool. *Par delicatesse j'ai perdu ma jeunesse.*

It was different in June 1944:

DEAR GALAHAD, – When I first heard how you had been parachuted into Lapérouse during the last days of the German occupation of Paris I was told that you had fought your way out. But I did not know that you carried away with you two bottles of Château Pichon-Longueville-Lalande, Pauillac, 1929, and a 10-lb. amphora of pâté de foie gras. Nor did I know then that these were presents for me. Later, when you came to London to receive the second bar to your VC, and we dined together, you never reproached me for drinking both bottles, and eating all the foie gras, when you had momentarily left the table to wash your hands. We shall meet again when you bring me the Rocquefort you captured and put in a cage: and once more I shall feel guilty.

1945. I have been given some votes to use by several of our readers who think my opinion best and I am going to use them for Labour. *Perimeter* is non-political, in spite of numbering among its readers several MPs, an ambassador or two, and a permanent under-secretary to the Board of Trade. Labour has not done anything to help *Perimeter* yet, but Mr Morrison and Mr Bevin have faces of the right kind. They may now have a chance to show their metal. Free Algerian for all editors of literary magazines would be a good start, by way of marking interest in the Arts; and, as the wine situation improved, a move might be made towards less astringent vintages.

Tramping one behind the other, elephants trunk-linked-to-tail, we move towards the sunset. *Angst* is my *mahout.*

Ja będę palit podczas gdy pan piszesz listy. How often on the way home to my terminary, I find myself thinking I will put those words into practice. Perhaps it is true that *Minha lanterna precisa d'uma trocida nova.*

Anyway, Sainte-Beuve says somewhere that poetry and eloquence are never found in those totally destitute of that richness of the senses which is the body's organ of expression. How can English writers have any richness of the senses when many of them do not know the difference between a café and a cafeteria?

1947. The fact is that the Socialist Government has betrayed the writer; especially the 'engaged' writer. The Goncourts relate that Turgenev once went in sixtieth to dinner. Even with that place the Russian novelist would have been well ahead of the editor of *Perimeter*

the other night at the party given to the Minister of Superdiction. No
new talent has come to birth in this country under Labour rule. What
novel on this side of the Atlantic can be seriously considered beside a
work like *Save Me the Bebop*? The Golden Age that seemed about to break
in 1945 has turned into a mere scrimmage in the fish queue. Meanwhile
the circulation of *Perimeter* shows no improvement. The steep rise in
income tax has had the direct effect of reducing postal-orders sent as a
mark of affection to the editor.

Fortunately my vein of stoicism still allows me to dip into the classics.
When Demetrius besieged Rhodes he refused to set fire to a part of the
city which might have made him master of the whole, becase he knew
that Protogenes, the painter, was working in that quarter. When the
town was taken Protogenes was found finishing a picture. The
conquerer asked why he showed no more concern at the general
calamity. He replied: 'Demetrius makes war against the Rhodians, not
against the fine arts.' How many VIPs of today could say the same?
They would be more like Mnasilus, that youth who assisted Chromis to
tie the old Silenus, whom they found asleep in a cave. The moral is,
don't go to sleep in caves, I suppose. In fact, one way and another,
looking round at our contemporaries, we must ponder the ambivalent
lament attributed to Petronius, that disinherited Roman clubman:
Pueri mater amica optima est.

1953
Punch

BARBARA SKELTON

Barbara Skelton has written three novels. They might be called slight, rather haphazardly organized, but are expressed with a peculiar wit and savagery. *Tears Before Bedtime*, a characteristic Skelton title (in fact borrowed from Cyril Connolly), has the same qualities and imperfections in its mixture of memoir and diary. It stands out from other books of a similar sort on account of the author's boundless indifference to what anyone thinks about her. This self-abandon projects some extremely amusing passages of autobiography.

She was the daughter of a regular army officer, who married a beauty from the chorus. Her mother's family had Danish blood, Barbara Skelton's own good looks reflecting this Scandinavian strain. After a childhood no more than ordinarily stormy, in the circumstances of her family background, she was found a job as model at a dress shop in Knightsbridge; a firm of which a rich friend of her father's happened to be director. She calls him Sidney.

Here the fun started. Sidney, who, although married, was a man of relatively regular habits in his indiscretions, set her up as his mistress in a Crawford Street flat. There she remained for a while finally (after an abortion) getting bored. The affair, regarded not without disapproval on the part of Barbara Skelton's mother, was terminated amicably.

The next step, almost routine at the time, was for the Skeltons to send their daughter to India, where her father's brother was a Major-General in the Royal Army Medical Corps. There she fell in love with Charles, a Captain in the Royal Engineers. He read T. S. Eliot and disliked the army. Charles became ill; Barbara Skelton sailed back to England. Great was her surprise early in the voyage to find that Charles had stowed away on the ship. They stuck it out together, with surreptitious raids on the dining-saloon, until Aden, where, not surprisingly, Charles was arrested.

At the subsequent court-martial General Skelton's medical evidence carried such weight that Charles, whose temporary loss of responsibility was attributed to recent illness, was merely ordered to active service on the North-West Frontier. The Fakir of Ipi was making trouble at the time, and Charles was killed.

Barbara Skelton resumed her life as a model in London, gravitating naturally enough to the more bohemian end of intellectual society; though a society by no means bigotedly intellectual. Familiar names began to crop up. Those being the days when such things could be done, she bought herself a cottage in Kent for £400. This retreat, known as The Cot, was to play a great part in her life.

The war was marked by association with a Free French figure working under the name of Monsieur Boris, 'a balding stocky man with a pale reptilian face'. (Barbara Skelton makes the point early on that male good looks do not attract her, her ideal being Erich von Stroheim.) She and Monsieur Boris set up house in Shepherd Market. Luckily Sidney, her original seducer, reappeared when calling-up for jobs was becoming difficult, finding her a place (not without humorous implications) in a nuts-and-bolts factory.

Life was soon enlivened by a transfer to employment with the Government of the Free Yugoslavs, whose office in Kingston House was conveniently near the flat in Brompton Road where she was by then living. Her Yugoslav experiences are convincingly described, while her diary records a contemporary private life that was, to say the least, complicated; to call it hectic would be no exaggeration. It was at this period that she encountered Cyril Connolly, then editing the magazine *Horizon*, whom in due course she was to marry.

Before that took place official machinery came into action again, resulting in her being ordered to Egypt as a cipher clerk – a cipherine – at the Embassy. While she was dining in the same Cairo restaurant as King Farouk, an equerry was sent across inviting her to join the royal party. Friendship with Farouk (which was to have a later renewal, when the King whipped her with a dressing-gown cord) was not well looked on by the Foreign Office. Barbara Skelton was transferred to the Athens Embassy, where she underwent the siege when Communist elements tried to take over Greece.

The diary entries relating to the events leading up to marriage with Cyril Connolly, followed by the marriage itself, are perhaps the remarkable part of *Tears Before Bedtime*. Connolly had an extraordinarily strong will; so too did Barbara Skelton. They were a well-matched couple. Anybody contemplating a plunge into bohemian intellectual life should study these pages before taking an irrevocable decision.

Of the Connollys' stay with Bernard Berenson at I Tatti we are given a straightforward account, one that might have been supplied by any guest there; Berenson saying that Roman painting was only derived from Greek, or the Frescoes of the Villa of the Mysteries at Pompeii were copies, etc.

Such is not Barbara Skelton's forte. No special gifts are required for that. Where she has dreadful aptness is in presenting everyday things like Connolly refusing to get up in the morning, lying in bed chewing the sheets; weekends with friends that went badly wrong, trips to France that went worse; the stupefying boringness of Sir Oswald Mosley holding forth at dinner (1950) which she defines as 'like listening to Radio Luxembourg'.

Tears Before Bedtime, Barbara   1987
Skelton, Hamish Hamilton.   *Daily Telegraph*

EVELYN WAUGH

I

Evelyn Waugh was born in 1903. This opening volume of his autobiography begins with family origins and background, closing about 1926, after he had come down from Oxford, and was employed – lowest ebb of his fortunes – as assistant master at a boys' preparatory school.

One takes a deep breath with a view to describing the book, which covers a great many fields; then pauses, wondering whom to address. People who know little or nothing of Waugh except that he is a superlatively gifted writer? Others, who have formed some relatively grotesque picture of his background, from gossip columns, lampoons, his own sometimes eccentric utterances?

Then there are old Oxford contemporaries, like myself, too close to be unprejudiced, yet the only ones fully to appreciate the interest of some of the material. All categories will find plenty of entertainment here; and much to correct an inaccurate view of the author.

When I went up to Oxford in 1923, Evelyn Waugh, then in his third year, was already a famous figure in undergraduate life. One was immediately told stories of his exploits. All the same, it is the other parts of *A Little Learning* rather than the Oxford section that I found most absorbing.

For Waugh (who came there from Lancing, of which he gives a gloomy picture) Oxford of that time was a Kingdom of Cokayne. 'Those of my contemporaries who were bored at Oxford were mostly of foreign origin or had been oddly educated,' he remarks in one of those generalizations which he loves to indulge. '. . . Few had any serious interest in women.' Although failing to qualify in either of the two first groups, bored at Oxford was, alas, what I was; while, if the last statement is admitted to be some limited extent true, that was surely principally because the University authorities descended like a ton of bricks on anyone seen so much as saying goodnight to a pretty waitress.

Accordingly, the picture of Oxford seems to me too rosy, undeniably exotic as was that particular vintage. Looking back, one now sees the undergraduate world of which Waugh chiefly writes as unusually brilliant, socially ambitious, intellectual, yet choosing on the whole a consciously anti-intellectual approach to life. To these he adds sketches of some fine eccentrics.

Here will be found plenty of subject for controversy. I shall add no more than the suggestion that the chronology sometimes dovetails the years in a manner to blur the minutiae of undergraduate social history.

Although there are enjoyable things recorded about Oxford, I preferred the account of Waugh's family antecedents with which the book begins.

> There is an element of fantasy [he writes] in the thought of those four totally dissimilar men [four of his great-great-grandfathers], quite unknown to one another, entering, as it were, into a partnership to manufacture my brother and myself, who, apart from a common aptitude in story-telling, are antithetical – though not antipathetical.

The four men were Alexander Waugh, DD, Minister of the Secessional Church of Scotland; William Morgan, FRS, an impoverished Unitarian Welsh coal-owner of ancient family; Lord Cockburn, a Judge of the Scottish court, like Boswell's father; Thomas Gosse, an itinerant portrait-painter of (what was then wrongly supposed) Huguenot lineage, who was led by the spirit to become a Plymouth Brother.

The sober ability coming in contact with writing, painting and visionary religion in these and other forerunners is striking, those connected with the Law and the Church tending to produce books more than the common run of parsons and lawyers.

The religious orientation of so much of this background may have been the cause of Waugh's own quite serious wish, as a boy, to become a clergyman. This account of his relations and early life, told at some length, is of the greatest interest, both as a record of how people once lived, and, in a more personal way, of the circumstances which helped to form the very individual writer – and man – that Waugh became.

Over and over again in the book one is impressed by the author's innate seriousness, his indomitable determination. He is on the whole better at delineating himself than at conveying the character of other people, because the broad effects in which he deals cut out the minor embroideries of egotism that can cloud a self-portrait. With other people, this simplification can sometimes lead to apparent unfairness, on the one hand; on the other, to perhaps uncritical acceptances.

However, the best autobiographies are made not of elegantly turned opinions, but by saying what the writer really thinks. Waugh presents a mass of this best sort of documentation. The result is an illuminating, at times even ruthless picture.

There are many notable vignettes. Edmund Gosse, for example, was a kinsman:

> 'I held Gosse in disdain. His polished art of pleasing was not effectively exercised on children. I remember him once, when I was,

I suppose, eight or nine, greeting me with: "And where do you carry those bare knees?"

'I answered pertly: "*They* carry *me* wherever I want to go."

' "Ah the confidence of youth! To be able to envisage an attainable destination!" '

That, in a sense, seems just what Waugh has always been able to do, a characteristic which makes this foundation promise a full autobiography of extraordinary interest, these quiet beginnings already, by the end of the volume, dissolving into scenes of comic horror overshadowed by Captain Grimes.

A Little Learning: The First   1964
Volume of an Autobiography,   *Daily Telegraph*
Evelyn Waugh, Chapman &
Hall.

II

It is sometimes alleged that writers in this country are not sufficiently regarded. A more valid objection might be that they are too often relegated to the gossip-column. Evelyn Waugh is a case in point. The persona he deliberately presented to the world is no doubt partly to blame, but surely the time has come to abandon trivialities and treat him as a great writer.

Waugh died in 1966. What has happened since then? Christopher Sykes, it is true, is at work on a biography of Waugh. Clearly this must take some time. It is not unreasonable that seven years should have passed, and that further time should still be required before the work is done. Meanwhile, odds and ends about Waugh appear in a happy-go-lucky fashion, usually taking a form unlikely to make Sykes's task any easier.

Waugh's Diaries – the most cursory glance should have revealed these as a documents of quite exceptional interest – are allowed to appear as newspaper snippets. It is first stated that no more will be published. Then the policy is for some reason changed. The Diaries will be published as a whole. In that case, why produce them in a mutilated form?

Evelyn Waugh and his World (apparently bearing the blessing of the Evelyn Waugh Estate) produces yet more piecemeal material. It is a symposium of essays by (in order of sequence) Alan Pryce-Jones, Roger Fulford, Peter Quennell, Dudley Carew, Lady Dorothy Lygon, Father Martin D'Arcy, SJ, Eric Newby, Penelope Chetwode, Douglas Woodruff, (Sir) Fitzroy Maclean, the Earl of Birkenhead, Malcolm Bradbury, David Lodge, Handasynde Buchanan, John Jolliffe, Anne Fleming.

These pieces are of differing approach and competence, some are chatty, personal reminiscence, others provide brief critical examination of a few of the books. The former often pass judgments that need a presentation of the whole story of Waugh's life to assess their value; the latter, in the same limited manner, ought to stand beside a general consideration of Waugh's writing. In fact, most of this material, personal and critical, should have been absorbed into the biography.

The usefulness of short personal accounts of certain specialized aspects of Waugh's life is chiefly when the writer of the reminiscence has something to say which requires a certain amount of talking about him or herself in a manner inappropriate to a biography. For example, Lord Birkenhead, who was with Waugh on the military mission to Tito's Yugoslav partisans, gives an interesting account of their time together, his own experiences acceptably filling in the picture in a manner not suitable for a book solely about Waugh.

In a different, but equally informative way, Douglas Woodruff (the best piece in the collection) describes his relations, when editor of the *Tablet*, with Waugh as a contributor. Here, again, the writer's own presence is required, some of the point being likely to be lost if the account were absorbed into the biography. At the termination of one row Waugh sent Woodruff a postcard saying: 'The Pop [*sic*] is an ass and so are you.'

Peter Quennell puts straight some of the Oxford picture, which *Brideshead* has left more than a little out-of-hand so far as realities of that period were concerned.

There are regrettable lapses in captioning the photographs. To say 'extreme right Anna May Wong' (p. 199) may not matter much, because obviously it is Waugh's second wife, Laura, on the extreme right, not Anna May Wong. On the other hand, there is no chance of the reader guessing that 'Mother, wife and first-born' (p. 198) is not Waugh's mother, and his wife and first-born, but Laura Waugh and her first-born, with Laura Waugh's grandmother, Lady de Vesci.

More serious, because involving Waugh's approach to an event that closed one of the chapters in his life, is the editorial note below the facsimile of a letter from Waugh to Lord Kinross (p. 185). The letter says:

145, North End Road,
N.W.11.

Dear Patrick,

Thank you so much for the advertisement. As soon as I see any hope from my window in the Slough of Despond I will let you know.

As a matter of fact I think there will probably be an elopement quite soon.

Yours,

Evelyn.

The note adds: 'A letter written from his parents' house; its envelope is postmarked 20 February 1928 . . . The last sentence refers to the end of his first marriage.' But this postmark is nearly four months before the date of Waugh's first marriage, which took place on 17 June 1928. The sentence refers not to the end of his first marriage, but to its probable beginning. Apart from getting this fact wrong, there is the totally erroneous implication as to the nature of the break-up, and how Waugh himself felt and spoke about it. Looked at from this last angle the howler is altogether inexcusable.

Evelyn Waugh and His World,   1973
David Pryce-Jones, ed.,   *Daily Telegraph*
Weidenfeld & Nicolson.

III

It is an unusual piece of luck that someone quite so well qualified as Christopher Sykes was available to undertake the biography of Evelyn Waugh (1903–1966).

Sykes is not only himself an accomplished writer, a Roman Catholic (interested in doctrine, but of tolerant views), a wartime soldier (with gallant record), a man born into the world to which Waugh aspired (and eventually achieved), but also a lifelong friend, who actually served side by side with Waugh in the army, and is able to see his subject with an eye always deeply affectionate, but never in the least uncritical. To say that one ends up by knowing almost as much about Sykes as one does about Waugh is no disparagement of a first-class biography.

Sykes makes two shrewd generalizations. He says that Waugh was an arrogant man, but never in the least a conceited one. That was essentially true. Sykes's other comment is even more revealing. He suggests that had Waugh (like his father) been at all stage-struck (which he was not) he might have become a great comedian. This opinion gives meaning to much of Waugh's behaviour – both the way he managed his life in general, and his demeanour at any given moment. He was almost always playing a part into which he had thrown himself with absolute self-identification.

The publication in extracts of the Waugh Diaries at a moment when Sykes must have been well on in writing this biography can have made his task no easier, but he has absorbed much of that information into his narrative with complete success. Considering how people behave today, I am surprised how shocked some were by the Diaries. Even Sykes himself is not altogther immune from holding up his hands at the amount Waugh recorded himself as drinking as a young man, though

I should have thought that it was not inordinately more than most in the bohemian circles the early Diaries chronicle; but Waugh wrote it all down.

When Sykes was at Oxford, a year or two later, Waugh's name as an undergraduate was forgotten and I think perhaps he does not altogether appreciate how much Waugh was always – even at the depths of his unhappy schoolmastering period – regarded as a bright boy by his own Oxford contemporaries. The reason that Duckworth's published Waugh's book on Rossetti was simply that I brought him in there as a potential writer. One of the directors had already decided that a book on Rossetti would be a hopeful project, and it was a coincidence that Waugh happened to have produced a privately printed essay on the Pre-Raphaelites.

Evelyn Waugh's early successes were contemporaneous with his first brief marriage, which lasted hardly more than a year. Sykes speaks a little as if no marriage, either before or since, had ever broken up (and somewhat soft-pedals some of the the circumstances), but there is no doubt this was a great blow. The reason why no papers could be found regarding the disposal of the Canonbury Square flat is explained by the fact that the first Mrs Evelyn Waugh (who continued to live there for several years) was its lessee.

Some of the most absorbing pages of this book describe Waugh's experiences in the armed forces. Apart from being almost certainly the only man who ever served in both the Royal Marines and the Royal Horse Guards (The Blues),* he was present at operations in Crete, and a member of the military mission sent to Yugoslavia to make contact with Marshall Tito.

Characteristically, Waugh also underwent some of the most dreary sides of army life as well as these adventurous interludes. Towards the end of the war – during the unedifying period when the British Government was exchanging its former allies for their Communist successors – he so much aroused the ire of the Foreign Office by a report on the persecution of Yugoslav Catholics that he came near being court-martialled.

The many flamboyant aspects of Waugh's life are, of course, secondary to his importance as a writer. Sykes examines the *oeuvre* in detail, and always has interesting observations to make. My own serious critical disagreement with him is regarding *The Ordeal of Gilbert Pinfold*. Sykes thinks this a good minor work. I find it possibly the

---

* Various letters were written giving instances of other Horse Marines, notably from Major Alastair Donald, later Royal Marine Archivist, who was commissioned into the Royal Marines, and on the last day of his demobilization, joined the 3rd Carabiniers (Prince of Wales's Dragoon Guards) with an emergency commission.

best thing Waugh ever wrote. The beginning and end of *Pinfold* may be open to criticism; the 'voices' on the boat seem to me to make a sequence unequalled in their combined funniness and macabre horror.

Evelyn Waugh could be a man of astonishing kindness and generosity, but he had a very unpleasant side, which he himself recognized. Sykes makes no attempt to conceal this strain of deliberate cruelty, especially to those who were not in a position to hit back.

Sykes does not invoke the strong possibility of a hereditary failing. Waugh himself (in *A Little Learning*) describes the spiteful and sadistic habits of his Waugh grandfather, who, among other things, crushed a wasp on his wife's forehead with the knob of his stick. In the capricious manner of inherited family traits, this particular one seems to have skipped his mild father, and good-natured brother Alec, descending appreciably on Waugh himself.

Some of the best pages of this excellent book transcribe verbatim superbly comic conversations held between Waugh and Christopher Sykes. They convey with the utmost verisimilitude Waugh's talk; at once unexpected, logical, perverse, wildly laughable, annoying and altogether of the man himself.

Evelyn Waugh: A Biography, Christopher Sykes, Collins.

1975
Daily Telegraph

IV

The extracts offered from Evelyn Waugh's Diaries three years ago are now expanded to what is to all intents and purposes the full text, except for a few libellous remarks, and 'about twenty phrases' that the Editor considers would have been 'intolerably distressing'.

This civilized principle stops a long way short of removing all disparaging comment. Michael Davie has done an excellent job, but, for a book of this sort that will be consulted for future reference, the index is altogether inadequate, omitting many names, and giving careless references to some of those included.

Waugh's Diary, of which few if any of his friends knew, was kept, with certain gaps, from childhood to death. He is not a diarist in the tradition of, say, Amiel or Kilvert, a man who can suddenly light up some trivial activity by setting it down in his own words on paper. The importance of Waugh's Diary is its unvarnished picture of himself. Had he never written any books, these Diaries would have given him a measure of fame.

It may be objected that some of the purely social entries are too numerous, or that the sections dealing with African or South American journeys are material for a volume of travel, but here we have the whole panorama – which seems to me far the best. The result is an extraordinary document.

Davie points out that a schoolboy diary such as Waugh kept is all but unknown. It is impossible not to be struck by Waugh's early powers of expression, his ability to set down what he felt about things at the age of fifteen or sixteen with freedom from the typical clever-boy's introversion. His first two unhappy years at Lancing remain unrecorded, but latterly he was a success there, all the ambition, irritability, odd combination of anarchism and conformism, being already apparent.

At Oxford, too, the opening years are missing, possibly destroyed because their activities sounded banal, but there are flashing accounts of times when Waugh visited the University during his three years as a schoolmaster (and of the strange schools themselves). This was a rackety period, prelude to an even more dissipated one – Waugh's life in London before his first marriage.

When extracts appeared describing these goings-on during the late 1920s many people were shocked. Why they should have been, considering 'permissive' behaviour today, is hard to understand. Probably because Waugh chronicled debaucheries in a detached way, and without expressing any high-minded sentiments about rebelling against bourgeois standards, or the getting rid of moral inhibitions.

Waugh leaves no account of the break-up of his first marriage, and the social snippets that follow are the least interesting of the Diaries, though they show the way his life was developing. During his war service with the Royal Marines, Commandos, and Royal Horse Guards, he kept a diary, though this was strictly forbidden by army regulations. Some of the entries at this time were written up after the event, indeed consist of a kind of report (beginning like an official summary with numbered paragraphs) on his own employment with – finally exclusion from – the Commandos.

Waugh was eye-witness to the Cretan campaign, of which he here gives his impressions. His personal courage was never in the smallest doubt. Waugh was a very brave man. At the same time he was in a comparatively privileged position in Crete, attached to an officer senior to himself, not at that moment responsible for troops.

Waugh makes many strictures about what was taking place, and no doubt much of the withdrawal was disordered. At the same time it never seems to have occurred to him, either then or later, that, if some sort of a line was not being held, the enemy would have been where he himself was moving about, or that the German Parachute Corps is reputed never wholly to have recovered from the casualties inflicted on Crete.

Waugh includes here the 'demi-official' letters leading up to his posting away from the Commandos (a correspondence that suggests Combined Operations discipline was more relaxed than the Army's), and, for the best part of three years, he was in military doldrums. Then came the extraordinary experience of being sent, with Randolph Churchill and Lord Birkenhead, in a mission to Tito's Yugoslav partisans. Of this interlude Waugh leaves an inimitable account.

When Waugh was demobilized he emerged into great literary success. His name was famous. Among many fairly startling entries in the Diary, the only one that really staggered me was the recording that he seems to have thought seriously of standing for Parliament. There could be no better example of his complete lack of all self-awareness regarding himself and his own behaviour. This was the moment when he seems deliberately to have set out to acquire the unaccommodating *persona* for which he was later known – not always justly, though entirely through his own fault.

The Diary of the wartime period suggests this was the time when various strains loosened Waugh's grip, never very strong, on his own capriciousness. From then on, no matter how successful he was, his melancholy increased. Over and over again comes the entry: 'Low spirits'. The last section consists of what Waugh calls 'irregular notes of what passes through my mind'. It is rather a sad ending, but gives shape to the continuous interest of what he had already set down.

Perhaps I may be allowed to note that I was not the unidentified 'Tony' described as taking part in an Oxford 'orgy' (p. 189), nor was that, I think, the often mentioned Tony Bushell, but another of the name. 'Miss Karsima' (p. 167) is probably 'Miss [Barbara] Ker-Seymer' and 'Marcus Clarke' (p. 270) should read 'Marcus Cheke' (later Minister to the Holy See). John Greenidge, elder brother of Waugh's Oxford friend, Terence Greenidge, was called 'The Bastard', but was not really illegitimate, as a note states. His parentage was eminently respectable. It was a joke deriving, I think, from his having got very drunk on burgundy, and being described later as the 'Bastard of Burgundy', on the Shakespearian analogy of the Bastard of Orleans.

The Diaries of Evelyn Waugh,   1976
Michael Davie, ed., Weidenfeld   *Daily Telegraph*
& Nicolson.

V

One would agree with Mark Amory in his Preface to this collection that Evelyn Waugh may or may not have foreseen that his diaries would be published, but expected correspondents to retain his letters with such an end in view.

To that extent some of the Letters here might be thought to have an eye cocked on posterity, but in fact Waugh the letter-writer is not substantially different from Waugh the diarist. Those (like myself) who found the Diary absorbing will find the Letters no less compulsive reading, while those who disapproved of the Waugh persona in the Diary are unlikely to change their minds after reading the Letters.

Amory has chosen about 840 letters from a potential 4,500 and manfully tackled the formidable task of identifying individuals and explaining private jokes. Very few survive from Waugh's schooldays and undergraduate period, not many from before the break-up of his first marriage, but at least one of the former group is of great interest in its firmness of expression and early grasp of how a novel should be written. The date is January 1921, when Waugh was only seventeen and still at Lancing, the recipient Dudley Carew, a Lancing friend, later an author himself:

> I like the idea immensely. The whole conception of Jimmie and his rising out of the rut for the moment only to slip back again and the ever delightful cynicism that contentment is the only failure is well brought out. But as it stands now it is too frail a scaffolding to support the theme (I'm afraid I'm mixing a metaphor but I want to be sincere rather than technically unimpeachable). I can see it rather degenerating into long conversations and descriptions of the weather. That was all right just to fix Jimmy but won't do for 10,000 words . . . Try and bring home thoughts by action and incidents . . . Make things happen.

From the start Waugh was fond of laying down the law about behaviour, and after becoming a Roman Catholic in 1930 his religious fanaticism knew no bounds. John Betjeman (22 December 1946 to 14 January 1947) is literally threatened with Hell, not for being an atheist, but for his devout Anglicanism ('a handful of homosexual curates'), while Nancy Mitford (October 1951) is asked: 'Would it not be best to avoid any reference to the Church or your Creator? Your intrusions into this strange world are always fatuous.' To which she snapped back: 'I can't agree that I should be debarred from ever mentioning your Creator. Try and remember that He also created me.'

Some of the best letters are to Waugh's long-suffering second wife Laura Herbert, though often these are not much different from entries in his diary of the same period. There can be no doubt that he was very devoted to her, but that did not prevent severe dressings-down when her own letters seemed dull. Those to his children, Victorian in tone, if that was his mood, are at the same time models of good advice well expressed.

The *amitié amoureuse* was the area in which Waugh took most pleasure as a correspondent; bullying, gossiping, complaining about his own troubles, in letters to what he himself describes as 'faded ladies of fashion'. These groups of letters vary a good deal in quality, but all have their place in illustrating the tenor of Waugh's way of life.

A side of Waugh rather different from his preoccupation with the beau monde, though in its way just as characteristic is revealed in a letter (17 October 1944) to Laura Waugh from the wartime Yugoslav military mission in which he was serving:

> I must write to you about an exciting new idea that has come to me and ask what your opinion of it is is. For some time now I have been worried about how, after the war, we are going to reconcile your wish to farm and my wish to have the children brought up on a farm and in the country with my own ineradicable love of collecting bric-a-brac and my need for a harmonious place to write in. This is my idea. Why should we not dispose of Stinkers [their house, Piers Court, Stinchcombe, Gloucestershire] and buy you a simple farm-house and property near Bridget [her sister] for yourself and the children where I would live when not working, and for my work and collecting mania and your frequent visits retain my aunts' house at Midsomer Norton.
>
> This will presumably be left equally between Alec, myself, and my Tasmanian cousins. They would obviously wish to sell their shares . . . I could then make the house into a museum of Victorian art . . . I could keep my library there and write my novels there. It would be a secret house to which no guest would come. I have photographs of the rooms in 1870 and could gradually restore them to that splendid state . . .
>
> After my death if none of my sons-in-law or spinster daughters want to live there, I could make it into a public museum and memorial to myself. It will by that time supposing I live to 1970 be a unique spectacle.

It was not to be. Waugh's last years were rather sad. The policies of the Vatican were by then deeply unsympathetic to him, and he even wrote to a Monsignor who answered queries in the *Clergy Review* to enquire what minimum church attendance was needed from him in hearing the new liturgy. Nevertheless some of the letters of this period are still full of biting comments that make one laugh aloud.

There cannot be many people whose collected (or rather selected) letters would not produce a tangle of inconsistencies. Waugh was no exception, and one of the amusing aspects of proceeding through this volume is the manner in which people Waugh knew go up and down in favour, few if any escaping his sharp tongue. In the light of that it is surprising how many old friendships were in fact maintained to the end.

Mark Amory has done pretty well. Yet the following might be noted: the letter to Laura Herbert of summer 1936 (when they were walking out) saying: 'I was sad leaving you at Gower Street' is more likely at the period to have reference to her attendance at RADA than to the Duff Coopers' house. The note on p. 90 should read Lady Diana Bridgeman, not Bradford, the Princesse de Caraman-Chimay on p. 430, the same as she on p. 559, was née Hennessy, not Hamilton; the dog that acted in *La Dolce Vita* belonged to Iris Tree, not Mrs Taffy Rodd.

The Letters of Evelyn Waugh,   1980
Mark Amory, ed., Weidenfeld
& Nicolson.   *Daily Telegraph*

VI

The year 1903 produced some accomplished journalists, for instance Orwell, Connolly, Muggeridge, contemporaries who all find a place in this fat volume of Evelyn Waugh's journalism. It was a field in which Waugh was well equipped to hold his own.

Whether he would have wished all the pieces here to be reprinted is another matter. There is, however, plenty that is of interest. An author's journalistic sundries often reveal more, anyway on the surface, about the writer than do the books.

Waugh himself remarks that enthusiasm is the essence of journalism; and even if enthusiasm is not always quite the word to describe the attitude, he is never indifferent. A point is always made. Usually, anyway in the less serious pieces, he adopts the *persona* he invented for himself, sometimes absurd from its sheer unreality, at the same time always providing a defined basis from which to argue.

The extent to which Waugh exercised complete control of what he was writing is well illustrated by his short contribution (1940) to the *Globe and Laurel*, the corps magazine of the Royal Marines. The style of regimental magazines is completely caught, though the mention of 'immature conifers' and 'the Anatolian Jute industry' might alert the reader to the fact that a brighter officer than usual had been detailed to do the job.

There is a decided irony in the earliest article, written at the age of fourteen, being 'In Defence of Cubism' (printed, November 1917, in *Drawing and Design*), a remarkable achievement for a schoolboy both in opinion and expression, even if Picasso ('taking his place among the masters') was in later life to be Waugh's major *bête noir*. The remaining school and university stuff is equally competent, if a shade pompous.

This collection is extremely well edited by Donat Gallagher, whose introductory notes on the various periods are helpful and sensible. The facility and tact with which he handles the subject of the Roman Catholic Church, often a thorny one with Waugh, suggest Gallagher may be a calmer co-religionist.

Gallagher prefaces his sections with epigraphs from Waugh's writings. These set the note of the period; for example in November 1928, Waugh wrote to his agent: 'I think it would be convenient if the editors could be persuaded that I embodied the Youth Movement so that they would refer to me whenever they were collecting opinions.'

This hope was more than fulfilled. A flood of articles followed, only a small proportion of which are reproduced here. Too much should not be expected from titles like 'This Sun-bathing Business', but they show how Waugh was earning as much as £2,500 a year, a very considerable sum, from freelancing during the period before the war. To this period also belong the visits as a newspaper correspondent to Abyssinia where Waugh showed himself capable of doing a normal journalistic assignment with efficiency, though occasionally individual methods, as when he cabled a scoop in Latin, alas unintelligible to the prosaic mind of the editor.

The energy with which Waugh poured out all this miscellaneous journalism is impressive (he was writing books as well), and his war-service did not by any means bring the flow to a stop. There were interludes when he was laid off from the army. In March 1942, he found a moment to write a letter to *The Times* to protest against the vandalism of tearing down gates and railings for 'scrap', negligible in the war effort, and (I speak from knowledge) bringing about such subsequent troubles as the collapse of church walls.

Waugh's withdrawal from the Commandos (p. 298, 'so popular as to be unemployable' should of course read 'unpopular', a misprint Waugh would have enjoyed for its implications in spite of the blow) resulted in his saying that up till then he had looked on himself as a 'man of the world', now he saw he must be only a writer. Disgust at the backing of Tito Communism in Yugoslavia, the squalors of post-war Great Britain, are reflected in the later journalism.

On the whole the viewpoint of the disillusioned old buffer (Waugh was only in his forties) is more effective journalistically than the rather shadowy smart pre-war young man. Much of the best stuff is in the later sections. Waugh had always done a good deal of reviewing, sometimes because he needed the money, sometimes because he wanted to express an opinion. Even when he dislikes a book he gives a fair account of what it is about and, far from being unwilling to praise, his tastes were considerably wider in scope than might be expected.

When Hemingway wrote one of his worst books *Across the River* . . . Waugh showed that he was not going to join the pack in leaping to attack a novelist who had once been a pioneer in the trade. Waugh always admired Compton-Burnett, and could pick out a new talent like V. S. Naipaul's. Complaining of the suppressions of disagreeable aspects of their subjects in the *Dictionary of National Biography*, Waugh suggested that there should be a set form: 'The above was sober, honest, chaste, maritally faithful, sexually normal, courageous, sweet-smelling, etc.', the omission of any quality being 'recognized as significant by regular readers'.

The first Post-Impressionist Exhibition (in London) was 1910, not 1908, and Nancy Mitford did not 'reign in the British Embassy'. She merely had a flat in Paris, where she was very hospitable to visiting friends.

The Essays, Articles and Reviews of   1984
Evelyn Waugh, Donat Gallagher,   *Daily Telegraph*
Methuen.

VII

Christopher Sykes's life of Evelyn Waugh (1975) had all the merits and some of the demerits of biography written by a close friend. It was subjective, giving a vivid picture of Waugh from the point of view of someone who knew him very well and, in spite of occasional rows, was devoted to him.

Since then Waugh's Diaries and Collected Letters have appeared, together with several fairly detailed accounts by other friends. There is, in short, room for a book which is simply the result of research.

The first volume of Martin Stannard's biography is much too long. Often repetitive, it could have been cut by a hundred, perhaps 200 pages. It begins with an excellent account of Waugh's background, the description of his parents being particularly good. I had always found his mother rather a mysterious figure. Apparently she was not at all literary, even after her younger son was an established writer regretting that he had given up the career he had once proposed for himself of furniture-maker.

It was true that Waugh himself said he was forced to become a writer, and would have preferred some other profession. The fact remains that a writer he became, living, sometimes very precariously, on his books and his journalism. It is, indeed, an extraordinary story, because he never lowered his own standard as far as the books were concerned, even if much of the journalism was essentially 'popular', and he was always extravagant.

Martin Stannard gives a less one-sided account of the break-up of Waugh's first marriage than has been recorded hitherto, carrying the narrative on to Waugh's second marriage and the outbreak of war in

1939. He recounts Waugh's various journeys in Africa and South America, which were often incredibly uncomfortable and fairly dangerous.

On the whole these are much as chronicled by Waugh himself, but his Arctic adventure is made more interesting by providing also the point of view of one of his companions. In addition, Stannard tells us that by leaving the expedition prematurely, Waugh missed the scoop of a Nazi spy in the area.

I do, however, beg Martin Stannard, before his new volume appears, to have half an hour's talk with some informed person about titles: the difference between Lord Snooks and Lord John Snooks, Lady Snooks and Lady Mary Snooks. This is not merely to obtain a veneer a social sophistication, but to avoid the actual misinformation which results from the hash that is made here.

The worst instance of this among many is Mells, the country house belonging to Mrs Katharine Asquith, where Waugh often stayed. Mells was the seat of the Horners. Katharine Asquith (née Horner), who inherited it, had married Raymond Asquith, son of the Prime Minister. When her husband was killed in action, she became a Roman Catholic. The Prime Minister was created Earl of Oxford and Asquith, a title inherited by his grandson. Katharine Asquith, although offered the rank of Dowager Countess, preferred to remain as she was.

Stannard makes a terrible muddle of all this. He says that Lady Horner was a Roman Catholic convert, and makes her the mother of the present Lord Oxford and Asquith. He refers to Katharine Asquith as Lady Katharine Asquith, which she could in no circumstances have been. (Incidentally, he also refers to Waugh's second mother-in-law, Mrs Herbert, as Lady Herbert, for no ascertainable reason.)

It is no doubt a very difficult business to sort out Waugh's closely-knit friends and acquaintances after fifty or more years for somebody quite unfamiliar with that sort of world. All the same, many facts got wrong are in books of reference. For example, John Heygate, who ran away with Waugh's first wife, was a baronet's nephew, not a baronet's younger son. The brothers Alfred Duggan and Hubert Duggan are perpetually confused; as are the brothers Richard and David Plunket Greene.

Alfred Duggan was the alcoholic who cured himself and became an historical novelist; Hubert may have drunk a fair amount, but was an MP and social figure. Richard Plunket Greene was the racing-car driver. David never did anything more dangerous than play the piano. Frank Pakenham had not become a Roman Catholic convert in 1930; while Christopher Sykes was not a convert, but had been born a Catholic.

In rather a different vein, the very last thing on earth Gerald

Duckworth, the publisher, could be called was 'garrulous'. It was very difficult to get more than a few grunts out of him. So far from being an expensive restaurant, Previtali's was one of the cheapest places in London to have a decent meal.

The Yorkes' house in Gloucestershire was Forthampton, rather than Fulhampton. There seems some ambiguity on p. 286 as to whether the dramatizer of *Vile Bodies* was called Boscastle or Bradley. Finally, the photograph, captioned 'Lady Dorothy and Lady Mary Lygon arriving for the wedding', in fact shows the Hon. Betty Askwith (not Asquith) and the Hon. Theodora Benson.

Martin Stannard has sensible things to say about Waugh's books, and he is quite tough in recognizing Waugh's tenuous hold on the society to which he aspired, but these errors do mar his study, and should be avoided in the second volume.

Evelyn Waugh: The Early Years,
1903–1939, Martin Stannard,
Dent.

1986
Daily Telegraph

CHRISTOPHER ISHERWOOD

I

The writing of a straight autobiography presents difficulties to a novelist of ability, both because of the complications of deciding what to put in, and of the ingrained habit of creative invention. Every person in the autobiographical story seems to require full development, every incident to be set in its right perspective, the temptation to dramatize hard to resist. Such an approach implies enormous length.

No doubt this is true of all autobiographers up to a point, but professional writers are particularly vulnerable. Christopher Isherwood most ingeniously avoids some of these pitfalls by using as frame to his own story that of his father and mother. In doing this he was exceptionally well supplied with basic material. Not only did letters survive and his mother keep a diary, but both parents were, in their own way, capable of far more than average self-expression.

One must begin by saying that the book would have been greatly improved by an index and simple chart pedigree. Everyone is called by a christian name, and, from time to time, the reader wants to look back to link up earlier happenings.

The Bradshaws, a family of which the best-known member is William Bradshaw the Regicide, but which included other Cromwellian notables, became possessed of Marple Hall and Wyberselegh Hall, Cheshire, at the beginning of the seventeenth century. The former was a country house of considerable distinction. In the first half of the eighteenth century, the Bradshaw heiress married Nathaniel Isherwood, a felt-maker, from whom the writer of *Kathleen and Frank* descends.

Possibly Isherwood, at times a little old fashioned in his social history, rather exaggerates this marriage as a come-down. Felt-making was a great Midlands industry, in which many squires were involved, prejudice against 'trade' being a later invention. Either way, the Isherwoods became a 'county family', though latterly rather a ramshackle one.

Isherwood's father, Frank (b. 1869), a younger son, married Kathleen, only child of a brewer called Frederick Machell-Smith and his wife, née Greene, thereby connecting Graham Greene as a cousin. Frederick Machell-Smith sounds unusually nasty, stingy and bad mannered. He made every sort of difficulty about his only child's marriage, although she was attractive, well behaved, already into her thirties. Frank was a regular soldier, and, as junior officers were abominably paid, poor; but there was no reason to suppose he would not have a reasonably good future.

Frank, within the terms of reference, seems to have been outstandingly agreeable, honourable and quite talented. He plugged away at getting married to Kathleen in the face of his tiresome father-in-law's opposition; hoped to become OC the Royal Military School of Music (full-colonel's appointment); thought of resigning from the army to become a professional painter; read a lot of poetry and other books with pleasure; commanded one of the battalions of his regiment (the York & Lancaster) with distinction; and was killed in action at Ypres in 1915.

Kathleen was also very reasonably well read, and a person of enormous vitality. She lived to ninety-one. Her great emotional tie-up was obviously with her mother, also a woman of notable liveliness, who, rather dashingly, spent her widowhood in a flat in the Adelphi, then, one would have thought, rather a raffish neighbourhood.

Isherwood, himself, of course, comes in all the time, if only by implication. The book is an extraordinarily vivid record of what it was to be an army family; Aldershot and Ireland; Strensall and Camberley; pushed round the country, from pillar to post. It is hard to imagine that it could be better described in an oblique manner.

There is, as Isherwood himself recognizes, a certain irony in this reconstruction; one of the reasons for his writing the book being to exorcize the past, which he early 'learnt to hate and fear, because it threatened his future'. This menace manifested itself in two forms: first the existence of the family mansion, with its tapestry, armour, traditions of ghosts; secondly, the compulsory imposition of the figure of a Dead-Hero-Father.

The latter problem seems to have been fairly well resolved when the author became a citizen of the United States in 1946; the former, by total eradication. When Isherwood inherited the property in 1940, he made it over to his brother Richard. Marple Hall appears then to have been put in the hands of a caretaker, which did not prevent burglars, vandals and mere sightseers from removing its contents and reducing the building itself to a ruin. The local authorities stepped in, as it had become unsafe, and the place was demolished.

Christopher Isherwood seems occasionally to cast blame when only an idiom of the period is concerned. For example, to say one had given someone a 'good character' was surely a typical facetious phrase of the time, not 'condescending' because servants were given 'characters'; and it is a little severe to his mother to object to her calling Harold Monro's Poetry Bookshop 'quaint'. I think she wrote 'careered up and down on her bicycle', rather than 'careened' (turn a ship over for cleaning), an American solecism. What were Christopher's reactions when Richard was born seven years after himself? It is the one psychological point omitted.

The picture is an absorbing one. It is autobiography handled in a truly original manner. Did Uncle Henry contribute something to Mr Norris?

Kathleen and Frank, Christopher   1971
Isherwood, Methuen.   *Daily Telegraph*

II

I met Gerald Hamilton once at a party for a brief moment, introduced, I think, by the writer, J. Maclaren-Ross, quoted here as calling him (characteristically) 'the last of the dangerous men'.

John Symonds, in this very amusing and well-handled series of 'conversations', thinks Gerald Hamilton better described as a 'child searching for he did not know what'. Even allowing for that, the Maclaren-Ross estimate is not to be entirely ruled out.

Christopher Isherwood put Gerald Hamilton on the literary map – he was on other maps, including those of various police forces, already – by immortalizing him as Mr Norris in *Mr Norris Changes Trains*, the classical novel of pre-Hitler Berlin. In due course Mr Norris came not far short of establishing a Frankenstein monster's hold on his creator. We are shown Gerald Hamilton here, for example, complaining that Isherwood has come to London, and not got in touch, supposedly fearing that a projected musical of the novel, if it came off, might entail giving his puppet (Hamilton) a cut.

Although Gerald Hamilton wrote two autobiographies, it is hard to speak with certainty about much of his life, the facts of which he treated imaginatively, rather than realistically. His true surname was Souter (Hamilton a middle name); he was educated for three years at Rugby and inherited a comfortable amount of money as a young man. He ran through this in about three years. Thenceforth he lived in a world of homosexuals, gourmets, dubious international aristocrats, and, one imagines, double agents, working for assorted political causes. During the 1930s his affiliations were Communist. When war broke out, he was interned under 18B.

John Symonds, biographer of Aleister Crowley (one time friend of Gerald Hamilton), puts over his subject's conversation and daily life with vividness and ease, the consequence of what must have been hard work, all traces of which have been removed. We hear about many odd encounters – with all sorts of persons, from Rasputin to d'Annunzio – his occasional memorable meals, his frightful money troubles. From the last of these he usually somehow extricated himself.

As always, when reading about this sort of adventurer, one is astonished by the way that personality, charm, bluff, invariably carry the field against sober fact. Hamilton (naturally a Jacobite, and author of a book called *Blood Royal*) gave chapter and verse of his own male line descent from the ducal family of that name, when all that had to be done to disprove his claim was to look it up in any book of reference, when the father and grandfather named by him would not be found.

In the early 1920s Gerald Hamilton, through unwise manipulations of a pearl necklace, landed himself in an Italian prison for a year – he was lucky not to serve three. In Brixton, where he paid more than one visit, somebody sent him (when in the privileged block) a bottle of Chambertin 1916 – a little old by then for burgundy, it might be thought – which the warder decanted into a tin, bottles not being allowed.

Gerald Hamilton on food and wine always sounds absolutely genuine (more than can be said for all who pontificate on the subject), and there is at least one recipe quoted, risotto, which would be worth trying. I think it unlikely that he was the original poet of the verses, dating well into the past, that begin:

> Uncle back from Evensong
> Rang for cook and did her wrong.

He tells the well-known story of the Prince Regent saying, 'Harris, a glass of brandy', after the presentation to him of his bride, Caroline of Brunswick, seeming to think Harris was the Prince's valet. Harris was, of course, our envoy to Brunswick, later Lord Malmesbury. This is not quite clear in Symonds's note. It is also odd that Gerald Hamilton, something of an authority on trafficking in foreign decorations, told Symonds that a CB was no better than an OBE, certainly not true, especially in the context of the question.

The illustrations, in the George Grosz manner, by the late James Boswell, although they afford a good likeness, seem not quite appropriate to the fastidious tastes of their subject. One feels he would have preferred something less openly brutal. He died in June 1970, at the age of seventy-nine, having been ill apparently for only a few days. Strangely, he gave Symonds the date of his birth as two years earlier than the apparent truth.

How did he live? Several people seem to have been very charitable in handing out relatively large sums from pure kindness of heart. There also seems to have been a small Spanish governmental pension. In the past money had certainly been earned in all sorts of murky ways, including two *mariages de convenance*.

Conversations with Gerald, John   1974
Symonds, Duckworth.   *Daily Telegraph*

III

This slice of autobiography between the years 1929 and 1939 might be looked on as a second volume, following up Christopher Isherwood's account of his parents, *Kathleen and Frank* (1971), which began the story.

In dealing with a work of an autobiographical sort, reviewers are apt to base their judgment on whether the writer sounds the sort of person they would themselves like; coupling that with an avalanche of moral, political, and social judgments, together with a word of advice on how it could have been better done.

I shall restrict myself to very tentative comments on the last theme: Isherwood's habit of using the third person – only sometimes the first – runs the risk of archness. Besides which, when he refers to the Narrator of the Berlin novels as 'Isherwood', the reader has to distinguish between the trinity of 'Isherwood' (in inverted commas), 'Christopher' and 'I' (the last two not placed in inverted commas).

Having registered these complaints, I was absorbed with Isherwood's chronicle of his early days, even if it would have been preferable in the first person. It has the clearness of narrative he brings to his novels and is full of characteristic adventures. Some events have been related before, but one feels like a child at bedtime: 'Tell me again about Mr Norris in the brothel, Uncle Christopher'; or 'Let's hear the one about the nice film director when you were in pictures.'

Incidentally, we learn at least as much about the author from the comment that he immediately took to the film world at his first attempt at scriptwriting, as from the many pages about homosexuality – especially homosexuality in pre-Hitler Germany. It is very believable when Isherwood says that he came to be fascinated by the Berlin male-prostitute world, not so much for its individual members, as for 'their slang, their girls, their thefts, their quarrels, their jokes, their outrageous unserious demands, encounters with the police'.

Isherwood could be called obsessed with 'telling the truth'; he frequently contrasts what he wrote in novels with 'what actually happened'. This moment of 'truth' in novels, as opposed to the 'truth' attempted by reportage, is an interesting and controversial subject. I am not at all sure that reportage always wins.

Let me give two small instances. I happened to know the 'Francis' of this book slightly at Oxford who plays a considerable part in Isherwood's account of Berlin life. In a novel Isherwood said that 'Francis' had a 'kind of contemplative repose' and 'could have posed for the portrait of a saint'. He now goes back on the description but (possibly another sort of 'truth') that is just what I remember 'Francis' looking like.

In a similar way Isherwood now regrets that he did not represent his Narrator in the Berlin novels as homosexual – which in those days would have made the book scarcely publishable. But surely no one of the smallest grasp ever supposed the Narrator was anything else but homosexual? To have made this explicit (something equally avoided by Proust) would have been to risk writing a tract.

I mention these points not to lessen the qualities of *Christopher and His Kind*, but to draw attention to what constitutes much of its interest; that is to say the competition between two different art-forms to convey an individual 'myth' – which is the only 'truth' an autobiographer can hope to put over, and then only in an individual way.

Isherwood became deeply involved with a German boy called Heinz. They tagged round the world together – Denmark, Belgium, Portugal, many other places. By this time Hitler had come to power and war began to loom. Owing to a blunder in filling up a form, Heinz was unable to come to England. For a variety of reasons he became *persona non grata* in almost every other European country, and, through a technicality, had to cross the German frontier. He was arrested for avoiding conscription – an exciting story – and then followed an extraordinary sequence – imprisonment, serving on both fronts during the war, marrying, and living happily ever after.

It had been hoped to buy Heinz Mexican citizenship at the price of £1,000; negotiations were in the slippery hands of Gerald Hamilton ('Mr Norris'). When all fell through Isherwood wondered whether Hamilton (though for certain reasons this seems unlikely) had deliberately arranged the arrest and kept at least some of the money. That could indeed have been a good alternative ending to *Mr Norris Changes Trains*; Mr Norris turning out a genuinely sinister clown, who brings tragedy rather than comedy.

Christopher and His Kind draws to a close with Christopher Isherwood and his old friend W. H. Auden embarking for America in October 1938. Neither of them had ever belonged to the Communist Party, but both had been ardent 'fellow travellers' for many years.

One morning, when they were walking on the deck, Christopher heard himself say: 'You know, it just doesn't mean anything to me any more – the Popular Front, the party line, the anti-fascist struggle. I suppose they're okay but something's wrong with me. I simply cannot swallow another mouthful.' To which Wystan answered: 'Neither can I.'

Christopher and His Kind, 1929–1939, Christopher Isherwood, Eyre Methuen.

1977
Daily Telegraph

NANCY MITFORD AND
HAROLD ACTON

This cannot have been an easy Memoir to write. The background, ostensibly a story of gaiety, social whirl, fantastic success, is darkened by petty vexations, loneliness, eventually ghastly tragedy – yet unless these elements are treated in the subject's own bright and smiling idiom, a wrong impression of how she lived her life would be given.

Harold Acton grapples with these difficulties successfully by adopting an informal approach. There is much quotation from letters. The reader is not always told to whom these letters are written, but it was certainly preferable to sacrifice anything that threatened too ponderous an approach, in favour of keeping a quickly moving narrative. No one knows better than Acton the people concerned, and the life described. He can appreciate the social froth, while handling the dreadful last years in a moving manner.

Nancy Mitford (1904–73) was the eldest child of the 2nd Lord Redesdale. The family, of diplomatic and legal traditions, was old, eccentric, not outstandingly rich. Acton mentions, but does not, I think, sufficiently emphasize, that her maternal grandfather was Thomas Gibson Bowles. Bowles, founder of the Victorian paper *Vanity Fair*, a journalist of notable gifts and attack, was of well-to-do but illegitimate birth. From him Nancy Mitford certainly inherited her own journalistic brilliance, and instinct for gauging the popular taste of the moment. Her tendency to be a little insistent on her other aristocratic side – even if that aspect, too, had to be treated as a joke – may also have been influenced by mixed feelings about those contrasted origins.

After a broken engagement, Nancy was not married until she was twenty-nine. Acton speaks with moderation when he categorizes her husband as a 'first-class bore'. Nevertheless, she behaved to him with great loyalty, her early writings helping to support a ménage that was chronically short of cash.

By the end of the war the two of them had become estranged, and she began an association with 'the Colonel' – as Nancy always called him – Gaston Palevski, a member of General de Gaulle's Free French entourage. This connection was to become the centre of her life. Two things emerged from it: Nancy Mitford's other lifelong love affair, which was with France (where she settled after the war); and her two novels, *The Pursuit of Love* and *Love in a Cold Climate*. She wrote other novels before and after, but it is on these two that her reputation for wit, originality and creation of character will rest.

Speaking of 'the Colonel', Acton says: 'He admired Nancy and was deeply attached to her, but he had always been candid about not falling in love with her. He was a devoted companion on whose sympathy, advice and intellectual refreshment she could steadfastly rely.' In addition to that 'the Colonel' was unquestionably the inspiration that gave the two novels named above a lyrical touch that she never achieved again.

In 1958, she made a trip to England, staying successively with L. P. Hartley, Evelyn Waugh, and myself. 'Leslie had the warmest house and warmest heart. Evelyn by far the coldest house and Tony Powell the coldest heart . . . I find all these writers take themselves very seriously.'

If kind hearts are more than coronets, cold ones are certainly less than bestsellers; but taking oneself seriously is perhaps another matter. Acton makes the point that it would be hard to argue that writers on this side of the Channel take themselves more seriously than in France; while Nancy herself – as may be seen from many of the letters – was far from being unserious about her own work. It would, however, always seem a surprise to her that she could write at all, or that successful writing – and she was very successful with her public – naturally resulted in consequences like fan-mail or newspaper interviews. Her books were to her not so much a form of art as a passionate emotional upheaval in herself; particularly her historical works.

'In spite of her intellectual bent she could not be described as an intellectual, nor could she be described as sensual or worldly,' writes Acton; and later on he says with great truth: 'Nancy had the naivety of the pure in heart'. This did not prevent her books selling, and she speaks of the sales of her illustrated study of Louis XIV, 'The Sun King', as 350,000; a figure not to be sneezed at.

She had a house of great charm in Paris, but, contrary to what many supposed, did not 'go out' a lot; partly because she worked very hard, partly to be available if 'the Colonel' decided to visit her. She was a person who aroused great devotion in those around her. For example, she fell into the habit of staying in Venice most years, going to write in the island of Torcello. I can vouch for the fact that her name, mentioned casually in the bar or restaurant of the Torcello hotel, would arouse an immediate reaction of remembrance and affection among the staff.

Her historical books do not seem to me to have the interest of most of her novels. Harold Acton judges *Voltaire in Love* the best. She never learnt that what is excellent journalism is not necessarily good history;

but at the same time she felt – in a sense rightly – that her own individual touch, with its smattering of schoolgirl slang, gave them their particular cachet, without which they would be merely humdrum.

Latterly, she left Paris for Versailles, and there she was assailed by a malady that the doctors could not diagnose. The last four years of her life were tortured with pain, and the worries of being in and out of hospital. She behaved, as one would have expected, with the greatest courage, but these pages make painful reading.

Nancy Mitford: A Memoir, Harold   1975
Acton, Hamish Hamilton.   *Daily Telegraph*

GRAHAM GREENE

I

In his excellent Introduction, both informative and amusing, to this reissue of *Night and Day*, the comic magazine which ran from July to December 1937, Christopher Hawtree rightly points out that it was a kind of counterblast, in its light-hearted gaiety (in the true sense), to the half-baked Communist cant of W. H. Auden & Co.

That confraternity is still, sometimes, inexplicably spoken of as 'The Writers of the Thirties', as if no other views than theirs existed at that period, nor any superior talent.

There had long been plans to supersede the vapid philistinism of *Punch* with something better and at last several persons, of whom Graham Greene and the Hispanophile John Marks were the moving spirits, really got a paper under way. I have the impression that Greene first mentioned the project to me towards the end of 1936, or even as late as the beginning of 1937, and, hilarious as that might now appear, suggested that I might do the film criticism.

As it happened I had plans (never realized) to become a scriptwriter in Hollywood, and was away from London from April until August 1937, the period of *Night and Day* coming to birth. On my return from California Greene had decided to take on film criticism himself. This was most fortunate, because lacking the burning puritanism of Greene, in certain moods I should never have done more than say that I thought *Wee Willie Winkie* was an awful picture – and one of the great comic incidents of the century would have been lost.

Instead came the famous alleged libel in Greene's notice of the child-star Shirley Temple (reproduced in the book). *Night and Day*, already tottering to its fall, went down like the Fighting Téméraire in a blaze of laughter. It was a Far, Far Better Thing . . . and, like those heroes who die young, meant the paper never had to descend to hack-writers and routine jokes, the inevitable fate of long-lived publications of its kind.

In his Preface to this edition Graham Greene, I think rightly, emphasizes that, in spite of the dazzling cast of writers, the drawings in *Night and Day* were perhaps its strongest feature. This was largely due to Selwyn Powell (so far as I know, no relation). In this field especially – dare one hint it? – was the magazine's undoubted touch of chic, a characteristic very much to seek in the periodicals of today. Among the artists (H. Botterill, Walter Goetz, Nicolas Bentley, Barbosa, several more) one would particularly mention, for his originality, Paul Crum, whose real name was Roger Pettiward and who was killed in a Commando raid a year or two later.

It is possible only to pick out things here and there among the written material because so much might be commented upon. For instance, John Hayward, the scholar and bibliographer, close friend of T. S. Eliot's and regarded by the poet as of notable assistance in commenting on his uncompleted poems, did the *Night and Day* Broadcasting and Television column. Osbert Lancaster wrote on Art; Constant Lambert on Music. Cyril Connolly, through the eyes of the daughter Felicity, observed in a serial the middlebrow family of Arquebus.

Evelyn Waugh did the regular lead book review. These are well worth reprinting. They vary between recommending the still perhaps not adequately recognized novel about the 1914 War, *In Parenthesis*, by David Jones, to a now forgotten but by no means ungifted short-story writer Peter Chamberlain. For those interested in the craft of reviewing I would particularly recommend a notice by Waugh, which includes Edith Sitwell's novel *I Live Under a Black Sun*, Ernest Hemingway's *To Have and Have Not*, and *Tinpot Country* by Terence Greenidge.

Waugh was well disposed towards Edith Sitwell, but her novel was not an easy one to review in a manner the writer would herself find satisfactory. Hemingway was admired by Waugh, but the latter did not consider *To Have and Have Not* anything like as good as *The Sun Also Rises*. Terence Greenidge was a dotty Oxford friend (and, I believe, cousin) of Waugh's, who produced novels from time to time that were, to say the least, eccentric. Anyone who wants to know how to deal with a package like that in an elegant manner can here learn a lot.

Peter Fleming, then renowned as a young explorer, wrote a gossip commentary signed Slingsby; the last, I think, more of an 'in' joke than because the *Night and Day* premises were near Slingsby Place, though that may also have played a part. His brother Ian Fleming (begetter of Bond) may have helped to raise money for the magazine in the City.

Among less expected contributors were the French writer Paul Morand, friend of Proust's, later to be one of Vichy's ambassadors; the poet Stevie Smith making an early appearance; and Gerald Kersh, whose novels about serving in the ranks of the Coldstream Guards and the prostitute/ponce world of London are still worth a glance.

The early numbers of *Night and Day* were made a shade too like the *New Yorker*, but that was to show the difference from *Punch* rather than resemblance to the American paper, in spite of including a drawing by

Thurber. In short *Night and Day* was a wholly original production, and this reprint should make a perfect Christmas gift.

Night and Day, Christopher   1985
Hawtree, ed., Chatto.   *Daily Telegraph*

II

The first volume of Norman Sherry's life of Graham Greene is – to use a favourite phrase of our Balliol tutor Kenneth Bell, when one of his pupil's essays was interminable – 'a most portentous length'. Bell had been, as it happened, also educated at Berkhamsted, of which Greene himself was alumnus; his father headmaster; older brother head of the house.

This last concatenation of circumstances does not seem to have worked out well for Greene, who hated his schooldays, felt himself at once persecuted and betrayed by individual boys, resulting in his running away (naturally rather a difficult thing to do as his home was also his school), finally suffering a nervous breakdown.

Greene's parents (in a manner decidedly go-ahead for the period) sent their difficult son to a psychoanalyst. Their choice turned out to have three strings to his bow, being at the same time a Spiritualist and an alcoholic. On the face of it these contending professional, religious and physical states might have seemed to threaten any possible cure. On the contrary, the triune effect appears to have been dramatic. From being a boy scarcely able to sit down without fear of a pair of dividers being thrust into his bottom, Greene became henceforth the energetic forceful personality now internationally celebrated.

So far as I can remember – in the Balliol manner of everyone living his own life – Greene and I met only once there, although he was merely a year (1922) ahead of me. That was in Sligger's rooms. Greene, with several others, was wearing a dinner-jacket. Probably some club dinner had taken place. I addressed a remark to him, at which he replied rather sharply. No doubt it was foolish or frivolous. We did not meet again until 1933 or 1934, when we saw a certain amount of each in the years just before the war, and he was later briefly to become my publisher.

At Balliol, Greene showed a lively interest in social life, editing the *Oxford Outlook*, which brought him indirectly into touch with quite a few literary figures of the time like Edith Sitwell and Edmund Blunden. His own collection of poems, *Babbling April*, was published while he was still up at Balliol. He also appeared in a group of Oxford poets in a radio programme of the newly established BBC. More important, perhaps, was a visit to Germany, with the aim of making trouble for the French authorities, France having recently reoccupied the Ruhr in order to extract Repatriation Payments; an early step on Greene's part into the world of espionage and intrigue.

Meanwhile Greene had fallen desperately in love with Vivien Dayrell-Browning, who worked in Blackwell's bookshop. Her parents were separated, her father in Africa. At one moment her mother had been governess to the Rudyard Kiplings. (Of that one would like to hear more. Was she Miss Blake in *Puck of Pook's Hill?*) Vivien Dayrell-Browning was an intensely devout Roman Catholic convert. Greene's own conversion, with its far-reaching literary consequences, was in the first instance due to her refusal to marry him unless he converted. A celibate marriage was seriously discussed.

As the time for going down approached, the question of a job loomed. There was the possibility of Insurance (like Kafka, Aubrey Beardsley, Wallace Stevens, Roy Fuller); Asiatic Petroleum; *The Times*; while Kenneth Bell favoured (indication of his perspicacity) the Levant Consular Service. In the end it was journalism, with a depressing job on a paper in Nottingham. From there Greene progressed in due course to *The Times*.

All the while, of course, the ambition to write was at the back of his mind. He was obviously regarded as unusually efficient at the *Times* job (on the strength of which he married), but he had also written three novels, the last of which was accepted by a publisher. *The Man Within* (first of all to be called *Dear Sanity*) proved a winner when it appeared in 1929, selling 8,000 copies (exceedingly successful for a first novel of those days), and was translated into German, Dutch, Norwegian, Danish, Spanish.

Norman Sherry, who perhaps somewhat over-extends paraphrasing Greene's books in his own words, is first-rate on statistics. He always records a book's circulation, or the rent of accommodation occupied. It was news to me that Greene's second and third novels had been (by the standards of *The Man Within*) relative failures, putting him into a financially parlous state.

From these embarrassments Greene extracted himself with *Stamboul Train* (1932), where J. B. Priestley, ludicrously, considered himself libelled, on that account making a bit of trouble. A more serious case of libel resulted from a film review during Greene's shared editorship of the short-lived magazine *Night and Day*, when the (then) child-star Shirley Temple (upon whose sex-appeal Greene too freely adumbrated) objected, through her employers in Hollywood, to what he had written. Priestley and Shirley Temple make a hilarious duo in this field.

Sherry guides his readers through the penitentially uncomfortable journeys taken by Greene to Liberia and Mexico, and the later novels:

A Gun for Sale (1936), *Brighton Rock* (1938), *The Power and the Glory* (1940). The last was outside the scope of this volume, though often referred to in connection with its Mexican *doppelgänger The Lawless Roads* (1939). I don't think Sherry quite appreciates what a terrible condition the book trade was in during the two or three years leading up to the war. Every time Hitler marched into a new place book sales in Great Britain slumped. Greene, like every other writer, was affected to some degree.

All this time Greene was making an impact on the film world, paving the way to 'the legitimate', together with producing a mass of effective journalism. All these aspects of building a writer's career, far too many to be mentioned in the space available here, are conscientiously dealt with by his biographer.

Where one has doubts about Sherry's judgment is in his repeated insistence on Greene's taste for privacy, his shunning of publicity, withdrawal from the everyday world, although Sherry does go so far as to admit: 'His letters to his agents reveal him as cool, clinical and business-like, keeping them up to scratch. . . .'

Secretive, yes, but surely to arrange for a biography to appear in one's lifetime in which love letters, an intimate diary, every sort of personal detail, has been provided for the biographer, is the antithesis of being a private person, anxious to keep himself to himself. Indeed – dare one say so? – some of the information supplied (such as prostitutes and the part they played in Greene's early married life) borders on the exhibitionist.

In short, one would have thought Greene revealed himself from the start as a master of publicity – why not? To be sparing in accepting interviews in a well-known figure is to be that desirable thing hard-to-get, a manner of drawing attention to oneself, rather than the opposite. Such ploys as these which were to be used later like the 'open letters' about other notabilities (Charlie Chaplin, Colette), not to mention a steady stream of correspondence to the papers on usually controversial subjects, which continues until this moment, do not suggest a man who abhors publicity. This might be worth a moment's thought on the part of Norman Sherry, while we eagerly await further revelations in his next volume.

The Life of Graham Greene: Volume
One: 1904–1939, Norman
Sherry, Cape.

1989
Balliol Register

III

THE DRYING ROOM: or, The Termination of the Predicament

by GR*H*M GR**N*

When the curtain rises FATHER FLESH *is sitting at a table in the Drying Room, pasting photographs into an album. To leave his hands free he has strapped his ear-trumpet to the side of his head with one of his suspenders. He is eighty. There is a rattling at the door. This noise continues for ten minutes. Then the door comes off its hinges, and his sister,* MISS FLESH, *steps over it into the Drying Room. She is some years older than her brother. She wears lavender satin and a mob cap.*

MISS FLESH (*shouting into his ear-trumpet*). There is another letter from the Bishop.

FR FLESH (*without looking up*). What does he want this time?

MISS FLESH. It is about incense again. Two hundredweight in three months! He's guessed you're reselling it.

FR FLESH. Rats!

MISS FLESH. You'll be unfrocked.

FR FLESH. Perhaps it would be better if one *were* unfrocked.

MISS FLESH. How should we live then?

FR FLESH. One thinks one would find a way. Have the new photographs from Paris arrived yet?

MISS FLESH. Nipcat is bringing them. That young man is after our niece.

FR FLESH. If she *is* one's niece.

MISS FLESH. Whether she's your niece, or whether she isn't, she is to leave Nipcat alone.

FR FLESH. You want him for yourself.

MISS FLESH. Why not?

FR FLESH. Why not, indeed?

MISS FLESH. There are only sixty-seven years between us.

FR FLESH. It should be enough. Here *is* Nipcat.

Enter NIPCAT. *He is about twenty, with a wooden leg and a false hand. He wears a zoot suit and two pairs of spectacles. He is carrying a large parcel.*

FR FLESH. Where are the photographs? I can't wait all night. I have Sin to commit.

NIPCAT (*handing over the parcel and sitting down to adjust his wooden leg*). Take 'em. (*Wearily*) How sick one is of Sin!

FR FLESH. Naturally, one is sick of Sin. Do you suppose one can sit in a drying room all day long, pasting pictures like this into a scrap-book, without getting sick of Sin?

NIPCAT. Why doesn't one stop, then?

FR FLESH. One can't spend *all* one's time selling incense on the Black Market, can one? When does Benita's turn end at the Blue Belfry?

NIPCAT. She is due here at any moment. One hopes one will not slash her across the face with one's rosary to-night.

FR FLESH. That depends on one's Sin quota. She is bringing a sample of the new blended incense with her – it goes twice as far as the ordinary kind. (*Dreamily*) But does it smell as sweet as in the old days of one's innocence? One remembers the scent so well when one was an acolyte. But here she is.

> *Enter* BENITA. *She has come straight on from her night-club turn, and wears a bikini bathing dress, top hat, and black silk stockings.*

FR FLESH (*sternly*). Do you consider those suitable clothes in which to appear before one? Put on your gloves!

BENITA. Stow it! Do you want to try some of the blended incense? I've got a sample here.

> *She places a large rubber bag full of incense on the table. Then she crosses the room and takes* NIPCAT *by the hand.*

MISS FLESH (*giving a shriek*). Leave Nipcat alone!

NIPCAT (*to* BENITA). It can't be.

BENITA. Why not?

NIPCAT. I belong to her.

BENITA. But we were to be married by the Cardinal!

FR FLESH. Stop arguing and show me the incense.

> NIPCAT *shrugs his shoulders.*

BENITA (*passionately*). Oh, why do we have to lead this awful life, half-way between the Third Man and the Third Programme? I can't stand it much longer!

FR FLESH. It's all a question of Sin. How is one to pack in one's Sin quota otherwise? Light the incense.

> BENITA *suddenly pours a handful of incense into his ear-trumpet, and ignites it with a match. There is a deafening explosion. All the water pipes burst and flood the Drying Room.* FR FLESH, MISS FLESH, *and* NIPCAT *are blown from the stage.* BENITA *removes her top hat and begins to make up her face. A gentle perfume of incense pervades the auditorium. Off-stage the deep notes of a church organ begin to play.*

BENITA. I do believe I've lost my sense of Sin.

> [*curtain*]

1953
Punch

GEOFFREY GRIGSON

I

At first sight it seems strange that, in 1764, when asked by his patron, Lord Hardwick, for '*real views*', Gainsborough replied that, if the Earl wanted anything from him but a picture 'out of his own brain', he had better buy something of the 'good Old Masters'. When one comes to think of it, a 'real view' might be almost as hard to extract from some painters of distinction today, if by that a particular sort of naturalistic treatment were required.

As a matter of fact, from other letters of Gainsborough – excerpts from which are given in the notes of Geoffrey Grigson's enjoyable book – it looks rather as if Gainsborough had professional reasons for discouraging Lord Hardwicke from buying straightforward land-scapes, because, when writing to his own friends, the painter mentions time and again his enjoyment in doing landscape, and getting away from 'People with their damn'd Faces'.

Great Britain has a tremendous tradition of landscape painting, which goes back to the sixteenth century, and it was an excellent idea to run through some of the artists to whom this tradition is owed; saying a word about each, and giving an example or two of his work.

Grigson rightly takes a landscape where he finds it, not necessarily expecting landscape, as such, to be the immediate focus of the eye designed for the viewer by the painter himself. Thus we begin with a St George and the Dragon by Rubens (1577–1640), in which Charles I is shown as St George and Henrietta Maria as the rescued Princess. But they are not the main point in the illustration here reproduced, which is the panorama of the Thames, and distant London in the background.

Skipping a couple of hundred years to Jacques-Laurent Agasse (1767–1849), we find another picture painted primarily as a figure-subject (a lady stepping from a boat at Westminster Bridge about 1817), which gives a self-supporting landscape (again London) in the background, using a formula that has appealed to many painters, that is to say, a view seen through the arch of a bridge. Agasse, a Swiss (like Fuseli), had an admiration for the great figure and animal painter, Stubbs, and he brings a curious continental view of English hunting and coaching scenes – like hearing some familiar English happening described by a keen-eyed foreign friend.

There are the usual examples here (Turner being of course the greatest) of painters who used techniques comparable with those of the Impressionists and Post-Impressionists without arousing the same rage those schools at first evoked. This was perhaps simply because these painters were too few in number to come to the notice of the public in general. Turner was not only linked to an accepted Romantic tradition but supported by aristocratic patrons who did not care what others thought. Both facts help to explain why he did not suffer the same sort of indignation. He is a giant who has emerged from the sneers of petty detractors.

Here, also, will be found Francis Towne (1739–1816), who painted rocks rather like Cézanne's; and the Norfolk artist, John Sell Cotman (1782–1842), whose *Distant View of Greta Bridge* has some of the same Cézanne-like quality. Cotman's *The Marl Pit*, reproduced here in colour, is also extraordinarily 'modern', though the treatment of the sides of the pit slightly suggest Richard Wilson's somewhat 'Cubist' mountains. Another interesting, and not much known, painter capable of innovation was George Barret (1767–1842), represented here by *View of the Coast seen through a Window*. This must have been a daring way to portray the Isle of Wight in 1840.

Richard Wilson (1713–82), one of the greatest of them all, is of course present with the most famous of his mountain pools, *'Cader Idris'*, in the Tate. Wilson, even when painting his native Wales, would habitually add romantic touches like a distant temple or monastery. For that reason the *View of the River Wye* (Plate 20) is hard to be sure about in the suggested reference 'perhaps above Hay-on-Wye', though the buildings are so individual that one would have thought they should be identifiable.

Coming to later times, Grigson mentions that excellent painter, Paul Maitland (1863–1909), a hunchback, who often painted in Kensington Gardens. Sickert speaks of him with warm feeling. Maitland had learnt his art from the London Frenchman, Théodore Roussel, friend of Whistler. It would have been nice to have had one of the Kensington Gardens Maitlands rather than two of Chelsea, attractive as they are.

Grigson has a good word for William Nicholson, whom he reasonably regards as underrated – anyway at his best – and produces what looks like a very pleasing snow scene, the termination of a stretch of balustrading at a Yorkshire country house.

Victor Pasmore (b. 1908) is the last exhibit in a collection that gives a great deal of pleasure, and from which it is possible to learn a good deal about painting – and about Great Britain as well.

Britain Observed: The   1975
Landscape through Artists' Eyes,   *Daily Telegraph*
Geoffrey Grigson, Phaidon.

II

This thorough, but not too solemn, exploration of the position held by
Aphrodite of the classical pantheon, in art and poetry, takes in a great
many interesting – and often disregarded – facets of the goddess.

Aphrodite appeared from the East as Astarte or Ashteroth. Her
Greek name means 'risen from the foam', which Aphrodite did when
she first stepped from the waves (perhaps in a scallop shell) on the coast
of Cyprus. The Romans changed this name to Venus, an epithet of
somewhat obscure origin that seems to denote the magic element of
worship.

In her Asiatic beginnings Aphrodite was primarily a deity of fertility
rather than the Queen of Love. The Romans, when they transmuted
her to Venus, also made certain subtle alterations in her character, the
nature of which Geoffrey Grigson goes into. The curious thing is that
even classical dictionaries are apt to call Aphrodite the 'Greek name for
Venus', rather than vice versa.

Indeed Venus has triumphed over the more beautiful Aphrodite who
was goddess of love in all its forms, including love for sale, and physical
love between those of the same sex. Grigson – who becomes at times
almost frenzied in his anti-puritanism – gets particularly cross with
those who attempt to diminish the claims of Sappho (who invoked
Aphrodite in a poem) to being a lesbian in the clinical sense. It is not
clear from the footnote here exactly what Maurice Bowra said on this
subject, but I feel certain that, whatever it was, it had nothing to do
with prudish feelings. Bowra would have been much more likely to
suggest ingenious reasons for Clytemnestra or Phaedra really preferring their own sex.

There is no doubt that homosexual lovers offered up prayers to
Aphrodite and that some of her temple prostitutes included males,
but it is perhaps worth mentioning that, so far as she represented
fertility, homosexuality would surely have irked her. At least that
seems to be suggested by Petronius in the case of Aphrodite's son,
Priapus (by the wine god, Dionysus), whose shrine was usually close
to that of his mother. Incidentally, I am not so confident as Grigson
that temple prostitutes were such an absolute feast of physical
attractions.

Temples to Aphrodite that remain are rare. Her cult was particularly
obnoxious to Christians, and Constantine, although he did not in
general actively persecute those faithful to the old gods, rooted out
many of Aphrodite's images. One of the few left is at Baalbek in the
Lebanon, where a dozen or more gigantic columns of a temple to
Aphrodite still stand, with carvings dedicated to Priapus.

Grigson quotes Valéry on the subject of the impossibility of making any satisfactory representation of a goddess of beauty because 'what captivates us in some being or other is not this highest perfection of beaty; it is not generally of grace, but always some special feature'.

As would be expected from Geoffrey Grigson, the illustrations here of how various sculptors and painters have conceived Aphrodite are first-rate. Astarte, even in Cyprus as late as 500 BC, was a grotesque shapeless figure, though the Greeks had already by then begun to produce likenesses of a beautiful goddess – as opposed to a beautiful woman.

What one thinks of today as a typical Aphrodite (or Venus) seems to have begun to take shape about the fourth century BC. There are a great many examples of these 'Hellenistic' Aphrodites here, and they are well worth comparing, to see the marked differences between them. Most books show the statues of one museum or one period, rather than bringing together many examples of one individual figure-subject, which this one does with powerful effect.

Archaeology begins at home, and I should particularly like to draw attention to the Aphrodites (perhaps one should say Venuses) that have been excavated in this country, with one of the same Celto-Roman period found in France.

The first of these is a second-century AD bronze statuette of the goddess from Verulamium, St Albans. This was no doubt imported. Immensely sophisticated, it shows her with a huge bow tied well below her waist, and might have been executed by a Renaissance contemporary of Benvenuto Cellini.

Then, from High Rochester, Northumberland, is a third-century relief, Romano-British – decidedly more British than Roman – which has retained all the earlier crudity of the Celts' representations of their own gods. Nevertheless at just about the same date (AD 230–240), near Orleans, was found a Gaullish bronze figure of Venus that seems almost in the style of Reg Butler. Here the distortion is, in its way, just as sophisticated as the naturalistic Verulamium Venus.

In the two mosaics of Venus at the Roman villa at Low Ham, Somerset – one in which the goddess stands between two cupids, the other, between Aeneas and Dido – she looks, especially in the former, rather like a young repertory actress, and something genuinely British seems to have become attached to her.

The gem of the collection, however, is undoubtedly the fourth-century Rudston Venus, from a village in Yorkshire, only discovered in 1933. Grigson remarks with truth: 'Perhaps no more bizarre Venus has survived from antiquity.' He suggests that her extraordinary shape (which recalls ivory figurines of 25,000 BC, found in the Haute-Garonne, though more comically grotesque) was envisaged by some British apprentice or slave who had once worked for a Greek master.

The Goddess of Love: The Birth,	1977
Triumph, Death and Return of	*Daily Telegraph*
Aphrodite, Geoffrey Grigson,	
Constable.	

I I I

Geoffrey Grigson opens this book with a poem (not one of his best) as epigraph:

> My goodness, they're already starting to remember!/I thought they weren't three decades old, but now/They're fifty. Some are bald. Some launch bad breath/Across club luncheon tables, fixing labels./ Some teach. Some write lead reviews each week,/Some nest inside the littlest little magazines,/As ever. And only yesterday the whole platoon/Appeared (but not to me) so clever, etc.

It is not clear whether this is intended simply as a personal apology for moving into the Memoirs-and-bad-breath belt or as a challenge.

If it is a challenge thrown down at last to show how deftly a septuagenarian can handle his *Recollections*, then readers are in for a disappointment. Grigson's earlier volume of autobiography, *The Crest on the Silver* (1950), was a coherent, at times striking, account of the start of a writer's life. The present book is scrappy, repetitive, above all lacks an index. The last is a disaster, because the author's views on the people dealt with are by no means always consistent, and without an index it is almost impossible to collate what he really thinks about, say, T. S. Eliot, who crops up here quite often.

There is nothing wrong with the subjects themselves, chapters being devoted to Eliot, Wyndham Lewis, Clere Parsons, Ruthven Todd, Herbert Read, W. H. Auden, Louis MacNeice, Stephen Spender, Norman Cameron, Henry Moore, Cyril Connolly, Bonamy Dobrée, Geoffrey Taylor, George Barnes, John Piper, John Betjeman, Nikolaus Pevsner, Roy Campbell, Basil Taylor, Ben Nicholson (the last perhaps the best in conveying an idea of its subject). The trouble is that Grigson is far more interested in awarding marks than capable of transmitting, to a reader, something of the subject's essence.

The admired figures – notably Wyndham Lewis (whose accommodation address was the Pall Mall rather than Piccadilly Safe Deposit), W. H. Auden, Henry Moore, Ben Nicholson – are treated with something not much short of gush. But it should be added that lesser names like Clere Parsons, Norman Cameron, Geoffrey Taylor and others, get their due. The etymology of Auden's second name,

Wystan, is pondered. I suspect, from the counties concerned it is simply a corruption of Winston, Anglicization of the Welsh name Trewyn (Whitehouse). There is an amusing account of how Ruthven Todd, a fairly obscure literary man, used to pay Grigson ten bob a week for a room in the Grigson house; sell Grigson books for that amount to a bookseller, from whom the same books would be covertly bought back by the owner for the exact sum.

The last, however, is one of the rare light moments. Grigson, although a paid-up member of the 1920s and the Modern Movement, has little or none of the buoyancy with which the period has rightly or wrongly been associated. On the contrary his dictatorial self-righteousness suggests more some fanatical religious sect.

Naturally the unrighteous are given a bad time. Roy Campbell, for instance, appears to have chased Grigson with a knobkerry, for which he is rightly censured. Cyril Connolly also comes in for obloquy, but there was surely no reason why Connolly, any less than Grigson, should not take an interest in Dylan Thomas as a new young poet.

In this last connection Grigson has been wholly misinformed about the Connolly dinner-party where, among others, the older critic Desmond MacCarthy was present, also Dylan Thomas:

Dylan was scared, as he often was; Dylan was uncertain of how to handle his knife and fork. Not altogether free of his last drinking of beer in the Fulham Road, he began filling up once more and gaining courage and telling dirty old chestnuts which Cyril and his guests had known since childhood.

I was one of the guests at that dinner, and can put Grigson's mind completely at rest. Nothing remotely like that happened. Lord Chesterfield himself could not have behaved with more aplomb at dinner than Dylan Thomas. Everyone thought (as it turned out not wholly correctly) what a nice young man Dylan Thomas was, who knew how to drink just the right amount, and just what degree of literary ribaldry to indulge in.

As a matter of fact Grigson is often less than accurate. You could hardly call the publisher Tom Balston 'little'. Balston must have been well over six foot, and I am sure he never carried 'a silver-topped cane'. An umbrella would have been much more his form.

When it suits him Grigson can be snobbish, but to write 'I have been told that Evelyn Waugh's father, the publisher Arthur Waugh, spoke with a poor command of the King's English' argues a positive fog of misapprehensions. If one wanted to give an example off the cuff of someone who did speak the King's English, worse examples could be found than Arthur Waugh.

John Betjeman incurs Grigson disapproval too. Here I think the

Grigson Achilles heel can be localized. He does not think Betjeman serious. Many would certainly agree that Betjeman overdid his clowning, especially on television. I should have thought, on the other hand, that to suppose him not serious was a complete error. A case might even be made for Betjeman, as a poet, being gifted with a seriousness more subtle than Grigson's own.

To be fair to Geoffrey Grigson, he once perforce had to spend the night in the same double bed at the Royal Clarence Hotel, Exeter, with Betjeman and his teddy-bear Archie, so bitterness is perhaps justified, but what a cartoon for Max Beerbohm.

In the end the reviewer feels a little like a magistrate:

Look here, Grigson, this is the umpteenth time you've been up before the beak for Insulting Behaviour. A clergyman's son ought to know better, but you're not so young as you were, and in your day you have produced some good anthologies and collections of pictures, so this time you'll just be Bound Over in your own recognizances to keep the Peace. Next case.

Recollections: Mainly of Writers and Artists, Geoffrey Grigson, Chatto & Windus/The Hogarth Press.

1984
Daily Telegraph

EDWARD BURRA

I

Edward Burra (1905–76) was not only one of the most remarkable artists of his own or any other period in this country, but also a very extraordinary person. I never knew him at all well, but we used to come across each other occasionally after a first meeting in 1928, and I can think of no one who could be named as a parallel in answer to the question 'Who was Burra like?' That was true physically, socially, aesthetically, taking the last chiefly to mean his own painting and attitude towards it.

We first met quite by chance at Toulon, where Burra was on a holiday with two cronies, William Chappell, then dancer later theatrical director, and Irene Hodgkins (always called Hodge), an extremely pretty girl, also a painter, who died comparatively young, after a fairly romantic and adventurous life. They had all three been at the Chelsea School of Art, and belonged to a small but striking circle formed there, which this symposium, edited and principally contributed by William Chappell, puts deservedly on record.

Chappell provides not only a business-like account of Burra's career as a painter (including his accomplished designs for theatre and ballet), but, as a friend from the age of fourteen, is able to give a close-up – sometimes very funny – of Burra at home. His family life and background are described by Burra's sister Anne (Lady Ritchie of Dundee). Chappell's account of the painter's last days and death are moving. Frederick Ashton recalls Burra's décor for Constant Lambert's *Rio Grande* (Ashton choreography), and Dame Ninette de Valois also writes of Burra and the Ballet. Another old friend of Chelsea Art School days, Barbara Ker-Seymer, a gifted photographer, describes the pressure she had to put on Burra to make him visit his own Retrospective Exhibition at the Tate Gallery in 1973, at the entrance to which he put his hand in his pocket expecting to have to pay.

John Rothenstein says a word about Burra's painting, remarking with truth that 'it would be hardly possible to forge a work and convincingly attribute it to his hand'. The sales side of the paintings (in which Burra was hardly at all interested) was largely handled by Gerald Corcoran, his son and second wife, Corcoran's first wife Bumble

(Beatrice) Dawson, theatrical designer, being another Chelsea Art School friend.

John Banting, perhaps the only true English Surrealist painter, a less substantial artist than Burra but of comparable strangeness, is a contributor. George Melly in his Introduction records that Banting and Burra used to roam together the 'Old Town' pubs of Hastings, where the former lived.

The American poet and writer Conrad Aiken thought Burra the best painter of the American scene (anyway its more *louche* side) in the 1930s, and Aiken's widow Mary Augusta, and son (by an earlier marriage) John, give a lively vignette of Burra in the USA and Mexico. Burra as a traveller in Spain, a country he specially loved, is hilariously chronicled by Clover (née Pritchard) de Pertinez, yet another friend from Chelsea Art School.

The Burra family origins were in Westmorland, but Edward Burra's parents, who were comfortably off, lived in a house outside Rye, where most of their son's life was spent. In theory Burra hated Rye, calling it Tinkerbell Town, but one suspects he really rather loved the place, with its horse-brasses, grandfather-clocks, Breton plates, and lesbians.

Burra's health was never good – all his life he suffered painfully from arthritis – and, being as a boy in no state to go to Eton as planned, he was very sensibly brought up to be a professional painter. His whole life was painting, but, unlike any other artist I have ever heard of, he was quite uninterested in the paintings after they were finished. True he did not depend for his livelihood on painting (though sales latterly must certainly have made a difference to his income), but so far as I am aware there is no evidence that other relatively well-to-do painters (Manet, Matthew Smith) did not bother to attend their own exhibitions; though certainly painters sometimes prefer to keep their own works. Burra would not even allow his friends to hang one of his pictures in any room he frequented with them.

Burra was offered a CBE, but the award would never have been conferred had not a friend made him write a letter of acceptance, and he refused to attend an investiture. The decoration had to be sent by post. In the same way the Academy would have liked to make him an ARA, probably later an RA, but he would undergo none of the formalities. This was not particularly a gesture against conformity, but simply because he could not be bothered.

Burra was, as might be imagined, wholly uninterested in politics. He might be called antinomian, not revolutionary. He was in Spain at the beginning of the troubles there, and, having a meal in a restaurant, asked what the smoke he saw was, which he had noticed on earlier occasions. It was explained that the armed forces of the Left were burning churches. This greatly upset him, and, though inconceivable as a Fascist, he told John Rothenstein that after that he hoped Franco would win.

He liked Wyndham Lewis's writing, but did not care for his painting, though *Beelzebub* (1938), illustrated here, is not without a touch of the Lewis manner. John Aiken defines Burra's middle-period as 'apocalyptic, comic-horrific, sleazy, grim'.

This is a fascinating book, well edited, organized, illustrated. It was, by the way, Ravaillac, assassin of Henri IV, who was torn in pieces by horses (a picture Burra would pore over as a child), rather than Balzac's hero Rastignac, who was only socially torn in pieces by hostesses. The slip is one that Burra himself would have absolutely loved.

Edward Burra: A Painter   1982
Remembered by His Friends,   *Apollo*
William Chappell, ed., Deutsch.

II

It is always dangerous to recommend what has made one laugh, but I found *Well, Dearie! The Letters of Edward Burra*, though not without its sad moments, inexpressibly funny. It also conveys the atmosphere of the 1920s, at its particular level, better than any other book known to me.

Burra suffered all his days from arthritis and pernicious anaemia. He arrived at the Chelsea School of Art at the age of fifteen. There he found William Chappell, then fourteen, and, in due course, Hodge. Other friends made there were the photographer and artist Barbara Ker-Seymer; the stage designer Beatrice (Bumble) Dawson; Lucy Norton, translator of Saint-Simon; Clover (née Pritchard) de Pertinez, also adventurously inclined, who at one moment here found herself immured by a sinister husband in an Hungarian castle. Burra kept these friends all his life. There are others, too, but they constitute the hard core of the Letters, both as recipients and subject-matter.

William Chappell edits with deep affection, understanding and much quiet fun. He can supply notes on forgotten film-stars (the cinema played a great part in Burra's life), and he knows all about theatrical matters. Burra sometimes executed décor for the stage, notably ballets in which two other friends, Constant Lambert and Frederick Ashton, were involved. Another correspondent was the American poet, Conrad Aiken, with whom Burra would sometimes stay for several months in Massachusetts.

As a painter, Burra is not easy to place. He was not really a Surrealist (though latterly a friend of perhaps the only true English Surrealist

painter, John Banting) even if a taste for un-related objects sometimes
gives Burra's pictures Surrealist undertones. The Letters are illustrated throughout the text, and at first the influence of George Grosz
and Jean Cocteau is very apparent. Beardsley, too, made an impact.
Oddly enough, although Burra's general appearance was not in the
least like portraits of Beardsley, a photograph of Burra's profile taken at
Toulon (by Chappell? Ker-Seymer?) certainly resembles Beardsley
side-face. In temperament the two artists undoubtedly had something
in common. Burra's Old Masters were Bosch, Brueghel, Goya.

Often preferring to be a hermit, Burra also loved parties, bars,
night-clubs – the sleazier the better in each case. In this vein his
pictures are seen to equal advantage when portraying Harlem street-
scenes and snack-bars or, nearer home, The Agricultural Arms, Islington.
In the earlier pictures there is perhaps a rather too facile cynicism, though
very genuine horror is never far away, with an extreme sense of sexual
disquiet. Burra's own sexual experience remains enigmatic.

Osbert Lancaster (quoted in the Catalogue) shrewdly sees a kinship
between Burra and those anonymous artists who used to decorate
merry-go-rounds and ice-cream carts – genuine examples of popular
baroque art. For my own part, I prefer Burra's *natures mortes* and
landscapes to the more apocalyptic subjects. He did not concentrate on
landscapes much until his sixties when they become particularly
impressive. He himself lived within sight of the Romney Marsh, and
such huge expanses of country fascinated him, whether Northumberland, Wales, or Connemara. Burra almost always painted in water-
colour. At times the landscapes curiously recall another watercolourist,
the eighteenth-century painter Francis Towne, and, in a different
mood, the Pre-Raphaelite John Brett.

Dealing with Burra's epistolatory style, largely phonetic spelling,
little or no punctuation, is not unlike reading Chaucer in the original,
but none the worse for that. It is hard to do justice by quotation. As
Burra is particularly good on England during the war years, the
following, on a recent Blitz, perhaps gives the flavour. It was sent to
Gunner Chappell 979498 (William Chappell) in December 1940:

> Lightening strikes twice alright on Burton's Piccadilly a cavity in the
> road an elves grotto on the site of Burton Jermyn Street in a fearful
> state and that arcade between Piccadilly and Jermyn Street looked
> like Old San Francisco without Jeanette Mcdonald.

Well, Dearie! The Letters of   1985
Edward Burra, William   *Daily Telegraph*
Chappell, ed., Gordon Fraser.
Edward Burra: Complete
Catalogue, Andrew Causey,
Phaidon.

JOHN BETJEMAN

Constant Lambert was fond of quoting the dictum of a fellow musician: 'I'll try everything once, except incest and folk-dancing.' As an only child who got on badly with both parents, John Betjeman (1906–84) was under small temptation from the former. His Oxford lodgings were at Headington, centre of English Morris Dancing, and for a brief moment he came under the influence of the 'Red Vicar of Thaxted', who encouraged the Morris, but there is no record, so far as I know, that Betjeman ever succumbed. He did, however, try a great many unorthodox things, some of them more than once.

Of my contemporaries who have made some sort of a name in the world (for that matter those who have not, a few of them no less extraordinary) I have no hesitation in saying Betjeman was the most unusual, in background, talents, curious erudition and way of life. His will was of iron, his liking for domination (of his own particular sort) boundless. Bevis Hillier takes the story up to Betjeman's marriage in 1933 to Penelope Chetwode, herself no nonentity. He has tackled a lot of intractable material remarkably well, indeed brilliantly.

There appears little or no doubt that the Betjeman(n)s were of German origin (rather than Dutch), sugar-bakers who arrived here in the early nineteenth century, later founding a furniture business. This produced things like cocktail-cabinets for Maharajahs, Art Deco objects of horrific design, at once torture and poetic inspiration for Betjeman himself, who would have been fourth generation had he agreed to go into the family firm.

Betjeman, only eight months my junior, went up to Oxford (Magdalen) two years later, so that I did not share the bulk of his residence in a slightly different Oxford from my own. All the same Bevis Hillier gives the best impression I have read of Oxford in the 1920s, though it is scarcely just to include Wyndham Ketton-Cremer, Walpole's biographer, in his list of homosexual undergraduates. I knew Ketton-Cremer pretty well, and never heard a suggestion that he had physical relations with another human being, then or throughout his life.

Hillier devotes well-deserved space to Betjeman's contemporary at Marlborough and Oxford, John Bowle, including the hilarious story of their competition to be secretary to Sir Horace Plunket, Irish writer on agricultural economics. When Bowle (later an author and academic) was history master at Westminster, Betjeman took Lord Alfred Douglas to lecture to the boys there. Afterwards Bowle got so drunk that (it is said) Lord Alfred and (Sir) Angus Wilson, one of the then boys, had to carry him to bed.

Betjeman had perpetual rows with his father, who liked his business, shooting and golf; he was incapable of understanding a son of very different tastes who was also by nature extravagant. Ernest Betjeman, not without all humour of a rough and ready sort, had a good deal to put up with, but it should be remembered in his son's favour that, when Betjeman *père* interviewed Sir Horace Plunket to discover why Betjeman *fils* had been sacked, Plunket noted: 'A bounder of the worst kind! I must try to help the boy to get away from his father.'

It would be unrealistic to describe Betjeman as (to use an old-fashioned term) anything but a tuft-hunter in the top class. His capacity for charming those who might be useful to him was unrivalled. Only this determination to 'get on', to persuade whom he could to give him a roof over his head (usually at a goodish address), saw him through until a job turned up on the *Architectural Review*.

Hillier faces squarely the fact that, the *Architectural Review* standing above all for Modernism, Betjeman was, during his employment there, propagating the cause he most hated. ('Encase your legs in nylons/ Bestride your hills with pylons/O age without a soul.') This betrayal haunted him a bit in later life, because from his earliest days he had been fascinated by existing beauties, architectural and otherwise, that were then unrecognized.

All the time Betjeman was, of course, writing poetry. This early obsession that he must be a poet was in some respects almost a handicap at the start, as it left him closed to new ideas, his own being already formed. The other obstruction was his passion for buffoonery, a love of showing-off that never left him. In the short term this brought in good dividends, the British upper classes loving buffoons. In another way, for quite a long time, it prevented Betjeman being taken seriously as a poet.

Hillier makes exceedingly interesting comments on Betjeman's poetry, influences, development, borrowings. He shows certain striking resemblances to the nineteenth-century wit and scholar C. S. Calverley; though I would put Betjeman far above Calverley in the end. Hillier amusingly calls the now all but forgotten Humbert Wolfe the John Betjeman of his day, and one can see what he means, with much else of an acute kind.

Many Betjeman aspects cannot be touched on here, so that we must move on to marriage. Penelope Chetwode's father was baronet (later peer), Field Marshal, former C-in-C of the Army in India; his wife descended from the Lord Combermere of whom Wellington said 'He *is* a fool – a damned fool – but he can take Rangoon.' It would be nice to be able to say that this couple grasped the point of Betjeman at once. That, alas, was far from the case. One can only wonder at their surprise, after the way they had treated their son-in-law, that news kept on coming in of his vivid imitations of them both.

Young Betjeman, Bevis Hillier,   1988
Murray.   *Daily Telegraph*

PETER FLEMING

I

In the early 1930s, no writer did more than Peter Fleming (1907–71) to convince older people that the younger generation was 'all right'.

When other promising young men spent their time drinking, gossiping about art, or indulging in even more dubious activities, Fleming went on expeditions to Brazil and China, joined the Supplementary Reserve of the Grenadier Guards, and wrote a series of bestsellers that showed he could not only use a pen as skilfully as a ·275 Rigby Mauser, but make money out of it too.

Fleming himself was perfectly aware that there was a comic side to all that moral and physical virtuosity. He played Bulldog Drummond in the Oxford University Dramatic Society, and was always at pains to laugh at himself for sustaining that same role to the end of his life. Indeed, he laughed at himself so much, was so determined to understate everything he did, that his very considerable abilities as a writer are sometimes strained by this self-consciousness.

The Fleming background was a grandfather from Dundee, who had left school at fourteen, but, happening to be a financial genius, made a fortune and turned himself into an Oxfordshire landowner; a father, friend of Winston Churchill in the Oxfordshire Yeomanry, noted for his bravery in the First World War in which he was killed; mother, to whom her sons were devoted, but whose flamboyance and indiscretion were at times distressing to them.

One of the most interesting revelations in Duff Hart-Davis's workmanlike and enormously readable biography concerns Fleming's childhood illness, which left him with a stammer, very little sense of taste, and none of smell. The first of these disabilities wore off, but the others always remained. He was for a long time on a tedious diet, and not allowed to go to children's parties. He is on record as behaving with unusual stoicism about a régime that must have been very trying to a little boy.

At school (Eton), Peter Fleming was good at his books, and, although not a top-rank athlete, one of those all-rounders who are a great success. His puritanism must have been a little trying. This pattern was followed at Oxford (Christ Church), where he also got to work on his passion for acting, at which he was more adept in real life than behind the footlights.

Efforts were made to turn Fleming into a banker, but he greatly disliked business. His mother had been left a good deal of money but had absolute control of it (provided she remained unmarried) so that, contrary to what many supposed, money was handed out capriciously to her sons and sometimes cut off altogether. The Brazilian trip which made Peter Fleming's name with *Brazilian Adventure*, and a sizeable sum of royalties, was the consequence of answering an advertisement.

Fleming was an exceedingly brave man. He liked danger for its own sake. One might offer a distinction between the sort of danger that, say, Hemingway liked, and the sort of danger Fleming liked; quite apart from Hemingway's love of showing off, and Fleming's detestation of it. Fleming's kind of bravery was pressing on up the river into unknown country peopled by almost certainly unfriendly Indians as on that hopelessly ill-organized Brazilian expedition, or doing the later journey through Tartary (in *News from Tartary*) astonishing in its hardships. It was the capacity to endure discomforts and uncertainties alone, or as leader of a small group, rather than the wish to face, so to speak, the oncoming bull in front of a large audience.

When the last war broke out Fleming's celebrity, as Hart-Davis points out, immediately swept him into the more glamorous bypaths of army life. In consequence he got to Norway, but did not have a really adventurous time until Greece, where he was wounded, and nearly blown up, in the evacuation. Later he served in the Far East on the 'deception' side of Military Intelligence, where he showed great ingenuity.

Fleming's self-confidence – at times arrogance – was of a kind to make him irresistible to generals, admirals, editors (in his early days), and even to intractable material like Chinese officials. No one who knows anything of army life can doubt that the very favoured position he enjoyed with the Top Brass must have put many backs up. Fleming himself was conscious that, useful as his work was, it belonged to a side of war less sympathetic to him than the front line.

He got away from office work as much as he could, at one point crashing an aircraft behind the Japanese lines in circumstances that would certainly have led to court-martial, if brought to the ears of higher authority. Fleming, dealing with the position in which he and his dozen personnel found themselves (Japanese sentries observed 300 yards away from time to time in the jungle), appears at his best. One is a trifle shocked to find an officer whose job was concerned with security not only keeping a diary (strictly forbidden) but carrying it on such a jaunt.

Duff Hart-Davis takes all this at a canter of well-constructed narrative, tactful comment, and refusal to be over-impressed even if he is Fleming's godson. In the earlier pages he perhaps a little underplays the distinction as an actress of Celia Johnson (Mrs Peter Fleming). Of Fleming's character, Hart-Davis uses the telling phrase 'so little emotional confidence'. Eva Maillart, the Swiss girl who accompanied him (certainly platonically) on the journey through Tartary, spoke of his 'horror of distortion of facts'.

After the war Peter Fleming wrote some good historical books, farmed and shot, the last his great delight. One found him always good company, if a bit melancholic – this was certainly his burden throughout life, though much concealed. His death was all he could have desired, a right and left when grouse shooting, and his heart stopped beating before he reached the ground.

Peter Fleming: A Biography, Duff Hart-Davis, Cape.

1974

Daily Telegraph

II

A Day at the Zoo by P*t*r Fl*m*ng

There is little or nothing to say about this trip. It met with more success than it deserved. Such difficulties as we encountered were little worse than those experienced any day of the week by most *banderilleros* or all-in wrestlers. If I give an impression to the contrary, I have been unintentionally misleading. It began with an advertisement in the Entertainments Column of *The Times*.

'Zoo. Regent's Park, Open Daily, 9 a.m., Sundays, 2.30. Adults 2*s*. 6*d*., child, half-price. See the Aquarium.'

There was something intriguing about the words 'See the Aquarium'. I wrote to the Secretary for particulars. Even then I should probably have done nothing about it if I had not run into Tom Mackintosh-Joy in Pall Mall. Tom, in a bowler hat and Oppidan Wall tie, was carrying a pair of oars and a shooting-stick.

'Why oars, Tom?' I asked. 'I always thought you were a Dry Bob.'

In answer he pulled up his trouser leg, revealing a strip of Leander sock.

'Come to the Zoo,' I suggested, on impulse. 'There's an Aquarium. You might be able to row through it. It must be a matter of five kilometres. Call it four versts. We'll have to catch a 3 or a 53. You realize that at this time of year we may be the only white men on board.'

It is a relic of my schooldays that I always take a pair of grappling-irons about with me, so that with the help of these, and the shooting-stick, we managed to transfer ourselves to the first bus.

'*Oku de 'u*,' said one of the djellaba-clad figures around us on the top deck. He was wearing a *ffon chokoto* and an *owu-chon*.

'*Atyan*,' I answered, almost the only Dahoman greeting I could remember from African extras at school.

His name was Buku-no Uru. He explained by signs that the distance from the bus-stop to the Zoo entrance was considerable, and offered his services, which we gladly accepted.

It was already late in the afternoon when the three of us came in sight of the Mappin Terraces, unmarked on my obsolete map. We halted for a short rest, and I divided a piece of last year's pemmican stored in the pocket of my diary. Then we zigzagged towards the turnstiles. To my delight the man accepted the money we offered him.

Once inside, our task was comparatively easy – to find the Aquarium, and ask whether rowing was allowed there. I thought it wise, since such transport was available, to hire llamas. None of us knew how long our trek might be. We set off towards the Terraces, now plainly visible in the refulgent light of the evening sun.

I was determined that on the way we should locate the legendary Chimpanzees' Tea Party, and here there was some delay that was to cause us trouble later; for Tom then wanted to inspect the Reptile House. We entered the building successfully, but owing to his pigmentation lost poor Buku-no Uru in the darkness. Unfortunately he had the shooting-stick with him. However, we still possessed the oars.

At Monkey Hill, in the hope of getting a good photograph, I allowed two of the inmates to examine my compass. They were unwilling to restore it to me, and, as time was short, we had to press on without it. I had already begun to worry about the hour of closing, when we found we were lost in the Tunnel. I cursed myself for not having insisted on the return of the compass. Now we did not know whether we were travelling North or South.

An unbelievable piece of luck, a friendly keeper passed within hail. 'You've just time,' he yelled. 'But they don't allow any rowing.'

The bell was sounding as we left the Aquarium.

Something like eighteen months later I ran into Tom in the Club. In these sybaritic surroundings it seemed inappropriate to speak directly of what we had experienced together.

'But surely you used to be a Dry Bob?' I urged.

He fumbled in his trouser pocket and produced a yellow, crumpled piece of paper. It was Lower Sixpenny Choices, thirty years or more back. 'T. Mackintosh-Joy' was Keeper.

'I thought I'd change,' he said.

There was a click as his teeth met. The bowl of the pipe dropped with a thud to the heavily carpeted floor.

1955
Punch

OSBERT LANCASTER

I

I must have met Osbert Lancaster once or twice before the war, but only superficially. We did not get to know each other well until the later 1940s. After that we met often; when both of us moved out of London, staying regularly for mutual weekends. Lancaster was one of those friends with whom one wanted to discuss as soon as possible any comic event, whether connected with an individual or a grotesque happening of the world in general.

As a young man he had consciously modelled himself on Max Beerbohm, both in outward appearance and the duality of their art. Like Beerbohm, Lancaster was at home both in drawing and writing (also, in private, a bit of a musician). The surprising result of this mimesis (to use a word both would have appreciated) was to produce not a less effective duplication but, in life and work, an entirely original Lancastrian persona.

Times, need it be said, had greatly changed since Beerbohm's entry on the London scene in the 1890s, and both artists were intensely aware of the epoch in which they lived in their prime. At the same time a yearning for the past of his childhood was characteristic of each. Beerbohm (b.1872) declared that romance for him lay in the 1880s; Lancaster (b.1908) was similarly drawn to Edwardian days.

Those with a penchant for a particular style of life, whatever that may be, often find the taste satisfied without any special effort on their own part. When Lancaster went to live at Henley-on-Thames, the Edwardian Age would annually descend on the town for a week like a mirage.

That was during the regatta. Figures would appear on the streets, and along the river, who had not only walked straight out of Lancaster's drawings, but were quite unchanged from what they would have been in 1910: beefy young oarsmen in shorts, pink Leander socks, crested caps slightly too small for them, white-moustached, megaphone-grasping ancients, their flannel trousers sere and yellow, college blazers bursting at the seams; an aura everywhere of cider-cup, salmon mayonnaise, strawberries-and-cream; certainly of tea-time honey and clocks stuck at ten to three.

It would be wrong to suppose that Lancaster's preoccupation with a

362

comparatively recent past was more than a small section of his imaginative kaleidoscope. On the contrary, he was the most acute and graphic interpreter, in the pocket-cartoon (of which he was virtually the inventor), of his own contemporaries, whether they lived in Vogue Regency, Stockbroker Tudor, or Culture Cottage.

No doubt Lancaster fans differ in their favourite Lancaster period, or the specific personal vicissitudes of the varied career through which the Countess of Littlehampton passed. For myself I think I esteemed most the alleviation Lancaster cartoons brought to the grim years of war.

One of the reasons for his exceptionally felicitous treatment of the wartime world lay in Lancaster's mastery in delineation of military (indeed any other) uniform. This is something that few cartoonists in this country (they are usually more skilful on the Continent) can handle both satirically and correctly. Even the great Beerbohm, in the few examples of uniform to be found in his work, has no great turn.

The subtlety with which Lancaster could play with his effects in this line is perfectly illustrated in the vignette showing a young officer home on leave from the Army of Occupation in Germany. His girl-friend steps back aghast at the manner in which his (otherwise regimentally correct) British uniform has somehow become completely Teutonized; the ensemble completed by three small parallel duelling scars on his cheek.

Lancaster, having severely stylized his own exterior – bristling moustache, check suits, shirt and tie in bold tints – manipulates his puppets by a similar stylization of type. At first sight this might seem to threaten crudity by its simplification. In the end it achieves the traditional dramatic effectiveness of a greatly extended cast for a *commedia dell' arte* performance.

Lancaster's early interest in architecture (an art form from which his heart was never really parted) left its mark on all drawings where there is room for a background. I am particularly fond, for example, of a cover he executed for one of my own paperbacks, which conveys with extraordinary power the grimness of a Pimlico street, before that area of London underwent any smartening up. His architectural abilities are also noticeable (over and above the versatile costumes) in many stage-sets.

I spoke earlier of Lancaster being a friend to whom one immediately wished to report any funny happening. It would be a mistake, however, to convey by that impression that he was a better listener than talker. The number of acknowledged wits I have known of whom that might be said could be numbered on one hand, but any anecdote whatsoever would set Lancaster off effectively on his own wide experience of the social jungle.

His phraseology had been strongly influenced by the celebrated locutions of Maurice Bowra, a don in Lancaster's undergraduate days at Oxford. Of this explosive and prepotent delivery he was perhaps the last truly apostolic representative.

Although best known as a cartoonist, or for theatre décor, Lancaster's watercolours and lithographs – especially those of the Aegean – have an atmosphere very much their own. Greece exercised a powerful hold over him, both romantically, and purely pictorially; the last shown specifically in his *Sailing to Byzantium*.

The touch of melancholy, inseparable from all artists who give themselves, even fitfully, to the Muse of Comedy, was perhaps strengthened in him by a sense that he might have allowed her to seduce him too exclusively. His dandyism could have been intended as some consolation, if that were so. It was dandyism of possibly a rather old-fashioned kind; none the less it turned out an admirable basis for enlarging Osbert Lancaster's wit and gifts.

1986
Daily Telegraph, Obituary Appreciation.

I I

Osbert Lancaster (1908–86) was gifted in three of the Arts. It is, in my experience, unusual to find exceptional talent in more than two of them together. Lancaster, apart from drawing and writing, could perform on more than one musical instrument, and his grasp of architecture made him a first-class explicator of architectural styles.

He could do the last in a manner that was not merely unboring (less easy than might be imagined), but exceedingly funny. Indeed he had the extraordinary power of making you laugh aloud at what seems ostensibly to be a naturalistic drawing of a run-of-the-mill Victorian house in a terrace.

Edward Lucie-Smith's anthology of Lancaster's cartoons, watercolours, stage designs, writings and occasional verse, is adequate, if uninspiringly produced. Inevitably everyone has his or her own favourites, so it would not be fair to grumble at different tastes as to these, but margins are skimped and the printing is decidedly muddy. Perhaps a better paper might have been used.

Lucie-Smith remarks in the introduction that Lancaster's cartoons now 'seem the least important part of his achievement'. That is perhaps going a little far, even though one sees what he means. If this exaggeration draws attention to other sides of Lancaster's art, certainly insufficiently recognized, so much the better. In that respect this volume should be helpful.

Relating the cartoons in terms of fiction, Lucie-Smith compares them with the novels of Evelyn Waugh. This is understandable for someone who knew neither Lancaster nor Waugh personally. Except in the most superficial manner it is immensely misleading. Waugh and Lancaster shared, it is true, a severely stylized view of the British aristocracy. Both disliked any suggestion that social types are never quite so cut-and-dried as each represents them (to some extent necessarily in cartoons), but their temperaments (the overriding element in any artist) were wholly different.

Lancaster (who never cared for *Brideshead*, finding the film unviewable) had none of Waugh's mystique about the aristocracy, nor his fanaticism in religion. Lancaster was staunchly C of E, but tolerantly so; to him Lord Marchmain would have been a comic figure.

Waugh, for his part, was always a shade condescending about Lancaster. Waugh was, of course, a much more accomplished writer, but he also drew proficiently, and may well have felt rivalry. Lancaster passionately loved parties, in which, anyway momentarily, he may have scaled peaks Waugh failed to ascend. He would also delight in an evening at the Ruritanian Institute, which would have made Waugh's blood run stone cold.

All these feelings are reflected in their respective work. A closer approximation would perhaps be between Lancaster and John Betjeman, who shared Lancaster's architectural enthusiasms and fascination with variegated ecclesiastical types. A difference that set Lancaster apart from both Waugh and Betjeman was the keen interest he took (essential for a cartoonist) in current politics.

As a writer Lancaster was always happily baroque in phraseology, and can be extremely amusing. I think it was a mistake to include here two pieces written for the American press about what the English are like, which really says all the things the Americans expect to be said about the English. They show Lancaster in the unaccustomed light of skirting the edge of banality.

He is at his travelogue best writing of Byzantine Greece, about which he felt intensely romantic. More serious is the piece reproduced here, 'On Stage Design'. This is an altogether remarkable exposition of the theory of stage design, at which Lancaster was also so much a master in practice. It deals, for example, with such complicated questions as how costumes of an opera set in an historical period in the past should be modified by the manner in which that period was looked on when the opera was first produced.

It is of interest that both *The Rake's Progress* and *Les Mamelles de Tirésias*, both excellently designed by Lancaster, were more recently equally well executed in another manner by David Hockney. Lancaster's delightful scene for *Falstaff*, conceived in the manner of a Peter de Hooch picture and reproduced in the book, also deserves a mention.

Lancaster's architectural skills almost always influence what might be called his 'ordinary' landscapes, which are undoubtedly underrated. Again, he is usually at his best in Greece, although, in the series of *Afternoons* (in each of which a drawing accompanies a poem), 'Italian Afternoon' superbly suggests in black and white the blazing heat of a piazza in a small Italian town, where:

> Across the square a monsignore
> Late for his siesta goes:
> The prison scene from Trovatore
> Dies on a dozen radios.

Lancaster's light verse is as enjoyable as other manifestations of his *persona*. There is a private joke in the illustration to 'English Afternoon', represented by an infinitely depressing seaside resort. On one side of the picture appears the corner of a Private Hotel. It is called Yarnton. This was the name of the largish country house belonging, on retirement, to an Oxford academic called Kolkhorst, the host of a salon and favourite butt of Betjeman, who occurs as 'G'ug' in memoirs of those days.

The Essential Osbert Lancaster: An Anthology in Brush and Pen, selected and introduced by Edward Lucie-Smith, Barrie & Jenkins.

1988
Daily Telegraph

ROY FULLER

I

Roy Fuller opens with the reflection: 'Perhaps my whole life could be depicted in terms of the destruction or modification of public and private illusions . . . But mightn't I have been happier as a crank?' Instead he became an 'articled clerk' – what is now known as a 'trainee solicitor' – which led eventually to a job with the Woolwich Equitable Building Society.

Arrival in London, cramming for the Law Examination, digs in Guildford Street, Bloomsbury, resulted in his running across a schoolboy contemporary called Gilbert Waller. Waller was also setting out on a career, in his case, becoming a journalist, being paid for any line he actually had printed as a reporter for the *Daily Express*.

Waller was one of those eccentric figures most people have in their early backgrounds. The account of how he dragooned Fuller into being his assistant in helping to photograph a corpse in the morgue (allegedly deceased in suspicious circumstances) is one of the most macabrely funny incidents I have read about for a long time.

Fuller drove a kind of troika – the central horse his Law activities, at which he was obviously very capable – the two accompanying horses, his poetry and Left-wing enthusiasms respectively. The last occasionally involved him in selling the Communist *Daily Worker* in the street, an activity that went side by side with (and was perhaps a little vitiated by) being forced to collect money while Waller (with the hint of being an unemployed fisherman) stood in the gutter near The Angel singing 'Caller Herrin''.

Fuller married very young, a girl who had shared many of his own childhood scenes, though they had met only when grown up. When he got a job with a solicitor's in Ashford, Kent, they set up house in rooms at 16 shillings a week, soon producing another poet.

It was inevitable at this period for Fuller to find his poetry (with that of Larkin, Amis and many others) being published by R. A. Caton of the Fortune Press – not long ago hilariously described in print by Timothy D'Arch Smith. No money changed hands between Caton and his poets, and the former will certainly go down in history as one of the most grotesque gargoyles on the great baroque façade of publishing.

The job with the Woolwich came in December 1938, and Fuller is

367

justifiably cross with George Orwell for putting a Building Society into *Coming Up for Air*, the constitution of which would have been grossly illegal. War was only nine months away (we are reminded that while the Left railed against Munich it was then, as now, opposed to Civil Defence), and in April 1941, Fuller was conscripted.

He found himself in the Royal Navy more from distaste for the thought of trenches or flying than on account of any instinctive love of the sea. Yet in the end he quotes with what he describes as 'incomplete irony':

> There's a far bell ringing
>> At the setting of the sun,
> And a phantom voice is singing
>> Of the great days done.
> There's a far bell ringing,
>> And a phantom voice is singing
> Of renown for ever clinging
>> To the great days done.

The account of life at HMS *Ganges*, the training establishment opposite Harwich, later at Chatham, at Aberdeen and, learning to be an 'Air Fitter (D.F.)', at Lee-on-the-Solent, is splendid. On the way to *Ganges*, Fuller inevitably fell in with the ubiquitous Waller of an earlier incarnation, who insisted on celebrating in the train with a bottle of claret.

The memoirs are immensely enjoyable about the Royal Navy, known to those who serve as the 'Andrew' (possibly deriving from a former training ship *Andromache*), its 'figgy duff' (pudding) and 'tiddy-oggies' (snacks), both in generous helpings and excellent anyway at the beginning, and its indolent race of 'dockyard mateys'.

A page is rightly devoted to the intricacies of putting on a 'square-rig', the matelot's open-neck and bell-bottomed trousers with details as to how this outfit could be made even more chic.

When asked his religion, Fuller (perhaps rather naively) admitted to atheism. This resulted not only in more chores, but having ATH stamped on his identity disc, running the risk of being buried (at least consigned to the deep) with the religious ceremonies of some obscure sect deriving from St Athanasius.

Vamp Till Ready: Further Memoirs, Roy Fuller, London Magazine.

1982
Daily Telegraph

I I

The wrapper of this book is taken from a wartime painting by Eric Ravilious of a remote Royal Navy station of a few wooden huts on the shore of a creek or bay. Three or four ratings come and go, carrying the small green suitcases that play so considerable a part in Roy Fuller's life as a bluejacket.

Although the landscape could scarcely be the Africa of much of Fuller's experience in this book (more likely Orkney or the Shetlands) the symbolism is perfectly caught of much that is described here: bleak, trivial, boring, yet in spite of everything not entirely without a touch of something impressive in the background, perhaps even a touch of grandeur.

Vamp Till Ready got him into naval uniform and, via the training-ship HMS *Ganges*, ended with instruction in radar and its mysteries. The present book begins with leaving England in 1942 for duty with the Fleet Air Arm. *Home and Dry* is a vivid account of life with that branch of the Service, seen not only through the eye of a poet, but a poet who in civilian life happened also to be extremely good at his job as solicitor with 'the Woolwich', and eventually became an equally efficient naval officer at the Admiralty, dealing with radar equipment.

In short this is not the hard-luck story of an incompatible intellectual press-ganged into Service life, incapable of coping. The observation is therefore keener, and much funnier, when the author is – as not seldom – 'cheesed off'.

Unexpectedly Fuller spent the first part of his life as a sailor on land and in Africa. On the voyage out he was equipped with no more tactical reading matter (his own phrase) than *The Ring and the Book*, everything else being in the hold. Eventually he arrived at Durban, continuing to Mombasa, where Browning was exchanged for Thackeray's *Henry Esmond*. These records of wartime reading always have their own fascination.

All the time there are glimpses of messmates and the eternal routines of shipboard life. Some of this period was covered in Fuller's early novel *A Perfect Fool*, and he is perhaps too conscientious in emphasizing repetitions from that book – the row about the ladder, for example, eminently acceptable as a typical scene of its kind, is surely not really required in more than one version.

By the time he fetched up in Kenya, *The Middle of the War*, Roy Fuller's first published collection of poems, appeared in London, and was received with very satisfactory notices. That helped to make up for some of the excruciating boredom the poet himself was suffering in the hut housing personnel responsible for working IFF (Identification Friend or Foe). He was promoted Petty Officer, and the Petty Officers' Mess provides another series of Dickensian naval portraits.

Fuller makes the point that however much Dickens is criticized for drawing figures of allegedly crude caricature, you find when you are knocking about in the Services that a great many individuals you come across are remarkably like Dickens characters at that novelist's most exaggerated; or even like 'humours' in Ben Jonson's plays.

The record of books available is always welcome. At one moment Fuller had the luck to happen on a canteen where – what a treasure trove – there still existed volumes of Nelson's red sevenpenny fiction of thirty or forty years before: Henry Seton Merriman; William Le Queux, Jeffrey Farnol: 'I believe I would not have been above pinching any I fancied . . .'

Fuller's capacity for nailing down sensations is well illustrated by his sense of becoming a cocoon when sleeping in a slung hammock, 'rather as if one were on the stage to becoming a giant cockroach, like [Kafka's] Gregor Samsa.' In a similar manner he likens a gang of Petty Officers, skulking in the hillocks behind the camp with the object of avoiding daily jobs 'of a generally dubious nature', instead playing cards, to Act III in *Carmen*.

There was splendid moment when he was in charge of what amounted to a patrol of Naval Police armed with batons to deal with drunks and the like, but the inevitable took place, and he was put forward for a commission.

Fuller is always enjoyable describing clothes. He was determined to buy his officer's uniform from an 'ancient naval emporium in Portsmouth', therefore turned up in

> a dark green, single-breasted overcoat bought off-the-peg . . . the colour and style daring for the Thirties, even the final years; initial hesitation in the shop turned to self-congratulation when I wore the garment a few times, it seeming the sort of thing a literary man might wear without losing face as a solicitor.

However, the officer drilling the officer-cadets thought otherwise. He 'came irritably up to me':

> 'Haven't you got your uniform yet?'
> 'No.'
> 'At least you've no need to wear a hat.'
> 'I thought it would be appropriate, for the salute and so forth.'
> 'Not at all.'

Owing to wartime austerities, the gold stripe did not run all the way round the cuff when Fuller reached the Admiralty (a branch in Lower Regent Street). Then, to this new side of naval life, is added that curious phenomenon in the background of wartime London, poets and writers trying to carry on their pre-war avocations. There were also the difficulties of finding accommodation for wife and family.

Fuller brilliantly chronicles all sorts of tediums and absurdities without himself ever becoming tedious.

Home and Dry: Memoirs III, Roy   1984
Fuller, London Magazine.   *Daily Telegraph*

J. MACLAREN-ROSS

J. Maclaren-Ross, who died last year in his early fifties, was a remarkable figure. Many people have split personalities, writers especially, but few writers, even, have been so inconveniently divided within as Maclaren-Ross.

His outstanding talent was always burdened by quirks of personality that made him almost impossible to steer through the world of making a living by writing even by those determined he should not starve to death.

This book, *Memoirs of the Forties*, was only three-quarters finished at the time of his death, a typical piece of Maclaren-Ross ill fortune. It was going to be his definitive work so far as his own life was concerned. Even as it stands, it gives a very good idea of his gifts and failings.

The most important thing about him was his really passionate interest in writing as such. This, so it seems to me, far exceeded that of most members of the literary profession, creative or critical, and was backed up by a stupendous memory. It was almost impossible to mention a novel published in England during the last forty years that Maclaren-Ross had not read (remembering its essentials), and he was by no means unversed in American novels in that period.

His likes and dislikes were strong, and he could support them by great chunks of quotation. He was also a confirmed cinema addict, equally expert on films and their actors.

Tall, good-looking, with a knobbed stick and decayed camel's hair coat, he work dark green spectacles that alarmingly reflected one's own image in their orbs when talking to him. He was a well-known figure in the pubs of Fitzroy Street and Soho, a trifle absurd, yet in his way impressive.

How much this cult of his own personality handicapped his writing is hard to say, but certainly the rows he always managed to pick with publishers and editors – in which there was certainly a touch of uncontrollable paranoia – did not make getting his work into print any easier.

With all this went much that was amusing in his conversation and a good deal of simplicity and lack of knowledge of the world – in spite of much experience of the hard side of life. This simplicity is very evident in the present book.

Probably Maclaren-Ross's best work is in his collection of short stories, *The Stuff to Give the Troops*, in its own way as good a 'war book' as ever appeared. The present volume is appropriately made up to full length with some of these army pieces, like 'Y List' and 'I had to go Sick', which certainly deserve reprinting. 'They can't give you a Baby' belongs to the same vintage.

However, the intention of *Memoirs of the Forties* was obviously to give a picture of the writers and other personalities Maclaren-Ross came across from the period just before the war to the years that immediately followed. In this undertaking – although there is a lot that is of interest – the book was never able to receive the final pulling together that it certainly needed.

Whether Maclaren-Ross could ever have summed up the energy and application to do this, had he lived, is impossible to say. It is extraordinary enough that he managed to get so much on paper (in his fantastically minute hand-writing) harassed as he was by lack of money and uncomfortable circumstances.

We have, for example, a brief visit to Graham Greene, just before the outbreak of war; dealings with Cyril Connolly while he was presiding over *Horizon*; Alun Lewis encountered in the army; Dylan Thomas in a film unit. Lewis was killed on active service, so that the account of him is necessarily limited to the period of meeting, but the others seem to require some reappearance, if not in the flesh, then in the author's later consideration, to make their portraits at all complete in the setting.

Plenty of unknown names occur with the better-known ones. Again, it is hard to say whether Maclaren-Ross's indiscriminate interest in what happened round him was an advantage or not to him as a writer. He will sometimes use material that is not available to most authors, and use it very well. At other times he will seem impressed by persons and events that seem contrived and banal.

The fact was that Maclaren-Ross had, with his considerable powers of self-expression, something genuinely original about him. On one side, there was the broken-down 1890ish dandy; on the other a real impact with the horrors of contemporary life, in which he sold vacuum-cleaners for a living or was sent for three weeks' detention to the Glasshouse for being Absent Without Leave.

These things alone make *Memoirs of the Forties* worth reading. Over and above that, no one else has ever managed to put over the strong, not particularly agreeable atmosphere of those years so well. Finally, there are patches of excellent and unusual writing and that rare gift, a true sense of the comic that can exist even in tragedy.

Memoirs of the Forties,
J. Maclaren-Ross, Alan Ross.

1966
Daily Telegraph

KINGSLEY AMIS

I

On the face of it Light Verse is not a subject to cause loss of temper, and at first one smiles tolerantly at the black eyes and cauliflower ears exchanged by rival editors.

Gradually, however, hearing them argue, one begins to become unexpectedly heated oneself. Why has such-and-such been omitted? Why such-and-such included? What rules are being observed? The fact is that rules as to what constitutes good Light Verse are exceedingly hard to define.

The present volume, edited by Kingsley Amis, takes the place of that chosen by W. H. Auden, which appeared in 1938. Auden stated that he based his selection largely on common life and the speaking voice, thereby allowing admission of a lot of folk-songs, ballads, blues lyrics and the like. He also – astonishingly – included Kipling's 'Danny Deever', which Kingsley Amis justifiably describes as 'one of the most harrowing poems in the language', and about as far from Light Verse, it might be thought, as one could go – though not necessarily on account of its subject, one illustrated here by 'The Night before Larry was stretched' (Anon.).

Amis says:

> Light Verse is not one thing but many, so much so that I should hate to frame a single generalisation which would comprehend them all: every law I have laid down admits of the odd exception. Rough rules and limitations, some of which may seem personal or even idiosyncratic, are a different matter. These will appear as I proceed.

I go along pretty well with Amis's regulations. They quote A. A. Milne's in agreement that Light Verse is not the relaxation of a major poet, or a minor poet contributing to a little girl's album, but a precise art as difficult and demanding as any other. In fact I go rather further, and am not sure I hold with Amis saying that Light Verse can never be beautiful, only genial, memorable, enlivening, funny. I should have thought verses by the Poet Laureate [John Betjeman] for instance, have sometimes combined lightness with beauty.

Byron is absolutely pre-eminent in the game. Amis's choices are excellent ones from 'Beppo' and 'Don Juan'. Praed only falls short of

Byron in not being in not being the same sort of monumental figure himself, an archetypal tragic hero. Technically – up to a point emotionally – Praed is just as good, a very fine poet who left his mark for a century on competent imitators (among others the excruciating Austin Dobson) who were never anything but miles behind.

I cannot altogether share the universal admiration for C. S. Calverley (1831–84). No doubt his verses are of an immense facility, but they lack that inner melancholy which Byron and Praed always somehow imply to point up their own high spirits. Calverley is infinitely neat, but somehow thin and facetious. Perhaps that shows a failing in myself; just as Amis grumbles about Lear for what seem to me inadequate reasons.

Reaching more modern times the influence of John Betjeman – surely another great master of Light Verse in the best sense – is as noticeable as was Praed's on earlier generations, though it is striking how, when writing of often similar people and incidents, Philip Larkin and Kingsley Amis himself are free of any Betjemanian tone. Amis's own poems included here are enjoyable, perfectly accordant with all the requirements of Light Verse.

Amis says:

> Light verse in the late 1970s consists almost entirely of political ephemera, often written with great skill and force: exercises in the styles of the dead or ageing, for the most part in competitions in weekly journals; and limericks. I cannot see the situation improving much.

Among contemporary poems included here I took special pleasure in 'Royalties' (from publishers, rather than palaces) by D. J. Enright.

One poet I think should have been represented is Matthew Prior, not so much for his well-known things like 'My noble, lovely, little Peggy', but – if too serious, though I'm not sure it is – for 'The Secretary', that splendid account of going off for a quiet weekend with a book and a girl.

The wording of some of the limericks seem to me heretical, and at least one is wrongly attributed to Anon., when in fact it was written by Philip Heseltine (see *Peter Warlock* by Cecil Gray, 1934). The correct verses goes as follows:*

> Young girls who frequent picture palaces
> Don't hold with this psychoanalysis;
> And although Doctor Freud
> Is distinctly annoyed,
> They all cling to their long-standing fallacies.

---

* A correspondent wrote that the joke was missed if 'young girls' took the place of 'young men', but the girls were, of course, sitting next to the young men.

I should perhaps speak a word of excuse for a squib of my own included here, an eighteenth-century pastiche called 'Caledonia', which never expected to find itself in an Oxford Book of Verse. It was composed during a period of insomnia, and later Constant Lambert wrote the musical section. Much contemporary allusion has been omitted as altogether unintelligible today, and it should perhaps be explained that the moment was one marked by the publication of several rather self-applauding books by Scotchmen. It was, in short, a leg-pull, and, for example, so far from wishing the late Eric Linklater north of the border, I always regretted not seeing more of him south of it.

The New Oxford Book of Light   1978
Verse, chosen and edited by   *Daily Telegraph*
Kingsley Amis, OUP.

I I

Some explanation is required these days – as opposed to the nineteenth century – to define the object of an anthology with this title. I seem to remember a picture (possibly by Du Maurier, though I think a later artist) showing a curate breaking down in the course of a rendering of 'The Charge of the Light Brigade', and his hostess giving a helping hand by saying: 'Never mind, Mr Smith, tell us the rest in your own words.'

Such a situation would today be exceptional at a party, even if Betjeman or Larkin were substituted for Tennyson.

Kingsley Amis's Introduction deals with the various uses to which *The Faber Popular Reciter* may be put, emphasizing that he does not want the collection to be looked on wholly for educational purposes in schools, nor even at such twentieth-century occasions when public recitation does take place. The latter (at which he represses a shudder) would, in fact, be unlikely to make use of most of the poems on offer here, but he points out that family reading aloud has by no means died out (perhaps each member reading a poem) and it is therefore useful to have some old favourites in easy reach.

This is quite true, and his *Reciter* solves the comparative difficulty at a moment's notice of putting your hand on, say, Old Kaspar and his two forward-looking grandchildren, or the reactionary views of Mrs Hemans as to the stately homes of England. Both are to be found here, with lots more of about the same flavour. Comic verse has been omitted as inappropriate for this particular volume, I think rightly.

Excellent as is the present selection, everyone will have choices of their own they feel ought to have been included. Amis is rather defiant about putting in the whole of 'Horatius', but in my view he is absolutely right. He makes the percipient comment that for the reader to recover 'some of the strong emotions of boyhood' when he reads Macaulay, or any other example of successful heavy rhythms, strong rhymes, vigorous sentiments, is 'not a lapse from maturity but an endorsement of it'.

The difficulty comes with poets like Swinburne or Kipling, the former of whom offers at least half-a-dozen possibilities which must have meant a hard choice ('The Garden of Proserpine' winning here), while almost every successful poem Kipling wrote is suitable for recitation. I'm not sure that I agree with Amis that poems of this sort have necessarily disappeared 'never to return', but no poet to be found in this *Reciter* was born later than 1888.

Amis makes room for at least twenty well-known hymns, some interesting on account of verses here printed, but rarely if ever sung in church. For example, we note the changed meaning (anyway changed acceptance) of 'to condescend' in 'Abide with me':

> Not a brief glance I beg, a
> passing word;
> But as Thou dwellst with Thy
> disciples, Lord,
> Familiar, condescending,
> patient, free –
> Come, not to sojourn, but
> abide with me.

With most popular items, it is right to give a few less-well-known ones (perhaps one could have done with a few more of the little known), among which might be mentioned James Hogg's:

> Where the pools are bright and deep,
> Where the grey trout lies asleep,
> Up the river and over the lea,
> That's the way for Billy and me.

At my preparatory school, not a place of great enlightenment, the poetry-book in use was called *Poems of Action* (I don't remember the editor), and my chief pleasure was derived from poems there which were never recited. One of these, 'Ramon', by Bret Harte, began:

> Drunk and senseless in his place,
> Prone and sprawling on his face.
> More like brute than any man
> Alive or dead, –

> By his great pump out of gear,
> Lay the peon engineer,
> Waking only just to hear,
> Overhead . . .

In the end Ramon saved the situation, in spite of his drunkenness, but died. He might have found a place in Kingsley Amis's *Reciter*.

Where Longfellow is in question, *Poems of Action* had 'Robert of Sicily brother of Pope Urbane/and Valmond, Emperor of Allemaine', who said of the 'Magnificat': ' 'Tis well that such seditious words are sung/Only by priests and in the Latin tongue', the same night finding himself displaced from his throne for a period of months by an Angel. That too would have fitted in here.

The Faber Popular Reciter,
Kingsley Amis, ed., Faber.

1978
Daily Telegraph

III

In the course of newspaper interviews, writers are usually asked if they have any comments to make on contemporary writing. Perhaps four or five times during the last decade, when such a question has been put, I have answered that Roy Fuller is underrated as a novelist, because of his celebrity as a poet; Kingsley Amis underrated as poet, because of his celebrity as a novelist.

For some reason this comment always gets omitted. Too obvious? Not abrasive enough? A different view from that of some sub-editor? Anyway, here are Kingsley Amis's collected poems covering a period of thirty-five years for people to judge for themselves.

There is a moment when rich development suddenly seems to take place in the volume published in 1956. This, one might guess, followed the success – to some extent consequent change of mood – brought about by the appearance of *Lucky Jim* (1953). The earliest poems date back to when Amis was twenty-two, possibly younger. They always possess the familiar Amis flavour, but that becomes much more noticeable, more assured, by about 'A Bookshop Idyll', finally taking over entirely:

> We men have got love well weighed up; our stuff
> Can get by without it.
> Women don't seem to think that's good enough;
> They write about it . . .
> Women are really much nicer than men:
> No wonder we like them.

One night remark in passing that *Jake's Thing* (1978) presents in a novel an alternative view to the conclusion of the last two lines above, but that does not detract from the force of the poem.

'They only Move' also appears to belong to the moment, so to speak, of drawing a new deep breath:

> Tell me, will movement make or mar?
> Then root my body, tell my mind
> They only move, who travel far
> And take me where the good times are.

It should be at once added that a powerful sense of human mortality largely inspires such occasional (by no means pervasive) hedonism. Webster was not more keenly aware than Amis of the skull beneath the skin, as one of the earlier poems makes clear:

> In his low-ceilinged oaken room
> The corpse finds pastimes of the tomb
> Cramped into scratching nose
> And counting fingers, toes.

This awareness of death often returns:

> 'You saw old Kingsley's gone?' – 'Christ!
> I hadn't heard he was ill.' – 'No age
> To speak of, was he?' And the whole crew
> Try to conceal their glee at this
> Time it still isn't them.

Again, in 'A Reunion' and 'Drinking Song', among the latest poems in the collection, age and decay are sung as man's inevitable lot, though Amis's evident relish in writing these verses does not in the least lessen the impression that he himself is still in there punching.

Somewhat apart from the personal reflections indicated above are certain set-pieces. Of these 'The Evans Country' – a dozen poems – are the most sustained on one subject, Dai Evans, a Glamorganshire Don Juan. Here Dai Evans is dissected, rather than the poet himself, and there are some nice glimpses of South Wales landscape. Another of these more static poems is 'On a Portrait of Mme Rimsky-Korsakov', which I liked for its almost surrealist contrasts.

There are what might be called philosophic poems, too, for instance the world considered by the standards of literary criticism in 'The Huge Artifice: an Interim Assessment':

> . . . manifesting there
> An inhumanity beyond despair.

Amis asks questions about everything in life, but manages never to be banal. No one else is quite like him, least of all the novelists with whom he was inexplicably classed when he first appeared on the scene. He brings off in his poetry – something exceedingly difficult in all the arts – the appearance of being very ordinary, while not being ordinary at all.

> Then farmyards, and cobbled roads
> Full of sun, fresh fruit, village wells,
> Tents pitched in the leaf-strewn woods,
> Slow crossing of iced-up canals,
> Those seasons, that immutable scene
> Trodden through in the end – all that,
> Plus litres of lager and wine
> And a sniff or so at the frat.

In short, Kingsley Amis simply seems one of the very best of our poets.

Collected Poems, 1944–1979,
Kingsley Amis, Hutchinson.

1979
Daily Telegraph

PHILIP LARKIN

I

'Writers,' remarks Philip Larkin (in discussing Emily Dickinson and Walter de la Mare), 'are usually on surprisingly affable terms with their neuroses.' The comment is profoundly true, and by no means inapplicable to Larkin himself, who, one feels, treads with deft mastery a perilous tight-rope over an abyss of melancholic horror, balancing himself with art in one hand and good sense in the other.

Required Writing consists for the most part of introductions of an autobiographical kind to Larkin's own early books; a couple of long interviews; many reviews; a few articles on jazz, the last mostly written for the *Daily Telegraph*.

Larkin points out that his Oxford – he went up to St John's College in 1940 – has become a distinctive historical period. Normal dilemmas about a career were settled by the predestination of the Services (in his own case ruled out by bad eye-sight) or some other specifically wartime niche. The picture is a vivid one (not least the imaginary Yorkshire Scholar, invented by Larkin and a friend, who 'conversed in flat rapacious tones . . . "You're getting the best education in the land, lad"'), so is the striking vignette of the first sight of his fellow Johnian Kingsley Amis, slowly and painfully collapsing after a fanciful pistol-shot.

Interviews, in this case in the *Observer* (Miriam Gross) and the *Paris Review* (Robert Phillips), are never really satisfactory because they are simply by journalists trying, with greater or lesser efficiency, to extract what they think will be good points for their readers. The only true sparks in reporting such discussions would be struck between the subject and a person holding individual views and arguing the point.

There is, of course, rarely space for that, but one sees how much more stimulating such arguments might be if followed up when Larkin stings the *Paris Review* interviewer into momentary resentment (it never fails) by reference to that odd American illusion that there is 'no sense of class' in the United States. All the same, these two interviews produce some quite sharp Larkin cracks.

Naturally he is best on poets and poetry. There is some very good stuff, in a somewhat moving memoir of the poet Vernon Watkins, wholly devoted to poetry yet content to be a flight sergeant in the RAF

381

during the war, and returning to be a bank clerk in South Wales, as he found banking more acceptable than pot-boiling. In contrast we have a splendid excoriation of the Beats ('Hi, what's cookin'? Are yer gonna blow some poetry maybe?')

As it happens this last piece is followed by one on Francis ('Hound of Heaven') Thompson, who was something of a Beat himself. Incidentally, has it ever been noted that Francis Thompson and George Gissing must have overlapped at Owen's College, Manchester, from one angle a splendid pair of down-and-out literary alumni, even if Gissing was in his own way intensely respectable?

Among matters considered by Larkin is the reading aloud of poetry. No one who has heard a poem (or for that matter a novel) read aloud by an actor could doubt how unsatisfactory that can often be. There is almost always an element of not going the whole hog in poetry (or prose), but only too rarely is restraint shown by actors. On the other hand, poets themselves do not always read very well. Eliot, for example, was not regarded as a good reader, but Larkin chronicles how, just to show an Italian visitor what Eliot's voice was like, he put on a record of the poet reciting Prufrock, and found himself having to listen enthralled to the end.

Rupert Brooke (whose appalling quotability has certainly not diminished with time and hard knocks from the highbrows) provides a lively piece. Larkin suggests that 'so far from being Mrs Cornford's Apollo, or even the most distant relation of Percy Bysshe Shelley, Brooke was a vigorous, practical, and self-interested character whose short life was a continual approximation towards knowing this,' and he could well have become leader of the Liberal Party or headmaster of Rugby.

As might be expected, Hardy is thoroughly examined, and Larkin – who is more apologetic than one would think necessary in taking that view – says 'I am more conscious than I was, too, of an undercurrent of sensual cruelty in the writing.' Tennyson is sensitively treated, and the observation made that

> we [as opposed to the critics of fifty years ago] are not so impatient with his role of public poet, or Laureate. Tennyson did not enter public life through backing away from personal problems; he *believed* a poet should know as much as any spokesman of his time.

On the other hand, rather an opposite judgment is expressed on Marvell. Larkin says 'We no longer make much of adulatory poems, whether of national heroes or owners of big houses.' But surely Marvell's 'Horatian Ode upon Cromwell's Return from Ireland' is a splendid poem which sets Cromwell – a character I happen to find in general unsympathetic – in a light that does compel the reader to consider the Lord Protector's better qualities.

Otherwise, however, the piece on Marvell – like Larkin a fellow
worthy of Hull, of which Marvell was MP for eighteen years – is full of
enjoyable points, emphasizing how Marvell during the last half-
century has emerged from being classed with 'Herrick, Lovelace and
Wither' to a place of fame not far below the very top. Larkin pulls a
donnish leg for making elaborate heavy weather about what a
seventeenth-century contemporary might have understood by the
phrase 'vegetable love'. Of the lines:

> What wondrous life is this I lead!
> Ripe apples drop about my head;
> The luscious clusters of the Vine
> Upon my mouth do crush their Wine;
> The Nectaren and curious Peach,
> Into my hands themselves do reach;
> Stumbling on Melons, as I pass,
> Insnared with Flow'rs, I fall on Grass.

Larkin most aptly refers to the speaker in the poem as a 'Hulot-like
figure, with all the fruit crashing down on him'.

Required Writing: 1983
Miscellaneous Pieces, 1955–1982,   *Daily Telegraph*
Philip Larkin, Faber.

II

In the Gents at Hull University, the fuse-box, ten feet off the ground, for
a space bore the injunction: 'Knock three times and ask for Philip
Larkin.'

The tone and place of the message at once suggest the essential
privacy with which the poet (Librarian at that University) always
surrounded himself, and the recognition of that privacy among those in
academic contact with him.

We live in a world in which a public persona is almost universally
demanded. To lack one is running the risk of being thought stuck-up.
But Philip Larkin, widely judged as probably the finest poet writing in
English today, lacks that useful, almost essential mask. Accordingly,
producing a Festschrift embodying his characteristics has not been
easy, though there are several revealing items here, like that quoted
above from the piece by Douglas Dunn, some-time fellow librarian and
also poet.

One sees the precise reverse of Larkin's stance in the Poet Laureate's
contribution to this volume, a poem dedicated to Larkin, but all about
Betjeman – or rather Betjeman's Teddy Bear – which perfectly
expresses the Betjeman public persona. No doubt in a sense Betjeman

is no more – perhaps less – revealed in the poem than is Larkin in, say, 'Wild Oats' (*The Whitsun Wedding*, 1964), but there is always much more in Betjeman for the public to get hold of.

Kingsley Amis's account of Larkin at St John's, Oxford, throws light (they were not only at the same college but both reading the English School), and the grimness of Wellington Square is admirably suggested by a photograph of this period. Incidentally, a word should surely have been said of Larkin's own photography, in which he is master of the 'interval shutter', setting up the camera, then joining the group himself.

Robert Conquest raises an interesting point about Larkin's poem 'Naturally the Foundation Will Bear Your Expenses' in which the taxi of an academic flying to India to lecture is held up, it being:

> That day when Queen and Minister
> And Band of Guards and all
> Still act their solemn-sinister
> Wreath-rubbish in Whitehall

A well-known Leftist MP wrote agreeing with this supposed attack on remembering the war dead, but the irony was intended to embrace just such persons as himself, full of smug anti-patriotism. It will be remembered that the poem goes on in anticipation:

> And dwindle off down Auster
> To greet Professor Lal
> (He once met Morgan Forster)
> My contact and my pal.

It is a great pleasure to learn from Charles Monteith's piece (about publishing Larkin) that a real Professor Lal wrote delightedly from Calcutta – he ran the Writers' Workshop there. Larkin (who has only once left Great Britain, to receive the Shakespeare Prize at Hamburg) was confronted with the alarming obligation of having to travel to India to become his correspondent's contact and pal.

B. C. Bloomfield reveals that when Larkin came down from Oxford in 1943 the Ministry of Labour enquired what contribution he (unfit for military service) was making to the war effort. On the day the letter arrived Larkin saw an advertisement for the post of Librarian in the Public Library at Wellington, Shropshire (where the previous incumbent had been appointed in 1903), and was at once accepted, though his sole qualification was to have often used libraries. It is heartening that such things can happen.

Anthony Thwaite, the editor, points out that Larkin poems translate well. That is easily understood so far as goes 'Le nozze di Pentecoste' in Italy, but all is apparently equally smooth in Chinese. Donald Mitchell arranged for Larkin to become Jazz correspondent of the *Daily*

Telegraph, and he writes here of Larkin and music, a subject touched on by various other contributors, notably Clive James, writing mainly on the poet's wit.

Peter Porter ('Going to Parties') and Gavin Ewart ('An Old Larkinian') both offer poems. John Gross tackles the somewhat delicate subject of Larkin as an anthologist, especially *The Oxford Book of Twentieth-Century English Verse*, remarking that some felt 'To restore Thomas Hardy to his rightful position was one thing, but did it have to entail the reinstatement of J. C. Squire, Francis Brett Young, Susan Miles, Julian Birdbath?'

Noel Hughes plays the part of the school contemporary who inevitably knows a shade too much, but has kept within bounds, permitting himself no more than to doubt that Larkin was all that miserable at school. Harry Chambers describes a Person-from-Porlock call on Larkin, which was reasonably well received. Alan Bennett does not know Larkin personally, but writes about him with that fact in view, and possibly partakes of the Armistice Day heresy mentioned above.

Andrew Motion, George Hartley, Alan Brownjohn, Christopher Ricks, Seamus Heaney, all discuss the poems, and at times the novels; there are also recurrent references to Larkin's interest in cricket.

May I add my own word? Larkin seems to me to write with an amazing directness, which certainly conceals a great deal of art, but always appears just to flow out. He is a poet without contemporary nonsense, including the nonsense of having no nonsense about him. It is hard not to suspect that *Larkin at Sixty* is just a shade embarrassing for its subject, but is obviously a necessary volume for the shelf in 'fulfilment's desolate attic', and contains quite a lot for Larkin fans.

Larkin at Sixty, Anthony
Thwaite, ed., Faber.

1982
Daily Telegraph

JOHN BAYLEY

I

For the author of an academic study in literary criticism not only to write well but also obviously to enjoy books for their own sake, is so unusual that *The Characters of Love* immediately catches the reader's attention.

However, it is easier to praise John Bayley's style, even to disagree with some of his opinions, than to summarize his theme briefly. In any case, I found myself enjoying this work most as a general discourse on writing, which is touched here at all sorts of unexpected points.

All the same, *The Characters of Love*, as its title suggests, has a definite aim, which is to examine the literary approach to love now and in the past. In order to do this, Bayley takes three famous love stories and investigates their material. These are Chaucer's *Troilus and Criseyde*, Shakespeare's *Othello*, and Henry James's *The Golden Bowl*.

Troilus and Cressida are better known to most people through Shakespeare rather than Chaucer. It is a first-rate love story, dramatic, sad, inevitable. Cressida is left behind at Troy, when her father escapes with the Greeks. Troilus, the king of Troy's son, 'has an affair' with her.

Then arrangements are made for Cressida to be exchanged for a Trojan prisoner in Greek hands. Troilus can do nothing to prevent this since their 'affair' cannot be mentioned. Cressida, swearing undying love, goes to the Greeks, where she immediately falls for Diomed's elementary – but, as ever, effective – routine seduction methods.

In Shakespeare's play the lovers are somewhat overshadowed by the war and the surrounding Greek and Trojan heroes. Chaucer gives more of the bare bones of the story. It is splendid stuff.

Othello we know, of course, of old. Bayley's point here, as I take it, is that the play is not, as so often assumed, a rather crude melodrama, but has its own special kind of subtlety. The situation is not so much as if Col. (now Gen.) Mobutu had married a Belgian princess and found her wanting. It is that Iago is a kind of super-gossip-writer, out to make trouble at all costs through sheer love of power, and his own personal inability to grasp the intricacies of human relationships.

Troilus and Cressida, Othello and Desdemona, are comparatively simple stories to which Bayley applies sensitive treatment. That is reasonably easy. With *The Golden Bowl*, however, when he grapples with Henry James, they are like a pair of oiled and naked wrestlers.

Charlotte, an American girl, has been mistress of a Roman prince. They have not enough money to marry. The Prince marries Maggie Verver, whose millionaire father, Mr Verver, marries Charlotte. Obviously this is a piquant situation. Bayley never quite manages to throw James, but there is some excellent sport in the course of which he points out, what must be generally agreed, that Mr Verver is really much too good to be true. In *The Golden Bowl* one is always curious to know more of the sex-life of the Assinghams, the somewhat interfering observers of this *partie carrée*.

Bayley discusses the creation of individual personality in the character of a novel or play as a method of showing how love works; and the alternative approach – popular in our own day – of examining 'moral values'. In doing this, he skims lightly over a great number of absorbing literary questions.

He seems to me to put too high a value on D. H. Lawrence as a novelist. Lawrence is a writer whose powers lie, one feels, rather in the poetry of his descriptive passages, even as a critic rather than a novelist. Again, whether you like Joyce or not (and I would grant to him very remarkable powers indeed), I cannot see that 'of all modern authors, the closest to Shakespeare is certainly James Joyce'. Joyce, to my mind, is almost as far away from Shakespeare as you can get; although I willingly underwrite Bayley's claim for a Shakespearian buoyancy in P. G. Wodehouse. While registering disagreement, I must also point out that the Great Gatsby was in love with a girl named Daisy, not Alice.

These are small points. Much more important are such things as Bayley's remarks on 'realism':

> Nature and realism have little in common, for realism ignores the individual's, or the tribe's, sense of itself. An account of our daily lives, however remorselessly realistic, will seem as unfamiliar to us as our voices on a tape recording. An account of a miner's life which strikes us as wonderfully 'realistic' in a documentary book or film will seem totally unreal to the miners themselves, however much they recognise its accuracy. And it is an irritating kind of falsification, for realism is often a peculiarly arrogant kind of romanticism, creating and hugging to itself a dead accurate image of our external selves, and then saying: 'this is your life.'

In this connection, Bayley has some interesting things to say about Tolstoy. He put forward the theory that one can speak of 'Proust's world' or 'Dickens's world', because certain novelists create a vision of life which we accept, rather than a picture of life itself. We do not say 'Tolstoy's world', he suggests, because Tolstoy gives us 'the real thing'.

This is a fascinating question. Speaking for myself, I do not entirely accept John Bayley's findings, but clearly there is a great deal to be said for the statement on the face of it. He is scrupulously fair:

> This is not to say that fullness or inclusiveness for its own sake cannot be as tiresome an approach as contrast, and as disingenuous as the social aim of 'absolute frankness'. The idea that the whole truth can be told now and should be told, down to what contraceptives were used and what was the abortionist's fee, is deeply falsifying, for these matters not only acquire a disproportionate importance in the telling but are also so facile to record.
>
> It is easy for Tolstoy to let us know that Anna practised birth-control after the doctor had told her she could have no more children, but it is exceedingly difficult for him to intimate – as he does – how this throws light on the nature of her love and jealousy, and at a further remove on the relations of Stiva and Dolly and of Kitty and Levin.

Finally, this enjoyable book has some amusing things to say about 'novel-reading morality', in which connection I always think an absorbing study could be written on the moral standards of reviewers considered solely in relation to the novels they review.

The Characters of Love, John Bayley, Constable.

1961
Daily Telegraph

II

As an art-form (to use an old-fashioned phrase) I do not find the Short Story sympathetic. You are either given a naturalistic slice of life with a sting in its tail, which disconcerts me, or shown a man standing on a bridge contemplating a fish, which fails to hold my attention. There are, of course, other sorts of short story too, as demonstrated here. The taste is a matter of temperament. I simply put my cards on the table.

John Bayley, in what were presumably six lectures, gives an admirable account of the short story's nature in the hands of several first-class performers. He begins rather unexpectedly with poetry for illustrations of the difference between the short story and the novel.

Bayley sees Wordsworth's 'Tintern Abbey' as short story, and Larkin's 'Dockery and Son' as partaking of both short story and novel. Rather than either of these, Hardy's poetry can often be positively anecdotal. Charles Wolfe's 'The Burial of Sir John Moore after Corunna' lacks both the 'secret harmony' needed in a short story, and the 'exchange of confidences with the reader' required by the novel.

I am not sure that I fully understand the argument, but I can see it as well worth investigating when we come to individual authors who have written short stories. In this art, Bayley says, a 'latent element of comedy is essential,' thereby bringing up another interesting point. Many short stories are painful, even tragic. Must there be comedy too? I am inclined to think he is right.

One of the stories Bayley examines is Kipling's famous 'Mrs Bathurst', its narration pieced together against a background of undoubtedly comic naval slang, ending up with two charred bodies struck by lightning in an African teak forest. Incidentally, Bayley comes down fairly heavily on the side of those who think one of these was the charming hotel-keeper Mrs Bathurst (an example of a convincingly nice woman in literature), an ending which is still a matter of controversy.

We would agree that Conrad's *Lord Jim* is really a short story, even though it grew to novel length, Jim himself being what Bayley calls an 'anecdotal person'. Henry James largely earned a living by writing short stories – some of them decidedly indifferent in quality – but Bayley thinks highly of 'A Landscape Painter', which I should have thought, unlike *Lord Jim*, bordered on a very short novel.

Kipling's incredible virtuosity gave new life to the short story, this genre representing some of his very best and very worst writing, 'hypnotic brilliance and cocky assertiveness'. Kipling's are also a good example of Bayley's rule that the best short stories are immensely localized.

Kipling shows striking parallels in certain respects on the one hand with D. H. Lawrence; on the other with Ernest Hemingway, who learnt a great deal from him. Kipling and Lawrence were 'both emotional men and good haters', while they often used 'willed or imagined events' – for instance, respectively, 'Mary Postgate' and 'The Captain's Doll'.

One of the links with Hemingway is a need for love, 'Baa Baa Black Sheep' having a good deal in common with 'Indian Camp' – the hidden epiphany (to use Joyce's term) a boy's realization of a parent in both cases. Bayley comments that in spite of experiences undergone, the innocence of the heroes has survived, 'renunciation of overt curiosity, intention, the will' being necessary to the best stories.

I have not read Hardy's 'On the Western Circuit' (but shall now make a point of doing so), which Bayley much recommends; yet another of his rules being that 'no good short-story writer can be "realist" in the sense that novelists are, or have been'. Other stories specially mentioned are Chekhov's famous 'The Lady with the Little Dog' (apparently more correctly 'A Lady with a Doglet') and Elizabeth Bowen's wartime 'Mysterious Kôr'.

Bayley makes all sorts of amusing comments in the midst of his definition of the short story. He points out, for instance, that the popularity of Philip Larkin's poetry has something in common with the popularity of 'The Rubáiyát of Omar Khayyám' and Housman's 'The Shropshire Lad'. He also remarks (something that used to worry me as a child) that Sir John Moore's soldiers couldn't possibly have dug his grave with their bayonets; especially, incidentally, with the bayonets of the period.

All the same, in *Cymbeline* the Roman commander Caius Lucius says:

> The boy hath taught us manly duties: let us
> Find out the prettiest daisied plot we can,
> And make him with our pikes and partisans
> A grave.

Pikes and partisans would make scarcely better spades than bayonets.

As an authority on Russian literature, it must have been with a sense of self-denial on his own part that John Bayley doesn't deal with Lermontov's *A Hero of Our Time*, an undoubted novel made up of at least some undoubted short stories. But are they all short stories within the Bayley terms of reference? Some certainly are, while others seem to come dangerously near to being very short novels. I should have liked to hear him on that problem in relation to the various short-story writers dealt with here.

The Short Story: Henry James to Elizabeth Bowen, John Bayley, Harvester.

1988
Daily Telegraph

V. S. NAIPAUL

I

V. S. Naipaul, a Hindu whose family has lived for a couple of generations in Trinidad, is often spoken of as the best of the Caribbean authors. It is time for the regional epithet to be abandoned and for him to be quite simply recognized as this country's most talented and promising younger writer.

His novel about Trinidad, *A House for Mr Biswas*, was not only a rich and exotic chronicle, but also something of a masterpiece. An excellent and unusually well-read critic, too, Naipaul now comes along with a travel book about his home ground and those neighbourhoods. *The Middle Passage* would be hard to beat for descriptive power and cool assessment of the situation there.

There used to be a clerihew which went:

> Mr Stephen Gwynn
> Tells you what a mess Ireland is in;
> When you ask him to explain,
> He tells you all over again.

This approach is, in general, very much the case with the Antilles. Everyone recognizes the place is in a mess, but very few do more than repeat this fact. Naipaul is extraordinarily good at putting his finger on the situation. He has a keen social sense which gives bite to his accounts of individuals; at the same time he is humane. He can look at things dispassionately without becoming a merely critical observer.

The Middle Passage was the name given to the slave-carrying voyages between Africa and the Caribbean. Naipaul sees Caribbean problems as perpetually leading back to this slave-built society. I suppose, in fairness, one has to admit that Greece and Rome were slave-built too, just as horrible in that aspect, but they were not competing, as were the Antilles and the United States (and Russia) of the past, with non-slave civilizations.

Naipaul visited Trinidad, British Guiana, Surinam, Martinique and Jamaica. The difference of these places, close to each other on the map, is enormous in other respects.

In Dutch Surinam, slavery was only abolished in 1863. It used to be the threat of a British slave-owner that he would sell a badly behaved slave to a Dutchman; the threat of the Dutchman, that he would sell a badly behaved slave to a freed Negro.

However, in Surinam today government has few of the aspects we associate with the Afrikaners. The territory possesses – so Naipaul informs us – the only uncorrupt police force in that part of the world and a nationalist movement which is *inventing* a language for half a million people.

About Martinique, he is particularly interesting. The French, so different from ourselves, we are always told, have no instinctive difficulties about a colour bar. What did Naipaul find, but that Martinique was a region of colour differentiation to a degree unheard of in a British possession?

The *Martiniquois* was turned into a perfect Frenchman so far as education and taste went. He was perfectly all right when he went to France. While he remained in Martinique, where there is no daily paper and all local rum must be sent to France to be marketed, he would be graded as a Negro if one-sixteenth coloured – and pedigrees are carefully kept in Martinique.

In British Guiana, except for the architectural beauties of Georgetown a country of little facile appeal, no sides are taken in politics, yet there is at the same time no uncomfortable feeling that the writer is sitting on the fence. The account is vivid, without any of the nauseating smears and priggish assumptions that so often disfigure journalistic vignettes.

Naipaul is most penetrating about Trinidad, which he naturally knows like the back of his hand. He intersperses his description with random excerpts from the Trinidad newspapers.

Then he takes a look at Jamaica, with its uncomfortable situation *vis-à-vis* tourists and emigrants, its Rastafarian movement, of which the members believe that the world is ruled by the Pope (who is also head of the Ku Klux Klan) and that the Duke of Edinburgh is a reincarnation of Philip II of Spain.

Although very entertaining, it cannot be said that *The Middle Passage* is particularly cheering. Where one knew things were bad, one usually learns they are worse. Perhaps Naipaul's most important emphasis is on the fact, little understood in this country, that racialism in the Caribbean is not even principally between coloured and white. It is, in general, between African and Indian.

Even then, the situation is infinitely complicated by other considerations – the Chinese, for example. It is like an extraordinary panorama of human folly and cruelty designed by Swift. Naipaul unfolds the picture with irony and pity.

Thie Middle Passage: Impressions
of Five Societies – British, French
and Dutch – in the West Indies and
South America, V. S. Naipaul,
Deutsch.

I I

To say *The Loss of El Dorado* is a history of Trinidad is to suggest quite a different sort of study; while to speak of an 'historical reconstruction' immediately conjures up a confection of romantic inaccuracies. V. S. Naipaul's brilliant tapestry is neither, though it does, indeed, recount most of the history of Trinidad, illustrating this by examining in close detail certain all-important episodes.

The first of these is Sir Walter Ralegh's connection with Trinidad, and the near South American coast, which can be seen from the island on a clear day. These events are to some extent familiar from Ralegh's own words together with various records collected in Hakluyt's Voyages. Naipaul expands the Ralegh picture by filling in the Spanish side of the story.

Ralegh made his first raid in 1595. He returned to England to be confined later in the Tower, from which he was released after thirteen years so that he could look for 'El Dorado', or at least a legendary gold mine in those parts. Naipaul dryly remarks that the conditions under which James I released him were 'absurd, as in a parlour game. The mine was in Spanish territory; the Spaniards would be informed of his movements. He would have to find the mine without disturbing the Spaniards; and the penalty for failure would be death.'

As we know, that penalty was exacted, but there is much here that will be new to most people. The narrative gives a vivid picture of the way in which the Spanish overseas empire was run, and why even at this early stage it had begun to break up. Its problem was the quarrelsomeness of the colonial Spaniards among themselves.

It is an exciting and violent story, in which the adventurers of Great Britain were as prepared to use slaughter and treachery as the Spaniards, but it is rightly accepted by Naipaul in the terms of the period, as no more or less open to objection than making a journey to the moon today. This freedom from moralizing makes *The Loss of El Dorado* a most refreshing book to read.

Naipaul records the horrors ironically – in a manner that sometimes even makes the reader laugh aloud – but is at the same time neither flippant nor facetious.

For the latter part of the seventeenth century, and first three-quarters of the eighteenth, Trinidad sank back to a population of about 150 colonists, living more or less in the bush. Then – after the British had dropped a hint that they might be prepared to swop Gibraltar for Trinidad – the Spaniards took an interest and decided to colonize the island energetically.

This was to be done chiefly with French immigrants from other islands, who would bring their slaves – the most important point – but, although all immigrants had to be Roman Catholic, they were not necessarily Creole Frenchmen, some being free Negroes with slaves of their own. The French representative of the immigrants (writing in 1777) referred to the new American constitution, which 'must enchant the mind of every citizen by its fanatical attachment to liberty'.

During the wars with Bonaparte, Great Britain took Trinidad. This provides Naipaul with his second great set-piece, balancing the Ralegh story. The scene is once more set for this country to play a major role in the South American continent, where the colonies were rising against Spain.

Thomas Picton was sent to Trinidad as governor, and the scandal in which he became involved over the use of torture on Luisa Calderon, a Trinidadian girl of fourteen or fifteen, is investigated with attention. It is a hair-raising incident, against a no less hair-raising background. No one but Naipaul could have told it in quite the same cold-blooded, vigorous, understanding way.

One would like to put Picton's case as well as possible – he was Wales's greatest general since the Middle Ages, a brave soldier, who would have taken over command at Waterloo had Wellington, not Picton, fallen on the field of battle. Some even thought him Wellington's serious rival as tactician. He was not, however, a very nice man. That is even allowing for kid gloves being inappropriate when governing a Caribbean island at that period, and for prison conditions at home not conspicuous for their humanity.

A plea may, however, be put forward to refute contemporary complaints about Picton's 'low extraction' in an age that liked its eminent men to be both well born and rich. It may be true that none of the Picton family had enjoyed the title of Excellency 'before or since the days of Caractacus', but their house, Poyston in Pembrokeshire, not enormous, is at least respectably distinguished. No doubt Picton's troubles in Trinidad prevented him getting the peerage his fellow commanders were awarded.

The Loss of El Dorado: A History,   1969
V. S. Naipaul, Deutsch.   *Daily Telegraph*

III

A facile way out among reviewers is to equate, usually somewhat ineptly, any given contemporary writer with another. It saves the trouble of thinking about what the writer in question is really saying. In the case of V. S. Naipaul, this has not been done, simply because no other writer can be at all easily compared with him.

Reading *The Overcrowded Barracoon,* long essays in the higher journalism, which range from India to the Caribbean, Mauritius to Cannery Row, I tried to define just what quality it is which gives Naipaul his originality. In one sense, his Trinidadian-Indian background has little or no bearing. He has become one of this country's most important writers. In another, it is possible his particular dead-pan humour does belong to a definite Indian tradition. In India once or twice I was reminded of its particular tone.

Naipaul's unusualness, however, consists not so much in his humour or language, vigorous as these are, but in his own attitude. This attitude is specially hard to define. He has a point of view, very much so, and does not at all mind making himself disagreeable about circumstances of which he disapproves. On the other hand, he does not look at life from any explicitly political or social angle, least of all does he 'see things from both sides' in a bluff, understanding, middle-of-the-road manner. It might be said that he is utterly unimpressed by most of the popular present-day myths.

In addition, Naipaul possesses quite extraordinary powers of reproducing the way people talk, and doing so at considerable length. His splendid account here of the election in Ajmer, Rajasthan, might be dismissed by saying that the writer is, after all, an Indian, therefore knows about Indians. In rather the same way, the English-official-public-school conversation of the Governor of British Honduras might be put down to a Trinidadian's familiarity with British officials overseas.

But what about Norman Mailer running for mayor of New York? This is one of the best pieces in a volume full of good ones. There is an absolute rattle of tough American dialogue which certainly gives the impression of being authentic.

'I've been talking to taxi-drivers,' a foreign reporter said (he had joined us at the Electric Circus). 'They may know about *The Naked*. But they don't always know who the author is. I was talking to an old Jew in Brooklyn yesterday. I told him about Mailer. He said, "Isn't he the guy who stabbed his wife?" Nine years, and he's talking about it like he'd read it in the paper that morning.' 'He probably gets his papers late.'

In the same way Jacques Soustelle, Aztec scholar and once Gaullist henchman, is characterized in his exile from France; or the seedy political bosses of Anguilla shown in their home setting, and troubles with St Kitt's next door.

India is where Naipaul's heart really lies. He is always stimulating on the subject of the sub-continent; severe but loving. If he is a trifle too severe for some Indians themselves, they make a mistake, though an understandable one.

Unlike most who write about India, he dislikes the Lutyens New Delhi ('neither British nor Indian') and, equally unorthodox, finds a kind word to say for Calcutta (usually disparaged in comparison with Bombay) for what he calls its 'Calcutta Corinthian' palaces. He comments on the absence, owing to the Indian manner of looking at life, of Indian autobiographies. 'Gandhi drops not one descriptive word about London in the 1880s, and even Mr Nehru cannot tell us what it was like to be at Harrow before 1914.'

An exception is, of course, Nirad Chaudhuri (author of *Autobiography of an Unknown Indian* and *The Continent of Circe*), with whom Naipaul deals in one of the essays here, called 'The Last of the Aryans'.

Naipaul is a great admirer of Chaudhuri, though they are writers of a very different sort; Chaudhuri far more polemical. Chaudhuri is full of controversial ideas – that people who become obsessed with religion, inevitably become obsessed with sex; that caste is the only thing that holds India together; that 'there are few delineations of the Indian character more insultingly condescending' than E. M. Forster's *A Passage to India*; that Hindus are militarists and always have been.

One of V. S. Naipaul's own acute descriptions of the Indian countryside is:

> divisions not strictly racial and not strictly social: more as if, in an English village, where everyone more or less looked alike, spoke the same language and had the same religion, every man yet remembered that he was a Dane or a Saxon or a Jute and stuck to his kind.

The Overcrowded Barracoon: and   1972
Other Articles, V. S. Naipaul,   *Daily Telegraph*
Deutsch.

IV

In the old colonial days it was not at all uncommon in this country to hear those whose employments took them to Asia or to Africa praise (sometimes to the disadvantage of local Christians) the Mohammedan sections of the population with which they were brought in contact.

These were alleged to live by a few simple rules, to be on the whole well behaved, above all easy to deal with as man to man. Lately the picture seems less simple. One reads of floggings for tasting alcohol, stonings for adultery, attitudes that are simple, easy to deal with only in their return to seventh-century dispensations of the law. More understanding is clearly required in the West as to what is going on in the Islamic states. Islam, incidentally, means Surrender – that is Surrender to God.

V. S. Naipaul, who has already written absorbingly about Africa, the

Antilles, Argentina, made a journey with the object of finding out
something about the New Islam – the movement being consciously a
revival and redistribution of Islamic forces – something that required
on his part a great deal of trouble; and, one might add, in Iran, for
example, a certain amount of courage.

Amongst the Believers is a book with two sides: first, the personal
reactions of the author – appreciative listener, pertinacious investigator, exasperated hotel guest – which are often immensely funny.
Secondly, the picture that unfolds, as he crosses Asia, of what is so often
what Naipaul calls a 'religion of resentment'.

We begin with Iran, visited in August 1979, and again in February
1981. In a sense Iran needs no introduction. It is always with us. Of his
first visit Naipaul says:

> I telephoned the editor-in-chief of *Iran Week* and he asked me to
> come over right away. I had to be careful though, he said: there
> were two buildings in the street with the same number, 61. And
> when I had found the right 61, I had to remember that if I took the
> lift, the office was on the sixth floor, but if I walked it was on the
> fourth.

Everything was emptier, quieter, eighteen months later, but in no
less of a mess. Iran is predominantly Shia Islam, Iranians recognizing a
special line, fourth in succession, to the Prophet; but there are other
religions there. Three hundred thousand Baha'is are regarded as
heretics of the worst sort who, so we read at this very moment, may
face massacre. Yet the flow of Iranian oil is still great enough to
prevent economic collapse in the face of every political and religious
madness.

In Pakistan, a poor country (also troubled by Islamic heretics),
things are very different. The concept of a separate Indian Moslem
state was formulated in 1930, the idea being that religion for a Moslem
is not that of private conscience (like Christianity), but a 'polity', which
includes certain legal concepts. The Moslems feared that in an
independent India they would be swamped, and that Islam would lose
its politico-social force.

Pakistan is now under a military government, and exists largely by
its population emigrating and sending back money. 'Our people
emotionally reject the West,' said one of Naipaul's informants, a
leading lawyer. 'Materially, we may depend on the West. Our people
may go abroad to better themselves. But however long they stay, they
will always come back, if only to die.' Naipaul comments:

> The West, or the universal civilisation it leads, is emotionally
> rejected. It undermines; it threatens. But at the same time it is

needed, for its machines, goods, medicines, warplanes, the remit-
tances from the emigrants, the hospitals that might have a cure for
calcium deficiency, the universities that will provide master's
degrees in mass media. All the rejection of the West is contained
within the assumption that there will always exist out there a living,
creative civilisation, oddly neutral, open to all to appeal. Rejection is
therefore not absolute rejection. It is also, for the community as a
whole, a way of ceasing to strive intellectually.

Again and again the woman question comes up; the necessity to
control women, get them back into the veil. In Malaysia Naipaul was
taken round by a keen worker for the Moslem cause:

'Social pollution?'
'Something that contradicts our customs and traditions. A man
cannot walk with a woman who doesn't belong to his family in the
kampong (village). It is forbidden.'
'Why is it wrong?'
'The very essence of human respect and dignity comes from an
honourable relationship of man and woman. You must have a law to
protect the unit of your society. You need your family to be protected.
When girls come from the village to K L [Kuala Lumpur] they don't
want to be protected by the law.'

In Malayasia there are a few Hinduized architectural remains in the
far north, but no great Indianized civilization grew up as in Java, one of
the islands of Indonesia.

Indonesia is under a military government, which came in after the
twenty years' rule of Sukarno, who had collaborated with the Japanese
when they invaded the islands. Here Islam is in great need of reform in
Islamic eyes because the villages have intermixed it with memories of
Hinduism, animism, touches of Christianity.

Naipaul was taken to a school, or rather an example of 'deschooling'
and the doctrines of Ivan Illich. It was exceedingly difficult to find out
what was going on. Naipaul objected that nothing seemed to be taught
except learning the Koran by heart:

'People didn't make beds at my school,' Prasojo said. 'They didn't
make them and sell them. That's a new idea.'
I said, 'I did woodwork at my school.'
'You did?' He went silent . . .
I said, 'Have you heard of an English writer called Charles
Dickens? . . . Well in 1837 or 1838 Charles Dickens wrote a novel
called *Nicholas Nickleby*, and he described a school like that. It was run
by a man called Mr Squeers. He believed in learning by doing. Botany –
go out and garden. Biology – go out and brush down the horse.'

'I have heard of Charles Dickens but I haven't read Michael
Nickleby.'
Among the Believers is one of V. S. Naipaul's best books, making you
laugh aloud while feeling at the same time intensely disturbed about
what is happening in Islamic countries.

Among the Believers: An Islamic   1981
Journey, V. S. Naipaul, Deutsch.   *Daily Telegraph*

V

Every morning when he got up Hat would sit on the banister of his
back verandah and shout across, What happening there, Bogart?" '

Nearly thirty years ago V. S. Naipaul typed those words on 'non-rustle'
paper in the freelance room of the BBC Caribbean Service, then located
in what had formerly been the Langham Hotel (favourite haunt, as it
happens, of the Victorian novelist Ouida). From the moment of that act
Naipaul himself became a writer.

Writers are perpetually asked by private persons, interviewers, and
the like, how it's done. The answer is, of course, that the writer does not
know. So far as the writer does know, Naipaul seems to me to give as
accurate an account as possible of a curious process that somehow
combines the imagination and the will; forcing yourself to get
something down on paper, 'non-rustle' or not.

The first of these two narratives, *Prologue to an Autobiography*, describes
childhood in an Indian family for three generations settled in Trinidad
– the scene of Hat's shout to Bogart quoted at the opening of this
review. Mystery surrounded the birth of Naipaul's grandfather who
had been taken to the Caribbean island as a child by his mother.
Naipaul's father, also possessing an ambition to write, and supporting
himself intermittently as a journalist, was an interesting and complicated figure.

The second narrative, *The Crocodiles of Yamousskro*, appears at first
sight to have no connection with the first except that it is written by the
man whose childhood, relations, early days with the BBC, have already
been chronicled.

That judgment would, however, be superficial. There are close, if
subtle, links between the two pieces. The second narrative deals with a
comparatively recent visit to the now independent former French
colony of the Ivory coast, ruled over by an aged, relatively beneficent
dictator whose country is prosperous. By now Naipaul is a celebrated

writer, well equipped to investigate, anxious to understand rather than judge.

The prosperity of the Ivory Coast, founded on good sense (unpenetrated by Marxism) rather than rich resources ('a little coffee, a little cocoa'), does not preclude the strange, sometimes sinister aspects, common to Africa. In these, the religious and mystic workings of 'animism', Naipaul is specially concerned; for example, the crocodiles of the title specially imported to an artificial lake in the Presidential garden, and ritually fed with a live hen every day – were finally explained as the President's family totem.

Naipaul writes:

> I travel to discover other states of mind . . . So while, when I travel, I can move only according to what I find; I also live as it were, in a novel of my own making, moving from not knowing to knowing, with person interweaving with person and incident opening out into incident. The intellectual adventure is also a human one: I can move only according to my sympathy.

If we return for a moment to the first narrative, two incidents (many more could no doubt be noted) offer a foretaste of the second narrative. Naipaul refers to his father's bookcase-and-desk made from packing crates (the unstained panel of one drawer stencilled *Stow away from boilers*), a piece of furniture of obvious use and origin. When, however, at the age of six, he asked a Negro carpenter what he was making, the fascinating reply was: 'The thing without a name.' The Ivory Coast was to provide many such things without a name.

To take another instance. Naipaul's father, as a Hindu and religious reformist, had written with disapproval of the practice of sacrificing a goat to the Indian god Kali. It appeared from his son's researches that Naipaul *père* – possibly under threat of his life – had been forced to retract, perhaps even to the extent of being compelled himself to sacrifice a goat. Without the episode we thus anticipate the live offering to the Presidential crocodiles, other matters too.

There are not wanting rumours in the Ivory Coast to suggest that when a chief dies his servants and wives are buried with him, and sanctuary villages exist to which dependants can fly if they are able to do so before his death. The alleged formula for the sacrifice of children as announced in the paper is said to be *après une courte maladie*. What at least is not denied is that Africans who accept animism commonly regard the period from sunset to sunrise as their own, giving them magical powers unvouchsafed to other races.

Naipaul relates this last belief to the Caribbean, where after dark the slaves had their own customs and hierarchies, some even said to be carried in litters by their fellows. One has read of such things, especially in connection with Haiti. Here their African roots are observed, and the widespread conviction that the African, by a magical concentration of energy, can carry 'another self' far afield.

An interesting point about this belief in being magically transported perhaps thousand of miles is its apparent similarity in medieval European witchcraft with accounts where persons seem firmly to have believed that they flew through the air. It has been surmised that drugs are the explanation of these states.

Naipaul suggests that some of the non-Africans who live among Africans do so because what is often a daily sense of discomfort and danger 'adds to the sense of self, the daily sense of personal drama'. V.S. Naipaul's writing is never quite like anyone else's. These two narratives are rich in good things, things to be found nowhere else.

Finding the Centre: Two Narratives,   1984
V. S. Naipaul, Deutsch.   *Daily Telegraph*

VI

The legend of the South is a potent one. We have to remind ourselves that the author of 'Way Down upon the Swannee River', 'My Old Kentucky Home', 'Massa in de Cold, Cold Grave', was a Northerner, who did not visit the South until his late twenties, and only rarely afterwards, and that the Civil War was fought at least as much over the right of a State to secede from the Union, and over tariffs (industrial versus agricultural), as over the question of slavery.

None the less the burning of Columbia by Sherman's dashing Yankee boys, on the march from Atlanta (city of *Gone With the Wind* and Coca-Cola) to the sea, is remembered as if it took place yesterday, and the statue of Washington, damaged by Union troops, remains unrepaired. Stickers on cars proclaim: 'American by birth, Southern by the grace of God.'

In *The Middle Passage* (1962) V. S. Naipaul considered the circumstances of the slave-trade, so there is a logical following up of the theme in an investigation of the old slave States of the South. Besides, that area of America has something in common with the land of Naipaul's own origins, Trinidad – origins, that is, after his family came there from India. The result is a most unusual and absorbing book.

Naipaul's method was to wander about examining places and people for himself; also to undertake interviews of every sort with black and white – such as a visit to the distinguished Southern writer Eudora

Welty, or exploring the Mississippi birthplace of Elvis Presley. On the
wall of the Presley family dwelling was a framed copy of Kipling's *If*.
This appeared not to date back to the birth of the great man, when 'the
paper on the walls would have been newspaper,' as Naipaul's guide
remarked, adding: 'He was the lowest of the low.'

One meets lawyers, politicians, agitators, backwoodsmen, farmers;
all, black or white, have their own point of view, with the only
characteristic in common a pride in being of the South.

One of the points that Naipaul notes is that in England the 1920s seem
yesterday; in the South the 1920s often represent the very beginning of
time. No doubt changes have been immense since those days, notably, of
course, desegregation – not always felt to be advantageous.

Then there were the Rednecks. Naipaul says that his general picture
of a Redneck was uneducated intolerance and toughness, basically
anti-black, determined to make no concession to polite manners. Then
he came across a semi-Redneck, who gave an almost lyrical account of
their cult. In this, dress plays a considerable part, especially cowboy
boots. The Redneck

> is going to live in a trailer . . . smoke about two and a half packets of
> cigarettes a day, drink about ten cans of beer at night, and he's going
> to be as mad as hell if he doesn't have some cornbread and peas and
> fried okra and some fried pork chops to eat . . . they love to hunt and
> fish . . . these redneck sons of bitches say they'd rather have one of
> these river catfish than one of those pond catfish. They say it's got a
> better taste.

The particular semi-Redneck Naipaul talked to was not specially
interested in religion, but one of the strongest impacts of the book is the
powerful hold of religion in the South; usually some form of Baptist.
One American in three is now said to be a born-again Christian. 'That
had been the great discovery of my travels so far in the South,' writes
Naipaul. 'In no other part of the world had I found people so driven by
the idea of good behaviour and the good religious life. And that was true
for black and white.'

V. S. Naipaul ends his story in the heart of the North Carolina
tobacco country. Tobacco was felt to be a gradually dying industry,
and again he was reminded of Trinidad, the family he visited having a
tradition that they had first emigrated to Barbados. Here too was one of
the Southern obsessions: the 'right to bear arms' embodied in the
Declaration of Independence.

Anyone who wishes to attempt to understand the problems that still
pursue the South should certainly read Naipaul's book. It provides an
extraordinary panorama; in a few places horrifying, but never loaded,
never taking sides, the author just presenting innumerable points of

view, conveying in a new and always personal manner the atmosphere of country that has been much written about. Does all this bear out the Legend of the South? It is hard to say.

A Turn in the South, V. S.   1989
Naipaul, Viking.   *Daily Telegraph*

Proust and Proustian Matters

BENJAMIN CONSTANT

Those who urge that the world would be a better place if politicians possessed less commonplace minds rarely pause to consider past examples, so often lamentable, of persons of imagination who have engaged themselves in problems that belong to the field of action. A few names in history possess undeniable claims in both spheres; but on the whole a good case could be made in support of the view that in government even the throng of cliché-ridden nonentities have often proved more effective in the long run than many of the men of intellectual brilliance.

Benjamin Constant is a case in point. From his earliest childhood his intelligence and powers of expression were recognized, in spite of the acceptance of him by his own relations as something of a problem-child. His short novel *Adolphe* (published in London in 1816) demonstrates incontrovertibly his powers as an imaginative writer. His pamphlets and draft constitutions are said to be models of their kind. He was an orator who could amuse the Chamber of Deputies, charm kings, and make an adventurer in decline like Bonaparte believe in the value of his support. And yet, in spite of these gifts, his political achievement reduced itself to a reiteration, under various governments, and in and out of season, of a plea that Press censorship should be relaxed in France.

It is, of course, not primarily as a politician that Constant is an absorbing figure, and much has been written of him that scarcely touches on that side of his life. All the same the fact remains that he came to regard politics as his profession and in politics the greater part of his life and energies were spent. If we disregard the elderly deputy from the Sarthe with his crutches and untidy papers and old round hat, we can only appreciate one side of his antics as a red-haired, green-spectacled young man, or his complicated relationships with Madame de Charrière or Madame de Staël.

Harold Nicolson, for example, has less to say of Constant's political career than of his personal life, which is in one way disappointing, not because the former is more interesting than the latter, but because Nicolson is adept in presenting such material in intelligible terms. He, if anyone, could have been Constant's political apologist and his tendency to reduce the narrative of the later years to a minimum seems to confirm their decided air of futility. This does not mean that he fails to relate Constant to the history of his times. On the contrary, he places him in perspective most successfully even when one may disagree with his judgments: and, although this new biography claims to add nothing original to what is already known of its subject (and sets out to be no more than 'a moral tale'), it is concise, balanced, and readable. Indeed, for those not yet addicted to the cult of Constant, Nicolson unquestionably provides the best introduction that has yet appeared in English. Readers already familiar with the story may become at times restive, at the unremitting certainty with which the biographer particularizes and explains every circumstance, however controversial, however delicate.

The son of a Swiss officer in the service of the States-General of Holland, Benjamin Constant was born in 1767. His French mother died at his birth and he was given an eccentric and inauspicious education which he has himself described most amusingly in his autobiographical fragment *Le Cahier Rouge*. Nicolson is severe to Colonel Constant, his father, no doubt justly, as a bad influence on Constant's early life, though he is perhaps too inclined to present the former as the heavy, military man of tradition (remarking that at least 'he never tried to induce Benjamin to adopt a military career'), whereas the Colonel's paternal failings were surely due to his being a crank: or even a highbrow. The family already possessed a tradition of intelligence (Constant's grandfather had been a friend of Voltaire), a sense of their own importance (as the descendants of the Artois *noblesse*) and a feeling that they were being kept out of their rights (as Vaudois gentry dominated by a Bernese oligarchy). The combination of these circumstances was calculated to produce a recognizable cast of character in a member of the family unusually well supplied with nervous energy.

It is tempting to suppose that the under-dog element bequeathed to him in this manner played an important part in Constant's development. Nicolson does not say much about the French origins beyond stating them: adding that the considerable fortune amassed by the Constants in Switzerland may have been made in the fruit trade. Constant himself (who did not care to be thought a Swiss) never satisfactorily proved their French descent, desired by him not merely as a genealogical foible but as an important requirement for entering French public life. There exists, in fact, an implication that the Constants had emigrated to better themselves in some way, rather than, as they themselves claimed, to avoid religious persecution. It might not be drawing too remote a parallel to compare Constant's position with that of a young man of Anglo-Irish stock, brought up in the intellectual atmosphere of eighteenth-century Dublin, deprecating his Irish connections, though never feeling himself entirely at ease in England. Certainly Constant came to France, if not with a feeling of inferiority, at least with determination, highly developed and proved by a score of duels, that he would not be put upon by anyone. The fascination that social success held for him and his sudden bursts of startlingly anti-social behaviour may well have had their roots in this proud but unassured family background.

Constant's association with Madame de Charrière has been described sympathetically, almost rhapsodically, in Godfrey Scott's *Portrait of Zélide*. Nicolson adds an excellent account of the bleak surroundings (the remains of which he has personally examined) in which this witty, selfish, attractive woman was living out the failure of her life when she met Constant in 1787. She was twenty-seven years older than he, an excellent conversationalist, and in the habit of taking too much opium. Nicolson does not like her: and it cannot be denied that with many gifts she had a disagreeably insensitive strain in her nature. Her effect on Constant at this early stage in his life was marked. She imposed upon him the severe critical standards of the eighteenth century, and it is perhaps due to her impatience with pretentious phrases that by the end of his life Constant 'denied the assumption of the natural equality of man and described Rousseau's formula of *la volonté generale* as "the evil ally of any kind of tyranny"'. Her reign was a short one and Constant passed into the hands of Germaine de Staël, daughter of Louis XVI's Finance Minister, Necker.

Nicolson gives it as his opinion that Constant was not a snob, rather paradoxically supporting this assertion by stating that he was a bohemian: as if the double condition were in some way incompatible. Certainly a ramshackle form of life was congenial to Constant, as the pattern taken by his two marriages shows. However, once having embarked on a career of seeking office, he could hardly do otherwise than make some effort to ingratiate himself with those who controlled the sources of power: and he was by no means inexpert at doing this, even when he held views conflicting with theirs. Be that as it may, there can be no doubt concerning another aspect of his conduct, that is to say his not very creditable atittude towards the money of his friends – and especially of his female friends. Though fairly ample funds were obviously required to live in the sort of circle he preferred there seems no reason to suppose that he was personally extravagant, except on account of his taste for gambling. This practice ate up all his capital and was indeed a bottomless pit for expending any wealth that came into his possession.

From the moment when at the age of nineteen he went to borrow from an elderly lady (who thought he had come to make a declaration of love) to that when Louis Philippe handed him 200,000 francs to pay his private debts, Constant never ceased to demand money from all with whom he came into contact. Madame de Charrière, in the days of their final disunion, reproached him with sums never paid back to her husband. His father complained that he did not mind Benjamin keeping Madame de Staël, but he could not approve Madame de Staël keeping Benjamin. Money was always placed first in Constant's own dreams of his life's requisites, and his long term with Madame de Staël ended with a financial wrangle of the most sordid kind.

With Madame de Staël we come back to the subject of Constant's role as a political force, and Nicolson calls her 'that splendid woman' and speaks of 'the purity of her political principles'. His book shows her as neither the one nor possessing the other; and it is hard to think of her influence on Constant – or anyone else – as anything other than wholly bad. 'It seems that Madame de Staël has written a novel in which both she and I are introduced disguised as women,' remarked Talleyrand; and there does not appear to have been a single stage in the career of this female embodiment of political irresponsibility when she would not have compromised her so-called liberalism for the realities of power. Her well-advertised antagonism to Napoleon was only the result of that shrewd man's resolution to have nothing to do with a woman whose mania for public affairs was not tempered by the smallest degree of discretion. Her scandalous private life was no less marked than her political intrigues by her insensate egotism; and the picture handed down of days and nights at Coppet, seat of the Neckers, is one to make quail the stoutest advocate of unrepressed behaviour.

Constant's subjection by this woman is painful to read of, and even Nicolson does not attempt to palliate much of her behaviour. However, the tolerance which he extends to her perhaps inclines him to attach more importance to her powers of attraction and less to her money as a means of holding on to Constant. However disagreeable it may be to admit this for those who feel warmly towards Constant, there can be little doubt that the latter consideration played an important part in keeping him at her side when love, or even sufferance, was long dead. In *Adolphe* the situation was romanticized by putting the tenacity of Madame de Staël into the body of another mistress, whose life the hero was represented as having ruined and whose circumstances were, indeed, of a tragic kind. It is, however, hard to imagine the man who could ruin Madame de Staël, and, although there can be no doubt that Constant, like Adolphe, felt he had been caught in a trap, in his own case it was a trap contrived largely by the wealth and notoriety of his mistress, both of which attributes he felt might be of help to him in his career.

As her lover *en titre* Constant was naturally forced to share her Napoleonic antipathies; and the narrative leads to a kind of climax when, at the time of the Hundred Days, Constant, completely reversing all he had said, and written, offered his services to the ex-Emperor. It is a deplorable story, the darker patches of which no amount of whitewash can conceal. Its only excuse could be that of the collaborationist in an occupied country: that without his efforts worse might befall. If Constant thought of himself as a moderating influence he was soon disillusioned concerning the extent of his importance in the eyes of Napoleon. At the Restoration, owing to the magnanimity of Louis XVIII, he was not treated as a traitor and shot like some of the insurgent soldiers, who at least had had excuse for their apostasy in that the Empire had in the first instance given them their high places.

For forty years he worked (like Mr Casaubon) at his history of religion; and, when at last this *magnum opus* was finished, it was found to be hopelessly out of date, failing to win him a place in the Academy. This was a bitter disappointment; but he could set against this the fact that he had become, if not a famous statesman, at least a popular figure in the eyes of the crowd. One can perhaps imagine him in the House of Commons – rarely without a few eccentrics – more easily than in a French setting, and his life ended much as it had begun, with general agreement in the eyes of the world that he was a clever fellow who lacked ballast. His funeral in 1830 was a public affair with troops and speeches. Rather appropriately, it was the scene of administrative muddle and an effort on the part of students to make it an occasion for political demonstration. It was an odd end after all the midnight conversations with Madame de Charriére, the ambitions, the scepticism, the aristocratic prejudices in favour of clear thinking and purity of motive. The whole chronicle might be one of Stendhal's novels – with their insistence on the forces of love and power – and Stendhal was, indeed, one of Constant's keen admirers.

There is much to be regretted in the story of Benjamin Constant's life, and it is surprising how he emerges, in spite of everything, as a brilliant – and even likeable – figure. His first-class intelligence was reinforced with detachment and humour, but he was the unhappy possessor of other traits that could prevent him from making the best use of his intelligence to the best effect. Ambition led him along paths which might be thought quite unsuitable for a man of his sort. He was himself aware of the malign effects of a split personality and was perpetually bemoaning the way his life was frittered away. In *Adolphe* he could objectify the circumstances of his love affairs: in real life he had no sort of control over his emotions, at the age of forty-six falling madly in love with Madame Récamier, an acquaintance of years.

The pattern of his political experience is no different. On paper he was moderate, clear-headed and full of common sense. When it came to making decisions or dealing with men he lost all grasp of reality. He was an almost classic example of Proust's observation: '*Ce n'est jamais qu'à cause d'un état d'esprit qui n'est pas destiné à durer qu'on prend des résolutions définitives.*' Trying in many ways as his life was, it is often surprising that he managed to extricate himself with such comparative success from the predicaments which he courted. He had neither the solid basis of unquestioned integrity nor the cynical agility of the truly professional politician or party man. His relations had expected him to make his name in literature. In a sense they were right, because it is for *Adolphe* that he is remembered. It is a thousand pities that – not much regarded by its author – this little book remained his single experiment in novel-writing.

Benjamin Constant, Harold   1949
Nicolson, Constable.   *Times Literary Supplement*

HENRI-FRÉDÉRIC AMIEL

I

It is perhaps not surprising that Hénri-Frédéric Amiel, who lived through the middle sixty years of the nineteenth century, the high noon of gloomy introspection, should have abandoned himself to self-pity of an unusually determined kind. By his very nature the diarist is especially addicted to this tendency, a powerful enough element in all literature. At the same time a more favourable background than his, or even one where his gifts might have proved a less tormenting burden, is not easy to conceive. To be born a Swiss was, after all, a wise choice on the part of a man who preferred to stand aloof from the tumults of Europe; while to become a don might be supposed an equally discreet decision, promising as undisturbed a retreat from life's bear-garden as a sensitive person in an imperfect world might reasonably expect. He had a private income, small but adequate; bearded, cadaverous good looks; a gift for pleasing women; an early reputation for brilliance. At the Académie de Genève he appeared as advantageously placed, at least outwardly, as any man of letters with (or indeed without) a fear of life might desire. But he seemed for ever unable to profit by his situation. His lectures were dull, his verse occasional and uninspired, his relations with his colleagues discordant, and his love affairs timid and inconclusive. Of these circumstantial inadequacies no one was more aware than himself. It was, in fact, from his consciousness of them and from his need to set down on paper a profound dissatisfaction with himself that proceeded the work for which he is still remembered – the now almost famous *Journal Intime*.

This diary, beginning in December 1847, runs to some 17,000 pages, of which the last sentence was written in April 1881. From being a record of his thoughts and a kind of intellectual exercise, it became gradually a refuge and a companion; at last almost his only interest. Into its pages poured everything, good, bad, and indifferent; and the result, in spite of weaknesses and repetitions, gives an analysis of his own character and dissects the human type to which he belonged – diffident and critical, ineffective and penetrating, unoriginal and yet gifted with a powerful sense of form – that in its own manner (comparable in some ways to that of Proust) could scarcely be bettered. In it he expresses perhaps as much as it is possible (at least in

413

an analytical form) to express of the workings of the human mind and of the human heart. The self-pity, it is true, rarely recedes; but it is as often as not relieved by a kind of self-deprecatory humour.

Parts only of the *Journal* have been published, the first edition, edited by his friend Edmond Scherer (translated into English by Mrs Humphrey Ward), appearing in 1882, the year after Amiel's death. Scherer's deliberately symmetrical selection consists of passages that show the author only at his best – or rather what Scherer considered to be Amiel's best – no excerpts being included that might be held in the eyes of the world to detract from the self-portrait of a high-minded Genevese philosopher. Blunt phrases are modified, incautious strings of adjectives whittled down. The expression of religious doubt is never allowed to transcend the limits permissible to an energetic and inquisitive, but essentially devout, mind. Nor were the dramatic values of the tableau less considered. The diary was presented as opening with the sentence: 'There is but one thing needful – to possess God'; while its equally apt closing quotation was: '*Que vivre est difficile, ô mon coeur fatigué!*'

If, from the great bulk of the manuscript, a book was to be produced in a saleable form some kind of doctoring was undoubtedly required; and, so far as it went, in spite of his liberal use of scissors and paste, Scherer's edition was good. It made available in a limited space material that introduced the *Journal* to the world, established Amiel's characteristics and qualities, and brought its author immediate posthumous distinction. Indeed, taking into consideration the date of publication and the public to which it was intended to appeal, the selection was judicious. Above all, the book that resulted was readable, a relevant aspect of its quality that might not be inferred from some of the many essays and critical studies that have since been devoted to it.

But although Scherer can hardly be charged with misrepresenting Amiel, he inevitably omitted much that showed sides of his life and personality, which, no less interesting, might be considered less conventionally appropriate to an idealistic professor occupying the chair of Aesthetics and Moral Philosophy; and it was more than forty years before a substantial alteration was made to the portrait that Scherer had built up. From time to time during this period further extracts were released from the diary, and letters appeared which enlarged and coloured the picture; but it was not until 1927, with the publication of a number of passages mainly referring to Amiel's views on love, that the clue was given to much of the higher pessimism of his perpetual self-examination. The figure of the writer that emerges from this additional material, if not an entirely different man, is certainly a man wearing a different (far more recognizable) suit of clothes. Before examining this more detailed likeness it may be well to consider some of the circumstances and early environment that contributed to Amiel's point of view and may have induced his persistent depression of spirit.

The Amiel family, French protestants from Languedoc, had come to Switzerland in the seventeenth century after the revocation of the Edict of Nantes. They were hosiers, but became clockmakers in their new country, where they intermarried with other commercial families, numbering a sprinkling of doctors and pastors among their relations. By the time the diarist was born they were well established in Geneva and had added a successful grocery business to the selling of watches; and it was with the former of these two trades that Amiel's father was chiefly occupied. His mother died when he was about eleven years old; and his father about two years later. He and his sisters were brought up in their uncle's family, where there seems no reason to suppose that he was unhappy. On the contrary the evidence seems to indicate that he was somewhat spoiled by these relations and that, if his father had lived, Amiel might not have found it easy to get on with this impatient, strenuous Swiss business-man, described as the possessor of 'une nature napoléonienne'.

From his earliest days Amiel himself and those who surrounded him had supposed that he was marked out for great things; although his successes at school were no more than might have been expected from any intelligent pupil. As a young man his brilliance and capacity were widely recognized, but already discouragement was there; and as the years passed the cloud of melancholy darkened, and his secret fears about himself grew ominously. The solid Swiss background, the intellectual adventures in Germany and elsewhere, his assured position in his native town, all these were already dust and ashes. There was a relentless force that gnawed at him within. In December 1849, he wrote in the *Journal*:

At twenty-eight years of age, not yet, as Pythagoras says, to have betrayed one's strength to any woman, or, as Goerres says, not to have tasted, or, as Moses says, not to have known, or as the French novelists say, not to have possessed, is a phenomenon, or rather a curiosity, of which none of my acquaintances of my age can offer a second example. Is it a good thing? Is it a misfortune? Is it stupidity? Is it a virtue? I have often debated this question. To have slept in all the beds in Europe from Upsala to Malta, from Saint-Malo to Vienna, in châlets and hotels, among the shepherdesses of Britanny and a step from the girls of Naples and to know sexual pleasure only in the imagination; to have had the most precocious temperament and to have read the most provocative books; to have had even the most seductive chances, and all this before twenty; curious even about crime, and, with greater reason, about love, inflammable,

always blundering, by what miracle did I bring home the innocence
of my childhood?

This then was the key to some – perhaps most – of his unhappiness. It
was a state of affairs that was not brought to a speedy conclusion; and
even when the difficulty was overcome the remedy came too late to be
efficacious. In the meantime there were a number of flirtations, some
supplied by 'Clot., Sar., Alex., Eriph.,' whose abbreviated names
remain their sole memorial; while there was 'Egeria', who stayed the
course better than the rest; but was written down at last a bad
influence. There were the Mercier sisters, too, whose mother kept a
girls' school, and to the elder of whom, Fanny Mercier, he left, when he
died, his diary and correspondence. He used to call her 'the little
Calvinist' and she provided much of the sentimental and domestic
relationship that he needed, and was intelligent as well. She used
sometimes to tell him that she was his 'widow'. Intellectual friendships
of this sort pleased him; but they were not enough. It was not until the
age of thirty-nine that he took the plunge, when the woman he calls
'Philine' (undoubted heroine of the later editions of the *Journal*),
became his mistress; and, at last on 6 October 1860, he was able to write
in his diary:

> But what am I to call the experience of this evening? Was it
> disappointing? Was it intoxicating? Neither the one nor the other.
> For the first time I have received a woman's favours, and frankly
> compared to what the imagination assumes or expects, they are a
> small matter. It was like a bucket of cold water. I am very glad of it. It
> has cooled even while it has enlightened me. Physical pleasure is
> three-fourths or more desire, that is to say, imagination. The poetry
> about it is worth infinitely more than the reality. But the keen interest
> of the experience is essentially intellectual; I can at least reason
> intelligently about women, without that semi-silliness of ignorance
> or that faulty idealisation of my thoughts, which has embarrassed me
> hitherto. I regard the entire sex with the calm of a husband, and I
> know now that, for me at least, the physical woman is almost
> nothing.

But it was not quite as easy as all that; and the entries in the months
that follow describe somewhat breathlessly the emotions of a lover,
emotions characteristic of a much younger man, but written with the
observation and acuteness of an intellectually mature mind – and
recorded with an unusual honesty. Sometimes the whole affair seemed
easy, agreeable, releatively unimportant; at other times a wearisome
entanglement, promising nothing but difficulties, dangers, and embarrassments; then, again, infinitely desirable, the most important thing in

the world. But his own egotism and self-consciousness were rarely absent, making enjoyment, even in passion, scarcely achievable. On 25 February 1861, he was back at the old subject and writes:

> Sexuality has been my Nemesis, my torment since childhood. . . . Disturbance of the sexual function is, I believe, one of the scourges of this nervous and enervated generation of ours. The whole of a woman's physical life revolves about this centre; the man's too, though less evidently. What is there surprising in that? Is not life the keyword of the universe, and generation the hearth of life, and sex the key of generation? For us, it is the question of questions. Whoever can neither reproduce himself, nor produce, is no longer a living being.

Not much is known of Philine herself, who was twenty-six when she met Amiel. Divorced and a widow with a small son, she had connections that were undesirable from Amiel's point of view. Her ineligible family seem to have offered certainly one of the positive reasons why he could never bring himself to marry her, although, about 1870, he came near to overcoming his hesitations. A passage dated 3 August 1868, throws a little light on the way he regarded Philine and on his own literary tastes:

> (11.30) I am finishing with a sad heart a novel by Theuriet (*Madame Véronique*). It is like a challenge. Véronique bears an astonishing resemblance to X [Philine] in appearance, character, and almost in her life story. These unexpected comparisons produce a cruel and fantastic impression. The important difference is that Mme La Faucherie resigned herself and that Véronique was only separated. On the other hand she had no impossible family. But this book has been like a vision to me; except for the ending which, God willing, will be otherwise.

Those who have the curiosity to disinter André Theuriet's novel will find a story of French provincial life, vapid in the extreme. Mme La Faucherie is a major's widow, living in the forests of the Argonne with her twenty-four-year-old son, Gérard, whom she decides to marry to Adeline Obligitte, the pretty, but worldly, daughter of a local timber merchant. The Obligitte family have staying with them a niece, Véronique, a young woman who had made a bad marriage in Alsace, and become a widow at the end of a year. Gérard falls in love with Véronique; and later, while visiting a distant farm belonging to his mother, he encounters Bernard du Tremble, Véronique's husband, still alive, forty years of age, but in appearance older, an impoverished, but proud and bitter, glass-blower. The plot creaks laboriously this way and that, until Véronique rejoins her husband, the murder of whom by a charcoal-burner (whose daughter du Tremble had seduced) brings the tale to a happy conclusion.

It is surprising that so discerning a literary critic as Amiel should have been able to endure these inanities, much less be deeply moved by them. The lapse must be regarded in terms of 'going to the pictures', a sphere where the action and psychology of Madame Véronique would not be out of place. Of greater interest is the question of how much can be learnt from the stiff, mechanical gestures of Theuriet's puppets that has bearing on Philine and her background, as seen through the eyes of Amiel. Véronique was small, pale-faced, and dark, with a high forehead, black eyebrows, and red lips. Her behaviour is melodramatic and her incompatibility with her husband never fully explained. She belongs to that gallery of haughty, sensitive, misunderstood ladies with husbands who are beastly to them, who reach their meridian at Irene in *The Forsyte Saga*, to disappear slowly from the literary scene as a changing way of life supplied them with compensations that brought in their turn a different series of problems to be argued out in a different sort of novel. Bernard du Tremble is the only figure in the book who shows any sign of coming to life. He is a 'gentleman glass-maker' (glass-blowing was the only trade in pre-Revolutionary France permissible to members of the *noblesse*), boasting of the letters patent conferred on his family by Henri IV in 1603, and presumably owing his description to some special knowledge of local types possessed by the author. He complains that women like only successful men and speaks of his wife's obstinacy, her reserve, and her pride, saying that she was not pretty but had '*je ne sais quoi d'attirant qui vous mettait le diable au corps*'. His business ventures had gone wrong, he drank too much, his health was bad. Worst of all he was in love with his wife; and his coarse manner of showing this had finally made her leave him.

To what extent this story resembled that of Philine's first marriage it is impossible to conjecture with any hope of accuracy from the facts available; but one cannot help feeling that Amiel in making the comparison may have allowed his romanticism to run away with him. That Philine loved him and was anxious enough to marry him seems plain; but his congenital indecision always made their relationship difficult in the extreme. It is not surprising to find that after some eight years he was full of doubts that she might be deceiving him. What form these fears took is not entirely clear from the *Journal*. In July 1868, some of the correspondence between them were missing from the file (where, with methodical sentiment, it was arranged), and he feared that Philine might have taken the letters for some undesirable purpose. Whether the letters were her own, which she wished to destroy in case they might fall into the hands of another lover, or whether they were Amiel's, and he feared some kind of blackmail is not apparent. An impression is conveyed by the cumulative effect of a number of related passages in the diary that Philine may, indeed, have had some other semi-permanent tie, which haunted Amiel's thoughts; and which gave his own relations some more or less substantial cause to object to any question of marriage. In September 1868, he burst out against them:

Oh, the Family! If the superstition with which loyalty and religion have surrounded that institution would allow the truth to be told, to what account would it not be called! What an innumerable company of martyrs it has sullenly, inexorably, forced into submission! What hearts it has stifled, lacerated, broken! What oubliettes, what death sentences, what dungeons, what abominable tortures in its annals, darker than those of the Spanish Inquisition. One could fill all the wells of the earth with the tears it has caused to be shed in secret, one could people a planet with the beings it has made wretched, could double the average of human life with the years of those whose days it has shortened. Oh, the suspicion, the jealousies, the slanders, the rancours, the hates of the family, who has measured their depth? And the venomous words, the insults that never cease to rankle, the invisible thrusts of the stiletto, the infernal second intention in speech, for that matter the mere irreparable slips of the tongue, the deadly chattering, what a legion of suffering have they not engendered? The family arrogates to itself impunity in abuse, the privilege of insult, irresponsibility in affronting. It punishes you alike for protecting yourself from it, for having confided in it . . .

The attack (one thinks of Samuel Butler) continues in this vein in equal length to the passage quoted above, and no doubt Amiel had had to put up with much from his sisters and their husbands. On the other hand, if he felt so strongly that a protest should be made against the tyranny of family opinion, here was an excellent opportunity for action. The fact was that in this as in all other questions that came to him he could not make up his mind. Would he have been a happier man if he had married Philine? If the *Journal* is to be believed he could hardly have been more wretched than he remained as a bachelor. Amiel would at least have had someone on the spot to look after him, been able to extend the scope of his acute observation to the sphere of married life and its psychological intricacies. This was not to be; and in July 1874, he noted 'when she kindly mended some of my linen for me' that the enchantment was over. However, Philine and Egeria had become friends by this time, and had arranged that when they died each should have half of Amiel's blue velvet waist-coat (which he had worn in Berlin) upon which to lay her cheek.

To Matthew Arnold, writing in 1887, Amiel's gift appeared to lie in the direction of literary criticism. Arnold found the assessments of

Sainte-Beuve, La Fontaine, and Victor Hugo, a great deal more
entertaining than the philosophy and psychology contained in the
Journal. He preferred Amiel's views on society, national characteristics,
and religion, to his self-examination and his despair; and it must be
admitted that when he allows himself to digress (which he does all too
frequently) on the subject of Maïa, the Great Wheel, and the Infinite
Illusion, Amiel is not at his best. Times and critics change; so that to
Middleton Murry in 1921, Arnold's essay seemed 'irrelevant and
superficial', and Amiel appeared 'a Stoic who had a clear intuition of
the insufficiency of Stoicism,' whose 'title to remembrance rests in the
last resort upon his profound conviction of the necessity of morality'.

Neither Arnold nor Murry had been in a position to read any but the
bowdlerized version of the diary when they wrote their articles. The
additional material would, perhaps, not have caused them to alter their
opinions; though resemblances to his own Swiss love affair could hardly
have failed to strike the author of the lyrical sequence to Marguerite.
Others may feel that the passages which refer to Amiel's emotional life
suggest that he was on the whole more concerned with, and influenced
by, his own individual problems than by any very remarkable grasp of,
or preoccupation with, those of the universe in general. He was not a
poet; nor, indeed, much of a philosopher. It is doubtful whether he
could have written a novel. He was not, in fact, what is called 'creative'.
On the other hand his critical faculty was exceptionally keen and, in
spite of indecisiveness, he had a power of anatomizing ideas with
extraordinary precision. Having given his views in one direction,
habitual vacillation (or unhappy sense of balance) caused him always
to provide the other side of the case, so that most of the best enunciative
passages in the diary close with a weak statement of the opposite point
of view. But although easy to disparage his diffuseness and other faults
of style, the *Journal Intime* remains a work of enormous talent. There is a
further aspect that is worth comment. In spite of the fact that its writer
never came to England, it is curious how often his thoughts and ideas
seem to take on an English tone. Indeed, although Amiel's mental
powers were of an infinitely higher order, he sometimes strangely
recalls his contemporary fellow-diarist, Kilvert.

1945
Cornhill Magazine

II

Throughout his life human nature continued to surprise and outrage
him by its inadequacies, and, although he never ceased to find in it
cause for complaint, Amiel never managed to accustom himself to the
vexations that almost inevitably accompany most personal relation-

ships. When he was forty-eight, for example, he could write (4 November 1869) after some crisis with his mistress, 'Philine':

> O inconstancy, O fragility, O contradiction, thy name is woman! I have never wished to admit this to myself. I have always acted as if women were constancy, loyalty, fidelity, and tenderness personified. But my simplicity has been punished more often than it has been rewarded. Like a people, a woman punishes equally him who speaks evil of her or him who thinks too well of her. She seems to care more for flattery than for esteem. She is under the lunar and Satanic influence, like a bad child who cannot be prevented from tormenting those who love him. One thing seems to be beyond her strength, that is, being consistent with herself, logical, firm, and faithful to an agreement. She inhabits the world of passion, of caprice, of suspicion, and cannot be at home in the superior world of serene wisdom. In fact, in spite of what I have said at other times, a good man is better than a woman, he is steadier, more upright, more considerate, and if he does not love better at least he loves more wisely. Woman is truly a weaker vessel who has need of a master, but of a beloved master.

As a don in Rousseau's city, fighting something of a rearguard action on behalf of the sentiments, Amiel might be expected to survey literature and politics through the same haze of fine feelings which enveloped Philine, Sorella, Egeria, and the rest of them in his eyes. However, he brought a kind of spiritual toughness to his consideration of these subjects which he was never able to command in his daily life. Where books or nations were in question he could be discriminating enough, and his views were far removed from the romantic liberalism that might in the circumstances have claimed him so unequivocally. His comparison (24 September 1857) of Chateaubriand and Rousseau shows the activity of his critical method:

> Essentially jealous and choleric, Chateaubriand from the beginning was inspired by mistrust, by the passion for contradicting, for crushing and conquering. This motive may always be traced in him. Rousseau seems to me his point of departure, the man who suggested to him by contrast and opposition all his replies and attacks. Rousseau is revolutionary: Chateaubriand therefore writes his *Essai contre les Révolutions*. Rousseau is republican and protestant; Chateaubriand will be royalist and catholic. Rousseau is bourgeois; Chateaubriand will glorify nothing but noble birth, honour, chivalry, and deeds of arms. Rousseau conquered Nature for French literature, above all the Nature of the mountains and lakes of Savoy and Switzerland. He pleads for Nature against civilization. Chateau-

briand takes possession of a new and colossal Nature, that of the ocean and America; but he makes his savages speak the language of Louis XIV, he makes his Atala bow before a catholic missionary, and, with a mass, sanctifies passions born on the banks of the Mississippi . . . Chateaubriand posed all his life as the wearied Colossus smiling pitifully upon a pigmy world, and contemptuously affecting to desire nothing from it, though at the same time wishing it to be believed that he could if he pleased possess himself of everything by mere force of genius. He is the type of a baneful race, and the father of a disagreeable lineage.

To Rousseau, naturally enough, Amiel often returns and (13 August 1865) he wrote:

For a man to make his mark like Rousseau, by polemics, is to condemn himself to perpetual exaggeration and conflict. Such a man expiates his celebrity by a double bitterness; he is never altogether true, and he is never able to recover the free disposal of himself. To pick a quarrel with the world is attractive, but dangerous . . . And yet, with all these extraordinary talents he was an extremely unhappy man – why? Because he always allowed himself to be mastered by his imagination and his sensations; because he had no judgment in deciding, no self-control in acting. Regret indeed on this score would be hardly reasonable, for a calm, judicious, orderly Rousseau would never have made so great an impression. He came into collision with his time: hence his eloquence and his misfortunes. His naïve confidence in life and himself ended in jealousy, misanthropy, and hypochondria.

Amiel's approach to contemporary writers was no less critical. His remarks on Victor Hugo (8 April 1863) provide a good analysis (not unlike Flaubert's) of that writer's imperfections and his qualities:

I have been turning over the three thousand five hundred pages of *Les Misérables*, trying to understand the guiding idea of this vast composition. – The fundamental idea of *Les Misérables* seems to be this. Society engenders certain frightful evils – prostitution, vaga-bondage, rogues, thieves, convicts, war, revolutionary clubs, barri-cades. She ought to impress this fact on her mind, and not treat all those who come in contact with her law as mere monsters . . .

It is great and noble, but it is a little optimistic and Rousseau-like. According to it the individual is always innocent and society always responsible, and the ideal before us for the twentieth century is a sort of democratic age of gold, a universal republic from which war, capital punishment, and pauperism will have disappeared. It is the

Religion and the City of Progress; in a word the Utopia of the
eighteenth century revived on a grand scale. There is a great deal of
generosity in it, mixed with not a little fanciful extravagance. This
fancifulness consists chiefly in a superficial notion of evil. The author
ignores or pretends to forget the instinct of perversity, the love of evil
for evil's sake, which is contained in the human heart.

Fourteen years later (26 April 1877) he had found no reason to
change his opinions on the same subject:

> I have been turning over again the *Paris* of Victor Hugo (1877). For
> ten years event after event has given the lie to the prophet, but the
> confidence of the prophet in his own imaginings is not therefore a
> whit diminished . . . Victor Hugo superbly ignores everything that he
> has not foreseen. He does not see that pride is a limitation of the mind
> . . . If he could but learn to compare himself with other men, and
> France with other nations, he would see things more truly, and
> would not fall into these mad exaggerations . . . But proportion and
> fairness will never be among the strings at his command. He is vowed
> to the Titanic; his gold is always mixed with lead, his insight with
> childishness, his reason with madness.

To hold these views on Hugo, so generally accepted in his own time
as the authentic voice of Liberty and of Letters, shows a considerable
independence of outlook. Amiel's remarks on politics (in the wider
sense of the term) and on the nations of Europe were no less at variance
with the optimistic daydreams of many of his distinguished contemporaries. It is not without interest that in a passage quoted earlier he
comments that 'a woman punishes equally him who speaks evil of her
or him who thinks well of her,' rather strangely prefixing this
observation with the words 'like a people'. In this way he reverses the
more common process of drawing an analogy between the way of a
nation and the way of an individual, as if he felt more at home with the
collective abstraction. This was, indeed, his habit of mind. Men and
women – even 'a Man' and 'a Woman' – were always a little remote
from him; while the European scene (although its scrutiny gave his
habitual melancholy plenty of substance upon which to dwell), was an
element with which he felt himself at ease . . .

An ironical pleasantry of fate had decreed that he should receive his
appointment as Professor of Aesthetics at the Académie de Genève in
1849, on the crest of the revolutionary wave that swept away (or, at
least, was intended to sweep away) the race of conservative preceptors
who had hitherto presided over that university. His acceptance of this
post involuntarily classed Amiel, in the eyes of local society, with these
revolutionary forces; and, accordingly, the old families of Geneva
refused to receive in their houses a man who not only believed as firmly

as any of them in the necessity of maintaining traditional standards; but who also possessed the particular brand of analytical intelligence most appropriate to the vivisection of a sentimental idealism. At an early age, indeed, he had begun to feel misgivings as to the path that democracy seemed to be taking, and he had written (17 June 1852) when he was thirty:

> Every despotism has a specially keen and hostile instinct for whatever keeps up human dignity and independence. And it is curious to see scientific and realist teaching used everywhere as a means to stifle all freedom of investigation as addressed to moral questions, under a dead weight of facts. Materialism is the auxiliary doctrine of every tyranny, whether of the one or of the masses. To crush what is spiritual, moral, human – so to speak – in man, by specialising him: to form more wheels of the great social scene, instead of complete individuals; to make society and not conscience the centre of life, to enslave the soul to things, to de-personalise man – this is the dominant drift of the epoch.

Again and again he returns in the diary to this theme, and a dozen years later (20 March 1865) he wrote:

> The only counterpoise to equalitarianism is military discipline. To the officer's stripes and the guardroom, the dungeon and the firing squad there is no reply. But is it not curious that the régime of individual rights should end simply in a respect for force? Jacobinism brings on Caesarism, pettifoggery ends in artillery, and the régime of the tongue leads to the régime of the sword. Am I protesting against democracy? By no means. Fiction for fiction, it is the least evil. But it is a good thing not to confuse its promises with its realities. The fiction is this: the democratic government postulates that virtually all the voters are enlightened, free, honest, and patriotic. And this is a delusion. The majority is necessarily composed of the most ignorant, the poorest and the least capable; therefore the state is at the mercy of chance and the passions and it always ends by succumbing at one time or another to the rash conditions that have shaped its existence.

Amiel's opinions were not of a kind to find wide popularity even at the period when they were committed to paper; and although time has not lessened the potency of much of their criticisms, they are perhaps still less likely to win any very ready appreciation at the present day. As a background to these views it may be of interest to consider what he has to say in the diary about some of the different countries of Europe. This observation of the contemporary world was one of the aspects of the *Journal Intime* which (even its truncated form) had greatly impressed Matthew Arnold.

Notwithstanding the happy years spent as a young man in Berlin, he was by no means unaware of sinister undercurrents in the apparently healthy development of Teutonic civilization. In the same way his generally astringent attitude towards France (where he rarely seems to have enjoyed himself) did not prevent him from recognizing the pre-eminent gifts of many Frenchmen. He allowed himself a latitude in expressing his feelings regarding the imperfections in the French character, almost as shocking to his friend and editor, Edmond Scherer, as the *Journal*'s account, omitted in the earlier editions of Amiel's emotional life.

They understand only black and white, yes and no, omitting all the colours and variations on either side . . . – They are logicians and not dialecticians. The mathematical tendency leaves them incapable before a higher degree of reality. In fact, they *understand* nothing, although they cavil at everything. – Skilful in distinguishing, classifying, and haranguing, they stop short on the threshold of philosophy, which consists in recognising the inanity of differences and finding the genesis. They leave descriptions only to rush into hasty generalisations. – They believe they truly represent the entire nature of man, while they cannot even break the hard shell of their own nationality, and they do not understand a single people outside themselves.

Ignorant, absolute, scholastic, formal, abstract – so you always find them when it is a question of explaining a social or ethnographical phenomenon. They pigeon-hole everything with the simplicity of savages. Their punishment is that they do not judge themselves and are stuffed with prejudices, in spite of their mocking incredulity. Mutinous spirits, they consider themselves free spirits. Witty, if you will, but limited to the last degree.

These are hard words; but few persons at all familiar with the people and literature of France would be prepared to deny that there is some measure of truth in them. On the other hand, after three hours spent on Hermann Lotze's *Geschichte der Aesthetik in Deutschland* (9 April 1868) almost anything seemed preferable to the German approach:

Erudition and even thought are not everything. A little wit, keenness, vivacity, imagination, grace, do not come amiss. Can one recall a single image, or a formula, or a striking or a new fact on setting down one of those pedantic books? No, one is only fatigued and befuddled. The terrible phrase, 'Sausage-eaters, idealists' (Taine), comes back to one with a vengeance. O, clarity, perspecuity, brevity! Diderot, Voltaire, even Galiani! One little article by Sainte-Beuve, by Scherer, Renan, Victor Cherbuliez, can inspire more enjoyment, revery, and reflection than a thousand of those German pages, crammed to the margin, in which one sees the labour but not the results. The Germans heap up the faggots for the pyre, the French apply the torch.

On the whole Amiel's disapproval of Germany tended to grow. The Franco-Prussian war and its aftermath had opened a number of eyes in this respect, even though the Germanophils were now louder than ever in their praise, because Germany had at last showed her power. On 30 July 1877, he entered some remarks on the subject which were to stand up well to the judgment of the next seventy years:

> In spite of all the ages that have passed, the mind alone in Germany has worked itself free; the statue has not emerged from its sheath of stone, and of the head itself only the brow is modelled. The German is a barbarian from the cheek-bones to the soles of his feet. Up to the ears he is a faun and nothing else. – One has only to look at the features of the great Germans of today – Bismarck, Molkte, Emperor William – to see of what clay they are made, and how crudely modelled, a race that is strong but crass, rude though calculating. Æsthetically, they are distressing, and the women are as imperfect as the men in appearance, bearing, form, in all that meets the eye . . . German vulgarity is vulgar ten times over, German corruption and blackguardry are ten times uglier than elsewhere. The Germans are condemned to being honest, solid, serious, under pain of being nothing else, in this resembling women, who lose everything when they lose their modesty.

Holding these somewhat severe views on the national characteristics of the French and the Germans, both of whom he knew so well, it is not surprising that there were moments when England (a country he had never visited, but for which he felt a certain attraction) fell into equal disfavour. On 2 May 1877, he wrote:

> News of the great world. England declares herself neutral in the Russo-Turkish war, but the first thing she has done is to lay hands on Egypt, holding the customs, the navy, the railways, the finances, the canal, as a preliminary to encamping her army of occupation . . . England has always identified what is useful to her with her right and has always found that her interest was a sufficient and legitimate reason. The effrontery of egoism becomes, with her, candour.

It might be argued that there has never been (nor, indeed, could be) anything notably altruistic in the foreign policy of any country, Switzerland included; also that the subject of England's relations with Egypt, for better or worse, could scarcely be excluded from the general consideration of disturbing German tendencies observed by Amiel himself. This is, however, a little beside the point and it is to be regretted that he never knew Great Britain better, as he would have excelled in examining those confusions of English thought and custom which have excited the wonder of every intelligent foreigner. There was much in English life that he found to admire, and he could have tested the good impression made upon him (9 October 1872) after taking tea with some English people:

These households in the English manner are very pleasing. They are the reward and the result of a long civilisation and an ideal followed with perseverance. What ideal? That of a moral order founded on a respect for oneself and for others, on a respect for duty, in a word on dignity. The masters of the house show consideration for their guests, the children are deferential to their parents, everyone and everything is in its place. People know how to command and how to obey. This little world is governed and seems to go along by itself; duty is the *genius loci*, but duty with that shade of reserve and self-mastery which is the British colouring. The children give the measure of their domestic system: they are happy, smiling, trustful and yet discreet. One feels that they know they are loved, but that they also know they are subordinate. Our children behave as if they were masters themselves . . .

How do the English mothers obtain this result? By an impersonal, unvarying, firm rule, in other words by law, which forms the mind in a free way, whereas giving orders only incites it to revolt and discontent. This method has the immense advantage of creating characters that are intractable to the arbitrary but submissive to justice, knowing where their duty lies and what is due to them, vigilant in conscience and trained in self-control. In every English child one feels the national motto, *Dieu et mon droit*. In every English home one also feels that the home is a citadel or, better, a ship. And so family life, in this world, is worth what it costs. It has its sweetness for those who bear the weight of it.

In the last two sentences he is thinking, no doubt, of his own problems and the family considerations which played the main part (or which, at least, he liked to feel played the main part) in preventing him from marrying Philine. He reverses his usual process of working from the general to the particular when writing (1 July 1856) on the subject of the Russians; but, although it seems clear that the entry is the result of contact with some individual Russian woman or Russian women, there does not appear to be any clue in the published diaries as to the person or persons concerned. Geneva had in any case a colony of

Russian exiles (portrayed by Conrad in *Under Western Eyes*), even a quarter known as *La Petite Russie*.

A man, and still more a woman, always betrays something of his or her nationality. The women of Russia, for instance, like the lakes and rivers of their native country, seem to be subject to sudden and prolonged fits of torpor. In their movements, undulating and caressing like that of water, there is always a threat of unforseen frost. Their humour freezes or thaws at a puff of wind that passes in the morning, a thought sets them bristling with sharp crystal or smoothes out a brow already freezing. The way they suffer or punish is to turn to stone. The Northern nature, a swift mobility, a centre that is always prepared to harden, winter, the frosts, are present, under the smiles and the ermine, at the bottom of the Russian soul. The high latitude, the difficulty of life, the inflexibility of their autocratic régime, the heavy and mournful sky, the inexorable climate – all these harsh fatalities have left their mark upon the Muscovite race. – A certain sombre obstinacy, a kind of primitive ferocity, a foundation of savage harshness which, under the influence of circumstances, might become implacable and pitiless; a cold strength, an indomitable power of resolution which would rather wreck the whole world than yield – the indestructible instinct of the barbarian tribe, perceptible in the half-civilised nation – all these traits are visible to an attentive eye, even in the harmless extravagance and caprices of a young woman of this powerful race. Even in their badinage they betray something of that fierce and rigid nationality which burns its own towns and keeps battalions of dead soldiers on their feet.

What terrible masters the Russians would be if ever they should spread the night of their rule over the countries of the South! They would bring us a Polar despotism – tyranny such as the world has never known, silent as darkness, rigid as ice, insensible as bronze, decked with an outer amiability and glittering with the cold brilliancy of snow, slavery without compensation or relief: this is what they would bring us.

Russian psychology was a subject to which he reverted a quarter of a century later (3 April 1881):

Nothing could be more moving than these recollections of a Polish political prisoner, deported to the banks of the Irtich, who contrived to escape from Siberia in 1846. This flight savours of the miraculous. And as for the picture of Siberia, it is enough to horrify one with the Russian régime and lead one to measure the mountain of crimes heaped up by the czars. – If the regicidal attempts are multiplying against the Romanovs, the iniquities of their house must not be forgotten. Muscovy is synonymous with ferocity, and the sovereigns have set the example for the subjects, *lupus lupis*. Monsters have brought forth monsters. The law of retaliation is the only law on a level with this inferior society, which has scarcely emerged from moral barbarism.

It will be seen from the passages that have been quoted that with all his love of abstractions Amiel was fully alive to the realities of contemporary European development. These passages are, of course, capable of giving only a general impression of what he thought. His habit of adding final qualifications to much that he said often weakens any single entry in such a way that, if left in, the qualification nullifies the point of the observation, while, if omitted, it might be objected that a *parti pris* extract is being provided. All that a commentator can do, therefore, is to recommend the *Journal Intime* and to try as far as possible to convey the firmer line of its thought by the quotations that are reproduced.

Inevitably one comes back to Amiel's own circumstances as the strength and the weakness of what he has to say, whether it is about literature or about international affairs. He never continued to make a satisfactory synthesis of his own life, he was always afraid of the world; and this, reinforced by his exceptional intellectual powers, inclined him to put an undue emphasis on generalizations. The result is not infrequently conflicting arguments, excellently put forward, which leave the reader without guidance as to what Amiel himself finally thought. But, just as he says that a 'calm, judicious, and orderly' Rousseau would be unthinkable, an Amiel untormented by half a dozen different points of view would, equally, be no Amiel.

1946
Cornhill Magazine

ITALO SVEVO

Although humour, melancholy and ability to convey individual character are qualities in a novelist that might be thought particularly to appeal to English taste, Italo Svevo is less widely read in this country than might be expected. The first English edition of his novel, *La Coscienza di Zeno*, appeared in 1930 – in a notably excellent translation, now republished by Beryl de Zoete – as *Confessions of Zeno*. Translations of other works followed. At present, however, he remains on the whole merely a name to many who would enjoy his robust, anti-romantic, and sometimes brilliantly comic approach to life. The circumstances of his career as an author are unusual, and the fact that he was never, in the ordinary sense, a professional writer has no doubt had something to do with the delay that has taken place in recognition of his talent.

He was born in Trieste in 1861, of a family of German-Jewish origin. Italo Svevo – Italus the Suabian – is a pseudonym indicating his mixed racial affiliations, his real name being Ettore Schmitz. His father, son of an Austrian official in a town north of Venice, moved to Trieste and married an Italian. Svevo was mainly educated in Germany, but the family's financial affairs took a turn for the worse, and he was brought home to be a bank clerk with his schooling unfinished. Later he left the bank, and became in due course a prosperous business-man. His first novel, *Una Vita*, influenced by Flaubert, and – as its title suggests – by Maupassant, came out in 1893, and had a small success. *Senilità*, published five years later, fell flat at the time: also translated by Beryl de Zoete, it appeared in England in 1932 with the title *As a Man Grows Older*.

One of the aspects of Svevo's business in Trieste is said to have been the preparation of a mysterious concoction to be applied to ships' bottoms for the removal of barnacles; and, as representative of his firm, he was accustomed to travel once a year to England, where, in a small and secret room at Woolwich, he is pictured supplying the appropriate authorities of the Royal Navy with the elements of this antidote. Svevo already spoke enough English to undertake these annual official visits without undue difficulty; but, wanting to improve his knowledge of English literature, he made enquiries for a tutor. He was recommended to a British subject living in Trieste, an Irishman, who had been teaching languages at the Berlitz School there, and had recently begun to give private lessons on his own account. The peril of acquiring 'an accent' seems to have been disregarded: for the Italian of Trieste was, after all, itself not above criticism. The young man was called James Joyce; and was himself, it appeared, interested in writing.

Svevo and his language teacher became friends; and it has even been suggested that Joyce drew some of his portrait of Bloom, the Dublin Jew in *Ulysses*, from the lineaments of his employer, apparently his only literary confidant for a large period of his life. Their talks may have encouraged Svevo to return to writing himself, and to embark on *La Coscienza di Zeno*, which shows every sign of being the result of prolonged thought and work – in spite of the statement by Joyce's brother, Stanislaus (in the introduction to *As a Man Grows Older*), that *Zeno* was written in a fortnight; a term of days in which reasonable industry would be required only to copy with a typewriter a manuscript of that length.

Whether Svevo and Joyce influenced each other as writers is an interesting and, naturally, a difficult question. Proust and Joyce are often – somewhat inexplicably – spoken of as if they wrote in a similar manner; and there is no doubt that in his treatment of characters Svevo sometimes resembles Proust. If Joyce, who read *Senilità* with appreciation, is held to write like Proust, possibly he might, therefore, be held to write like Svevo. However, Proust and Svevo are 'classical' writers, while Joyce, in spite of much window-dressing to prove the contrary, is really 'romantic', as his critics have not been slow to point out. Psychoanalysis may, however, provide a link. As early as 1898, in *Senilità*, Svevo was already toying with dreams as indications of hidden desires, and he is clearly interested in the father–son relationship which obsesses Joyce, with whom he almost certainly discussed the theories of the Vienna School; though Svevo always keeps abstract conceptions of this sort under a strict discipline in his writings. Perhaps by chance, and because all such ceremonies have more than a little in common, the account of Paddy Dignam's funeral in *Ulysses* somewhat suggests the obsequies of Guido Speier in *Confessions of Zeno*.

Svevo died in 1928, as the result of a motor-car accident. In the last few years of his life he was relatively well known as a novelist, and – although in Italy he had to contend with a prejudice (considered by some admirers of his work to be unjust) against the Triestine variant of Italian which he uses – his books were translated into several languages. The mark left on his work by French writers has been mentioned. This was followed by Russian impacts. Indeed, it is possible that a more potent and congenital ingredient than literary pastiche causes his books so often to remind the reader of Gogol or Goncharov: the mechanism of *The Hoax*, for example, his last published piece, owes something to stories like Gogol's *The Overcoat* or *The Nose*: while Zeno's hypochondria recalls the invincible lassitude of Oblomov. This additional element is to be considered in his polyglot background, the international port where Latin is brought up short against Slav and Teuton. Although he had the exactitude in expression of the Latin, Svevo is drawn to the introspective habits and delights in paradox of the Slav: however passionately he may have longed to be Italian, and nothing but Italian, there is almost always something of the Slav in the way he analyses a situation.

Confessions of Zeno, which appeared when he was over sixty years of age, shows Svevo in maturity as a man and a writer. The novel is told in the first person, and begins with the narrator Zeno Cosini's decision to cure himself of smoking by psychoanalysis. In order to give effect to this treatment, Zeno is told by his doctor to recall his past life. In this way his own development is recorded – parents, marriage, mistress and business relations. The result is an extraordinarily acute picture of life and of love. The novel is not without imperfections. In its earlier stages the author appears perhaps to have intended something more light-hearted than the narrative subsequently becomes; while the last section, which describes wartime scenes round Trieste in 1916, does not altogether successfully dovetail into the rest of the book: although both beginning and end of the novel contain good passages; especially the early chapter describing the death of Zeno's father. It is even possible that the psychoanalytical *raison d'être* was added later as an afterthought to what was to have been a straightforward account of Zeno's life.

In all Svevo's stories the central figure is a business-man with literary or intellectual interests living in Trieste. Usually the hero has written a book in his youth which has been a failure. Sometimes he is rich, sometimes poor. To this extent the material is autobiographical; but it would no doubt be easy to exaggerate the similarity between Zeno's life and Svevo's, although the illusion of reading memoirs is imposed on the reader (and was taken quite seriously by some critics when the book first appeared) by the author's adroit setting out of the story in this form.

Zeno, a bachelor of about thirty, not unsuccessful with the opposite sex (whose business affairs are managed for him by Olivi, dour and exacting representative of his father) decides that it is time to get married. He has conceived an admiration for Malfenti, a stockbroker, shrewd and insensitive, about twenty years his senior, who possesses all the business ability and will to get on in life which Zeno himself lacks.

Malfenti was about fifty, with a constitution of iron; a huge, tall man weighing about fifteen stone. The few ideas which he kept in his great head had been weighed, analysed and sifted by him with such care and lucidity, and their application to the numerous cases which arose each day so perfectly thought out that they seemed to have become part of himself, like his limbs or character. . . . He was very ready to help me and went so far as to write with his own hand in my notebook three commandments which he held should suffice to make any business prosper.

(1) It is not essential to work yourself, but you are lost if you can't make others work for you.

(2) There is only one great cause for remorse – to have failed to look after one's own interests.

(3) Theory is very useful in business, but only when the business has been already settled.

I knew these and ever so many other wise sayings by heart, but they were never any use to me.

After deciding that he would like to become Malfenti's son-in-law, Zeno first courts the pretty daughter, Ada; but finally, after many ludicrous episodes, marries her sister Augusta, quiet and kind, though less alluring outwardly. How all this happens is described with extraordinary dexterity and delicacy. Svevo has the capacity – so rare as to be almost unknown in the English novel – of handling emotional relationships with a combined tenderness, humour and realism. Zeno's acceptance of Augusta, his sudden feeling of warmth towards her after marriage, his subsequent associations with Ada as sister-in-law (who finally loses her looks, though not entirely Zeno's admiration) carry complete conviction. Zeno loves his wife but does not remain faithful to her. His connection with his mistress, Carla, the result of becoming involved in an act of charity, is equally well observed. Finally there is the account of Zeno's business life and partnership with the absurd Guido, Ada's husband, who, in his efforts to startle his family into submitting to his imbecilities, at last commits suicide by accident.

There has been a tendency on the part of critics in this country to regard Zeno as the portrait of a blundering, futile person, with whom everything that he touches goes wrong; and to imply that Svevo might have been well advised to choose a more decisive character for a hero. This is, at best, rather like complaining that Cervantes might have found a subject of greater edification in the adventures of a Spaniard of more progressive outlook than Don Quixote; and, in fact, the more Zeno's ups and downs are analysed, the more he is revealed as a universal figure whose fate is in some degree the fate of Everyman. Svevo scarcely deviates at all from a naturalistic approach. The sanatorium scenes at the beginning of the book perhaps come near farce, and Zeno's office life with Guido is not taken very seriously as a business partnership. It could hardly be urged, however, that there are no sanatoriums and no offices where the measure of daily life is not without some resemblance to events described by Zeno.

Proust's scope is, of course, much wider than Svevo's, who is in the comparatively rare – and on the whole happy – position of being a novelist who knows inside out a limited milieu unhaunted by men of letters; and who restricts himself to this milieu in its most normal manifestations. Svevo never indulges in the over-elaboration which mars some of Proust's best passages, that final running to seed, product of a prodigious literary fertility, allied to ill-health and other disrupting circumstances, which at times induces an almost overpowering sense of artificiality. He is also more successful than Proust in the difficult art of giving body to his narrator; though, again, it could not be suggested that Svevo attempts to emulate the mosaic of moods and sensations which Proust sets out so successfully to compose.

That Svevo, like Proust, possessed an unusual gift for examining the intricacies of love and jealousy can be seen from his earlier book, *As a Man Grows Older*, in which Emilio Brentani, a bachelor of forty, living in fairly straitened circumstances with his sister Amalia, becomes involved with Angiolina, a pretty girl, below him in the social scale. Angiolina, as it turns out, is not overburdened with moral prejudices. Emilio (who has had no previous practical experience with women) suffers alternations of love, irritation, affection, hatred and despair, in the course of the dance she leads him. At last Angiolina gives herself to him; and the account of Emilio's feelings after this conquest is strikingly similar to passages in the *Journal* of the Swiss diarist, Amiel, in which Amiel describes his first serious love affair, entered into at the same age and curiously reminiscent of Emilio's in some of its circumstances. Svevo could not have read of this parallel incident in Amiel's life, because it belongs to a section of the *Journal* which had not yet been published when he was writing *Senilità*: though he may well have known what had already appeared of Amiel's writings – which also have distinctly Proustian affinities. Angiolina, with her charm and her deceptions, is completely alive, a more feminine Albertine, and Emilio's sister Amalia, plain, hard-working, victim of her own goodness, is not without some similarity to Zeno's wife, Augusta.

Although Svevo writes about characters and situations of universal application, he manages at the same time to give a picture of life in Trieste, at once fresh and individual, and covering a period of some thirty years. *As a Man Grows Older* shows the town in the 1890s, and *The Hoax*, in which a commercial traveller heartlessly pretends that an elderly man's unsuccessful early novel is to be republished on highly favourable terms, depends for its climax on the confused state of currencies at the end of the First World War. Although Slavs and Germans are rarely introduced in the earlier stories they appear in *The Hoax*, and the atmosphere, disturbed though at the same time charged with a kind of fatalism, gives a good idea of the changes that had taken place in Trieste and in Europe since the turn of the century. The reader is conscious of a touch of nostalgia on the author's part for those quieter days, when patriotic Italians in the town could fulfil their duty merely by grumbling at the imperial administration.

One cannot help wondering whether Svevo ever came across Richard Burton, the explorer and translator of *The Arabian Nights*, when he was British consul at Trieste between 1872 and 1890. Such a meeting would be likely enough. It would, however, be, no doubt, too much to hope that as a small boy he met Burton's immediate forerunner in that post, Charles Lever. If so, Svevo might have boasted that he had bridged the literary gulf in writing of Irish life that divides *Charles O'Malley* from *Finnegans Wake*.

Confessions of Zeno, Italo Svevo;   1948
Beryl de Zoete, trans., with an   *Times Literary Supplement*
Essay on Svevo by Renato
Poggioli, Putnam.

MARCEL PROUST

I

Simultaneous reappearance in this country of *The Forsyte Saga* and *Remembrance of Things Past* in illustrated editions indicates a certain change in point of view regarding both art and letters. The occasion also provides an opportunity for comparing two novelists of very different aim and achievement, whose contrast provokes various reflections on the novel: especially the chronicle novel covering several generations. For that reason alone, therefore, the Forsytes are worth re-examination. Proust, after subjection to fires of severe criticism, has correspondingly consolidated his position. the Guermantes seem as assured of their place in literature as of their rank in society; while the worlds of which both authors wrote have passed, for better or worse, into the sphere of social history.

When these two books appeared, a quarter of a century or more ago, to call an artist 'illustrator' approached disparagement; and to suggest that Proust or Galsworthy might be interpreted through this visual medium would in those days have seemed to most of their admirers, to say the least, peculiar. It is true that at different times Van Dongen and Soutine tried their hands at subjects taken from *A la Recherche du Temps Perdu*, writer and draughtsman going their separate way according to the ideas of the period; so that the designs – pre-eminently in the Soutine series – remained well on the safe side of anything that could be accused of resembling genre painting. There was never any question of fusion of expression like that of Phiz and Cruikshank with Dickens, Leech with Surtees, or Tenniel with Lewis Carroll. Philippe Jullian and Anthony Gross, on the contrary, make no bones about their dependence on a literary foundation. Though the manner may be contemporary, they are illustrators in the old-fashioned sense.

The two novelists, totally dissimilar in most matters, possess a few unexpected characteristics in common. They were, in the first place, close contemporaries, Galsworthy born in 1867, Proust in 1871. Their rich middle-class families had risen fairly recently in the world, and were possibly not entirely unlike in some other respects, though no Jewish strain existed in Galsworthy's ancestry. (Incidentally, genealogy was a subject in which both were keenly interested; and Proust would scarcely have committed the heraldic howler made by Galsworthy in describing the coat-of-arms – appropriated by Swithin Forsyte – of 'the well-known Forsites with an "i"'.) Physically they present a complete antithesis, Proust from an early age suffering from poor health, while Galsworthy was robust and relatively athletic. Galsworthy was devoted to his father; Proust – it is scarcely necessary to recall – to his mother. Proust was always thought to show brilliant promise as a boy, Galsworthy was chiefly notable at school and university for sedate, unexceptional behaviour. Proust was intended for diplomacy or the Law, Galsworthy was actually called to the Bar, though he practised little, supporting himself for the most part during his early days by directorships in several of the companies in which his father owned interests.

Proust believed himself a writer from the beginning. By the time he was twenty-five he had already produced *Les Plaisirs et les Jours*, a volume of short pieces. Galsworthy was twenty-nine or thereabouts when he first seriously settled down to write; and when his first book, *Jocelyn*, a novel, appeared he was thirty-one. Both these volumes were published at the authors' expense. In due course each young writer decided to embark on a long novel that was to cover more than one generation and present a kind of panorama of society. *The Forsyte Saga* was, in the first instance, to particularize only certain sections of the rich middle class; though in other books Galsworthy dealt with different social groups. Proust, in an entirely different manner, set out to cover the whole of life as he knew it; in spite of which his work is almost always thought of – not altogether justly – as primarily concerned with scenes and characters from the *haut monde*. As it happens, both novelists, at about twenty years of age, completed 'confessions' in albums characteristic of the epoch. Galsworthy's answers are reproduced in H. V. Marrot's *Life and Letters of John Galsworthy*; Proust's in *The Quest for Proust* by André Maurois. The questions are not always identical in the two albums; but the following paraphrase of some of them could be considered applicable to both books. Some of the replies are not without interest:

Favourite Painter? Galsworthy: Turner. Proust: Leonardo da Vinci, Rembrandt.

Favourite Author? Galsworthy: Thackeray, Dickens, Whyte Melville. Proust: 'At the moment Anatole France, Pierre Loti.'

Favourite Poet? Galsworthy: Lewis Carroll. Proust: Baudelaire, Alfred de Vigny.

Favourite Composer? Galsworthy: Beethoven. Proust: Beethoven, Wagner, Schumann.

Favourite Colour? Galsworthy: 'the colour of Queenie's hair.' Proust: 'Beauty lies not in colours but in their harmony.'

Favourite Flower? Galsworthy: 'carnations, well wired.' Proust: 'hers – but apart from that – all.'

Favourite Heroes in Real Life? Galsworthy: Bayard, Damien. Proust: Monsieur Darlu, Monsieur Boutroux (professors at Condorcet and the Sorbonne respectively).

Favourite Heroines in History? Galsworthy: 'only heard of Florence Nightingale so suppose it is she.' Proust: Cleopatra.

Favourite Quality in a Man? Galsworthy: stoicism. Proust: feminine charm.

Favourite Quality in a Woman? Galsworthy: sympathy. Proust: 'a man's virtues and frankness in friendship.'

Favourite Amusement or Occupation? Galsworthy: grouse-driving. Proust: loving.

Obviously, no one should be trammelled by views inscribed in a confession book at the age of twenty – or, indeed, at any other period of life – but it would be fair to agree that, on the whole, Proust's entries are marked by that degree of frivolity for which friends sometimes blamed him: Galsworthy's by the gravity recorded as his salient quality as a young man. An awareness of his own seriousness allowed Galsworthy small inclination to attempt to become a 'pure artist'. He was always in his own eyes a writer 'with a purpose'; and among his own literary circle he himself could instance only Conrad as a novelist belonging wholly to the former category. Proust for his part intended to explore the mysterious workings of memory depicted through the mechanism of fictional characters. In the two novels, therefore, exists the same oppositeness as in the character and physique of the novelists. Once more, too, unexpected resemblances are to be found.

The foundations of *The Forsyte Saga* are laid on the unhappy emotional life of Soames Forsyte, a solicitor, belonging to the third generation of a family, similar to the author's, rising successfully in the world. Soames is madly in love with his wife, Irene; but she, after four years of married life, finds him, beyond all men, repulsive, refusing access to her room and taking as lover Bosinney, a young architect engaged to a Forsyte cousin. Soames, somewhat improbably, contracts with Bosinney to build a house; and, at a stage when Irene has already given herself to Bosinney, her husband finds her bedroom door unlocked, and insists on physical relations taking place. On hearing of this incident Bosinney is so distraught that, wandering half-mad through foggy London streets, he is run over and killed. (In the original draft of the novel Galsworthy made Bosinney deliberately commit suicide, and unwillingly allowed himself to be persuaded to leave the volition of the architect's death an open question.) Irene returns momentarily to Soames, leaving him almost immediately and living alone, teaching music, for a dozen years. She has £50 a year of her own, and inherits, towards the end of that period, a life interest in £15,000 from Soames's uncle, 'Old' Jolyon Forsyte, whose son, 'Young' Jolyon, she finally marries. Soames, too, remarries, and his second wife, a French girl, whose mother keeps a Soho restaurant, gives birth to a daughter. The latter section of *The Forsyte Saga* – and the associated volumes that followed it, on the whole greatly inferior in execution – is for the most part devoted to chronicling the far-reaching complications that result from a love affair between Soames's daughter, Fleur, and Irene's son by Young Jolyon.

This story, with many other threads, is set against the background of Forsyte family life, tenaciously clannish, and Forsyte desire for property, represented as an interest predominant over all others in every member – with the exception of a few blacklegs – of the Forsyte family. The spirit of the style is not unlike a blend of Marx and Meredith: constant reiteration, at least by implication, that the possession of property is morally wrong, interspersed with lively ornamental passages describing character and scenery. There are passages. Some of the dinner-parties, Soames *vis-à-vis* his parents, the death of Uncle Timothy to mention only a few, are written with skill; but the narrative always weakens when Galsworthy strays away from his own circle of relations and the society with which, as a young man, he must have completely identified himself.

When the author attacks the Forsytes for their materialism the reader feels again and again that Galsworthy is attacking a view of life never in his heart entirely rejected, and that his love-hate of the Forsytes is a love-hate of himself. His efforts to contrast with the typical Forsytes the behaviour of people who practise the arts professionally, or whose conduct or manner is light-hearted, are unsuccessful, sometimes to the point of being ludicrous. Although the 'modern movement' in painting was at times a fatal preoccupation, it remained totally unintelligible to Galsworthy, to whom creative ability seemed mysteriously vested in bad manners and personal untidiness. Bosinney, for example, conveys no sense of architectural accomplishment, and the circumstances of his professional life are often quite beyond belief.

Turning to *Remembrance of Things Past*, we find a framework formed on the emotional and aesthetic experiences of the narrator, Marcel, a personal analysis that has no parallel in the Galsworthy novel: though some faint similarity of effect might perhaps be traced between the blurred outlines of Soames's wife, Irene, and Marcel's mistress, Albertine: two utterly different images of desire who have this in common, that neither quite comes to life. Proust's novel looks backwards – and, as it were, sideways – through the medium of Swann, a rich Jewish connoisseur, received in the best society, and belonging to the generation of the narrator's father. From the technical point of view Swann plays a somewhat similar role in the construction of the story – if it may be so called – to that of the Forsyte uncles in supplying material for past happenings that have a bearing on the memories of Marcel. Like Soames, Swann is a picture collector; and, although his matrimonial troubles are of a different order, they are – again like Soames's – sufficiently disturbing. A close comparison of their taste in painting (*Swann*: Vermeer, Gustave Moreau, Elstir; *Soames*: Watteau, Turner, Josef Israels, Meissonier, Old Crome, Alfred Stevens, Goya, Gauguin, Matisse, etc.) might reveal further affinities. Each was unquestionably endowed with traits of his creator, Swann becoming on the whole less like Proust as the book progresses; Soames, at least in his processes of thought (as may be observed from the *Life and Letters*) becoming more like Galsworthy.

Snobbery, investigated so closely and with such skill in *Remembrance of Things Past*, is only touched on in the crudest terms in *The Forsyte Saga*: Soames, for some unaccountable reason, even supposes it necessary to explain its existence to his French wife, who, not surprisingly, replies that the phenomenon is not unknown in France. Finally, Proust's novel discusses the whole field of sexual abnormality, a subject never mentioned by Galsworthy (except by occasional implications of sadism) in spite of the book's preoccupation with the sexual relationship as such. Indeed, it would be possible to imagine Swann or Madame Verdurin described in Galsworthy's terms, or Soames and Old Jolyon in Proust's; but Charlus could never have strayed within the pages of *The Forsyte Saga*.

The improbability of some of the Forsyte episodes may be seen in the general account of the course of June Forsyte's engagement to Bosinney; in Soames's, a solicitor's, extraordinary negotiations with the private detective, or in the singing of the hymn about 'the hosts of Midian' at a fashionable wedding; or in the supposition that Fleur, as a girl of nineteen or twenty, would be normally found spending the morning in her club. Such examples are chosen at random, and an odd lack of familiarity with the ways of everyday life at times seems only thinly cloaked with a bustling display of practical detail. Proust, too, has his pages of pure unreality, particularly the scenes in which Albertine, an unmarried girl of ostensibly respectable background, visits Marcel at all hours of the night and even lives as a prisoner in his flat. Some of the coincidences that give Marcel opportunities to observe other characters – notably Charlus – are also hard to accept; or they would be if the author had not built up his material in a form that does not, in fact, lean too heavily on naturalism. Many novelists of distinction and power have handled improbable characters and incidents with success; but Galsworthy accentuates the naturalistic approach so strongly that his deviations are less easy for the reader to overlook.

The moment that all attempt at objectivity is abandoned in a novel a whole host of difficulties arise for the author in the way he handles his characters; and even from the standpoint of 'writing with a purpose', arguments, if over-emphasized, may easily rebound like a boomerang. Thus Galsworthy is forever informing the reader that Soames is utterly despicable and Irene infinitely desirable, without ever producing entire conviction that either premise is true. He cannot see – or is unwilling to see – where his own propositions lead, so that his 'artists' and 'bright young people' represent by their unreality a kind of Forsytean recoil from what such persons might in truth be like. The characters for whom the author feels affection never really lose their money, however imminent financial cataclysm may seem. In the depths of her penury, between husbands, Irene has a self-contained flat on the Embankment and, changing every night for dinner, is waited on by a maid: Young Jolyon, in spite of having made a mess of his early life, comes into his father's substantial fortune, his drawings fetch high prices, and he 'is in the very van of water-colour art, hanging on the line every-where'.

Like so much writing based on a nineteenth-century view of things, *The Forsyte Saga* basically assumes – at least in its earlier pages – that the old, comfortable world will go on, and that, although social changes are noted, it is perfectly safe to discharge heavy broadsides into such institutions as Property and Marriage: because, like the Poor (also a necessary adjunct), they will always be with us. This feeling of dissatisfaction with the established conventions was fairly widely known to persons of Galsworthy's generation and class, as may be seen by the Nineties movement; but how little he realized where lay the road along which he pointed may be judged by Galsworthy's letters. Conrad wrote: 'But, I say, the Socialists ought to present you with a piece of plate,' but Galsworthy himself always denied this political label; and it never seems to occur to him that property or marriage (as he attacks them) are merely forms of power that are capable of being translated by violent change into equally oppressive variations.

When Bosinney, already engaged to June, abandons her for Irene, her cousin's wife, he is – even from the romantic point of view – displaying a stronger will to power – and, in a sense, claim to property – than Soames, merely hoping to retain possession of his own wife. Indeed, Soames's obsessive love for Irene (which in a character of whom the author approves would no doubt have won him marks for being 'sensitive to beauty') is an element that Galsworthy has difficulty in explaining away. If Soames had, for example, suffered heart-failure

and died in one of his attempts to batter down Irene's door, it is hard
to believe that her union with Bosinney would have been a happy
one, even on her presumed inheritance of Soames's wealth. Bosinney
might well have become another rake like Monty Dartie. We are
given no indication how the author would treat a character who,
taking the first plunge for a noble passion, later lapsed into
promiscuity, of which Galsworthy would unquestionably have
disapproved.

Galsworthy is essentially a Forsyte novelist, a fact that makes the
Saga almost a book within a book. In many ways it is a work full of
hatred; and the curious consequence of contrasting its liberal humani-
tarianism with the much more sustained objectivity of *Remembrance of
Things Past* is to find that in the gallery of many unpleasant portraits
which the latter book contains none falls entirely outside the scope of
the author's sympathy. It is only necessary to think of Proust's
sentiments regarding the Dreyfus case, and his treatment of the *Affaire*
in the pages of his book, to appreciate the strength of his approach; and
it is an interesting comment – turning back for a moment to the
confession albums – that this objectivity was the product of apparent
frivolity; while Galsworthy's prejudice had its roots in high seriousness.

All this consideration of the two novelists has somewhat relegated
to the background the question of their illustrators. Gross has been
inspired to depict Soames with a shaved upper lip – an impression of his
appearance also almost undoubtedly conveyed to most readers by the
book, though for no definable reason – in spite of more than one
reference by the author to a moustache in later life. This firmness of
opinion on the part of the artist is surely to treat the question of
illustration correctly; and more than once in this excellent edition
it is possible to feel that the illustrations have taken charge of the
narrative.

One method of appraising these two sets of pictures would be to
return once more to the biographical works, already quoted, which
contain numerous pictorial records of Proust and Galsworthy at
different stages in their career. These photographs provide, therefore,
one indication of the spirit that might reasonably be demanded from
illustrations to their works. This test of examining the physiognomies of
the novelists' friends and relations is again favourable to Gross.
Jullian's delicate etchings seem more at home with Odette than with
Françoise or Swann. They scarcely rise to the full-blooded temper that
characterizes the photographs which survive of Proust's parents, or the
faces, for example, in the group taken at Princess Brancovan's
houseparty in the summer of 1899. All the same, they have a lyrical
quality that is in agreement with certain moods of the novel; and

consideration of the relative success of each artist in his respective task throws light on the contents of the books themselves.

The Forsyte Saga, John   1950
Galsworthy: with drawings by   *Times Literary Supplement*
Anthony Gross, Heinemann.
Remembrance of Things Past, 12
vols, Marcel Proust, C. K. Scott
Moncrieff, trans., illustrated by
Philippe Jullian, limited to 165
sets, Chatto & Windus.

II

One of the best features of George Painter's book is the manner in which priggishness is avoided. Proust liked high society in the purely social sense. Coming from a rich but irredeemably middle-class family, having a Jewish mother, his entry into the beau monde of that day was naturally something that required effort on his own part.

His own contemporaries were sometimes distressed that a young man of such obvious – but apparently unproductive – intelligence was so keen on getting to know dukes. Climbing of this kind may not be particularly attractive, but it is not the only sort of social penetration. People seem to forget that, and lose a sense of proportion. After all, it is not unknown for the ambitious to climb in such hierarchies as, say, the church or the Labour Party.

This point is worth making because Proust is often accused of writing about a 'narrow' world. I have heard this said even by Frenchmen. But his world would not have been less 'narrow' had Proust restricted himself to a novel about chartered accountants or rodent operatives: On the contrary it would have been – although, no doubt still fascinating – decidedly narrower.

Painter writes with the greatest coolness and good sense of this aspect of Proust's behaviour. Indeed, his book shows that, so far from being narrow, Proust's social life was astonishingly comprehensive; especially for someone with such bad health.

He knew, comparatively well, an enormous number of more or less celebrated persons, and he was, in fact, also brought in touch with innumerable 'ordinary' people in the political, professional and business worlds. One is almost tempted to wonder whether certain critics want to take it out of Proust simply because they feel that he attended more amusing parties than they themselves.

We are struck here by how much the highly conventionalized social life of nineteenth-century Paris lends itself to Proust's treatment. An entertaining section of this biography describes the various salons which helped to give Proust models for the households of the Duchesse de Guermantes and Madame Verdurin.

Certainly no one would attempt to deny that it was a tough society. For example, a well-known hostess, Countess Emmanuela Potocka (one of whose lovers was Maupassant) made 'a belated reply to a theological argument of the philosopher Caro; as he was leaving she leaned over the banisters and spat downstairs on his bald head, shouting: "Take that for your Idea of God!"'

At the same time, in this world the intelligence was (as even Countess Potocka's gesture indirectly shows) to some considerable extent respected. It was, as Painter points out, less exclusive than Proust suggests in his book. Proust himself, and other famous figures, would not have gained entry had it not been. The picture is absorbing on its own account. Proustians will take pleasure in the way Proust's special literary approach is investigated: the question whether he 'put people in' his novel.

Painter makes it clear that much earlier identification of the Guermantes, Charlus, St Loup and others had been done in too crude a manner. Proust would not only use traits of more than one individual (together with much rearrangement of circumstances) to make up characters of his novel; he would also redistribute the characteristics of one person 'in real life' among several of the dramatis personae of his book.

In other words, he wrote a novel rather than a thinly veiled fictional account of certain people who actually existed.

Proust's parents always deplored their son's 'weakness of will'. Although marked down at an early age as 'brilliant', he found himself unable to make headway in any profession. So much was this view of himself inculcated that he, too, accepted it. In fact, Proust's will must have been a will of iron. That is clearly shown by the case of his unfinished novel *Jean Santeuil*. This book of some 300,000 words (about the length of four ordinary contemporary novels) he simply put away as unsatisfactory.

Painter truly insists that *Jean Santeuil* itself, although greatly inferior to *A la Recherche*, would have been a very striking book had its author made the comparatively small additions required to round it off. This fact should not be forgotten. Its publication would, of course, have meant that the far greater work would never have appeared. But how many authors would have been prepared to scrap so immense a labour, and just start again?

Painter has done his work so well that it is hard to speak in moderate terms of his skill and unobtrusive wit in unravelling Proust's life and method. True, there is already a great deal of first-class material about the subject to draw on. That is not wholly to a biographer's advantage. The labour of collating this material, and adding to it, as George Painter has done, must have been prodigious. He is much to be congratulated.

Marcel Proust: A Biography: Vol I,   1959
George D. Painter, Chatto.   *Daily Telegraph*

I I I

George Painter's first volume of his biography of Proust took the reader to the year 1903. Now we are carried on to Proust's death on 18 November 1922. The second half is every bit as good as Painter's earlier work, with the same concentration of information and social atmosphere, absorbing yet never oppressive.

Perhaps the chief point that Painter emphasizes in the new book is the ambivalent nature of Proust's relationship with his mother. Everyone who has taken any interest at all in Proust as a writer knows that the novelist's mother greatly obsessed him, and that she is represented in *A la Recherche* as the narrator's grandmother.

Painter points out that this relationship had a cruel, even brutal side. It was by no means a matter of sentimentality and mutual admiration alone. Proust hated his mother, and her mental and moral domination over him, almost as much as he loved her; while she, for her part, was not without a kind of envy and hatred of her son.

To express so complicated a family connection in a few lines is of course to over-simplify its many complications; but Painter does add something to what has been said already on this subject, showing Proust had reason to feel guilty often about his immediate personal behaviour in small matters, as well as the general horrors he suffered from the sense of having let the family down by homosexuality and failure to become a successful diplomatist or lawyer.

Proust's homosexuality was not of a kind to preclude passionate affections for women. Another interesting facet of Painter's study is the manner in which it reveals that Albertine – often regarded as a mere reversal in sex, modelled on some good-looking chauffeur – was in truth largely drawn from now established female sources, girls who did in fact live in the house and visit Proust when he was in bed, though apparently only in one case as his mistress.

Painter's detective work in tracing the actual circumstances which Proust transformed into the magic of his story is remarkable. At the same time he never loses sight of the fact that Proust was writing a novel, not confessions. This is an aspect of Proust's work that even Gide never wholly grasped.

Gide felt that by not representing the Narrator as himself homosexual, Proust had taken the easy way out and missed a great opportunity. The flood of homosexual 'confessional' writings that has since appeared, in an increasingly permissive age, demonstrate that, critically speaking, Gide was quite wrong in supposing this. Indeed the view illuminates Gide's own relative failure as a novelist.

As this volume draws to a close, we are shown the extraordinary manner in which Proust, still under fifty, became a legend in his own lifetime. The extent to which *Swann's Way* was recognized as a work of genius when it first appeared is perhaps not generally appreciated. It should be noted, for example, that Henry James greeted Proust's work as the greatest French novel since Stendhal's *La Chartreuse de Parme*.

On the other hand, the subsequent volumes of *A la Recherche* encountered a good deal of critical opposition. As Painter comments, Proust suffered from the oldest trick of reviewers 'to blame an author for writing about the subject of his book'. Some amusing fan-mail is quoted, including an Italian journalist who wrote: 'I enjoy everything in your books, but my wife has a marked preference for the meeting between M. de Charlus and Jupien, though she also likes the scene between Charlus and the cabman.'

Proust did not at all avoid objections expressed by those who supposed they had been 'put in' his novel, although, as Painter is never tired of emphasizing, the derivations from actual individuals are almost always infinitely combined and adapted. Proust himself observed that authors had to be careful with their friends 'because if my characters turn out to poison people or commit incest later on, they'll think I mean them'.

After Proust visited Comte Greffulhe (one of the models for the Duc de Guermantes), the Count remarked: 'He left as pleased as Punch, but he didn't fool me, I could see what he was after, I'm no child.' In this field of derivations, the rather absurd young man, Octave, who turns up at Balbec as Andrée's fiancé, has something of Cocteau – to end up finally as a Member of the Academy.

The figure who took charge of Proust himself and became quite uncontrollable in his contribution to the novel, was M. de Charlus, modelled largely, if by no means entirely, on Comte Robert de Montesquiou, about fifteen years older than Proust, insanely proud of his ancient name, at the same time a poet and social figure.

Proust hoped that he would get away with certain differences he had included in the representation of Charlus, but the more he tried, the more hopelessly recognizable became the portrait.

Montesquiou is, indeed, one of those richly comic figures, who always have something tragic about them, and, if Charlus embodies one side of him, he also lived recklessly in his own right. Everyone was

afraid Montesquiou would get his own back when he published his
Memoirs, but these appeared posthumously and were self-applauding
and dull.

Mme Greffulhe (one of the models for the Duchesse de Guermantes)
was generally accepted as having pronounced the right verdict on
Montesquiou's Memoirs saying: 'It's not quite what one expects of a
dead man.'

Painter steers us through a sea of invitations, publishing arrangements, disreputable assignations and segregation in a cork-lined room,
with consummate skill. The static nature of most of the narrative must
have made the material very difficult to select, but the reader is never
given a hint of this, though perhaps an occasional sentence is slightly
overweighted with information.

Not long before his death, Proust considered himself insulted by a
reviewer and wanted to challenge him to a duel with sabres. 'But,' said
Paul Morand (who would have been his second), 'he doesn't want to
take his overcoat off.' The encounter never took place, partly because
Proust's opponent would have been going to bed just at the moment
when Proust himself normally got up.

When Proust moved from the Boulevard Haussmann, the cork walls
were sold to a manufacturer of bottle-corks. What a chance to combine
bibliographical association with wine snobbery! 'Smell the cork of this
Chambertin '23, my boy, not much of that noble vintage left now – and
the cork itself once lined Proust's bedroom.'

Marcel Proust: A Biography: Vol.
II, George D. Painter, Chatto.

1965
Daily Telegraph

IV

The larger part of *A la Recherche du Temps Perdu* was translated into
English by C. K. Scott Moncrieff. Scott Moncrieff did not live to
complete the last section, *Le Temps Retrouvé*, and this was translated by a
friend of Proust's, Sydney Schiff (whose pen-name was Stephen
Hudson), and, in America, by Frederick A. Blossom.

Scott Moncrieff's translation is justly famous though at times
idiosyncratic. For example, the title *Remembrance of Things Past* is
something rather different from *A la Recherche du Temps Perdu* and *The
Sweet Cheat Gone* adds a fanciful, not wholly Proustian tone to *Albertine
Disparue*. This in turn was to be re-edited in the French to *La Fugitive*,
which appears to have been Proust's own choice for that section.

The translation by Schiff (alias Hudson) was, one would say, a very
respectable affair – certainly more elegant than Blossom's – but, as

Schiff himself was aware, the French text of 1927 from which he had to work was riddled with errors. These were caused chiefly by the difficulty of deciphering Proust's manuscript – Proust himself having died in 1922 with three-sevenths of his work still unpublished – but editorial interference had also played a part.

Andreas Mayor's new translation, *Time Regained*, is taken from the French text of the Pléiade edition of *A la Recherche*, in which every effort has been made to present what Proust actually wrote and also what his notes show his intention to have been. In consequence, there is scarcely a page of the Mayor translation that is not an emendation of the earlier ones.

Let us look at three parallel passages:

The relations one has with a woman one loves can remain platonic for other reasons than the chastity of the woman or the unsensual nature of the love she inspires. [Hudson]

One's relations with the woman one loves (and this can apply also to love for a young man) may remain platonic for quite another reason than the chastity of the woman or the non-sensual nature of the love she inspires. [Blossom]

A man's relations with a woman whom he loves (and the same may be true of love for a young man) may remain platonic for a reason which is neither the woman's virtue nor a lack of sensuality in the love she inspires. [Mayor]

It will be noted that the homosexual reinforcement of the argument was omitted, perhaps deliberately, from the first translation, but reached the second. The well-known last paragraph of the novel affords a good illustration of variations of style:

If, at least, time enough were allotted to me to accomplish my work, I would not fail to mark it with the seal of Time, the idea of which imposed itself upon me with so much force today, and I would therein describe men, if need be, as monsters occupying a place in Time infinitely more important than the one reserved for them in space, a place, on the contrary, prolonged immeasurably since, simul- taneously touching widely separated years and the distant periods they have lived through – between which so many days have ranged themselves – they stand like giants immersed in Time. [Hudson]

If, at least, there were granted to me time enough to complete my work I would not fail to stamp it with the seal of that Time the understanding of which was this day so forcibly impressing itself upon me, and I would therein describe men – even should that give them the semblance of monstrous creatures – as occupying in Time a place far more considerable than the so restricted one allotted them in space, a place, on the contrary, extending boundlessly since, giant-like, reaching far back into the years, they touch simultaneously epochs of their lives – with countless intervening days between – so widely separated from one another in Time. [Blossom]

But at least, if strength were granted me for long enough to accomplish my work, I should not fail, even if the result were to make them resemble monsters, to describe men first and foremost as occupying a place, a very considerable place compared with the restricted one which is allotted to them in space, a place on the contrary immoderately prolonged – for simultaneously, like giants plunged into the years, they touch epochs that are immensely far apart, separated by the slow accretion of many, many days – in the dimension of Time.' [Mayor]

Apart from the textual emendations, Andreas Mayor is to be congratulated on a translation of lively, readable English particularly good in its rendering of Proust's pastiche of the Goncourt Diary.

Time Regained. Vol. 12 of 1970
Remembrance of Things Past, *Daily Telegraph*
Marcel Proust, newly
translated by Andreas Mayor
from the definitive French text,
Chatto.

V

The careers of writers under arms arouse conjecture. What were they like as soldiers? Tolstoy is to be envisaged without too much difficulty as a Gunner officer; Lermontov, anyway within his own terms of reference, as a Hussar. In contrast, Dostoevsky in the Engineers can never have been a run-of-the-mill Sapper subaltern, even if later, with the 7th Siberian Regiment of the Line, on the Chinese frontier, his saluting is recorded by the Chief Bugler as punctilious. One can picture Rilke (always, it appears, in parade uniform) silently ruling his parallel lines for the account books of the Imperial and Royal War Office. Poe, on the other hand, even in a rank that proliferates unusual characters, defies speculation as Regimental Sergeant-Major to the 1st United States Artillery. For that matter, during his four days' embodiment, did Kierkegaard give physical expression to the dread interrogatory *Either/ Or?* by mounting a charger, himself wearing the bright yellow coatee, enormously plumed black helmet, of the Danish Royal Horse Guards?

At the age of thirteen, Proust's favourite painter had been Meissonier, that somewhat facile master of the lonely cavalry piquet or off-duty troopers playing cards; and, as it happened, he continued throughout life to be keenly interested in military affairs. Indeed, treatment of soldiers and soldiering in Proust's work deserves fuller examination than that accorded in the present brief survey. The army also provides a clear-cut background from which to present examples of how Proust operated when he 'put people in his book'. His own fairly well-documented interlude with the French 76th Regiment of infantry, makes an appropriate introduction to the subject.

The mood is set by the Narrator's comments during the visit to Saint-Loup, then serving as *sous-officier* in the small garrison town of Doncières, where the roof of the Louis XVI cavalry barracks was surmounted by a weathercock. This was no doubt the sort of edifice, conjured up in *Jean Santeuil*, that had attracted the attention of 'a poet accused of espionage because he spent two hours looking at the changing colours on a barrack building at sunset'; suspicious behaviour that caused his judges to shrug their shoulders. A Proustian touch is added to this hypothetical situation by the Judge not only failing to see what can be beautiful in a barracks, but adding that he, too, from time to time writes poetry. The Judge's view, aesthetic or contemplative, was in no sense Proust's.

> The silence, though only relative, which reigned in the little barrack room where I sat waiting was now broken. The door opened and Saint-Loup, dropping his eyeglass, dashed in. 'Ah, my dear Robert, you make yourself very comfortable here,' I said to him; 'How jolly it would be if one were allowed to dine and sleep here.'
>
> And to be sure, had it not been against the regulations, what repose untinged with sadness I could have tasted there, guarded by that atmosphere of tranquillity, vigilance and gaiety which was maintained by a thousand wills controlled and free from care, a thousand heedless spirits, in that great community called a barracks where, time having taken the form of action, the sad bell that tolled the hours outside was replaced by the same joyous clarion of those martial calls, the ringing memory of which was kept perpetually alive in the paved streets of the town, like dust that floats in the sunbeam; – a voice sure of being heard, and musical, because it was in command not only of authority to obedience but of wisdom to happiness.

As it turns out, Saint-Loup has, of course, already approached the Squadron Commander (Captain de Borodino, of whom more will be said later), and obtained permission for the guest to lodge in barracks overnight. This arrangement so much delights Marcel that, long afterwards in the narrative, he compares its legacy of content with the famous occasion – almost the corner-stone of *A la Recherche* – when his mother allowed him as a child to spend the night in her bedroom.

It might very reasonably be urged that there is a big difference between being temporarily housed by a soldier friend – in possession of quarters decorated with Liberty hangings, eighteenth-century German stuffs and photographs of superlatively smart relations – and compulsory existence as an 'other rank', in a draughty barrack room, on a straw palliasse, between intervals of drill or fatigues, in a world where scepticism as to 'authority to obedience' bringing 'wisdom to happiness' might easily result in transference to the *Bat. d'Af.*; desert sands and Saharan forts taking the place of rotating weathercocks and classical pediments. The poet of the barracks might continue to argue that that were merely to exchange Fragonard and Hubert Robert for Delacroix and Fromentin, pastoral days for Arabian nights. Certainly Proust showed himself equally appreciative of his own service in the ranks, where, anyway for a season, he found moral and mental relief in being told what to do for most of the time.

Even though he wrote later of his months in the army as a 'paradise', there must have been bad moments as well as good, physical and temperamental discomforts, notwithstanding an understanding Commanding Officer who excused early morning parades, and jumping ditches during training in equitation. Those who have had any direct contact with the French army are familiar with an excellent tradition – on the whole to be admitted superior to our own – of having a good time when a good time is on offer. None the less British army regulations lay down certain basic standards of comfort pooh-poohed by the French. For example, the French ratio of man-to-room space is – or was – a modified version of the Black Hole of Calcutta; and, eighty years ago, in Proust's day, sanitary conditions in barracks may have been less than ideal. In this last connection, when, with incredible appropriateness, Alfred Jarry was appointed latrine orderly during his military service, he remarked of such duties: 'It is no mere bow to rhetoric to designate with the word "brush" these objects known in civilian life as brooms. They are, in reality, exceptionally suited for sketching decorative designs on the ground . . .', so that cloacal deficiencies may have been amply compensated by the graphic art of the author of *Ubu Roi*. That, however, was a year or two after Proust's own tour of duty.

Jarry was, of course, a conscript; Proust, a volunteer. George Painter – to whom the writer of this essay, like all Proustians, owes a considerable debt – gives a lucid account in his biography of Proust's military circumstances. They were not at all unfavourable. In 1889, the year he joined the army, administrative changes were taking place in the law governing conscription. Hitherto, service had been in theory for five years; in practice, few, if any, of the conscripts being retained so long. To make absolutely sure the period was no more than a year, it was possible to 'volunteer'; such an opening being available only to those of baccalaureate level in education, together with ability to call on a sum of about £60 to pay for uniform.

If Proust had wished to avoid the army entirely, he could no doubt have done so simply on the grounds that he was taking a university education. The additional fact of bad health, put forward through his father, a doctor with imposing Civil Service connections, would certainly have provided adequate grounds for exemption. At the same time, this was the last year of the volunteer system. It was, therefore, a question of moving quickly; doing a year, or arranging to keep out of the army altogether. Proust chose to join.

Volunteers served in the ranks, but were treated more or less like officer-cadets. It might be remarked *en passant* that in Great Britain that would have meant being given a much tougher time. In France things seem to have worked differently. For instance, volunteers, at least unofficially, were allowed to employ a comrade-in-arms to look after their uniform and equipment. If their period of training was satisfactory, they passed out in the rank of *sous-officier* of the Reserve, of which there is no precise British equivalent. This was apparently the status of Saint-Loup (who was preparing for a course at the Cavalry School of Saumur), when Marcel stayed with him in barracks. An annual calling-up for training was subsequently required, with possibility of promotion to lieutenant, captain or even higher rank. Saint-Loup's circumstances are not, in fact, absolutely clear, but we shall return to them.

The 76th were stationed at Orléans. Rather surprisingly, Proust does not mention that the Battle Honour '*Solferino*' decorated their regimental Colour, as to which one would have expected at least a short dissertation on the purplish tint dedicated to that battle, in contrast with Magenta's brilliant crimson. Some of the life Proust lived with his regiment is described in *Jean Santeuil*; an inchoate work of great interest to those concerned with the technique of novel writing, on account of the manner in which the army material, and much else of a directly autobiographical nature, is there presented; then, after more thorough digestion, remodelled in preferable form for *A la Recherche*, or excluded altogether from the narrative.

If Proust looked back with pleasure on his year in the ranks, that was certainly not because he was cut out to be a soldier. No doubt the duties were considerably less arduous than those of a wartime army, not such a grind and more leave; but there must nevertheless have been tedious moments. Later, Proust compared his inability to grasp the abstruse phraseology of a pretentiously 'modern' critic with his own former efforts to perform the exercise known in army gymnastics as the 'bridge-ladder', for which he 'never received any marks'. The 'bridge-ladder' sounds uninviting. Such occasions are not great fun at the time.

At one moment, he was appointed clerk at a Divisonal Headquarters but – 'not without reason', he says – the Chief of Staff could not tolerate the novelist's handwriting; and he lost the job. One likes to think of Part II Orders covered with the elaborate, spidery corrections of a Proustian manuscript; but that would probably be to expect too much of life. For the last few months of his service, as a matter of form, he was posted to the instruction squad for promotion to *sous-officier*; passing, George Painter tells us, sixty-third out of sixty-four or, according to Maurois, seventy-third out of seventy-four. One cannot help speculating about the candidate at the bottom of the list.

As against such stresses, and those that must have taken place on the square and in the field, were champagne parties given by the volunteers in rooms hired in the town – a practice expressly forbidden, but, in fact, watched rather enviously by less affluent officers, who were sometimes invited in to take a glass. In spite of such diversions, one feels there was justification when, a Confession Album having put the question: *What event in military history do you most admire?*, Proust wrote down: *My own enlistment as a volunteer.*

There was enough leave to allow him to make a habit of attending the Paris salons of hostesses like Madame Arman de Caillavet, in whose drawing-room, in blue *capote* too big for him, red epaulettes and red trousers, Proust would be seen somewhat embarrassed, clutching several parcels and his *képi* when he said goodbye. A photograph shows him in this turn-out, a figure from the albums of Caran d'Ache, whose comic genius so well expressed itself in military subjects of the day. Madame Arman (who contributes something to Madame Verdurin) had rather unwillingly added 'Caillavet' to her name, a decision of her rich husband, who owned a vineyard château of that name; and their son, a great friend of Proust's, was known simply by this additional latter half of the family surname. When Proust volunteered for the army, Gaston de Caillavet was already doing his service as a Gunner. Since he is one of the models for Saint-Loup, he may have played a part in persuading Proust to take the plunge.

These labels attached to Gaston and his mother – that he gave something of Saint-Loup, she of Madame Verdurin – raise a big subject, at which a glance may now be taken. Captain de Borodino, mentioned earlier as Saint-Loup's Squadron Commander, is one of the characters in the novel drawn from life. His prototype was Captain Walewski, a Company Commander in the 76th, grandson of Bonaparte by a Polish lady, an affair well known to history. As it happened, the Captain's mother, in addition to his grandmother's imperial connections, had been mistress to Napoleon III. That such a figure, with origins, appearance and behaviour all crying out for chronicling, should turn up in Proust's regiment illustrates one of those peculiar pieces of literary luck which sometimes attend novelists. Borodino represents the most extreme example of 'putting in' – that is to say, no doubt whatever exists as to his identity, owing to the exceptional nature of his background. At the same time, he is only an extra on the Proustian stage. He takes no emotional or dramatic part in *A la Recherche*. In fact, the manner in which he is 'put in' is organically different from that which applies to the always multi-composed characters who dominate the narrative.

If Captain de Borodino represents the furthest extremity of the process in his unequivocal perceptibility and lack of vital role, General de Froberville, also a minor character, is somewhat nearer the centre of the stage. He is less essentially a portrait, and plays some small part in the story. Froberville had, for example, put up Swann for the Jockey, and seconded him in more than one duel. General de Froberville's prototype in real life was General de Galliffet, a well-known personality in the world with which Proust deals. Galliffet, who had led the cavalry charge at Sédan, suppressed the commune with an almost Communist savagery, and (though not a Dreyfusard) insisted on a revisionist approach to the Dreyfus case, was also a wit and a womanizer. Painter mentions several stories about him: the silver plate covering the wound in his abdomen (received in the Mexican campaign) alleged to lend physical subtlety to his many love affairs: the distinguished lady archaeologist, rather masculine in dress, who insisted on joining the men after dinner, at which the General took her by the arm, with the words: 'Come along, my dear fellow, let's go and have a pee.' Froberville is allowed no such knockabout stuff. A novelist less disciplined than Proust might have devoted much more space to him as a comic character. Indeed, so far from Froberville being a caricature of Galliffet, Galliffet is a caricature of Froberville; the real man, far the more exotic creation.

Froberville first appears, an eyeglass jammed in his face like a shell-splinter, at a party of Madame de Saint-Euverte's. It is true that he tells Swann, also present, that he would rather be husband of Madame de Cambremer – whose appearance has taken his fancy – than be massacred by savages (a phrase that recalls a similar one used later by Dr Cottard in similar circumstances); but that is mild enough compared with what Galliffet himself would probably have said. The distinction with which Swann had served in the Franco-Prussian War, where (in the same regiment as Forcheville, his successor as husband of Odette) he had won a Légion d'honneur, had perhaps played a part in General de Froberville's regard for him. Swann had never bothered to wear the decoration in civilian dress until the time of the Dreyfus case, when he took to carrying its red ribbon in his buttonhole.

Froberville's aid had been sought by Monsieur de Charlus to obtain a Légion d'honneur of a rather different kind for his protégé Morel, in recognition of the musical talent of the violinist for whom he had conceived so deep a passion. Again, it is possible to imagine all sorts of witticisms from Galliffet; while, if he gave utterance to any at all, none by Froberville are recorded. A slip has been made on the subject by one of Proust's American translators, not without an aspect that might have appealed to General Galliffet's enjoyment of comic situations.

The efforts of Charlus to procure the Légion d'honneur for Morel were unsuccessful; but, when the war came in 1914, the violinist, after a chequered opening to his military career, behaved courageously in the line, and was awarded the Croix de Guerre. The Narrator comments: '*Il s'y conduisit bravement, échappa à tous les dangers et revint, la guerre finie, avec la croix que M. de Charlus avait jadis vainement sollicitée pour lui, et que lui valut indirectement la mort de Saint-Loup. J'ai souvent pensé depuis, en me rappelant cette croix de guerre égarée chez Jupien . . .*'

There is some obscurity in this passage, if it is not known that certain citations for the Croix de Guerre automatically carry with them a Légion d'honneur. The translator, for some reason supposing that to render '*la croix*' simply by 'the cross' would be insufficiently understood, goes out of the way to substitute the words 'Croix de Guerre', making nonsense of the sentence. Admittedly, the author is a little confusing by dragging in the incident of Saint-Loup losing his own Croix de Guerre in Jupien's homosexual brothel; but a moment's thought might have suggested that – however much awards for bravery were appropriate for those who frequented Madame Verdurin's salon – even Monsieur de Charlus would hardly have had the temerity to press General de Froberville for a Croix de Guerre to be conferred on his favourite merely for playing the violin. Nevertheless, Morel's situation was by no means that of Ludwig II of Bavaria, to whom, as a French newspaper said when he visited Paris in 1874, no patriotic objection could be raised, as during the hostilities of 1870 he had 'accompanied his troops only on the piano'.

Froberville/Galliffet therefore occupies a place similar to that of Borodino/Walewski, though more closely integrated into the novel. Both differ not only in degree, but in kind, from Saint-Loup/Caillavet. The divergence of these types of 'putting in', often misunderstood, cannot be too much emphasized. Since Saint-Loup's origins happen to be particularly complicated, we may turn for a moment from Proust's military characters, the better to pinpoint this matter. Some of its aspects are well exemplified in Philippe Jullian's biography *Robert de Montesquiou*.

From Jullian's book it may be seen that Proust, in his construction of Charlus, uses not only incidents and characteristics taken more or less directly from Montesquiou's life, but also – so at least one strongly suspects – includes large chunks of Montesquiou's actual conversation in Charlus's dialogue. At the same time, the biography makes it perfectly clear that the real Montesquiou, morally and physically, when closely examined, was hardly at all like Charlus. A glance at any of Montesquiou's innumerable portraits – say, the Boldini – at once confirms the latter.

To assert there is no resemblance is, of course, an exaggeration. Both were homosexual (Montesquiou with considerable reservations), cultivated, possessed of insane family pride; but there were many contrasts even in these respects. Montesquiou was quite a different sort of homosexual from Charlus, possessed a frenziedly 'fashionable' taste in the arts that would have appalled the Baron; and the Montesquiou dukedom dated only from the Restoration (in spite of the antiquity of the family), a fact about which Charlus felt particularly snobbish. Contemporaries are apt to be chiefly interested, when reading a novel, in the question 'Who is this meant to be?'; and in this case even the victim himself remarked: 'Shall I have to change my name to Montesproust?' In spite of that, comparisons and contrasts are, in truth, beside the point, almost frivolous, simply because Charlus is so effectively conceived as a character within the novel. The occasional resemblances borrowed from Montesquiou – if you like, the many resemblances to Montesquiou – are totally unimportant. In Charlus a new figure emerges; one that lives entirely on its own. The same is, of course, not true of Borodino, though had he not existed, an officer of illegitimate Napoleonic descent, serving obscurely in a regiment of the Line, would certainly be a happy conception in a novel. Froberville, again, is perfectly imaginable without Galliffet, though the knowledge that Galliffet was frequenting the beau monde at the Guermantes period, for readers who like a stiffening of social history, gives an authenticity to the narrative.

In the making of Saint-Loup, a far more formidable list of contributors has been put forward. There is Gaston de Caillavet mentioned above, Bertrand de Fénelon, Louis d' Albuféra, Jacques d' Uzès, George de Lauris – even Boni de Castellane and Lieutenant le comte de Cholet of the 76th, who presented Proust with a signed photograph 'from one of his torturers'. Again it may be said categorically that, in his fictional essence, Saint-Loup has nothing to do with them. He too, like Charlus, and the other main figures in *A la Recherche*, whatever has gone to the building up, emerges simply as a living figure in a great novel.

At Doncières, Saint-Loup and his friends in the regiment discuss the art of war with the Narrator. The aspect of Staff Duties that immediately catches Marcel's imagination is that concerned with Order of Battle. Saint-Loup explains:

> If it is not the first time an operation has been attempted, and if for the same operation we find a different Corps being brought up, it is perhaps a sign that the previous Corps have been wiped out or have suffered heavy casualties in the said operation; that they are no longer in a fit state to carry it through successfully. Next, we must ask ourselves what was this Corps which was now out of action; if it was composed of shock troops, held in reserve for big attacks, a fresh Corps of inferior quality will have little chance of succeeding where the first has failed. Furthermore, if we are not at the start of the campaign, this fresh Corps may itself be a composite formation of odds and ends withdrawn from other Corps, which throws light on the strength of the forces the belligerent still has at his disposal and the proximity of the moment when his forces shall be definitely inferior to the enemy's, which gives to the operation on which this Corps is about to engage a different meaning, because, if it is no longer in a condition to make good its losses, its successes even will only help mathematically to bring it nearer to its ultimate destruction . . .

Saint-Loup, who could hold his own as a talker, continues for several pages in this strain. His remarks about German theories of attack were, of course, written by the author after the First World War had taken place; but Saint-Loup's comment that the 'break-through in the centre at Rivoli' would crop up again, was 'no more obsolete than the *Iliad*', is not without bearing on tactics in the Second World War. In rather the same way, although he may in one sense have been wrong in disparaging *Field Service, 1895*, for its doctrine that cavalry was only useful for moral effect, in another he was right to foresee the mobile striking force of armoured vehicles that were to take the place of cavalry in attack. There are indications that, even for Marcel, Saint-Loup went on talking about his military theories rather too long, and when he got on to the subject of tactics and strategy, may have been regarded as a bit of a bore in the mess.

Was he at this time planning to make a career of the army? This is hard to decide. After his marriage, whenever homosexuality was discussed, Saint-Loup would remark: 'I have no ideas about such things. I am just a soldier, nothing more. I am as little interested in these matters as I am deeply interested in the Balkan War.' He would then go off into one of those rather pedantic dissertations on the great flank-turning attempt at the Battle of Ulm – to some extent personifying that tactical movement himself by changing the subject from one too near home for his own taste – finding parallels for this operation in the contemporary campaign in the Balkans.

These words seem to indicate that Saint-Loup was a Regular; but perhaps it was merely a whim of his to pose as such. In spite of the professional talk there, the Doncières interlude does not suggest a very serious attitude to the army on Saint-Loup's part. One pictures him as about the same age as the Narrator, possibly a shade older. In any case he would have been in his forties by the time of the Balkan War, and might be expected to have become a major or lieutenant-colonel though it might be argued that promotion tended to be slow in European armies before 1914. When the First World War came, he could even have been given command of a battalion. Perhaps he was. All we are told is that, finding the cavalry unlikely to be employed in action (in spite of his own earlier prophecies that the *arme blanche* was by no means out of date), he exchanged into the infantry, then again to the *Chausseurs à pied*; perhaps the equivalent of a posting to the Reconnaissance Corps in the Second World War.

Someone of Saint-Loup's background might be expected to have gone to Saint-Cyr, like young Létourville (relation of the duchess of that name), who had just graduated from the military academy, when Marcel met him, soon after the war. He seemed just the acquaintance to take the place formerly filled by Saint-Loup, another specialist who would talk amusingly about military matters. Like so many similar reminders of the ravaging of Time brought home at the princesse de Guermantes's party, was a note received from Létourville signed 'your young friend' – emphasizing a difference in their ages that had never, until then, struck Marcel. Perhaps the solution of the question is that Saint-Loup had retired early in a junior rank, but always continued to look upon himself as a professional soldier. That would fit in with his romantic side. Had he served continuously until he married Gilberte, something would probably have been said, at least in retrospect, about homosexual difficulties within his unit.

Saint-Loup's aristocratic and military affiliations did not prevent him, at the Doncières period, from being a Dreyfusard; mention of the case – an important underlying theme of Proust's novel – being avoided in the mess for that reason. Later, when the injustice done to Dreyfus was used without much scruple by the Left, to serve less worthy political purposes, and attack the army in a general way, Saint-Loup and others, who had faced the dire disapproval of friends and relations for their support of Dreyfus, to some extent withdrew into the background. The feeling that vilification of the army, as such, had gone too far, even resulted in General de Froberville's nephew, Colonel de Froberville (married to a distant cousin of the Guermantes), receiving some unexpected invitations to grand parties, merely because, although impecunious and not much 'asked out', he was a professional soldier.

The Dreyfus case, one of the most extraordinary cauldrons of human behaviour ever put on to stew, containing ingredients, moral and material, of almost every known variety to attract the interest of a writer, lacks, so far as I know (though I am at any moment prepared to find this incorrect) an element of homosexuality.* So much of *A la Recherche* turns on that particular axis that it is perhaps unexpected that Proust did not allot an aspect of inversion to haunt one of the byways of the *Affaire*. In *Jean Santeuil* he does, however, devote a good deal of space to Colonel Picquart, another good instance of Proust's approach to army matters, and also his technique for absorbing 'real people' into his writing.

Picquart's story should be briefly recalled. An Alsatian, sixteen years old when Alsace was annexed by Germany, he was regarded as an ambitious and very promising officer. Although no mention of him is made in *A la Recherche* in connection with Froberville, he had served on Galliffet's staff, been present at Dreyfus's court-martial, and, in due course, put in charge of the Secret Service Section – an outstandingly ramshackle one – at the French War Office. On taking over, Picquart re-examined the Dreyfus file held by his Section, coming to the conclusion that something had gone badly wrong in the Court's acceptance of evidence. He drew this fact to the attention of his superiors, with the consequence that he was himself posted to North Africa (stationed where there was a good chance of death in action), then, when he persisted in making further representations about Dreyfus, put under arrest, imprisoned, and placed in the running for condemnation to five years in a fortress.

All this is striking enough; but when it is added that Picquart, if not a rabid anti-Semite, was decidedly unfriendly towards Jews, he will at once be seen to be building up the sort of character upon which a writer likes to get to work. When Dreyfus was cleared, Picquart refused to meet him; and, when, in due course, Picquart rose in rank and was in a position to be of some assistance in Dreyfus's professional rehabilitation in the army, he would take no step to make things easier. Clemenceau, in a slapstick mood, appointed him his Minister of War, a post Picquart filled without great distinction, behaving rather badly to officers who had merely been carrying out orders issued by former anti-Dreyfusard superiors. Picquart remained unmarried all his life; dying, in consequence of being thrown from his horse, when in

---

* In fact, I believe the German Military Attaché in Paris was having a homosexual affair with the Italian Military Attaché.

command of an Army Corps, about six months before the outbreak of war in 1914.

Even this very truncated summary conveys some idea of the complexity of Picquart's character, and of the attraction it could exercise for a novelist. Conrad, for example, would surely have been in his element in dealing with its contradictions and Picquart's ups and downs of fortune. At the same time, the Dreyfus case, unique in itself, was something too extraordinary, too earth-shaking, to allow any real fictional parallel to be contrived. Proust was certainly aware of that. If Picquart was to be handled at all, he must be handled as himself. He does not appear in person in *A la Recherche*, although we are told that Madam Verdurin's guests flocked to see Stravinsky and the dancers of the Russian Ballet, just as they had once come to goggle at Picquart, when invited to her parties as a lion. In *Jean Santeuil*, on the other hand – an instance of material omitted in the more mature work – Proust gives an account, even if a trifle romanticized, probably as good a one as exists, of Picquart's appearance in court. It includes some of Proust's own musings on the state of being a soldier.

Jean had now made his way into the Courtroom and was listening to Colonel Picquart.

The Colonel was a friend of Monsieur Beulier, Jean's professor, and like him a man whose life, in spite of his sky-blue uniform, had been spent in seeking the light of reason, while he turned his horse at a corner, or was on his way to the barrack square for an inspection, the truth of everything which might, with some urgency, involve a degree of self-examination.

One cannot help noticing the Jamesian tone here – perhaps on account of the phrase 'with some urgency' – on the whole rare in Proust, in spite of his own involutions of expression.

As though he had only just dismounted, and still retained even on his feet the quick, light movement of a Spahi, walking quickly straight ahead, with that free and easy carriage which a man might show who had just dropped his reins and unbuckled his sword, and with a look of mild bewilderment on his face advanced to the President's seat, where he came to a stop and saluted, not in military fashion, but with a mingled air of timidity and frankness, as though his every gesture was free of all formality or merely external significance but was overflowing like his walk, the sideways carriage of his head and, as would soon be apparent, his well-bred voice, with the elegance and warmth of his personality.

Picquart under arrest at the time, appears sometimes to have attended the court *en civil*, because Jean noted, during the interval, when people were eating their sandwiches, that his rather superb top-hat was worn at an angle.

Colonel Picquart was a philosopher, whose thoughts, while he moved ahead of his men, were ceaselessly employed in trying to get a clear view of the problems with which they were engaged . . . And so in an assembly where Jean, himself a philosopher, found himself surrounded by some two hundred persons with nothing of the philosopher about them, he could not help smiling sympathetically when he recognized the true philosophic note in Colonel Picquart's voice, and heard him answer, 'Do you mind if I don't say anything more about that now? I will come back to it later' . . . We think of a colonel as of somebody cold-blooded and solemn, only to find a brother of whom to make fun at a distance, have as it were a game with, joking about his failings, about the way he wrinkles up his nose when he talks, but always with an undercurrent of true sympathy, so that should anyone want to do him a hurt, we should be prepared to give our life for him.

As not seldom in Proust, the picture trembles on the verge of absurdity; yet the balance is somehow preserved, and the effect is oddly telling. That the writer was prepared to sacrifice himself in a war is not to be doubted.

Proust's own earliest experiences of warfare had been during the siege of Paris, before his mother gave birth to him. Pre-natally, he must have been familiar with the thud of artillery fire. When invasion took place again, he was in his middle forties; and naturally the subject of the army comes once more to the fore. It is the army in Proust's life and work that is being examined here, rather than the general circumstances of war; but, of course, in the novel these circumstances had important consequences in showing the contradictions and paradoxes of human nature. Professor Brichot, for example, one of Madame Verdurin's 'faithful', an aggressive French patriot before the war, finds himself disapproving of 'militarism' after war breaks out, because 'militarism' has to be German. He praises a Swiss novel, because it ridicules a picture of two children admiring a dragoon. This irritates Monsieur de Charlus, who not only considers a dragoon a beautiful object, but welcomes the variety of exotic military personnel to be found in wartime Paris, especially representatives of Highland regiments wearing the kilt, and Sengalese with high red tarboosh.

The Allied armies fallen back, a German headquarters staff, followed by a 'regiment' – that is to say a German brigade – was quartered at Tansonville. Gilberte was full of praise in a letter for the 'correctness' of their behaviour. Saint-Loup himself wrote the kind of letter that would certainly have been drastically treated by the censor in the Second

World War. Still pondering his own tactical theories, he pointed out
that the old idea of a 'break-through' had been modified by the
necessity for devastating by shell-fire the ground held by the enemy;
how, having achieved that, it was impossible for infantry and artillery
to advance over such terrain honeycombed with shell craters. 'War,' he
wrote, 'does not escape the laws of our old friend Hegel. It is a state of
perpetual becoming.'

Marcel was disappointed at this too meagre discussion of military
problems. He would have liked to go into the situation far more
thoroughly, being particularly annoyed by the fact that names of
generals were not allowed to be mentioned in letters. Geslin de
Bourgogne, Galliffet, Négrier were dead – and, it must be admitted,
even if alive, would be getting a shade old for active service – and
Saint-Loup had never discussed with him their replacements, new
commanders like Joffre, Castelnau or Pétain. Incidentally, Saint-Loup
held in peculiar horror the use of the term '*poilu*', near equivalent in
French for 'tommy', dear to the popular Press of the period.

Speaking of the intellectually stimulating effect the war seemed to
have had on Saint-Loup, the Narrator makes one of those comments
that, from time to time, show how much Proust was child of his age,
unable – or unwilling – to advance far into the world of the Modern
Movement. This is already clear from his approach to pictures in *A la
Recherche*; but the firmness with which he sets his face against changes
that were taking place elsewhere is well illustrated by the comment that
'soldier poets' describe the war just as they would have done ten years
before, '*vol frémissant de la victoire*', and so on. No doubt there were
'soldier poets' of this sort; but, if worth mentioning, they should surely
be contrasted with the very different school, in this category, that
almost immediately developed. The label is certainly untrue of, say,
Apollinaire, and utterly inappropriate as to what was soon to be written
by the 'soldier poets' of our own country. The examples are, in short,
not at all representative of the way war poetry was shaping. This is an
interesting facet of Proust's approach. If such objections had been
raised, possibly he would have taken a stand on his own point of view –
finding its conservatism in itself absorbing – just as Marcel was unable
to believe that he had grown old, yet only too aware of age and decay in
others.

These musings on 'intellectual' soldiers recall to the Narrator an
incident involving Colonel du Paty de Clam. This officer, who had
played an unattractive part in the Dreyfus case, resigned from the
army, and, in 1914, was offered a lines-of-communication appointment. He refused, and enlisted in the *Chasseurs à pied*, Saint-Loup's
chosen corps. Subsequently, given the command of an infantry
battalion, he died of wounds received in action at the age of sixty-three.

Proust's reference to the quintessential military anti-Dreyfusard recalls the occasion at Zola's trial when du Paty de Clam, one of the witnesses, passed the violently Dreyfusard Symbolist poet, Pierre Quillard (whom du Paty did not know), and immediately recited some lines to him from Quillard's own play *La Fille aux Mains Coupées*.

In the old days, the sound of cavalry stationed at Combray going out for a military exercise had been a matter for great local excitement, the gardener's daughter overturning an orange tree in its tub, cutting a finger and breaking a tooth, in her anxiety that no one should miss any of the show. Françoise used to dissolve in tears at the sight – 'Poor boys, to be mown down like grass in a meadow' – while the gardener, to 'draw' her, would remark: 'A fine sight, isn't it, Mme Françoise, all these young fellows not caring two straws for their lives.' The helmets glittered, their horses scraped against the walls of the houses, the whole town was thrilled.

Now it was no exercise. Troops going into action moved through Combray all the time. The battle for Méséglise lasted more than eight months. The big field of corn there became Hill 307. The French blew up the bridge over the Vivonne, for eighteen months holding one half of Combray, while the Germans held the other.

When the Narrator met Gilberte at the princesse de Guermantes's party, where everyone had suddenly grown so old, they talked of Saint-Loup, and the subject of his obsession with strategy and tactics again cropped up. His final words spoken to Marcel, when they said goodbye for that last time, had been that he expected to see Hindenburg, '*général napoléonien*', fight a Napoleonic sort of battle, try and drive a wedge between the French and British armies. Saint-Loup had compared battles with plays, in which it is not always easy to know what the author has intended, probably because he himself changed his mind in mid-campaign. Marcel reflects – with great truth – that, as every critic can refashion a play or a campaign in his own way, there were some who saw the Hindenburg offensive as the prelude to a lightning attack on Paris; others who thought it meant a series of unco-ordinated hammer-blows against the British Expeditionary Force.

Gilberte appears to have been just as keen on these matters as her late husband, recollecting the time when he said that aircraft would make every army 'a hundred-eyed Argus'. This classical allusion leads to Xenophon, and to the campaigns in Mesopotamia, where the British Command had used the long narrow boat – the gondola of the country – that dated back to the time of the Chaldeans at the very dawn of history. It is not surprising that here, within about a hundred pages of the end of the novel, the question of place-names, playing such a part in the earlier sequences, arises finally in a military connection. The case in point is Kut-el-Amara (a British disaster, where, of 14,000 prisoners-of-war, 3,000 survived), the name meaning 'Kut-of-the-Emir'. This was to be compared with villages the curé of Combray used to speak of, such as Vaux-le-Vicomte or Bailleau-l'Evêque. General Townshend and General Gorringe find themselves named here in *A la Recherche* beside the Caliphs and Sinbad the Sailor.

Proust's own health was naturally far too precarious for there to be any question of serving again in the army. That did not prevent the routine requirements of medical boards, which he accepted – we recall the great to-do D. H. Lawrence made in similar circumstances – as inevitable consequence of a world war. All the same, there was one aspect of them that was exceedingly troublesome to Proust – the time the boards took place. He dreaded these orders to present himself, merely because they threatened the hour or two's sleep he could achieve only during the daytime. By one of those clerical errors endemic to military administration, certainly a classical example, he was ordered on one occasion to report to the Invalides for medical examination at 3.30 a.m., instead of the same hour in the afternoon. To many people such an instruction would have been disturbing. Proust was charmed. This nocturnal summons seemed just another example of how accommodating the military authorities could sometimes show themselves.

1971
*Marcel Proust 1871–1922: A Centenary
Volume*, Peter Quennell, ed.,
Weidenfeld & Nicolson.

VI

'I should prefer glycerine – yes, hot, excellent.' Marcel, dining with Saint-Loup in a Paris restaurant rather later than usual one foggy night, was horrified to hear these words spoken by a guest sitting behind him, instead of what was apparently the most normal order: 'Bring me a wing of chicken and a glass of champagne – not too dry.'

The statement turned out less daunting than at first appeared, being merely uttered by a doctor using the first-person singular in reply to an acquaintance, who, seeing his physician at one of the tables, had hoped to get some free medical advice. All the same, as the shadow of the sick-room hangs over so much of *A la Recherche du Temps Perdu*, one would not be altogether surprised if Marcel himself had indeed, even if apologetically, made glycerine his appetizer that evening. Tisanes and orangeade were more in his line than aperitifs and *vin ordinaire*. The gourmet, especially the amateur of wine, who hopes to be provided by Proust with the same subtleties on the subject of eating and drinking which he finds about, say, love, friendship, social life, writing, painting, music, will be disappointed. Nevertheless, investigation of their treatment is of interest, even when negative. We may regret that the local wines of France do not receive the attention devoted to place-names and their origin, churches and their architecture, but what is recorded about food and drink is well worth considering. I shall do no more here than indicate the lines along which an ambitious student might gain a PhD.

The classic mention of wine in the novel is, of course, Swann's gift of Asti Spumante to Marcel's aunts Céline and Flora; his grandfather's uneasiness that these ladies offered no apparent thanks for the present; the aunts' own self-satisfaction in having expressed their gratitude obliquely by reference to 'some people having nice neighbours'. Cyril Ray, in *Through a Glass Lightly*, records his surprise – which many must have shared – that a connoisseur like Swann should have presented an Italian wine, and especially Asti, even to a couple of elderly provincial maiden ladies. Ray goes on to say – quoting among other authorities the *Pink 'Un's* Dwarf of Blood and his collaborator Algernon Bastard in *The Gourmet's Guide to Europe* – that France was then, and still remains, Italy's best customer for sparkling wine. Swann was to be relied upon to produce just what was required, and it would certainly be true to say that Asti has something of its own in bouquet compared with even the sweetest French champagne.

A warning note is struck early in Proust's book by the fact that Marcel's grandfather is not allowed to drink liqueurs. On account of this, his great-aunt – to tease her sister-in-law – used to persuade him to take a few drops of brandy after dinner. This habitually upset Marcel's grandmother. However, the emphasis is on the pain caused to her, rather than on the quality of the brandy, about which we are told no more than that only very little was consumed, and it did not do the slightest harm.

Where food was concerned in Marcel's home at Combray, the presiding genius was their cook Françoise, one of the great figures of *A la Recherche*. She had come there from Aunt Léonie's, where she played an important *rôle* in discussing the neighbours, with special reference to such matters as who had been able to buy the largest branches of asparagus. Françoise, like most good cooks, was inclined to become bored with the uneventful routine of family cooking, and *bœuf à la casserole* seems to have been a fairly frequent item on the daily menu. Such humdrum dishes were varied, not only by the march of the seasons, but also by the moods of Françoise herself, who would serve up brill, 'because the fish-woman had guaranteed its freshness'; a turkey, 'because she had seen a beauty in a neighbouring village'; cardoons (a vegetable like the artichoke) with marrow, 'because she had never done them before'; roast leg of mutton, 'because the cold air makes one hungry'; spinach, 'by way of a change'; apricots, 'because they were hard to get'; gooseberries, 'because in another fortnight they would be over'; raspberries, 'which Monsieur Swann had bought specially'; cherries, 'the first to come from the cherry tree which had not yielded for two years'; cream cheese, 'because Marcel was extremely fond of it'; almond cake, 'because she had ordered one the evening before'; *crème chocolat*, 'because it was one of her specialities'.

As a boy at Combray, Marcel was usually sufficiently interested about dinner to go down to the kitchen beforehand to find out what was 'on'. Exciting arrangements of vegetables were always to be found set out there. The kitchen was also, of course, the scene of that 'solemn passover', the servants' midday dinner, though this is only referred to after the family had come to live in Paris in the house where they shared a courtyard with the Guermantes. Not even Marcel's father would have dared to ring during the celebration of that sacred congress, and, had he so far forgotten himself as to have done so by mistake, no one would have taken the slightest notice. The rite ended with Françoise undoing the napkin from round her throat, after which she wiped away the last traces of watered wine and coffee. So far as wine went, Françoise would always accept a glass offered between meals from time to time, by Jupien – not yet revealed to Marcel in his intimate role *vis-à-vis* Monsieur de Charlus and others – social occasions that also required a longish talk. At those awkward moments when Marcel inadvertently entered the kitchen to find Françoise entertaining her daughter to a complicated spread, this was always designated by her as 'just having a scrap'.

However, the most famous set-piece for a meal at Marcel's home is undoubtedly the dinner to which the former Ambassador, Monsieur de Norpois, was invited: partly to advise Marcel on the choice of a career. The *pièce de résistance* was *bœuf en daube*, that is to say cold beef spiced with carrots, 'lodged by the Michael Angelo of our kitchen upon enormous crystals of jelly, like transparent blocks of quartz'. M. de Norpois was delighted with the manner in which the beef was cooked:

'You've a chef in the top class, Madame,' he said. 'That is not an easy thing to achieve. I myself, when I was living abroad, had to maintain a certain style in entertaining, and I know how difficult it is to find a perfect master in the kitchen. This is a veritable banquet you've set before us.'

M. de Norpois uses the characteristically carefully selected term *agapes*, meaning a love-feast held by the early Christians:

'This is the sort of thing you can't get in a tavern, even the best of them,' he went on . '*A daube de bœuf* in which the jelly doesn't taste of glue and the beef has caught the flavour of the carrots. It's admirable. Invite me please again.'

At this point he made a sign to show that he wanted more jelly. 'I should be interested to see how your Vatel would manage a dish of a different sort,' he said. 'I should like, for instance, to see him tackle *bœuf stroganoff*.'

Bœuf stroganoff (mushrooms, sour cream, olives, onions, lemon) gives us further insight into M. de Norpois's tastes, though he was not always prepared to reveal these. For example, Marcel's mother was hoping for praise for the pineapple-and-truffle salad, but the Ambassador, 'after fastening on it for a moment the penetrating glance of a trained observer', ate it 'with the inscrutable discretion of a diplomat', without disclosing his opinion. However, a moment later he could not prevent himself from exclaiming: 'What do I see? Nesselrode pudding! After a Lucullan feast of this sort I shall have to take a cure at Carlsbad.'

Afterwards, when congratulating Françoise on the dinner (they never seem to have admitted to M. de Norpois that their cook was a woman), Marcel's mother said: 'The Ambassador assured me that he knows no place where he can get cold beef and soufflés such as yours'; so presumably a soufflé was also one of the courses of the dinner. It is, however, notable – and very regrettable – that we are told nothing of the wine given to M. de Norpois, who might be expected to rise to great heights of praise or sink to depths of blame, when speaking of vintages he had enjoyed or execrated.

The question why Françoise made better jelly than that supplied at the great restaurants opens up an interesting list of names. Her own explanation of the restaurants' relative failure in this direction was that they 'do it in too much of a hurry', though she was prepared to admit that she could mention 'one of those cafés where they knew a bit about cooking'. The ideal to be aimed at she described as beef that was 'like a sponge' and mopped up the juice. Marcel's father, who had joined the discussion, asked if the restaurant to which Françoise allowed this claim was Henry's in the Place Gaillon, where he regularly attended *repas de corps* – club dinners:

'Oh, no,' said Françoise, evidently feeling some contempt. 'I meant a little restaurant. Henry's is more like a soup-kitchen.'

'Weber's, then?'

'Oh, no, sir, I meant a good restaurant. Weber's, that's in the Rue Royale, that's not a restaurant, it's a *brasserie*. I don't even know if they serve you there. I don't think they have any table-cloths, they just throw it in front of you anyhow.'

'Ciro's?'

'Oh, there I should think the cooking's done by *dames du monde*' – meaning ladies of the *demi-monde* – 'they need that to get the young men in! No, I mean a restaurant where they have a good little *cuisine bourgeoise*. That's what brings the money in. Madame knows it, right along the *grandes boulevardes*, a little way back.'

This restaurant finally turned out to be the Café Anglais.

At about the same period as this, Marcel was receiving invitations to Swann's house, but we are told little about the food there. Odette's anglomania caused her to provide Christmas pudding at the appropriate season, and certainly on one occasion there was lobster *à l'Americaine*. One might have expected here a dissertation on the question whether this manner of cooking had not once been *à l'Armoricaine* – in the Breton way – but Proust does not tackle the issue. Incidentally, in Madame Prunier's Cookery Book, the 'Armorican' version is different from the 'American', though only very slightly, the sauce of the former being bound with egg yolks and cream before being poured over the lobster.

This brings us to the Grand Hotel at Balbec. Madame de Villeparisis, a great epicure, thought the food there indifferent, although she recommended the oysters, the very thought of which made Marcel feel sick. Among the guests staying at the Grand, with his mistress, was a Frenchman who had proclaimed himself 'king' of one of the Cannibal Islands. His goings-on in general caused a good deal of offence to the more staid residents of the hotel, and, among other things, he always drank champagne at luncheon. On a later visit to the same hotel, Marcel found himself having to cope with the manager, who was famous for his malapropisms. Doing his best to offer everything at his disposal, the manager suggested that he should bring up some of the 'old wine' he had downstairs in a *bourrique* (she-ass), meaning a *barrique* (hogshead). He goes on to explain to Marcel that this wine is 'not Château-Lafite', but is almost as 'equivocal' (meaning 'the equivalent'), and, as it is light, would go well with a fried sole. Although the whole sequence is Proust in one of his knockabout moods, one knows pretty well what the wine would have tasted like.

It was also at the Grand Hotel that Monsieur Nissim Bernard, great-uncle of Marcel's friend Bloch, was 'keeping' one of the waiters. M. Nissim Bernard liked to lunch in the dining-room every day and watch the young man rush about with trays, a situation Proust compares to sitting in the front row of the stalls for those having an affair with a ballet-girl. This favourite waiter was only a *commis*, but owing to M. Bernard's influence with the management, was singled out for promotion. At one moment he was offered the job of *sommelier*, but M. Bernard made him refuse that post because its duties meant that too little would be seen of him. Instead of charging about in and out of the kitchen, he would merely have approached each table discreetly with the wine-list. It is good to know that this reckless manner of appointing a wine-waiter was renounced from the start, if even for less than the best of reasons.

When Marcel lunched with Bloch's father, a 'light sparkling wine' was brought in a decanter, which purported to be champagne, but was decidedly not. In fact there seems to have been a strong tendency for champagne, or at least sparkling wine, to have been drunk in the middle of the day, and it is surprising that the King of the Cannibal Islands should have made any impression, good or bad, by doing so. For example, on a day's leave from the garrison at Doncières, when he takes his mistress, Rachel, to Paris for luncheon, Saint-Loup drinks champagne. Indeed, he drinks too much of it, because Rachel irritates him by ogling the other men in the restaurant. Incidentally, at Doncières, the officers' mess was at the Cocq-Hardi; the sergeants' (where they drank Sauterne), at the Faisan Doré.

Marcel and Saint-Loup also drank champagne when they dined together at Rivebelle, near Balbec. Marcel, forgetting for once his grandmother and her anxieties about his health, apparently drank a lot of beer, as well as the champagne; also some port. The passage describing these potations is obscure, so that one is not absolutely certain that he did not actually add a few drops of port to the beer itself, since he says later that he could hardly taste the port. One hopes – indeed, it is much the most likely – that the figure of speech means merely that the port was taken as a digestive – rather than more normally in France as an aperitif – and that by that time it made little impression. In any case Marcel got rather tight. Here, again, the champagne appears to have been unsatisfactory, for several of the diners sent it away as 'not fit to drink', which for some reason gave positive pleasure to the young waiters.

When Albertine became part of Marcel's life, they used to tour the neighbourhood by car, looking at churches. To refresh themselves while doing this they would stop at farms and buy a bottle of 'calvados or cider'. The cider was always described as non-effervescent, but when opened would usually drench both of them from head to foot. Calvados, one feels, might be a little strong for such outings, and it is no surprise to learn that such powerful liquid restoratives ultimately suggested love-making. For shorter trips on foot from the hotel, they would take a bottle of champagne into the forest, or, on a fine evening, enjoy an alfresco no further away than among the dunes. Albertine was never easy to deal with, and, in spite of Marcel's dislike for oysters, always wanted to eat bivalves when she heard them cried for sale in the street. Marcel felt inclined to say that they would be better at Prunier's, but before he could give any such advice, she was tempted by other street-criers: shrimps, skate, whiting, mussels, mackerel. The vendor of the last of these announced his wares with the cry: '*Il arrive le maquereau!*', which always sent a chill down Marcel's spine – not merely because he disliked that particular fish.

Before we depart from the Grand Hotel, another friend of Marcel's must be called to mind in relation to Proust and wine. This is Monsieur Pierre de Verjus, Comte de Crécy, who turns out in due course to be none other than the former husband of Odette. Comte de Crécy was of very ancient family, related to the English bearers of that title (possibly the Cressys of Lincolnshire), though the connection is puzzling, as the Count's patronymic is later said to be 'Saylor'. He himself was extremely hard-up, living in fact on a pension paid by Swann. Comte de Crécy was also unusually good company, and, although modest about his own family, a notable authority on local pedigrees, also the gastronomic arts. Accordingly, Marcel used often to invite him as a guest.

The Verjus coat-of-arms, in punning reference to the name (it is not clear where 'Saylor' came in) was *a branch of verjuice slipped and leaved sinople* (one translator renders this in English as *vert*, also meaning green, but Proust writes *sinople*, the rarer and more exotic heraldic term); though Marcel, no doubt rightly, judged that M. de Crécy would not have liked to be given verjuice (extract of sour grapes used for cooking) when asked out to luncheon or dinner. Indeed, so far was that from the case that the Count preferred only the most expensive wines in the list, about which he knew a great deal and for which he possessed a notable capacity. Here a real chance is missed of hearing what M. de Crécy ordered, preferably with the price. The suspicion that Proust himself was not deeply interested in wine is to some extent confirmed by the fact that he thinks it worth mentioning that M. de Crécy made the wine-waiter *chambrer* or *frapper* the wines, if so required, and always specified the date when he ordered port or brandy.

The Verdurins' table will be estimated later, but for the moment they are named only in connection with that party of theirs which Monsieur Charlus attended as a consequence of his passion for the violinist Morel. M. de Charlus is a dominating figure from whom one might reasonably hope for a strong lead in the matter of wine, as on almost every other subject, but the incident in which he is first mentioned as selecting a drink is not encouraging:

'Have you tasted my orangeade?' Madame Verdurin asked him.

'No, I prefer its neighbour, the strawberry juice,' replied the Baron.

He said this in a voice so high that it once suggested his feminine side, even if the choice of beverage, in some eyes, might not have gone far

towards prejudicing a reputation for masculine tastes. However, M. de
Charlus somewhat redeems himself from the implication of liking sickly
drinks on a subsequent occasion, when he is giving Morel dinner at a
little restaurant at Saint-Mars-le-Vétu on the Normandy coast; no
doubt a contrast in price with the *Guillaume le Conquérant* at Dives,
which Marcel thought very expensive; an opinion that half a century
later I myself saw no reason to disallow. At the restaurant chosen
by M. de Charlus the waiter brought them two glasses of frothy
liquid:

'But I ordered champagne?' said M. de Charlus.
   On this occasion, too, he spoke in an unusually shrill voice.
   'But, sir . . .'
   'Take it away, this horror which has no connection with the worst
known champagne. It is the emetic called *cup*, which is usually made
of three strawberries rotting in a mixture of vinegar and seltzer
water.'

M. de Charlus uses the English word 'cup', and he evidently felt
strongly about it; as well he might. Later on in the meal he upset the
staff of the restaurant again by saying fiercely:

'Ask the head waiter if he has a Bon Chrétien.'
   'A good christian, I don't understand.'
   'Can't you see we've reached the dessert? It's a pear.'

Morel was as much at sea as the waiter, and the Baron, after quoting
the example of various members of the aristocracy who grew prize
pears, together with references from Molière on the subject of the same
fruit, tried to find out what was available in that line:

'Waiter, have you any Doyennée des Comices?'
   'No, sir, there aren't any.'
   'Have you Triomphe de Jodoigne?'
   'No, sir.'
   'Any Virginie-Dallet? Or Passe Colmar? No? Very well, since
you've nothing, we may as well go. The Duchesse d'Angoulême is
not in season yet; come along, Charlie.'

M. de Charlus's preoccupation with Morel eventually involved him
in the question of fighting a duel, which, although something of a sham
from the start, required a second. The Verdurins' friend, Dr Cottard,
who had a great medical reputation, and had treated Marcel as a boy
for his asthma, occupied this *rôle*. Cottard was, indeed, immensely
excited about the duel. When it fizzled out, he and Charlus were left
confronting each other with nothing to do but go home. The Baron took
Cottard's hand – which filled the Doctor with fear that a sexual assault

was about to be made on him – but all M. de Charlus suggested was that they should 'take something' together. 'What used to be called a *mazagran* or a *gloria*, drinks one doesn't find any more, like archaeological curiosities . . . a *gloria* would be distinctly suitable to the place and the occasion.'

A *mazagran* (named after the once famous Café Mazagran) is simply coffee in a glass, but a *gloria* is coffee laced with brandy. Here, we may again invoke Cyril Ray, who (in his section referring to 'Irish Coffee', mingled, of course, with whiskey) quotes Eliza Acton's *Modern Cookery* as to how to produce 'Burnt Coffee or Coffee *à la militaire* (*in France vulgarly called gloria*)'. Miss Acton (1799–1859), daughter of a brewer, which may have directed her mind towards food and drink, first published her *Modern Cookery* in 1845. She is probably better remembered for that work, or her treatise on bread, than for her fugitive poems. She never married, but whilst in Paris became for a time engaged to an officer of the French army, who perhaps taught her the term for – and the method of making – the drink that so much took M. de Charlus's fancy. However, Cottard disappointingly replied that he was President of the Anti-Alcoholic League, and that he could not risk some ass of a country doctor coming past and blaming him for not practising what he preached. In fairness to Cottard, it should be remembered that he had ordered 'no alcohol' for Marcel's asthma, when other practitioners had recommended beer, champagne and brandy to produce 'euphoria'.

We must now return to the Verdurins, whose food and drink, as such, might almost be said to play the predominant part in the book. Madame Cottard, early on, had asked if one of their salads was a 'Japanese salad', but that was a joke with obvious reference to a current play by the younger Dumas. We know that they sometimes had bouillabaisse, because Monsieur Verdurin once said that 'the bouillabaisse must not be kept waiting'. Perhaps they rather went in for fish, since one of Monsieur de Cambremer's stock remarks, when an appropriately large one appeared on the Verdurin table, was to say: 'That fish is a fine animal.' He considered this comment sufficiently amusing and charming to absolve him from ever inviting the Verdurins themselves to eat in his own house.

At one of the Verdurin dinners, the Polish sculptor Viradobetski (who was always called 'Ski' because his name was regarded as too difficult to pronounce) asked: 'What is this pretty coloured thing we are eating?' Madame Verdurin replied that it was strawberry mousse.

'It's rav-ish-ing,' said Ski. 'You ought to open bottles of Château Margaux, Château Lafite, port.'

The thought of this prodigal outlay greatly alarmed Mme Verdurin, who at once pointed out that this reference to wine was a very good joke on Ski's part as he himself never touched alcohol. However, Ski was not to be laughed off as easily as that.

'But not to drink,' he said. 'You shall fill all our glasses. They will bring in marvellous peaches, huge nectarines, set out there against the sunset. It will be as luxuriant as a beautiful Veronese.'

'It would cost almost as much,' murmured M. Verdurin.

'But take away those cheeses with their dreadful colour,' said Ski.

He tried to remove his host's plate, who defended his Gruyère with all his might. We must infer from this incident that the Verdurins' wine was nothing very remarkable, perhaps also in short supply. At the same time, in fairness to the Verdurins, the great Goncourt pastiche in which they appear, towards the end of *A la Recherche*, shows them in a rather different light. The reader must make up his own mind as to whether Marcel or the Diarist is to be believed.

Goncourt is fancied as recording that M. Verdurin dropped in to escort him to dinner, mentioning at the same time (something one forgets) that Verdurin was a former critic of *La Revue*, who had written a book on Whistler, and – how very up-to-date – was, or had been, a morphine addict. The 'Venetian' wineglass in front of the Diarist at the dinner table, *'une riche bijouterie de rouge est mise par une extraordinaire Léoville acheté à la vente de M. Montalivet'*. Montalivet (1800–80) was a Minister of Louis-Philippe, who promoted musuems and published a book of memoirs. One does not know the precise implications of a Léoville bought at his sale. The immediate thought is that the bottle might have been a bit on the old side, but the question deserves closer study, with more information. It should be borne in mind that the double-edged epithet 'extraordinary' is employed.

The food is described as an 'exquisite repast' and a detailed account is given of the crockery off which it was eaten. The menu appears to have included *foie gras* and turbot – the sauce a 'white sauce', not made like 'flour paste', but with butter 'costing five francs a pound'. When Goncourt remarked that her husband must be very proud of his beautiful china, Mme Verdurin replied in a melancholy tone:

'It's easy to see you don't know him,' she said.

She described him as an absolute maniac, indifferent to these refinements.

'A maniac,' she repeated. 'Absolutely that, who would rather drink a bottle of cider in the rather degraded (*encanaillée*) coolness of a Normandy farm.'

Mention of cider is a reminder that the Duchesse de Guermantes was in the habit of inflicting on her luncheon guests a horrible (*affreux*) cider inported from Guermantes.

The last two examples I chose of having a drink in *A la Recherche* are
'*encanaillés*' too, both scenes in houses of ill fame. The first was in the
smart brothel a little way up the coast from Balbec, which so impressed
strangers by its size and air of convenience that they supposed it would
be a good hotel in which to stay. M. de Charlus went there with Jupien
to spy on Morel. While he was waiting, a 'clever little lady' was sent to
amuse him, and, to prevent her taking off her clothes, Charlus had to
buy her champagne at forty francs a bottle. The second incident is
when Marcel, quite by chance, found himself in the house of
homosexual prostitution run by Jupien during the war; frequented, as
it turns out, by M. de Charlus, in his more violently sado-masochistic
interludes.

'Could somebody kindly tell me to whom to apply to get a room and
have something to drink sent up?' asks Marcel, in all innocence. After
negotiation, the boss appears, carrying coils of ominously heavy chains.
Marcel explains that he is not feeling well and would like something to
drink. Sinister, even hair-raising, things are being said and done all
round. The boss's order is something of an anti-climax. 'Pierrot, go
down to the cellar and get some *cassis* . . .'

The Complete Imbiber, 1970, Cyril   1970
Ray, ed., Hutchinson.

VII

About twenty years ago Mina Curtiss wrote a book about Bizet, the
world of the composer of *Carmen* having abutted in several ways on to
that of Marcel Proust. She had previously edited and translated into
English a selection of Proust's letters.

An American, now in her eighties, her energies not in the least
diminished, she had the excellent idea of basing a memoir (which takes
in much else of her life) on the search for Proust's letters; the people she
met in the course of that, and the way she dealt with them. The result is
an extremely entertaining book.

Mina Curtiss, clearly a formidable personality, begins by describing
how she always had a passion for reading other people's letters, dating
from the moment, when at the age of seven or eight years old, she came
on a packet of her parents', written when they were engaged. Since then
she has seized every opportunity to read everybody else's letters,
whether by their permission or not, and has the honesty to admit to
what many others have done surreptitiously. Proust's letters naturally
opened up a festival in terms of compulsive letter reading.

One of the earliest, and most pathetic, that has been preserved was
written by Proust at the age of about sixteen to his grandfather, asking

for a small sum of money to pay for a chamber-pot he had accidentally broken in a brothel, where he had been sent by his father for purposes of 'hygiene'. Some of the letters from Proust's mother indicate that she must have been aware of his homosexuality when her son was still quite a young man.

Mina Curtiss, a widow, was professor at Smith College (*'Ah, mais c'est pour les jeunes filles. C'est très chic,'* commented Prince Antoine Bibesco when she introduced herself on the telephone). She was comfortably off, and knew a lot of key people. That made her job easier, but it was undertaken during the appalling post-war winter of 1946–7, the cold and discomforts of which find a deservedly horrid memorial in her book.

The most remarkable of her achievements was to become intimate with Céleste Albaret, Proust's maid, who had married Proust's former chauffeur. By this time the Albarets were running a very down-at-heel hotel in Paris off the Boulevard Saint-Germain. Mina Curtiss had a good introduction to them, but even so her later friendship with Céleste must have been due to remarkable powers of sympathy in herself. The picture she gives of both the Albarets is absorbing.

If the dealings with Céleste required, in the one sense, the greatest delicacy, and are perhaps the most interesting part of the story for example, in showing how utterly wide of the mark is the view of Proust that he knew only about duchesses (for that matter that Mina Curtiss herself was only equipped to deal with the smart world), far the funniest episode, which has the suspense of a play or novel, is her account of coping with Antoine Bibesco. The Prince, one of Proust's close friends who belonged to the large Rumanian contingent of Proust's world, was known to be a great womanizer and not too keen on spending money. This part of Mina Curtiss's book takes the form of the diary she kept at the time.

At their first meeting (she was fifty-one, he sixty-nine) Bibesco tried to go to bed with her and the reader is on tenterhooks to learn whether she will or she won't. In the end she did – and it appears to have been a great success – but there, she decided, the matter was to rest; though quite a long time later Bibesco proposed to her. The point was that she got the Proust letters from him, and managed to read most of what Bibesco had altered or blacked out in them.

Céleste Albaret and Antoine Bibesco, with others like Comtesse Greffulhe, Daniel Halévy, the Duchesse de Clermont-Tonnerre, Madame Scheikévitch, Princess Marthe Bibesco (married to a cousin of Antoine's), are well known to Proust fans, and Mina Curtiss invariably adds that little something that brings them more alive. She also trafficked with persons quite unknown to fame, who are no less well described; for example, Madame Sibilat, a Danish lady married to a

Frenchman, by then a widow. Madame Sibilat, for complicated reasons, had inherited Proust's letters to the famous hostess, Madame Straus (née Halévy, widow of Bizet), though Madame Sibilat herself was chiefly interested in racing.

Fortunately Madame Sibilat developed a schoolgirl 'pash' for Mina Curtiss, but even so things were not always easy. Among other eccentricities, Madame Sibilat sent three croissants (a form of bread Mina Curtiss happened not to like) every day in a hat-box delivered by an hotel *chasseur* in buttons and pill-box cap.

Other People's Letters: A Memoir,   1978
Mina Curtiss, Macmillan.   *Daily Telegraph*

VIII

Before Philip Kolb brought Proust's letters together under the title *Correspondence générale de Marcel Proust* the novelist's letters had suffered a rather scrappy fate. They had appeared only piecemeal in France.

Proust did not want his letters published (indeed quite often asks the recipient specifically to destroy a letter), and he writes with no eye on style or posterity. Accordingly translation is not easy, the combination of formality and colloquialism setting problems.

On the one hand, 'Sir', 'Dear Sir', 'Dear Friend' have none of the ring of 'Monsieur' or 'Cher Ami', either in the former two's stiffness in English, or the latter's dreadful folksiness. On the other hand, Ralph Manheim's 'to bother you some more', 'today I'm fine', 'feeling good' (convalescent), 'come to think of it', 'boned up on', 'phoned', strike an uneasy note for *la belle époque*, even if such infelicities are only occasional.

The notes are excellent, telling the reader who everyone is with just the right amount of detail, and giving innumerable useful references where some sentences or some experience of Proust's has been reproduced in *A la recherche*

Marcel Proust: Selected Letters, 1880–1903 takes the novelist up to the death of his father, when Proust himself was thirty-two. Once in a way a letter from someone else – usually his mother – is included to make a contemporary situation clearer, and the whole sheds a good deal of light on matters that can never quite be conveyed by a biography however subtle.

One is immediately struck by the early age at which most of the models (or near models, for after Proust had finished with them in *Remembrance of Things Past* they bore comparatively little resemblance to their originals) came into the novelist's life. His own relations figure naturally enough, but at seventeen he was receiving the present of a book with an arch inscription from the *poule de luxe* Laure Hayman, who had been his uncle's mistress and contributed something to Odette.

At nineteen he was writing 'Don't scold me for the chrysanthemums' to Mme Straus (Bizet's widow) to whom the Duchesse de Guermantes owed her wit; at twenty-one he was confirming with Count Robert de Montesquiou that he might call for the first time. They had met at the salon of Mme Lemaire, who had some of the characteristics of Mme Verdurin.

Even allowing for French conventions of the period, and the fact that Proust wanted to get to know the aristocracy because they were the sort of people he liked to write about, Proust's letters to Montesquiou strike a dizzy level of obsequiousness. He worked off steam, however, by giving apparently brilliant Montesquiou imitations, which took some explaining away when the subject got to hear about them.

Proust's homosexuality and his attitude towards it, which was a somewhat complicated one, is of interest in the Letters. The fact seems to have been accepted to some extent even by his parents, but at the same time he writes to his close friend Daniel Halévy: 'Don't call me a pederast, it hurts my feelings. If only for the sake of elegance I try to remain morally pure.' He was then about seventeen, and these words seem to deny what in other respects that letter (as do others) appears to affirm.

The letters indicate strongly that Proust's health and his neurasthenia became very much worse a year or two before he was thirty. To what extent the nerves brought on the asthma, or the asthma attacks caused the nerves, is impossible to say, but already he was refusing to go out at all during the day, and having his meals at the strangest hours.

This is very much in contrast with his earlier grown-up years when one is struck by his liveliness and energy. No one without superhuman energy of a kind could have written a novel of the length of *Jean Santeuil*, abandoned it, then written another the length of *Remembrance of Things Past*. He was at work on the former during the period covered here, and sometimes makes an oblique reference to a book he was writing.

It was no good his mother saying that other people felt just as rotten as he did, and they had to get up and go to work. Proust (as it turned out rightly) would have none of that, and even in his thirties was bothering her about the safety pin to keep up his drawers. Some of the references to his clothes are enjoyable, such as: 'The Crystal Palace trousers have been delivered. They are too tight.' 'About the hat I'll do whatever you say, but the rain has straightened the straw and it's as good as new. It would break my heart and give me no pleasure at all to spend more money on a mediocre hat.'

If Montesquiou was touchy, so too was Proust, increasingly so as his nerves deteriorated. That is particularly shown with Antoine Bibesco, who was not above pulling Proust's leg in his letters. In fact some of the diatribes about betrayed friendship delivered by Charlus, and commonly attributed to Montesquiou, were not very different from what Proust himself would write when wrought up.

Proust fights two duels in the course of this volume – pistols are after all always dangerous if pointed at anyone – and his friend Gaston de Caillavet (with several others, a model for Saint-Loup) was actually wounded fighting with sabres.

Marcel Proust: Selected Letters,   1983
1880–1903, Philip Kolb, ed.,   *Daily Telegraph*
Ralph Manheim, trans.,
Introductions by J. M. Cocking,
Collins.

IX

Since C. K. Scott Moncrieff made his justly celebrated translation of *A La Recherche du Temps Perdu* in the 1920s an enormous amount of work has been done on the chaotic manuscript of Proust's million-and-a-quarter-word novel, of which in France a definitive edition, with voluminous notes, appeared in 1954 in Gallimard's Bibliothèque de la Pléiade.

Even in this French edition not all Proust's extraneous passages, apparently intended for inclusion, could be accommodated in the main text, and at times the novelist's handwriting proved beyond elucidation.

Scott Moncrieff died before his translation was finished, and the last section of the novel, *Le Temps Retrouvé*, was translated by Stephen Hudson (Sydney Schiff) in this country, in America by Frederick A. Blossom, and in 1970 again by Andreas Mayor, the best of the three. A new translation was therefore needed to incorporate the many required corrections and give unity to the whole. Terence Kilmartin provides this while retaining the basic structure supplied by Scott Moncrieff.

Scott Moncrieff had a tendency to elaborate Proust's language which, apart from admittedly long and complicated sentences, is natural in expression. Perhaps the worst example of Scott Moncrieff getting out of hand is his rendering of the section called *Albertine Disparue* as *The Sweet Cheat Gone*, which Kilmartin rejects, returning to what was in fact the original sub-heading *The Fugitive*.

To give anything like a scholarly opinion on Kilmartin's revisions would really require a re-reading of the whole of *A la Recherche* (together with the Pléiade notes) in French, again in the Scott Moncrieff and Mayor translations, and finally in the present one. Scarcely a paragraph is without at least some minor alteration. My impression is that Kilmartin carries the reader along at a distinctly swifter pace, with the result that possibly one's sensations by the end of the book might be appreciably different.

All that can be done here is to draw attention to a few particular aspects of the new version. These are especially hard to collate because re-arrangements have taken place such as the opening pages of *Time Regained* being put in a different place by all three translators. In the section *The Captive* both Scott Moncrieff and Kilmartin have a practically identical paragraph opening: 'As I listened to Albertine's footsteps with the consoling pleasure of thinking that she would not be going out again that evening . . .' but passages both before and after this are widely different in their actual material – no doubt owing to closer study of Proust's manuscript. There are many such examples.

In certain places Scott Moncrieff slipped up in small matters and these have often been put right. When Marcel visits Saint-Loup in barracks at Doncières, Saint-Loup's squadron-commander, the Prince de Borodino, cultivates a Napoleonic air. Scott Moncrieff writes of Borodino as 'followed by the adjutant and the quartermaster, as though by Berthier and Masséna'. Kilmartin alters this to 'sergeant-major and quartermaster', *adjutant* meaning not English 'adjutant', an officer, but in fact something more like a warrant-officer.

During this same visit Saint-Loup introduces Marcel to his mistress, Rachel, and, says Scott Moncrieff, 'She never stopped talking about books, new art and Tolstoyism.' Kilmartin adjusts this to 'books, Art Nouveau and Tolstoyism' – Rachel was in fact speaking of that contemporary art of which, say, Beardsley was representative.

On the other hand in *Le Temps Retrouvé* section neither Mayor nor Kilmartin get the heraldic term *quartiers de noblesse* quite right; they both render it as 'quarters on his escutcheon'. This simply means the sixteen quarterings (*seize quartiers*) – that is the arms of his sixteen great-great-grandparents of noble birth – and needs no more than 'quarterings of nobility'. One must, however, regret that Scott Moncrieff's correct reference to Saint-Loup's 'eye-glass' has been altered to 'monocle', a term certainly regarded as a solecism in the England of Proust's day, nor would 'trilby' have been used. If a soft hat had to be specified, it would have been called a 'Homburg.'

Although it has not been possible to include the textual and other notes of the Pléaide edition, which would have added another volume to these three, some very useful notes are appended with regard to certain references in the narrative, also a useful synopsis of incidents (which is a great help when reading Proust).

The Addenda here are most interesting. They contain a number of complete incidents the author intended to use – or at least he had not yet made up his mind on the subject. One of these (Vol. I) describes how Mme de Marsantes (Saint-Loup's mother) shows rudeness to Odette by leaving her alone while Mme de Marsantes shows over the house Lady Israels (later referred to in the same passage as Lady Jacob, though one would take her to be the wife of Sir Rufus Israels in the main body of the novel).

An even longer and more striking additional passage (Vol. II) touches on the Princesse de Guermantes's love for M. de Charlus – something I find difficulty in accepting, anyway in the near-suicidal form it took – and on Charlus's indifference to her frantic notes, since they arrived at a moment when he was about to be introduced by Jupien to a bus-conductor he particularly wanted to meet. The bus-conductor thought Charlus was a professional photographer, a scene all Proustians will enjoy.

Remembrance of Things Past: Vol I, *Swann's Way*: *Within a Budding Grove*. Vol II, *The Guermantes Way*: *Cities of the Plain*. Vol III, *The Captive*: *The Fugitive*: *Time Regained*, Marcel Proust; Terence Kilmartin, trans., Chatto & Windus.

1981
Daily Telegraph

X

When I began reading his book I wondered whether Montesquiou would run to a full-scale biography. These doubts were quite unjustified. Philippe Jullian has done a brilliant job.

Montesquiou, like Anatole France, is to be investigated at two levels: first, as the man he was; secondly, as the fictional character novelists modelled on him.

The man – perhaps one should say the nobleman, because Montesquiou was very keen on his family origins – was a striking enough figure in his particular way. Good-looking, gifted, with an overpowering personality, he fell always short of being what he really wanted to be, a great poet or artist.

Verses, indeed, poured from him; he lectured, propagated, organized, where the arts were concerned. He was witty, intensely malicious, determined to be the last word in modernism. In the end all the result was to be left messing about with odds and ends of his own work that nobody much wanted to read.

He wrote on the last page of his Memoirs: 'An impression which is even more extraordinary than painful is that which consists of suddenly observing, without any warning, that one's life is over.'

Robert de Montesquiou was born in 1855. Doubts have been cast on the genuineness of the Montesquiou lineage before the end of the tenth century; but they claimed Merovingian descent by way of the Dukes of Aquitaine. They were not only ancient, but very genuinely distinguished, with amusing ramifications like the historic D'Artagnan.

At an early age Montesquiou became the outstanding figure in the social area where the great families of the Faubourg St Germain were beginning to mix with those who represented the extraordinary richness of French intellectual life that came into being after the Franco-Prussian War. A group of predominantly Jewish hostesses played the part of impresario to this new world of *Tout-Paris*.

Montesquiou, Jullian emphasizes, was that rather un-French figure, a dandy. His eccentricities were soon notorious. Although he was not in principle attracted by the opposite sex, not a few of them were fascinated by him. There was a brush with Sarah Bernhardt. Although this appears to have been in itself a fiasco, they remained firm friends throughout life.

In 1884, Montesquiou made his first important appearance as a character in a novel, that is to say as Des Esseintes in Huysmans's *A Rebours*. Various lesser novelists also used him, until finally he reached an apotheosis as Charlus in Proust's *A la Recherche du Temps Perdu*.

There is a great deal here that is worth examining from a literary point of view. Des Esseintes, a Baudelairian ideal of decadence, is probably, as Jullian points out, the last of the romantic heroes in a novel that holds reasonably high claims still to be read. There is a great deal of well-invented detail in Huysmans, but his Des Esseintes is not a 'real person'. He is a projection of the author, doing a lot of things the author would no doubt have liked to do.

Charlus is quite another matter. Jullian shows convincingly that Proust inserted great chunks of Montesquiou's actual conversation into his novel, while various incidents there described could well have taken place between the two of them.

In examining the differences between Montesquiou the man, and Montesquiou/Charlus, Jullian throws a lot of light on the way novelists create characters – the important point being that, although Proust did indeed use an immense amount of actual Montesquiou material in presenting Charlus, Charlus really emerges as quite a different person from Montesquiou.

Charlus has all Montesquiou's overweening pride in his family (though Montesquiou's mother, in fact, came of rich bourgeois stock rather than being a 'Bavarian duchess'). Charlus has also Montesquiou's intelligence, cruelty and wit. Where they differed was that Charlus, a pillar of the Jockey Club (as opposed to Montesquiou, who detested conventional womanizing and racing men), was a secret homosexual, whose habits become increasingly degraded as the novel progresses.

Montesquiou was quite different from this. He was always shocking conventional people by saying outrageous things, wearing exotic clothes, giving ornate parties – but he was too fastidious to indulge in sordid adventures. Indeed he gets rather castigated by Jullian for being too prim.

The striking conclusion one arrives at is that Charlus has real life and tragedy about him, while Montesquiou, talented as he was, remains a trifle absurd, almost a figure in cardboard. In other words, Proust used that extraordinary power that is called art to create Charlus. He breathed something into this invented character which no amount of documentary facts drawn from his prototype could ever have given him.

In justice to Montesquiou, pompous, ludicrous, odiously spiteful as he could be, he did remark towards the end of his life: 'Will I be reduced to calling myself Montesproust?', a joke that redeems a good deal of narcissistic tiresomeness.

Philippe Jullian's book is packed with information, but one wishes there were a few references saying where the stories come from. For example, the one that describes Oscar Wilde arriving to dine with Proust, but leaving before dinner because he could not face the Proust parents when he saw them.

Montesquiou's vitality was extraordinary. He emerged from *la belle époque* to preach the wonders of Diaghilev's Russian Ballet, involving himself in an extraordinary emotional triangle with D'Annunzio and Ida Rubenstein, the dancer.

In the end he admitted despair where Picasso, 'Czechoslovakian aestheticism' and African art were concerned, but it is satisfactory to think that Montesquiou's portrait by Boldini dominated the recent excellent Art Nouveau Exhibition at Ostend. He deserved that.

Robert de Montesquiou: A Fin-de-   1967
siècle Prince, Philippe Jullian;   *Daily Telegraph*
John Haylock and Francis
King, trans., Secker &
Warburg.

XI

In his day, Anatole France (1844–1924) was a towering figure. White-bearded, skull-capped, dressed with just the right amount of eccentricity, a member of the Académie, recipient of the Nobel prize, with international sales and well-advertised love affairs, he seems – and, indeed, was – a caricature of the successful French literary man.

David Tylden-Wright, creditably in a biographer, will not hear a word against France's writing, but, although energy, scholarship and wit are undoubtedly to be found there, many people will feel that it would be a heavy task to re-read them.

Mannered, arch, sentimental, their banality seems personified by the short story which ends by Pontius Pilate saying: 'Jesus of Nazareth. I cannot call him to mind.' However, France himself was far from being a boring man so far as his career was concerned.

His grandfather was a cobbler, whose son joined the Royal Guard of Charles X. When he was twenty-one, France's father could neither read nor write, but he eventually established himself as a well-known bookseller on the Paris *quais*. His shop was frequented by famous people like the Goncourts. In this eminently appropriate atmosphere France was brought up.

The family name was Thibault, and it was a mere chance that the writer chose the pen-name 'France' – merely an abbreviation of 'François' – for his early efforts. Again, one feels the pseudonym was essentially that of an author destined to become a bestseller.

However, if France's own works now seem more than a little faded, he himself lives on, so to speak, in another dimension, with curious vigour. This is because he is the prototype of 'Bergotte' in Proust's novel. The theme of a writer of France's stature becoming, as it were, himself a lesser figure than a novelist's picture of him, is a fascinating one – perhaps to appeal to Henry James – but in France's case that is almost what has happened.

Bergotte, of course, has other elements than France to make up his portrait – Renan, for example. Proust himself, as the Narrator, writes of his own extraordinary admiration as a young man for Bergotte (France), and, in justice to France, the germ of many of the elements that make *A la Recherche* outstanding are to be found in France's pages.

Tylden-Wright's appreciative, serious and painstaking biography does not, I think, give quite sufficient critical attention to this influence of France on Proust. Proust, describing Bergotte, speaks of the 'rare, almost archaic phrases which he liked to employ at certain points,' when he would speak of the 'vain dream of life', the 'inexhaustible torrent of fair forms' or 'the sterile, splendid torture of understanding and loving'.

This is all France's style to the life, and George Painter in his biography of Proust points out that many of France's themes, 'the unreality of the phenomenal world, the poetic nature of the past in which the only true reality is hidden, the impossibility of knowing another person, the continual feeling of change in the self, feelings and memory', were all to give Proust subjects with which he dealt with far greater genius.

The more one reads Tylden-Wright's biography, the more one feels how hopelessly entangled France and Bergotte have become. For example, France's first marriage broke up comparatively early, and, although he married again as a very old man, his life-long attachment was to Mme Arman, who conducted a salon. 'On entering the drawing-room of Mme Arman,' wrote one of her guests, 'one had the impression of being in a railway-station, of which Anatole France was the stationmaster.'

As we read about Mme Arman and her husband – who seems to have been only too thankful that France was prepared to keep his wife quiet – the Verdurins come soon to mind. Sure enough, it turns out that Proust frequented this salon too, and obviously collected much of his material there for this preposterous couple.

The Armans' son also provided some of the military material for St Loup in *A la Recherche*. It is interesting that – probably on account of the too great closeness to life – Bergotte was not a frequenter of Mme Verdurin's salon in Proust's novel, but of Odette's.

France was an early and energetic supporter of Dreyfus, and, as he grew older and more famous, became increasingly drawn into politics, though not with any great distinction.

He did not live in the same house as Mme Arman, but worked and had all his meals there. On the two days a week when she 'received', France would come downstairs at the correct moment carrying his top-hat and a bunch of violets. The hat he would hand to the butler, the bouquet to Mme Arman, saying he could not resist buying this humble offering on the way to visit her. It will be remembered that in the novel Bergotte picks up a top-hat in the hall (to give an impression of having just arrived, rather than sojourning in the house), of which Marcel later relieves him, seeing the hat is his own.

France seems always to have been strongly attracted to the opposite sex, a taste that increased with age. It was generally agreed that the form this indulgence took verged latterly on the sordid. It was not unknown for Mme Arman to set out for his residence and knock him up at, say, five o'clock in the morning to make sure all – from her point of view – was well.

When he went to South America in his middle sixties a lot of publicity was given to France's affair with a middle-aged actress on the boat. She was a member of a theatrical company which was to spread French culture in that continent, while France lectured on Rabelais.

France had a row with his secretary, Brousson, at Buenos Aires, and sacked him, giving him his ticket home but no additional money. Brousson managed to get a job on the return journey tutoring two South American boys.

When France arrived home there was hell to pay with Mme Arman (who had in any case wanted to come with him to South America) and, in reconciliation, they made a trip together to Bordeaux. In the Chapon

Fin Restaurant, whom should France and Mme Arman find but
Brousson and his two pupils?

The fact is that France, in many respects, was a richly comic
personality. Tylden-Wright does not accentuate this side, perhaps,
from his point of view, with good reason. All the same one prefers to the
world-famous *cher maître*, the France who, instead of using his bath for
the normal purpose, threw complimentary copies of books sent him
into it, then sold them, when the bath was full.

Anatole France, David Tylden-   1967
Wright, Collins.   *Daily Telegraph*

XII

'Nisard fell silent, and looked at me with his sharp, searching eye.
Then, in a slow, precise voice, as if weighing every word, he said:

'Perhaps we now have the leading thread in our hands – the thread of
Ariadne . . . But what shall we find in the labyrinth?" '

The scene was, of course, the Quai D'Orsay: the year 1897. The
couple, deep in debate, Maurice Paléologue and a colleague in the
French Diplomatic Corps. They were discussing the sinister undercurrents of the Dreyfus case, then just beginning its fourth year.

Paléologue, who later had a career of some distinction in diplomacy,
will perhaps be chiefly remembered as supplying the model for
Monsieur de Norpois in Proust's *A la Recherche du Temps Perdu*: that
suave, ambassadorial figure, stting permanently on the fence, whose
oracular and prolix sayings were absolutely impossible to disentangle
for those in search of what he really thought. In these extracts from his
diary we have the man to the life: often one might be reading the urbane
harangues of his fictional prototype, so much does one resemble the
other.

He was in his middle thirties when the Dreyfus case began, serving
with the branch of the French Foreign Office in contact with War Office
Secret Service. In addition to that, he was a lieutenant on the Artillery
Reserve, so that during his annual recall to the colours he was posted to
the department of military intelligence. In this latter capacity he was
actually present, in uniform, at the ceremonial degradation of Dreyfus.

The diary is admittedly touched up; and it would probably be safer
to regard it as Paléologue's personal account of the case, written up
from notes made at the time, rather than as a document showing what
the diarist recorded when those events were taking place. Certainly the
writer, on revision, was not going to allow himself to appear in an
unfavourable light. Even so, however artificial, the book is enormously
readable and vivid; and it is a pity that the translator sometimes vitiates

the period flavour by the use of words or phrases characteristic of more recent years.

But if Paléologue is three-parts Proust he is at least one part Phillips Openheim:

> Thanks to the influence of General de Cissey – who was to be ruined a few years later in the shameful adventure of the Baronne de Kaulla – he [Maurice Weil] secured a posting as a captain of the reserve to the intelligence department.

This Maurice Weil is Paléologue's main contribution to the history of the *Affaire*, together with an unnamed officer of high rank. These two, together with the known traitor, Esterhazy – that really extraordinary figure who took flight to England, where he lived to a ripe old age – had been at work since 1886, according to Paléologue, selling secrets to the German, Austrian and Italian General Staffs. Two officers in the French Secret Service (Henry and Lauth), although not themselves acting as spies, had personal reasons for covering these other sinister figures in the background.

The accusation of Dreyfus was, therefore, not entirely the result of stupidity and prejudice; there was in it – if Paléologue is correct – a strong measure of deliberate 'framing'. If a man could be found to be blamed for what had taken place, there was a better chance of the real traitors escaping notice.

The extraordinary thing is that we still do not know the true story. After sixty or more years, with shelves and shelves of every library devoted to the Dreyfus case, much that is of mystery yet remains. Paléologue does not tell us the name of the senior officer said to be deeply involved; while Maurice Weil is, in fact, dismissed in Guy Chapman's excellent book on the *Affaire* (which came out in 1955) as a somewhat contemptible but harmless figure. Presumably the general could be run to earth without too much difficulty; perhaps this diary will alter opinions about Weil. The fact remains that there is still much to clear up.

However, for those who read this diary – which for some reason has been given here quite unnecessarily large day-to-day headlines – without undue concentration on the detail of the case, there is a great deal of entertainment. Not least D'Annunzio at a luncheon party:

> 'You asked me just what my method was in love, *madame*. It is silence and action . . . I have never known either remorse or regret; I live only in the present; I perpetually need new pleasures and new sensations . . . Being *immoral*? What could be more simple! But only a genius can be *moral*.'

How rightly the French sometimes call it *la belle époque* – even though it wasn't that for the unfortunate Dreyfus.

My Secret Diary of the Dreyfus   1957
Case, Maurice Paléologue,   *Punch*
Secker & Warburg.

XIII

When in 1861 Isaac Singer, inventor of the Singer sewing machine came to Paris, he was in several respects, the prototype of the Henry James American exploring Europe – many times a millionaire, interested in the arts, anxious to widen his horizons.

In one point, however, Singer was very unlike a Jamesian hero. So far from being an innocent, corrupted by the bad Old World, he had fathered sixteen illegitimate children back home, and soon after arrival in Paris, he seduced an upper-middle-class French girl thirty years his junior, whom he subsequently married, producing six more, legitimate, offspring.

One of these legitimate children was Winnaretta (supposedly an American Indian name), a daughter of unusual promise, even among a gifted family. From her earliest years Winnaretta Singer was devoted to music, but as she also possessed a talent for drawing it was decided to send her to be trained by an academic artist who took a few selected pupils.

Before she was twenty her paintings were being accepted every year by the Salon, but she had already grasped that the Impressionists (then generally regarded as a bad joke) represented the true path of modern painting, and it is clear from reproductions in this book that her own later painting in the Impressionist style was completely professional.

Winnaretta Singer never seems to have had any doubt that what she wanted to do was live a high-powered life in Paris that was both smart and intellectual. She was financially equipped to do this owing to the vast extent of the Singer fortune, but it would be necessary to marry. The only difficulty about settling the sort of arranged marriage normal in France was Winnaretta's condition of being congenitally lesbian. A first marriage had to be annulled on this account, but her second, to Prince Edmond de Polignac, thirty years older than herself, also homosexual, a musician of great talent, was a complete success.

Winnaretta de Polignac now moved into the position she held all her life of being one of the predominant figures in that world of *la belle époque* which lives on most vividly in the pages of Proust. As its members are often decried as 'decadent' the extraordinary gifts possessed by some of them are worth remembering. Edmond de Polignac himself, for example, had submitted an opera to the Conservatoire in 1869 when out of forty-two competitors he came fifth, with Massenet second, Bizet seventh.

Michael de Cossart describes all this in a usefully informative manner, without great sparkle, and with at times rather odd phrases. There are inevitably a few stories that have been told before, such as the female archaeologist of masculine dress, who insisted on staying behind with the men after dinner to smoke, whose arm General Galliffet took, with the words: '*Et maintenant allons pisser.*' But it is an amusing addition to know that Comtesse Mathieu de Noailles (née Anne de Brancovan), the poet, was angry at having this anecdote told in front of her.

The appearances of Proust here are also of interest, as he got on badly with Winnaretta de Polignac, and it is possible to glimpse rather a different view of him from that given in books where Proust himself is the main subject. De Cossart emphasizes that Mme de Polignac's parties were in many respects very unsnobbish in terms of the period, being easy-going about changing for dinner. He draws attention to the fact that 'Prince' is not a French title (royal family apart), Polignac's being Papal and Bavarian.

When de Cossart settles down to the narrative of Winnaretta de Polignac's life (apart from her lesbian relationships, which are perhaps not of outstanding interest, except that we learn she liked whipping her ladies), the chronicle is chiefly an astonishing record of musical and ballet patronage. In this respect what she did takes an important place in musical history. Apart from assistance to Diaghilev without which his company could not have survived, encouragement of Nadia Boulanger's undertakings, a long list of famous composers assisted, her unknown benefactions must have been on an immense scale too.

Isaac Singer had developed a strong affection for the west of England, and caused to be constructed a large and baroque Singer family tomb at Torquay Cemetery. In August 1939, when attending the obsequies of one of her brothers, Winnaretta de Polignac was caught by the outbreak of war. In England, therefore, she was to spend the years of life that remained. Her financial circumstances were somewhat reduced by now, but on the whole it is possible to feel that avoidance of the circumstances of Vichy France may have been for the best.

Winnaretta de Polignac must have been one of the last major figures of her particular society to survive into the very different sort of life lived during the Second World War. It was a constant irritation to her that the only thing everyone she met wanted to hear about was Proust. She was not without wit, and when a young man who did not know her well shouted '*Bonsoir, tante Winnie!*' she replied: '*Tante vous-même!*' At the news of Mme de Polignac's death a friend of mine adapting Edward

Lear's lines on himself remarked: 'Long ago she was one of the Singers. But now she is one of the dumbs.'

The Food of Love: Princesse Edmond   1978
de Polignac (1865–1943) and her   *Daily Telegraph*
Salon, Michael de Cossart,
Hamish Hamilton.

XIV

George Sand has been written of endlessly, but André Maurois approaches her from an unusual angle. His interest grew from the fact that her novels were the first grown-up books given to Marcel Proust by his mother and grandmother. Even in his maturity Proust liked Sand's writing. That certainly lends her work a new interest. In addition to this, Maurois discovered unpublished Sand material. He set out to write a book about her that would avoid the hostility and ridicule that her life and ideas almost inevitably arouse. He has been successful. It is possible to disagree with some of his conclusions, but from start to finish the story (well translated) is absorbing.

Madame de Staël and George Sand have always seemed to me the two most dreadful women of the nineteenth century: perhaps of any age. Their energy, pretentiousness, egotism, vulgarity, lack of principle, inability to know their own minds, and delight in meddling with matters which had nothing whatever to do with themselves, made them a blight on the whole epoch in which each lived. Any attempt to mitigate the lamentable impression either of them still wafts across the years is therefore welcome. In George Sand's case let us glance at the facts.

Born in 1804, Aurore Dupin de Francueil was the daughter of an army officer married to a woman more or less a prostitute. Much play is made by Maurois (as by Sand herself) that she was a great-granddaughter of Marshal Saxe, illegitimate son of Augustus of Saxony, King of Poland, by a lady of the Koenigsmark family. No doubt this was a remarkable heredity, but it must be remembered that of her sixteen great-great-grandparents only one was a king and one a Koenigsmark, the remaining fourteen being a mixture of minor nobility and, at times, perhaps rather unusually disreputable lower-middle class. This point seems worth mentioning as her behaviour is perpetually ascribed to her royal blood, when in fact, there must have been scores of people about then with the blood of Augustus II or many other minor potentates flowing in their veins.

Aurore was an heiress with a country house and a comfortable, if not enormous, income. At eighteen she married the illegitimate, but recognized, son of a baron of the Empire, thus keeping up the extraordinary tendency of her family to prefer the wrong side of the blanket. It soon turned out that her husband, a simple, good-natured, perhaps rather coarse fellow, was quite inadequate for such a woman. She had always a taste for wearing men's clothes and smoking cigars. It was not long before she was installed in Paris, living with a lover called Sandeau (from whom the pseudonym 'Sand' ultimately derived) and producing the first of her seventy or more novels.

From the moment that she appeared in Paris, George Sand became identified with the fascinating literary life of that era in France. She had a string of lovers of whom Musset and Chopin are perhaps the best known, although she by no means restricted herself to men of genius. Maurois takes episode after episode, telling it frankly yet sympathetically. Every time, we begin to feel that, after all, there is something we can like about her; the past can be forgiven; on this occasion she is going to behave well. Yet again and again Maurois's skilful advocacy breaks down. Sand acts so abominably that it is impossible to sustain the great scaffolding of excuses that have been built up.

She was, when it came to the point, inordinately dishonest with herself. Never was a woman given greater opportunities to test her high pretentions. In the end it was her lovers who hated her most of all. The men who behaved well towards her were Mérimée, who had had a somewhat embarrassing encounter with her (in fact failed to come up to scratch), and Vigny, who disliked her, suspecting lesbian relations with his beautiful mistress, Marie Dorval. Baudelaire, moving in rather different circles, loathed her. 'She is no artist,' he wrote, 'She has that famous, easy style so dear to the bourgeois heart. She is stupid, she is heavy, she is garrulous. There is in her moral ideas about as much depth of thought, as much sensibility, as you would find in a concierge or a kept woman.' She was certainly Queen of the Middlebrows.

Sand gave scarcely veiled accounts of her own love affairs in her novels, including even letters actually written or received. She put an offensive picture of poor Chopin into one book, and then read it aloud to him; but he was too polite to comment. At the height of her 'Communist' political period she kept eight or nine servants, to say nothing of innumerable 'dailies'; and, although she did not like to hear people talking of *masters* and *servants*, she was very insistent that the domestic work was not scamped. As she grew older she settled down at her country house, Nohant, surrounded by a horde of young men.

Théophile Gautier stayed there in 1863, and left an account of it.

The subject of these morning dissertations is usually linguistic – how, for instance, *d'ailleurs* and *meilleur* should be pronounced, with much jollity and a great many lavatory jokes. Ugh! But not a word, mark you, about sex. I got the idea that if one so much as mentioned the horrid thing, out one would go!

Lélia: The Life of George Sand,   1953
André Maurois; Gerard   *Punch*
Hopkins, trans., Cape.

XV

In Martin Seymour-Smith's *Guide to Modern World Literature* (1973) Pierre Loti's novels are described as 'never quite awful'. This is higher praise than might be thought on the face of it, because the particular kind of exotic romanticism which Loti goes in for has not worn well, and from Istanbul to Tahiti, Tokyo to Algiers, the landscapes have taken on perspectives very different from those seen through Loti's eyes.

Oddly enough, he is chiefly remembered in this country for *Pêcheur d'Islande*, the sentimental yet rather moving story of Brittany and the Breton fishermen who sail to Iceland, much used here as a school textbook, Iceland itself being, as it happens, one of the few places Loti had never visited.

Lesley Blanch, no doubt sensibly, meets Loti more than half-way so far as romanticism is concerned. She lets him off lightly on the subject of glamorously presented bisexual love affairs some of which must have been pretty squalid, while she comments only occasionally on Loti's ferocious egotism and phenomenal lack of humour. It would indeed have been impossible to carry on the way Loti did without the two last characteristics.

Having said that, one must admit that Loti was an extraordinary man whose life was unusual by any standards. He possessed altogether exceptional reserves of energy within his small frame, and people found hard to describe his mesmeric powers of attraction over and above his fame in writing novels, admired by, among others, James and Proust, the latter choosing Loti as one of his two favourite novelists in the Confession Album he contributed to in 1892, the other being Anatole France.

He was born Julien Viaud (1850–1923), of Protestant parents (his father converted in order to marry his mother) coming from the neighbourhood of La Rochelle and the island of Oléron. There were naval traditions on both sides: an admiral, a grandfather who served as a gunner at Trafalgar, an uncle rumoured, at the age of fourteen, to have been one of those eaten by their comrades on the notorious raft of the *Méduse*.

Loti was enormously fussed over by his parents (who had lost an older son and were not at all well off), and in general the only respect in which he does not sound like a typical child who would turn out to be a writer is that he was good at mathematics. The fact that he was undersized was painful to him all his life but, although his family wanted him to become an engineer, he was determined to go into the navy. This he did, and one side of him was devoted to that profession about which he speaks in terms that recall his contemporary and unexpected fellow literary sailor, Conrad.

Off the cuff I can think only of Marryat as a British naval officer who became a novelist of any distinction, but the French Navy can point to Claude Farrère (b. 1876) as well as Loti and, in that coincidental manner so often to be noticed, they served together and were friends. In the Royal Navy one might have qualified the last by adding that friendship was in spite of difference of rank, but Loti totally disregarded such matters and himself frequently wore a rating's uniform, with the red pompom cap, when going out on the tiles and even to the Opera when invited here by his friend (possibly mistress) Sarah Bernhardt.

The tolerance of the French Navy towards Loti is indeed breathtaking. One admiral noted a prejudice against Loti's use of make-up, later withdrawing and admitting he was a competent officer. On another occasion thirty officers signed an objection to Loti being posted to their ship, but they too seem to have been won over. Even allowing for Loti's first sexual experience at the age of sixteen with a gypsy probably being nothing very unusual, and for that matter his having a Tahitian or Japanese mistress, the affair he had with a Turkish married woman has curious aspects.

These adventures tended to be represented in Loti's novels as the experiences of a British naval officer, though he was intensely anti-British, a matter about which Edward VII pulled his leg. Loti was very keen on Royalty.

The good nature of the French Navy towards Loti is illustrated at quite another level by allowing him six months leave for physical development. This was on account of his dissatisfaction with his own physique, but he did not stop at merely producing an adequate improvement, he carried the training so far as to be an acrobat in a circus where he appears to have done double somersaults on the back of a horse.

He was in any case an excellent rider, and it was only chance which prevented him taking part in a Moorish equestrian display which would have combined his passion for dressing up (wherever he went he wore local costume when on leave) with drawing attention to himself as a a performer.

In spite of all the episodes with exotic mistresses, burly sailors,

Levantine dragomen and the like, Loti wanted to be respectably married. It is not surprising to hear that his wife had rather a rough time – especially as he established a Basque mistress in the neighbourhood because he wanted to have some Basque children since he felt romantic about the Basques. The mistress had a fairly rough time too.

Loti also built a mosque and various other bizarre additions to his old home, an otherwise modest house but did not improve the dungeon-like kitchen or the sole privy until pressure came from a younger generation.

If Loti himself lacked humour one certainly cannot say the same of the French naval authorities who eventually appointed him naval attaché at Constantinople. There he became involved in a hoax played by some Turkish ladies, which resulted in his bestselling novel *Les Désenchantées*. Here again Loti must be agreed to have shown the qualities of his defects because, after they had made a fool of him the Turkish women so-to-speak defected from their harem, and Loti was put to a fearful amount of trouble and expense when they arrived on his doorstep to stay with him, disrupting his household by their malice and bone-idleness.

Lesley Blanch tells a most entertaining story – though one gets a shade fed up with Loti himself in the end. Something has gone amiss in the attribution of the epigraph to Chapter 2, which does not come from *The Waste Land* and I should be surprised to hear was written by T. S. Eliot at all.

Pierre Loti: Portrait of an Escapist,   1983
Lesley Blanch, Collins.   *Daily Telegraph*

XVI

In 1972 work began on a project to turn Proust's great novel sequence *A la Recherche du Temps Perdu* (*Remembrance of Things Past*) into a film. The English title is worth emphasizing because, as Cyril Connolly wrote with some truth, Proust's work became so much read in translation that it almost took on the shape of an English book.

This point seems to be worth making at the start in the light of an Englishman, rather than a Frenchman, doing an adaptation for the screen. Harold Pinter was a bold choice. Certainly he is one of the most accomplished of contemporary dramatists, yet his plays are, at least outwardly, in subject matter and treatment, about as far from Proust's style as you could get. It is possible, though, to imagine Proust finding plenty to interest him in, say, *The Caretaker*.

We are now presented with Pinter's script to be read as a book, since, so far, sufficient money has not been raised to make the film. Naturally what we are offered here is only part of the ultimate work that would be for consideration if *The Proust Screenplay* ever reached the screen. There would be the actors, who might or might not rise to the occasion, while what reads well in print might not be equally effective as a film.

A vast amount would depend on good direction. Notwithstanding all that, Pinter has produced something that should be read not only by all Proustians as a fresh illumination of the novel but also by all enthusiasts of the art of the film interested in seeing how intractable material can be deftly handled.

Proust's novel consists very largely of an analysis of what it feels like to be unhappily in love, this sensation viewed chiefly through the eyes of the tart-fancying womanizing man-about-town, Charles Swann, or those of the narrator himself, Marcel. A man in love is not an easy subject to photograph for several hours on end, but there are innumerable other themes in the novel, so that, at the other extreme, an embarrassment exists in the luxuriance of incident.

The time-sequence required to chronicle the growing up of Marcel, and his passing from the state of a sensitive child to that of an experienced middle-aged man not far from death, creates yet another technical problem.

In his Introduction, short and much to the point, Pinter says:

> We decided that the architecture of the film should be based on two main and contrasting principles: one a movement, chiefly narrative, towards revelation, rising to where time that was lost is found and fixed for ever in art.

This seems an excellent summary of one – probably the best – approach.

For the Proust addict an enormous effort is required to accept that, if *A la Recherche* ever reaches the screen, the overwhelming majority of those who see it will start entirely from scratch, without the smallest knowledge of the writer, or his characters. So certain simplifications in the story must take place.

Harold Pinter begins with a series of unconnected shots, without dialogue, which show more or less what the viewer is going to be involved with as the story unfolds. We are then, with the visit of Swann to Marcel's parents, almost immediately introduced to the theme of lesbianism, which plays such an obsessive, at times almost unbalanced, part in the novel. Swann, so it seems to me, is the chief casualty, the only one of the main characters to play appreciably less part in the screenplay than he does in the novel. There was probably no avoiding this. After all, Proust at first presents the story through Swann, then to some extent changes his mind and uses Marcel instead.

One feels that Marcel's love affairs with Gilberte, Andrée and

Albertine might be a trifle confusing on the screen, but they are no less enigmatic in the novel. Here no doubt a great deal would depend on the three individual actresses playing these parts. In the novel the girls are to some extent substitutes for Proust's male love affairs (though he undoubtedly experienced female loves too), and here they never quite come alive.

That cannot be said about M. de Charlus who shows every sign of taking over the screenplay to the same extent that he does the novel. The scene in which Charlus waits for just the right cabman (eventually choosing a drunken one), and Marcel destroys Charlus's top-hat, should both be immensely effective. The rescue of Charlus by the Queen of Naples at the Verdurins' party also possesses great possibilities.

The language of the dialogue seems just what is required. When (p. 80) Albertine uses the affirmative 'That's right', no doubt the phrase correctly suggests the way she talked, though perhaps a shade anachronistically. On p. 63, Mme Blanche Leroi (at whose house the Duchesse de Guermantes speaks of having met the Queen of Sweden) is misprinted 'Blanche Lord'.

Pinter went specially to Cabourg, model for Balbec, and the Grand Hotel where Marcel stayed. His stage directions give only one lift there. I had the good fortune to see the two lifts described by Proust before the renovation took place, and hope that they will be shown when Pinter's adaption reaches the screen, a production to which we must all fervently look forward.

The Proust Screenplay: A la   1978
Recherche du Temps Perdu, Harold   *Daily Telegraph*
Pinter, with the collaboration
of Joseph Losey and Barbara
Bray, Eyre Methuen/Chatto.

XVII

I arrived, as it happened, unusually early in the morning at the Marcel Proust Commemorative Exhibition; and, at first I thought I was alone in the Wildenstein Gallery. Then, as soon as I entered the inner room, I saw him. He was standing in front of Boldini's rather unrestrained portrait in fawn and grey of Count Robert de Montesquiou, gazing at the picture with a look of mingled admiration and annoyance.

I was surprised that I recognized him so easily. His hair was white now, of course, but under the rather battered top-hat the arched eyebrows, hooked nose and prominent cheekbones, that had once reminded Swann of Bellini's Mahomet II, were curiously ageless. There could be no doubt whatever that he was Bloch.

It was evident, too, that he was impatient for someone to turn up on whom to vent his views. Almost at once he began to speak in excellent English which he must have mastered at last after his early difficulties with that language. 'If a suppliant newly escaped from the wine-dark sea may be permitted to address a total stranger, I must remark the coincidence that brings both of us to this place at an hour when the Mother of Morning, Rosy-fingered Dawn, has but lately laid her finger on New Bond Street (where in the past, and in the ardour of my youth, I have erstwhile sacrificed to the fair-tressed nymphs still shrouded by Stygian night) for, that you have risen betimes, must presage more than common interest in the little person to whom these altars are dedicated, in short the young Marcel.'

I agreed; at the same time asking if I had the honour to speak with Monsieur Albert Bloch. He swept his hat from his head and held out his hand: 'Your very humble servant,' he said, 'whose humbleness is not lessened by the treatment he has received on this occasion. My heart has had its fill of weeping and my spirit is given over to the horrible Avengers.'

He made a gesture with his hand towards the exhibits. Then, seeing I did not understand his meaning, he went on: 'All are here, but I. *Etiamsi omnes ego non.* That was the motto of one of the noble families in the book, though I cannot at the moment remember which. But at least it is a statement appropriate to my present position. Of the author's parents, for example, there are any number of photographs; and that extraordinary oil painting of his father skilled in medical knowledge in the guise of a Renaissance doctor. I believe the father was a more interesting man than you would ever guess from the novel.'

'Indeed?'

'Then the Baron de Charlus of the flashing eyes – it doesn't say anything about it in the catalogue, but you may observe at least one side of him in Boldini's portrait here and those admirable caricatures by Sem. . . .

Particularly the one of noble, long-enduring Count Robert de Montesquiou reading his poems. . . .

In the room you have come from you saw Charles Swann, beloved of kings and princes, in Tissot's big group of *Le Cercle de la Rue Royale.* It is like him, I can assure you. Some of his smart friends are there, too, by the way. He knew a lot of dukes and counts, I can assure you. I, too, was a friend of the Marquis de St Loup-en-Bray, tamer of horses, you will remember. In these rooms you will find certain attributes of St Loup-en-Bray, too.'

'And the other Guermantes.'

'Naturally, Madame Straus, rich in vitamins, Comtesse Greffulhe, golden-haired like Aphrodite as well, though it would perhaps be less than charitable in me to point out where that famous host and hostess are chiefly commemorated. Some of their lineaments were perhaps taken from close friends.'

'And Gilberte.'

'There are some charming photographs of Mademoiselle Bernadacki, later Princesse Radziwill. She is generally agreed to have been the model for that young lady red-haired like Menelaus.'

'And her mother?'

'Laure Haymann certainly had something of Odette. She was also the prototype of Bourget's Gladys Harvey. Here you may see a copy of that book bound in the silk of her petticoat with an inscription to Marcel warning him against such women. She was fair as Helen, wife to Atreus' son.'

'No doubt in Céleste we see at least something of the maid Françoise?'

'The handmaidens, too, have their offerings. There are even photographs of all those female wearers of the high buskin whom his uncle loved.'

'The actresses?'

'Yet I, former friend of the author's ingenuous boyhood, who was his companion when, with swift sandal, we paced the groves of the Paphian Aphrodite, I am left out. His waistcoat is shown but not my hat. Look round these walls, and in these showcases, and tell me if you can see a trace of him who was once Marcel's *fidus Achates*.'

'Well, look here,' I said. 'I quite see your point, but they couldn't cover absolutely everyone and everything. For example, there is a canvas by Le Sidaner, who is said to be the origin of Elstir, but they didn't arrange for Vinteuil's "little phrase" to be played over and over again on the gramophone. As a matter of fact there was, musically speaking, something of the sort at the Diaghilev exhibition, so I suppose it would have been possible. You might as well say they ought to serve tea and madeleines every half-hour.'

I thought it an excellent show, and did not see why Bloch should run it down, egotistically, just because he happened not to be included.

'Anyway,' I said, 'you might be held to be represented, one way or another, in the genre pictures by Béraud that hang on the walls.'

'Between you and me,' said Bloch, 'Béraud is an artist I do not greatly admire, cunning though he may be to ornament the halls of kings and heroes.'

'There is nothing about Cottard, if it comes to that, or Jupien.'

Bloch smiled.

'Nor Albertine!' I said.

This seemed to cheer him up. 'True,' he said. 'There is nothing about little Albertine Simonet. She, like me, is without a memorial here,

Albertine worthy to be hymned by her whose father Herodotus calls Scamandronymous.'

He held out his hand in farewell. Then a thought struck him.

'Cattleyas,' he said, slowly. 'They should have had some cattleyas.'

'They should indeed.'

He bowed again, 'Perhaps I shall buy some cattleyas, as little Marcel might express it,' he said, still thoughtfully, 'in the leafy pasture round high Olympus, to which I now wend my way.'

Marcel Proust and His Time,   1955
Wildenstein Gallery.   *Punch*

INDEX